PHILLIPS EXETER ACADEMY

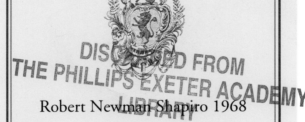

Robert Newman Shapiro 1968

ΧΑΡΙΤΙ ΘΕΟΥ

1983

HISTORICAL DICTIONARY

The historical dictionaries present essential information on a broad range of subjects, including American and world history, art, business, cities, countries, cultures, customs, film, global conflicts, international relations, literature, music, philosophy, religion, sports, and theater. Written by experts, all contain highly informative introductory essays on the topic and detailed chronologies that, in some cases, cover vast historical time periods but still manage to heavily feature more recent events.

Brief A–Z entries describe the main people, events, politics, social issues, institutions, and policies that make the topic unique, and entries are cross-referenced for ease of browsing. Extensive bibliographies are divided into several general subject areas, providing an excellent reference for students, researchers, and anyone wanting to know more. Additionally, maps, photographs, and appendixes of supplemental information aid high school and college students doing term papers or introductory research projects. In short, the historical dictionaries are the perfect starting point for anyone looking to research in these fields.

HISTORICAL DICTIONARIES OF ASIA, OCEANIA, AND THE MIDDLE EAST

Jon Woronoff, Series Editor

Malaysia, Second Edition, by Ooi Keat Gin. 2018.
Tajikistan, Third Edition, by Kamoludin Abdullaev. 2018.
Postwar Japan, Second Edition, by William D. Hoover. 2019.

Historical Dictionary of Postwar Japan

Second Edition

William D. Hoover

ROWMAN & LITTLEFIELD
Lanham • Boulder • New York • London

Published by Rowman & Littlefield
A wholly owned subsidiary of The Rowman & Littlefield Publishing Group, Inc.
4501 Forbes Boulevard, Suite 200, Lanham, Maryland 20706
www.rowman.com

6 Tinworth Street, London SE11 5AL

British Library Cataloguing in Publication Information Available

Library of Congress Cataloging-in-Publication Data

Name: Hoover, William D., author.
Title: Historical dictionary of postwar japan / William D. Hoover.
Description: Second edition. | Lanham : Rowman & Littlefield, 2019. | Series: Historical dictionaries of Asia, Oceania, and the Middle East | Includes bibliographical references.
Identifiers: LCCN 2018027758 (print) | LCCN 2018027920 (ebook) | ISBN 9781538111567 (electronic) | ISBN 9781538111550 (cloth : alk. paper)
Subjects: LCSH: Japan—History—1945 to—Encyclopedias.
Classification: LCC DS889 (ebook) | LCC DS889 .H569 2019 (print) | DDC 952.0403—dc23
LC record available at https://lccn.loc.gov/2018027758

Printed in the United States of America.

Contents

Editor's Foreword

Unlike most other country historical dictionaries, what is most interesting about Japan is not how much it has changed over the years but how much it has remained the same, be it political parties and trade unions, schools and universities, economy and corporate structures, and even relations between parents and children and men and women. This volume starts with an updated chronology that outlines the events of the modern period, and the list of acronyms and abbreviations identifies the players. The key to the front matter is the introduction, which provides a necessary overview, establishing links between the entries in the expanded and updated dictionary section. Here readers can find more details on political parties, major corporations, sectors of the economy, facets of society, cultural features and concepts, and some essential vocabulary. Numerous appendixes present statistical information, and an extensive bibliography lists sources with further information.

This second edition, like the first, was written by William D. Hoover, professor emeritus of the University of Toledo in Ohio. He joined the History Department in 1968 and was its chair for 15 years. Among his teaching specialities were 19th-, 20th-, and 21st-century Japan. He visited Japan periodically, spending six years teaching and researching there, with a long stay from 1994 to 1996. His lectures covered a broad spectrum of topics, and he has written many papers on Japanese history, with an emphasis on prewar internationalism and pacifism and postwar historiography.

Jon Woronoff
Series Editor

Acknowledgments

FROM THE FIRST EDITION

As a professor of Japanese history for many years, I used to lament the fact that by the time my classes had finished World War II and briefly treated the American Occupation of Japan, the semester was over. Any attention given to the years after 1945 were cursory in nature.

Having seen colleagues who taught courses on the United States and Europe after 1945, I decided to do the same with Japan, feeling that the Japan of this time period was at least equally important and interesting. Returning from Tōkyō in the fall of 1996 after spending two years in Japan on a sabbatical and a Japan Foundation fellowship, I began to construct a course devoted exclusively to postwar Japan. By concentrating on this fifty-plus-year period of time, I could develop an in-depth study for my students and satisfy my own curiosity at the same time. Such a course would allow me to indulge my various interests in the period. I could deal with more than just the political outlines, the economic developments, and the foreign policy issues, which had been themselves treated with great brevity and vagueness.

In the writing of any book, many people play a role in shaping the final product. First, I wish belatedly to acknowledge my parents, Kenneth D. Hoover and Florence I. Montgomery Hoover, for making it possible to have the educational opportunities that they afforded me. Likewise, I would like to thank my Aunt Pauline for her intellectual encouragement, academic rigor, and inspiration. Finally, in my family, thanks to my sister, Becky, for her interest and help proofreading.

Second, I want to acknowledge my Muskingum College professors. Among them special mention should be made of the late Professor David R. Sturtevant who stimulated my interest in East Asia and Professor William L. Fisk who inspired me to study history. In graduate school at the University of Michigan, I want to thank Professor Roger F. Hackett who taught me much about Japanese history and the late Professor Robert E. Ward who encouraged my interest in Japanese politics.

Librarians make it possible for scholars to do their work. For this project, I would like to thank the librarians at the University of Toledo, the University of Michigan, International House of Japan, and the Library of Congress. The University of Toledo, my employer for many years, has been generous in supporting research trips to Japan and allowing me to teach courses in my modern Japan specialty. The Japan Foundation provided a generous fellowship that enabled me to explore many aspects of postwar Japan. Thanks to both.

Students are often an inspiration and sometimes an actual help with projects such as this. In particular, I would like to express my appreciation to Andrew Lindsay for his help with the sections on sports; to Jill Nussel for her help with music; to James Cotton for his help with anime, manga, and games; and to Paul DeCorte for his valuable editorial assistance. I also owe a debt to Shirley Green, Melinda Seegart, Nathan Delany, and Justin Pfeifer for help as research and as graduate assistants. I also appreciate the encouragement, questions, and stimulation of undergraduate students who have shown great interest in postwar Japan.

My primary debt, however, goes to my wife, Marie. I want to thank her for all her help reading and discussing materials, editing and proofreading, and answering questions about style and substance. This book is partly hers. As always, traveling with her makes any journey infinitely more pleasant.

FOR THE SECOND EDITION

Although some of the people whom I acknowledged in the first edition have passed away, my debt to all people and organizations mentioned in the earlier edition still remain.

Beyond these earlier acknowledgments, I would like to thank three general sources for their materials. First, many scholars have produced a huge number of books on postwar Japan. One only needs to peruse the bibliography to see how the field of Japanese studies has flourished in recent years. Thank you to all the scholars from whose work I have borrowed.

Second, I have used various newspapers extensively in this edition. Particularly I would note the *New York Times*, *Japan Times*, and *Nikkei Daily News*. These and other newspapers and journals have enabled me to keep up to date with events in Japan.

Finally, the internet and numerous websites have made it much easier to track events, individuals, businesses, and other developments. The world has indeed become much smaller.

Preface

Japan not only remains an important country but also its role in the world has grown. It has become much more of a player on the international scene, expanding contacts around the world, making more and stronger trade deals, and playing a greater role in international security. On the world stage, Japan has grabbed an even larger role in pop culture, sports, literature, film, and music.

Japan's economy, while slipping to number three in the world, is still quite vibrant and a major force. That China has since surpassed Japan in economic standing is due to the sheer difference in size and not to the overall quality of the economy. Japan seems to have recovered from the lost decades and is moving ahead.

Thus, I am pleased to share with readers the major changes experienced by Japan in the past decade and perhaps hint at future developments. I have updated materials from the first edition, added new topics and areas to the dictionary, brought the chronology up to date, and greatly expanded the bibliography. However, this second edition follows the same format as the previous edition with the dictionary being the core section. Within individual dictionary entries, terms with their own entries are **boldface** the first time they appear. Related terms that do not appear in the entry are listed in the *See also* references at the end of an entry. *See* entries refer to other entries that deal with the topic.

Map

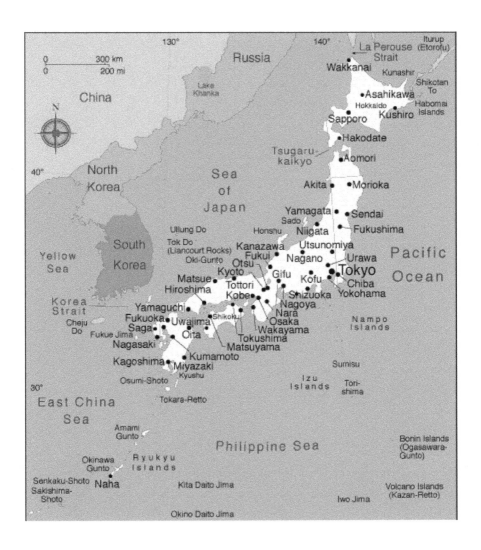

Abbreviations and Acronyms

ABD	Asian Development Bank
ANA	All Nippon Airways
APEC	Asia-Pacific Economic Cooperation
ASDF	Air Self-Defense Force
ASEAN	Association of Southeast Asian Nations
BoJ	Bank of Japan
CDP	Constitutional Democratic Party of Japan (Rikken Minshutō)
CEFP	Council on Economic and Fiscal Policy
CGP	Clean Government Party (Kōmeitō)
DLP	Democratic Liberal Party (Minshu Jiyūtō)
Dōmei	Japanese Confederation of Labor
DP	Democratic Party (Minshintō)
DPJ	Democratic Party of Japan (Minshutō)
DSP	Democratic Socialist Party (Minshu Shakaitō)
EEOL	Equal Employment Opportunity Law
EPA	Economic Planning Agency
FM	Foreign Minister
FNN	Fuji News Network
G-7	Group of Seven Industrialized Nations
GATT	General Agreement on Tariffs and Trade
GDP	Gross Domestic Product
GNP	Gross National Product
GSDF	Ground Self-Defense Force
HoC	House of Councillors
HoR	House of Representatives
IBRD	International Bank for Reconstruction and Development
IMF	International Monetary Fund

IMTFE	International Military Tribunal of the Far East
JAL	Japan Airlines
JAMA	Japan Automobile Manufacturers Association
JAS	Japan Air System
JAXA	Japan Aerospace Exploration Agency
JCCI	Japan Chamber of Commerce and Industry
JCP	Japanese Communist Party (Nihon Kyōsantō)
JETRO	Japan External Trade Organization
JNP	Japan New Party (Nihon Shintō)
JNR	Japan National Railway
JNTO	Japan National Tourist Organization
JR	Japan Railway
JRP	Japan Renewal Party (Shinseitō)
JSP	Japan Socialist Party (Nihon Shakaitō)
JTB	Japan Travel Bureau
JVC	Victor Company of Japan
Keidanren	Japan Federation of Economic Organizations
KM	Kōmeitō (Kōmeitō)
LDP	Liberal Democratic Party (Jiyū Minshūtō)
LP	Liberal Party (Jiyūtō)
MBS	Mainichi Broadcasting System
METI	Ministry of Economy, Trade, and Industry
MEXT	Ministry of Education, Culture, Sports, Science, and Technology
MHLW	Ministry of Health, Labor, and Welfare
MITI	Ministry of International Trade and Industry
MOF	Ministry of Finance
MOFA	Ministry of Foreign Affairs
MSDF	Maritime Self-Defense Force
MUFG	Mitsubishi UFJ Financial Group
NEC	Nippon Electric Company
NFP	New Frontier Party (Shinshintō)

NHK	Nippon Hōsō Kyōkai (Japan Broadcasting Corporation)
NIK	Japan Innovation Party (Nippon Ishin no Kai)
Nikkeiren	Japan Federation of Employers' Association
Nikkyōso	Japan Teachers' Union
Nisshō	Japan Chamber of Commerce and Industry
NKK	Nippon Kōkan (Japan Steel)
NKP	New Kōmeitō (Kōmeitō)
NLC	New Liberal Club (Shin jiyū kurabu)
NPS	New Party Sakigake (Shintō Sakigake)
NTT	Nippon Telegraph & Telephone Corporation
ODA	Official Development Assistance
OECD	Organisation for Economic Co-operation and Development
OPEC	Organization of Petroleum Exporting Countries
OSMP	Okinawa Social Mass Party (Okinawa Shakai Taishūtō)
PH	Party of Hope (Kibō no Tō)
PJK	Party for Japanese Kokoro (Nihon no Kokoro)
PM	Prime Minister
PRC	People's Republic of China
Rengō	Japanese Trade Union Confederation
SCAP	Supreme Commander for the Allied Powers
SDF	Self-Defense Forces
SDP	Social Democratic Party (Shakai Minshūtō)
SDPJ	Social Democratic Party of Japan (Shakai Minshutō)
SMFG	Sumitomo Mitsui Financial Group
Sōhyō	General Council of Japanese Trade Unions
SU	Soviet Union
TBS	Tōkyō Broadcasting System
TSE	Tōkyō Stock Exchange
UN	United Nations
UNESCO	United Nations Educational, Scientific and Cultural Organization
UNICEF	United Nations International Children's Emergency Fund

USDP	United Social Democratic Party (Shakai Minshu Rengō)
WTO	World Trade Organization
Zenrōren	National Confederation of Trade Unions

Chronology

1945 14 August: Emperor Hirohito proclaims Japan's surrender. **15 August:** Emperor Hirohito broadcasts his "bear the unbearable" surrender speech. **17 August:** The Diet names Prince Higashikuni Naruhiko as prime minister. **28 August:** Allied Occupation begins, and U.S. forces arrive in Tōkyō and fleet at Yokosuka. President Harry S. Truman approves Initial Post-Surrender Policy for Japan. **30 August:** General Douglas MacArthur receives guidelines to administer the Occupation when he arrives in Tōkyō as Supreme Commander for the Allied Powers (SCAP). **2 September:** Japan formally surrenders on the USS *Missouri*, and the U.S. occupation of Japan officially begins. **4 October:** SCAP issues Civil Liberties Directive. Officials order release of political prisoners. **9 October:** Prince Higashikuni resigns as prime minister. Shidehara Kijūrō becomes prime minister. **November:** MacArthur approves Yasuda Plan for the breakup of the zaibatsu. **1 November:** The Japanese government legalizes the Japanese Communist Party (JCP). **December:** Trade Union Law guarantees workers the right to organize and strike. **1 December:** The government abolishes the ministries of war and navy. **15 December:** The government disestablishes the state Shintō religion. **27 December:** Allies create the Far Eastern Commission and Allied Council for Japan at the Moscow Conference.

1946 1 January: Emperor Hirohito disavows his own divinity. **4 January:** First purge directive removes political rights of 220,000 people. **April:** Japan introduces universal suffrage, and women gain the vote and right of candidacy for the first time. **10 April:** Japan holds its first postwar House of Representatives elections. Liberals win 140 seats, and Progressives win 94 seats. Seventy-two percent of eligible people vote. **3 May:** International Military Tribunal for the Far East (IMTFE) opens proceedings in Tōkyō. **22 May:** Yoshida Shigeru, leader of the conservative Liberal Party, becomes prime minister and forms his first cabinet. **21 October:** SCAP-promoted Farm Land Reform Law passes. **3 November:** Japan proclaims new Shōwa Constitution to become effective on 3 May 1947.

1947 Toyota starts producing passenger cars. **1 February:** MacArthur bans general strikes. **31 March:** The Diet enacts the Fundamental Law of Education. **20 April:** Japan holds its first postwar House of Councillors elections; independents win 111 of the 250 seats, the Japan Socialist Party (JSP) wins 47 seats, the Liberal Party wins 38 seats, and the Democratic Party wins 28 seats. **25 April:** Japan holds House of Representatives elections where Liberal, Democratic, and Japan Socialist parties each win 25 percent of the vote. The JSP forms a coalition government. **May:** The Diet adopts the Labor Standards Act. **3 May:** New Shōwa Constitution goes into effect. **24 May:** Katayama Tetsu, JSP leader, becomes prime minister of a socialist coalition. **December:** Fundamental Law of Education revises the prewar education system. The Diet passes the De-Concentration Law and plans dissolution of 300 companies to reduce excessive concentration of economic power.

1948 1 January: New Criminal and Civil Codes come into effect. **February:** Katayama resigns, but a coalition continues under Prime Minister Ashida Hitoshi, leader of the conservative Democratic Party. **April:** IMTFE war crimes trial ends. **1 June:** The Diet passes Labor Relations Act. **July:** The government offensive against labor begins with the ban on strikes in the public sector. **September:** Politically active students form the National Student Federation (Zengakuren). **October:** Washington adopts NSC 13, which places priority on economic revival and political stability in Japan. Shōwa Denkō scandal leads to Ashida's resignation. **15 October:** Yoshida Shigeru again becomes prime minister. **November:** IMTFE condemns seven class A defendants to death, including wartime prime minister Tōjō Hideki. National Public Service Law denies civil servants the right to strike and bargain collectively.

1949 January: The Ministry of Commerce and Industry becomes the Ministry of International Trade and Industry (MITI). The government implements financial reforms under the Shoup Plan. "Reverse course" begins in earnest. An "anti-red" purge dismisses thousands of left-wing sympathizers from the public sector. The anti-zaibatsu program winds down. **23 January:** Japan holds its third postwar lower house elections where Yoshida Shigeru's Liberal Party gains a plurality of seats. **16 February:** Prime Minister Yoshida forms third cabinet. **April:** The government fixes the yen at ¥360 to the US$1. **15 April:** Joseph M. Dodge calls for budgetary retrenchment and implements "Dodge Line," which brings about economic stabilization but leads to large-scale Japanese unemployment. **12 May:** Reparations program ends. **October:** SCAP formally ends censorship.

1950 The Diet enacts Local Civil Service Law. **6 April:** The United States appoints John Foster Dulles to negotiate the San Francisco Peace Treaty. **4 June:** Japan holds its second postwar House of Councillors elections with the Liberal Party winning 52 and JSP 36 of 132 seats at stake. **6–7 June:** The government carries out Communist purge. **25 June:** Korean War begins and stimulates Japan's economy. **10 July:** Japan creates the 75,000-man National Police Reserve. **12 July:** Labor leaders establish a new labor federation called Sōhyō, General Council of Trade Unions of Japan. **7 September:**

Nihon Keizai Shimbun begins calculating the Nikkei index, a measure of the stock market average. **October:** The Japanese government de-purges 10,000 military and political people connected with the war.

1951 11 April: President Truman dismisses MacArthur and appoints Matthew Ridgway as SCAP. **20 June:** The government lifts political purge on 69,000 people. **8 September:** Japan signs the San Francisco Peace Treaty with 48 nations. Japan and the United States sign the United States–Japan Security Treaty continuing U.S. military in Japan. **September:** Japan renames the National Police Reserve as the National Safety Force. **24 October:** The Japan Socialist Party strongly disagrees with colleagues over the security treaty.

1952 Japan joins the International Monetary Fund (IMF). Japan gains admission to the International Bank for Reconstruction and Development (IBRD). Japan licenses transistor technology from the United States. **22 February:** The United States and Japan sign an administrative agreement on military bases in Japan. **28 April:** San Francisco Peace Treaty goes into effect, and Japan regains sovereignty. The United States officially ends occupation of Japan. **1 May:** Anti-American riots disrupt Tōkyō. **July:** The Yoshida government enacts Subversive Activities Prevention Law. **18 September:** The Soviet Union vetoes Japan's admission to the United Nations (UN). **1 October:** Japan holds its fourth postwar lower house elections. **15 October:** National Police Reserve officially becomes the National Safety Force. **30 October:** Prime Minister Yoshida forms his fourth cabinet.

1953 Japan's economic productivity reaches prewar level. The government eases restrictions brought about by Occupation policies. Minamata disease first appears in Kumamoto. Japan's economy begins a period of rapid economic growth. **19 April:** Japan conducts fifth postwar lower house elections. **24 April:** Japan holds its third House of Councillors elections with the Liberal Party winning 46 of 128 seats. **21 May:** Yoshida Shigeru forms his fifth cabinet. **27 July:** Cease-fire in Korea comes into effect.

1954 TTK electronic company, soon called Sony, introduces the world's first transistor radio. **12 January:** Japan Cotton Spinning Association reports that Japan ranked first in cotton textile exports in 1953. **1 March:** U.S. nuclear test fallout near Bikini Island hits the fishing boat *No. 5 Fukuryu-maru*, sparking anti-American feelings. **8 March:** The United States and Japan sign the Mutual Defense Assistance Agreement and other pacts providing for increased American military and economic aid. **19 March:** The *Koan-maru*, the second Japanese repatriation ship from the Soviet Union, reaches the port of Maizuru. **3 June:** The upper house passes Self-Defense Forces (SDF) Bill and Defense Board Establishment Bill. **23 June:** Economic Commission for Asia and the Far East (ECAFE) formally admits Japan. **1 July:** The government reorganizes the National Safety Force as the SDF under the Defense Agency, a civilian-controlled operation. **August:** The government creates the National Police Reserve. **26 September:** Prime Minister Yoshida travels to the United States, Canada, and Europe on a goodwill mission. **24 November:** Politicians, under the leadership of Hatoyama Ichirō and Shigemitsu Mamoru, inaugurate the Japan Democratic Party after dissolving the Progressive and Japan Liberal parties. **7 December:** Yoshida cabinet resigns en bloc due to a shipping scandal and fear of no-confidence vote. **10 December:** Japan Democratic Party elects Hatoyama Ichirō, a purged politician, as president; he soon becomes prime minister and forms a cabinet.

1955 The Diet establishes the Economic Planning Agency (EPA). Period of high-speed growth begins. **27 February:** Japan holds its sixth postwar House of Representatives elections; Democrats win 185 seats, Liberals win 113 seats, leftist Socialists win 89 seats, and rightist Socialists win 66 seats of the 467 seats. **19 March:** Hatoyama forms his second cabinet. **6 August:** First World Conference against Atomic and Hydrogen Bombs meets in Hiroshima. **10 September:** Japan joins General Agreement on Tariffs and Trade (GATT). **13 September:** Start of struggle over expansion of Tachikawa Air Base (Sunagawa) where 33 policemen and five townsmen are injured in a clash. Japan and the Soviet Union hold a meeting where Japan expresses shock that the Soviet Union failed to account for more than 11,000 missing people. **13 October:** The reunification of the left and right Socialists forms the Japan Socialist Party after a four-year split. JSP elects Suzuki Mosaburō chair. **17 October:** Japan and People's Republic of China (PRC) agree to a communiqué calling for the normalization of diplomatic relations. **15 November:** The Democratic Party and Liberal Party join forces to create the Liberal Democratic Party (LDP), which holds 299 of 467 seats in the lower house. **21 November:** Second Hatoyama cabinet resigns. **22 November:** Hatoyama forms his third cabinet. **5 December:** The government's Advisory Council on Economic Affairs submits a comprehensive six-year economic development plan.

1956 Japan becomes the world's leading shipbuilder. Japan sells its first Japanese-made car in the United States. **31 March:** Long coal mine strike ends when both sides accept a compromise settlement. **16 April:** The Diet approves two defense bills in a six-year defense buildup program that will add 40,000 ground troops, jet planes, and naval vessels. **3 July:** The *Kōan-maru* returns with 335 Japanese war criminals released by the PRC and a list of 7,000 Japanese who died in China after the war. **8 July:** Japan conducts fourth postwar House of Councillors elections where LDP wins 61 and JSP 49 of the total 127 seats contested. **12 October:** Police clash with Sunagawa villagers and labor unionists, injuring more than 1,000, when government surveyors try forcefully to survey land for an extension of the Tachikawa Air

Base. **19 October:** Japan and the Soviet Union issue joint statement normalizing relations, ending the technical state of war, but leaving the Northern Territories question unsettled. **14 December:** Prime Minister Hatoyama Ichirō resigns. LDP leaders select Ishibashi Tanzan, MITI chief, as president of the party and thus prime minister. **18 December:** The United Nations admits Japan as its 80th member. **26 December:** Around 1,025 Japanese are repatriated from the Soviet Union. This makes 453,849 returned, but 11,068 are still missing.

1957 17 January: Japan Socialist Party holds its first convention since merger of left and right wings. **4 February:** Foreign Minister Kishi Nobusuke pledges efforts to base Japan's foreign policy on cooperation with the United States. **23 February:** Prime Minister Ishibashi resigns due to ill health. **25 February:** The Diet chooses Kishi Nobusuke, a "depurged" politician, as prime minister. **11 March:** General Council of Japanese Labor Unions (Sōhyō) orders the third wave of its spring offensive and directs its three million members to struggle for higher wages and a minimum wage law. **20 May:** Kishi leaves on a 14-day tour of Southeast Asia. **16 June:** Kishi travels to the United States where the United States and Japan issue the Eisenhower-Kishi communiqué. **18 September:** Ceremonies mark the completion of the first experimental atomic reactor at Tōkaimura. **1 October:** The UN elects Japan to a non-permanent member seat on the Security Council. **6 December:** Japan and the Soviet Union sign the Treaty of Commerce.

1958 18 April: The lower house unanimously adopts a joint antinuclear test resolution and upper house approves similar resolution. **25 April:** Japan Socialist Party's no-confidence motion against the Kishi government leads to dissolution of House of Representatives. **13 May:** Japan protests U.S. nuclear testing and the production and stockpiling of nuclear weapons. **21 May:** Japan and Nationalist China sign a one-year trade agreement. **22 May:** LDP wins 287 and JSP 166 of the 467 seats in the seventh postwar lower house elections. The LDP gains 57.8 percent of the vote, in this, its first election. The election produces the highest voter turnout ever, with 76.99 percent of the eligible population voting. **24 May:** Third Asian Games open in Tōkyō with 20 countries participating. **12 June:** Prime Minister Kishi forms his second cabinet. **21 July:** JCP opens its seventh party congress, the first in 11 years. **21 August:** The government and LDP decide to enforce teachers' efficiency rating system and take strict measures against illegal protests. Japan Teachers' Union conducts 100 percent protest walkout.

1959 1 January: Japan officially implements the metric system. **17 February:** Lloyd's Register of Shipping reports that Japan led the world in shipbuilding in 1958. **10 April:** Crown Prince Akihito marries Shōda Michiko, a commoner, but from a prominent family. **16 April:** The United States accepts Japan's compromise proposal for voluntary restrictions on cotton exports. **1 May:** Japan authorizes a 12,000-man increase, bringing the SDF to a total of 231,000 troops. **2 June:** Japan holds its fifth postwar upper house elections with LDP winning 71 seats and Socialists 38. **11 July:** Kishi leaves for a month's visit to 11 countries in Western Europe and Latin America. **31 July:** The limited express Kodama sets a world speed record of 163 kilometers per hour. **16 October:** JSP reopens its 16th national convention in Tōkyō and reelects Chairman Suzuki Mosaburō and Secretary-General Asanuma Inejirō. **27 November:** Some 12,000 leftists demonstrate against the U.S.-Japan Security Treaty, injuring 300 Tōkyō policemen and 100 demonstrators. **16 December:** Supreme Court unanimously reverses the Tōkyō District Court decision that the stationing of U.S. forces in Japan is unconstitutional.

1960 Japan begins phenomenal economic growth rate of 14–15 percent, elevating the country to the world's second-largest economic power. **5 January:** Mitsui Mining notifies 1,278 workers of layoffs at Miike Coal Mine, and the union begins a strike. **19 January:** Japan and the United States sign revised United States–Japan Mutual Cooperation and Security Treaty. **24 January:** Some 300 right-wing socialists, including 32 Diet members, found the Democratic Socialist Party (DSP); they elect Nishio Suehiro chairman. **28 March:** Clash between Miike unionists and strike breakers kills one person and injures 100 others. **19–20 May:** LDP pushes ratification of the United States–Japan Security Treaty through the Diet despite socialist boycott and public demonstrations. **15 June:** Giant anti-treaty demonstration results in the death of a University of Tōkyō student and injury to more than 300 students and 278 policemen. **19 June:** House of Councillors automatically ratifies the United States–Japan Security Treaty. **15 July:** Prime Minister Kishi resigns under pressure. **19 July:** The Diet selects LDP president Ikeda Hayato as prime minister; he appoints the first woman to cabinet. **11 August:** NHK discloses Japan has five million TV set owners and is the world's fourth-leading TV country. **5 September:** Prime Minister Ikeda promises to improve living standards in Japan and proclaims his 10-year income-doubling plan. **12 October:** A right-wing crazed youth assassinates Asanuma Inejirō, leader of the JSP, on national TV. **20 November:** Japan holds its eighth postwar lower house elections where LDP wins 296 seats, JSP 145, and DSP 17. More than 73 percent of possible voters turn out. **25 November:** Miike miners and Mitsui Coal Mine sign a contract ending the long, bitter strike.

1961 21 February: Japan's ambassador to the UN argues that Japan should send the SDF abroad to strengthen Japan's UN voice, but he encounters strong criticism. **2 May:** The World Bank lends Japan National Railways

US$80 million, the bank's second-largest loan. **1 November:** Japan opens new National Diet Library in Tōkyō. **16 November:** Prime Minister Ikeda leaves on a 15-day goodwill mission to South and Southeast Asia.

1962 9 January: Japan becomes the world's fourth-largest steel producer. **12 March:** MITI paper on economic cooperation records that Japanese economic assistance to foreign countries in 1960 totaled $1 billion, ranking Japan seventh among nations giving aid. **20 March:** Around 4.5 million workers hold limited strikes, rallies, and demonstrations in the spring labor offensive. **26 April:** Labor leaders create Dōmei Kaigi, a federation of Zenrō, Sōdōmei, and Zenkankō moderate labor unions, to counter more totalitarian unions. **1 July:** Japan holds its sixth postwar upper house elections, and LDP wins 69 and JSP 37 of the 127 seats. **10 July:** Japan launches the world's biggest tanker, the 131,000-deadweight-ton *Nisshō-maru.* **5 August:** Sōhyō adopts a new policy placing priority on unionism over political action. **27 October:** Japan becomes the world's seventh most populous nation with a total population of 95,010,000. **4 November:** Prime Minister Ikeda leaves for a three-week trip to Great Britain and Western Europe. **9 November:** Japan and PRC sign memorandum on a five-year trade agreement. Nationalist China soon suspends talks on loan and trade with Japan.

1963 1 January: First broadcast of *Tetsuwan Atomu*, Tezuka Osamu's famous anime. **16 February:** Kumamoto University presents the theory that the cause of Minamata disease is mercury dumped by the Chisso Fertilizer Company. **10 June:** The government white paper shows Japan leads the world in percentage of individual savings. **5 September:** Honda opens the first wholly owned Japanese factory in Europe at Aalst, Belgium. **23 September:** Prime Minister Ikeda starts a 14-day tour of the Philippines, Indonesia, and Australia. **26 October:** The Japan Atomic Energy Research Institute makes Japan the 11th country to generate electric power by atomic energy at Tōkaimura. **21 November:** Japan holds its ninth postwar lower house elections where LDP wins 283 and JSP 144 of 467 seats. **9 December:** Ikeda appoints his third cabinet after being reelected prime minister by the Diet.

1964 20 January: The king and queen of Belgium arrive as the first reigning European monarchs ever to visit Japan. **10 February:** Toyota Motor Company opens a car and truck assembly plant in Bangkok, its first in Asia. **1 April:** Japan joins the IMF. **8 April:** Japan and West Germany sign a trade protocol. **28 April:** The Organisation for Economic Co-operation and Development (OECD) admits Japan as a member. **15 May:** Lower house approves ratification of the partial nuclear test ban treaty signed in 1962. **10 July:** Prime Minister Ikeda Hayato is reelected president of LDP for a third consecutive term. **2 September:** Japan proclaims that it will not permit entry of U.S. nuclear-powered submarines into its ports without prior approval. **1 Octo-**

ber: Bullet Train (Shinkansen) begins operation. **10–24 October:** The Tōkyō Olympic Games, the 18th Olympiad, begin for 94 teams. Japanese athletes win 16 gold, five silver, and eight bronze medals. **9 November:** Ikeda resigns due to poor health. The Diet selects Satō Eisaku prime minister, and he begins the longest tenure as prime minister in postwar Japan. **11 November:** Labor organizations form the Japanese Confederation of Labor (Dōmei), Japan's second-largest labor organization after Sōhyō, in Tōkyō. **17 November:** Sōka Gakkai, a Buddhist group, founds the Kōmeitō (KMT, Clean Government Party).

1965 13 January: Prime Minister Satō and President Lyndon Johnson confer in Washington and agree to maintain "close consultation" on the issue of the PRC. **17 February:** Lloyd's Register of Shipping announces that Japanese shipyards led the world in ship production for the 10th time, launching 4.1 million tons of shipping in 1964, or 40 percent of the world's total. **22 June:** Japan and South Korea sign a peace treaty and other agreements, thus normalizing relations. **4 July:** LDP retains control of the House of Councillors in the seventh postwar elections but loses four seats. LDP holds 140 seats, JSP 73, KMT 20, DSP 7, JCP 4, and independents 5. **15 August:** Emperor Hirohito leads a memorial service to pay tribute to Japanese war dead to commemorate the 20th anniversary of the end of World War II. **19–21 August:** Satō makes the first postwar visit of a prime minister to Okinawa. Some 10,000 demonstrators demand return of the Ryūkyū Islands to Japan.

1966 6 October: More than 100 firms form a Sino-Japanese Trade Promotion Federation in order to improve trade between the two countries. **23 October:** Foreign Minister Shiina Etsusaburō addresses the UN and states Japan will strive to spend 1 percent of GNP to aid developing nations. **24 November:** Inaugural meeting of Asian Development Bank opens in Tōkyō with 500 representatives from 32 countries attending. **29 December:** The Ministry of Labor reveals that Japan has 53,985 unions with 10,403,742 members (35.4 percent of the labor force).

1967 29 January: Japan holds its 10th postwar House of Representatives elections where LDP gains 277 seats (only 48.8 percent of popular vote), JSP 140 seats, DSP 30, KMT 25, JCP 5, and independents 9. A full 74 percent of eligible voters cast ballots. **11 February:** Some 600 places observe the first National Founding Day holiday, the old Empire Founding Day. **17 February:** Prime Minister Satō forms his second cabinet. **15 May:** Japan and the United States hold the seventh meeting of the US.-Japan Security Consultative Committee in Tōkyō, where they affirm the U.S. stance in Vietnam and Japan's support. **7 June:** Japan makes concessions at the Kennedy Round of GATT's tariff schedule where 1,600 items are reduced, some by as much as 50 percent. **30 June:** Prime Minister Satō visits Seoul to attend the inauguration of South Korean president Park Chung-hee; Satō is the first Japanese prime minister in office to visit South Korea since the war. **7 September:** Prime Minister Satō visits Taiwan and has a conference with President Chiang Kai-shek. **20 September:** Satō leaves on an 11-day official tour of five Southeast Asian countries. **12 November:** Some 3,300 Zengakuren students clash with police near Tōkyō International Airport in a demonstration to prevent Satō from departing for the United States, resulting in 170 casualties. **11 December:** Prime Minister Satō declares Japan's three nonnuclear principles in a Diet speech.

1968 Japan's GNP rises to second after the United States. **19–23 January:** The U.S. nuclear-powered aircraft carrier *Enterprise* visits Sasebo, and Prime Minister Satō reiterates Japan's three nonnuclear principles. **5 February:** MITI recounts that Japanese aid to developing nations increased 150 percent from around $120 million to $290 million during 1964–1966. **8 February:** JSP, JCP, and KMT agree on a joint Diet resolution designed to prevent Japan from being armed with nuclear weapons. **6 March:** Japan and the PRC extend the Liao-Takasaki trade pact. **21 March:** LDP resolves to promote peaceful use of atomic energy, abolish nuclear weapons, maintain the United States–Japan Security Treaty, and follow the three nonnuclear principles. **6 May:** The EPA reports that Japan's GNP in 1967 totaled ¥41.6 trillion, an 18.7 percent annual increase, ranking Japan the third-largest GNP after the United States and West Germany. However, per capita income was only $922, ranking Japan 20th in the world. **26 June:** The United States returns the Ogasawara (Bonin) Islands to Japan after 23 years of U.S. rule. **7 July:** In the eighth postwar House of Councillors elections, the JSP receives a bitter setback when Satō's LDP maintains its power. **11 July:** Japan's population reaches 101,988,020. **30 September:** The Tōkyō Stock Exchange soars to an all-time high of 1,843, topping the record of 18 July 1961. **27 November:** LDP elects Satō to a third term as president. **10 December:** Kawabata Yasunari becomes the first Japanese to receive the Nobel Prize in Literature.

1969 14 January: The University of Tōkyō decides to conduct its spring entrance examination after seeking police intervention to remove dissident students. **16 January:** The government announces that Japan has become the world's fourth-largest exporter after the United States, West Germany, and Great Britain. **17 January:** The Japan Automobile Manufacturers Association reveals that Japan produced 4,085,826 cars in 1968, making it the second largest in the world. **18–19 January:** Riot police evict dissidents from the University of Tōkyō. **31 January:** The Ministry of Finance declares that Japan's balance of payments surplus for 1968 totaled $1.1 billion in the overall accounts, the biggest favorable figure ever recorded. **6 March:** Yawata Iron & Steel Company combines with Fuji Iron & Steel Company to create the giant called Shin Nihon Steel Corporation. **21 November:** Satō-Nixon communiqué outlines the reversion of Okinawa by 1972. Under this agreement, the United States is to retain its rights to bases on the island, but these are to be nuclear free. **27 December:** Japan holds its 11th postwar House of Representatives elections where the LDP gains more seats but again fails to obtain 50 percent of the vote.

1970 14 January: Prime Minister Satō Eisaku forms his third cabinet. **15 March:** The 1970 World Exhibition opens in Ōsaka. **3 May:** Kōmeitō proclaims its separation from Sōka Gakkai. **22 June:** Japan confirms the automatic renewal of the U.S.-Japan Security Treaty after expiration of the 10-year period, provoking large anti-treaty demonstrations. **29 October:** Satō is elected to an unprecedented fourth term as LDP president. **25 November:** Novelist Mishima Yukio commits ritual suicide at Ichigaya Headquarters after an abortive appeal to the SDF for insurrection.

1971 1 February: Japan becomes one of the five largest subscribers to the World Bank's authorized capital stock and is thus entitled to appoint an executive director. **27 February:** Compulsory expropriation of land for the new Narita Airport sparks protests against the project. **17 June:** Japan and the United States sign treaty for Okinawa reversion to take place on 15 May 1972. **27 June:** Japan holds its ninth postwar upper house elections. LDP fills 62 and JSP 39 of the 125 open seats. **15 July:** First "Nixon shock" comes from the United States with the announcement of the president's plan to visit China with no prior Japanese consultation. **15 August:** The second "Nixon shock" of a 10 percent surcharge on imports and non-convertibility of the U.S. dollar leads to higher duties on Japanese exports. **October:** The emperor visits Queen Elizabeth in Great Britain. **15 October:** Japan accepts quotas in a textile agreement with the United States. **20 December:** Japan agrees to fix the value of the yen at ¥308 to the US$1, a 16.88 percent increase in value of the yen.

1972 Japan's literacy rate reaches 98 percent. **3 February:** The Winter Olympic Games open at Sapporo. **15 May:** Okinawa reverts to Japan and becomes a prefecture. **30 May:** The Japanese Red Army—left-wing student terrorists—attack passengers at the Tel Aviv (Lodi) airport in Israel and kill 24 people. **7 July:** The Diet chooses Tanaka Kakuei as prime minister, and he forms his first cabinet. **29 September:** Prime Minister Tanaka visits China to normalize relations and restore diplomatic ties. **2 October:** The government creates the Japan Foundation. **10 December:** Japan holds its 12th postwar lower house elections where both the JSP and the JCP make gains. **22 December:** Prime Minister Tanaka forms his second cabinet.

1973 15 February: Japan places the yen on a floating exchange rate system. **20 February:** The Bank of Japan and the IBRD sign a loan agreement by which the Bank of Japan loans ¥35 billion to the World Bank, the largest single loan in its history. **14 November:** Japan opens Kammon Bridge between Honshū and Kyūshū and Kammon Tunnel four months later. **November–December:** The Arab oil boycott has a profound impact on Japan and produces an "oil shock" as prices quadruple. **8 December:** The UN decides to locate the headquarters of the United Nations University in Tōkyō.

1974 Japan experiences acute inflation. Hello Kitty first appears on the scene. Japan begins to suffer a severe economic recession. **15–16 January:** Hostile demonstrators confront Tanaka's tour of Thailand, Indonesia, and the Philippines. **18 March:** OPEC ends a five-month oil embargo against the United States, Europe, and Japan. **7 July:** Japan holds its 10th postwar House of Councillors elections; LDP retains a narrow majority but slips in overall count. **6 October:** Admiral Gene La Rocque reveals that U.S. naval vessels carry nuclear weapons in Japanese waters. **10 October:** *Bungei Shunjū* brings allegations of financial corruption against Tanaka Kakuei. **18–22 November:** Gerald Ford visits Japan; he is the first incumbent American president to do so. **9 December:** The Diet chooses Miki Takeo as prime minister.

1975 16 January: The Soviet Union proposes Japan-Soviet treaty of good-neighborliness and cooperation. **May:** Queen Elizabeth visits Japan; she is the first reigning British sovereign to come to Japan. **2–13 October:** Emperor Hirohito visits the United States. **15–17 November:** The leaders of the six (soon to be seven) major industrial democracies meet near Paris in their first summit. Prime Minister Miki participates in this first meeting.

1976 4 May: The court indicts Chisso executives at the first criminal proceedings in the Minamata pollution case. **8 June:** Japan ratifies the Nuclear Nonproliferation Treaty that was signed in February 1970. **16 June:** Japan and Australia sign a treaty of friendship and cooperation. **25 June:** Kōno Yōhei forms New Liberal Club (NLC) in the wake of the Lockheed scandal as the LDP experiences its first split when six members join NLC. **27 June:** The government arrests former prime minister Tanaka Kakuei in connection with the Lockheed scandal. **5 December:** Japan holds its 13th postwar lower house elections, and LDP gains only 42 percent of the vote and a one-seat majority of the 511 seats. **24 December:** Fukuda Takeo replaces Miki Takeo as president of LDP and soon becomes prime minister.

1977 Japan's average life expectancy, 73 years for men, surpasses Sweden to become the world's longest. **26 March:** Eda Saburō deserts the Socialists to form a new party but dies on 22 May. **8 May:** Narita Airport faces major clash with one fatality. **1 July:** Japan begins enforcement of 12-mile territorial waters and a 200-mile economic zone. **10 July:** Japan holds its 11th postwar House of Councillors elections where LDP gains a majority of four. **6 August:** Prime Minister Fukuda Takeo announces Japan's Southeast Asian policy, the so-called Fukuda Doctrine, where he promotes relations with Southeast Asian countries. **16–18 August:** Fukuda tours Southeast Asia and promises more aid. **12–14 November:** First Conference of the Association of Southeast Asian Nations (ASEAN)–Japan Dialogue meets in Japan.

1978 MITI sets voluntary restraints on auto exports. **20 May:** Narita Airport finally opens, seven years behind schedule, amid continuing opposition. **12 August:** Two leading East Asian countries sign Japan-China Treaty of Peace and Friendship in Beijing. **17 October:** Yasukuni Shrine enshrines 14 class A war criminals. **26 November:** Ōhira Masayoshi wins the first LDP primary for party president. **7 December:** Ōhira forms his first cabinet, bringing out the bitter factional rivalry between Tanaka Kakuei and Fukuda Takeo.

1979 Japan settles textile trade dispute with the United States. Sony launches the Walkman portable stereo. **13 January:** Japan holds its first uniform national university entrance examination. **22 April:** The courts find Chisso executives criminally responsible for the Minamata pollution case. **24–27 June:** U.S. president Jimmy Carter visits Japan. **28–29 June:** Tōkyō hosts the fifth Group of Seven meeting. **2 October:** Japan lodges a protest against the Soviet Union over military buildup on Kunashiri and Etorofu and the deployment of military forces on Shikotan. **7 October:** Japan holds its 14th postwar House of Representatives elections where LDP wins 248 of the 511 seats. **9 November:** Ōhira forms his second cabinet. **27 November:** Kōmeitō officially confirms its support of the United States–Japan Security Treaty.

1980 15–20 January: Prime Minister Ōhira tours Western Pacific nations speaking of a Pacific Rim Alliance. **1 May:** Ōhira visits Washington. **2 May:** Asukata Ichio, chair of the Japan Socialist Party, discloses that JSP will drop its opposition to the U.S.-Japan Security Treaty. **16 May:** The lower house votes no confidence in Ōhira, and he calls a new election. **12 June:** Ōhira suddenly dies from a heart attack, 10 days before the House of Representatives elections. **22 June:** Japan jointly holds 15th postwar lower and 12th upper house elections in which LDP wins strong majorities in both. LDP wins 284 of 511 seats in the lower house and 135 of 252 seats in the upper house. **9 July:** President Jimmy Carter and representatives from more than 100 nations attend the memorial service for Ōhira. **17 July:** The Diet chooses Suzuki Zenkō as the next prime minister.

1981 Japan becomes the world's largest carmaker with 11.2 million vehicles. **1 May:** Japan agrees to self-restraint on car exports to the United States of 1.7 million units in fiscal year 1981. **7–8 May:** Prime Minister Suzuki Zenkō visits Washington and confirms with President Ronald Reagan the "alliance relationship" between Japan and the United States. **17 May:** Former U.S.

ambassador Edwin Reischauer's statement that American nuclear weapons should pass through Japanese waters stirs up great controversy. **15 August:** Suzuki and 18 cabinet members visit Yasukuni Shrine. **1 December:** Kōmeitō recognizes SDF as a constitutional entity.

1982 Sony launches the compact disc. **26 March:** The U.S. secretary of defense, Caspar Weinberger, calls for a 100-mile radius of defense by Japan, which it accepts on 14 September. **14–18 April:** French president François Mitterrand visits Japan. **31 May:** Chinese premier Zhao Ziyang comes to Japan and asks for Japan's help in China's modernization. **17 July:** The average life span, 74 years for Japanese men and 79 years for women, is the world's longest. **26 July:** The PRC protests wording of textbooks that appear to play down Japanese aggression in World War II. **17 September:** British prime minister Margaret Thatcher arrives in Japan for a six-day visit. **26 September:** Prime Minister Suzuki begins six-day tour of China. **12 October:** Suzuki resigns as LDP president. **24 November:** Nakasone Yasuhiro wins the LDP presidency and soon forms his first cabinet in what will be a five-year run as prime minister.

1983 11–12 January: Nakasone consults with President Chun Doo-hwan in South Korea and promises $4 billion in aid. **17–21 January:** Nakasone travels to Washington where he declares Japan "an unsinkable aircraft carrier." **21 April:** Nakasone visits Yasukuni Shrine as prime minister. **26 June:** Japan convenes 13th postwar upper house elections. **12 October:** The Supreme Court sentences Tanaka to four years in prison and fines him $2 million for taking a bribe in the famous Lockheed scandal. **9–12 November:** Ronald Reagan visits Japan and becomes the first U.S. president to address the Diet. **18 December:** Japan holds its 16th postwar House of Representatives elections where LDP falls from 286 to 250 seats and needs help of independents to gain a majority. **27 December:** Prime Minister Nakasone forms his second cabinet, a coalition with the NLC, the first coalition cabinet since the LDP formed in 1955.

1984 19 January: Professor Ienaga Saburō files his third legal suit over the government's textbook-authorization system. **31 January:** Japan's unemployment rate in 1983 hits 2.6 percent, the highest since statistics began in 1953. **27 April:** Japan records a $34.6 billion trade surplus and $24.3 billion in balance of current account in 1983. Nippon Steel Corporation leads the world in steel output in 1983 for the 14th consecutive year. **10 August:** The Ministry of Education says that 94 percent of the nation's junior high school graduates advanced to senior high school in 1984. **26 August:** According to a prime minister's poll, two-thirds of Japanese consider themselves middle class, and 70 percent of them are satisfied with their lives. **1 November:**

Prime Minister Nakasone reshuffles his cabinet and appoints the first woman in 22 years. **21 December:** The EPA says that Japan ranks 10th in the world in per capita GDP.

1985 25 January: The Japan Automobile Manufacturers Association discloses Japan made 11.5 million cars and that Japan has become the world's largest vehicle maker. **21 March:** GATT states that Japan has become the world's largest manufacturer of export goods. **30 April:** Prime Minister Nakasone leaves for Bonn to attend the 11th summit of the Group of Seven nations. **17 May:** Japan adopts Equal Employment Opportunity Act. **21 May:** The House of Representatives passes a resolution calling for a total ban of nuclear weapons, similar to the 1978 and 1982 bans. **8 June:** Japan spends $4.3 billion in 1984 for foreign aid, the second-largest aid contribution in the world. **25 June:** The government adopts a package of tariff cuts of 20 percent or more on 1,850 import items as part of its effort to further open Japanese markets. **3 July:** The World Bank announces that Japan had the 13th-highest per capita income in 1983. **12–21 July:** Prime Minister Nakasone leaves for a tour of France, Italy, and Belgium to discuss trade issues. **15 August:** Nakasone and his cabinet officially worship at Yasukuni Shrine on the 40th anniversary of Japan's surrender in World War II. **18 September:** The government sets the defense budget at 1.04 percent of GNP, but Nakasone says it will respect the spirit of the 1976 decision to hold defense spending to less than 1 percent of GNP.

1986 15 January: Soviet Union foreign minister Eduard Shevardnadze arrives in Japan, the first visit by a Soviet foreign minister in 10 years, and discusses arms control but rejects the Northern Territories issue. **19 March:** The Tōkyō High Court upholds the legitimacy of the school textbook screening system and dismisses the appeal of Ienaga Saburō filed 20 years ago. **12–15 April:** Prime Minister Nakasone visits Washington to seek economic and defense cooperation. **4–6 May:** Group of Seven leaders meet in Tōkyō and agree to set up a G-7 finance ministers' conference to promote coordination of economic policies. **6 July:** Japan concurrently holds 17th postwar lower house and 14th upper house elections. LDP wins 304 seats in revised 512-seat lower house, the biggest margin since 1969; JSP wins 86 seats, KMT 57, JCP 27, and DSP 26. LDP wins 72 of 126 upper house seats, its largest margin since 1963. **6 September:** In a landslide victory, Doi Takako becomes Japan's first female party leader as JSP secretary-general. **8 September:** Nakasone dismisses Education Minister Fujio Masayuki for his disparaging remarks about Koreans. This is the first time in 33 years that a prime minister fires a cabinet member. **19 September:** The government adopts a ¥3.6 trillion package of economic measures to rejuvenate an economy hard hit by a slump in exports. **16 October:** The UN elects Japan as a member of the Security Council for a two-year term. **2 November:** An opinion poll by the Prime Minister's Office shows nearly 90 percent of Japanese people regard themselves as middle class, but they are not necessarily content with their quality of life.

1987 21 February: Finance Minister Miyazawa Kiichi pledges that the government will take steps to stimulate Japan's domestic economy at a G-7 meeting in Paris. **29 April:** Prime Minister Nakasone visits the United States to discuss economic issues with President Reagan. **26 May:** The balance of Japan's net foreign assets was a record $180 billion in 1986, making Japan the largest creditor nation for the second year. **3 June:** The Nikkei index of the Tōkyō Stock Exchange exceeds 25,000 for the first time. **26 June:** Japan's foreign currency reserves reached $68.6 billion in April, making Japan the world's largest holder of foreign reserves. **27 August:** Prime Minister Nakasone says that sending Japanese SDF on a mine-sweeping mission in the Persian Gulf is constitutional. **3 September:** The International Labour Organization (ILO) reports that Japanese worked 30 percent more hours than workers in other industrialized countries. **21 September:** Prime Minister Nakasone meets President Reagan in New York and addresses the UN General Assembly where he says Japan is prepared to take a positive role in helping end the Iran-Iraq war. **20 October:** Share prices on the Tōkyō Stock Exchange plummet by a record 3,836, or nearly 15 percent, the largest drop ever. **31 October:** The LDP formally elects Takeshita Noboru president with the backing of Nakasone, and he assumes the office of prime minister. **20 November:** Labor organizations form Japan's largest labor federation, the Japanese Trade Union Confederation (Rengō), with 5.39 million members in 55 major unions.

1988 22 April: Land agency minister Okuno Seisuke creates an international furor by claiming that Japan was not the aggressor in the China war in the 1930s. In May, public opinion forces his resignation. **July:** Scandal over insider trading in stocks of real estate subsidiary of Recruit Company starts persistent criticism of Takeshita, Nakasone, Miyazawa, and other politicians in "Recruitgate." **19 October:** Japan and the Soviet Union unsuccessfully end a conference to resolve the issue of the Soviet-held islands known as the Northern Territories. **30 October:** Foreign Minister Uno Sōsuke pledges to the United States that Japan will bear a bigger burden of foreign aid in a non-militaristic role. **8 November:** Japan's per capita savings reaches $38,439, making it the world's leader in individual savings. **7 December:** The Nikkei index of the Tōkyō Stock Exchange breaks the 30,000 level for the first time.

1989 Asian countries form APEC to unite the area. **7 January:** Emperor Hirohito (1901–1989) who had reigned since 1926 dies of duodenal cancer. **4 March:** The Tōkyō District Prosecutor's Office indicts four individuals, including former Recruit Cosmos chairman Ezoe Hiromasa, over the transfer of unlisted shares from Recruit to politicians. **25 April:** Takeshita resigns as prime minister, a victim of Recruitgate and the 3 percent consumption tax. **1 June:** LDP selects Uno Sōsuke as president and later the Diet elects him prime minister. **23 July:** In the 15th postwar House of Councillors elections, LDP loses 33 seats and JSP gains 24; it is the first time LDP loses its majority. **24 July:** Prime Minister Uno resigns due to election loss and a tarnished geisha scandal. **8 August:** LDP elects Kaifu Toshiki as president, and he forms his first cabinet, which includes two women. **August:** Japan has all the world's top ten banks and is the largest creditor nation. **5 October:** The International Institute for Strategic Studies (London) reports that Japan has become the world's second-largest defense spender. **15 December:** The World Bank reports Japan (at $21,040) topped the United States (at $19,780) to rank second in per capita annual income for 1988, behind only Switzerland. **29 December:** The Nikkei index reaches a record high of 38,916, up 29 percent this year.

1990 The government authorizes the SDF at its largest troop number of 274,652. However, the actual number never reaches more than 247,191. **18 February:** Japan holds its 18th lower house elections in which LDP wins 275 seats (54 percent), JSP 136, CGP 45, JCP 16, DSP 14, and independents 21. **26 February:** The Nikkei index plunges 1,569 points to 33,322, the second-largest drop ever. **27 February:** The Diet reelects Kaifu prime minister, and he forms his second cabinet the next day. **6 May:** The Japan Personnel Administration Institute shows that nearly 80 percent of respondent firms now set mandatory retirement age at 60. **9 June:** Japan's 1989 birth rate plummets to an all-time low. **22 June:** The OECD records that with $8.96 billion given last year, Japan surpasses the United States as the world's largest donor of official development assistance (ODA). **24–28 September:** LDP and JSP leaders visit North Korea where Prime Minister Kaifu apologizes for Japan's colonial rule and urges normalization of relations. **19 October:** White paper on crime says Japan experienced 2.26 million crimes last year, a postwar record high. **12 November:** Japan enthrones Akihito as the Heisei Emperor, its 125th. **20 December:** The EPA announces Japan's GNP, $23,296 per capita, is second only to the United States. **28 December:** The Nikkei index ends the year at 23,849, dropping 48 percent from 38,916 at the end of 1989.

1991 The Japanese "bubble economy" bursts with stock prices starting a 10-year decline. **February:** The Japan Socialist Party changes its name to the Social Democratic Party of Japan (SDPJ). **6 April:** The National Defense Academy first admits women. **16–19 April:** Soviet president Mikhail Gorbachev arrives in Tōkyō, the first Soviet head to visit Japan. **24 April:** Japan decides to dispatch Maritime SDF minesweepers to the Persian Gulf. **10–13 August:** Prime Minister Kaifu visits the PRC to normalize relations. He is the first major leader to visit China since the Tiananmen Square incident. **11 September:** Members of antinuclear groups, peace organizations, political opposition parties, and labor unions, as well as local residents—some 4,000 people—protest the arrival of a U.S. aircraft carrier at Yokosuka. **19 September:** The Japanese government approves a SDF peacekeeping operations bill. **24 September:** The EPA confirms continued economic expansion, and the "Heisei Boom" records the 58th month of economic growth extending since December 1986, the longest growth period on record. **5 October:** Kaifu resigns, taking responsibility for having failed in his effort to revise the political reform laws. **27 October:** Miyazawa Kiichi wins the LDP presidential election, and the Diet designates him as prime minister. **27 December:** Japan's organized workers hit a postwar low of 24.5 percent.

1992 7–10 January: President George H. W. Bush meets Miyazawa in Tōkyō for talks on economic issues and to adopt the Tōkyō Declaration on the U.S.-Japan Global Partnership. **13 January:** For the first time ever, a Japanese government spokesman, Cabinet Secretary Katō Kōichi, apologizes for wartime forced prostitution. **6–10 April:** Secretary-General Jiang Zemin arrives in Tōkyō as the first Chinese leader to visit Japan since the Tiananmen Square incident in June 1989. **22 May:** Hosokawa Morihiro announces the formation of a new political party, the Japan New Party (JNP). **26 May:** Japan surpasses Germany to become the world's largest holder of net foreign assets. **26 July:** The LDP makes an impressive showing in the 16th postwar upper house elections, winning 67 of 126 seats. **13 August:** The Nikkei index plunges to a six-year low of 14,768. **28 August:** The government adopts a ¥10.7 trillion economic stimulus package, the largest ever. **14 September:** The government admits, for the first time, that the Japanese army ran brothels during World War II. **16 September:** Three Japanese join a UN peacekeeping mission to monitor Angolan elections, and 423 troops and three vessels go on Cambodian mission. **23–28 October:** The emperor and empress visit the PRC in the first-ever imperial visit. He expresses deep regret over the "great sufferings" Japan inflicted on China.

1993 27 January: The Sumō Association promotes Akebono, an American, to *yokozuna*, the first foreigner to reach the top spot in Japan's national sport. **7 April:** SDF sends 600 troops to Cambodia on a UN peacekeeping operation. **15 May:** Japan's first professional soccer league, the J.League, kicks off its inaugural season. **7–9 July:** Tōkyō hosts the 19th summit of G-7 nations, which calls on members to rescue the world's economy. **18 July:** In the 19th postwar House of Representatives elections, the LDP loses its majority, ending 38 years of continuous rule and forcing the LDP to organize a coalition government. **29 July:** The Japan New Party elects Hosokawa Morihiro as president, and he becomes prime minister as head of a non-LDP coalition of eight parties, the first time LDP has not held power since 1955. **6 August:**

The House of Representatives elects Doi Takako as speaker, the first woman speaker of the house. **15 August:** In his first Diet speech, Hosokawa apologizes to Asian countries for Japan's actions in World War II, the first prime minister to publicly declare Japan the aggressor and express sympathy for the victims. **18 August:** The National Tax Administration Agency discloses the first drop in land values since 1955. **25 September:** The SDPJ elects Murayama Tomiichi its chair. **10 December:** The Ministry of Labor says one in three male university graduates quits his corporate job within 10 years, contradicting the lifetime employment concept.

1994 29 January: Both chambers of the Diet approve political reform bill with 500 seats in the House of Representatives, 300 of which are to be elected in single-seat electoral districts and 200 by proportional representation. **8 April:** Hosokawa suddenly resigns due to allegations about his financial deals. **25 April:** The Diet elects former foreign minister Hata Tsutomu as prime minister; he forms the first minority cabinet in four decades. **25 June:** Prime Minister Hata resigns in the face of a no-confidence vote. **29 June:** Murayama Tomiichi, chairman of the SDPJ, forms a socialist-led coalition government of LDP, SDPJ, and New Party Sakigake. He is the first socialist prime minister since 1947. **14 July:** The Ministry of Health and Welfare confirms Japan has the world's highest life expectancy for the eighth year, 82.51 years for women and 76.25 for men. **18 July:** Prime Minister Murayama, in a dramatic shift, tells the Diet that SDPJ recognizes the SDF as constitutional and necessary. **13 October:** Ōe Kenzaburō receives the Nobel Prize in Literature, only the second Japanese to win this prize. **17 November:** The EPA proclaims that the recession ended in October 1993 after continuing for 30 months, making it the nation's second-longest postwar economic downturn since the 1980–1983 recession. **10 December:** The New Frontier Party, composed of former members of Japan Renewal Party, KMT, and JNP, holds its inaugural convention with 214 Diet members with Kaifu Toshiki as president and Ozawa Ichirō as secretary-general; it becomes the second-largest force in the Diet. **16 December:** Data from the EPA places Japan first among industrialized nations in per capita GDP for 1993 with a figure of $33,764.

1995 17 January: "The Great Hanshin Earthquake," Japan's worst earthquake in 60 years, kills more than 6,000 and destroys about ¥14 trillion in property. **20 March:** Twelve die and 5,500 are hurt in the Tōkyō subways where Aum Shinrikyō, a religious cult, releases sarin nerve gas. **19 April:** The yen rises to ¥79.75 to the US$1 in world trade markets, the highest figure ever. **2 May:** Japanese pitcher Nomo Hideo makes his successful U.S. Major League debut with the Los Angeles Dodgers. Nomo fever sweeps Japan as he becomes the first Japanese to win the National League rookie of the year award. **16 May:** Police arrest Asahara Shōkō, the Aum Shinrikyō leader, and 16 other people for masterminding the Tōkyō subway nerve gas attack. **3 July:** The Nikkei index dips to its lowest level since 1986 when it hits 14,295. **23 July:** Japan holds its 17th postwar upper house elections where LDP wins 46 seats, SDPJ 16, Shinseitō 40, KMT 51, DSP 15, JNP 35, and JCP 15. **15 August:** Prime Minister Maruyama calls Japan's war aggression a mistake on the 50th anniversary of the war's end. He expresses "deep remorse" and offers a "heartfelt apology." **22 September:** Hashimoto Ryūtarō, minister of international trade and industry, wins election as president of LDP. **15–19 November:** The APEC forum holds its summit meeting in Ōsaka and agrees on an agenda to liberalize trade. **28 November:** The Diet approves a new National Defense Program with a stepped-up role in natural disasters and in UN peacekeeping operations. **23 December:** Japan's nominal per capita GDP in 1994 is the highest in the world despite the recession. **27 December:** The Management and Coordination Agency reports the unemployment rate hit 3.4 percent, the highest since 1953 when Japan began keeping such records.

1996 5 January: Prime Minister Murayama Tomiichi resigns, but the three-party ruling coalition continues when Hashimoto Ryūtarō forms a coalition government six days later, becoming the first LDP prime minister in over two years. **16 January:** The Social Democratic Party of Japan reelects Murayama its chairman by 85 percent. **31 January:** An SDF contingent to transport supplies sets off to Israeli-held Golan Heights to help in a UN-sponsored peacekeeping mission. **16 February:** Health and welfare minister Kan Naoto admits the government's responsibility for the spread of the HIV virus among hemophiliacs due to the use of unheated blood products and formally apologizes to the victims. **18 April:** President Bill Clinton visits Japan and, with Prime Minister Hashimoto, works out the Japan-U.S. declaration on security alliance. **29 July:** Hashimoto visits Yasukuni Shrine and signs the register as prime minister, the first such occurrence since Nakasone in 1985. **14 August:** The Asian Women's Fund pays out its first "atonement" money to four former "comfort women," as controversy continues over the government-initiated private effort. **29 September:** Doi Takako formally returns to the helm of the SDPJ and promises to end the LDP coalition. **20 October:** In the 20th postwar House of Representatives elections, LDP wins the first election under a new system of 300 single-seat constituencies and 200 proportional representation seats, but it fails to secure a majority. **7 November:** Hashimoto is reelected prime minister and forms his second cabinet, with all LDP members. **29 November:** Japan's population growth slows to its lowest rate since 1945, with a total of 125,570,246 people.

1997 7 January: Prime Minister Hashimoto leaves for a trip to Southeast Asia, where he proposes expanding top-level dialogue between Japan and ASEAN members. **1 April:** The government increases consumption tax to 5 percent. **26 April:** In an *Asahi Shimbun* survey on the constitution, more than two-thirds say they support the war-renouncing provisions of Article 9. **9 May:** The EPA states that Japan's economy is growing for the 43rd consecutive month, the third longest in the postwar period. **19–21 June:** Prime Minister Hashimoto visits Denver for a G-7 meeting where world leaders urge Japan to stimulate its economy. **29 August:** Ienaga Saburō's 32-year legal school-textbook battle ends with an unprecedented Supreme Court ruling that screeners acted unconstitutionally. **7 September:** Representatives of 19 Asia-Pacific nations and 11 international organizations meet in Kōbe to examine ways to encourage economic development in Asia; called "Eco Asia 97." **24 November:** Yamaichi Securities, one of the nation's top brokerages, announces it will voluntarily shut down; with ¥3.5 trillion in debt, it is the largest corporate failure ever in Japan. **9 December:** The Diet approves a bill establishing a nursing care system for the elderly in 2000. The system, supported through payments from people aged 40 or over, will provide government-sponsored nursing care for the elderly. **11 December:** An international conference on global warming concludes an agreement in Kyōto among 160 nations to reduce greenhouse gas emissions. **16 December:** The EPA reports Japan's per capita GDP in 1996 is $36,521, the third highest after Luxembourg and Switzerland. **30 December:** The Nikkei index closes the year at 15,259, shrinking 21 percent for 1997.

1998 7–23 February: The 18th Winter Olympic Games are held in Nagano Prefecture with approximately 3,500 athletes and officials from 72 countries. Japan wins 10 medals, half of them gold. **27 April:** Four parties, an earlier Democratic Party of Japan, the Good Governance Party, the New Fraternity Party, and the Democratic Reform Party, merge to form the new Democratic Party of Japan (DPJ), headed by the charismatic Kan Naoto. The DPJ, with 93 members in the lower house and 38 in the upper house, offers a middle-of-the-road alternative to the LDP. **18 June:** Japan, which contributed $9.36 billion in 1997, remains the world's top ODA donor for the seventh straight year. **12 July:** Japan holds its 18th postwar House of Councillors elections where LDP suffers a stinging defeat, winning only 44 seats. DPJ wins 27, and JCP garners an all-time high of 15 to become the third-largest party. Hashimoto resigns to take responsibility for the election defeat. **24 July:** Foreign Minister Obuchi Keizō wins the election for the LDP presidency. Six days later, the House of Representatives elects him prime minister. **8 September:** Using frank language, the EPA admits that Japan's economy is in "a prolonged slump, a very severe situation." **7 November:** Two parties backed by the lay Buddhist group Sōka Gakkai, New Peace Party, and Kōmeitō reunite as New Kōmeitō after a four-year separation, creating Japan's second-largest opposition party with 65 seats in the Diet. **16 November:** The government adopts its largest-ever economic stimulus package, totaling ¥24 trillion.

1999 13 January: The LDP and Liberal Party agree to allow Japanese SDF to participate in UN "Peacekeeping Operations" not involving the use of force. **14 January:** The LDP and Liberal Party form a coalition government with Obuchi Keizō as prime minister. **12 February:** The Financial Reconstruction Commission says it will inject ¥7.45 trillion into 15 major banks to strengthen the financial system. **22 July:** The lower house adopts controversial legislation designating the *Hinomaru* Japan's national flag and "Kimigayo" Japan's national anthem. The upper house does likewise on 9 August. **30 July:** The Management and Coordination Agency reports that the jobless rate hit a record 4.9 percent. **5 October:** Obuchi launches a new coalition cabinet with ministers from LDP, the Liberal Party, and the New KMT. Through the coalition the government establishes a majority in the House of Councillors and controls 357 of the 500 seats in the House of Representatives. **24 December:** *Asahi Shimbun* reports that 80 percent of the 50 largest companies use a performance and ability system to determine wage scales.

2000 6 February: Ōta Fusae becomes Japan's first female governor by winning the election in Ōsaka. **3 March:** Japan calls for a change in the dues structure of the UN where it presently pays 20.6 percent of the total, second only to the United States' 25 percent but more than the rest of the Security Council members together. **2 April:** Prime Minister Obuchi falls into a coma and dies 12 days later. **5 April:** LDP selects Mori Yoshirō as its president and thus prime minister. He cements the ruling coalition and reappoints all the Obuchi cabinet. **25 June:** Japan holds its 21st postwar House of Representatives elections. LDP wins 233 seats and DPJ 127 of the 480 seats, giving the DPJ a major boost. **4 July:** The LDP, New KMT, and New Conservative Party again elect Mori Yoshirō as prime minister. **21–23 July:** G-8 Summit takes place in Okinawa where leaders issue the G-8 Communiqué Okinawa 2000, the first official summit document to call for reform of the UN Security Council. **5 August:** Japan puts into operation a national computerized registry of all citizens who are each assigned an 11-digit number. **24 September:** At the 2000 Olympic Games in Sydney, Australia, Takahashi Naoko wins the women's marathon in 2 hours, 23 minutes, and 14 seconds to set a new Olympic record and become the first Japanese woman to win a track and field gold medal. **13 December:** Ozawa Ichirō wins reelection as leader of the opposition Liberal Party, which adopts a platform calling for a revision of the war-renouncing Constitution, the first major party to favor its amendment.

2001 6 January: Government reorganization, the first major overhaul since 1949, streamlines offices and gives the prime minister more power and reduces the cabinet ministries and agencies from 23 to 13. **6 April:** Prime Minister Mori resigns. **26 April:** The Diet elects LDP president Koizumi Jun'ichirō as prime minister. He names only a few cabinet members from the three main factions, chooses a record-high five female ministers, and selects several younger Diet members and nonpoliticians. **21 June:** The Council of Economic and Fiscal Policy finalizes Prime Minister Koizumi's economic reform guidelines with a call for final disposal of bad loans and seven key reform programs. **30 June:** Prime Minister Koizumi meets with President George W. Bush at Camp David where they emphasize the U.S.-Japan partnership. **29 July:** Japan holds its 19th postwar House of Councillors elections. LDP wins a landslide victory when it garners 64 of the 121 contested seats. **13 August:** Prime Minister Koizumi visits Yasukuni Shrine arousing great protest in Korea and China. **11 September:** Japan gets first reports of the 9/11 terrorist attacks in the United States. Koizumi quickly convenes his national security panel and pledges help. **15 October:** Koizumi visits Seoul and apologizes for his country's brutal colonial past. **29 October:** The upper house votes to allow use of SDF to support U.S. troops against terrorism despite the objections of opposition parties. **14 November:** Suzuki Ichirō receives the American League Rookie of the Year Award after leading in batting average (.350), hits (242, the most in the majors in 71 years), and stolen bases. A week later he wins the league's Most Valuable Player Award. **28 December:** Japan's unemployment rate reaches a record high of 5.5 percent.

2002 1 April: Crime, an indicator of social alienation, jumps by 60 percent since 1996. **April:** Fiscal year 2001 is the worst for bankruptcies in 18 years and the second worst on record. **21 May:** The lower house approves ratification of the Kyōto Protocol on prevention of global warming, and the upper house approves on 30 May. **31 May:** Japan and South Korea begin cohosting the World Cup soccer tournament; it is the first World Cup held in Asia and the first cohosted tournament. **May:** Japan introduces the five-day school week, but some groups prepare "Saturday school" classes to offset the loss of educational time. **17 September:** Prime Minister Koizumi travels to North Korea, the first Japanese premier to do so, for talks on normalization of relations. North Korea admits kidnapping 11 Japanese since the late 1970s. **26 October:** Consumer prices fall nationwide for the 35th consecutive month as deflation continues. **5 November:** Prime Minister Koizumi attends an ASEAN meeting in Cambodia where he pledges increased trade. **28 November:** Nonsmoking zones appear outside some public places in Japan; 50 percent of Japanese men, but only 14 percent of women, smoke. **29 November:** Japan's public-sector debt level—at 140 percent of GDP—is the highest in the industrial world. **3 December:** Hatoyama Ichirō resigns as president of the DPJ. A week later, the DPJ elects Kan Naoto. **13 December:** Japanese elementary and junior high school students' performances on standardized tests decline, especially in math and social studies. **31 December:** The Nikkei index drops to 8,579, a 20-year low.

2003 29 January: The Sumō Association promotes Mongolian-born Asashōryū to *yokozuna* (68th), only the third foreigner after Akebono and Musashimaru. **1 April:** Japan charges that North Korea fired a test missile over its airspace. **16 April:** Japan launches the Industrial Revitalization Corporation, a government-backed entity to assist businesses in financial difficulty. **30 May:** Koizumi meets with Hu Jintao, president of the PRC; they agree to cooperate in dealing with the North Korean nuclear threat. **7 June:** Japan's parliament passes a series of war contingency bills that give the government significantly increased military powers. **26 July:** Despite strong resistance from the opposition, the Diet adopts the Iraq Reconstruction Assistance Law allowing Japan to send troops to Iraq. **24 September:** The Liberal Party chaired by Ozawa Ichirō formally agrees to merge with and adopt the name of the Democratic Party of Japan (DPJ) headed by Kan Naoto. **9 November:** The DPJ makes major gains in the lower house elections, increasing its seats from 127 to 177. The LDP and its coalition partners, the New KMT and New Conservative Party, drop from 287 to 275 seats but still hold a solid majority. The SDP and JCP are the biggest losers. **13 November:** Doi Takako steps down as SDP president to take responsibility for her party's poor election performance. SDP elects Fukushima Mizuho as its new leader. **12 December:** Prime Minister Koizumi meets with leaders of 10 ASEAN member countries and signs the Tōkyō Declaration, pledging to expand cooperation.

2004 14 January: An advance team of SDF leaves for Iraq, the first Japanese troops deployed since World War II; the 550 SDF troops provide medical relief and water purification. **22 January:** Toyota becomes the world's second-largest automobile manufacturer with 6.78 million vehicles in 2003, behind General Motors' 8.59 million. **27 February:** Court sentences Asahara Shōkō, leader of the Aum Shinrikyō cult that released the deadly sarin gas in the Tōkyō subways, to death. **10 May:** Prompted by gaps in his payments into the public pension system, DPJ president Kan Naoto resigns as head of the main opposition party. **11 May:** Some 54 of the Diet's 725 members admit failing to pay their mandatory pension premiums since 1986 when Japan adopted the national pension fund. **21 May:** Prime Minister Koizumi visits North Korea and meets with Kim Jong-il to secure the release of Japanese kidnapped 20 years ago. **1 June:** Japan now has 15 million subscribers to high-speed internet connection services, making Japan the second largest after the United States. **25 June:** Japan states that its outstanding debt rose to 1.4 times the country's GDP in 2003, the highest in the industrialized world. **11 July:** Japan holds its 20th postwar upper house elections where the LPD wins 49 of 121 seats while the opposition DPJ wins 50 seats, giving it 82. **7 August:** Prime Minister Koizumi's top policy panel unveils plans to privatize Japan's mammoth postal operations into four separate entities. **1 October:** Suzuki Ichirō breaks the 84-year-old Major League record for the most hits (257) in a single season. **1 November:** Japan hosts an international conference to expand exports from Africa to Asia with representatives of 60 countries.

2005 18 January: The Japan Iron and Steel Federation says Japan's crude steel production in 2004 rose to 112.68 million tons, the highest in 30 years. **26 January:** China surpasses the United States as Japan's top trading partner for the first time, accounting for 20.1 percent as compared to 18.6 percent for the United States. **25 March:** The 2005 World Exposition opens at Seto in Aichi Prefecture for six months. **22 April:** Prime Minister Koizumi Jun'ichirō expresses "deep remorse" and conveys a "heartfelt apology" for Japanese wartime atrocities during a speech at the Asia-Africa Conference. **4 May:** The number of children under 15 years of age in Japan falls for the 24th year in a row to an estimated 17.65 million to reach its lowest level since the census began in 1920. **11 September:** In a landslide victory, the LDP sweeps 296 of the 480 seats in the lower house. **21 September:** The Diet reelects Koizumi as prime minister. **14 October:** A set of bills to privatize the Japan Post, the centerpiece of Prime Minister Koizumi's reform initiatives, clears the upper house and becomes law. **26 October:** Japan and the United States realign military bases in Japan, including plans to relocate the Marine Corps' Futenma Air Station in Okinawa. **24 November:** A government panel on imperial succession recognizes female imperial family members as candidates for succession.

2006 20 March: Japan beats Cuba 10–6 in the championship game of the inaugural World Baseball Classic. **1 June:** According to the Ministry of Health, Labor, and Welfare, Japan's total fertility rate falls to a record low of 1.25 in 2005, the lowest in Japanese history and for any major country. **29 June:** Prime Minister Koizumi and U.S. president George W. Bush talk in Washington, issuing a joint declaration to emphasize the importance of Japan-U.S. ties. **30 June:** Japan reports that the population aged 65 or older reaches 21 percent, Japan's and the world's highest. **17 July:** Ground SDF troops complete withdrawal from Samawah, Iraq, ending humanitarian and reconstruction assistance. **15 August:** Prime Minister Koizumi visits Yasukuni Shrine, drawing protests from China and South Korea. **6 September:** Princess Kiko, the wife of the emperor's second son, gives birth to a boy, Hisahito, providing the imperial family with its first male heir in years. **20 September:** Chief Cabinet Secretary Abe Shinzō wins the ruling LDP's presidential election. **26 September:** The Diet elects LDP president Abe Shinzō as prime minister, and he forms a cabinet. **8 October:** Abe visits the PRC for talks with President Hu Jintao and Premier Wen Jiabao where the leaders agree that the two nations should build a strategic, mutually beneficial relationship. **12 October:** In its monthly economic review, the government maintains that "the economy is recovering." The current economic expansion stretches into its 57th month, the longest postwar expansion.

2007 9 January: For the first time since 1945, Japan upgrades the Defense Agency to ministerial status and appoints Kyuma Fumio as director-general. **26 February:** The Nikkei index hits a 21st-century high to date of 18,300. **11 April:** Prime Minister Abe and Chinese premier Wen Jiabao, the first Chinese premier to visit Japan since 2000, encourage economic cooperation. **3 May:** Foreign Minister Asō Tarō holds talks with his Russian counterpart, agreeing to strengthen strategic relations in the development of oil resources in Russian territory. **9 June:** The Japanese government adopts measures to reduce the suicide rate of more than 30,000 annually, the highest in the industrialized world. **25 June:** The national debt rises to a record ¥834 trillion, the largest in the world, at the end of fiscal year 2006. **29 July:** The Liberal Democratic Party suffers a major defeat in an upper house election, winning only 37 seats, while the DPJ wins 59 and becomes the largest party. **7 August:** The DPJ elects Eda Satsuki as president of the upper house. **21 August:** Prime Minister Abe visits India to promote economic and political ties. **12 September:** Prime Minister Abe, plagued by scandals, electoral defeat, and opposition to support of American military actions, abruptly resigns. **23 September:** The LDP elects Fukuda Yasuo as party president, and the Diet names him prime minister. **19 November:** Japan and the ASEAN members sign an economic agreement. **20 November:** A new law goes into effect by which Japan takes fingerprints and photographs of foreign nationals when they enter the country. **4 December:** Japanese first-year high school students rank lower than previously in all subjects in an international assessment survey conducted by the OECD. **26 December:** The Japanese economy accounts for 9.1 percent of the world's GDP in 2006, the lowest in 24 years.

2008 1 January: The Health Ministry estimates that 1.09 million babies were born in Japan in 2007, the second fewest in the postwar period. **11 January:** The government passes a special law authorizing its navy to resume a refueling mission in the Indian Ocean as part of the American-led military effort in Afghanistan. **22 January:** The Nikkei index plunges 5.7 percent on this day and has lost a third of its value since July 2007. **3 April:** The lower house approves a special bill setting the Japanese share of the cost of U.S. military forces stationed in Japan. **7 May:** Chinese president Hu Jintao visits Prime Minister Fukuda, the first visit by a Chinese leader in a decade; they jointly issue a statement agreeing to cooperate in environmental and energy matters while improving relations. **13 August:** The government announces that Japan's economy contracted 0.6 percent in the April–June quarter, reinforcing views that Japan's economy had slipped into a recession after its longest postwar expansion. **21 August:** The finance minister announces that exports to China reached ¥1.28 trillion in July, topping shipments to the United States for the first time since the end of World War II. **24 August:** The Beijing Olympics ends with Japan winning 25 medals. **18 September:** The Land Ministry data shows that the average nationwide land prices as of 1 July fell 1.2 percent from a year earlier, the 17th straight year of decline. **22 September:** Asō Tarō is elected president of the ruling Liberal Democratic Party and launches a new cabinet two days later. **25 September:** According to the Finance Ministry, Japan's trade balance in August fell to ¥324 billion in the red, the first time in 26 years for Japan to post a trade deficit in a month other than January, when exports fall during the New Year holidays. **10 October:** 225-issue Nikkei index tumbles to 8,276 at the close, down 881 points or nearly 10 percent from the previous day and marking its third-steepest decline ever. The Nikkei index has dropped 46 percent for the year 2008. **18 October:** Japan, the second-largest contributor to the United Nations budget after the United States, is elected to a two-year seat on the United Nations Security Council. **23 October:** Japan's trade surplus falls 94.1 percent year on year to ¥95.1 billion in September alone, or 85.6 percent, to ¥802.0 billion in the first half of fiscal year 2008 from a year earlier, the lowest level in 26.5 years, says the Finance Ministry. **24 October:** The 225-issue Nikkei index plunges to 7,649.08 at the market close, down ¥811.90 from the previous day, nearing the level recorded immediately after the collapse of the economic bubble. **28 October:** Share prices on the Tōkyō Stock Market "hit a 26-year low and are down 50 percent this year." **31 October:** Japan plans a $51 billion stimulus package to the economy, the second stimulus package in two months. **17 November:** Japan's economy, the world's second largest, is in recession. For the first time since 2001, Japan's economy contracted for two consecutive quarters, the definition of a recession. **12 December:** Prime Minister Asō Tarō announces emergency measures totaling ¥23 trillion to deal with worsening economic and employment conditions, including ¥1 trillion in reserve funds that the government may use at its discretion. **14 December:** Leaders of Japan, China, and South Korea meet in Dazaifu, Japan, to promote measures to deal with the East Asian economic crisis. This is the first such independent summit.

2009 6 February: The government acknowledges the world's largest public debt of nearly $10 trillion or 180 percent of its annual economy. **16 February:** Japan's economic minister acknowledges the worst recession in the postwar period with a 13.1 percent quarterly drop, the worst since 1974. **1 April:** The government admits that the Tankan Report has slipped to its lowest level since its inception in 1974. **9 April:** The government adopts a $154 billion stimulus package. **16 May:** Democratic Party of Japan elects Hatoyama Yukio, former secretary-general of the main opposition party, as its new president. **20 May:** Economic leaders admit that Japan's real gross domestic product shrank by an annualized 15.2 percent in the January–March period, the steepest postwar decline. **21 May:** A survey released by the Labor Ministry shows the average household income in Japan fell 1.9 percent on the year to ¥5.56 million in 2007, the lowest level in 19 years. **6 August:** Prime Minister Asō Tarō signs a document making all 306 plaintiffs who have sought recognition as suffering from atomic bombing–related illnesses eligible for a government relief package. **28 August:** The Ministry of Internal Affairs and Communications reports that Japan's seasonally adjusted unemployment rate rose 0.3 percentage points month on month to 5.7 percent in July, surpassing the previous record high set six years and three months earlier. **31 August:** The Democratic Party of Japan defeats the Liberal Democratic Party in a landslide vote for the 45th House of Representatives election. **17 September:** Hatoyama Yukio takes office as prime minister. **28 September:** The Liberal Democratic Party elects Tanigaki Sadakazu its 24th president as he becomes the opposition leader. **28 September:** Japan, China, and South Korea hold a meeting of foreign ministers in Shanghai, in which the three participants agree to work together toward the formation of an East Asian community. **7 November:** The Yomiuri Giants of the Central League win the Japan Series professional baseball championship for the first time in seven years, and the 21st title overall. **13 November:** U.S. president Barack Obama visits Prime Minister Hatoyama Yukio in Japan where the two leaders agree to strengthen the Japan-U.S. alliance and to relieve the pressure of the U.S. Marine base in Futenma on Okinawa. **27 November:** The yen, at ¥85 to the US$1, reaches a 14-year high against the dollar; not since April 1995 was the yen higher than ¥79 to the US$1. **9 December:** Prime Minister Hatoyama Yukio promotes an $81 billion stimulus plan.

2010 19 January: As the day marks the 50th anniversary of the signing of their security treaty, Japan and the United States issue a joint statement saying their alliance remains the anchor of regional stability. **19 January:** Japan Airlines Corporation files with the Tōkyō District Court for bankruptcy protection. **26 January:** The National Police Agency announces that the number of suicides in Japan grew 1.6 percent on the year to 32,753 in 2009, topping 30,000 for the 12th consecutive year. **27 January:** The Ministry of Finance reports that Japan's exports rose 12.1 percent year on year to ¥5.41 trillion in December, their first increase in 15 months. **29 January:** The Japan Automobile Manufacturers Association reports that domestic automobile production plunged 31.5 percent to 7.93 million units in 2009, marking the sharpest decline on record and dipping below eight million units for the first time in 33 years. **15 February:** The Cabinet Office reports that Japan's real-term GDP grew an annualized 4.6 percent in the October–December period for the third consecutive quarter of expansion. **26 February:** The Ministry of Internal Affairs and Communications reports that Japan's consumer price index, excluding perishable food prices, fell 1.3 percent year on year in January, the 11th consecutive month of decline. **2 March:** The Ministry of Internal Affairs reports Japan's unemployment rate declined to 4.9 percent in January, falling below 5 percent for the first time in nearly a year. **18 March:** The Japan Automobile Manufacturers Association says it projects domestic sales of new automobiles to shrink to 4.64 million units in fiscal year 2010, which would be the fewest since about 4.23 million cars were sold in fiscal year 1977. **24 March:** The fiscal 2010 budget, worth a record ¥92.29 trillion in general-account expenditures, is approved by the upper house of the Diet. **26 March:** A bill to provide monthly benefits to families with children is enacted, with passage by the upper house of the Diet. **30 May:** The Social Democratic Party leaves its coalition with the Democratic Party of Japan over the American air bases decision, thus voiding the DPJ's two-thirds majority necessary to guarantee passage of bills rejected by the upper house. **2 June:** Prime Minister Hatoyama announces his resignation. **8 June:** Kan Naoto becomes Japan's fifth prime minister in four years. **11 July:** The Democratic Party of Japan loses 10 seats in the House of Councillors election and its three coalition partners, thus costing the DPJ its majority. **14 September:** Kan Naoto is reelected leader of the Democratic Party of Japan and thus prime minister, defeating Ozawa Ichirō. **7 December:** The spacecraft *Akatsuki* reaches Venus but fails to enter orbit around the planet.

2011 13 January: The United States secretary of defense, Robert M. Gates, meets with Prime Minister Kan Naoto and Japanese foreign and defense officials and agrees to follow Tōkyō's lead in working to relocate the American base on Okinawa, discusses a sophisticated new antimissile system, and consults with Japan concerning North Korea. **26 January:** Toyota, the world's largest automaker, announces that it will recall 1.7 million vehicles because of defective fuel lines and high-pressure fuel pumps. **15 February:** The Bank of Japan raises its assessment of the country's economy for the first time in nine months as exports and production improve. **11 March:** The Great East Japan Earthquake, also called the Fukushima or Tōhoku Earthquake, with a magnitude of 9.0, devastates Fukushima Prefecture. The quake triggers a huge tsunami that causes tremendous destruction, damages the Tōkyō Electric Power Company, and melts down and releases radiation from all four units. The catastrophe causes nearly 16,000 deaths and another 3,000 people still missing. **18 May:** Economists report that Japan's economy shrank at an annual rate of 3.7 percent in the first quarter of 2011, tipping the country into a recession. **1 June:** International nuclear regulators issue a critical report saying Japan underestimated the danger of tsunamis and failed to prepare adequate backup systems at the Fukushima Daiichi Nuclear Plant. **1 July:** The Tankan Report for April–June shows that large Japanese manufacturers' confidence in Japan's economy dropped drastically after the devastating Tōhoku Earthquake. **17 July:** The Japanese women's soccer team, known as Nadeshiko, wins the Women's World Cup in Germany, defeating the United States on a penalty shoot-out after a 2–2 tie. **29 July:** The Japanese government, desperate to pull the economy out of a massive recession, proposes an aggressive plan to spend $167 billion over the next five years to generate a swift recovery. **26 August:** Prime Minister Kan Naoto announces his resignation after just 15 months in office. He is the sixth prime minister to step down in the past five years. **29 August:** Finance Minister Noda Yoshihiko is elected the new head of the Democratic Party of Japan and is confirmed as prime minister the next day. He faces the problems of cleaning up the Fukushima Earthquake mess, a stagnant economy, a huge national debt, and a yen that is overly strong. **21 November:** Fukuoka Softbank Hawks capture the Japan National Baseball title, their first in eight years. **25 November:** Hakuhō wins his 21st sumō championship in Fukuoka. **25 December:** Prime Minister Noda Yoshihiko goes to Beijing for a two-day state visit focusing on improving bilateral ties and the dangers of North Korea.

2012 18 January: Yu Darvish, a highly talented pitcher with the Hokkaidō Nippon Ham Fighters, signs a six-year deal for $60 million with the Texas Rangers. **25 January:** Japan reports its first annual trade deficit in 31 years due to surges in fuel imports in the wake of the Fukushima nuclear disaster. **18 February:** Emperor Akihito has coronary artery bypass surgery. **8 March:** Itō Daiki, with a ski jump of 463 feet, wins his fourth World Cup in Trondheim, Norway. **26 April:** The United States and Japan reach an agreement to reduce the number of Marines on Okinawa by 9,000 and begin returning land, thus easing a long-simmering dispute. **27 April:** The Bank of Japan increases expenditures by $62 billion to continue its inflation target and thus jump-start the country's long-stagnant economy. **5 May:** Japan shuts down the last of its nuclear reactors, making it without atomic power for the first time in 42 years. **13 May:** East Asia's three leading economies—China, Japan, and South Korea—agree to seek ways to strengthen regional trading ties and work to ease political tensions. **16 June:** Prime Minister Noda Yoshihiko and his Democratic Party of Japan agree with the country's two largest opposition parties, the Liberal Democratic Party and the New Kōmeitō Party, to attack the growing debt problem by doubling the country's consumption tax. **29 June:** Tens of thousands of demonstrators protest the government's decision to restart a nuclear power plant. Two days later, officials at a western plant reactivate the reactor for the first time since the

Fukushima disaster. **12 August:** Japan's government announces its economic growth slowed to an annual rate of 1.4 percent in the second quarter. **26 September:** Former prime minister Abe Shinzō is elected to lead the Liberal Democratic Party, the main opposition group in Japan. **16 October:** Authorities arrest two U.S. sailors charged with raping a woman in Okinawa. The incident fans anger over the presence of American forces on the islands. **2 November:** For the 14th straight day, Chinese patrol ships enter waters around the disputed island group in the East China Sea, causing further rifts between Japan and China. **14 November:** Prime Minister Noda Yoshihiko announces that he is ready to dissolve parliament and calls for a December election. **16 December:** The Japanese people hand the Liberal Democratic Party a landslide victory. Prime Minister Noda has not been successful in cleaning up the Fukushima Earthquake mess, or solving the problems of a stagnant economy, a huge national debt, *and* a yen that is overly strong. **25 December:** Prime Minister Noda Yoshihiko resigns, and Abe Shinzō becomes prime minister for the second time.

2013 7 January: Japan, with the world's sixth-largest military budget and one of Asia's most advanced militaries, announces that it will increase its defense spending. **13 January:** Japan approves a $116 billion economic stimulus package on public works and disaster mitigation. **16 January:** Prime Minister Abe Shinzō makes his first official visit overseas to Vietnam, Thailand, and Indonesia. **28 January:** Toyota surpasses General Motors and Volkswagen to regain the title as the world's top-selling automaker in 2012. **1 February:** The Nikkei has its best week in 54 years when the stock index rallies for the 12th straight week. **13 February:** The Japanese economy shrinks and remains in recession. However, 2012 recorded a 1.9 percent growth after a .6 percent contraction in 2011. **22 February:** Japan and the United States reaffirm their close ties. Prime Minister Abe meets President Barack Obama at the White House. **17 March:** Itō Toyō wins the Pritzker Prize, architecture's top award. **4 April:** The United States and Japan agree on returning land in Okinawa. With a timetable for returning 2,500 acres as early as 2022, both countries hope that Okinawans will drop their opposition to the air base. **4 April:** Tōkyō Skytree, at 2,080 feet, sets a new record for the world's tallest freestanding tower. **15 May:** The Nikkei breaks 15,000 for the first time since 2007. **1 July:** Japan's business sentiment hits its highest point in two years when the Bank of Japan's *Tankan Report* rose to 4 from a negative 8 in the previous quarter. **21 July:** The LDP wins 65 of the 121 seats being contested and, with 11 seats won by Kōmeitō in the House of Councillors election, strengthens the party's grip and promises to accelerate changes in Japan's economy. Altogether the LDP coalition has a majority in the 242-seat chamber. **24 July:** President Barack Obama nominates Caroline Kennedy to be the U.S. ambassador to Japan. She is sworn in as the U.S.

envoy to Japan, the first woman to serve as the American ambassador. **9 August:** Japan's debt reaches $10 trillion. **21 August:** Suzuki Ichirō gets his 4,000th hit in Major League baseball. He has 2,722 hits with the Mariners and Yankees and 1,278 hits in Japan. **7 September:** The selection of Tōkyō to host the 2020 Olympic games brings hope for renewal in Japan, but it also brings a host of challenges. **15 September:** Wladimir Balentien of the Yakult Swallows breaks Oh Sadaharu's single-season home run record of 55 set in 1964 (also shared with Tuffy Rhodes and Alex Cabrera) with 57 home runs. **26 December:** Prime Minister Abe Shinzō visits Tōkyō's controversial Yasukuni Shrine, reigniting strong criticism in China, South Korea, and other countries.

2014 17 January: Prime Minister Abe Shinzō visits Mozambique, the Ivory Coast, and Ethiopia. **19 January:** Nago residents reelect Mayor Inamine Susumu, a leftist who continues to block the move of the U.S. Marine Corps Air Station Futenma to Henoko, a small fishing village in his city. **22 January:** Prime Minister Abe plays a major role in the World Economic Forum that meets in Davos, Switzerland. He champions his success called "Abenomics" with its big fiscal stimulus. **22 January:** The New York Yankees purchase the contract of Tanaka Masahiro—owner of a startling 24–0 record and a 1.25 ERA in 2013 in Japan—for a sum of $155 million over seven years. **14 February:** Hanyu Yuzuru, a 19-year-old figure skater from Sendai, becomes the youngest men's Olympic champion since Dick Button in 1948. **19 February:** Prime Minister Abe's nationalistic remarks send a chill to Japan's relations with the United States. Abe's right-wing government tries to stir up patriotism while glossing over Japan's wartime history. **22 February:** Japan and the United States take part in military exercises in California. The United States seems to be increasingly allied with Japan over China's flexing its military muscle. **3 March:** Diplomats from Japan and North Korea talk for two hours in Shenyang, China, the first dialogue since North Korea tested a rocket in December 2012. **1 April:** The International Court of Justice rules against Japan in its quest to continue whale hunting. Japan's "research" is considered to be mere commercial whaling. **1 April:** Prime Minister Abe decides to discard the half-century ban on the export of weapons and military hardware. **22 April:** About 150 conservative lawmakers led by Prime Minister Abe visit Yasukuni Shrine, angering Japan's neighbors and frustrating the coming visit of President Barack Obama the next day. **23 April:** President Obama, the first American leader to visit in nearly 20 years, arrives in Tōkyō on his four-country tour of Asia. **21 May:** Tanaka Masahiro loses his first game after 21 months and 42 starts. This Japanese pitcher, now with the New York Yankees, went 24–0 in Japan with the Rakuten Golden Eagles and won six straight with the Yankees. **1 July:** Prime Minister Abe announces a reinterpretation of the country's pacifist Constitution, freeing its military for a more assertive role in East Asia for the first time in 60 years. **3 September:** In reshuffling his cabinet, Prime Minister Abe names five women to leadership posts, an effort to raise the status of women. **8 September:** Tennis star Nishikori Kei, the first Japanese man to reach a Grand Slam singles final, makes it to the finals of the U.S. Open but loses in the championship match. **25 September:** Prime Minister Abe addresses the United Nations and attempts to counter the deep-seated anger among Asia-Pacific countries over his government's militaristic shift. **1 October:** The volcano Mount Ontake, one of Japan's most celebrated peaks near Ōtaki, Japan, erupts. This is the worst volcanic disaster in recent history with 47 people known dead. **10 November:** Prime Minister Abe Shinzō and Chinese president Xi Jinping meet and promise to work toward a "mutually beneficial" relationship. **18 November:** Prime Minister Abe calls for early elections, causing fears that his "Abenomics" program, the high-profile program for economic revival, is failing. **14 December:** Abe's Liberal Democratic Party, winning 291 of 475 seats, scores a landslide victory in the snap parliamentary election.

2015 24 January: ISIS decapitates Japanese hostage Yukawa Haruna. A few days later, ISIS beheads Gotō Kenji, a journalist. **8 February:** Ishiba Shigeru, holder of the new cabinet post of overcoming population decline and revitalizing the regional economy, reports that rural Japan is shrinking in population and families are even abandoning ancestral graves. **15 February:** The Cabinet Office announces that Japan emerged from recession at the end of 2014. **21 March:** Japan, China, and South Korea hold talks for the first time in three years. Their greatest concern is stopping North Korea's nuclear weapons program. **9 April:** Emperor Akihito and Empress Michiko visit the remote island of Peleliu to offer flowers and prayers to mark the coming 70th anniversary of World War II. **22 April:** Prime Minister Abe Shinzō meets with China's President Xi Jinping in Indonesia, a signal of slight warming in relations between the two Asian powers. **27 April:** President Barack Obama welcomes Prime Minister Abe to Washington where they reach an accord to tighten defense cooperation and to reduce trade barriers. **29 April:** Abe Shinzō is the first Japanese prime minister to address a joint meeting of the U.S. Congress. He praises Japan's "quantum leap" in economic reforms but offers no specific concessions as he appeals to skeptical lawmakers concerning the Trans-Pacific Partnership arrangement. **22 June:** The ruling coalition—the Liberal Democratic Party and its junior coalition partner Kōmeitō—extends the parliamentary session by an unprecedented 95 days, the longest under the postwar constitution, seeking to expand Japan's defense powers. **24 June:** The Bank of Japan announces that its loan support program to financial institutions is about to hit the $241 billion mark, roughly a fourfold increase over two years. **16 July:** The Japanese Diet votes to allow

Japan's military to exercise limited powers to fight in foreign conflicts, the first time since World War II. **11 August:** Four years after the disaster at Fukushima, an electric utility company restarts its nuclear reactor in Kagoshima Prefecture. Most of Japan's 48 nuclear reactors have been shuttered since the Fukushima accident. **14 August:** Prime Minister Abe reiterates Japan's official remorse for the catastrophe of World War II on the 70th anniversary of the war's end. **18 September:** Japan's parliament approves an overseas combat role for its military. **29 September:** In speaking to the United Nations, Prime Minister Abe Shinzō announces that Japan will triple its aid to Mideast refugees. **28 December:** South Korea and Japan reach a landmark agreement to resolve their dispute over Korean women forced to serve as sex slaves for the Japanese army. In the agreement, Japan apologizes and promises a payment of $8.3 million.

2016 26 January: Kotoshōgiku wins the January sumō tournament, the first Japanese to win in ten years. **4 February:** Ministers from the 12 member countries sign the Trans-Pacific Partnership in Auckland, New Zealand. **12 February:** Share prices plummet on the Tōkyō Stock Exchange amid serious concerns about the global economic outlook. The Nikkei closes at 14,952.61, dropping below 15,000 for the first time since October 2014. **27 March:** The Democratic Party of Japan and the Japan Innovation Party merge to become the Democratic Party (Minshintō), the largest opposition force with 156 politicians in both houses. **10–11 April:** The Group of Seven foreign ministers meet in Hiroshima. **16 April:** Earthquakes rock southern Kyūshū, killing at least 40 people, injuring about 1,000 more, and causing widespread damage. **4 May:** The Ministry of Internal Affairs and Communications releases data showing the ratio of children through age 14 to the overall population slipped to a record-low 12.6 percent, down for the 42nd consecutive year. **12 May:** Japan announces that its current account surplus doubled in fiscal year 2015 from the previous year to $166 billion. **27 May:** President Barack Obama visits Hiroshima, the first sitting president to do so. **9 June:** At a Group of Seven summit in Ise-Shima, Prime Minister Abe pledges to invest $200 billion in the coming five years to build roads, power plants, and ports around the world. **15 June:** Suzuki Ichirō gets his 4,256th career hit (Japan and the United States combined), which moves him past Pete Rose as the all-time hit leader in pro baseball. **19 June:** Tens of thousands of people in Okinawa protest American military bases in the largest demonstrations in 20 years. **11 July:** The Liberal Democratic Party and its allies capture two-thirds of the seats in the House of Councillors election. **13 July:** The Ministry of Internal Affairs and Communications announces that Japan's population had dropped to 125,891,742. **31 July:** Tōkyō elects Koike Yuriko as its first female governor. She asks for greater transparency and a reexamination of the ballooning costs of the 2020 Summer Olympics. **6 August:** Swimming star Hagino Kosuke wins the Olympic 400-meter individual medley, a first for any Japanese swimmer. **8 August:** Emperor Akihito speaks publicly for the first time of his desire to step down as emperor. **19 August:** SMAP, the aging boy band popular for thirty years in Japan, announces that it is dissolving its longest-running music group. **25 August:** Prime Minister Abe leaves for Kenya to attend the Japan-led African development conference. Soon after, Japan hosts the Sixth Tōkyō International Conference on African Development. **1 September:** Saudi Arabia's Deputy Crown Prince Mohammed bin Salman meets Prime Minister Abe Shinzō in Tōkyō where Japan agrees to support efforts to transform his country. **3 September:** At a meeting in Vladivostok, Prime Minister Abe implores Russia's President Vladimir Putin to settle disputes over the Northern Territories. **5 September:** China's President Xi Jinping welcomes Prime Minister Abe Shinzō to Hangzhou, China, where they resume talks after an 18-month interruption. **13 September:** Japan's Welfare Ministry announces that Japan's centenarian population has reached a record high of 65,692 people with 87 percent of them being females. **15 September:** The Democratic Party selects Murata Renhō, known simply as Renhō, as its leader, making the 48-year-old House of Councillors member the first woman to lead Japan's main opposition party. **22 September:** Prime Minister Abe visits Cuba and meets with President Raul Castro where they discuss the expansion of bilateral trade. **6 November:** India's Prime Minister Narendra Modi visits Japan and receives economic assistance for an Indian bullet train and nuclear power technology. **17 November:** Prime Minister Abe Shinzō meets with president-elect Donald Trump in New York, the first major leader to meet the new president. **15 December:** A special government panel approves a one-time exception to the abdication rule opening the way for Emperor Akihito to retire. **23 December:** Japan adopts an all-time high defense budget of $43.6 billion for fiscal year 2017.

2017 10 January: Japan's land, infrastructure, transport, and tourism minister reports that Japan hosted more than 24 million foreign visitors in 2016, a record for the fifth straight year. **12 January:** Prime Minister Abe Shinzō announces a five-year $8.66 billion foreign aid package for the Philippines just prior to his visit. **31 January:** The Ministry of Health, Labor, and Welfare reports that Japan's job availability hit a 25-year high with unemployment at a 22-year low. **2 February:** The Japan Sumō Association promotes Kisenosato to the rank of Grand Champion (*yokozuna*), the first Japanese-born man to reach this rank since 1998. **16 February:** Takanashi Sara, Japan's premier ski-jump champion, won her 53rd World Cup event, topping the all-time record for men or women. **6 March:** The Liberal Democratic Party revises its party rules allowing Prime Minister Abe to serve a third term for a total of nine years or until September 2021. **15 March:** As a result of Saudi Arabian king Salman's visit to Japan, several Japanese corporations sign agreements for a wide range of economic projects with Saudi partners. **19 March:** Prime Minister Abe travels to Germany, France, and the European Union headquarters in Brussels to lay the groundwork of the Group of Seven summit to be held in Italy in May. **25 March:** Tōhō announces that its film *Your Name* became the second-highest-grossing Japanese film ever. **1 April:** Hanyu Yuzuru wins the World Figure Skating Championship. **6 April:** According to a cabinet report, Japan's economy just completed its third-longest postwar growth period, a 52-month growth cycle. **13 April:** The Defense Ministry announces that during the past year it scrambled jets a record 1,618 times, 20 percent more than at any other time, thus demonstrating the unrest over China. **20 April:** The Ministry of Finance announces a $37 billion trade surplus in 2016, the first surplus in six years. **27 April:** Prime Minister Abe begins a four-day trip to Russia and Britain. **28 May:** Satō Takuma wins the Indianapolis 500 making him the first Japanese winner. **26 June:** The Ministry of Finance announces that direct foreign investment in 2016 topped $26.9 billion, the highest ever. **2 July:** Tōkyō governor Koike Yuriko's Tōkyōites First Party wins a sweeping victory over the LDP in the metropolitan assembly election. **18 August:** Japanese military and diplomatic leaders pledge a greater defense role in Japan's alliance with the United States. William Hagerty, the new United States ambassador to Japan, promises an "ironclad" tie with Japan. **23 August:** The Ministry of Defense seeks a record budget for 2018. **8 September:** The Ministry of Finance announces a record-high $21 billion in current account surplus, the 37th straight month in the black. **14 September:** North Korea threatens to use nuclear weapons to "sink" Japan and reduce the United States to "ashes and darkness." **25 September:** Prime Minister Abe dissolves the House of Representatives and calls for a snap election. Tōkyō governor Koike Yuriko announces a new party, the Party of Hope, to challenge the LDP. The Democratic Party, under the leadership of Maehara Seiji, joins the opposition party. **22 October:** Prime Minister Abe and his LDP win a landslide victory in the lower house election. Together with its Kōmeitō partner, the LDP has a two-thirds majority in the House of Representatives. **1 November:** Abe Shinzō is reelected prime minister. With its disastrous defeat, the Democratic Party replaces Maehara Seiji with Ōtsuka Kohei as its leader. **6 November:** President Trump visits Japan for three days. **9 November:** The Nikkei index tops 23,000, its highest level since 1991. Government data reveals the 58th consecutive month of economic expansion, the second-longest recovery in postwar Japan. **14 November:** Tōkyō governor Koike Yuriko announces her resignation as leader of the Party of Hope after poor election results. **16 November:** With Japan's leadership, the Trans-Pacific Partnership reaches an agreement with eleven participating nations, minus the United States. **1 December:** The Japanese government announces a 2.8 percent jobless rate, the lowest since January 1974. **1 December:** A special government panel sets 30 April 2019 as Emperor Akihito's official retirement date. The cabinet approves one week later. **9 December:** Japan and the European Union approve an economic partnership agreement that will include approximately 40 percent of the world's trade. **14 December:** The Japanese High Court blocks the restart of nuclear reactors after the Fukushima Daiichi nuclear disaster of 2011. **15 December:** The Bank of Japan's Tankan Report announces that business sentiment has just hit an 11-year high. **16 December:** The Japanese government plans a record $46 billion defense budget in 2018. **23 December:** The Cabinet Office publishes a report showing Japan's per capita GDP at $38,968, ranking Japan 18th among 35 developed economies.

Introduction

People have been fascinated by Japan since the end of the war. Japan, or Nihon in the Japanese language, means the land of the rising sun. Japan's history, arts, and culture, as well as its economy and foreign relations, have attracted strong interest in countries around the world. After scholars got beyond consideration of World War II, its causes, issues, and outcome, and a consideration of the American Occupation, their curiosity about Japan blossomed.

In the 1990s, the number of scholars studying more diversified topics in the postwar period grew. By focusing on the years after 1945, they could examine important topics in a more complete way. They could treat more than just the political outlines, the economic developments, and the foreign policy issues, which had been the main topics of consideration in earlier days.

In addition to the politics, economy, and foreign policy, scholars wanted to learn about social issues, the arts, culture, and sports. Who were the great Japanese writers and what were their major works? What Japanese movie directors had made world-famous films? Which Japanese architects were making a dynamic impact on the world of architecture? Which Japanese fashion designers were shaping the world of fashion? Who among the Japanese were winning Nobel Prizes? What were the leading technological accomplishments? Who were the Japanese sports stars gaining international recognition? What Japanese musicians had risen to international renown? Who among the popular culture figures had opened the doors to anime, manga, and other forms of youth culture? Indeed, there was much to examine in postwar Japan.

PHYSICAL FEATURES

The first thing that strikes one about Japan is its small physical size. Japan is only the 62nd-largest country in the world. Covering 145,925 square miles, Japan is about the size of the state of California. It is 70–80 percent mountainous and heavily forested, and as of 2015, only about 12 percent of the land is used for growing crops. Japan suffers from frequent earthquakes of a destructive nature as well as being in the line of typhoons and the target of devastating tsunamis. Mount Fuji, a volcanic mountain, is not only Japan's highest mountain but also its symbol. Japan's seasons are temperate, paralleling the United States from Maine through Georgia, but somewhat milder.

Japan consists of four major islands, Hokkaidō, Honshū, Shikoku, and Kyūshū, from north to south. In addition, there are nearly 7,000 smaller islands although they make up only about 3 percent of Japan's land. The Japanese islands, although rich in natural beauty, are poor in natural resources. Lacking in major metals and ores, having almost no petroleum, and being short in most natural resources, Japan would not appear to be a likely candidate for economic success.

The islands of Japan, located in the Pacific Ocean, lie off the northeast coast of Asia, across the sea from Korea and its larger neighbor, China. Japan is very much a part of the East Asian sphere and reflects that culture and history. To the southwest are the countries and cultures of Southeast Asia, which have also added their influence to Japan. To the north and west of Japan lies Russia, a country with which Japan has had a difficult relationship for more than two centuries. Finally, stretching across the broad Pacific lies the United States, whose distance may be far but whose influence has been strong in the postwar period.

Japan is divided into 47 prefectures or the equivalent of states. As of 2018, Japan has 12 cities with a population of more than one million people, including Tōkyō, Yokohama, Ōsaka, Nagoya, Sapporo, Kōbe, Kyōto, Fukuoka, Kawasaki, Saitama, Hiroshima, and Sendai. It also has 24 cities of more than a half million people.

POPULATION

Japan has a population of just over 126.5 million people, making it the 10th-largest country in the world in terms of people. However, its population has declined by nearly a half million in the last decade. Japan's population is unevenly distributed with the major portion living on Honshū and most of these on a strip of land 50 miles wide running from Tōkyō through Kyōto along the old Tōkaidō Road and extending on to Shimonoseki. Japan's overall population density is 870 people per square mile, ranking it 38th in the world. As of 2016, Greater Tōkyō has a population of nearly 38 million people, making it the largest metropolitan area in the world.

The people of Japan are rather homogeneous, most of them having been assimilated into the Japanese race many generations ago. Only about 1.5 percent of the people living in Japan are non-Japanese, most of them coming from China, Korea, Southeast Asia, and the United States. Although there are considerable variations in the physical features of the Japanese people, compared to the United States and Western European countries, there appears to be great similarity.

The Japanese are an aging people. As of 2015, the Japanese people have the world's longest life span with females living to be an average of 86.8 years and males an average of 80.5 years with the overall average being 83.7 years. Not only are Japanese people living much longer than the people of many countries, but the birth rate in Japan is much lower than in almost all countries. Japan has not only the world's highest life expectancy but one of the world's lowest infant mortality rates. As of 2015, the average Japanese woman had 1.46 children; thus, today the people of Japan are not even reproducing themselves.

Health care in Japan is of high quality, extending the life span of the Japanese people. Japan's high-quality national health care program, together with its healthy diet and quality of life, enables Japanese people to live both long and well. As of 2014, about 26 percent of Japan's population is 65 years of age or older.

HISTORY

Japan has a long and rich history. Although this volume focuses on Japan only since 1945, Japan's history is probably at least five millennia old. Japan's pre-historic period is well documented. Its first permanent capital in Nara dates to the eighth century. Together the Nara Period (710–784) and the Heian Period (794–1185), which centered in Kyōto, flourished under the imperial system with the emperor exercising a reasonable degree of power over the country. In 1185, Japan entered the era of military rule where three different sets of military rulers, the Kamakura shogunate (1185–1333), the Ashikaga shogunate (1336–1573), and the Tokugawa shogunate (1600–1868), controlled the political, economic, and military aspects of the government while the imperial family continued its ceremonial vestiges in Kyōto.

In the mid-19th century, Japan embarked on a vigorous program of transformation, or what some have called modernization. In a generation or two, Japan went from being an isolated, rather limited country into being one of the major world powers. Indeed, the Meiji Period (1868–1912) saw Japan vault from a rather unnoticed nation to one of the top 10 nations in the world. During this period, Japan's economy, political system, military capacity, and world status changed dramatically. Japan became a truly modern world power.

The transformation that Japan experienced led to problems. As Japan became more modern and more involved in the world, it acquired competitors that grew to be adversaries and, together with Japan's own rise of imperialism, led to Japan's attacks on China, the United States, and European colonial possessions in Southeast Asia and the Pacific. For 15 years or more, Japan was a perpetrator of World War II in Asia, or what many called the Pacific War. Japan's actions during this time brought justified criticism from many Western nations and from the people and areas devastated by the Japanese military juggernaut.

POLITICS

Japan is a constitutional monarchy with Emperor Akihito having been on the throne since 1989. Recently, the Diet honored his request to step down in 2019, a development not seen in Japanese royalty in 200 years. Political power, however, rests with the National Diet, a dual legislative body consisting of the House of Representatives with 465 members, each elected every four years or more frequently, and the House of Councillors with 242 members, half of whom are elected every three years for six-year terms. In 2016, Japan lowered the voting age to 18 years. For most of the postwar period, the Liberal Democratic Party (LDP) has dominated Japanese politics. In 2009, the Democratic Party of Japan made remarkable gains. Having dominated the 2009 lower house election, it controlled the government for three years. However, in 2012, the LDP regained control. As of the 2017 elections, the LDP and its coalition partner, Kōmeitō, control 67 percent of the seats and are firmly in charge. The coalition also controls 60 percent of the seats in the upper house.

Although fraught with difficulties, Japan has grown into a modern political power. Japan is one of the most democratic countries in the world. Replete with laws, a constitution, political parties, elections, a prime minister with a cabinet that serves as the executive branch of government, a bicameral parliament that is the legislative body, and a judicial system, Japan has a thoroughly modern political system. However, sometimes Japan's political system seems slow to act, lacks innovation, or is not immediately effective.

Japan's political system has at times been plagued by scandals and individual failures. Leaders call for action and reform, but Japan's political system does not seem to achieve any dramatic breakthrough or innovative success. However, compared to most countries in the world, Japan has achieved many political accomplishments.

In 2016, the Japanese government had the world's third-largest expenditures with nearly $2 trillion, trailing only the United States and China, but took in only $1.7 trillion in revenues. Japan continues to carry a large public debt.

ECONOMY

Leaving aside the period from roughly 1992 to 2009 when the country experienced a degree of economic stagnation, Japan has been one of the world's economic success stories in the last 60 years. Devastated by World War II, Japan, with the help of the United States, has picked itself up and developed into one of the world's top economic powers. Surpassing all other countries except the United States in the 1980s, Japan seemed to be on the fast track to be the world's premier economic leader. Indeed, one scholar exuberantly predicted that the 21st century would be the Japanese century. However, in the 1990s, Japan's planned economy encountered difficulties, which its leaders were not able to correct easily. In the most recent years, Japan appears to have turned the corner on its economic problems. Although no longer designated as *the* premier economic power, Japan is one of the top three economic countries in the world today.

In the postwar period, Japan has been a leader in the production of automobiles, electronic equipment, machine tools, steel, ships, chemicals, textiles, computers, and robots. Historically, Japan has flourished in banking, insurance, real estate, retailing, transportation, telecommunications, and construction. As of 2012, Fortune Global 500 lists 68 Japanese companies or 13.6 percent of the world's leading companies as being in Japan. In 2017, it ranked Toyota as the world's fifth-largest company. Names such as Nissan, Honda, Panasonic, Sony, Toshiba, Mitsubishi, Mitsui, and Canon are well known throughout the world.

As of 2017, Japan is the world's third-largest economy with $4.84 trillion, trailing only the United States and China, according to the International Monetary Fund's World Economic Outlook. Using a 2013 Gallup poll, Japan ranks 15th in the world in gross annual household income with $34,822. In short, Japan, while suffering a recent downturn, is still doing very well economically.

From the 1990s onward for the next 20 years, Japan's economy faced serious problems with a shrinking workforce, a high debt level, and sometimes less than creative responses to economic problems. Japan's public debt is nearly double its annual gross domestic product, a bad situation for any country. As of 2017, Japan's unemployment rate stood at an unusually low

2.8 percent, making it the lowest among the developed nations. While most Japanese consider themselves middle class, perhaps as many as 16 percent of the people live below a reasonable poverty line.

FOREIGN POLICY

Japan is the only Asian country in the G-8, a distinction it relishes. It is a member of the United Nations and a non-permanent member of the UN Security Council, a position it hopes to turn into a permanent seat. Japan is also a member of the Association of Southeast Asian Nations (ASEAN) and of Asia-Pacific Economic Cooperation (APEC). Japan is one of the top 10 countries in living standards.

Japan has struggled with its image in foreign countries. Indeed, foreign policy, although not given a premier spot in Japan's postwar transformation, has attracted considerable attention. Originally Japan placed foreign policy on the back burner and paid little attention to the matter. Economic development took top priority, and foreign policy was considered no better than an also-ran. Having been unsuccessful in its foreign policy in the early 20th century and having aroused the ire of much of the world by its war efforts, Japan wanted as little as possible to do with foreign policy issues. It largely followed the advice of the United States on foreign policy for the first 50 years of the postwar period. The United States continued to have a strong control of Japan's economy and political policy. The bonds and connections between the two countries will become readily understandable throughout this book.

Well into the 21st century, Japan has exhibited more interest and involvement in the wider world. It has expanded its focus beyond East Asia and the United States. Today, Japan cultivates diplomatic relations, cultural exchanges, and economic assistance, to say nothing of the vast international trade missions. Japan is deeply involved in Southeast Asia, highly committed to European affairs, and increasingly involved in Africa, the Middle East, and Latin and South America. Japan has indeed become a world player.

DEFENSE

Japan's defense budget for 2018 has risen to $46 billion, the sixth straight year it has increased. Concern over the growing North Korean aggression is the driving force behind the increases. Although well behind the expenditures of the United States, which spends 13 times that amount, still it is a significant amount for Japan. It represents 1 percent of Japan's gross domestic product as compared to 4 percent of GDP spent by the United States. Make no bones about it, Japan is one of the world's leading military powers. In absolute terms, the Japanese military is small but, nonetheless, extremely well equipped. In 2015, Credit Suisse ranked Japan the world's fourth-strongest military power with a budget then of $41.6 billion and 247,173 men under arms.

SOCIETY

Japan has one of the world's highest standards of living. Its standard of living ranks in the top 10 among the countries of the world. Its life expectancy is the highest in the world. Its literacy rate exceeds 99 percent. Its cities are clean and safe. Although not reaching the level they desire, women have achieved a high level of political and social equality and are growing in economic capacities.

The health care system in Japan is very good with services provided by both the national and local governments. Japan has a universal health care insurance system and a strong medical staff. If employers do not provide health care, the local government sponsors health care insurance. In 2015, the World Health Organization ranked Japan first in its health systems while the United States stood at 37th.

A number of social problems, however, have recently come to the fore. Japan has the sixth-highest suicide rate in the world, the second worst among the major industrialized nations. In 2003, it had 34,427 suicides, a Japanese record. However, in 2016, Japan's suicides had dropped to 21,897, the lowest in 22 years. Suicide is still the leading cause of death among people under the age of 30.

In an interesting study published in early 2018, *U.S. News & World Report* ranks Japan fifth overall in "Best Countries" after Switzerland, Canada, Germany, and the United Kingdom.

ENVIRONMENT

Although known for being close to nature, the Japanese did a poor job in protecting their environment during their race to economic domination after World War II. They polluted their air and seas with industrial waste. However, they soon realized that they could not continue to pollute the small amount of land and space that they occupied. Thus, they adopted strict laws to protect the environment and today are among the more progressive nations when it comes to environmental protection. In 2018, the Environmental Performance Index ranked Japan 20th in the world, seven spots ahead of the United States and the first non-European country on the list.

RELIGION

Although Japan is not especially religious, nearly 90 percent of its people are in some way connected with a Shintō shrine or a Buddhist temple. However, no more than one-third participate in any religious group on a regular basis. Around 2 percent of the Japanese are practicing Christians.

EDUCATION

Japan has a highly developed, highly competitive educational system. Since 1947, it has had nine years of compulsory education. The students attend school for 240 days a year and graduate from high school in high numbers with a strong academic background. After junior high school, almost all students continue to high school. Although highly successful, the Japanese educational system has been plagued recently by decreasing scores on international tests, bullying of students, children who refuse to attend school and even to leave their own room, and a lack of creative initiatives.

Of the high school graduates, about 70 percent continue on to university, junior college, trade school, or some other postsecondary institution. That means Japan has about three million men and women enrolled in their 700 universities and colleges, the second-largest enrollment in the world. Yet many Japanese admit that their university system is weak compared to other countries as courses are not rigorous, professors are not engaged, and university time is largely a period of social adjustment.

CULTURE

Japan is very strong in its cultural programs and opportunities for all people to enjoy art and culture. Japan's growth in stature is not limited to the economic realm. It has established itself as a leader in fashion, architecture, literature, film, and other arts. In fashion, who has not heard of Hanae Mori, Miyake Issey, or Kawakubo Rei? Architects such as Andō Tadao, Tange Kenzō, and Maki Fumihiko are world famous. The writings of Kawabata Yasunari, Ōe Kenzaburō, Endō Shūsaku, and Murakami Haruki are read around the world. The films of Kurosawa Akira, Ozu Yasujirō, and Mizogu-chi Kenji, as well as the works of younger directors Miyazaki Hayao and Koreeda Hirokazu, are popular worldwide.

Japanese athletes have gained international fame in golf (Aoki Isao), swimming (Kitajima Kōsuke), figure skating (Itō Midori), and baseball (Suzuki "Ichirō" and Matsui Hideki). Japan also plays a leading role in the creation of computers, games, and animation.

JAPAN'S ROLE IN THE MODERN WORLD

Based on its long list of historical accomplishments, its period of modernization under the Meiji regime, its 20th-century growth and development, and despite the wartime interlude, Japan has emerged as a major world player in the postwar period. It is this period of time, from 1945 to the present, that this book will examine.

After recovering from the war, lifting itself onto the stage of the late 20th-century world, and jettisoning its cheap, bizarre goods, Japan began to extend its influence into the wider world. The impact was first felt in the economic arena. Japan's production and marketing of high-quality products gained it an important foothold in the world's economy. Japanese products became increasingly recognized for their high quality and reliability. Japan came to dominate several major technological fields.

In 2015, Japan was one of the top five nations in its contributions to official development assistance (ODA). Japan contributed $9.32 billion dollars to ODA. It has grown to exercise a leadership role in science and technology. It ranks fourth in internet usage (93.3 percent), barely trailing Germany, the United States, and the United Kingdom. Even with a much smaller population, Japan ranks eighth in the world in mobile telephones. It is fourth in fixed-line telephones with 64 million.

Japan has traveled the road to a modern destination without totally losing sight of its traditions and values. Although some in Japan lament the passing of old ways, Japan has held on to a reasonable amount of its traditions and values. This is easier to find in its arts and crafts and its literature and films as well as in its social habits.

Japan is a mix of the old and the new, traditional and modern, and old-fashioned and innovative. This book will introduce the broad sweep of people, events, and trends, including the successes and failures, of postwar Japan.

ABE KŌBŌ, 安部公房 **(1924–1993).** Abe Kōbō, a famous novelist with strong international recognition, was one of Japan's outstanding literary personalities in the second half of the 20th century. The main theme of his writings is the alienation of modern man from urban society. In general, Abe focused on contemporary culture and modern industrial society. Although his official registry was in Hokkaidō, Abe was born in **Tōkyō**, brought up in Mukden, and worked mainly in Tōkyō. He opposed Japan's fascist-like policies and its militarism in World War II but still wanted to participate in the national effort. Abe originally studied medicine at Tōkyō Imperial University but immediately turned to **literature**.

Abe's *Tanin no kao* (*The Face of Another*, 1964) tells of a man who tries to regain the love of his wife by putting on a plastic mask to hide his own burned and disfigured face. His *Suna no onna* (*Woman in the Dunes*, 1962) focuses on an entomologist who falls into a sand pit and the clutches of an insect-like woman. From his early novels on, Abe, an avant-garde writer, was consistently preoccupied with the stultifying effect of urban isolation on modern man. For him, contemporary urban living was dangerous as well as destructive and something to flee from, for it crushed man and rendered him impotent.

ABE SHINTARŌ, 安倍晋太郎 **(1924–1991).** Abe Shintarō was a politician and Prime Minister **Nakasone Yasuhiro**'s foreign minister from 1982 through 1986, the longest-serving foreign minister of the postwar period. He was also minister of international trade and industry under the **Suzuki Zenkō** government; agriculture, forestry, and fisheries minister in the **Miki Takeo** cabinet; and chief **cabinet** secretary for **Fukuda Takeo**.

Born in Yamaguchi Prefecture and a graduate of the **University of Tōkyō** in 1949, Abe became a political reporter for the *Mainichi Shimbun*. He served as the right-hand man of Prime Minister Fukuda. He then became the private secretary to and the son-in-law of Prime Minister **Kishi Nobusuke**. Elected to the first of 10 terms in the **House of Representatives** in 1958, he belonged to the Fukuda faction. He later headed the second-largest faction in the **Liberal Democratic Party** (LDP) and held all three top LDP posts: secretary-general, executive council chairman, and chair of the Policy Affairs Research Council. In 1982, he finished behind Nakasone and **Kōmoto Toshio** in the party **election** for **prime minister**. In 1987, **Takeshita Noboru** defeated him to become prime minister.

In diplomacy, Abe was a tough negotiator and strong advocate for Japan. One of his primary policies was the advancement of close relations with the **United States**. Accused of involvement with the **Recruit scandal**, an insider-trading episode, Abe was forced to resign as secretary-general of LDP in December 1988, ending his political career. *See also* FOREIGN POLICY.

ABE SHINZŌ, 安倍晋三 **(1954–).** Abe Shinzō became Japan's youngest postwar **prime minister** when he took office on 26 September 2006 at the age of 52. He was the first prime minister born after the war, as well as the first after the end of the **Occupation**. Abe was born into a distinguished Yamaguchi Prefecture political family. His father was **Abe Shintarō**, a secretary-general of the **Liberal Democratic Party** (LDP), and his grandfather was former prime minister **Kishi Nobusuke**.

After graduating from Seikei University in 1977, Abe studied politics at the University of Southern California. On his return to Japan, he began work at the Kōbe **Steel** Company and continued there until 1982. Turning to politics, he served as executive assistant to the foreign minister, as private secretary to the chairperson of the LDP general council, and then as private secretary to the LDP secretary-general.

In 1993, Abe received the highest vote count in the Yamaguchi 1st District in his first run for the **House of Representatives**. He was appointed to the House's Committee on Foreign Affairs, and he also served as director of the LDP Social Affairs Division, where he focused on the pension and social security systems. Abe became the LDP secretary-general in 2004 under the **cabinet** of **Koizumi Jun'ichirō**. In the 2005 general **election**, he was re-elected to the **Diet** for a fifth term.

In September 2006, Abe was elected president of the ruling LDP and consequently prime minister. His rather strong right-wing stances—including supporting the **textbook controversy**, redefining Japan's aggressive wars, denying any government coercion in the **"comfort women"** issue, visiting **Yasukuni Shrine**, calling for revision of Article 9 of the **Constitution**, and opposing any change to Japan's imperial succession law—produced a shaky administration that lasted only one year. Abe favored a strengthening of Japan's military, reforming its **economy**, following close relations with the **United States**, and pursuing an active foreign policy. However, he was not able to show much progress in these areas. **Fukuda Yasuo**, who also served only one year, replaced him as prime minister.

Like a phoenix, Abe would rise again. On 16 December 2012, the Liberal Democratic Party won a landslide victory in the election. The LDP again selected Abe Shinzō as prime minister. He quickly launched his "Abenomics" growth plan, which utilizes massive monetary easing, government spending, and red-tape slashing. He adopted strong measures to revive Japan's economy. He introduced his "three arrow" policy where he pushed for monetary expansion, accepted a flexible fiscal policy, and adopted a growth strategy focusing on structural reform and private-sector investment to achieve long-term growth.

Abe supported educational reforms, policies that promoted population growth, a more international foreign policy that elevated Japan's status in the world, and military policies that gave Japan a stronger defense and better security.

In his third term as prime minister (2014–2017), Abe sought to strengthen the economy, **agriculture**, health care, and other sectors. But in 2017, Japan's growth remained fragile and inflation stood above the 2 percent goal.

Abe, a proponent of amending the war-renouncing constitution, also followed a policy of "taking a practical step towards proposing amendments to the constitution." The LDP sought to revise the postwar constitution that prevents Japan from using any military force except for a strict definition of defense.

Abe remains an outspoken nationalist but has agreed to uphold the 1993 apology to "comfort women." He continues to project an image of being closely aligned with the United States. There are signs that Abe is shifting to the right in his international policy. In 2015, Abe pushed Japan to the right when he took steps to allow Japan's military to send soldiers on overseas missions for the first time since World War II. Although severely limited, even this simple gesture set off alarms for many Japanese who fear that Japan will again be led down the path to war. On 14 August 2015, Abe again apologized for Japan's aggression in World War II, upsetting the more nationalistic and offering minimal succor to the internationalists.

In 2017, Abe faced controversy over an alleged land deal involving a primary school linked to his wife. The deal involved the bargain-price sale of public land to the controversial new school, where Japan's first lady briefly held a role as honorary principal.

On 5 March 2017, the LDP extended its term limits for prime ministers from two to three, three-year terms. Having been successful in the October 2017 election, Abe could serve until September 2021 and could thus become the longest-serving prime minister ever.

As of 1 January 2018, Abe is the third-longest-serving postwar prime minister (2,183 days) after **Satō Eisaku** (2,797 days) and **Yoshida Shigeru** (2,614 days), but ahead of Koizumi Jun'ichirō (1,979 days) and **Nakasone Yasuhiro** (1,805 days).

ACTORS AND ACTRESSES. Japan's outstanding postwar actors include Hayakawa Sesshu, **Ryū Chishū, Shimura Takashi, Mifune Toshirō, Takakura Ken, Nakadai Tatsuya, Yakusho Koji,** Sanada Hiroyuki, and **Asano Tadanobu.**

Kitano Takeshi (1947–) is a multitalented comedian, **television** personality, actor, director, and author. Known by his comedy name, Beat Takashi, he starred in several gangster films, directed the popular **film** *Hanabi*, and worked on the crime trilogy *Outrage*.

Many other exceptional actors deserve mention. Ishihara Yujirō (1935–1987), brother of **Tōkyō**'s governor, **Ishihara Shintarō**, was a leading man in the late 1950s and through the 1960s. Yamazaki Tsutomu (1936–) played the lead in outstanding films including *Tengoku to jigoku* (*High and Low*, 1963), *Kagemusha* (1980), *Ososhiki* (*The Funeral*, 1984), and *Tampopo* (1985). Watanabe Ken (1959–) often played samurai roles and in 1987 starred in the 50-episode **NHK** drama *Dokuganryu Masamune* (*One-Eyed Dragon, Masamune*). He also had a role in the American-produced film *The Last Samurai*. Toyokawa Etsushi (1962–) starred opposite Russell Crowe in the thriller *No Way Back*. In his career, he costarred with some of Japan's most beautiful leading ladies. Nagase Masatoshi (1966–) is best known for his many popular movies and dramas and television commercials, especially for his Cup Noodle ads.

Some of Japan's most famous actresses include Sawamura Sadako, **Tanaka Kinuyo, Takamine Hideko, Kyō Machiko, Hidari Sachiko,** and **Wakao Ayako.** Other slightly less well-known actresses include Shimada Yoko (1953–) who played the role of the beautiful Mariko in the film *Shōgun*. Yamaguchi Tomoko (1964–) appeared in several television series including *Junchan no oenka* (*Sweet Home*), *Osama no restoran* (*Long Vacation*), and *Kanojo no tabi no monogatari* (*Letters*). Koizumi Kyoko (1966–) and Nakayama Miho (1970–) were 1980s popular idols who successfully made the transition to film. Fujiwara Norika (1971–) has been called the female face of the late 1990s. She is often seen in magazine, **newspaper**, and television advertisements selling various commercial products including J-Phone. Matsushima Nanako (1973–) is a beautiful young actress who started as a model. She has had leading roles in the television drama *Himawari* (*Sunflower*) and in *Ringu* (*Ring*), *Gurēto Tichiā Onizuka* (*Great Teacher Onizuka*), and *Hyakunen no Monogatari* (*The Story of One Century*). Given the success of the Japanese film industry, there is virtually no end to the number of actors and actresses that could be mentioned.

As of 2016, the motion picture industry ranked Japan fourth in the world for the production of feature films. Japanese actors and actresses are known worldwide. Some of the bright young stars include Matsuda Ryūhei (1983–), who has 40 films to his credit in less than 20 years; Tsumabuki Satoshi (1980–), who has appeared in 50 films with spectacular performances in

Tōkyō! and *Dororo*; Oguri Shun (1982–), who has appeared in many films and directed a few others; Sometani Shōta (1992–), a popular young actor; and Nagayama Eita (1982–), a very popular actor, as well as several other rising stars.

ADVERTISING. Advertising is big **business** in Japan, the third-largest advertising market in the world. In 2015, its advertising expenditures totaled nearly $70 billion. **Television** remains the main advertising medium with **newspaper** advertising declining. However, the digital media is growing. The Japan Advertising Review Organization, a self-regulatory body for advertising, is the primary organization handling complaints. Japanese advertising companies all make use of celebrities, stylized language, novel aesthetics, impressive visual designs, and catchy music.

As of 2014, Dentsū controlled 25 percent of ad spending in Japan. It had approximately $746 million in capital and nearly 56,000 employees worldwide. Dentsū is about 80 percent larger than Hakuhodo DY Holdings, Japan's second-largest ad agency. No other agency anywhere has such influence in its home market. It is listed on the **Tōkyō Stock Exchange**. Dentsū directs the advertising for leading companies such as **SoftBank Corporation**, **Toyota Motor Corporation**, Suntory, and Coca-Cola.

On 25 December 2015, Takahashi Matsuri, a 24-year-old female employee of Dentsū, committed suicide due to *karoshi*, or death due to overwork. She had been exceeding the 70-hour monthly overtime limit. A year later, Ishii Tadashi, the company's president and CEO, resigned to take responsibility for the tragedy. As of January 2018, Yamamoto Toshihiro (1958–) is president and CEO of Dentsū.

Hakuhodo DY Holdings, the second-largest advertising agency, is less than half Dentsū's size. Most other agencies are even smaller. Headquartered in **Tōkyō**, as of 2016, Hakuhodo had nearly 15,000 employees in 21 countries and a capital of $100 million. It is the oldest advertising agency in Japan, having its start in 1895. Its Cup Noodle campaign is legendary. It is listed on the Tōkyō Stock Exchange. In 2016, it had revenues of approximately $395 million. The group is ranked by *Advertising Age*, a leading international trade magazine, as being among the world's top 10 agency groups and the second-largest agency group in Japan.

Today, Cyber Agent Incorporated, a new company, is threatening for advertising supremacy, having risen meteorically. A web media goliath, it is technologically creative and uses celebrities from the fashion world, TV personalities, and media stars to heighten its appeal. It uses online advertising, electronic business cards, and an electronic filing system. As of 2016, it employs nearly 4,000 people and had a gross profit of $113 billion.

AGRICULTURAL COOPERATIVES. Japan's Central Union of Agricultural Cooperatives (Nōgyō kyōdō kumiai), or Nōkyō for short, is an agricultural association that combines cooperatives to gain advantages in finances, sales, and procurement for farmers. Nōkyō is a cooperative to assist farmers in marketing their products, purchasing supplies in large quantities, and providing inexpensive, ready credit. It is a strong organization contributing to the welfare of farmers.

Nōkyō, first organized in 1947 during the **Occupation**'s land reform, blankets the entire agricultural scene in Japan. It is a mammoth economic entity that provides almost every kind of service to rural areas. Among other things, it seeks to maintain price supports on rice and other crops and protect the Japanese farmer from the importation of cheaper agricultural products. Rice is particularly important to Japan and as of the early 1990s, Japan was nearly self-sufficient in rice. Since the late 1990s, Japan has found it increasingly impossible to maintain a "Fortress Japan" in the production and sale of rice.

Nōkyō, one of Japan's most powerful political and economic organizations, has strongly supported the **Liberal Democratic Party**. The mid-1990s appeared to be a turning point for Nōkyō. Its position of strength had been based on its privileged position in financial services, creating stability in its operations in the 1970s and 1980s. Since fierce competition began in Japan's financial markets in the mid-1990s, Nōkyō's influence has declined.

The National Federation of Agricultural Cooperative Associations (Zennō) is Japan's—and one of the world's—largest federations of agricultural cooperatives. Most of Japan's three million farm households belong to one of the association's 1,000 primary level co-ops. Working with prefectural and primary level co-ops, the association serves its members by purchasing and distributing the materials and equipment for agricultural production and necessities for daily farm life. It is also involved in the collection, distribution, and marketing of agricultural products. The association works to develop **agriculture**, to improve farm life, and to provide food for Japan. *See also* BANKING.

AGRICULTURE. Agriculture dominated Japan's **economy** in the early 20th century but declined in overall significance in the 1940s. The percentage of people involved in agriculture and the amount of revenue these people generated declined from 80 percent to 50 percent of the total workforce by the end of World War II. Since the end of the war, there has been a steady decline in the amount of land farmed, the number of farm households, the number of full-time farmers, and the income from farming.

The economic boom that began in the 1950s left Japan's farmers behind in income and **technology**. Relatively few farm families engaged exclusively in agriculture, and most derived more than half their income from jobs outside farming. Today, agriculture occupies only about 13 percent of the entire area of Japan. However, Japanese farmers practice intensive agriculture, producing far more from a small amount of land than the average farmer around the world. Japanese farm productivity is high due to technically advanced fertilizers, sophisticated farm machinery, and careful management.

Raising livestock is a rather minor activity in Japanese agriculture. With the increased import of foreign beef and meat products, stock farming is now a dwindling enterprise.

Agricultural production as a percentage of GDP has declined dramatically from about 9 percent in 1960 to only a little over 1 percent in the early 21st century. The farming population, because of the nature of the enterprise, continues to age more rapidly than that of employees in modern industries.

Japan has long maintained a policy of promoting self-sufficiency in rice and allowing imports only to offset shortages in domestic production. However, in 1999, the government removed the ban on the importation of rice, allowing foreign rice, although heavily taxed, to be sold in Japan. Japan has increased its imports of all farm products 40-fold over the past 40 years. *See also* AGRICULTURAL COOPERATIVES.

AINU, アイヌ. The Ainu people were among Japan's earliest settlers and distinguished themselves by their hairy appearance. Today, living mainly in Hokkaidō and the nearby islands, the Ainu are an indigenous people who can be traced archaeologically to the Jōmon peoples. Probably a mix of cultures and races, the Ainu were caught between the expanding pressure of the Japanese and **Russian** peoples. Beginning with the Meiji era, the Ainu frequently became the targets of discrimination. Threatened by acculturation and the relentless progress of modernization, there were some 50,000 Ainu as of the beginning of the 21st century. An Ainu rights organization, the Utari Kyōkai, has tried, with only limited success, to represent Ainu interests and culture. Kayano Shigeru (1926–2006), an Ainu author and spokesperson, produced Ainu cultural programs, studies, and performances. The first Ainu elected to government, he also served five terms in the **House of Representatives** and ended his political career by finishing a term in the **House of Councillors** from 1994 through 1998.

AKAO BIN, 赤尾敏 **(1899–1990).** Akao Bin, whose real name was Akao Satoshi, was a right-wing ultranationalist who headed the Greater Japan Patriotic Party. Akao publicly defended an assassination attempt on a **newspaper** publisher who criticized the **imperial system**. He saw the press as being under the influence of communism and therefore open to violent attack.

Elected to the **House of Representatives** in 1942, Akao was expelled for publicly criticizing Prime Minister Tōjō Hideki. In 1952, Akao founded the Greater Japan Patriotic Party and practiced radical politics for many years. In 1960, one of his followers assassinated **Asanuma Inejirō**, the **Japan Socialist Party** leader. A perennial losing candidate for the House of Representatives, Akao was a colorful political figure with his harangues against left-wing politicians and politics.

AKATSUKA FUJIO, 赤塚不二夫 **(1935–2008).** Akatsuka Fujio, who was born in **China** but returned to Japan after the war, was one of Japan's original **manga** pioneers. In the prewar period and even into the first 20 years of the postwar period, comedic manga were nothing more than pictorial adaptations of the tales told by comedians and *rakugo* artists. In the late 1960s, however, Akatsuka came along to change all that, with wildly popular works like *Osomatsu-kun* and *Tensai Bakabon* (*Genius Bakabon*). The characters in these works were truly warped, both in looks and personality. It was not uncommon for the supporting characters to be more active than the protagonists, and the laughs came more from spontaneous humor than from punchlines with long buildups.

AKEBONO TARŌ, 曙太郎 **(1969–).** In 1993, Akebono Tarō became the first foreign **sumō** wrestler to reach the rank of grand champion or *yokozuna*. Akebono, the 64th *yokozuna*, was born in Hawaii as Chad George Rowan. He entered sumō in 1988 after being a high school basketball player. At 6 feet, 7 inches tall and weighing 480 pounds, he was very powerful. He rose rapidly through the ranks, equaling the record for the most consecutive *kachikoshi* (majority of wins in a sumō championship) from his debut, reaching the rank of *sekiwake* before suffering his first *makekoshi* or losing record. He was promoted to the Jūryō Division in March 1990 and to the Makuuchi Division in September 1990.

Akebono competed at the rank of *yokozuna* for nearly eight years. His career highlights include the rare achievement of winning the top division championship in three consecutive tournaments. He also beat **Takanohana** and Wakanohana in consecutive matches to win a *basho* when all three ended up tied at the end of the 15-day tournament. After winning his 11th championship in November 2000, Akebono retired to become an elder in the Japan Sumō Association and an *oyakata*, or trainer/parent, at the Azumazeki stable. In 2003, Akebono completely retired from sumō.

Since his retirement from sumō, Akebono has had a checkered career at best. He tried professional wrestling and won some awards. He appeared in **television** commercials, did talk shows, and opened a restaurant that failed. He gave interviews in *Hustle* magazine, made appearances in **films**, and promoted various wrestling endeavors. Given these post-retirement involvements, it is understandable why he lost his network supporters (*koenkai*). However, he did become a Japanese citizen in 1996.

AKIHITO, EMPEROR, 明仁天皇 **(1933–).** The fifth of seven children and the elder of two sons of late **Emperor Hirohito**, Akihito became emperor of Japan in 1989 under the reign name Heisei. Representative of the world's longest-serving monarchy, he is the 125th Japanese emperor. Born in 1933, he spent much of the wartime period in the mountain resort of Karuizawa. With the end of the war, he returned to **Tōkyō** and his studies at Gakushūin High School (Peers' School). At the same time, he studied English and Western culture under the tutoring of Elizabeth Gray Vining, a Quaker, librarian, and noted author of children's **books**.

Akihito's coming-of-age ceremony and his investiture as heir to the Japanese throne took place in 1952, the year that he graduated from high school and entered Gakushūin University. Like his father, he specialized in marine biology, particularly the classification of Japanese fish. In 1959, he married Shōda Michiko (1934–), a commoner. Although not coming from a family of royal rank, she is the daughter of Shōda Eizaburō, the wealthy president of Nisshin Flour Milling Company. The courtship and marriage created a stir because this was the first instance of an heir to the imperial throne marrying outside the circle of the traditional nobility.

While serving as crown prince, Akihito visited 37 countries as the official representative of Japan and tried to humanize the role of emperor by interacting more with the people. After becoming emperor, Akihito has visited 30 countries, and royal family members have made at least 400 visits to as many as 100 countries, spreading Japan's presence around the world.

Akihito's role as emperor focuses mainly on acting as the "symbol of the state and the unity of the people." The Japanese monarch is largely a ceremonial figurehead. His powers are strictly limited by the constitution and by tradition. He appoints the **prime minister**, ministers of state, and other high officials on the advice of the **National Diet**. He convokes the Diet, promulgates laws and treaties, awards honors, attests the credentials of foreign ambassadors, and receives foreign dignitaries. Since the **Constitution of Japan** vests executive power in the **cabinet** and prime minister, Akihito is not even Japan's nominal chief executive. He acts both as a symbol and a spokesman for Japan. Since ascending to the throne as emperor, he has visited all 47 Japanese prefectures. The emperor and empress host many ceremonies, audiences, and social functions on an annual basis. The emperor and empress have demonstrated a special concern for children, the elderly, and the disabled. They have consoled victims of natural disasters such as the **Kōbe**

Earthquake. Maintaining the tradition of his father, Emperor Akihito annually plants and harvests a rice crop showing links to the past and to the god of **agriculture**.

Emperor Akihito has brought world attention to Japan on several occasions. In 1992, he toured **China** seeking to improve relations with that country. In 1994, he made an important trip to the **United States** where he met with President Bill Clinton to emphasize the strong ties between the two countries. He has frequently expressed remorse over Japan's military aggression in World War II. In an interview in 2001, Akihito revealed a feeling of kinship with Koreans and noted the historical and perhaps biological ties with **Korea**. In 2005, he visited the United States territory of Saipan where he honored Japan's war dead as well as American casualties. He has taken steps to bring the **imperial family** closer to the Japanese people.

Akihito's wife, Empress Michiko, graduated from the English Literature Department of Sacred Heart University in Tōkyō. Emperor Akihito and Empress Michiko have three children: Crown Prince Naruhito born in 1960, Prince Akishino born in 1965, and Princess Sayako born in 1969. The crown prince and his wife Princess Masako have a daughter, Princess Aiko, born in 2001. Prince Akishino and his wife Princess Kiko have three children: Princess Mako born in 1991, Princess Kako born in 1994, and Prince Hisahito born in 2006. Young Prince Hisahito is the first male in the imperial line in more than 40 years.

Following the devastation wreaked by the **Great East Japan Earthquake** in 2011, Akihito spoke to the people of Japan via television to comfort his shell-shocked citizens, and he also met with survivors. He continues his long interest in marine biology and published a 350-page paper on the gobiodei fish in 2013.

In July 2016, Akihito expressed his desire to abdicate due to his age and declining health. This has created constitutional, political, and historical issues. Crown Prince Naruhito would succeed him. The last time an abdication occurred was in 1817. In order to avoid interference with the Imperial Household Act and the line of succession law, a one-time exception is being considered. The one-time succession would avoid the trouble of altering the Imperial House Law that says the emperor reigns for life. It also side-steps the need to consider the possibility of female succession. The abdication will take place on 30 April 2019.

National Diet law governs imperial succession. The current law excludes women from succession. A change to this law had been considered until Princess Kiko gave birth in 2006 to her and Prince Akishino's son, Prince Hisahito. Prime Minister **Koizumi Jun'ichirō** appointed a special panel composed of judges, university professors, and civil servants to study changes to the Imperial Household Law and to make recommendations to the government. However, the matter was dropped after the birth of an imperial grandson. *See also* FOREIGN POLICY.

AKIYOSHI TOSHIKO, 秋吉敏子 **(1929–).** Akiyoshi Toshiko is a pianist and composer, the leader of her own jazz orchestra, and the first Japanese to be inducted into the International Jazz Hall of Fame. Based in New York, she is internationally famous as a jazz pianist and conductor. She won a **music** scholarship to the University of California at Los Angeles in 1956 and led a jazz band from the mid-1970s until 2003.

An innovator in jazz and big band music, Akiyoshi created her unique style of composition by fusing elements of Japanese culture with American jazz into an elegant blend that has been called "majestic, haunting and hard-driving." She was the first **woman** to win *DownBeat* magazine's Best Arranger/Composer poll category. Trained in classical piano, she has been praised for her conducting style; she has been identified by the *New York Times* as perhaps "the most physically articulate conductor since Duke Ellington." Her work has won 14 Grammy awards. Akiyoshi made her farewell conducting performance in 2003 and now concentrates on her piano performances.

ALL NIPPON AIRWAYS (ZEN NIPPON KŪYU KABUSHIKI-GAI-SHA, 全日本空輸株式会社**).** All Nippon Airways (ANA) is one of Japan's major airlines. Incorporated in 1952 and expanded in 1958, ANA concentrated on domestic flights but also developed international routes. It also operates hotels and promotes international travel. ANA enjoyed a period of gradual growth in the 1960s when it added several new planes. ANA first appeared on the **Tōkyō Stock Exchange** in 1961.

In 1971, ANA inaugurated its first international service, a charter flight from **Tōkyō** to Hong Kong. In 1986, it started international flights from Tōkyō to Guam and soon to Los Angeles, New York, London, Paris, and Frankfurt.

In 2004, facing a surplus of gates due to the **construction** of new airports and the expansion of **Haneda**, ANA announced a fleet renewal plan that would replace some of its larger aircraft with a greater number of smaller planes. In July 2005, ANA signed a deal with Nippon Yūsen Kabushiki-Gaisha (NYK), Japan's leading shipping company, to sell its 28 percent share in Nippon Cargo Airlines, in order to pursue its own cargo business.

ANA is now Japan's largest domestic and international carrier, just ahead of **Japan Airlines**. ANA's main international hub is at **Narita International Airport**. As of 2016, ANA employed more than 20,000 people. It flies 35 international routes and to nearly 50 domestic cities with its fleet of more than 200 planes, many of the newer ones being Boeing aircraft. ANA has an excellent safely record, having had no fatal accidents since 1971. ANA has codeshare agreements with approximately 40 airlines.

AMANO TEIYŪ, 天野貞祐 **(1884–1980).** A philosopher and educator, noted for his studies on Immanuel Kant and advocacy of democracy in **education**, Amano Teiyū was born in Kanagawa Prefecture. After graduating from the First Higher School and Kyōto Imperial University, he went to Germany and studied philosophy at the University of Heidelberg during 1923–1924. On his return to Japan, he was appointed to the faculty of Kyōto Imperial University where he developed his theory of human morality. In 1937, he published *Dori no kankaku* (*The Sense of the Right*), a highly controversial book that was denounced by military and right-wing groups for its antiwar theme.

Amano was a member of the Japanese committee that dealt with the first of the **United States** Education Missions to Japan and the Education Reform Council. After serving as principal of the First Higher School, he was named minister of education in **Yoshida Shigeru**'s third **cabinet** (1950–1952). During his tenure, he criticized the left-wing tendencies such as unionism, socialism, and anti-imperial themes then prevalent in educational circles and stressed the necessity of moral education in the schools. He also worked for implementation of the school lunch program and passage of the law requiring the government to underwrite a portion of compulsory education expenses. After retiring as a minister of education, he founded Dokkyō University in 1964. From 1955 to 1963, he served as chairman of Japan's Central Council for Education.

ANDŌ TADAO, 安藤忠雄 **(1941–).** Andō Tadao, one of Japan's leading architects, received the prestigious Carlsberg Architectural Prize in 1992, the Pritzker Architecture Prize in 1995, the Royal Gold Medal in 1997, the American Institute of Architects Award in 2002, and the International Union of Architects Award in 2005. Born in **Ōsaka**, Andō traveled through Europe, the **United States**, and Africa in the 1960s, becoming largely self-taught in **architecture**. He opened his private practice in Ōsaka in 1969. His creations combine Western influence with traditional Japanese style, yet they have a contemporary appearance. In 1997, Andō became a professor at the **University of Tōkyō**.

Andō's creations are relatively free of consumerism and show a connection to the setting's landscape. He uses concrete and glass to set off his designs and creates spaces of enclosure rather than openness. He is known for his exquisitely poured and crafted concrete done in graceful geometric shapes. He incorporates a lot of stairs and reinforced concrete in his buildings and defines space in new ways. He allows for constantly changing patterns of light and wind in all his structures. His works combine traditional and modern forms and Western and Eastern styles. He is sensitive to the forces of nature and the **environment** with many of his works having a spiritual quality.

As of today, Andō continues to work but at a somewhat slower pace. Since 2010, he has designed 10 major buildings around the world. In 2016, he received the Isamu Noguchi Award given to "individuals who share Noguchi's spirit of innovation, global consciousness, and East-West exchange." Among his many buildings, Andō's most famous works include Row House in Sumiyoshi, Church of Light in Ōsaka, Suntory Museum in Ōsaka, Omotesando Hills in Tōkyō, and **Tōkyō Skytree**. Andō Tadao is indeed one of the world's great architects.

ANIME, アニメ. Anime refers to animated **films** and comes from the Japanese word for animation. Japanese animation has become dominant around the world. Cartoons such as ***Doraemon***, ***Pokémon***, *Digimon*, *Dragon Ball*, *Dragon Ball Z*, *Sailor Moon*, *Hamtaro*, *Yu-Gi-Oh*, and their many spinoffs, have become quite famous. There are many kinds of animation including action, adult, biography, children's, comedy, **crime**, documentary, drama, fantasy, female, historical, horror, musical, mystery, racing, **robots**, romance, science fiction, **sports**, war, and westerns. While a few major anime and **manga** (a cartoon or comical picture) are treated separately, what follows is a sampling of some of the major anime series.

Tetsujin 28 go (*Iron Man #28*) is a science fiction anime that portrays a giant robot operated by remote control. Aired in Japan (1963–1965), this is an early masterpiece of animation. It appeared on **United States** television in 1966 under the title *Gigantor*. This anime, containing nearly 100 episodes, is based on Yokoyama Mitsuteru's manga.

Saraba uchū senkan Yamato ai no senshitachi (*Farewell to Space Battleship Yamato*), produced by Voyager Entertainment in 1978, was perhaps Japan's most popular anime film. Influenced by *Star Wars* and other science fiction movies, the film "reflects the very Japanese aesthetic of the tragic beauty of youth dying for a cause."

Mezon ikkoku (*Maison Ikkoku*), a **television** show, is one of anime's greatest romantic comedies, having been adapted from **Takahashi Rumiko**'s manga. In this leading female comical presentation, the heroine is trying to enter a good university while living in a boarding house called the Maison Ikkoku. This television series, which was popular in the mid-1980s, is a love story.

Ginga tetsudō no yoru (*Night on the Galactic Railroad*) is an anime based on **Mizoguchi Kenji**'s 1927 novel of the same name. Directed by Sugii Gisaburō and produced by Central Park Media in 1985, the film is about a boy, Campanella, living in poverty in a small town. He travels by train across the Milky Way and thus frees his spirit. Giovanni, a young cat, travels through the galaxy in a magical steam engine train, visiting planets and their strange inhabitants with his friend Campanella.

Kōkaku kidōtai (*Ghost in the Shell*) is a 1995 anime hit movie based on the popular artist Masamune Shiro and directed by Oshii Mamoru. It combines advanced **computer** graphics with traditional cell animation. Set in 2029, the world is rendered borderless by super humans who live in virtual environments, watched over by law enforcement people able to download themselves into superpowered crime-busting agents. The ultimate secret agent of the future is not human, has no physical body, and can freely travel the information highways of the world, hacking and manipulating wherever and whenever.

Tranzor Z is a story about a giant robot that struggles against villains. *Space Battleship Yamato* is a cartoon where young astronaut-soldiers have one year to save the earth from destruction. *Ranma 1/2* shows an androgynous character who turns into a girl when splashed with cold water and then into a boy when hit with warm water. *Ōritsu uchūgun: Oneamisu no tsubasa* (*Royal Space Force: The Wings of Honneamise*) explores human emotions in space. *Rurōni Kenshin* presents an anime hero who leaves his friends to fight for justice in the 19th century. *Patlabor* shows police who have their own robots to combat crime and accidents of giant robot workers. *Tenchi mūyo* (*Tenchi Universe*) brings us a young hero who is meek and kindly but surrounded by attractive, sometimes bizarre **women**. *Yu-Gi-Oh* is a popular children's animated character series. *Dr. Slump* portrays an android created by a "genius" Senbei. *Hagane no renkinjutsushi* (*Fullmetal Alchemist*) uses alchemy to create fantasy situations. *Shinkidō senki Gandamu uingu* (*Mobile Suit Gundam Wing*) features giant robots that fight the forces of evil. And finally, Akamatsu Ken's *Mahō sensei Negima* (*Magical Teacher Negima*) reveals a young wizard who helps people. These are representative of the Japanese anime world.

One Piece was originally a manga series, but in 1998, the series was adapted as an anime series. Over the next decade, nearly 800 episodes entertained anime enthusiasts. The young hero has properties of rubber that enable him to accomplish all sorts of amazing feats. He searches for the ultimate treasure, which is the "one piece." This anime has amazing spinoffs offered for sale to excited fans. To date, the manga *One Piece* has sold more than 350 million copies, making it the best-selling manga in history.

Naruto Shippūden debuted in 2007 and ran until March 2017 with more than 500 episodes. Ninjas carry out numerous adventures and pranks popular with hyperactive youngsters. All the while Naruto struggles to become the greatest ninja ever.

Briefly searching the web brings a plethora of new anime presentations. *Full Metal Alchemist Brotherhood* (2010) features two brothers trying to revive their dead mother, but the effort leaves them in damaged physical form. *Angel Beats* (2010) takes us to the afterlife where rebellious teens struggle against an over-dominant young woman with superpowers. *Gosick* (2011) features a girl with superpowers who solves mysteries in the 1920s. *Hunter x Hunter* (2011) shows a young boy who strives to become a great hunter. *Mirai Nikki* (2011) introduces a young man who competes with people around the world to become the new god with his diary telling the story. *Steins;Gate* (2011) frightens everyone when university students try to defend the universe against evil aliens. *Sword Art Online* (2012) shows intercontinental intrigue. *Attack on Titan* (2013) features a young man seeking revenge after terrorists destroy his hometown. *Parasyte* (2014) terrorizes when worm-like creatures take over the brains of people. *Zankyō no Terror* (2014) reveals a bizarre internet video with clues to a terrorist attack on **Tōkyō**. *Tōkyō Ghoul* (2014) frightens with terrifying creatures that feed on human flesh. *One Punch Man* (2015) is all about a fun person who dispatches his foe with, yes, one punch.

The year 2016 was filled with a host of new anime with some of the best being *21 Days*, a fast-paced mafia drama with a revenge theme; *Kabaneri of the Iron Fortress*, in which a pandemic strikes during the industrial revolution turning humans into horrifying, infectious corpses; *Orange*, which features a high school girl who receives letters from her future self; *Mob Psycho 100*, in which a middle school student has extraordinary psychic powers; *Bungo Stray Dog*, in which a boy is kicked out of an orphanage and forced to make his life on the streets until a detective agency takes him in and he helps solve mysteries; *The Great Passage* involves the unlikely exciting adventure of making a dictionary; *Kiznaiver*, where seven very different students are kidnapped and bound together by a device that makes them feel each other's pain; *Shōwa Genroku Rakugo Shinjū*, which features a man just released from prison who learns *rakugo*, the ancient art of storytelling, and finally *Ajin* about a boy killed by a truck who becomes an *ajin* or an immortal who can endlessly regenerate.

One has only to look at the number of anime shows and films, well over 1,000 in 2005, the countless number of manga volumes, the television programs and series, the **games**, and the toys to get an idea of the tremendous popularity of this art form, not only in Japan but around the world. The anime possibilities are endless! *See also* FUJIKO FUJIO, 藤子不二雄.

ANPO. *See* UNITED STATES, RELATIONS WITH.

AOKI ISAO, 青木功 **(1942–).** An internationally famous golfer, Aoki Isao first won a **golf** tournament in England in 1978 and has been a national hero ever since. Japan's great golf legend was born in Chiba Prefecture and commenced his professional career on the Japanese tour in 1964. During his many years of play, Aoki has won nearly 80 tournaments around the world. For many years, Aoki represented his country on the Professional Golfers' Association (PGA) circuit, winning the 1983 Hawaiian Open and finishing second to Jack Nicklaus in the 1980 U.S. Open. Playing on the senior tour, Aoki continued his success, winning eight Japan Senior Opens and nine titles on the American PGA senior tour. In 2004, Aoki was elected to the prestigious World Golf Hall of Fame.

AOSHIMA YUKIO, 青島幸男 **(1932–2006).** Aoshima Yukio served as governor of **Tōkyō** from 1995 through 1999. He strongly promoted an **environmental** agenda. Originally a **television** personality, Aoshima coined the term *ecoship* and vowed to make Tōkyō more green, but he did not achieve as much as he planned. Aoshima's **election** in 1995 was something of a turning point for Tōkyō.

A former television comedian, Aoshima pledged during his campaign to scrap a planned $1.6 billion world cities exposition, a pledge that he kept. He scaled back, but did not halt, a controversial waterfront development project. Aoshima ran with no party backing and won, but he declined to run for a second term.

ARAHATA KANSON, 荒畑寒村 **(1887–1981).** A journalist and activist in the socialist and **labor** movements, Arahata Kanson was born in Kanagawa Prefecture. Based on his work at the Yokosuka Naval Arsenal and his reading of antiwar pamphlets by Kōtoku Shūsui, Sakai Toshihiko, and other leading socialists, Arahata converted to socialism in 1904. After the Russo-Japanese War, Arahata wrote for numerous socialist publications, and many consider his account of the Ashio Copper Mine incident a classic of Japanese journalism. In 1922, Arahata helped found the **Japanese Communist Party**.

After World War II, Arahata took part in the labor movement, serving on numerous labor committees, and was elected the first chairman of the National Trade Union of Metal and Engineering Workers. He also helped found the **Japan Socialist Party**, joining its Central Committee in 1947 and winning **election** to the **Diet** on its slate in 1946 and 1947. In 1948, his opposition to the party's approval of postal, tobacco tax, and train fare increases led him to leave its ranks. After a vain attempt to create a new socialist party, he was defeated in the 1949 election. In 1951, Arahata withdrew from active involvement in the labor and socialist movements, but he continued to write and exercise influence on socialist and labor movements.

ARAKAWA SHIZUKA, 荒川静香 **(1981–).** Arakawa Shizuka was the 2006 **Olympic** gold medal winner in **women's figure skating** at Turin, Italy. She was Japan's only medal winner in the 2006 Winter Olympics. She defeated the favored Irina Slutskaya (**Russia**) and Sasha Cohen (**United States**). Arakawa is the first Japanese woman to win gold in this event. In 1992, **Itō Midori** finished second to Kristi Yamaguchi. Arakawa won the world title in 2004 but dropped to ninth in 2005. She finished 13th in the 1998 Nagano Olympics and did not make the team in 2002.

ARCHITECTURE. Postwar Japan has achieved international recognition for its contributions to the field of architecture. With the internationalization of the architectural profession, Japan has seen its architects accepted as leaders in the field. Antonin Raymond (1888–1976), a long-time practitioner and participant in Japanese architecture, claimed that "the Japanese are the best architects in the world today."

Japanese architecture is deeply rooted in its own traditions. **Construction** principles from the past still survive today in various forms. For example, wooden pillars, light panels, sliding doors, and verandas around buildings are all features of the past. The link between the interior and the exterior, "living" rooms linked to nature, divisions by screens and sliding doors, and simplicity are all tendencies from the past. Yet, Japan has introduced a plethora of new architectural forms in its buildings.

Modern Japanese architecture displays various characteristics including a strong effort to design and construct buildings to fit the location in both natural and urban settings. Japanese architects strive to make the man-made architecture coexist or blend with the area's natural surroundings. The buildings also show flexibility in design while placing great importance on function.

In the postwar period, Japan struggled to provide for its people and to right its **economy**. Thus, distinctive architectural contributions in the early postwar period were nearly nonexistent as Japan struggled just to meet the bare necessities of life. Anyone who saw the drab, box-like buildings of the 1950s can attest to the architectural void. It was not until the 1960s that the creative genius of Japan came forth in its architecture.

The creation of more earthquake-resistant building techniques enabled architects to reach skyward with their creations. The construction of Japan's first super high-rise in 1968, the 36-story Kasumigaseki Building, opened the way for much larger, grander creations. Japan now has many skyscrapers with **Tōkyō** leading the way. Tōkyō presently has 46 buildings of at least 185 meters (607 feet) with **Tōkyō Skytree** rising 634 meters or 2,080 feet. By the time of the 2020 **Olympics**, Tōkyō plans to add 45 new skyscrapers with the Sky Mile Tower to reach more than a mile high. Japan is said to have the most skyscrapers in Asia and possibly in the world. The tallest building in

Japan is presently **Ōsaka**'s Abeno Harukas, which stretches to 300 meters or 984 feet. Other tall buildings in Japan include the Ringu Gate Tower Building in Izumisano (256 meters), Ōsaka World Trade Center (252 meters), and JR Central Towers in **Nagoya** (245 meters). Tōkyō City Hall in West Shinjuku stretches 243 meters into the sky.

Metabolism was an architectural movement established by **Tange Kenzō** in 1960 at the World Design Conference held in Tōkyō. Participants in this movement believed that architecture should not be static but, instead, should be "metabolic," meaning to be able to change its form and function. These architects concentrated on changeability of space and function. The key members of the group, along with its leader Tange, were Kikutake Kiyonori, **Maki Fumihiko**, Otaka Masato, and **Kurokawa Kishō**. The most striking features of Metabolism were its emphasis on **technology** and machines that coexisted with organic and biological interchangeable parts and changeable modular structural units.

The 1970s saw a struggle to regain independence in architectural matters and freedom from commercial and technological demands. **Andō Tadao**, Shinohara Kazuo, and Kurokawa Kishō led this decade's architects.

The boom in the economy in the 1980s gave rise to more innovations in architecture. More freedom and more creativity appeared in architecture. Designs became more artistic and more innovative. Architecture showed more ephemeral and more sensual qualities. Buildings appealed more to the human sensitivities.

The Tōkyō Metropolitan Government headquarters, which opened in 1991, demonstrated Japan's new architecture with classical form. The 1990s saw an increase in international collaboration. International buildings such as Peter Eisenman's NC Building, Norman Foster's Century Tower, Philippe Starck's Asahi Super Dry Hall, and Mario Botta's Watarium show the international infusion. The names Andō Tadao, **Itō Toyō**, and Kuma Kengo, along with Kishi Waro, Takamatsu Shin, Yamamoto Riken, Kitagawara Atsushi, and **Hasegawa Itsuko**, dominated Japanese architecture.

Exciting new faces have recently appeared on the Japanese architectural scene. **Sejima Kazuyo** and her creative partner Nishizawa Ryue have gained international recognition for their work. Recently, Japanese architects have launched incredibly innovative designs with an avant-garde appearance. Modernity and sustainability are the watchwords of Japanese architecture. *See also* HOUSING.

ARIYOSHI SAWAKO, 有吉佐和子 (1931–1984). Novelist Ariyoshi Sawako was born in Wakayama Prefecture and graduated from Tōkyō Women's Christian University, where she majored in English literature. Recognized for her persistent emphasis on, and adept handling of, social issues, Ariyoshi was one of Japan's most popular **women** writers. Early stories, such as *Jiuta*

(*Ballads*, 1956), brought to life the traditional world of Japanese entertainers and artists. In the 1960s and 1970s, her work increasingly approached nonfiction as she began dealing with social problems. *Kinokawa* (*The River Ki*, 1959), her first long novel, is a sensitive record of four generations of women of Kii Province. She took a similar vein in *Hanaoka Seishu no tsuma* (*The Doctor's Wife*, 1966), an account of the 18th-century surgeon Hanaoka Seishu and his devoted wife.

Ariyoshi's *Kōkotsu no hito* (*The Twilight Years*, 1972), a novel about problems of the elderly, and *Fukugō osen* (*Compound Pollution*, 1975), a look at pollution in Japan, became bestsellers. Suffering health problems of her own, Ariyoshi drew a vivid portrait of a dying parent and his caregiver. Her novels championed the ill and generated popular support for improving welfare for the elderly. *See also* LITERATURE.

ASADA AKIRA, 浅田彰 **(1957–).** Asada Akira is a prominent postwar intellectual who writes on trends in **advertising** and consumer spending. He deals with consumer economic issues. He is one of the most prolific editors and curators in Japan. At the Inter-Communication Center in **Tōkyō**, Asada works on large-scale urban design projects with people like **Isozaki Arata**. He strongly believes that it is important to support young artists who explore gender- and communication-related concepts. Asada's *Kōzō to chikara kigōron o koete* (*Structure and Power*, 1983) became a national bestseller. His writings are problematic and involve him in ongoing debates with a number of Western intellectuals. Besides making extensive lecture tours throughout Europe and the **United States**, Asada teaches economics at Kyōto University and is the dean of its graduate school.

ASADA MAO, 浅田真央 **(1990–).** Asada Mao is presently Japan's best-known and most competitive **figure skater**. Winner of the silver medal in the 2010 **Olympics**, she is famous for her triple axel jumps. A three-time World champion, three-time Four Continents champion, and four-time Grand Prix champion, Mao holds the world record for the women's short program score. She is a native of **Nagoya**. As of 2016, she was ranked as the world's 10th-best skater but has been ranked as high as second. **Itō Midori**, Japan's first world champion, a silver medalist in the 1992 Olympics, and also from Nagoya, is Asada's mentor.

ASAHI SHIMBUN, 朝日新聞*.* The *Asahi Shimbun* is a leading Japanese **newspaper**. Its circulation is around 11 million, far less than *Yomiuri Shimbun* but with considerably greater influence. Its views are generally on the liberal side. Its readers are more likely well-educated, white-collar people. Founded in 1879 by Murayama Ryōhei in **Ōsaka** as a small illustrated paper, it continued to grow by concentrating on the dissemination of information rather than opinions. Murayama founded a **Tōkyō** branch in 1888 by purchasing and combining three small newspapers. In the postwar period, **Ogata Taketora** was a leading figure in advancing the *Asahi Shimbun*. His innovations, combined with his political influence, made the paper a powerful force.

Asahi Shimbun, the second largest of Japan's five national newspapers, has a circulation of eight million in the morning and three million in the evening. In 2001, Asahi ceased publishing the *Asahi Evening News*, its English-language newspaper, but linked with the *International Herald Tribune* to jointly publish an English-language paper. Asahi owns and publishes *AERA*, a news magazine, and *Shūkan Asahi* (*Weekly Asahi*); it also owns and operates TV Asahi. The Asahi Group is engaged in publishing, radio and television broadcasting, printing, **advertising**, and marketing, as well as operating a news service.

On 26 June 2007, *Asahi Shimbun* named Funabashi Yōichi its third editor in chief. Ueno Shōichi, a co-owner of the paper since 1997, died on 29 February 2016. He was the great-grandson of Ueno Riichi, who jointly started the newspaper in Ōsaka with Murayama Ryōhei in 1879. Wakamiya Yoshibum, editor in chief of the daily *Asahi Shimbun*, died 28 April 2016 while in Beijing.

A rather left-leaning newspaper, the *Asahi Shimbun* has opposed altering Article 9 of the **Constitution**, has been harsh on political scandals, and has been critical of those who deny the **"comfort women"** issue. Although it later retracted the article, the paper was critical of the cowardice of people in charge of the Fukushima Daiichi **Nuclear Power** plant.

ASAKURA DAISUKE, 浅倉大介 **(1967–).** Born in **Tōkyō**, Asakura Daisuke is Japan's youngest musical million-hit performer. He is not so much a musician as he is a **music** producer. He was the synthesizer manipulator for the group TMN when it was famous. He organized the group Access as well as the group Iceman, a J-Pop band. Known as DA, Asakura produced many compositions and synthesizer pieces. He did the music for the **anime** and the **television** series *Gravitation*. Although his music is mainly electronic, his work has gone through many phases. Asakura has also written hundreds of songs for many bands as well as producing the T.M. Revolution.

ASANO TADANOBU, 佐藤忠信 **(1973–).** Asano Tadanobu, an **actor**, was born in **Yokohama** to a Japanese father and a mother of Navajo American ancestry. His fair complexion and lighter-than-black eyes drew attention from his male and female schoolmates. His father, an actors' agent, suggested he take on what became his first role, in the **television** show *Kimpachi Sensei* at the age of 16.

Asano's **film** debut was in *Bataashi Kingyo* (*Swimming Upstream*, 1990), though his first major critical success was in *Fried Dragon Fish* (1993). His first success in the West was in Koreeda Hirokazu's *Maboroshi no hikari* (*Phantasmic Light*, 1995), in which he plays a man who inexplicably throws himself in front of a train, widowing his wife and orphaning his infant son. His best-known works internationally are the samurai films *Gohatto* (*Taboo*, 1999) and *Zatōichi* (2003). In 2007, Asano starred in the blockbuster *Mongol*, where he plays the role of Temujin, or Genghis Khan. Recently, Asano has played major roles in *Battleship* (2012), a military science fiction action film; *47 Rōnin* (2013), where he plays Lord Kira; and *Silence* (2016), based on the powerful novel by **Endō Shūsaku**, in which he is the interpreter.

Although his characters are psychologically offbeat, if not downright psychotic, in real life, Asano is described as a down-to-earth family man.

ASANUMA INEJIRŌ, 浅沼稲次郎 **(1898–1960).** Asanuma Inejirō was a prominent socialist politician who championed economic change in Japan and strongly criticized the intrusion of the **United States** into his country. His left-wing positions greatly frustrated Japan's conservative elements, especially Prime Minister **Ikeda Hayato**. Born in Miyakejima, **Tōkyō** Prefecture, he graduated from Waseda University in 1923. While still a college student, he joined the fledgling **Japanese Communist Party** and took part in numerous social movements. He was elected to the **House of Representatives** on the Socialist Masses Party (Shakai Taishūtō) slate in 1936 and served a total of 20 years in the **Diet**.

Immediately after World War II, Asanuma helped organize the **Japan Socialist Party**, eventually becoming its secretary-general and chairman. He opposed the **United States–Japan Security Treaty** and favored immediate recognition of **China**. During a visit to Beijing in March 1959, he denounced American imperialism as the common enemy of both Japan and China in what would come to be called the "Asanuma statement." This speech aroused considerable controversy in Japan. Very popular with workers and shopkeepers, he lived in modest public **housing** his entire life. Asanuma is best remembered for being stabbed to death by a right-wing **student** while giving a speech, all caught graphically on **television**. *See also* FOREIGN POLICY.

ASASHŌRYŪ AKINORI, 朝青龍明徳 **(1980–).** Asashōryū Akinori, whose birth name is Dolgorsuren Dagvadorj, is a Mongolian-born **sumō** wrestler. Although not a huge man by sumō standards, Asashōryū relies on speed and technique to defeat his opponents. After his debut in 1999, Asashōryū needed only 24 tournaments to win his first top division championship, the quickest that any wrestler has achieved this. The Japanese Sumō Association promoted Asashōryū to the rank of grand champion (*yoko-*

zuna) after he won the January 2003 championship. In 2004, Asashōryū had two consecutive perfect 15–0 tournaments, had a streak of 35 unbeaten matches, and won five tournaments. From November 2004, Asashōryū won seven straight tournaments, a modern record. In January 2010, Asashōryū won his 25th tournament championship, giving him the third-highest total in the postwar period and trailing only sumō greats **Taihō** with 32 championships and **Chiyonofuji** with 31.

Asashōryū's career ended abruptly when he was forced to retire due to a barroom altercation, which followed on the heels of other indiscretions. Sumō aficionados roundly criticized him. They charged him with bad behavior in and out of the ring. The press accused him of not living up to the proper standards of behavior. They criticized him for skipping a tournament, missing expected public appearances, and failing to uphold the proper dignity of a sumō star. The Japan Sumō Association even levied one of its severest sanctions on Asashōryū. After retirement, he returned home to Mongolia and is now pursuing a business career. Subsequently, Asashōryū has been praised for his philanthropy, especially helping Mongolian **Olympic** athletes.

ASHIDA HITOSHI, 芦田均 (1887–1959). Ashida Hitoshi was a politician and, in 1948, the **prime minister** of Japan for seven months. A native of **Kyōto**, he graduated from Tōkyō Imperial University in 1912 and entered the **Ministry of Foreign Affairs**, but he resigned after the Manchurian incident over policy disagreements. He entered the **Diet** in 1932 as a Seiyūkai member. He was elected 10 times subsequently, including once in 1942 as a nongovernment-sponsored candidate. He lectured at Keiō University and, as president of the *Japan Times* (1933–1939), spoke out against military involvement in political affairs.

In 1945, Ashida became minister of welfare. Subsequently, he helped **Hatoyama Ichirō** form the **Liberal Party**, but in March 1947, he participated in the founding of the **Democratic Party**, of which he became president. Advocating moderate policies, he cooperated with the **Japan Socialist Party** (JSP) and, in June 1947, became foreign minister and deputy prime minister under **Katayama Tetsu**. On 10 March 1948, he succeeded Katayama as prime minister, heading a coalition **cabinet** of Democratic Party, JSP, and National Cooperative Party (Kokumin Kyōdōtō) members. Ashida served as his own foreign minister. He promoted the import of foreign capital to aid economic recovery and firmly opposed communism.

However, Ashida's cooperation with the Socialists alienated the conservative wing of his own party. The Socialists also became divided, and the cabinet resigned on 15 October 1948 over accusations of corruption among cabinet members in connection with the **Shōwa Denkō scandal**. Ashida himself was acquitted in 1958. He remained active in politics during the early 1950s but spent much of his time writing diplomatic history. *See also* FOREIGN POLICY.

ASŌ TARŌ, 麻生太郎 **(1940–).** After serving in various ministerial positions, **Liberal Democratic Party** (LDP) politician Asō Tarō became **prime minister** on 24 September 2008. Asō, who has a strong political legacy, was born in Fukuoka where his father was chairman of the Asō Cement Company and was closely linked to Prime Minister **Tanaka Kakuei**; his grandfather was **Yoshida Shigeru**, and his wife is the daughter of **Suzuki Zenkō**. After graduating from Gakushūin University, Asō studied at Stanford University and the University of London. He was a member of the Japanese shooting team at the 1976 **Olympics** in Montreal. He entered his father's company in 1966, and he served as president of the Asō Mining Company from 1973 to 1979 when he was elected to the **House of Representatives**. In 2003, he joined **Koizumi Jun'ichirō**'s **cabinet** first as the minister of internal affairs and then from 2005 to 2007 as foreign minister, where his pugnacious nationalism offended many of Japan's neighbors.

In 2007 and 2008, Asō served briefly as secretary-general of the LDP and on 22 September 2008 was elected as president of the party, succeeding **Fukuda Yasuo**. Two days later Asō was named prime minister but served only a year, being replaced on 16 September 2009. In response to the flagging world economic conditions, Asō offered a large economic stimulus package but was not successful. He extended the naval refueling mission, allowing Japan to maintain its small but symbolic presence in the U.S.-led military action in Afghanistan.

Asō was conservative on **foreign policy** issues and took confrontational stances toward **North Korea** and **China**. He frequently made controversial statements that led to trouble. In 2003, he remarked that Koreans wanted to change their names to Japanese names during colonial rule. In 2005, he praised Japan for having "one nation, one civilization, one language, one culture and one race." In January 2006, he called for the **emperor** to visit the controversial **Yasukuni Shrine** and, later that year, praised Japan's colonization of **Taiwan** and suggested that it was independent from the People's Republic of China. In 2007, he belittled *burakumin* people by a flippant comment about their suitability to hold political office. Further, he was also known to misread speeches or mispronounce words, providing a source of glee for his opponents. Finally, despite evidence to the contrary, he refused until recently to admit that Asō Cement Company had used some 300 Australian, British, and Dutch prisoners of war to work in his grandfather's company.

Asō belongs to the Roman Catholic Church but irritated other Japanese Christians when he prayed at Ise **Shintō** Shrine on New Year's Day in 2009. He enjoys good gourmet food and expensive wines at high-class restaurants. He is a big fan of **manga**. Given his tastes, his frequent slips of the tongue, and his erratic stewardship over the shaky **economy**, Asō's approval ratings reached an all-time low in the summer of 2009, dropping below 20 percent, thus providing justification for his ouster from the prime minister's office.

Despite continuing to be gaffe-prone—suggesting that the elderly were a drain on the country's finances (January 2013) and remarking that Japan could learn from Nazi Germany about how to change its **constitution** (August 2013)—Asō continues to hold great political influence and power. Since 1979, he has been elected to the House of Representatives 13 times. **Abe Shinzō** appointed him deputy prime minister and **minister of finance** in December 2012, positions he still holds as of January 2018. Asō Tarō is Japan's longest-serving finance minister ever.

ASTRONAUTS/SPACE EXPLORATION. In 1985, Japan's Institute of Space and Aeronautical Science launched the *Sakigake* probe, becoming the first interplanetary flight to rendezvous with Halley's Comet, and starting Japan's space program. Also in 1985, the Japan space program launched *Suisei* ("Comet") into heliocentric orbit also to fly by Halley's Comet. In 1989, Japan successfully launched its first private-sector communications satellite, JCSAT-1.

Akiyama Toyohirō (1942–), a former **television** reporter for TBS, became the first Japanese citizen in space when in 1990 he traveled to the Mir space station aboard a **Russian** Soyuz spacecraft. Mōri Mamori (1948–) was Japan's first shuttle astronaut who flew on the *Endeavour* in 2000 and on an eight-day mission in 1992. Other astronauts include Mukai Chiaki (1952–), a female cardiovascular surgeon; Doi Takao (1954–), who flew on the space shuttle *Columbia* in 1997; Wakata Koichi (1963–), the first Japanese astronaut to travel with Americans on the *Endeavour* in 1996 and in 2000 on the *Discovery*; and Noguchi Sōichi (1965–), who flew on the American *Discovery* mission.

In 1998, Japan launched *Nozomi* (Hope), its first unmanned space probe. It was a Mars orbiting aeronomy mission designed to study the Martian upper atmosphere and its interaction with the solar and wind power, and to produce technologies for use in future planetary missions.

Japan Aerospace Exploration Agency (JAXA) is Japan's leading space investigation body. It was formed in 2003 by the merger of Japan's Institute of Space and Aeronautical Science, which was responsible for space and planetary research; the National Aerospace Laboratory of Japan, which focused on aviation research; and Japan's National Space Development Agency, which created rockets, satellites, and other experiments.

In 2012, new legislation extended JAXA's sole objective from peaceful purposes only to include some military space development, such as missile early warning systems. Political control of JAXA passed from the **Ministry of Economy, Trade, and Industry** to the **prime minister**'s cabinet office of Space Policy.

Japan has had a total of eight astronauts travel to the International Space Station. Wakata Koichi made trips in 2000, 2009, and again in 2013; Noguchi Shōichi made trips in 2005 and 2009, Doi Takao in 2008, Hoshide Akihiko in 2008 and 2012, Yamazaki Naoko (the only female) in 2010, Furukawa Satoshi in 2011, Yui Kimiya in 2015, and Onishi Takuya in 2016.

In June 2014, Japan's Ministry of State for **Science and Technology** Policy said it was considering a space mission to Mars. It indicated that unmanned exploration, manned missions to Mars, and long-term settlement on the moon were objectives requiring international cooperation and support.

JAXA launched a successor mission called Hayabusa2 in December 2014. The spacecraft is en route to a carbonaceous asteroid called 162173 Ryugu, where it will arrive in mid-2018 and deploy several small **robots** on the surface. The spacecraft is expected to leave the asteroid in late 2019 and come back to Earth in late 2020.

JAXA became a National Research and Development Agency in April 2015 and took a new step forward to achieve optimal R&D achievements for Japan. JAXA launched the ASTRO-H/Hitomi X-ray observatory in early 2016, but the mission lost contact with Earth and was declared lost in April of that year.

JAXA is reviewing a new spacecraft mission to the Martian system, a sample return mission to Phobos called Martian Moons Explorer whose primary goal is to determine the origin of the moons of Mars. The launch of the Martian Moons Explorer is expected to be in 2022.

ASUKATA ICHIO, 飛鳥田一雄 (1915–1990). Asukata Ichio was a politician and chairman of the **Japan Socialist Party** (JSP) from 1977 until 1983. Born in **Yokohama**, Asukata graduated in 1937 from Meiji University Law School and represented many **labor** unions. In 1945, he helped reorganize the JSP. After serving on the Yokohama city council and in the Kanagawa Prefectural Assembly, he was elected to the **House of Representatives** in 1953, where for 10 years he opposed the **defense** and **foreign policies** of the **Liberal Democratic Party** (LDP). Elected mayor of Yokohama in 1963, the following year Asukata formed the National Association of Progressive Mayors and encouraged citizen participation in local affairs. While chairman of the JSP, he sought to unite its various factions and cooperate with other opposition parties against the ruling LDP. He rejected armaments buildup and nuclear weapons.

AUM SHINRIKYŌ, オウム真理教**.** Matsumoto Chizuo, alias Asahara Shoko (1955–2018), founded Aum Shinrikyō, a religious cult, in 1984. Aum Shinrikyō members practiced aggressive, paranoid, militant-style activities in the 1990s. Asahara, nearly blind, used his charismatic powers to attract bright, college-educated, middle-class adherents to this **new religion**. He provided a network of social relations for people adrift in the world. Many of them led spartan lives in communes at the Aum headquarters in the village of Kamikuishiki near Mount Fuji. They practiced acts of violence, sought to create Armageddon, manufactured chemical weapons, and formed alliances with people from **Russia**.

Aum members released sarin gas in four **Tōkyō** subways on 20 March 1995, killing 12 people and injuring more than 6,000. The police have closely watched its activity since the 1995 incident. The authorities arrested Asahara and forced Aum to dismantle. In 2004, after an eight-year trial, the Tōkyō District Court found Asahara guilty of masterminding the attack and sentenced him and several other Aum members to death for their terrorist attacks.

In July 2018, the government executed Asahara and six of his co-conspirators. Aum has split into two groups, Aleph and Hikari no Wa. Many countries, even **North Korea**, have formally designated Aum a terrorist organization, and Russia has cracked down on the group. In January 2015, the Japan Public Security Examination Commission renewed its surveillance on Aum, which continues to have about 1,000 members.

AUTOMOBILE INDUSTRY. In the years since World War II, Japan's automobile industry has evolved dramatically. Not only has Japan become thoroughly motorized, but the globe has become heavily dependent on Japanese cars. Indeed, Japan has become a world leader in the manufacturing of automobiles.

In the early 1950s, the **Ministry of International Trade and Industry** (MITI) promoted new **technologies** in the domestic production of cars. Working with automotive leaders, Japan set out to build better cars. It sponsored automobile shows, imported new technologies, and streamlined the production facilities. MITI took the lead in promoting an infrastructure for a motorized society. In the early postwar period, most Japanese cars were produced through tie-ups with foreign firms, but MITI began to encourage the production of purely domestic cars.

Automobile makers worked together to encourage the manufacture of small, fuel-efficient cars. The Japan Automobile Manufacturers Association (JAMA) was established in 1967 and took the lead in promoting high-quality, efficient automobiles throughout the Japanese auto industry. JAMA helped lead Japan into becoming one of the world's premier auto manufacturers.

In the 1970s, Japan became an important exporter of automobiles. Quality, reliability, fuel efficiency, and style made Japanese cars highly popular on the international market. In the 1980s, Japan began manufacturing cars abroad and working in partnership with Western manufacturers. Today, Japan is part of a global automobile industry.

By the 1990s, **Toyota, Nissan, Honda,** and **Mitsubishi Motors** were four of the top 10 automobile producers in the world. Other leading Japanese automobile companies include **Mazda, Isuzu,** Fuji, **Daihatsu, Suzuki,** Hino, and **Yamaha.**

In 2015, worldwide automobile production figures showed **China** producing 24.5 million units, the **United States** making 12.1 million units, and Japan manufacturing 9.3 million units. These top three countries were followed by Germany with 6 million units, **South Korea** with 4.6 million, and India with 4.1 million.

In terms of world carmakers, in 2016, Toyota and Volkswagen were virtually tied for first with just over 10 million vehicles. Nissan ranked fourth; Honda, sixth; Mazda, 14th; Suzuki, 18th; Subaru, 26th; Mitsubishi, 27th; and Daihatsu, 29th. In that year, Japan's eight automakers increased North American sales by 11 percent to 1.9 million vehicles. *See also* ECONOMY.

AYUKAWA YOSHISUKE, 鮎川義介 **(1880–1967).** Also known as Ayukawa Gisuke and Aikawa Yoshisuke, Ayukawa Yoshisuke was a creative businessman who founded **Nissan** Enterprises. He graduated from Tōkyō Imperial University with a degree in engineering, after which he worked in various engineering positions. One of Japan's leading industrialists, he assumed the presidency of a company that would become Nissan Enterprises in 1928. He also headed a firm in Manchuria and for this was convicted of war crimes and purged in the postwar period. However, after his release from prison, he was elected a member of the **House of Councillors** while continuing to serve as a leading **business** promoter. *See also* AUTOMOBILE INDUSTRY.

B

BABA SHŌHEI, 馬場正平 **(1938–1999).** Baba Shōhei, at nearly 7 feet tall and well over 300 pounds, was truly deserving of the nickname "Giant Baba." Coming from Niigata Prefecture, he played a variety of **sports** as he was growing up. After high school, he played professional **baseball**, pitching for the **Yomiuri Giants**, then for the Taiyo Whales. However, it was in professional **wrestling** that Baba would make his lasting mark. At the advice of the great wrestler Rikidōzan (1924–1963), he entered the professional wrestling world in 1960. He became the first and only Japanese to win the National Wrestling Alliance world heavyweight title three times. He holds the Japanese record of 5,759 wins.

Baba nearly single-handedly saved the sport of professional wrestling from extinction in Japan. When Rikidōzan was murdered while clashing with the *yakuza*, Japanese wrestling took a heavy loss. However, several young Japanese wrestlers whom Rikidōzan had taken under his wing, including Baba and Antonio Inoki, managed to revive the sport. Baba was one of the world's elite wrestlers. He won 16 different tournaments, often defeating 8–10 men in one night. However, in 1971–1972, Baba had a series of disagreements with leaders of the Japan Wrestling Association and left the group to start his own promotion, All-Japan Pro Wrestling, which crowned him heavyweight champion in 1972.

BAMBOO SHOOT TRIBE (*TAKENOKOZOKU***,** 竹の子族**).** "Bamboo Shoot Tribe" was a popular name applied to a large group of Japanese teenagers in the 1970s and 1980s who gathered Sunday afternoons in the Harajuku section of **Tōkyō** to play **music**, dance, and perform in colorful costumes. The name came from a popular clothing store in the area. The Bamboo Shoot Tribe, with its teenage, punk-style **fashion**, hip-hop music, and rockabilly dancers, was a youthful expression of independence and a desire to act out and challenge the traditional mores of Japanese society.

BANDAI, バンダイ. Bandai, headed by Yamashina Mokoto, was founded in 1950 and originally made primarily tin-plated toys. Now it is Japan's largest and the world's fourth-largest toy company after Mattel, Hasbro, and the LEGO group. With 53 subsidiaries in 18 countries, Bandai has global interests in video game software, multimedia, **music**, full-length feature **films**, **vending machines**, trading cards, and popular toys. After the merger with video game developer and producer Namco, Bandai is now under the management of Namco Bandai Holdings Inc.

Bandai also operates in the **United States** and has grown to be the master toy licensee of some of the most popular properties in children's toys and entertainment, including the Power Rangers, Strawberry Shortcake, and **Hello Kitty** lines. It manufactures and sells games and toys, action figures, children's **television** programs, and many cartoons, dolls, and toys, including Sailor Moon, **Gundam**, Power Rangers, Digimon, Ultraman, Super Sentai, Super Robot, Kamen Rider, Tamagotchi, *Doraemon*, Dragon Ball, and many others.

BANK OF JAPAN (NIHON GINKŌ, 日本銀行**).** The Bank of Japan (BoJ) is Japan's central bank and the only institution that issues Japanese money. It functions as the treasurer of Japan and directs its monetary policy as well as shapes its **banking** structure. Established in 1882, the BoJ is the primary fiscal institution of the Japanese government today. Historically, the BoJ has been a major factor in Japan's economic development. Directed by the **Ministry of Finance**, the bank regulates the value of the yen and oversees the yen in the foreign exchange market. It issues and manages banknotes, implements monetary policy, provides settlement services, ensures stability of the financial system, compiles economic data, and runs the treasury and government securities operation. Thus, it has an immense impact on Japan's **economy** and monetary policies.

Japanese bankers, guided by the **Occupation** authorities, restructured the BoJ into a more independent entity. However, even though in 1997 there was a major rewriting of the Bank of Japan Law intended to give it more autonomy, the BoJ has been criticized for its lack of independence.

In 1986, Prime Minister **Nakasone Yasuhiro** entrusted Maekawa Haruo, the president of the BoJ, with preparing a "Report on the Long-Term Restructuring of the Japanese Economy," which came to be known as the "Maekawa Report." It urged Japan to become more dependent on its domestic markets rather than on exports for its economic growth. Recent BoJ governors include Hayami Masaru (1998–2003), Fukui Toshihiko (2003–2008), Shirakawa Masaaki (2008–2013), and **Kuroda Haruhiko** (2013–).

In 2012, at Prime Minister **Abe Shinzō**'s urging, the BoJ took steps to curb monetary deflation. The Bank of Japan's Governor Kuroda stepped up the purchase of securities and bonds in an attempt to increase Japan's money base within a two-year framework. However, as of 2016, the policies have had little effect on deflation.

The BoJ is the largest holder of Japanese government bonds in the domestic equity market. In March 2017, it held $3.79 trillion or about 40 percent of the total. As of early 2017, Japanese government bonds are considered less risky than U.S. Treasuries, the first time this has happened in seven years.

BANKING. In Japan, banks hold a large portion of individual wealth and supply a major part of the capital to run Japan's corporations. Banks have a long history in Japan, dating from at least the beginning of the 17th century. During the 19th century, banks experienced new developments and expansion of activity. In the postwar period, the **Bank of Japan** (BoJ) plays the central role as it issues currency, serves as the bank for the government, implements monetary policy, and oversees fiscal policy. Commercial banks collect huge amounts of savings and funnel these into businesses.

The Dai-Ichi Bank, established in 1873, was Japan's first state bank. In 1971, it merged with Nippon Kangyō Bank to form the largest commercial bank in Japan. With about 400 branches, it was Japan's only bank with branches in every prefecture. In 1999, it consolidated with the Industrial Bank of Japan and Fuji Bank to form, at that time, the world's largest bank.

The Fuji Bank, formerly known as the Yasuda Bank, started in the 1870s but became the Fuji Bank in 1948. It opened a branch in London in 1952 and, in 1987, became the first Japanese bank listed on the London Stock Exchange. It has approximately 300 domestic branches and about 50 foreign-based offices. In 1999, it consolidated with the Industrial Bank of Japan and **Dai-Ichi Kangyō Bank** to form one of the world's largest banks.

The Sumitomo Bank, established in 1895 by Sumitomo Kichizaemon VII, was one of the largest city banks in Japan, and the third largest in Asia as of 2000. Sumitomo was the first Japanese private bank to expand overseas, opening branches in San Francisco and Hawaii as early as 1916. In 1999, Sumitomo entered a strategic alliance with Daiwa Securities Group. Later that year, it merged with Sakura Bank and, by 2002, became the second-largest bank in the world. This merger was unusual in that it marked the first time that major firms from two rival *keiretsu* groups joined together. The **Sumitomo** headquarters is in **Ōsaka**.

The Industrial Bank of Japan, formed in 1902, specialized in long-term credit to industry. In the 1970s, it played an important part in the international financial market, underwriting bonds issued by foreign governments and issuing yen-based bonds. By 2000, it was the eighth-largest bank in Asia. Soon thereafter, it consolidated with Fuji Bank and Dai-Ichi Kangyō Bank to form one of the world's largest banks under the name of the latter.

The Sanwa Bank, started in 1933 by the merger of three smaller banks, has become one of the leading city banks in Japan. It has a network that extends to 31 countries, including key capital markets in Europe, Asia, and America. It provides a wide variety of commercial banking and financial services as well as international banking services. As of 2000, it ranked as the fifth-largest bank in Asia. Sanwa Bank is closely associated with **Nisshō Iwai Corporation** and Nichimen Corporation.

The Bank of Tōkyō, organized in 1946, served as Japan's foreign exchange bank with many offices operating overseas. It played an important part in Japan's rapid economic growth during the 1950s. It merged with Mitsubishi Bank to form the Bank of Tōkyō–Mitsubishi. As of 2000, it was Asia's largest and the world's third-largest bank. It has more than 400 offices worldwide. Much of its **business** is international. It is the only Japanese financial institution listed on the New York Stock Exchange.

The Long-Term Credit Bank of Japan, incorporated in 1952, was the second-largest private bank specializing in long-term credit to industry. It provided financial aid for industrial recovery following World War II. It initially specialized in **steel**, coal, electric, and shipping industries but eventually became involved in other sectors.

Nippon Credit Bank was one of the three long-term credit banks established after the war to encourage the rebirth of industry. First incorporated as the Japan Real Estate Bank in 1957, it changed its name to Nippon Credit Bank in 1977. Nippon Credit has 30 domestic and six overseas offices. In 1998, the government nationalized the bank and took control of it the next year.

Sakura Bank was established in the early 1990s through the merger of Mitsui Bank and Taiyo Kōbe Bank. By 2000, Sakura had more than 16,000 employees and more than 500 offices in Japan and abroad and was the fifth-largest bank in Asia. In 2002, it merged with Sumitomo Bank.

In the countryside, **agricultural cooperatives** play a major role in providing banking and financial services to farmers.

Japan has been a leader in the international banking scene. In 1952, it joined the International Monetary Fund. It is also a leading participant in the World Bank. The Asian Development Bank (ADB) is a nonprofit financial institution with Asian governments as shareholders who are also the recipients of funding where appropriate. It was founded in 1966 with 31 member states and has now grown to include 63. The ADB is a multilateral financial institution dedicated to reducing poverty in Asia and the Pacific. Headquartered in Manila, the Philippines, the president of the ADB is always from Japan and is appointed by the Japanese government.

In the late 1980s, the top 10 banks in the world were located in Japan. Since the 1990s, Japan has experienced three downturns of the **economy**. While Japan suffers from a variety of structural problems, the most acute problem has been the crushing debt burden carried by the banks from bad loans caused by the collapse in asset prices. Yet as of the early 2000s, eight of the top 20 banks were Japanese (refer to appendix N).

In 2017, **Mitsubishi UFJ Financial Group** (ranked fourth in the world), **Mizuho Financial Group** (13th), and **Sumitomo Mitsui Financial Group** (15th) were the leaders among Japan's megabanks. According to a 27 February 2017 report in *Nikkei*, they are also the leaders in world banking, ranking at the top. They have all invested in bitcoin exchanges and seem to be joining the digital technology in finances. These companies are using more technology including the use of artificial intelligence to screen personal loan applications. In the April–June 2017 period, the assets at the country's three megabanks, together with the smaller Sumitomo Mitsui Financial Group and Resona Holdings, reached nearly $7.43 trillion. *See also* FOREIGN POLICY; SECURITIES COMPANIES.

BASEBALL. First introduced to Japan in the 1870s, baseball became quite popular. High school and college games first captured fan attention with the National High School Baseball Tournament, which started in 1915, and strong college competition in the 1920s. **Shōriki Matsutarō**, owner of the *Yomiuri Shimbun*, founded the **Yomiuri Giants** in 1934, and soon seven teams, many sponsored by **newspapers** or **railroad** lines, formed the Japan Professional League in 1936.

Although interrupted by the Pacific War, professional baseball resumed soon after the end of the conflict. The two-league system, with several new teams and the Japan Series, started in 1950. During the years 1965–1973, the Yomiuri Giants dominated professional baseball in Japan, winning nine straight championships. Overall, the Giants have won 34 pennants and 22 Japan Series, more than the **Seibu** Lions with 21 pennants and 13 Japan Series. Since 1982, the Seibu Lions, now known as the Saitama Seibu Lions, have won 16 pennants and 10 Japan Series titles. **Department store** owner **Tsutsumi Yoshiaki** built the fine Seibu Lions team and its modern ballpark. Operating on a small budget, the **Tōkyō** Yakult Swallows won five pennants and four Japan Series championships between 1992 and 2001.

From 2010 through 2017, the Fukuoka SoftBank Hawks won four Japan Series titles with one each for the Chiba Lotte Marines, Yomiuri Giants, Tōhoku Rakuten Golden Eagles, and Nippon-Ham Fighters.

Professional baseball features two leagues. The Central League has the Chūnichi Dragons (**Nagoya**), Hanshin Tigers (**Ōsaka** area), Hiroshima-Toyo Carp, Yakult Swallows (Tōkyō), **Yokohama** DeNA BayStars, and the Yomiuri Giants (Tōkyō). The Pacific League has the Chiba **Lotte** Marines,

Fukuoka **SoftBank** Hawks, Hokkaidō Nippon Ham Fighters, Orix Buffaloes (Ōsaka and **Kōbe**), Saitama Seibu Lions (Tokorozawa), and the Tōhoku Rakuten Golden Eagles (Sendai).

Oh Sadaharu was the world's leading home run hitter with 868 to his credit, but hitters such as Doi Masahiro, Harimoto Isao, **Nagashima Shigeo**, **Nomura Katsuya**, Ōsugi Katsuo, and Tabuchi Koichi all hit more than 400 home runs in their careers.

Only two Japanese have ever played more games than Harimoto Isao's 2,752 games. Harimoto was Japanese baseball's all-time leader in hits with 3,085, giving him a career average of well over one hit per game for his 23 seasons of play. **Suzuki "Ichirō"** surpassed this record in 2009. Harimoto was also third in runs scored, with 1,523 to his credit. His final batting average was .319, placing him a bare fraction behind only two others. His career totals of 420 doubles (fourth), 72 triples (ninth), and 1,676 runs batted in (fourth) place him in elite company as an offensive threat. He is one of only four Japanese baseball players who are in the all-time career top 10 in six categories.

Fujimoto Hideo (1918–1997) was one of Japan's greatest pitchers ever. He holds the best-ever ERA in the history of Japanese baseball at 1.9. He was the first-ever player in Japan to pitch a perfect game, which was on 28 June 1950. Winner of the best ERA award three times, he was the Giants' ace pitcher during the late 1940s and early 1950s.

Bessho Takehiko (1922–1999) was a leading baseball pitcher who holds several career records. Pitching for 17 years, mostly with the Yomiuri Giants, he had the seventh-best ERA (2.18) and winning percentage (.635) of all Japanese pitchers. The fifth-greatest pitcher ever in wins (310) and innings pitched (4,351), he stands behind only three others in shutouts with 72, and complete games, with 335. He was the most valuable player (MVP) for the Japanese Series in 1952 and 1955.

Inao Kazuhisa (1937–2007) entered professional baseball in 1956 and pitched for 14 seasons, hurling 3,599 innings in his career, 10th among pitchers. He tossed 2,574 strikeouts (seventh), pitched in 756 games (seventh), and won 276 of them (eighth). Only Fujimoto Hideo and Noguchi surpass his all-time ERA of 1.98. His astonishing winning percentage of .668 (276–137) makes him one of only two pitchers who won more than two-thirds of their games. A three-time, 30-game winner, Inao had an incredible 42 victories in 1961 and was a major star in the Lions dynasty. Inao stands in the top 10 of six different Japanese baseball categories. He later managed the Nishitetsu Lions and the Lotte Orions.

Yoneda Tetsuya (1938–), similar to Nomura Katsuya (1935–), would be king of the pitching mound if not for the presence of an unparalleled legend in the game. Eighth in career complete games (262) and seventh in shutouts

(64), Yoneda finished at or near the top in four different categories. He is second in all-time wins (350), innings pitched (5,130), and strikeouts (3,388). In his 22 seasons on the mound, he appeared in an unequalled 949 games.

Some Americans have made a name for themselves in Japanese baseball. Karl "Tuffy" Rhodes (1968–) became a superstar in Japan. He shares the home run record for a season with 55. Rhodes has played 14 seasons (1996–2009) in Japan, first with the Ōsaka Kintetsu Buffaloes and then with the Yomiuri Giants. Born in Hawaii, Wally Yonamine (1925–2011) played for the Yomiuri Giants (1951–1961) and then for the Chūnichi Dragons (1961–1962), winning the MVP award once and the batting title three times. He also managed the Dragons for six years. He was inducted into the Japanese Baseball Hall of Fame in 1994. Bobby Valentine (1950–), former manager of the Texas Rangers (1985–1992) and New York Mets (2000–2002), has twice been manager, in 1995 and again from 2003 to 2006, of the Chiba Lotte Marines. In 2005, Valentine's Lotte team won the Japanese World Series.

Outstanding Japanese baseball players have long sought to test their mettle in the American Major Leagues. Murakami Masanori (1944–) was the first Japanese to play baseball in the Major Leagues. He pitched for the San Francisco Giants in 1964 and 1965. **Nomo Hideo** gained great popularity in Japan by not only making the Los Angeles Dodgers team in 1995, but by being the National League's starting pitcher in the All-Star Game. In 2001, Suzuki "Ichirō" took American baseball by storm. "Ichirō," after winning seven consecutive batting titles in Japan with a .353 career average, helped lead the Seattle Mariners to one of the most successful seasons ever.

Matsui Hideki signed with the New York Yankees and became an immediate success with that star team. Homering in his first game, Matsui has proven that Japanese can not only play but also star in the Major Leagues. As of 2009, more than a dozen Japanese players are key participants in the Major Leagues. In total, 33 Japanese pitchers and 10 Japanese position players have played in the Major Leagues.

College baseball is also fiercely competitive with Tōkyō's Big Six university baseball teams (Tōkyō, Waseda, Keiō, Meiji, Hōsei, and Rikkyō) drawing the most attention. Not only are professional, college, and high school baseball games very popular, but recreational and company baseball attracts many participants. In 2006, Japan won the inaugural World Baseball Classic and repeated as champions in 2009, confirming Japan's status as a leading baseball country. In 2013 and again in 2017, Japan finished third. Some consider baseball an American game, but many Japanese enjoy and participate in the game. *See also* SPORTS.

BOOKS AND BOOKSTORES. Books and bookstores are a vital part of Japanese life. The Japanese literacy rate is nearly 100 percent, and Japanese people are avid readers. Books, first printed in the 17th century and greatly expanded in the 19th century, flourish today. Publishers produce more than 60,000 new titles each year. Sales are very strong, and Japanese readers devour many books each year. Kodansha publishes dozens of books in English each year. Kinokuniya operates bookstores in **Tōkyō** and in other Japanese and international cities. A visit to the Kanda district of Tōkyō reveals many used bookstores.

Not only does Japan publish a huge number of books each year, but it stands to reason that it would have numerous bookstores. In addition to the ones previously mentioned, several stand out. Yaesu Book Center specializes in **science and technology**, philosophy, **economics**, politics, **business**, and information science. Maruzen Nihonbashi sells many English-language books as does Kitazawa Bookstore in Jinbōchō, which dates to 1902. Isseidō Booksellers specializes in antiquities and second-hand books. Junkudo Ikebukuro, the Barnes and Noble of Japan, fills 10 floors with books. *See also* LITERATURE.

BUDDHISM (*BUKKYŌ*, 仏教). Buddhism is a **religion** imported to Japan from India through **China** and **Korea** in the sixth century. In its early form, it received state support and endorsement. In postwar Japan, Buddhism has a heavy influence, at least statistically. The majority of the Japanese people profess association with the Buddhist faith, with the country having 13 principal sects, 80,000 temples, and approximately 150,000 priests. Several new Buddhist sects have emerged in the postwar period giving vitality to Japanese Buddhism. In everyday life, most Japanese are deeply attached to Buddhism as well as to the **Shintō** faith.

Buddhist priests conduct a majority of Japanese funerals and inter the ashes of the deceased in Buddhist burial grounds. Today, most Japanese belong to either the Nishi Honganji Sect, Higashi Honganji Sect, Zen, or the Nichiren Sect. Obon, a summer Buddhist commemorative festival honoring the dead, unites families and the community with its traditions. *See also* KŌMEITŌ, 公明党; NEW RELIGIONS; SUZUKI DAISETSU TEITARŌ, 鈴木大拙貞太郎 (1870–1966).

BULLET TRAIN (SHINKANSEN, 新幹線). The "Bullet Train," officially known as the Shinkansen, opened between **Tōkyō** and **Ōsaka** on 1 October 1964, just before the start of the Tōkyō **Olympic** Games. The Shinkansen was extended to Fukuoka in March 1975. Service on the Northeast (Tōhoku) Shinkansen, from Tōkyō to Morioka, started on 23 June 1982. There are now other Shinkansen lines. Bullet Trains are universally recognized for their speed, comfort, punctuality, and efficiency. Sixteen-car trains reach speeds of 160 miles per hour and were the world's fastest for many years. *See also* RAILROADS.

BUNRAKU, 文楽. Bunraku, the most sophisticated form of puppetry in the world, is the Japanese professional puppet **theater** where three puppeteers operate two-thirds life-size figures. The subject matter of Bunraku is usually conflict between social obligations and human emotions. Beginning in the early 17th century, the Bunraku theater developed a distinctive Japanese flavor. Presently, the best representation of Bunraku can be found at Awaji Island in the Inland Sea, at the National Theater in **Tōkyō**, and the National Bunraku Theater in **Ōsaka**. **Yoshida Tamao** (1919–2006), a master puppeteer, provided great vitality for the puppet theater.

However, in the postwar period, Bunraku languished and now struggles to maintain its popularity and performance in a changing society that does not always appreciate the traditional arts. The decline of popular interest in Bunraku is due to its lagging subject appeal, more modern tastes, and fewer craftsmen and actors to promote the theater. Today, there are fewer than 30 active Bunraku troupes in Japan.

BURAKUMIN, 部落民. *Burakumin*, or "hamlet people," refers to the low-status social group set socially and historically as an outcast class. As Japan's largest minority group, *burakumin* are physically indistinguishable from any other Japanese, but when identified, are subject to prejudice and discrimination. Because of their work and ancestry, *burakumin* are considered unclean and hereditarily different from the majority of Japanese people. *Burakumin* handled the bodies of dead people and animals, dug graves, tanned hides and worked with leather, butchered animals, or collected trash. "Good people" were discouraged from associating with, living near, or marrying *burakumin*.

In 1871, the new Meiji government legally abolished the names *eta* (great filth) or *hinin* (nonhuman) and made these people part of the "commoners" class, but the stigma against them continued. In the 1920s, a movement to liberate the *burakumin* flourished, but did not completely solve the problem.

After World War II, the liberation movement pushed for people's rights. The new **constitution** gave what should be referred to as the former *burakumin* full legal equality, but they still face problems with job discrimination and full social equality. Marriage to a *burakumin* is still considered taboo in many quarters of Japan, and even touching a *burakumin* requires ritual purification by a **Buddhist** priest for some people.

Several well-known industrial companies discriminate against *burakumin* in hiring, and if hired, in promotion and pay. *Burakumin* are more likely to be unemployed, work in a lower-paying job, be associated with the *yakuza* or

Japanese mafia, be illiterate, live in overcrowded slums, or exist at a subsistence level. Shortly before taking office, Prime Minister **Asō Tarō** made disparaging remarks about the suitability of a person of *burakumin* roots serving as prime minister.

The Buraku Liberation League, which worked vigorously to eliminate discrimination, has accomplished some of its goals such as securing financial aid to assist communities that experience discrimination, making it harder for third parties to access family registers, and creating human rights promotion centers. However, issues such as employment equality and marriage discrimination still exist for today's estimated three million *burakumin*. Noted successful *burakumin* include Nakagami Kenji, a well-known writer, critic, and poet, and **Liberal Democratic Party** politician Nonaka Hiromu (1925–2018), who served in three government agencies, including as chief **cabinet** secretary in 1998–1999, and was viewed as a possible contender for prime minister in 2001.

BUSINESS. Japan has always had a high reputation for its business skills. Although the Confucian philosophers denigrated merchants as contributing little or nothing and placed them at the bottom of the social scale, businessmen made important contributions to Japan as of the 17th century. In the late 19th and early 20th centuries, business activities accelerated, taking Japan to the world stage. The postwar period would see Japan become one of the world's premier business countries. (Refer to appendixes F, G, H, and K.)

Obviously, Japanese business has connections to many sectors of the **economy** including manufacturing, **banking**, finance, **general trading companies**, the service industries, and auxiliary enterprises such as **shipping**, storage, delivery, and supply. In the early 20th century, the **zaibatsu** played a major role in advancing Japanese business interests. However, the **Occupation** found much to object to in this structure. In the postwar period, the zaibatsu gave way to the *keiretsu* system, which altered the economic structure.

Japanese business, its organizations, operations, and accomplishments attracted worldwide attention in the 1970s and 1980s. For example, the **Japan Federation of Economic Organizations** (Keidanren), Japan's most important business association, grouped most of Japan's leading business figures with politicians who promoted Japan's economic growth and development. The **Japan Business Federation** (Nippon Keizai Dantai Rengōkai), the replacement for Keidanren in 2002, represents companies, industrial associations, and regional employers' associations in an attempt to accelerate growth of Japan's and the world's economy.

In 1958, the **Ministry of International Trade and Industry** (MITI) organized the **Japan External Trade Organization** to promote Japan's economic growth and development, to encourage exports, and to secure international trade information to assist businesses. In 2001, MITI reorganized to become the **Ministry of Economy, Trade, and Industry**.

Postwar Japan saw the rise of several other organizations to promote business interests. The **Japan Chamber of Commerce and Industry** (Nihon Shōhō Kaigisho) strives to encourage trade domestically and internationally. The **Japan Association of Corporate Executives** (Keizai Dōyūkai), a group of non-*keiretsu* businessmen at the managing-director level, works to encourage economic growth. Finally, the **Japan Federation of Employers' Association** (Nihon Keieisha Dantai Renmei) is an organization that coordinates business and trade union interests.

Japanese stock exchanges, **securities companies**, and general trading companies play an important role in Japan's business success. Japan also has a long history of **department stores**, which have been a solid base for Japan's businesses. Today, **convenience stores** carry some of that role.

The role of banking has been essential to the growth of business in Japan. Throughout the postwar period, the **Bank of Japan** has directed Japan's monetary policy in such a way as to support Japan's economic development. Early in the postwar period, banks such as Fuji, Yasuda, Sumitomo, and Dai-Ichi provided strong support for business. Although on a somewhat lesser scale, the insurance and transportation industries have given an important support base to Japanese business. Japan's leading banks, including **Mitsubishi UFJ Financial Group**, **Mizuho Financial Group**, **Sumitomo Mitsui Financial Group**, and Sumitomo Trust, contribute much to Japan's business sector.

Labor organizations have provided an indispensable component of the business world in postwar Japan. The **Japan Confederation of Labor** (Dōmei), formed in 1964 and serving primarily public-sector workers, represented a leftist-centrist force in cooperation with the government. In the 1950s, the **General Council of Japanese Trade Unions** (Sōhyō), turning away from socialist politics and moving more toward the center, worked energetically for a more economically oriented business unionism. Sōhyō's leadership role in peace and democracy would continue to decline in the early 1980s with Prime Minister **Nakasone Yasuhiro**'s promotion of the **imperial system** and administrative reforms. Furthermore, Dōmei came to adopt a policy of working with business leaders to expand foreign markets and promote Japan's international economy. In the 1990s, the **Japanese Trade Union Confederation** (Rengō) became Japan's leading union confederation.

No treatment of Japanese business would be complete without the mention of various Japanese business techniques and procedures. Much has been made of the Japanese propensity for high savings rates and the role that such capital has provided for business development. The recognition of the value of **technology**, its development and promotion, and its cutting-edge contributions are quite important. The spirit of cooperation between government, labor, and business has often caught the attention of people who assess the accomplishments of Japanese business. Each of these factors may have played a role at some time in Japan's successful business development.

Entrepreneurial skill has been a definite factor in the successful business development of Japan. Names such as **Honda Sōichirō**, **Matsushita Kōnosuke**, and **Morita Akio** are universally recognized. Hundreds of other Japanese business leaders greatly swell the list of Japan's postwar entrepreneurs.

Japan has enjoyed and even gloried in prestigious world rankings for its businesses. The success of **Nippon Steel**, **Sony**, **Toyota**, **Honda**, **Nikon**, and many other internationally famous companies bring a strong sense of pride to Japanese people.

Japan has succeeded in business in part by investing large amounts of research and development (R&D) in its products. Many Japanese businesses are willing to make the investment of the company's resources on R&D, and this has paid off in the long run.

Having a large-scale, long-term commitment to business is another reason behind Japan's success. Although perhaps overstated, the concept of total national commitment to business is a factor contributing to this. Scholars and journalists have written many books and articles to explain the reasons for Japan's economic success. They range from claims that "the Japanese know how to do everything" and are "taking over the world" to those who see the Japanese business structure as an economic sham.

With all the success stories, there are still numerous negatives in the world of Japanese postwar business. About 95 percent of all Japanese businesses are family firms, but only one-sixth survive to the third generation. Many of these firms lack monitoring, proper supervision, and appropriate governance, which causes their eventual downfall. One only needs to point to Japan's pollution, its failure to address social issues, the poor treatment of women, the stress found in its people, the strange phenomenon of death by overwork (*karoshi*), the lack of balance in Japanese lives, and the over-concentration on business matters to see that all is not well in the wonderful world of Japanese business.

According to **Nikkei**, Japanese businesses experienced $28 billion in impairment losses in fiscal year 2015. This is the highest figure in the past seven years. Commodity prices were sluggish. **Mitsubishi** lost heavily in its

Chilean mines investment. **Mitsui & Company** also had big losses. Oil refiners and resource developers such as JX Holdings and **Sumitomo** Metal Mining saw big drops.

Losses from foreign subsidiaries also caused staggering impairments. **Toshiba** lost many dollars in its Westinghouse nuclear business. Mitsui Chemicals had large losses in its materials business. Kirin Holdings lost more than $1 billion in its Brazilian subsidiary. Analysts conclude that Japanese companies lost at least at least $100 billion in acquisitions. However, Japanese business remains a vital part of Japan's success.

BUTŌ, 舞踏. *Butō* is a unique type of avant-garde dance developed in the late 1950s with shocking and disturbing aspects. Originated by Hijikata Tatsumi (1928–1986) and Ōno Kazuo (1906–2010), *butō* combines traditional forms of dance with modern Japanese dance. Using extensive makeup, borrowing body movements from traditional folk dances, and inspired by experimental **theater**, *butō* offers a variety of new experiences.

Butō is often difficult to fathom. While violent or sedate, slow or frantic, embarrassingly intimate or extremely spectacular, totally improvised or highly choreographed in stylized gestures, *butō* seems to resist definition or explanation, yet provides a profoundly transforming encounter. Violent and sexual, irrational and frightening, *butō* is often labeled scandalous.

C

CABINET (*NAIKAKU,*** 内閣).** Japan formed its first cabinet system of executive leadership in 1885 with a government headed by a **prime minister**. Today, the cabinet continues to be headed by a prime minister who both appoints and dismisses the 19 ministers of state. The cabinet is collectively responsible to the prime minister and must resign if it loses a vote of confidence. A majority of the cabinet, including the prime minister, must be selected from members of the **Diet**, and none may be connected with the military.

Under Japanese cabinet law, all cabinet members must resign if the government loses a vote of confidence, if the prime minister resigns, or when a new Diet is formed after an **election**. The cabinet provides "advice and approval" to the **emperor** and collectively exercises executive authority with the prime minister. With the emperor, the cabinet convenes the Diet, proclaims general elections for the Diet, dissolves the **House of Representatives**, and confers honors. As general powers, the cabinet executes the law, conducts **foreign policy**, concludes treaties with the consent of the Diet, administers the civil service, issues cabinet orders, grants general amnesty, signs laws and cabinet orders, and administers the **judicial system**.

The Diet still names the prime minister, and the emperor approves its selection. The prime minister chooses the other 19 ministers. The cabinet exercises two kinds of power—power granted by the emperor and power explicit under the law. As of October 2017, there is a full complement of 20 ministers. **Asō Tarō** serves multiple positions as deputy prime minister, minister of finance, minister of state for financial services, and minister in charge of overcoming deflation. Other important cabinet positions and their heads include **Minister of Foreign Affairs** Kōno Tarō, **Minister of Economy, Trade, and Industry** Sekō Hiroshige, and **Minister of Defense** Onodera Itsunori.

Cabinet positions are viewed as a grooming opportunity for higher office, and rising politicians regularly cycle through the various positions. Recently, cabinet positions have often changed on a yearly basis.

CAMERA INDUSTRY. In the postwar period, Japan became the producer of the world's most attractive and popular cameras. Today, **Nikon** and Canon control 80 percent of the single-lens reflex sales, and **Sony** is a major force in digital cameras. Pentax, Olympus, and Fuji FinePix have lost most of their market share. However, some of these camera companies are in decline. With the switch to digital imaging, the camera industry in Japan is rapidly changing. Camera companies like Minolta, Konica, Mamiya, **Kyōcera**, Contax, and Yashica are disappearing.

As of 2005, of the largest companies in Asia, Canon ranked 32nd with sales of $22.8 billion and Nikon 382nd with sales of $3.1 billion. Canon specializes in imaging and optical products, including cameras, photocopiers, and optical products. It is one of the world's largest digital camera and office equipment makers. Fuji Film Company expanded into cameras in 1948, magnetic tape in 1960, and more recently, videotape and digital products. It is Japan's largest and the world's second-largest film maker and one of the world's major digital camera sellers.

Smartphones are killing the camera industry. Across the world, people purchased 130 million cameras in 2011, but by 2015, that number had dropped to 47 million. People are using smartphones for everything. Nikon, Canon, Olympus, and Sony have experienced a decline in sales. Most affected are point-and-shoot cameras and less expensive SLR cameras while high-end professional cameras have held their own. Camera makers seek to offer higher-quality pictures and features not found on smartphones.

Sony and **Panasonic** are working with German rivals to provide better-quality pictures, Olympus is moving more to medical equipment photography, and Konica Minolta has dropped its camera line to move to print and optical equipment. Fujifilm has also shifted its focus to a Polaroid-like product and other businesses. Financial figures released at the end of 2015 reflect this shift. The advantages of an all-in-one smartphone with computer, camera, and internet service make them a very attractive device to today's technologically savvy young people. *See also* ECONOMY.

CHINA, RELATIONS WITH. Historically, the relationship between Japan and China has been very important to Japan, which owes much of its writing system, **architecture**, philosophy, culture, and **religion** to its older neighbor. However, from the late 19th century through 1945, China felt the bitter sting of Japanese imperialism. In the postwar period, the history of foreign relations between Japan and the People's Republic of China (PRC) has been fraught with difficulties but also filled with opportunities. Hampered by both a long, aggressive war against China and its close ties with the **United States**, Japan found it difficult to restore relations with the PRC. Early efforts focused on small-scale trading, fishing rights, and repatriation of prisoners of war.

The Liao-Takasaki Memorandum of 1962 provided for considerable unofficial **trade** between Japan and China. This five-year trade memorandum brought Sino-Japanese relations to a semiofficial status. In 1971, when President Richard Nixon visited China, Japan and the world felt the "shock" of this visit, spurring dramatic change in Japan's **foreign policy**.

After the Nixon visit, representatives of Japan and China began to discuss the possibility of restoring diplomatic and trade relations. In 1972, Prime Minister **Tanaka Kakuei** went to Beijing to meet with Premier Zhou Enlai and do just that. Trade and cultural exchanges began to expand, but Japan's close security relations with the United States provided a major stumbling block for the Chinese. In 1978, Japan signed the Treaty of Peace and Friendship between Japan and the PRC. This eliminated any remaining official ties between Japan and **Taiwan**. Unofficial connections to Taiwan continued, however, and the Tōkyō-Taipei-Beijing relationship remained a tricky one.

In the 1980s, Japan provided considerable economic support to China as part of its ODA program. However, starting in the late 1980s and continuing in the 1990s, China experienced tremendous economic growth. This led Japan to adopt a much more favorable policy toward the PRC. In 1992, **Emperor Akihito** visited China and expressed Japan's desire for closer economic, strategic, and cultural relations. By the early 21st century, Japan was in the process of eliminating its economic assistance as China moved toward major power status.

The residue of Japan's wartime aggression in China, particularly the Nanjing Massacre of 1937, continues to cloud the relationship between China and Japan. Statements and actions by leading Japanese figures have exacerbated relations. In 1994, Nagano Shigeto, the justice minister in **Hata Tsutomu**'s **cabinet**, publicly claimed that the Nanjing Massacre was a fabrication. Although public opinion forced his resignation, great damage had been done by these remarks. China has frequently expressed frustration over the way Japanese history presents Japan's war in China in the **textbook controversy**, official visits by the prime minister and government officials to **Yasukuni Shrine**, and the handling of an ongoing dispute over a chain of islands in the East China Sea. The legacy of World War II is still sensitive.

In 1995, Prime Minister **Murayama Tomiichi** offered an official apology for World War II saying that Japan had followed "a mistaken national policy" and "ensnared the Japanese people in a fateful crisis, and, through its colonial rule and aggression, caused tremendous damage and suffering to the people of many countries" for which he as prime minister of Japan offered Japan's expression of "deep remorse and . . . a heartfelt apology."

Prime Minister **Koizumi Jun'ichirō** greatly frustrated the Chinese by his frequent visits to Yasukuni Shrine. Such actions had grave negative consequences for relations between the two countries. Prime Minister **Abe Shinzō** did not visit the shrine but did make offerings to the shrine. **Fukuda Yasuo,** who was openly pro-Chinese, never visited the shrine. In April 2009, hawkish prime minister **Asō Tarō** presented Yasukuni Shrine with an expensive tree, again setting off a round of protests in China as well as in **Korea**.

However, in the 1990s and early 2000s, trade between Japan and China flourished. By 2000, China's international trade was the sixth-largest in the world, and Japan was deeply involved in this trade. China became the biggest exporter to Japan, replacing the United States as its leading exporter by 2002. Some 22,000 firms did $168 billion in trade. By 2006, Japan exported $118.4 billion, or nearly 17 percent of its total exports, to China, making it the second-leading trade partner. In return, Japan bought $92.9 billion or 20 percent of its imports from China.

By 2006, more than 500,000 Chinese lived in Japan and nearly 114,000 Japanese lived in China. Some four million people travel between the countries yearly, including many students. China and Japan have formed 313 pairs of sister city relationships. Public surveys carried out in both Japan and China suggest that people in both countries see relations as improving between the two countries. People of both nations see their ties as important and seem willing to work to further encourage better relations. The opportunities for economic development are overriding the conflicts of the past.

As of 2012, relations between Japan and China were strained, at least as bad as in 2005. The two countries disputed territory in the East China Sea, and neither appeared willing to yield on the matter. Territory that Japan calls the Senkaku Islands and China calls Diaoyu are in the controversy. Fishing and energy rights are central in the dispute. Domestic considerations inspire supporters in both countries. People in both countries want to ameliorate the situation. A delegation from the Japan-China Friendship Association visited Beijing and spoke with political leaders. Former foreign minister **Kōno Yōhei** led the Japanese delegation.

The dispute over the islands escalated when Japan purchased the islands in September 2012 from the Kurihara family. Newly elected **Liberal Democratic Party** leader Abe Shinzō advocated asserting sovereignty over the islands. Businesses and restaurants of both countries experienced difficulties in the other country. **Nissan Motors** saw its sales in China drop by 9 percent, **Toyota**'s dropped by 18 percent, and **Honda**'s fell by 10 percent.

China claims that it has owned the islands for centuries. Japan contends that it took control of them in 1895, lost authority there after World War II, and had them returned by the United States in 1972. Both countries are acting out of nationalistic sentiments. Both have had patrol boats in the area. Prime Minister **Noda Yoshihiko** and Hu Jintao failed to lower the tensions at the Asia-Pacific Economic Cooperation Summit in August 2012.

Since China and Japan are the world's second- and third-largest economies, and are major trading partners, this presents the potential for real problems. Relations between the two countries remain mired in tensions stemming from World War II. The potential for conflict should be taken seriously.

Mutual dislike, hatred, and hostility between Japanese and Chinese people have flared recently. A 2014 BBC poll showed that 3 percent of Japanese viewed China positively but 73 percent had negative views of them. Similarly, 5 percent of the Chinese viewed Japanese positively, and 90 percent saw them negatively.

As of 2017, the Senkaku/Diaoyu controversy continues to stir. Chinese incursions into the islands seem to be the new normal. Increasingly, Japan and India are finding common ground in countering the potential threat of China.

However, there are numerous signs of cooperation between Japan and China. The Renault-Nissan Alliance and Dongfeng Motor Group are teaming up to produce electric cars. Kawasaki Heavy Industries is shifting a large part of its commercial shipbuilding to China. Prime Minister Abe declined to visit Yasukuni Shrine in October 2017 to avoid offending China and South Korea. While meeting in Vietnam in November 2017, Prime Minister Abe Shinzō and Chinese president Xi Jinping agreed to promote improved bilateral ties and are gingerly moving toward rapprochement. Business leaders from both countries oppose U.S. president Donald Trump's protectionism.

CHIYONOFUJI MITSUGU, 千代の富士貢 **(1955–2016).** Chiyonofuji was an outstanding **sumō** grand champion (*yokozuna*). A native of Matsumae in Hokkaidō, he was born Akimoto Mitsugu. An all-round athlete despite being a thin child, he was recruited and trained in the Kokonoe sumō stable of former *yokozuna* Chiyonoyama and Kitanouji. He began competing at age 15 in 1970 and, early on, caught the imagination of both male and female fans, displaying a lightning speed that allowed him to defeat much larger opponents. Chiyo scored a stunning upset as a *sekiwake* over a *yokozuna*, **Kitanoumi Toshimitsu**, in 1981. When he repeated this victory later that year, he was promoted to the highest level. Chiyo remained a *yokozuna* from 1981 to 1991, continuing to excel into his mid-30s. His longest winning streak of 53 bouts is second only to Futabayama, a pre–World War II *yokozuna*. In 1986–1987, he won five consecutive championships. Chiyonofuji garnered 31 in all, second only to **Taihō Kōki** at that time. He garnered more than 1,000 wins, a record until Hakuhō Shō broke it in 2017. Chiyonofuji, known as "Wolf," did all this despite weighing only 265 pounds.

CHRISTIANITY. *See* RELIGION.

CINEMA. *See* FILMS AND FILMMAKING.

CLEAN GOVERNMENT PARTY. *See* KŌMEITŌ, 公明党.

"COMFORT WOMEN" (*IANFU*, 慰安婦). During the Pacific War, the Japanese military, with government support, brutally forced thousands of young **women**, later (mis)identified as "comfort women," to serve as prostitutes in many military camps where they sexually served the soldiers under shameful conditions. Perhaps a quarter million young women, **Koreans**, as well as women from the Philippines, Thailand, Vietnam, Singapore, **China**, **Taiwan**, and the Dutch East Indies, were forced into such humiliating experiences. It was not until the early 1990s that the Japanese government admitted to official involvement in such activities. Prior to that time, it had refused to take responsibility for the policy, to apologize, or to compensate the victims, many of whom have been left in difficult financial, social, and emotional positions.

The Japanese government argued that all World War II compensation claims have been settled. The South Korean government has agreed, but its people have not. Moreover, in 1990, the Korean Council for Women Drafted for Military Sexual Slavery filed suit, demanding apologies and compensation. Several surviving "comfort women" also independently filed suits in the Tōkyō District Court.

The government initially denied any official connection to wartime brothels, and in 1990, the government declared that all brothels were run by private **businesses**. However, in 1992, the historian Yoshimi Yoshiaki of Chūō University discovered incriminating documents in the archives of Japan's National Defense Agency indicating that the military was directly involved in running the brothels. The Japanese government has finally admitted "moral but not legal" responsibility.

In 1995, Japan set up an Asia Women's Fund for atonement in the form of material compensation and to provide each surviving "comfort woman" with an unofficial signed apology from the **prime minister**. But because of the unofficial nature of the fund, many women have rejected these payments and continue to seek an official apology and compensation.

In 2014, when a cabinet secretary said that Japan should reconsider its apology to "comfort women," Prime Minister **Abe Shinzō** resolutely said that Japan would not alter or weaken its apology to these women. On 28 December 2015, Abe and his South Korean counterpart formally agreed that Japan would contribute approximate $8 million to a fund supporting surviving victims in exchange for which Korea promised to refrain from criticizing

Japan regarding the issue and to remove a statue memorializing the victims erected in front of the Japanese embassy. However, the ugly incident occasionally still raises its head.

COMPUTER INDUSTRY. Japan began its computer industry in the late 1950s but lagged behind many countries. Today, Japan ranks only behind the **United States** in its computer **technology**. Major leaders in Japan's computer industry include Canon, **Fujitsu, Hitachi, Matsushita, Mitsubishi** Electric, **NEC** (Nippon Electric Company), Oki Electric, **Ricoh**, Seiko Epson, and **Toshiba**. Japan recognized the value of computer technology for competitiveness in industry, including the production of **automobiles**. It has become a leader in developing computer software dealing with communications, **games**, and electronics.

Encouraged by the **Ministry of International Trade and Industry** and driven by talented researchers, Japan has made considerable progress in advancing Fifth-Generation computer systems and is significantly involved in artificial intelligence research.

Uenohara Michiyuki (1925–2007) was a major factor in Japan's computer chip industry. Uenohara spent much of his early career as a researcher at Bell Laboratories in the United States. He returned to Japan in 1967 to improve Japan's computer chip industry. He worked to mass-produce high-quality chips and did much to promote the work of Japan's young researchers. Uenohara became the research director for NEC.

In today's fast-paced world, where almost everything is digital, programming has gained significant attention both as a career and as an educational tool. Almost all industries use IT, and thus knowing how software works is an extremely important tool. Web services like Google, Twitter, and Facebook make extensive use of computer technology. Today, digital programming is a key to much of the world's successes.

The top Japanese computer systems vendors in sales volume are Matsushita ($70 billion), Toshiba ($47 billion), NEC ($37 billion), Fujitsu ($34 billion), Mitsubishi ($32 billion), Canon ($19 billion), Hitachi ($14 billion), Ricoh ($10 billion), Oki ($6 billion), and Seiko Epson ($4 billion). Sharp and Vaio are near the top 10.

In 2011, Japan's "K Computer" became the world's fastest computer, three times faster than its Chinese competitor. However, Chinese and American companies soon passed it. Japan is presently building the world's fastest supercomputer, expected to run at a speed of 10 petaflops and able to perform 130 million billion calculations per second. Targeted for completion in April 2018, it will be one million times faster than a personal computer. It will be used to improve driverless cars, robotics, and medical diagnostics. *See also* ECONOMY.

CONSTITUTION OF JAPAN (*NIHONKOKU KEMPŌ*, 日本国憲法). The Constitution of Japan, or sometimes called the Shōwa Constitution, provides for extensive postwar change in the legal status of the Japanese government. Prepared under the guidance of the **Occupation** authorities, the so-called MacArthur Constitution has strong elements of Western values and an English-language flavor. Adopted in 1946 and implemented in 1947, the constitution is the supreme law of Japan. It has a preamble and 103 articles grouped into 11 chapters. Articles 1 and 8 eliminate the divinity of the **emperor**. Article 2 separates church and state. Articles 10–40 grant extensive human rights.

Matsumoto Jōji (1877–1954), a **University of Tōkyō** law professor, oversaw the first revision of the draft of the Japanese constitution during the Occupation period. Satō Tatsuo (1904–1974) was an important government official who helped with Japan's postwar constitution and its personnel policies. Satō helped prepare the draft of the 1947 Constitution. His book *Nihonkoku kempō seiritsu shi* (*History of the Creation of the Japanese Constitution*) was an instructive account of the Japanese negotiations with Occupation leaders over the postwar political structure.

The Constitution of Japan is written in the name of the Japanese people and declares that "sovereign power resides with the people," who exercise their power through elected representatives. The constitution establishes a system of parliamentary government like that of Great Britain. It identifies numerous popular rights including liberty, equality, assembly, association, speech, due process, protection from unlawful detention, and fair trial.

Of considerable controversy in Japan's constitution, Article 9 seems to limit Japan's ability to maintain and use military force. The article states that "the Japanese people forever renounce war as a sovereign right of the nation and the threat of force as means of settling international disputes," and claims "land, sea, and air forces, as well as other war potential, will never be maintained."

While seemingly clear enough, the article has since been interpreted in such a way as to allow Japan to maintain its **Self-Defense Forces** (SDF) and to permit Japan's linkage to the **United States** in a **defense** pact. Despite the existence of Article 9, Japan has a powerful military force. Yet that military force is under strict civilian control and has its spending capped at 1 percent of Japan's GNP. Needless to say, given Japan's present level of military capability, Article 9 has been and continues to be a matter of controversy. Some Japanese argue that since the constitution is an imposed American document, it should be thoroughly revised to make it more truly Japanese in nature, value, and language.

Any change in the constitution requires a two-thirds vote in both houses of the **Diet** as well as popular approval, but conservative and nationalistic forces have not been able to garner sufficient support for even a single change in the past 70 years.

Prime Minister **Abe Shinzō** and some of his **Liberal Democratic Party** (LDP) members would like to revise Japan's 70-year-old constitution. If the LDP grows stronger, this may be a possibility. Many LDP members claim that the current constitution is no longer suited to recent social and political changes. In particular, some would like to revise the war-renouncing Article 9. The Japan Conference (Nippon Kaigi) is the largest citizens' group advocating nationalistic policies including a change in the constitution. The conservative journalist Sakurai Yoshiko, who chairs this forum, claims that the constitution does not protect Japan. Advocates for change say that the United States alliance and the SDF are what protect Japan, not the constitution.

However, public opinion polls as recent as 2016 show that 56 percent of the people oppose the idea of revising the war-renouncing constitution, and only 33 percent support its change. Opposition politicians believe that Abe is trying to remove the self-imposed ban by changing the constitution. Many fear a return to Japan's era of militarism. *See also* TAKAYANAGI KENZŌ, 高柳賢三 (1887–1967).

CONSTITUTIONAL DEMOCRATIC PARTY OF JAPAN (RIKKEN MINSHUTŌ, 立憲民主党). The Constitutional Democratic Party of Japan (CDP) is a center-left party headed by Edano Yukio (1964–). A spinoff from the **Democratic Party of Japan** in 2017, it threw its support behind **Koike Yuriko's Party of Hope** in the Tōkyō **election**. The CDP won 55 seats and thus became the leading opposition party in the **Tōkyō** government. As of 2018, the CDP has 56 seats in the **House of Representatives** and six seats in the **House of Councillors**. With a relatively liberal stance, the CDP favors maintaining Article 9 of the **Constitution**, phasing out the use of **nuclear power**, reducing the disparity between the rich and the poor, and building a more just **society**.

CONSTRUCTION INDUSTRY. The Ministry of Land, Infrastructure, Transportation, and Tourism, having superseded the Ministry of Construction, assists the construction industry by establishing criteria for qualifying contractors to bid for public works projects, by promoting research and development (R&D), and by maintaining the national building code. In Japan, engineers and **architects**, who are familiar with the specific **technology** used on their projects, lead the construction companies. Like their **United States** counterparts, they are concerned about productivity and safety. To ensure these measures, the large Japanese contractors conduct substantial R&D. Of

Japan's annual construction volume, 0.51 percent is spent on construction R&D, compared with under 0.1 percent in the United States for comparable sectors.

Industry, government, and universities generally work independently, yet there is cooperation in setting goals and working on certain priority areas. Partly through application of research findings, Japanese construction companies have moved ahead of their U.S. counterparts in many areas, including soft-ground tunneling, design and construction of intelligent buildings, deep foundation construction, construction **robotics**, and long-span bridge construction.

Japanese companies have also invested heavily in developing automated equipment, although they have produced very few practical pieces. Much of their motivation to automate stems from their desire to improve the image of the construction industry among workers, make construction safer, and ease the cost of increasingly expensive labor. Despite their push to automate construction equipment, Japanese companies do not use **computers** for scheduling or cost control as widely as U.S. companies do. However, Japanese companies are actively exploring ways to transfer information from computer-assisted design models to field equipment, and then manipulate that data from the surrounding environment using artificial intelligence.

Improving Japan's infrastructure has depended on efficient development and use of space. The Japanese have sought new space by building up, building out, and building down. They attack the construction of office and apartment buildings from a new perspective: the building is a system and needs systems solutions. The boom in office building and home construction markets offers an excellent opportunity to apply high-technology concepts to building construction to improve the **environment**.

Today's largest construction companies in Japan are Kajima, Obayashi, Sekisui House, Shimizu, Taisei, and Takenaka. These firms are among the top 100 companies of all types in all of Asia. The Japanese construction industry is expected to expand slowly over the next five years, with investments in infrastructure, health care, **education**, and housing construction projects driving growth. Japan's Vision 2020, under which the government aims to develop road, rail, airport, and other infrastructure projects, will also be a major force promoting the construction industry. Preparation for the 2020 **Olympic** Games will be a source of growth. Reconstruction of earthquake-damaged properties across the country is also stimulating the construction industry.

According to a 2015 report, the Japanese government has allocated $29 billion for the construction of bridges, roads, tunnels, rail, and other related infrastructure to support economic growth by 2020. The government is focusing on the reconstruction of properties damaged by earthquakes and tsunamis in northern Japan, as well as the nuclear waste problems of Fukushima. *See also* ECONOMY.

CONSUMER ELECTRONICS. By all measurements, Japan is the home of consumer electronics. Who has not used or at least heard of such electronic giants as **Sony**, Casio, **Hitachi**, **Tōshiba**, **NEC**, JVC, Panasonic, **Fujitsu**, Canon, **Sharp**, Pioneer, **Kyōcera**, **Ricoh**, **Nintendo**, San'yo, Epson, **Nikon**, **Yamaha**, and Seiko. Japanese electronics companies lead the world in televisions, music players, video game consoles, compact disc players, **cameras**, pianos, and **computers**, as well as other products.

Although having a prewar base, Japan specialized in electronic products after the war in order to jump-start its industry and to offset its lack of natural resources. Sony and other companies led the way in making high-quality products for the international market. The story of the first pocket transistor radio is universally famous. In the early 1990s, Japan exported nearly half of all its color televisions and more than 80 percent of its video-cassette recorders.

Japan is probably the largest top-quality electronics manufacturer in the world today. Not only are its offerings numerous, but Japan is universally recognized for the high quality and the inventiveness of its products. By the 1980s, Japan's prowess in electronics superseded that of the United States. This led to problems in Japan's relations with the **United States**. Japan has endeavored to solve the trade problems by establishing factories in the United States.

Japan continues to maintain the largest consumer electronics industry in the world, but its share is declining due to competition primarily from **South Korea** and **Taiwan**. Several Japanese companies still produce televisions, camcorders, and audio and video players. After all, Japan was the leader in developing the transistor radio, the Sony Walkman, the Tōshiba mass-produced laptop, the VHS recorder, and LCD screens.

Japan's consumer electronics sales have declined in recent days. This has been due to consumers' economic uncertainty, population decline, and an ongoing shift toward smartphones. Japanese customers use smartphones to go online, communicate, play media, capture images, and read e-books. Thus, many consumers have bought less of a wide range of consumer electronics. As of 2016, smart wearables such as smart watches, optical glasses, health-tracking systems, and entertainment devices seem to be the trend.

Since 2013, many Japanese companies have faced serious competition from South Korean, Taiwanese, and Chinese electronics companies. The Japanese electronics companies no longer dominate the world market as they did a decade ago. As of 2016, Apple continues to lead in consumer electronics sales in Japan. The future of the Japanese electronics industry is not as bright as it once was. *See also* ECONOMY; FOREIGN POLICY.

CONVENIENCE STORES. Convenience stores, or *konbini* as the Japanese call them, have become a way of life in Japan. With 60 franchise chains and more than 50,000 stores nationwide, it is hard to ever be very far from a *konbini*. Much smaller than **supermarkets**, *konbini* offer all the daily necessities, from food to drinks, from prepared meals to snacks, from rice balls to instant noodles, from cosmetics to magazines, from **banking** services to fax machines, from **video games** to DVDs, from ticket reservations to photo prints, from utility and insurance payments to bill paying, and from e-commerce to delivery services. Typically, each convenience store is laid out in a similar way. Chains with the largest number of convenience stores in Japan are 7-Eleven, Lawson, and Family Mart. 7-Eleven and Lawson are among the top 30 Japanese companies in brand-name recognition. Most convenience stores are usually open 24 hours a day, seven days a week. *See also* DEPARTMENT STORES.

COUNCIL FOR PEACE AND AGAINST NUCLEAR WEAPONS (KAKKIN KAIGI, 核禁会議). The Council for Peace and against Nuclear Weapons is an antinuclear federation founded in the early 1960s. Even the **Liberal Democratic Party** supported some of its activities, and in 1967, Prime Minister **Satō Eisaku** introduced the "**three nonnuclear principles.**" The council struggles against ideological and factional divisions within the peace movement. However, as recently as 24 February 2006, it cosponsored a **Tōkyō** protest rally against subcritical nuclear testing by the **United States** and Great Britain. *See also* DEFENSE; JAPAN CONGRESS AGAINST ATOMIC AND HYDROGEN BOMBS (GENSUIKIN, 原水禁).

COUNCIL ON ECONOMIC AND FISCAL POLICY (KEIZAI ZAISEI SEISAKU TANTŌ DAIJIN, 経済財政政策担当大臣). Founded by Prime Minister **Koizumi Jun'ichirō** in 2001, the Council on Economic and Fiscal Policy (CEFP) is strongly linked to the **prime minister**'s office. It was designed to carry out a major reorganization of the central government, strengthen the prime minister's leadership in economic matters, and serve as a major shaping force of economic policy while working with the **cabinet**. The CEFP seeks to improve the **economy** and fiscal performance through an integrated approach, a worldwide economic view, and, in short, with greater transparency, to cure Japan's economic stagnation. A fairly new institution when compared to the **Ministry of International Trade and Industry**, the **Ministry of Finance**, and the **Economic Planning Agency**, the CEFP does not have an established track record.

The CEFP gives the prime minister more of a leadership role in the nation's economic and fiscal policies. Its specific role is to conduct studies and deliberations and to present reports and suggestions to advance the overall economic and fiscal well-being of Japan, and to develop a comprehensive plan of action to resuscitate Japan's economy.

In 2001, the CEFP set out to produce sweeping economic reforms. These included finding a solution to the bank's non-performing loans and planning for structural reform, changes in the policy-making process, and long-term economic and fiscal management practices. Prime Minister Koizumi summed up the situation by saying, "There can be no growth without reform." He was right in his assessment but only partially successful in producing the needed reforms.

The members of the CEFP include the prime minister as chair, the minister of state for economic and fiscal policy, the chief cabinet secretary, the minister of finance, the minister of economy, trade, and industry, the minister of internal affairs and communications, the governor of the **Bank of Japan**, and four members selected from the private sector.

After a brief stint with **Asō Tarō** as its first minister, Koizumi selected Takenaka Heizō (1951–) to be minister of state for economic and fiscal policy, a position he held from 2001 until 2005. As such, Takenaka, the major driving force behind the CEFP, was the key spokesperson for the privatization of Japan's postal system. Successive heads of the CEFP include Yosano Kaoru (1938–), who served from 2005 to 2006; Ōta Hiroko (1954–), a woman politician and economic researcher with a specialty in finance, from 2006 to 2008; Yosano Kaoru again for seven months under Prime Minister Asō; Hayashi Yoshimasa (1961–), from July through September 2009; and **Kan Naoto**, from 2009 to 2010. Motegi Toshimitsu (1955–) is the present minister of the CEFP.

CRIME. Japan has a reputation for low crime rates in the postwar period, but it has experienced modest crime increases in recent years. The National Police Agency, which is Japan's chief crime-fighting body, categorizes crime into six groups: felonies, larceny, moral offenses, intellectual crimes, crimes against unlawful assembly, and miscellaneous offenses. The two most frequent crimes have been larceny and negligent homicide or injury stemming from accidents.

The present **judicial system** in Japan began with the Penal Code and Code of Criminal Instruction, both adopted in 1880. In 1907, the Penal Code was significantly revised to follow the German model. Modest changes were made to the Penal Code again in the postwar period.

Japan's criminal justice system functions well as seen through the performance of the police, the government prosecutor's office, the courts, and correctional institutions. These institutions cooperate to keep crime at a low level in Japan. Further, the Japanese people work with these institutions and participate in various crime prevention programs and take a negative view toward criminal behavior. Finally, the criminal justice system is flexible enough to allow for effective dealing with criminals.

Japan's justice system has a very high rate of conviction. Japan does not use a jury system but relies on judges to determine guilt or innocence. Although Japan has the death penalty, it is not used often. Prosecution and punishment are separate phases in the Japanese criminal system. Since the predictability of the criminal trials are high, many people confess their guilt in order to get reduced sentencing. Individual and international organizations have raised doubts over Japan's "voluntary" confessions and called for more careful oversight in the Japanese justice system.

The mention of crime in Japan immediately brings to mind the *yakuza*. A factor in Japanese society for more than a century, the *yakuza* use force and money to influence decisions and control people. It is estimated that there may be as many as 3,000 *yakuza* groups with perhaps 100,000 members. They operate largely in cities, have political connections, and are typically consolidated into syndicate-type groups.

In the last few decades, foreigners have been accused of committing crimes at a higher rate than Japanese citizens. The Chinese are said to work with organized crime groups to carry out their illegal activities. Other racial groups also have frequently been criticized for criminal actions. Brazilians have been identified in higher numbers than others. In 2006, Japan's National Police Agency reported 18,895 crimes involving foreigners. The most serious crimes were murder, rape, arson, kidnapping, and robbery. Less serious offenses included visa violations, drug use, illegal weapon possession, and prostitution.

Japan has had its share of high-profile crimes in the postwar period. In 1948, a robber killed 12 bank workers by posing as a doctor and telling them to take a "dysentery medicine" that was really cyanide poison. In 1971–1972, the **Red Army** tortured and murdered 12 gang members in a purge in Gunma Prefecture. In 1982, a deranged man forced the crash of a **Japan Airlines** flight, killing 24 people. In 1984–1989, *yakuza* gang wars resulted in 29 deaths. In 1995, the doomsday cult **Aum Shinrikyō** released sarin gas in Tōkyō's subways killing 12 people and sickening thousands. In 2001, a nurse murdered at least 10 people in a Sendai medical facility. In 2001, a former janitor stabbed eight children to death with a kitchen knife in an elementary school in **Ōsaka**. In 2001, a suspected arsonist killed 44 people in the Kabukichō section of **Tōkyō**. In 2007, Saga and Fukuoka Prefecture gang members killed seven members in battles. In 2008, a deranged truck driver killed seven and injured 11 people in the Akihabara section of Tōkyō. These, however, are the rare and bizarre incidents of crime in Japan.

However, world murder rates for 2015 demonstrate the safety of Japan. With .31 homicides per 100,000 people, this compares very favorably to the **United States** with 4.88 deaths. In other words, the U.S. homicide rate is more than 15 times that of Japan.

A number of factors account for Japan's low crime statistics. Prosecution and conviction rates are much higher in Japan and are less likely to be challenged successfully. Informal sanctions, group pressure, and social sanctions make it less likely that Japanese people will commit crimes. In spite of the recent worldwide economic difficulties, Japan's relatively prosperous **economy** has helped to prevent extensive criminal behavior. The relatively small gap between the rich and the poor in Japan makes crime less likely. Japan's homogeneous population also contributes to its low crime rate.

Strong gun control laws are also an important deterrent to crime. Ownership of handguns is strictly forbidden. The government regulates the manufacture and sale of guns and ammunition. The government licenses firearms, and people seeking authorization must undergo rigorous screening and must be of legal age and mentally stable. In 1987, only 319 crimes were committed in Japan using guns, and 90 percent of these involved street gangs.

There are two crimes that the Japanese police pursue with great vigor. One is drunk driving, and the other is illegal drug usage. Both are severely punished, and few people escape detection. Everyone is advised to avoid such activities in Japan.

Recently, crime in Japan has grown more sophisticated and more high-tech. One type of crime that has proliferated is white-collar crime including computer and credit card theft, illegal access to cash machines, insurance fraud, and minor drug violations.

An unusual crime in contemporary Japan is known as *chikan* or "grouping." Grouping consists of unwanted touching or feeling of one another's private parts in public places such as rock concerts, crowded trains, subways, or buses, where the victim is inhibited from responding.

In 2014, there were just six gun deaths, compared to 33,599 in the United States. Japan has a large number of tests and conditions before you can own a gun. Handguns are banned outright. Japan's current gun laws date from 1958, but their roots are even older. Japan has 0.6 guns per 100 people while the United States has 89 per 100 people. Many police do not carry guns, but when they do, the use of guns by police is strictly regulated, and the number of citizens shot is infinitesimal.

Japan claims to be "the safest country in the world." It may be right. The murder rate, already quite low, has declined steadily for a half century. The overall crime rate is low due to prosperity in Japan, relatively low economic inequality, strict gun laws, a tough criminal justice system, a rejection of violence, a distinct culture and disciplined population, intolerance to illicit drugs, and a social stigma against criminal activity. Japan is even revising its laws on organized crime so that anyone involved in acts of terrorism can be prosecuted for criminal conspiracy. *See also* ISHII SUSUMU, 石井進 (1924–1991); KANEMARU SHIN, 金丸信 (1914–1996); LOCKHEED SCANDAL (*ROKKIIDO JIKEN*, ロッキード事件); OKINAWA PREFEC-TURE (OKINAWA-KEN, 沖縄県); PACHINKO, パチンコ; RECRUIT SCANDAL (*RIKURŪTO JIKEN*, リクルート事件); SECURITIES COM-PANIES.

DAIHATSU MOTOR COMPANY (DAIHATSU KŌGYŌ KABUSHIKIGAISHA, ダイハツ工業株式会社**).** Daihatsu Motor Company is an **automobile** manufacturing company that specializes in the K-car and off-road vehicle market and is also a small *keiretsu*. Daihatsu produces small, inexpensive passenger cars, including electric models that sell worldwide under such names as Cuore, Sirion, and Terios. The company makes about 750,000 cars per year, including about 85,000 **Toyotas**, which it assembles on a consignment basis. The company, which was formed in 1907, has four factories in Japan and exports to more than 140 countries. In August 2016, Daihatsu became a wholly owned subsidiary of the Toyota Group *keiretsu*. Daihatsu's goal is to produce cars that are convenient for people and place little damage on the **environment** while retaining their individuality and consumer appeal.

In 2012, Daihatsu was Japan's sixth-largest automobile manufacturer with 633,887 units produced. In 2016, it ranked as the 29th-largest auto manufacturer in the world. It has nearly 12,000 Japanese employees and 43,000 workers worldwide. It has overseas production facilities in Malaysia and Indonesia and a worldwide auto network on all the continents except Antarctica. *See also* ECONOMY.

DAI-ICHI KANGYŌ BANK GROUP (DAI-ICHI KANGYŌ GINKŌ GURŪPU, 第一勧業銀行グループ**).** The Dai-Ichi Kangyō Bank Group, formed in 1971 by the merger of Dai-Ichi Bank and Kangyō Bank, was considered the newest of the Big Six horizontal *keiretsu*. The bank had assimilated a loose-knit group that included many of the firms originally part of the Furukawa and Matsukata **zaibatsu**. It was one of Japan's largest commercial banks, with branches throughout the country and in 30 other countries. Among the businesses the bank developed were commercial **banking** services, bond underwriting, financing and financial advisory services, and international **business** services, including the euro currency market. It merged with Fuji Bank and the Industrial Bank of Japan in 2000 to create the **Mizuho Financial Group**, one of the world's largest banking and financial institutions.

DAN IKUMA, 團伊玖磨 **(1924–2001).** Dan Ikuma was an orchestral composer but was also well known for his vocal compositions including his classical "Goodbye Forever." His work often featured Nagata Yoriko. As the composer of six symphonies, seven operas, choral works, and more than 200 **film** scores, Dan Ikuma's use of folk-infused melodies colored his approach. Dan came from a wealthy family and was able to devote his life to composition. His last work, *Black and Yellow* for string quartet, was finished just before he suddenly died while in **China**. *See also* MUSIC.

DARVISH YU, ダルビッシュ有 **(1986–).** Yu Darvish was a sensational **baseball** pitcher for the Texas Rangers, and now with the Los Angeles Dodgers in the Major League. He was considered by many to be Japan's best pitcher prior to signing a $60 million contract with the Rangers in 2012.

Darvish, born in **Ōsaka**, is the son of an Iranian father and a Japanese mother. A phenomenal high school pitcher, Darvish led his team to the national championship game. Drafted by the Nippon Ham Fighters, he pitched for them from 2005 through 2011. In Japan, Darvish was twice the Pacific League's most valuable player, the Sawamura Award winner in 2007, and a three-time strikeout king. He played for the Japanese national team in the 2008 Beijing **Olympics** and the 2009 World Baseball Classic. In Texas, he was an all-star three times and the American League strikeout leader in 2013. After undergoing Tommy John surgery in the off-season, Darvish was 7–5 with the Texas Rangers in 2016. However, the Rangers traded him to the Los Angeles Dodgers where at the end of the 2017 season his won-lost career record was a very good 56–42 with a total of 1,021 strikeouts.

DATE KIMIKO, 伊達公子 **(1970–).** Born in **Kyōto**, Date Kimiko was introduced to tennis at age six by her parents, both tennis players themselves. In 1989, she made the transition from champion high school tennis player to professional competitor on the **women**'s tour. Over the next eight years, Date rapidly progressed up the women's ranking ladder, climbing to number four in the world in 1995.

Date won eight Women's Tennis Association titles and 14 International Tennis Federation championships. Date competed well on her home soil, taking the Japan Open four times including three years running, 1992–1994. She broke into the top 10, the first Japanese player ever to do so, in 1994 by finishing second in a major tournament in Sydney, Australia. She also triumphed at the 1996 Toshiba Tennis Classic in San Diego. Her best performances in Grand Slam tournaments were at the 1994 Australian and 1995 French Opens where she reached the semifinals. She made the semifinals at Wimbledon in 1996 as well as the quarterfinal of the U.S. Open twice (1993 and 1994). Date represented her country in the 1992 **Olympics** and played for Japan's Federation Cup team for several years. During her career, she won 450 matches on the tour and purses of almost $4 million.

After playing in her second Olympic games, Date announced her retirement in September 1994. However, in 2008, after being away from tennis for many years, she unexpectedly made a tour comeback and won several more tournaments. Finally, at age 47, she retired in September 2017. *See also* SPORTS.

DAZAI OSAMU, 太宰治 **(1909–1948).** Dazai Osamu, a novelist, is considered one of Japan's most important fiction writers of the 20th century. He wrote about such depressing topics as family losses and the disappearance of an older way of life. Born Tsushima Shuji, the son of a wealthy landowner and politician in northern Honshū, Dazai was constantly at odds with his family over his drinking, philandering, and dabbling in Marxist politics. He found release in writing, especially about the despair of the postwar era. Alienated from society, influenced by alcohol and drugs, and dissatisfied with all politics, Dazai wrote *Shayō* (*The Setting Sun*), which portrayed the decline of an aristocratic family, and *Ningen shikkaku* (*No Longer Human*), an attack on Japanese traditions. His leading figures followed lives of dissolution as did Dazai himself. Self-destructive, after several failed attempts, Dazai and his lover took their own lives by jumping into the Tamagawa Reservoir. *See also* LITERATURE.

DEFENSE. The Self-Defense Forces (SDF), or Jieitai (自衛隊) in Japanese, is the formal name for Japan's military force. Started as the National Police Reserve in July 1950, it was renamed the Self-Defense Forces in September 1951. The Self-Defense Forces Law of 1954 created the SDF. This law guaranteed that there would be civilian control of the Japan Defense Agency (Bōei-chō) and that it was a **cabinet** office under the **prime minister**. The National Defense Council (Kokubō Kaigi), a civilian agency that advises the government on military matters, was created in 1956. In 2006, the **National Diet** elevated the Japan Defense Agency to a cabinet-level position, the Ministry of Defense (Bōei daijin). Kyuma Fumio became Japan's first minister of defense on 9 January 2007. Prime Minister **Hatoyama Yukio** appointed Kitazawa Toshimi minister of defense on 16 September 2009, and **Kan Naoto** continued him in that position. Prime Minister **Abe Shinzō** appointed Onodera Itsunori minister of defense on 3 August 2017.

Although the postwar **constitution** denies the "right of belligerency of the state," Japan has maintained a civilian-controlled military first under the cabinet-level Defense Agency and now under the Ministry of Defense. Constant at about 250,000 men, this well-trained, well-equipped force is among the 10 strongest in the world.

In the mid-1970s, under Prime Minister **Miki Takeo**, Japan articulated a military spending limit of "1 percent of gross national product," a self-imposed limit of the Japanese government on defense spending. Successive prime ministers have pledged to apply this principle. However, given the size of its **economy**, this provides for considerable military investment. (Refer to appendix F.)

While many individuals and groups have challenged the constitutionality of the SDF, the courts have upheld its legitimacy. Efforts to revise the constitution have failed thus far.

The **United States–Japan Security Treaty** (1951) and its revision as the **Treaty of Mutual Cooperation and Security between the United States and Japan** (1960) provide a major building block in Japan's defense. These agreements have given Japan the support and confidence to face a hostile world more easily and more confidently. Although highly controversial within various groups, the alliance has enabled Japan to achieve greater security at a lower cost.

The Ministry of Defense oversees the Ground Self-Defense Force, the Maritime Self-Defense Force, and the Air Self-Defense Force. Its collective responsibility is to defend the nation and to protect Japan's independence and peace. The inherent contradiction with Article 9 of the Constitution, which prohibits the existence of military forces, was overridden by the argument that all countries possess the right of self-defense. Starting with Prime Minister **Yoshida Shigeru**, Japan gradually developed a sophisticated military force.

In 1982, at the urging of **United States** secretary of defense Caspar Weinberger, Japan accepted the idea that its defense perimeter extends 1,000 miles from its shores and was referred to as the "1,000-Mile Radius of Defense." In November 1982, when the Defense Agency's former director-general, **Nakasone Yasuhiro**, became prime minister, there were strong efforts for an increase in Japan's military appropriations. Antimilitary forces steadfastly resisted this. However, the Japanese government did not seriously deviate from the "1 percent of GNP" limitation on military spending.

In 1992, the Diet passed a **United Nations** Peacekeeping Cooperation Law that allowed the SDF to participate in UN medical, refugee aid, transportation, infrastructure repair, election-monitoring, and policing operations under strictly supervised conditions. This allowed 600 SDF forces to monitor elections in Cambodia and 53 to aid in peacekeeping operations in Mozambique in 1993.

The phrase "free ride" was often used to refer to Japan's low expenditure on military armaments while plunging full speed into more remunerative economic endeavors. Although initially opposed to any military force in the early postwar period, the United States came to argue that Japan should spend more in its own defense and in the protection of the international scene. The phrase "free ride" is hardly correct as Japan spends nearly $40 billion in its annual defense budget and maintains a military force of 250,000 people under arms as of 2016. To avoid any semblance of a revival of militarism, Japanese leaders emphasize civilian control of the armed forces and use nonmilitary terms when possible.

The cabinet approved draft security legislation to give legal teeth to its decision in July 2014 to enlarge the role of the SDF. The law ensures the right to exercise collective self-defense in such a way as to mount a counter-attack in support of an ally under fire. The legislation lays out preconditions for the use of deadly force by the SDF. The situation must threaten national survival and pose a clear danger of fundamentally undermining the Japanese people's rights to liberty and the pursuit of happiness.

In April 2015, Prime Minister Abe met with a group of visiting U.S. congressmen and stressed the need for these lawmakers to strengthen the Japan-U.S. security alliance. Japan is expanding the scope of possible SDF activities due to growing tensions with **North Korea** and **China**. Because he is concerned that the United States might not protect Japan, Abe wants to strengthen the Japanese military.

Abe seeks to gain wider authority for Japan to deploy SDF troops to extended parts of the world to give logistical support to partner countries, to provide materials, and to transport these materials as well as troops. In short, these actions would allow Japan more military involvement and support. This would be part of what Abe calls "proactive pacifism."

In May 2015, Prime Minister Abe submitted a package of bills that would drastically increase Japan's postwar defense posture. These bills enable Japan to exercise collective self-defense in certain circumstances to help the United States or other allies under attack. This same month, Japan and the Philippines held joint naval exercises in the South China Sea, territory over which Japan has a dispute with China. These sea-lanes are crucial for ships bringing much-needed energy **petroleum** from the Middle East. Thus, we see an expansion of Japan's area of strategic importance.

The Ministry of Defense has announced that it plans to deploy security troops and anti-aircraft units to Miyako Island, which is 200 kilometers from the Senkaku Islands, known as the Diaoyu Islands in China. This shows the growing tension between Japan and China. This area is in Japan's vital shipping lanes.

Since the terrorist attacks against the United States on 11 September 2001, Japan's SDF has gradually expanded its overseas operations. It has supplied fuel to multinational forces engaged in Afghanistan and supported multilateral efforts in Iraq. Many Japanese fear that their country may be dragged into a U.S. war. Abe would like the authority to allow Japan's forces to exercise greater collective self-defense. But as Japan considers a wider military role, Asian neighbors have expressed growing concerns.

Nakatani Gen, former defense minister, says Japan would consider sending its Self-Defense Forces to the South China Sea to monitor Chinese island-building activity in cooperation with the American military. The **Diet** has deliberated on new national security legislation that would greatly expand the SDF's defense capabilities. Japan is cautiously and slowly beginning to flex more military muscle. It has donated $2 million in military aid to Cambodia and East Timor. Japanese-Chinese relations remain volatile. Japan's military is superior to China's in weaponry and training, but China's forces are much larger and growing faster.

Japan has a full-fledged military force and thus is one of the more powerful countries in the world. Yet, Japan still considers the U.S. nuclear deterrence an important force in its security. Japan is gradually becoming more international, not more isolationist. Japan increasingly plays a larger role in international affairs.

In February 2017, after much blustering, U.S. president Donald Trump reaffirmed America's commitment to the mutual defense treaty with Japan. Nuclear provocations by North Korea have reenergized the need for the longtime treaty commitment between the United States and Japan. Trump's provocative statements have led many Japanese to question the validity of the United States to continue to provide a nuclear shield for Japan. The United States claims it will continue to support an "unwavering alliance" with Japan. Prime Minister Abe promised U.S. defense secretary James Mattis that Japan will strengthen its defense capabilities.

As of 2017, Japan continues to spend about 1 percent of its gross domestic product on defense. Given the difference in GDP, China's military expenditure is much larger, probably at least three times greater. In 2016, Japan's defense budget totaled $46.1 billion but authorities raise it to $48.1 billion for 2018. (Refer to appendix S.)

DEMOCRATIC PARTY (MINSHINTŌ, 民進党). Founded on 27 March 2016 by the merger of the Democratic Party of Japan and the Japan Innovation Party, the Democratic Party became the main opposition party in Japan. It held 97 seats in the **House of Representatives** and 49 seats in the **House of Councillors**. Its general political stance was to the left of center and toward social liberalism. The party's platform called for the protection of the existing pacifist **constitution**, rejected the use of nuclear weapons and power, favored an increase in the minimum wage, and opposed Prime Minister **Abe Shinzō** and his policies of "Abenomics."

On 27 July 2017, Democratic Party leader **Murata Renhō** announced her resignation in the face of a crushing defeat in the **Tōkyō** Metropolitan Assembly election earlier in the month. The Democratic Party won only five of the 127 seats up for contention. On 1 September 2017, the Democratic Party picked former foreign minister Maehara Seiji (1962–) as its new leader. His tenure in office lasted only two months, and he was replaced on 31 October by Ōtsuka Kōhei (1959–). The party leaders faced a tough task of rebuilding the party.

The Democratic Party's main organized supporter was the **Japanese Trade Union Confederation** (Rengō). In addition to Maehara Seiji, other important figures included Okada Katsuya, Edano Yukio, Yamao Shiori, and Murata Renhō.

The Democratic Party was young, and it struggled. Some of its official candidates for the Tōkyō Metropolitan Assembly election dropped out. The support rate for this one-time leading opposition party dropped to an abysmally low 6.7 percent. Analysts suggested that the poor showing of the Democratic Party was due to a lack of clear identity, the appearance of being only a critic to Prime Minister Abe's policies, and a failure to consolidate its power. Toward the end of 2017, the party split into three groups: the **Constitutional Democratic Party**, the **Party of Hope**, and independents.

DEMOCRATIC PARTY OF JAPAN (MINSHUTŌ, 民主党). The original Democratic Party of Japan (DPJ) was formed in 1947 and cooperated with the **Japan Socialist Party** (JSP) and the People's Cooperative Party to form a government later that year. Prime Minister **Ashida Hitoshi** headed the party but resigned after being implicated in a bribery scandal. This DPJ dissolved in 1950.

An early version of the present DPJ won 52 seats in the October 1996 **election**. The present version of the DPJ was founded as a progressive democratic party in March 1998 and was headed by **Kan Naoto** and **Hatoyama Yukio**. The Good Governance Party, the Amity Party, and the Democratic Reform Party, three post–**New Frontier Party** groups, agreed to merge with the DPJ, making it the second-largest force after the **Liberal Democratic Party** (LDP). The new DPJ had a total of 139 members, the combined force of the four parties plus three independents, in both chambers of the **Diet**. Fifty-two **House of Representatives** members and five **House of Councillors** members attended the inaugural convention. Many of the DPJ participants were former members of the **Japan New Party**, the JSP, the **Demo-**

cratic Socialist Party, the **New Party Sakigake**, and the Citizens Action League. In 2003, **Ozawa Ichirō**'s center-right Liberal Party merged with the DPJ.

Although the DPJ was not riddled with factions like the LDP, the DPJ did have differences and disagreement among its members over various polices. Due to its mixture of conservatives and socialists, members differed on the issues of what **defense** and **foreign policies** to follow. Faced with serious problems in the **economy**, the DPJ presented a series of spending measures and tax cuts to help with the recovery but did not develop a viable strategy for long-term growth. The DPJ offered new faces and new rhetoric but not necessarily a truly new plan of action.

The DPJ, a liberal **political party** with moderate socialist leanings, strived to replace the staid, old LDP and to create a two-party system. It campaigned against the status quo and the governing establishment. It challenged the inefficiency of the political bureaucracy and promoted a new, self-reliant Japan. It sought to make the government more open and less centralized. In short, the DPJ attempted to bring a breath of fresh air to Japanese politics.

With the July 2004 House of Councillors election, the DPJ held, with carryover seats, 79 of the 252 seats, making it the second-largest party behind the LDP's 114 seats. Gaining strength, the DPJ soundly defeated the LDP in the 2007 upper house election to gain 109 seats to the LDP's 83 seats. However, this was not enough to give the DPJ a majority of the 242 House of Councillors seats.

Contradicting the growing trend of the DPJ, in the September 2005 House of Representatives election the LDP easily outpaced the DPJ. The DPJ got 31 percent of the votes and 113 out of 480 seats, making it the second-largest party after the LDP's 296 seats.

On 30 August 2009, voters handed the DPJ an overwhelming victory in the lower house election. The DPJ outpaced the LDP by a stunning 308 to 119 count. Postwar Japanese politics had never experienced such a drastic vote swing. Fed up with years of economic recession, bureaucratic domination, political scandals, stagnation, and malaise, the voters turned to the DPJ in droves. The DPJ captured more seats than the LDP ever enjoyed, and the LDP fell to only a little more than half the seats it held at its lowest point ever. However, it was obviously too early to tell what impact this dramatic political shift would have on the country.

In addition to Kan Naoto (who had served twice as president of the DPJ) and Hatoyama Yukio, Okada Katsuya (1953–) was elected president of the DPJ in May 2004 when Kan resigned over a lapse in payments into the national pension system. Other important leaders of the DPJ included **Hatoyama Kunio** and Matsuzawa Shigefumi (1958–). When the DPJ suffered a significant election loss in 2005, Maehara Seiji (1962–) replaced Okada in September only to be replaced by Ozawa Ichirō as president of the party in

April 2006. Ozawa stepped down in May 2009 after an aide was arrested on charges of taking an illegal political donation from a **construction** company. The DPJ chose Hatoyama Yukio as its president for the third time, and the Diet named him **prime minister** after the dramatic August 2009 election. However, Hatoyama would prove incapable of governing, and Kan Naoto replaced him in nine months.

On 27 March 2016, the DPJ merged with two smaller parties to form the **Democratic Party** (Minshintō).

DEMOCRATIC SOCIALIST PARTY (MINSHU SHAKAITŌ, 民主社会党). The Democratic Socialist Party (DSP) broke away from the **Japan Socialist Party** (JSP) in 1960. Members of the DSP disagreed with the hard-line doctrine of the JSP and at times cooperated with the **Liberal Democratic Party** (LDP). Unlike the JSP, the DSP supported the **United States–Japan Security Treaty**. The DSP opposed totalitarian rule, called for a welfare state, and aligned with **labor**. In 1970, the DSP changed its Japanese name to Minshatō but kept its English name the same.

Nishio Suehiro, who left the JSP over renewal of the security treaty with the United States, helped found the DSP in 1960. He served as the DSP chairman until his retirement in 1967. **Kasuga Ikkō** was elected in 1952 to the **House of Representatives** as a JSP candidate, but he left the party in 1960 and helped form the DSP, becoming its secretary in 1967 and later its chairman from 1971 to 1977. In 1955, **Sasaki Ryōsaku** was elected to the House of Representatives as a JSP member but left the JSP to help form the DSP in 1960. He served as party secretary-general and chairman of the party's **Diet** Policy Committee and became vice chairman of the DSP in 1975 and chairman in 1977. Yonezawa Takashi was also secretary-general of the DSP. Under Yonezawa, the DSP leadership resigned en masse in 1990 over the party's devastating defeat in the House of Representatives **election**. Ōuchi Keigo served as chairman of the DSP from 1992 until 1994.

In the 1970s and 1980s, the DSP typically won 6 to 7 percent of the national vote, but thereafter, its power declined precipitously. In 1994, the DSP dissolved and joined the **New Frontier Party**, which would eventually join the **Democratic Party of Japan**. *See also* POLITICAL PARTIES.

DEPARTMENT STORES. Japan has had a long history of department stores dating back to the 17th century. In Japanese department stores today, you can find anything you want to buy. These department stores have many floors with each featuring special products. The sales staff provides excellent service, the merchandise is of high quality, and the presentation is attractive.

Beyond marketing merchandise, Japanese department stores provide many services such as ticket sales, travel reservations, foreign exchange, and the sale of gift certificates. Many serve as pseudo museums with the display and sale of traditional pottery and lacquerware, as well as arts and crafts. Most have nice restaurants on the top floor and food courts and grocery stores in the basement.

Mitsukoshi is Japan's largest department store, with roots dating back to 1673. Its main store is still in Nihonbashi in **Tōkyō**. Mitsukoshi, which is a central part of the **Mitsui Group**, has 14 stores and 28 outlets around the world. First listed on the stock market in 1949, it has paid dividends yearly until financial difficulties caused a major restructuring in 1999. In 2007, Isetan merged with Mitsukoshi.

One of Japan's leading department stores, Daimaru originated in 1717 as a drapery shop. It is now one of Japan's largest department stores with 15 upscale stores, primarily in western Japan. Takashimaya is another of Japan's largest department store chains. The **Tōkyū Corporation** consists of approximately 400 companies, including Tōkyū Department Stores. Japan's other leading department stores include **Seibu**, Odakyū, Hankyū, Parco, Marui, Matsuya, and Matsuzakaya. *See also* CONVENIENCE STORES.

DIET, NATIONAL (KOKKAI, 国会). The Diet is "the highest organ of state power" and "the sole lawmaking organ of the state." according to the 1947 **Constitution**. The Diet, Japan's legislative body, consists of the **House of Representatives** (Shūgiin) or lower house, which wields the most power, and the **House of Councillors** (Sangiin) or upper house. The Diet building is located in the Nagatachō section of **Tōkyō**.

Japanese nationals aged 18 and older can vote for House of Representatives candidates, who must be 25 years of age to hold office. The term of office is four years, but the **prime minister** can dissolve the Diet at any time. The opposition can also call for a nonconfidence resolution, and if successful, Japan must hold an election. If there are disagreements between the two houses, the House of Representatives prevails on the choice of prime minister, fixing the budget, or making laws if it obtains a two-thirds vote. The House of Representatives now consists of 475 members with 295 people elected from single-seat constituencies and 180 elected from 11 separate electoral blocs under the "party list system of proportional representation."

Eligible voters also elect House of Councillors members, who must be 30 years of age to run for office. The term of office is six years with half of the members elected every three years. The House of Councillors elects 146 members from the 47 prefectural constituencies by means of a single nontransferable vote and the other 96 from an open national list.

The House of Representatives held its 48th election 22 October 2017, while the House of Councillors held its 25th election 10 July 2016.

The Diet selects the prime minister, makes the laws, approves the budget, ratifies treaties, and directs the **judicial system**. Each house of the Diet has its own standing committees that oversee the running of Japan's government. Under the Meiji Constitution, the **emperor** held sovereignty, but under the present constitution, the people of Japan exercise full sovereignty. Today, the Japanese emperor fulfills a purely ceremonial role. The Japanese National Diet has been an effective governing instrument for 70 years. *See also* ELECTIONS; POLITICAL PARTIES.

DIPLOMACY. *See* FOREIGN POLICY.

DISCOUNT STORES. Discount stores are making a bigger mark in Japan as budget-minded consumers look for ways to reduce their expenditures. The casual clothing retailer Shimamura has launched more than 250 new stores in recent years. Shimamura has linked with general merchandise stores that sell clothes.

Seria, the second-largest 100-yen operator in Japan, has opened 150 stores as of 2017. Daiei planned to boost its Big-A discount stores by 10 times by 2017. Aeon stores will continue adding around 100 Big-A locations annually until reaching 500 stores by 2018.

In the restaurant industry, Yoshinoya Holdings planned to add about 50 new locations to its mainstay Yoshinoya beef bowl chain by the end of 2017, its largest expansion in seven years. Torikizoku, a yakitori grilled-chicken chain known for its low prices, planned to open a record 100 locations, mainly in the **Tōkyō** area, by the end of 2017.

Since 2015, consumers have become more price conscious and are looking for cheaper purchases. However, with rising construction costs at high levels, setting up new locations is expensive. To offset the high cost, chain operators look to become tenants of bigger stores or take over shuttered sites with useful equipment.

DOI TAKAKO, 土井たか子 (1928–2014). Doi Takako was a populist **woman** politician and a major leader in the **Japan Socialist Party** (JSP). Born in **Kōbe** to a doctor's family, Doi graduated from Dōshisha University in 1955 and later became a professor at Dōshisha. In 1969, Doi was elected to the **House of Representatives** where she defended the Japanese **constitution** and women by organizing grassroots movements.

JSP members elected Doi chairperson in 1986, the first woman ever to lead a Japanese **political party**. She served as JSP chairperson until her resignation in 1991. In 1993, Doi was elected the first female chairperson of the Japanese **House of Representatives**, the highest political position a woman has held in the modern era. In 1996, she succeeded **Murayama**

Tomiichi as chair of the renamed **Social Democratic Party of Japan** (SDPJ) and served until 2003 when Fukushima Mizuho became chair. Doi tried to bring the party more into the mainstream on such divisive issues as national **defense** and **nuclear power**. A favorite of the voters, the "Doi boom" referred to her popularity, but she could not translate her popularity into a political rejuvenation of the ailing SDPJ. Doi retired from politics in 2005 after losing in the **election** and passed away in 2014.

DOKŌ TOSHIO, 土光敏夫 **(1896–1988).** Dokō Toshio was a businessman and the fourth president of the **Japan Federation of Economic Organizations** (Keidanren) from 1974 to 1980. Born in Okayama Prefecture, Dokō graduated from Tōkyō Technical Higher School and worked in an engineering firm. He became president of Ishikawajima Heavy Industries, which became Ishikawajima-Harima Heavy Industries (IHI) in 1960. Dubbed "Japan's **business** prime minister," Dokō pioneered the growth of IHI shipbuilding. In 1965, he accepted the presidency of the faltering **Toshiba Corporation** and in eight years rebuilt the company as its president.

DŌMEI, 同盟. *See* JAPAN CONFEDERATION OF LABOR (ZEN NIHON RŌDŌ SŌDŌMEI KAIGI, 全日本労働総同盟会議).

DORAEMON, ドラえもん. *Doraemon* is the best-selling **manga/anime** series in Japanese history. The title character, Doraemon, known and loved throughout the world, is an impish blue robot cat with the ability to make children's wildest dreams come true. He has a magical pocket full of high-tech gadgets such as a time-traveling *take-copter* (bamboo helicopter), a time *furoshiki* (time-wrapping cloth), and a *dokodemo* door (anywhere door).

First appearing in 1969, Doraemon and his 10-year-old human friend, Nobita, became national institutions. Immensely popular and profitable, Doraemon and Nobita are the Japanese equivalent of Charles M. Schulz's Snoopy and Charlie Brown. Nobita, a fourth-grade boy, is always looking for the easy way out. He is often seen as lazy, a poor student, bad at **sports**, and often subject to ridicule. Yet he is quite popular in Japan.

In addition to the *Doraemon* manga, there have been a long series of **television** shows and at least 19 *Doraemon* **films**. Fujimoto Hiroshi and his collaborator, Motō Abiko, originated *Doraemon*. Together, this productive duo created 49 manga series over 30 years. Nobita represents suburban Japanese youth, and *Doraemon* demonstrates a titanic struggle against evil powers. This manga and anime series, although set in the 22nd century, brings freedom and happiness to children all over the world today. Doraemon's image can be seen on books, backpacks, stuffed animals, telephones, and a myriad of other products.

EBIHARA HIROYUKI, 海老原博幸 **(1940–1991).** Born in **Tōkyō**, Ebihara Hiroyuki began boxing professionally in 1959 and in his first 33 bouts reeled off 31 wins (18 knockouts) with only one loss and a draw. On New Year's Eve 1962, Ebihara won the Orient Flyweight title. After four more wins, he challenged for the World Flyweight title and won it by a knockout in the first round. He lost his title four months later by decision in Bangkok. Fifteen consecutive victories (1964–1966) put Ebihara in a position to again contend for a flyweight crown, this time the World Boxing Association version, but he dropped a decision to Horacio Accavello in Buenos Aires in July 1966 and the rematch in August 1967. When this title became vacant in 1969, Hiroyuki beat Josh Severino in **Sapporo** by a decision. Seven months later, he lost his second world crown to Bernabe Villacampo in Tōkyō by a decision. All told, Ebihara had a stellar record of 63 wins (34 by knockout) against only five losses and a draw.

ECONOMIC PLANNING AGENCY (KEIZAI KIKAKUCHO, 経済企画庁**).** The EPA guided Japan's high-speed economic growth in the 1950s and continued to operate until its absorption into the **Council on Economic and Fiscal Policy** (CEFP) in 2001. With antecedents from 1946, but officially started in 1955, the EPA was responsible for Japan's economic planning. The EPA often worked in cooperation with the **Ministry of International Trade and Industry** to encourage worldwide growth.

In 1955, the EPA issued a white paper declaring that the postwar years were over and began to promote economic change. By the 1960s, Japan's **economy** had entered a period of phenomenal growth. The **steel**, shipbuilding, machine, electrical, and petrochemical industries made huge investments in plants and spurred on Japan's already rapidly growing economy. The EPA collected and provided information on the economy, helped guide Japan's economic development, directed long-term planning for growth, and led government assistance.

The most famous of the EPA plans was the 1960 Income Doubling Plan in which Prime Minister **Ikeda Hayato** promised to double Japan's GNP in 10 years. Miraculously, Japan accomplished the income doubling in just seven years.

Until 2001, the EPA was an agency under the jurisdiction of the **prime minister**'s office. Although not a **cabinet** ministry, its director-general was officially a cabinet member.

With **Koizumi Jun'ichirō**'s cabinet reorganization the EPA was turned over to the newly organized cabinet office, the successor to the prime minister's office. The director-general title was changed to minister of state for economic and fiscal policy. The newly reorganized office is called the CEFP and is a cabinet office under the **Ministry of Finance**. The change was completed in order to strengthen the prime minister's leadership in economic and fiscal matters.

ECONOMY. Japan's postwar economy developed from the prewar period where in the 19th century a dual structure had evolved. Major corporations, endowed with significant capital, a large number of employees, and extensive **technology**, produced goods on a huge scale. Such corporations thrived by joining with others in a **zaibatsu** or financial and industrial conglomerate. The original leading big four zaibatsu were **Mitsui**, **Mitsubishi**, **Sumitomo**, and Yasuda. Other newer zaibatsu included **Nissan**, Nomura, and Furukawa. These large **business** concerns exercised considerable political power. On the other side, small to medium-sized businesses followed more traditional ways of doing business.

After World War II, the government abolished the zaibatsu system and many of the holding companies. However, the larger companies remained loosely affiliated in *keiretsu* business groupings. These groupings usually included their own financial, insurance, and transportation operations.

In the early postwar period, two individuals were influential in shaping the Japanese economy. Nakayama Ichirō (1898–1980), an economic consultant, convinced Japanese leaders that they should concentrate first on expanding exports as the fastest way to build the economy. W. Edwards Deming (1900–1993), a world-famous statistician, educator, and consultant, introduced quality control circles to Japan. In 1964, Japan was admitted to the Organisation for Economic Co-operation and Development (OECD), a world institution to stimulate economic growth.

Following the **Occupation** and the Korean War, Japan entered a period of unprecedented economic growth. In 1956–1957, Japan experienced the "Jimmu boom," so named because no such prosperity was remembered since Emperor Jimmu ascended the throne in 660 BCE. By 1968, Japan had become the second-largest economy in the world after the **United States**. The government and business worked together to develop the textile, **steel**, shipbuilding, chemical, and **automobile** industries. The phrase "Japan's Industrial Policy" refers to Japan's industrial efforts in the 1960s and 1970s where business, government, and **labor** cooperated to provide the best possible environment for Japanese economic growth. All through the oil crises of 1973 and 1978, the privatization of the **railroads** and telecommunications systems, and the strengthening of the yen against the dollar were all important because of Japan's export-driven economy. (Refer to appendixes F, G, H, and K.)

Trade was a major factor in Japan's economic growth. One of the world's first major export-oriented economies, Japan used its profits from international exports to pay for its needed imports and to generate economic development. Aggressively planning, organizing, and promoting the sale of high-quality products enabled Japan to become one of the world's leading economies. **General trading companies** were instrumental in promoting international trade. (Refer to appendixes I and J.)

The extraordinary growth rate, exceeding 10 percent per year into the 1970s, slowed to a more modest 5 percent in the following years. Economic rates followed on a more moderate pattern, but Japan continued its economic gains. In achieving these economic gains, Japan had the benefit of self-sustaining **agriculture**, a well-organized **banking** system, a growing **construction industry**, and a ready supply of **energy**. The **Nikkei 225** tracked the rise of the average of the most actively traded stocks on the **Tōkyō Stock Exchange**.

Businessmen worked closely with **political parties** to form a symbiotic relationship. In the 1960s, Prime Minister **Ikeda Hayato** delivered on his promise to "double the income" in Japan. Political leaders followed a **foreign policy** designed to encourage Japan's overseas economic growth. The **Economic Planning Agency** gave assistance in Japan's economic growth. The growth of the stock market made investment easier, and **securities companies** led to further investments. The **computer industry** also contributed to technological innovations.

During the boom years of the economy, several social problems emerged. Japan's population shifted dramatically from the countryside to the cities and suburbs, causing a number of issues for the cities. Pollution also became a serious problem that was largely ignored until the late 1960s.

The 1990s saw the bursting of the economic bubble, causing a prolonged recession that lasted a decade. Between 1990 and 1996, Japan encountered a $7.3 trillion loss in business and household incomes. Household spending shrank 0.8 percent every year from 1991 through 1993. The financial system was largely stymied, and distribution and employment trends changed dramatically. The recession forced major banks to merge, go bankrupt, or be purchased by foreign companies, and foreign businesses and investments became more prominent. Corporate racketeers forced payoffs from banks and securities firms.

Companies from different *keiretsu* saw it in their interests to merge. Restructuring, or what the Japanese call *risutora*, became a common part of the vocabulary. *Risutora* generally has come to mean layoffs of older workers, company restructuring, higher unemployment, part-time work, changing jobs, venture capital, new startups, and social and economic problems.

Some common phrases used in discussing the Japanese economy include the following: "hollowing out" refers to the elimination of productive capacity on Japanese shores by exporting production through building plants abroad, "GNP-ism" suggests the exaggerated dependence that Japan placed on economic development in the 1960s and 1970s, and the phrase "big bang" was used to describe the financial decontrol movement in Japan during 1998–1999. It sought sweeping deregulation of Japan's financial markets.

"Japan Inc." is a concept applied by foreigners to interpret the unusually close working relationship between government and business interests to control and direct Japan's economy. The concept suggests a symbiotic power relationship between business and government. The **Ministry of International Trade and Industry** (MITI) worked particularly hard at providing a strong interface between government and business. In 2001, MITI was restructured to become the **Ministry of Economy, Trade, and Industry**, which continued to play a role.

Given the crisis in Japan's financial and business world, the Japanese government created the Industrial Revitalization Agency in November 2002. Headed by **Tanigaki Sadakazu**, this organization was supposed to reinvigorate Japan's economy. It decided which of Japan's heavily indebted companies should be resuscitated and which should close.

In May 2003, Prime Minister **Koizumi Jun'ichirō** organized the first meeting of the Financial Crisis Council, a group of bureaucrats who were to help him work through the financial morass of Japan. Takenaka Heizō, an economist and finance minister for Koizumi, worked with this group in an attempt to solve Japan's financial problems. The **Bank of Japan** also tried, without much success, to correct the matter by keeping interest rates low.

According to *Fortune* magazine, the 149 Japanese companies on the list of the world's largest 500 companies in the mid-1990s dropped to 82 by 2004. The value of stock in Japan's trading giants such as Mitsubishi, Mitsui, and **Itōchū** all dropped precipitously. By 2008, Japanese companies occupied only 10 percent of the top 200 companies although many other companies ranked in the top 500. At this time, **Toyota Motors** ranked fifth in the world, **Honda Motors** ranked 53rd, **Nippon Telegraph and Telephone** was 58th, **Nissan Motors** 61st, **Hitachi** 67th, Matsushita Electric 80th, and **Sony** 91st.

Japan's economy expanded by 2.7 percent in fiscal year 2003. Much of the growth was due to growing Chinese demand. Japan's economy improved, but for 12 years, since the bubble period, there was very little sustained growth. As of 2007, Japan's economy measured $3.7 trillion, the world's third-largest. It had displayed no signs of rising consumer prices or inflation and was again showing signs of successes.

A cursory perusal of newspaper headlines in 2009 reveals the economic difficulties faced by Japan. Headlines such as "*tankan* reflects lack of confidence," "Nikkei drops sharply," "Nomura reports $3.8 billion quarterly loss," "Japan accumulates largest public debt in the developed world," "bankruptcies surge," "Japan's economy plunges at fastest pace since 1974," and "Japan in worst recession in the postwar period" all underscored Japan's precarious situation. There were few positive headlines to offset the negative ones. One no longer saw projections of Japan as the world's master economy; however, most objective analysts were not yet ready to write Japan off as a has-been economic player. (Refer to appendixes N and Q.)

In 2016, Japan's economy seemed to continue in the doldrums, but one should be reminded that Japan continues to have the world's third-largest economy after the much larger, in both population and area, giants of the United States and **China**.

Political leaders in Japan regularly undertake economic stimulus measures to jump-start the Japanese economy, which continues to lag behind. Since the so-called lost decades, which started with the stock market crash of January 1990, the Japanese people have continued to do well. The Japanese still enjoy an affluent lifestyle. Housing prices remain well below their ridiculously high levels before the crash.

The Industrial Competitiveness Council outlined Japan's new growth strategy. It focused on dealing with supply constraints by improving industrial productivity, using the Internet of Things, big data, artificial intelligence, and other advanced technology to revolutionize industry. This strategy sought to strengthen Japan's competitiveness. The plan included a national innovation system aimed at deepening collaboration between industry, government, and academia by designating research universities and top graduate schools that can compete with leading overseas institutions. The strategy also called for promoting **robotic** technology as well as implementing reforms dovetailing into the 2020 Tōkyō **Olympics**.

In 2010, China replaced Japan as the world's number two economy. Japan's economy stood at $5.47 trillion while China's rose to $5.88 trillion. However, Japan was far richer than China on a per-capita basis, but its economy had been stagnant for 25 years while China's had grown considerably.

As of early 2018, there were signs that Japan's economy was looking up. Exports had risen, consumer confidence had grown, and economic expansion increased at 2 percent a year. Large companies were hiring, and salaries were rising. Japan had just enjoyed eight quarters of uninterrupted growth, the most since 1980. Things appear to be looking up for Japan's economy.

EDUCATION. Japan provides free public education for all its children through junior high school. The success of that educational system is demonstrated by the country's literacy rate of 99.9 percent, one of the highest in the world. Following junior high school, 97 percent of students go on to three-year senior high schools. Nearly 95 percent of Japanese students finish high school as compared to about 83 percent in the **United States**. Japanese high school graduates achieve about the same level of education as the average American student after two years of college. Competition for entry into the best Japanese universities is very rigorous.

In 1947, Japan adopted the Fundamental Law of Education that formed the basis for postwar education and set the primary principles of education, providing equal opportunity for education, nine years of free compulsory education, and a wide variety of education-related laws. Japan also adopted the School Education Law that defined the system as having six years of elementary school, three years of junior high school, three years of high school, and two or four years of university.

Japan has approximately 60,000 schools with about 25 million students. Each of the 47 prefectures has a five-member board of education appointed by the governor with the approval of the prefectural assembly. Financial support for schools comes from the national, prefectural, and municipal government levels. Japan's teachers are well trained and well paid. The **Japan Teachers' Union** (Nikkyōso) provides solid support for the educational system. Nearly three million students attend approximately 1,200 universities and junior colleges, giving Japan the second-largest higher education system in the world.

The Japanese school year begins on 1 April and has three terms running throughout the year. Until 2002, students attended school five and a half days per week, but this was reduced to five full weekdays. The school year lasts a legal minimum of 210 days, but most local school boards add another 30 days for school festivals, athletic meets, and ceremonies. The government provides free textbooks for all compulsory education. Schools are mostly public.

Approximately 50 percent of high school graduates go on to some type of university training. About 75 percent of higher education institutions are private. The Ministry of Education, Culture, **Sports, Science, and Technology**, working with the local people and teachers, exercises a strong hand in the education of Japan's youth. Worldwide, Japanese children score highly on international examinations. Japan's postwar educational system has been an important factor in the country's success.

Several additional features shape Japanese education. A *juku* is a private academy for makeup or acceleration of study programs. The *juku*, some starting in elementary school and running through high school, help students improve their chances of getting admitted to a more prestigious university. Additionally, a *kyōiku mama*, or "education mother," is a Japanese mother who puts heavy pressure on her children to achieve academic success.

Japanese students regularly rank among the highest performers in the Organisation for Economic Co-operation and Development tests for reading, math, and sciences. Thus, Japan has one of the best-educated **labor** forces in the world. Its education programs enable students to be successful in a highly competitive world. Success in education is one of the keys to Japan's economic strength. However, Japan's educational success is not dependent on large expenditures of money as it spends only 3.5 percent of GDP on education. Higher education is readily available with 59 percent of the people age 25–34 holding bachelor's degrees. Today, 75.9 percent of high school graduates attend a university, junior college, trade school, or other higher education institution.

Bullying and truancy are two problems that Japanese educators are trying to overcome. Although the Japanese educational system is highly ranked, it has come under criticism for too much focus on standardized tests, conformity, bullying, and overly strong academic pressure on students.

In higher education, the **University of Tōkyō** and Kyōto University always rank very high, domestically and internationally. Thirty-three Japanese universities rank in the top 100 in Asia.

Japanese students do not take any exams until they reach grade four. The goal for the first three years of school is to establish good manners and to develop proper character. Children are taught respect, to be gentle to animals and nature, to be generous, compassionate, and empathetic. They also learn grit, self-control, and justice.

Japanese students clean their classrooms, cafeterias, and even toilets. Japanese educators believe that requiring students to clean up after themselves teaches them to respect property, work as a team, and help each other. Public elementary and junior high schools prepare nutritious lunches for students, teaching the students to eat healthy and balanced meals. All classmates eat in their classroom together with the teacher. This helps build positive teacher-student relationships.

Most junior high schools require their students to wear school uniforms. While some schools have their own attire, a traditional Japanese school outfit consists of a military style uniform for boys and a sailor outfit for girls. The uniform policy is intended to remove social barriers among students and get them into a working mood. Besides, wearing a school uniform helps promote a sense of community among the children.

EKUAN KENJI, 榮久庵憲司 (1929–2015). Ekuan Kenji was a Japanese industrial designer, best known for creating the Kikkoman soy sauce bottle. Born in **Tōkyō**, Ekuan spent his youth in Hawaii. He returned to **Hiroshima**, in time to experience the atomic bomb, where he lost his sister and his father, a Buddhist priest. He attended Tōkyō National University of Fine Arts and Music (today's Tōkyō University of the Arts). In 1957, he founded GK Industrial Design Laboratory. In 1970, he became president of the Japan Industrial Designers' Association, and in 1975, he was elected president of the International Council of Societies of Industrial Design. He later would serve as chair of the Japan Institute of Design, dean of Shizuoka University of Art and Culture, and a trustee of the Art Center College of Design.

ELECTIONS. Elections have been a regular part of Japanese political life since the first national election was held in 1890. As of September 2017, Japan has had 26 elections since 1945 for **House of Representatives** members, or an average of one election every two years and nine months. The government must conduct an election for the lower house at least once every four years. However, it must hold elections more frequently if the ruling party loses a vote of confidence or if the ruling party chooses to dissolve the lower house before the end of its four-year term. When there is an election for the lower house, all seats are vacated, and their holders run for office.

Throughout the postwar period, an average of about 70 percent of eligible voters cast ballots in national elections. In the election of 22 May 1958, a high of 77 percent of eligible voters cast ballots. In the 16 elections since then, nearly 70 percent of the people have voted. In the dramatic election of 30 August 2009, 69 percent of the eligible people voted.

As of 2017, the **House of Councillors** has had 24 elections since its inception in the postwar period. Upper house elections are held on a regular schedule every three years in July. An average of about 65 percent of eligible voters have participated in these elections. At its high point, 77 percent of those eligible participated in the election of 2 June 1959. At its low point, only 45 percent voted in the 23 July 1995 election. Members of the upper house are elected to a full six-year term, with half the members subject to voter review every three years. Candidates for the upper house must be at least 30 years of age, but those running for the lower house need be only 25.

In the 16 December 2012 House of Representatives election, the **Liberal Democratic Party** (LDP) won a landslide victory. Continuing in the 14 December 2014 elections, Abe's LDP won but did not command a strong mandate from voters. However, he appeared to be making a record as one of Japan's strongest postwar **prime ministers**. The LDP won 291 seats and its coalition partner, **Kōmeitō**, won 35 seats. The **Democratic Party of Japan** did poorly, with even its leader, Kaieda Banri, losing his seat, the first time a party leader has been dropped since 1949. However, Abe's win was small enough to deny him claim to a rousing success of his economic program called Abenomics.

In Japan's 48th general election, held 22 October 2017, **Abe Shinzō** returned to lead the government and holds the prime minister's office as of January 2018. As of October 2017, the 465-seat House of Representatives is composed of the following parties: Liberal Democratic Party (283 seats), the **Constitutional Democratic Party of Japan** (54 seats), the **Party of Hope** (51), Kōmeitō (29), Group of Independents (14), **Japanese Communist Party** (12), **Nippon Ishin no Kai** (11), Independents (7), **Liberal Party** (2), and **Social Democratic Party** (2).

Politically, Prime Minister Abe Shinzō and the Liberal Democratic Party won a huge victory in the 10 July 2016 House of Councillors election and continued to dominate politics in Japan. The results (with holdovers) of the 2016 House of Councillors election are as follows: Liberal Democratic Party (126 seats), Democratic Party (50), Kōmeitō (25), Japanese Communist Party (14), Innovation Party (12), Hope Coalition (6), Independents Club (4), Okinawa Whirlwind (2), and Independents (3) for a total of 242 seats.

Abe has called for a fresh economic stimulus package and gradually reveals further plans for economic growth. Gaining a supermajority, the question of constitutional revision is a major topic of consideration. The LDP is in a position to change the **Constitution**. This recent election was the first in which people 18 years of age, rather than 20, could vote. The upper house will hold an election in July 2019.

Japanese voters are generally well informed. They have a broad knowledge of issues and candidates through extensive reading materials, an abundance of political literature, frequent campaign announcements, and discussion with friends and colleagues. However, many people are still inclined to vote based on personal relations.

Japan has had a multiparty system with at least five **political parties** running candidates for election and often as many as a dozen, not including candidates from minor parties. The Liberal Party, the **Japan Socialist Party** (JSP), the Reform Party, the first DPJ, and the Democratic Liberal Party dominated the first six elections.

In the 12 elections from 1958 through 1990, Japan had primarily a one-and--a-half-party system with the LDP dominating and the JSP being the "half party." Other minor parties have drawn votes but have not been a major factor. In the 17 elections from 1958 through 2005, the LDP has averaged 267 seats per election with a high of 300 seats and a low of 223 seats. From

1960 through 1993, the **Democratic Socialist Party** drained off approximately 22 percent of the socialist vote from the JSP. The Kōmeitō has averaged 42 seats for the 13 elections from when it first ran candidates in 1967, and its successor, the **New Kōmeitō** (NKP), averaged 29 seats in each of its four campaigns but hit a low of 21 seats in the 2009 election.

In 1996, the DPJ first ran candidates for the lower house, winning 52 seats. After that it grew dramatically, winning 177 seats in the 2003 election, and skyrocketing to be Japan's dominant political power capturing 308 of the 480 lower house seats in the 30 August 2009 election. However, since then it has declined at an astonishing rate.

In the last six elections, the JSP has become insignificant while the NKP has averaged 32 seats, the JCP 16 seats, and Independents 15 seats. (Refer to appendixes D and E.) *See also* DIET, NATIONAL (KOKKAI, 国会).

EMPEROR (*TENNŌ*, 天皇). The emperor of Japan was traditionally the head of state and exercised all political powers. Some emperors were supreme rulers, but many have been under the control of outside forces such as the shogun. For nearly 11 centuries, the emperor resided in **Kyōto**, but in 1868, his residence was moved to the newly named **Tōkyō**.

Today, the emperor is the ceremonial figurehead of a constitutional monarchy. According to the 1946 **Constitution of Japan**, he is "the symbol of the state and of the unity of the people." Unlike most constitutional monarchies, the emperor is not the nominal chief executive. Instead, the Constitution of Japan states that the emperor has "no powers related to government" and vests executive power in the **cabinet**, the **prime minister**, and the legislative power collectively in the elected members of the **Diet**. Sovereignty rests with the people of Japan. However, in diplomatic situations, the emperor acts as the head of state.

The constitution limits the duties of the emperor to appointing the prime minister from candidates "designated by the Diet of Japan without being given the avenue to decline appointment." This is quite different than the emperor's status under the 1889 Meiji Constitution where he was the embodiment of all sovereign power.

Historically, the succession of the Japanese throne was usually passed to male descendants. During the postwar period, Japan has had only two emperors, **Emperor Hirohito** and **Emperor Akihito**, the 125th in the line of succession. According to the present constitution, the imperial throne shall be dynastic, and succession will occur in accordance with the Imperial Household Law passed by the Diet. The law stipulates that only legitimate male descendants in the male line can be emperor, that imperial princesses lose their status as **imperial family** members if they marry outside the imperial family, and that the emperor and other members of the imperial family may not adopt children. Thus, the current law excludes **women** from succession. A change to this law had been considered until Princess Kiko gave birth to a son on 6 September 2006.

Emperor Akihito has been in poor health, and the duties of being emperor have weighed heavily on him. In January 2017, a government-appointed panel recommended special legislation that would allow him to abdicate. This recommendation applies only to the present emperor. The panel set 30 April 2019 as the beginning date for the new era. Although it continued to be discussed, the ruling did not deal with the possibility of admitting a woman as heir to the throne.

EMPEROR AKIHITO. *See* AKIHITO, EMPEROR, 明仁天皇 (1933–).

EMPEROR HEISEI. *See* AKIHITO, EMPEROR, 明仁天皇 (1933–).

EMPEROR HIROHITO. *See* HIROHITO, EMPEROR, 裕仁天皇 (1901–1989).

ENCHI FUMIKO, 円地文子 **(1905–1986).** Enchi Fumiko was a female writer whose works concentrated on the problems faced by women due to the repressive social structure dominated by men. Enchi "published brilliant, chilling novels that condemned the behavior of men and unveiled the hatred of women wronged." Enchi was the daughter of a Japanese-language professor at Tōkyō Imperial University. She attended Japan Women's University but did not receive her degree. She was a prolific writer.

ENDŌ SHŪSAKU, 遠藤周作 **(1923–1996).** Endō Shūsaku was an influential novelist, known in Japan both as an author of novels and plays on religious themes and as a humorist. Born in **Tōkyō**, Endō lived in **China** until he was 10 years of age. He was baptized a Roman Catholic at age 11. He studied French literature at Keiō University and became one of the first Japanese to study abroad after the war. He suffered from respiratory illness and spent time in hospitals, which would provide the setting of several of his novels.

After he returned to Japan, Endō began writing fiction. *Shirōi hito* (*White Man*, 1955), awarded the Akutagawa Prize, compared Western and Japanese attitudes toward Christianity, sin, and guilt. In his gripping novel *Chimmoku* (*Silence*, 1966), a study of the persecution of 17th-century Japanese Christians, Endō tries to resolve the conflict he felt as a Japanese embracing a foreign **religion**. This novel won the Tanizaki Prize.

Endō received the Noma Prize for his novel *Samurai* (1980), which is both a historical novel and a self-styled "I-novel" tracing the arduous journey that a Japanese must make in order to accept Christianity. In addition to his serious works, Endō sprinkled his writings with a wide array of unique humor. Though some critics were irritated by his extra-literary activities, Endō's willingness to collaborate with the mass media made him the most admired and widely read Christian writer in postwar Japan. *See also* LITERATURE.

ENERGY. Japan, the world's third-largest economic engine, runs primarily on imported sources of energy. Having very little domestic oil or natural gas resources, Japan is the world's second-largest importer of oil and the largest buyer of liquefied natural gas. In short, Japan produces less than 20 percent of its required energy supply. Thus, since the oil crisis of 1973, a strategic national priority has been to increase the national energy supply.

Japan's consumption of energy has grown dramatically in the postwar period, virtually doubling every five years. Oil has been the largest source of energy, but its usage has declined in relative terms by about 30 percent since the 1970s. Coal continues to be an important source of energy, but natural gas and **nuclear power** have shown the greatest increase as energy sources. Only the **United States** and France consume more energy from nuclear power.

Japan, the world's third-largest producer of electricity, has 10 major regional power utilities, which generate about 75 percent of all of Japan's electricity. The **Tōkyō Electric Power Company** is one of the world's largest producers of electricity.

In 2016, Japan was the world's third-largest user of nuclear power. Its 43 nuclear reactors produced an increasing percentage of its electricity needs. Even with substantial numbers of people opposed to nuclear power for fear of an accident or because of terrible memories of the atomic bombs, Japan plans to increase its use of clean nuclear energy. Although shut down due to the **Great East Japan Earthquake** of 2011, nuclear energy companies are gradually bringing these plants back on line.

Japan is the world's largest importer of liquefied natural gas. In 2006, Japan purchased 22 percent of its natural gas from Indonesia, 20 percent from Australia, 19 percent from Malaysia, 12 percent from Qatar, 10 percent from Brunei, 8 percent from the United Arab Emirates, and 5 percent from Oman.

In 2013, Japan imported about 83 percent of its oil, with most coming from the Middle East. The largest sources of imported oil for Japan are, in descending order, Saudi Arabia, United Arab Emirates, Iran, Qatar, and Kuwait.

Japan's largest refineries in order of capacity are Nippon Oil, Tonen-General, Cosmos Oil, Shōwa Sekiyu, Idemitsu Kōsan, Fuji Oil, and Japan Energy Company. These companies not only run the bulk of the domestic refineries but also have joint ventures with other countries in developing and operating refineries abroad.

In recent years, Japan has attempted to exploit geothermal energy with some measured success. It is also one of the leaders in photovoltaic electricity. Japan has recognized the need for renewable energy sources.

On the negative side, Japan is one of the top producers of carbon emissions, generating as much as 5 percent of the world's total emissions. Japan is working to reduce its carbon emissions to be in line with the Kyōto Protocol, thus seeking to solve pollution problems rather than contribute to them. Further, Japan previously experienced two serious nuclear accidents, the **Monju** reactor in Fukui Prefecture in 1995 and the 1999 **Tōkaimura accident** in Ibaraki Prefecture, both of which threatened a possible nuclear holocaust.

Japan imports a substantial portion of its energy, at least 84 percent as of 2010. It was the world's largest importer of coal and natural gas. Before the Fukushima Daiichi nuclear disaster caused by the Great East Japan Earthquake, Japan used nuclear power for about 30 percent of its energy needs, but when all nuclear reactors were shut down, the output dropped to zero. Gradually, despite a lot of public protest, these are going back on line and producing electricity. As of late 2015, the Sendai Nuclear Power Plant restarted its nuclear power plant. Government plans call for a 20 percent increase in the use of nuclear energy.

In 2014, Japan was the world's fifth-largest electricity producer, behind the United States, **China**, **Russia**, and India. However, it is only 18th in per capita usage. Japan is fourth in the world in its use of solar energy behind Germany, Italy, and China.

Japan's supply of liquefied natural gas is minimal, so it imports large amounts of oil that it converts into LNG. Japan plans to invest at least $700 billion into renewable energy by 2030. Japan also depends heavily on energy from hydroelectricity. With large geothermal reserves, Japan is putting serious efforts into developing geothermal power stations. By 2011, it had 18 geothermal plants. Although there are drawbacks, Japan has 1,807 wind turbines as of 2011. Japan also has developed numerous waste and biomass energy plants. It is also beginning to experiment with ocean energy. *See also* ECONOMY.

ENVIRONMENT. Motivated by the goal of rapid economic growth, Japan showed little concern for the environment in the early postwar period. Environmental negligence, driven by economic greed, caused numerous problems; among the most serious environmental catastrophes were the mercury poisoning in Minamata Bay causing the **Minamata disease** tragedy, cadmium poisoning in Toyama Prefecture producing the itai-itai disease crisis, and devastating air pollution in Yokkaichi.

Belatedly, in response to environmental pollution, the government established the Environmental Agency (Kankyō-chō) in 1970. Pushed by popular concerns, Japan began the regulation of its industries, adopted emission controls for automakers, and undertook oversight of waste disposal. By the 1990s, Japan was making significant progress in dealing with environmental problems by adopting some of the world's strictest environmental protection laws.

In 2001, Japan upgraded the Environmental Agency to the new Ministry of the Environment (Kankyō-shō), a **cabinet** position. **Koike Yuriko** served as an outstanding minister of the environment under Prime Minister **Koizumi Jun'ichirō**. Japan also created "Green Associations" in an attempt to protect the natural environment. It established Greenery Day in 1990 as a **national holiday** to encourage the planting and cultivation of trees.

Care and protection of the environment has become a popular theme for the Japanese. Today, Japan boasts a number of programs, organizations, and agencies that champion environmental causes. Among the organizations are the Japan Environment Association, the Nature Conservation Society of Japan, the Global Environmental Forum, the World Wide Fund for Nature Japan, and the Japan Environmental Education Forum. **Political parties** such as the Environmental Green Political Assembly, Greens Japan, and Rainbow and Greens, although not major political forces, at least awaken the public to environmental issues.

Japan, plagued by climate concerns and eager to share its technical knowledge with the world, took a leading international role by sponsoring the Kyōto Climate Conference, which produced the Kyōto Protocol on global warming in December 1997. With 168 participating nations, the **Kyōto** meeting was the largest international gathering to focus on the world's environmental problems. Faced with divergent interests not only between environmentalists and industrialists, but also with differences between developed and underdeveloped countries, the discussion was heated. The protocol that was adopted stipulated that different countries should diminish their CO_2 gas emissions by various amounts over the next decade. However, as of 2008, Japan was the world's fifth-largest producer of carbon dioxide and still struggled to meet its carbon-emissions goals.

Despite its efforts, Japan still faces many environmental problems, from being the world's second-largest consumer of fossil fuels and a major whaling nation, to deep involvement in deforestation in countries in Southeast Asia. Japan has had to struggle with issues around global warming, atmospheric deterioration, waste management, urban sprawl, soil and water pollution, the disposal of radioactive waste from its **nuclear power** plants, and chemical impurities. Thus, while Japan has made progress in handling some environmental issues, it must still regard others as a major threat.

Japan has become cleaner and more environmentally responsible in recent decades. It has made significant progress in dealing with these problems. Japan is working toward a low-carbon economy, the use of clean technology, smart material-cycle measures, and equilibrium in the use of natural resources.

Japan remains the world's leading importer of both exhaustible and renewable natural resources and one of the world's largest consumers of fossil fuels. This obviously presents environmental problems. With more than half the world's waste incinerators, Japan burns approximately two-thirds of its waste in municipal and industrial incinerators. This produces a high level of dioxin in its air. Recently, the Ministry of the Environment admitted that bleaching has destroyed 70 percent of the Sekisei lagoon in **Okinawa**, Japan's biggest coral reef. Even Japan's beloved cherry blossom trees are not doing as well as in the past due to global warming trends. *See also* ECONOMY; ENERGY.

EQUAL EMPLOYMENT OPPORTUNITY LAW. Passed by the government in May 1985 and coming into effect in April 1986, the goal of the EEOL is to improve **women**'s employment opportunities. The law tries to prohibit discrimination in the workplace, particularly as it affects women.

This law formally abolished discrimination, guaranteed women equal opportunity in entering the workforce, provided equal opportunity in training, and organized committees to ensure equal opportunity for women. Under this law, employers must offer equal opportunity to enter the workforce, avoid discrimination in recruiting or hiring, base promotions on performance and work ethic, and avoid using sex as a factor in making assignments or transfers. Women are given equal rights in training and in **education**. The law also prohibits discrimination based on age.

However, the EEOL has not been very successful in stopping job discrimination and improving women's chances of winning top jobs in major companies. The law has little in the way of penalties for companies that do not observe the employment guidelines. A "glass ceiling" still exists in Japan. As of 1976, the gender-based wage differential stood at 56 percent, but with the EEOL, the situation has achieved modest improvement. As of 2017, women filled only 5.1 percent of executive positions. Government itself has not done much better than **business** in this respect.

Women's groups have hotly debated the usefulness of EEOL and have both good and bad things to say about the law. Some women see the law as opening doors and assisting women in job opportunities and in other fields, while a few others interpret the law as restricting their chances to rise to the top. *See also* LABOR ORGANIZATIONS.

EXPOS. Expo '70 (Nihon bankoku hakuran-kai, 日本の万国博覧会) was a grand international exposition, which was also known as the Ōsaka International Exposition. It symbolized Japan's reemergence as a modern economic power and celebrated its affluence. The Ōsaka International Exposition, the first such fair held in Asia, championed its theme of Progress and Harmony of Mankind. Exhibitions included a moon rock, the latest commercial products, and modern living and transportation systems. Seventy-seven countries participated, and 60 million visitors came to **Ōsaka**, making it one of the largest and best-attended expositions in history.

Much smaller in size, Expo '75 was known as the **Okinawa** International Ocean Exposition and promoted marine life and cultivation of the sea. The next major international exposition hosted by Japan was Expo '85, which promoted **Science and Technology** for Man at Home. Located at Tsukuba, two hours northeast of **Tōkyō**, Tsukuba Academic New Town was a university-science-industry complex established to promote research. Government and private interests cooperated to advance scientific efforts.

Expo 2005 took place in Aichi Prefecture and stressed the **environment** and technology. Covering 427 acres, the theme was Nature's Wisdom. Here the area around Seto was transformed into a futuristic metropolis. It attracted more than 22 million visitors and had the participation of 121 countries. With extensive planning and a tremendous amount of infrastructure to support Expo 2005, Japan presented an excellent exhibition. *See also* FOREIGN POLICY.

F

FASHION. Recognized internationally, Japanese fashion seen on the streets of **Tōkyō** competes favorably with that of Paris, London, Milan, and New York. Fashion success stems from a variety of factors. Japan is financially able to develop and sustain a first-class fashion industry. Its artistic ability, creativity, sense of color, and quality of fabrics, as well as its presence and flair, all make for a leading role in the fashion industry. Japan has the places and occasions to wear high fashion. It also boasts some of the world's leading designers, manufacturers, models, and stores.

Giving some measure of the Japanese fashion presence, a leading website for fashion lists 44 outstanding designers from Paris, 14 each from Tōkyō and Milan, eight from New York, and seven from London. One sees the sophistication of the Tōkyō fashion world during a stroll down Omotesandō from Aoyama to Harajuku. Known as the Harajuku Champs-Élysées, one not only passes Gucci, Chanel, Yves Saint Laurent, Louis Vuitton, and other European high-class fashion stores, but one also sees the names of famous Japanese designers. **Mori Hanae** was the first Japanese designer to garner international fame in the fashion industry with her Japanese flavor in Western-style clothes. **Kawakubo Rei** is known throughout Europe and the **United States** for her stylish fashion sold under the label Comme des Garçons. **Takada Kenzō** (the first Japanese to open a boutique in Paris in the 1970s), **Miyake Issei** (the first fashion designer to establish an avant-garde, Japanese-Western reputation on an international level), and **Yamamoto Yōji** (one of the world's top fashion designers) have all pioneered international fashion.

In addition to these, Takahashi Jun (1969–) with his "Under Cover" line of clothing, Yanagida Takeshi (1968–) with his "NAiyMA" line, Maruyama Keita (1965–) selling under the brand name "Ray Beams," and Hosokawa Shin (1949–) with his men's clothing are among these 14 Japanese designers.

Younger Japanese fashion designers have already made a name for themselves. Higa Kyōko (A Rose Is a Rose), Ōta Norihisa (C'est Vrai), and Abe Kenshō (Kenshō) are all well known in the ladies' fashion world. Onozuka

Akira (Odds On), Kobayashi Yukio (Monsieur Nicole), Hosokawa Shin (Shin Pashu), and Katō Kazutaka (Tete Homme) have enriched the male fashion scene. Other young Japanese fashion leaders include Hanai Yukiko, the Koshino sisters, Watanabe Yukisaburō, and Suzuki Norio. Watanabe Junya, Hishinuma Yoshiki, Yanagida Takeshi, Homma Yū, and Takahashi Jun are among Japan's most active designers today.

Prominent younger fashion designers include Limi Feu, daughter of Yamamoto Yohji; Ashida Tae, daughter of Ashida Jun; Kubo Yoshio with his exotic designs for men's clothing; Amatsu Yu, who designs for Mori Hanae; Iwaya Toshikazu; and Koshino Yuma, the daughter of Koshino Yuma, among others. Japanese fashion design seems to run in families.

Harajuku is the Tōkyō center of young fashion. Takeshita-dōri, a small "alley" running between Harajuku Station and Meiji-dōri, is a good place to find what's popular at the moment. Big shoes and bright clothes, the trend in young fashion, can be readily found at Love Girls Market. Youth fashion is sold at stores such as Uniqlo, which features inexpensive but high-quality clothes, or Laforet, with more eccentric fashions. The Candy Stripper is a clothing store with a bright red front and bubble-mirror windows. Give Life specializes in clothes made strictly from natural products. Mujirushi Ryohin is Japan's original no-brand designer store, and 109 is a mecca the the fashion-minded teenage girl.

Harajuku street fashion in Japan, for both males and females, is focused on the youth culture. Bubbles-Harajuku is one of the most popular brands and stores. Souvenir jackets with kanji patterns are quite popular along with items decorated with favorite characters inspired by **anime**, **manga**, **video games**, or **otaku**. The increase in foreign tourism has made the Japanese fashion world more international.

FEDERATION OF ECONOMIC ORGANIZATIONS. *See* JAPAN FEDERATION OF ECONOMIC ORGANIZATIONS (NIHON KEIZAI DANTAI RENGŌKAI, 日本経済団体連合会).

FEDERATION OF INDEPENDENT LABOR UNIONS (CHŪRITSU RŌREN, 中立労連**).** The Federation of Independent Labor Unions, with 1.6 million members, was a trade union federation from 1961 until 1987. Its members were primarily employed in private enterprise. Although some union members identified with **political parties**, the federation itself was independent. It often cooperated with the **General Council of Japanese Trade Unions** (Sōhyō) in economic matters. It was one of the four national unions to dissolve in 1987, and it encouraged its private-sector unions to join counterparts in Sōhyō to form the National Federation of Private-Sector Trade Unions (Rengō). When the majority of the public-sector unions joined Rengō in 1989, the Japanese labor movement was unified for the first time.

FIGURE SKATING. Competitive figure skating began in Japan nearly a century ago. However, the first postwar skater to achieve fame was Satō Nobuo who won 10 consecutive national titles from 1957 to 1966. He placed fourth in the 1965 World Championships, the highest mark by a Japanese up to that time. He would become one of Japan's leading coaches, training three-time national champion Kozuka Tsuguhiko and his son, Kozuka Takahiko, the 2011 World silver medalist. Sano Minoru won the bronze medal at the first World Championships held in **Tōkyō** in 1977.

Among Japan's male figure skaters, Honda Takeshi was the first to achieve international prominence when he won bronze in the World Competition in 2002 and 2003. Takahashi Daisuke won the bronze medal in the Vancouver Olympics in 2010; he was the first Japanese and the first Asian male to medal in the Olympics.

Hanyu Yuzuru is a young figure skater from Sendai, who lifted the spirits of his hometown after the 2011 earthquake-tsunami by his outstanding performance in the 2014 Sochi Olympics. At 19 years of age, he became the youngest men's Olympic skate champion since Dick Button won the event. He is also the first Asian man to win the Olympic gold medal. Hanyu won the Olympic gold medal again in 2018.

Watanabe Emi was Japan's first female star, winning the bronze in 1979 at the World Championships. **Itō Midori** far surpassed Watanabe and became Japan's first real international star. Itō, the first woman to complete a triple axel jump, finished second to America's Kristi Yamaguchi in the 1992 Winter **Olympics**. Her success inspired many skaters in Japan.

Arakawa Shizuka skated for Japan in the 1998 Nagano Games. In 2004, she won the world title in Dortmund, Germany. In 2006, she won the Olympic title, the first Japanese and the first Asian to win an Olympic gold in skating. Like Itō, Arakawa's success inspired other Japanese skaters. **Asada Mao** won three world titles and came to dominate the international skating stage. Her triple axel inspired many Japanese skaters.

FILMS AND FILMMAKING. Japanese film genres can be identified as period films (*jidaigeki*), **yakuza** films, monster (*kaijū*) films, animation (**anime**), J-Horror films, comedies, and pink (pornographic) films.

Many Japanese films with a traditional setting and a historical theme are called period films. Films such as *Chūshingura* center on samurai loyalty. *Ran* splendidly displays clan warfare. *Rashōmon* is a medieval detective story. *The Seven Samurai* is a wonderful samurai-type western. *Ugetsu* is a hauntingly beautiful feudal tale.

Anime has generated much international interest in Japan. **Ōtomo Katsuhiro**'s science fiction movie *Akira* and **Miyazaki Hayao**'s international award–winning *Princess Mononoke* and *Spirited Away* have been at the forefront of the anime industry.

Two fantastic film series have captivated the Japanese in recent years. **Yamada Yōji**'s 45 movies about Tora-san and the 26 films centering on Zatōichi, the blind swordsman, have become Japanese film classics.

Japanese film companies are often referred to as the "Big Six," identifying the six major companies that have dominated the film industry from the beginning of the 20th century to the present. With some modest changes, the "Big Six" are Shōchiku and Nikkatsu, which are the oldest companies; Tōhō, which started in 1932 and is still going strong; the postwar Tōei and its spinoff Tōei Animation; and Shin Tōhō and Daiei, both of which are now defunct.

Starting in the 1950s, Shōchiku and Tōhō became Japan's largest film companies. Shōchiku produced movies by such leading directors as **Ozu Yasujirō**, **Kurosawa Akira**, and various New Wave people. Tōei, Japan's largest studio, is best known for its Kurosawa, monster, and animated films.

Nikkatsu grew to become a major filmmaker but was a theater-holding chain until 1954, when it assumed the role of a leading film production studio. Two years later the huge popularity of *Taiyō no kisetsu* (*Season of the Sun*) and *Kurutta kajitsu* (*Crazed Fruit*), both based on novels by **Ishihara Shintarō** that dealt with revolt against tradition, raised its profile. When the director **Mizoguchi Kenji** joined Nikkatsu, its prestige increased.

Japan has earned international renown for its films, and its list of directors with world-famous stature, in addition to Mizoguchi, Ozu, and Kurosawa, includes **Ichikawa Kon**, **Imamura Shōhei**, **Hani Susumu**, Fukasaku Kinji, Yamada Yōji, **Ōshima Nagisa**, **Itami Jūzō**, and Kitano Takeshi.

Other leading directors produced a rich array of cinematic masterpieces. Kinugasa Teinosuke (1896–1982) directed the 1952 film *Jigoku mon* (*Gates of Hell*), which is based on Kikuchi Kan's story of the Heiji Revolt of 1159. Yamamoto Satsuo's (1910–1983) *Shinkū chitai* (*Vacuum Zone*, 1952) is a moving antiwar film. Kinoshita Keisuke's (1912–1998) films often deal with social problems and show human frailties. Kinoshita's best-known films are *Nijūshi no hitomi* (*Twenty-Four Eyes*) and *Narayama-bushi kō* (*The Ballad of Narayama*), a powerful film that explores the sorrowful consequences of tradition as a spirited old woman prepares to sacrifice herself to the mountaintop gods. Imai Tadashi (1912–1991) provided a serious and sympathetic study of the oppression of women. Suzuki Seijun (1923–2017), in *Tōkyō nagaremono* (*Tōkyō Drifter*), gives us one of Japan's best *yakuza* films. Fukuda Jun (1924–2000) is best known for his work as the director of the *Godzilla* film series. Shinoda Masahiro (1931–), a politically and aesthetically conservative film director, created *Shōnen jidai* (*Childhood Days*), a film centered on the World War II bombing that sent the urban population fleeing to the countryside, thus producing a creative meeting of urban and rural cultures.

Ogawa Shinsuke (1935–1992) directed the film *Magino Village: A Tale* (1986), a story about protests at Sanrizuka, the site of **Narita International Airport**. Yanagimachi Mitsuo (1945–) directed *Himatsuri* (*Fire Festival*), a 1984 film that shows a small traditional Japanese village's battle against industrialization and one man's efforts to halt construction of a tourist park. Harada Masato (1949–) directed *Baunsu ko gaurusu* (*Bounce Ko Gals*), a film about the fetish that Japanese men have for young schoolgirls. Finally, Suō Masayuki (1956–) directed the popular 1996 film *Shall We Dance?*, an entertaining comedy that focuses on a middle-aged businessman who learns to ballroom dance in order to escape the bonds of conformity in his society.

Postwar Japanese films treat many social issues, including the position of **women**, as in Miike Takashi's *Deddo oa araibu* (*Dead or Alive*), where women are still subjugated; the fate of minorities in Sumii Sue's *Hashi no kai kawa* (*The River with No Bridge*), about the **burakumin**; problems concerning modern family life, as in Ozu's gripping film *Tōkyō Monogatari* (*Tōkyō Story*); aging, as seen in Kurosawa's brilliant movie *Ikiru* (*To Live*); work-related matters, in such films as Kurosawa Kiyoshi's *Tōkyō Sonata*; sexual liberation, as in Ōshima Nagisa's *Ai no koriida* (*In the Realm of the Senses*); and World War II, as seen in Kobayashi Masaki's *Ningen no jōken* (*The Human Condition*) and in Imamura Shōhei's study of the **Hiroshima** tragedy, *Kuroi ame* (*Black Rain*).

In 1997, Imamura Shōhei's *The Eel*, Kawase Naomi's *Suzaku*, and Kitano Takeshi's *Hana-bi* won international film festival awards. Hayao Miyazaki's *Princess Mononoke* became the highest-grossing movie ever released in Japan, while Suo Masayuki's *Shall We Dance?* became the highest-grossing Asian movie ever to show in America.

In the 2000s, Japanese films experienced an astonishing resurgence. The number of Japanese films made increased substantially, and box-office sales soared. Outstanding films included Koreeda Hirokazu's *Our Little Sister*, Miike Takashi's *Yakuza Apocalypse*, Hosoda Mamoru's *The Boy and the Beast*, and Yonebayashi Hiromasa's *When Marnie Was There*.

Statistics provided by the Motion Picture Producers Association of Japan confirm that filmmaking in Japan continues to thrive. The years 2012–2015 were the largest on record. Admissions continued to run high even though admission fees have increased. The number of theaters remains at the highest level, and Japanese films represent about 60 percent of the viewers' interest. Leading films for 2014 still focus on social issues, gangsters (*Tōkyō Tribe*), romance (*Hotori no Sakuko*, *Goodbye Summer*), and a few comedies (*Koi no Uzu*, *Be My Baby*).

Recent films to receive international recognition include Wakamatsu Kōji's *Caterpillar*, Kitano Takeshi's *Outrage*, Sono Sion's *Himizu*, and Miike Takashi's *Hara-Kiri: Death of a Samurai*. However, it is Shinkai Makoto's *Your Name* (*Kimi no Na wa*) that has set all kinds of records. It was the highest-grossing film of 2016, bringing in $162 million, more than twice that of the second film, *Shin Godzilla*. In 2016, Japanese moviegoers hit a 42-year high with animated films being a major driving force.

FOREIGN POLICY. According to Japanese law, foreign policy is led by the **prime minister**, guided by the **cabinet**, and supervised by the **Diet**. In the early postwar period, Japan concentrated on economic growth, while following pacifist principles, adopting a low profile and a rather passive role in world affairs, and maintaining a neutral stance on foreign policy issues.

In the 1950s and 1960s, Japan sought to regain economic viability while cooperating closely with the policies of the **United States** and following the lead of the **United Nations** (UN) in international security matters. Caught in the throes of the Cold War, Japan sided very closely with the United States, allowing it to maintain a strong presence in Japan and use the country as a base of military operations in East Asia. The **United States–Japan Security Treaty**, signed in San Francisco in 1951, cemented a connection between the two countries. With U.S. sponsorship and support, Japan joined the UN in 1956.

On 19 January 1960, Japan and the United States signed the **Treaty of Mutual Cooperation and Security between the United States and Japan** in Washington. This treaty, which superseded the security treaty of nearly a decade earlier, made both Japan and the United States responsible for the **defense** of Japan by establishing a guarantee of mutual defense support. This treaty created an inevitable conflict because it called for Japan to come to the military aid of the United States even though Japan was not supposed to maintain military forces.

In the 1970s, Japan initiated a somewhat more independent foreign policy with the rise of a stronger East Asia. Japan signed the Nuclear Nonproliferation Treaty in 1970 and ratified it in 1976. The "Nixon shocks" of change in U.S. policy toward the People's Republic of **China** (PRC), shifts in U.S. economic policy, as well as America's earlier disastrous Vietnam adventure, caused Japan to begin to seek a more autonomous foreign policy line. Further, Japan's economic success led to a demand for greater independence in its foreign policy.

In the 1980s, Japan, while maintaining most of its earlier approach to international relations, explored a more hawkish stance in foreign policy under the leadership of Prime Minister **Nakasone Yasuhiro**. Since Japan had become the world's largest creditor nation and the second-largest donor of foreign aid, several Japanese leaders pushed for a more assertive, more independent role in world affairs. Japan's huge economic success and its shift to a more independent foreign policy led to criticism abroad with Japan being condemned as an "economic animal" and identified as a potentially rearmed military threat. In 1985, Japan participated in the Plaza Agreement, an international **trade** arrangement that tried to reduce trade barriers, strengthen the yen, and bring down Japan's trade imbalance. Japan's military expenditures continued to grow despite its self-imposed restraint of not exceeding 1 percent of the budget. (Refer to appendixes P and S.)

In the 1990s, Japan's role in the world became more mature as the United States–Japan relationship shifted to one of greater equality and the Soviet Union's collapse gave way to the reemergence of **Russia**. Japan's growing economic power gave it more importance in the international arena. At the urging of Washington, Tōkyō gradually accepted a new global partnership role. Japan's meager participation in the Persian Gulf War of 1990–1991 generated criticism of Japan for its reluctance to become involved and its inadequate support of the international forces. This was particularly pertinent since Japan got 60–70 percent of its oil from the region. Prime Minister **Kaifu Toshiki** sought to encourage Japan to greater participation in the Persian Gulf War and to make Japan more internationally minded. Japan, led by the **Liberal Democratic Party**, contributed $13 billion to the Gulf War effort but was unwilling to contribute soldiers to help with the military mission. This led some international leaders to charge Japan with conducting "checkbook diplomacy." Critics of Japan's previous military adventures and supporters of the no-war clause in the **constitution** opposed sending any troops abroad, but Kaifu did manage to involve some nonmilitary personnel in the international effort.

Growing economic power gave Japan a greater role in international economic circles. In the 1990s, Japan became a major participant in the World Bank, the International Monetary Fund, and other international economic organizations. Japanese foreign aid and national investment gave the country the status of a major player in world affairs. Although adamant against assuming any military role in world affairs, Japan's leaders saw its status as a world economic leader increasingly evident abroad and accepted at home.

The PRC and the Soviet Union were major players and **Korea**, **Taiwan**, and countries of Southeast Asia minor players in shaping Japan's foreign policy. Political, economic, and social changes in the foreign policies of these countries as well as shifts in the U.S. approach have significantly affected Japan's role in international affairs. Like a kaleidoscope, the patterns of relationships between these countries of East Asia are always shifting. However, the largest consistency has been that of a close relationship between Japan and the United States, even while Japan has exercised more independence in its foreign policy.

Since the end of the Cold War, Japan has participated in UN peacekeeping operations in Cambodia, Mozambique, the Golan Heights, and East Timor. However, its role has been to provide support and assistance troops, not combat troops. Always fearful of their painful 15-year war experience, Japan has been reluctant to place its troops in harm's way.

Late in 2003, Japan decided to deploy ground troops to assist in the American-led war in Iraq. This was Japan's most ambitious military operation since World War II. In 2004, Japan sent 600 ground troops to southeastern Iraq for a year of service. These troops, though considered noncombatants, were the most heavily armed since Japan began tentatively dispatching its Self-Defense Forces overseas a decade earlier. They engaged in humanitarian efforts, including providing water and medical services and rebuilding schools and infrastructure.

Japan in the 21st century has become more active in its foreign policy. It has expanded its ties worldwide, especially into areas of Southeast Asia, the Middle East, Africa, and Latin America. It has official diplomatic relations with approximately 150 countries. Modest territorial disputes continue to exist with Russia over the southern Kuril Islands, with South Korea over the Liancourt Rocks, and with China over the Senkaku Islands. In addition, there are still disputes over natural resources in these regions, especially over **petroleum** sources.

Critics of Japan's foreign relations complain that Japan has not issued a satisfactory apology for the reign of terror it spread in Asia and the Pacific in the first half of the 20th century. A cursory examination of the record reveals that this is not accurate. Starting with a couple of oral apologies in the 1960s and 1970s, in the decades that followed more than 40 apologies have been issued by leading Japanese officials. From the time of Prime Minister Nakasone until the present, nearly every one of Japan's leaders has offered some kind of an apology. Japan's critics, when they admit that there have been such apologies, have charged that these are insincere and inadequate. They also make the point that the Japanese government has not issued an official written apology. The issue of an apology remains a sticking point in Japan's foreign relations.

Overseas Development Assistance (ODA) is the international measure of assistance provided by rich nations to poorer countries. Japan led the world in total ODA from 1992 through 2001, when the United States reclaimed the top position in total dollars contributed. Japan's ODA fell substantially due to a depreciation of the yen and other financial problems. With $932 billion in 2015, Japanese ODA ranked fifth among the world's 22 major donors in total amount but 20th among nations as a percentage of national income.

The **Ministry of Foreign Affairs** (MOFA) has been an important training ground for postwar prime ministers. A dozen prime ministers have previously served as minister of foreign affairs including most prominently **Yoshida Shigeru**, **Kishi Nobusuke**, **Ōhira Masayoshi**, **Miyazawa Kiichi**, and **Koizumi Jun'ichirō**. In 2008, Nakasone Hirofumi, the son of former prime minister Nakasone Yasuhiro, became the minister of foreign affairs.

In recent years Japan has spread its involvement in the international world far beyond its relations with the United States, China, Taiwan, Korea, Russia/Soviet Union, and the United Nations. India has become a major focal point for Japan. In 2016, Japan's direct foreign investment hit a record $169.6 billion. Kōno Tarō, who became head of the MOFA on 3 August 2017, is laboring to expand the horizons of Japan's foreign policy.

In January 2017, Prime Minister **Abe Shinzō** visited the Philippines and signed an $8.66 billion aid package with that nation. At the same time, many Japanese companies, including **Honda Motor Company** and **Toyota Motor Corporation**, are investing heavily in Myanmar, seeing great economic potential there. Abe and Deputy Crown Prince Mohammed bin Salman of Saudi Arabia recently exchanged visits and emphasized mutual economic growth for their countries.

Although Abe has approached the new leadership in Washington with energy but with a bit of subservience, Japan's relationship seems to be in a somewhat precarious position. Japan is learning the need to stake its own path in international affairs. However, William F. Hagerty, the new U.S. ambassador, proclaimed the U.S. alliance with Japan as "ironclad."

Japan's foreign policy continues to face problems with an aggressive North Korea, a South Korea where not everyone is satisfied with the **"comfort women"** settlement, territorial disputes with China, and lingering issues with Russia over the Northern Territories.

Japan does not have a strong voice on the global stage. It is a member of the Group of Seven (G-7) and frequently holds a nonpermanent seat on the United Nations Security Council. However, in the most important discussions in those international arenas, Japan supports or simply follows the directions of the United States, leaving the impression that it has no independent opinions to contribute to global discussions. Japan, and the Japanese, appear satisfied but silent.

Private organizations further Japan's image abroad. First established in 1972, the **Japan Foundation** is an independent institution focusing on the promotion of international cultural exchanges and mutual understanding between Japan and other countries. Within the Japan Foundation, the Center for Global Partnership operates grant programs in intellectual exchange, grassroots exchange, and education, as well as self-initiated projects and fellowships. Supporting an array of institutions and individuals, including nonprofit organizations, universities, policy makers, scholars, and educators, the organization seeks to promote a more formal collaboration between Japan and other countries.

Japan is a member of the G-7 and frequently holds a nonpermanent seat on the United Nations Security Council. However, Japan's voice is not strong on the global scene. Tōkyō frequently follows the lead of the United States. However, this may be changing gradually.

Spats with China continue to cloud relations between the two Asian powers. When the international tribunal at The Hague ruled in Japan's favor over islands in the South China Sea, Japan seemed pleased, but such a ruling did not gain favor with China. Japan continues to reassert its control over the southern islands.

The United States continues to maintain 47,000 troops in Japan. One half of these troops is stationed in **Okinawa**, thus making for difficult relations. Japan and the United States continue to have problems with U.S. military forces stationed there. Base relocation continues to be a major topic of discussion. Yet, the United States continues to be Japan's leading world partner.

Japan is reaching out to all parts of the world with a realistic effort at an international approach. The examples are abundant. Prime Minister Abe Shinzō attended the Asia-Europe Meeting in Ulan Bator, Mongolia. Electronics giant Hitachi works to expand its business in Myanmar. Japanese fashion designers are creating modern garments for Muslim **women**. The **Japan External Trade Organization** is working with two international agencies to promote water projects in Africa. Mitsubishi Aircraft has secured its first European sales. Sumitomo Rubber seeks to expand its operations in Brazil with a $141 million investment in the tire industry. Several Japanese automobile companies are showing interest in Brazil. Sumitomo has built a warehouse in Indonesia.

The leasing giant Orix has become the first Japanese company to create a financial product to fit within Islamic law and has begun to do business with Pakistan. Takasago Thermal Engineering has signed a contract to build a $95 million plant in Malaysia. Zensho and Yoshinoya, two Japanese fast-food beef bowls, are opening restaurants in China and Southeast Asia. Dai-ichi Life Insurance is opening an office in Phnom Penh, Cambodia.

Nationalist themes run close to the surface. Hawkish politicians frequently visit **Yasukuni Shrine**, the resting place of Japanese military forces, to honor Japan's war dead. This antagonizes not only the Chinese and Koreans but also more liberal and internationally minded Japanese. Acting with some restraint, no sitting prime minister visited Yasukuni during the period 2006–2012.

Japan and China continue their dispute over South China Sea Islands with Japan claiming the Senkaku Islands and China the Diaoyu Islands, both the same place. Japan also wrestles with Korea over the Takeshima/Dokdo Islands and with Russia over the Northern Territories/Kurile Islands.

The United States has had many distinguished ambassadors to Japan including Mike Mansfield (1977–1988), Walter Mondale (1993–1996), Tom Fowley (1997–2001), Howard Baker (2001–2005), John V. Roos (2009–2013), and Caroline Kennedy (2013–2017). On 27 July 2017, President Trump appointed businessman and political contributor William F. Hagerty to this important position.

Japan and the United States had very positive relations during the Obama administration. In 2015, the two countries agreed to revisions in the Guidelines for U.S.-Japan Defense, the first change in 18 years. In 2016, Abe became the first Japanese prime minister to address a joint session of the U.S. Congress. As of 2017, the Japanese leaders are perplexed over how to relate to President Trump who has threatened tariffs, called on Japan to become nuclear, accused Japan of currency manipulation, and demanded that Japan pay more for its defense.

Japan and France have moved slowly toward more security cooperation. In January 2017, they held their third joint meeting of the Ministers of Foreign Affairs and the Defense Ministers. They discussed joint action around the world and broadened their interests and cooperation. Japan has also recently increased its engagement with various Caribbean countries. It seeks to expand its leadership in Southeast Asia, partly to contain Chinese infringements.

The International Olympic Committee chose Tōkyō as the host for the **2020 Summer Olympics**, giving Japan a much-needed boost in the international arena.

FUJIKO FUJIO, 藤子不二雄. Fujiko Fujio is the pen name of the two men who, as a team, drew many popular comics. The two men, Fujimoto Hiroshi (1933–1996) and Motō Abiko (1934–), began drawing together in elementary school in Toyama Prefecture shortly after the war and continued to work together until 1987. Branching out into **anime**, the two were among the most popular comic artists in postwar Japan. They produced ***Doraemon***, *Tenshi-no Tamachan*, *Obake no Qtaro*, *Ninja Hattori-kun*, and a host of other **manga**. *Doraemon* alone sold at least 100 million copies in 20 years.

FUJISANKEI COMMUNICATION GROUP (FUJI SANKEI GURŪPU, フジサンケイグループ). Fujisankei Communication Group is Japan's largest media conglomerate with approximately 100 member companies and 12,000 employees. Its **business** activities include **television**, **news-**

papers, radio, publishing, **music** and video, direct marketing, and real estate. Fuji Television and the *Sankei Shimbun* are the group's two most prominent companies.

FUJITSU (FUJITSŪ KABUSHIKI-GAISHA, 富士通株式会社). This is one of the world's leading **computer** industry companies. By the late 1970s, it was Japan's largest IT company and sold more machines in Japan than did IBM. In the early 1980s, it became the largest computer company in the world after IBM. Fujitsu manufactures and sells personal computers, data processing systems, telecommunications equipment, and electronic components. The Fujitsu Group includes more than 500 companies and has about 175,000 employees in more than 70 countries. It currently runs Nifty Serve and At Nifty, both internet access **businesses**.

FUJIYAMA AIICHIRŌ, 藤山愛一郎 (1897–1985). Fujiyama Aiichirō was a politician, diplomat, and a **business** leader who was president of Dai-Nippon Sugar and chairman of **Japan Airlines**. Born in **Tōkyō**, he was a Keiō University graduate in 1918. He helped bring about the fall of Prime Minister Tōjō Hideki but was himself imprisoned for three years as a suspected war criminal.

Fujiyama was elected to the **Diet** in 1957 for the first of five terms. He served as foreign minister during **Kishi Nobusuke**'s first and second **cabinets** and headed Japan's first delegation to the **United Nations**. Fujiyama also helped revise the **United States–Japan Security Treaty** in 1960. He had to deal with the issue of borrowing of patents and designs. He served as the chairman of an international **general trading company**. Fujiyama was also director-general of the **Economic Planning Agency** under the second **Ikeda Hayato** and the first **Satō Eisaku** cabinets. *See also* FOREIGN POLICY.

FUKUDA KEIKO, 福田敬子 (1913–2013). Fukuda Keiko was an internationally famous **jūdō** master. She was the highest-ranked jūdō expert in both Japan and the **United States**. Born in **Tōkyō**, she grew up in a family with samurai roots and martial spirit. At 4 feet, 11 inches tall and weighing only 100 pounds, she thrived at jūdō despite her small stature. She studied Japanese literature at Showa Women's University, but jūdō was her first love and she became a jūdō instructor after graduation.

In 1953, she traveled to Oakland, California, and established jūdō in the United States. She taught jūdō at Mills College from 1967 to 1978. She later founded a jūdō school near San Francisco.

The last surviving student of Kanō Jigorō, the founder of jūdō, she was known as the pioneer of women's jūdō. She was the only woman promoted to the rank of 10th *dan*. She received many awards and honors for her contributions to jūdō worldwide. Her personal motto was: "*Tsuyoku, yasashi-ku, utsukushiku*" ("Be strong, be gentle, be beautiful"). She died in 2013, just two months short of her 100th birthday.

FUKUDA TAKEO, 福田赳夫 **(1905–1995).** Fukuda Takeo, a politician and **prime minister** of Japan from 24 December 1976 to 7 December 1978, was known for his hawkish, pro-American policy. A native of Gumma Prefecture, Fukuda graduated in law from Tōkyō Imperial University and entered the **Ministry of Finance** where he held top offices after the war. In 1948, he was accused of corruption with the **Shōwa Denkō scandal** but was acquitted in 1958. In 1952, he was first and then continuously elected to the **Diet** and subsequently became a member of **Kishi Nobusuke**'s faction in the **Liberal Democratic Party** (LDP). After serving as agriculture, forestry, and fisheries minister in the second Kishi **cabinet** during 1959–1960, he was head of the party's political affairs section under **Ikeda Hayato** and a strong supporter of **Satō Eisaku**.

Despite his criticisms of factionalism, Fukuda took over former Kishi adherents to create his own faction. He served as finance minister in the Satō (1965–1966) and **Tanaka Kakuei** (1973–1974) cabinets when he had to cope with the effects of the oil shock, and as foreign minister in the third Satō cabinet (1971–1972). In 1974–1976, Fukuda was deputy prime minister and later director of the **Economic Planning Agency**. He is known for the Fukuda Doctrine, which pledged Japan never to become a military power and to build international trust and cooperation, especially with Asian countries.

In December 1976, the LDP elected Fukuda president after which he became prime minister. Fukuda had close contacts both with the bureaucracy and the financial world, and he was regarded as being among the more conservative elements in his party. He resigned as prime minister and party leader in December 1978 after a nationwide ballot of the LDP membership expressed a preference for the leadership of **Ōhira Masayoshi**. Fukuda's greatest achievement as prime minister was probably the Peace and Friendship Treaty with the People's Republic of **China**. *See also* FOREIGN POLICY; FUKUDA YASUO, 福田康夫 (1936–).

FUKUDA YASUO, 福田康夫 **(1936–).** Fukuda Yasuo was the longest-serving chief **cabinet** secretary in Japanese history, being in office for 1,289 days under prime ministers **Mori Yoshirō** and **Koizumi Jun'ichirō**. Thought to be a master at politics and the art of compromise, Fukuda, a consensus candidate, became **prime minister** on 26 September 2007. However, he served exactly one year before resigning in the face of ineffectual leadership and plunging popularity.

Fukuda was born in Gumma, the eldest son of former prime minister **Fukuda Takeo**. He graduated from Waseda University in 1959. He then joined Maruzen **Petroleum** and rose to section chief. While his father was prime minister from 1976 to 1978, Yasuo served as his political secretary.

In 1990, Fukuda was elected to the **House of Representatives**. He was elected deputy director of the **Liberal Democratic Party** in 1997 and became chief cabinet secretary in 2000. He resigned this position in 2005 amid a large political scandal related to the pension system. He served as a representative in the lower house of the **Diet** until 16 November 2012.

One of Fukuda's most noted policy goals was to end visits of the prime minister to **Yasukuni Shrine**. In June 2008, Fukuda joined 134 other lawmakers in proposing a secular alternative to the shrine, citing **constitutional** concerns. However, he resigned as prime minister before anything came of this measure as well as any of his other proposals.

FUKUHARA AI, 福原愛 **(1988–).** Called Ai-chan, Fukuhara Ai is Japan's outstanding table tennis player. She played in the national championships at a very young age. She won the Bambi division three times in a row. By November 2015, the International Table Tennis Federation ranked Fukuhara fourth in the world. The Japanese **Olympic** committee chose her as their flag bearer in the 2008 Beijing Olympics. She also represented Japan in the 2012 London Olympics and the 2016 Rio Olympics where she finished third. Very popular in Japan, she has won many international events. *See also* SPORTS.

FURUHASHI HIRONOSHIN, 古橋廣之進 **(1928–2009).** Furuhashi Hironoshin was a swimming star, known as "the flying fish of Fujiyama." He was one of Japan's greatest postwar heroes. He broke the world record in the men's 1,500-meter freestyle in 1949. This record stood until 1956. He did not have the chance to perform at the **Olympics** in his heyday because of the war. In total, Furuhashi set 33 world records during his career. He served as honorary president of the Japan Olympic Committee, president of the Asian Swimming Federation, and vice president of the International University **Sports** Federation.

Furuhashi, more than any other athlete, lifted the pride and confidence of the Japanese after the Pacific War. He symbolized the Japanese hopes for a return to greatness from the total defeat in World War II. Although lacking in sufficient nutrition because of war hardships, he burst into the postwar world with excellent performances in middle distance freestyle swimming that inspired the people of Japan.

FUTENMA AIR BASE (KAIHEITAI FUTENMA KŌKŪ KICHI, 海兵
隊普天間航空基地**).** Whether it's **United States**–Japan relations, U.S. military forces in Japan, or domestic controversies, Futenma Air Base is frequently the center of attention. This United States Marine Corps base, located in Ginowan, six miles northeast of Naha on **Okinawa**, has been a major U.S. air base since the end of World War II. The Marine Corps Air Station Futenma, or MCAS Futenma as it is called, is a major part of the United States military presence in Japan.

Futenma is the focal point of political controversies as the local people rub shoulders with U.S. military personnel. Noise pollution, safety concerns, and inappropriate social interactions cause frequent crises. Protestors and supporters of the military base clash frequently.

In 1995, three U.S. troops gang-raped a 12-year-old girl, severely threatening United States–Japan relations. In response, the U.S. military took strict measures to ensure that such a heinous crime would not be repeated. In 1996, the United States agreed to return control of the base to Japan. Limited repairs have been made to the base, but the return of control has not been completed.

Working in tandem, Americans and Japanese have drawn up plans to relocate Marine Corps Air Station Futenma, but transitions have not occurred. Under the Japan–United States agreement, the base is supposed to be moved to a less populated part of the island. Political **elections** in Naha and Okinawa have been waged over the Futenma Air Base issue, but nothing substantial has yet been achieved.

In May 2016, Japanese authorities arrested a United States civilian military worker for the alleged murder of a young Japanese woman, again jeopardizing United States–Japan relations. Ambassador Caroline Kennedy apologized and announced steps to prevent a repeat of the atrocity. Defense Minister Gen Nakatani met with Lieutenant General John Dolan, commander of U.S. Forces Japan, in Tōkyō to express outrage. In Washington, White House spokesman Josh Earnest promised full cooperation with Japan over the investigation.

Meanwhile, there are concerns among national and Okinawan **Liberal Democratic Party** members that opponents of the bilateral plan to move U.S. Marine Corps Air Station Futenma farther north to Henoko will now have the upper hand. But continued opposition to the base for nearly two decades has prevented its completion. Even Okinawa people who support Prime Minister **Abe Shinzō** want the Futenma base closed within five years, as he promised. But if the government continues to try to promote the Henoko plan now, opposition will likely become stronger.

FUYO GROUP (FUYŌ GURŪPU, 芙蓉グループ). The Fuyo Group is one of Japan's leading *keiretsu*. It emerged after World War II as a continuation of the Yasuda zaibatsu, but centered on Fuji Bank, which did the majority of its financing. After Fuji Bank merged with **Dai-Ichi Kangyō Bank** and Industrial Bank of Japan to form Mizuho Bank, Fuyo Group's central firm became Yasuda Life Insurance, which would become part of the **Mitsubishi Group** of companies. The Fuyo Group is made up of 29 core companies with more than 200 affiliates. **Marubeni** is the **general trading company**.

The core members of the Fuyo Group are Yasuda Trust & Banking (asset management), Yasuda Mutual Life Insurance, Oki Electric Industry, **Nissan Motors**, **Hitachi** (electronics, capital goods), NKK (**steel**), Canon (**cameras**, copiers, printers), and Sapporo Breweries.

Although the Fuyo Group struggled financially in the late 1990s, it has rebounded in the early 21st century. It allowed Yamaichi Securities to fail in 1997, a sign of weakness, but that helped to recover its financial stability. The Fuyo Group is a leading part of the **Nissan Group** or *keiretsu*. Corporations in the Fuyo Group have a very high degree of interdependence in mutual stock holding and close linkages. *See also* BANKING.

G

GAINAX (KABUSHIKI-GAISHA GAINAKKUSU, 株式会社ガイナックス**).** Gainax is a leading Japanese **anime** studio that was founded in the early 1980s. Okada Toshio (1958–) was president of the company but now is a lecturer at the **University of Tōkyō**. Okada argues that the best anime come from original scripts and are not merely remakes of **manga**. Gainax represents the first generation of animators and early pop culture. Sadamoto Yoshiyuki (1962–), a cofounder of Gainax, is primarily a character designer. He was the creator of *Neon Genesis Evangelion*, and he was also the character designer for *Nadia: Secret of Blue Water* and producer of *Nausicaa of the Valley of Wind*.

GAMES. Japanese video and **computer** games dominate today's world game market. Names like PlayStation, **Nintendo**, Sega Dreamcast, and Game Boy are famous worldwide. Japanese companies make many of the world's games.

Kutaragi Ken (1950–), an engineer, began work on **Sony**'s PlayStation in the mid-1980s, and Sony released the first PlayStation in 1994. Gamers quickly made it their favorite gaming system.

Founded in 1951 but having adopted its present name in 1965, Sega Enterprises was Japan's third-leading video game manufacturer. It achieved worldwide success with its SegaSaturn machine, which it replaced with the 128-bit Dreamcast, developed with Microsoft and **NEC** in 1999. Sega also produced game software and game center amusement machines, and operated theme parks, movie **theaters**, and **karaoke** rooms. However, Sega was unable to compete with the other game-making companies.

At present, the popularity of the game companies, based on sales, appears to be PlayStation, Nintendo, and Microsoft, in that order. In the mid-1980s, Nintendo dominated the game world. Sega, the second company, had no console as of 2000. Sony PlayStation took over first place in the 1990s. Other leading game makers include Namco, Taito, Tekken, Sanrio, Capcom, Square Soft, and Enix Corporation. Japan has produced a mind-boggling number of video games. Among the older, more popular games are *Space*

Invaders, *Pac-Man*, *Donkey Kong*, *Super Mario Bros.*, *Dragon Quest*, and *Final Fantasy*. Among the newer games are *Puzzle and Dragons*, *Demon's Soul*, and a variety of PS4 games.

Created by Hasbro in 1984, Transformers were originally a collection of shape-shifting toy **robots** that captured the imagination of children. Power Rangers (*Jū rengā*) were popular Japanese **television** superheroes who with some modest transformation became superstars for Western children, too. Kawamori Shōji (1960–) and Studio Nue in 1983 created *Chojikū Yōsai Macross* (*Super Dimensional Fortress Macross*), a long-running television animation series. Their efforts gave rise to many sequels as well as **video games**, **manga**, toys, collectibles, **music** CDs, and models. *Robotech* was a spinoff of *Macross*. Well-drawn characters, vivid backgrounds, and powerful fighters make this an excellent animation.

However, in the first decade of the 21st century, Japan faced a decline in its video game **business**. Yet by 2017, Japan had experienced a renaissance in the video game industry. Leading new games include *Final Fantasy XV*, *Resident Evil 7*, *Gravity Rush*, *Yakuza 0*, and *The Legend of Zelda: Breath of the Wild*.

GENERAL COUNCIL OF JAPANESE TRADE UNIONS (NIHON RŌDŌ KUMIAI SŌHYŌ GIKAI, 日本労働組合総評議会, COMMONLY KNOWN AS SŌHYŌ). Sōhyō, established in 1950 with 4.4 million members, represented public-sector employees and was Japan's largest **labor** federation. The major affiliates of Sōhyō included unions of government workers, teachers, national railway workers, communications workers, and metal industry workers. Under Japanese labor laws, government workers did not have any bargaining ability or the right to strike. Sōhyō's best-known political tactic was the annual spring struggle (*shuntō*), which was an intensive campaign of street demonstrations, mass meetings, and other pressure tactics. Such unions frequently used political action in place of economic action.

Sōhyō was most concerned with labor issues and less concerned with social and political issues. Sōhyō strikes and work stoppages antagonized many people, and its public-sector workers generated opposition from many quarters. Sōhyō was more militant and left leaning than the **Japan Confederation of Labor** (Dōmei), and after Dōmei's early development, it merged with the right-leaning unions to promote Dōmei's agenda and work more closely with the **Democratic Socialist Party**.

Sōhyō rapidly changed from a moderate labor organization to the most powerful labor organization in postwar Japan, which formed close ties with the **Japan Socialist Party** (JSP). It opposed the **Yoshida Shigeru** government and its ties with the **United States** and supported the JSP. During the 1950s, Sōhyō was the largest trade-union federation in Japan. Key leaders of

Sōhyō included Takano Minoru (1901–1974), its first secretary-general; **Ōta Kaoru**, chairman of Sōhyō from 1955 to 1966; and Iwai Akira, who served as secretary-general of Sōhyō from 1955 through 1970. In 1989, Sōhyō merged with the **Japanese Trade Union Confederation** (Rengō). Most of its affiliated members joined Rengō, which now represents 65 percent of all organized workers.

GENERAL TRADING COMPANIES (*SŌGŌ SHŌSHA*, 総合商社). General trading companies (*sōgō shōsha*) are large, diversified Japanese conglomerates that include corporate groups, **banks**, manufacturers, and other businesses. *Sōgō shōsha* began in the 1870s to import raw materials and sell Japanese products abroad. By the early 1980s, Japan had 6,000 general trading companies, but a dozen of these did the vast majority of the international **business**. As of the end of 2015, Japan's largest general trading companies are **Mitsubishi Corporation**, **Mitsui & Company**, **Sumitomo**, **Itōchū**, **Marubeni**, Toyota Tsūshō, and **Sojitz**. These and other trading companies have become more involved internationally and have accepted more financial responsibilities, helping to promote Japan's economic growth.

Japan's general trading companies strengthen the ties of companies to their suppliers and thus reduce the risk of takeovers. They also engage in the practice of cross-shareholding to protect themselves against takeovers.

Japanese general trading companies are companies that trade in a wide range of products and materials. They engage in logistics, plant development, and other activities, as well as acquire international resources. While general trading companies in other countries are more specialized, Japanese trading companies have very broad business involvements. Japanese general trading companies buy materials from large companies and distribute them to other medium- and smaller-sized companies. They handle a major portion of Japan's imports and exports.

GOLF. A number of Japanese golfers, including **Aoki Isao**, Ozaki Naomichi ("Joe") (1956–), **Ozaki Masashi "Jumbo,"** and Katayama Shino (1973–), have reached the top ranks of professional golf. Maruyama Shigeki (1969–) won the national collegiate golf championships twice and the Asian Games in 1991 as an amateur. He has won seven professional tournaments in Japan and is well loved for his warm, funny character. Nakajima Tsuneyuki ("Tommy") (1954–), a professional golfer of international reputation, has garnered some 60 career victories. One of Japan's best professional golfers, he was the top prize money winner in 1982, 1983, 1985, and 1986.

Young, rising stars include Ishikawa Ryo (1991–) who has won 15 tournaments and is ranked #86 in the world. He has already won more than $4 million. Matsuyama Hideki (1992–) seems to be in the spotlight having risen as high as fourth in the world. In the later part of 2016, he won or challenged for five tournaments around the world. He has won more than $10 million. In June 2017, he tied for second in the U.S. Open.

Japan has a number of outstanding female professional golfers. Fukushima Akiko (1973–) won the Best Amateur women's golf title 11 times. In 1996, she was the Japanese Ladies Professional Golfers' Association (LPGA) leading prize money winner, the youngest ever to top the prize money list and the youngest Japanese woman golfer to pass ¥300 million career earnings. Higuchi Hisako (1945–) was an outstanding woman golfer and, in 1967, was among Japan's first group of **women** golfers to turn professional. In 1977, Higuchi was the first Japanese to win a **United States** LPGA tournament. She has won the most prize money in Japan in 11 different years and holds the Japanese women's record for tournament victories at 72. Okamoto Ayako (1951–), who became a professional in 1974, won 48 tournaments in Japan and 18 abroad. Other young rising Japanese female golfers include Ueda Momoko (1986–), Miyazato Miki (1989–), Miyazato Ai (1985–), Yokomine Sakura (1985–), and Morita Rikako (1990–). *See also* SPORTS.

GOTŌ MIDORI, 五嶋みどり **(1971–).** Gotō Midori is a world-renowned violinist, famous enough to be known simply as "Midori." Born in **Ōsaka**, she started studying violin with her mother at age two. At age 11, Midori entered the Juilliard School of Music where her performance earned her a concert debut with the New York Philharmonic under the direction of Zubin Mehta. At age 15, Midori gave a legendary performance at Tanglewood where the conductor Leonard Bernstein spoke of her performance in glowing terms.

In 1992, Midori left Juilliard and formed Midori & Friends, a group dedicated to introducing quality **music** to inner-city schoolchildren. In 2000, she graduated from New York University's Gallatin School with a degree in psychology. Not long after graduation, she was appointed to the Jascha Heifetz Chair in music at the University of Southern California's Thornton School of Music. She has received a host of awards and honors including the Japanese government's Best Artist of the Year, the Suntory Hall Award, and the prestigious Avery Fisher Prize for outstanding musician. In 2012, the University of Southern California named her a Distinguished Professor, and Yale University awarded her an honorary doctorate in music. In 2018, Midori will join the violin faculty of Philadelphia's Curtis Institute full time.

GREAT EAST JAPAN EARTHQUAKE (*HIGASHI NIHON DAISHIN-SAI*, 東日本大震災**).** The Great East Japan Earthquake, also called the 2011 Tōhoku Earthquake (*Tōhoku-chihō Taiheiyō Oki Jishin,* 東北地方太平洋沖地震) or the 3.11 Earthquake, had a profound effect upon Japan. The Great

East Japan Earthquake caused more death and destruction, produced more problems for Japan, and generated more news than any other single event in postwar Japan. Prime Minister **Kan Naoto** lamented, "In the 65 years after the end of World War II, this is the toughest and the most difficult crisis for Japan." It is the largest earthquake to hit Japan since the **Kōbe Earthquake** of 1995.

On 11 March 2011, at 5:46 a.m., a 9.1 magnitude earthquake savaged northeastern Japan and violently shook the area around Sendai in Fukushima and neighboring prefectures. In less than an hour, it unleashed a dreadful tsunami with waves up to 130 feet high and extending inland for six miles. It flooded 217 square miles of territory. The Japan National Police Agency has set the tragedy at 15,894 deaths, 6,152 people injured, plus 2,500 people still missing who will probably never be found. Approximately 230,000 people lost their homes. More than 125,000 buildings totally collapsed, more than twice that many were seriously damaged, and nearly 750,000 buildings were partially damaged. The total damage has been estimated at $300 billion. The effects of the earthquake have been felt around the world with the rumblings found far from Japan, at least five million tons of debris carried out to sea, and some materials washing up on the coast of North America. Japan experienced at least 5,000 aftershocks.

The tsunami, generated by the earthquake, caused a series of nuclear accidents in the Fukushima Daiichi Nuclear Power Plant complex. The accidents knocked out the electrical generators, which destroyed the cooling capacity causing at least three nuclear explosions. All residents within 12 miles were evacuated. The insured monetary losses were estimated at about $35 million, but the World Bank put the total cost at $235 billion, making it the most costly natural disaster in world history.

This Great East Japan Earthquake has had a profound impact on Japan. It has obviously caused much pain and suffering as well as a great deal of economic loss. However, it has shaken the Japanese psyche and, coming with the loss as the world's second economic power, caused the Japanese people to reassess their standing and security in the world.

Naturally, the issue of **nuclear power** has dominated the news in Japan. Several studies have been done to determine if the nuclear disaster could have been prevented. Critics of the government say "yes," but many government officials claim the earthquake and tsunami were acts of God, too huge to prevent. Both sides seem to have some legitimacy in their conclusions.

GUNDAM (ガンダム). If you visited the thriving new district of Odaiba in **Tōkyō** between 2012 and the spring of 2017, a 55-foot-tall robot statue of Gundam would have blown you away. Who, or what, was this Gundam that dominated the harbor and generated such interest? Gundam helped create a new genre of **anime** and became a key in robotic **technology**. *Mobile Suit*

Gundam became a trendsetter in Japan and the wider world. Gundam has become an icon in the entertainment world as well as a generator of interest in engineering and **robotics**.

Gundam is a franchise of an animation **television** series, OVAs, and movies, along with anime, **manga**, models, **video games**, and other merchandise. **Bandai** owns the franchise. The original Gundam TV series, which debuted in 1979, was known as *Mobile Suit Gundam* and was the brainchild of anime legend Tomino Yoshiyuki (1941–). The name Gundam denotes not only the original series but also any work that came after it. The Gundam franchise has generated well in excess of ¥80 billion in movies, manga, video games, and plastic models, as well as the Odaiba theme park.

The objects are large humanoid combat vehicles originally developed for outer space conflict. The first Gundam was developed as part of the Earth Federation V-Project to counter the Principality of Zeon's technological superiority. Gundam can be used to refer to any of the derivatives of the Gundam, or any copies in alternate universes. One can recognize Gundams by their signature V-Antenna, two eyes, and blocky anthropomorphic design.

Gundam shows are basically war dramas. Their stories revolve around the mobile suits and their pilots fighting in a war involving the destruction and dehumanization of mankind. Gundam includes political battles and debates on various philosophical issues and political ideals. These often result in fierce duels. Gundam is a popular cultural icon of Japan that has spread through the world. Its realistic scientific setting has inspired a generation of scientists and engineers.

GYMNASTICS. Japan has always had outstanding competitors in gymnastics. Tsukahara Mitsuo (1947–) won two gold, one silver, and three bronze medals in **Olympic** gymnastics competition. He earned a bronze in the rings and a gold in the horizontal bar at Munich. Four years later, Tsukahara was the bronze winner in the parallel bars and combined event, took a silver in the vault, and won gold in the horizontal bars. Tsukahara's name is used to identify a particular vault maneuver.

Nakayama Akinori (1943–) won four gold, two silver, and two bronze in Olympic gymnastics. He received gold three times in Mexico City, in the parallel bars, horizontal bars, and rings, and he added a silver on the floor and a bronze in the combined. In Montreal, he had another strong performance, earning bronze in the combined, silver in the floor exercise, and gold on the rings.

Gushiken Kōji (1956–) was an Olympic gymnast who won the all-around medal in the 1984 Los Angeles Games. He also won gold in the rings, silver in the vault, and bronze in the horizontal bars. He was third in the 1981 World Championships in Moscow and second in the World Championships in Hungary in 1983.

In 2005, Tomita Hiroyuki (1980–) became the first Japanese gymnast since 1974 to win the men's World Championship all-round title after a superb display in Melbourne. The 25-year-old went into the final rotation more than one point ahead and dazzled the crowd with his high bar routine to finish at 56.698 points.

Japanese female gymnasts have not been as much in the spotlight as their male counterparts. They won the bronze medal in the 1964 Olympics for their best-ever finish. In 2008, they placed fifth, in 2012 they were eighth, and in 2016 they just missed the podium, finishing fourth. Murakami Mai (1996–) won the gold medal in the floor exercise at the 2017 World Championships, the first Japanese woman to accomplish this. Other rising stars include Hatakeyama Airi (1994–) and Teramoto Asuka (1995–). *See also* SPORTS.

H

HABU YOSHIHARU, 羽生善治 **(1970–).** Habu Yoshiharu is the undisputed champion of *shōgi*, a complex game that is the Japanese equivalent of chess. As the world *shōgi* champ as of 1995, Habu is a top celebrity in Japan today. He was invited by the prestigious NAO Chess Club in Paris to participate in its international tournament. Since joining the professional *shōgi* ranks, Habu has been known as one of the most gifted players in the history of this ancient game.

Born in Saitama Prefecture, Habu learned how to play *shōgi* when he was six years old and quickly became proficient at the game. He later came under the tutelage of a *shōgi* master, and by the time he was 15, he had entered the professional *shōgi* ranks. He became the youngest champion ever when he won his first tournament in 1989 at the age of 19. He continued to do very well and, in 1995, won six of *shōgi*'s top seven titles. In 1997, he won all seven of *shōgi*'s biggest titles, an accomplishment never done before or since. Holding all seven crowns at the same time, Habu became a popular celebrity in Japan, and his fame renewed Japan's interest in *shōgi*. In 2003, Habu became the 11th *shōgi* player to notch 800 victories. By the end of 2017, Habu had won 1,380 official games, becoming the fourth player to do so, and the youngest player to accomplish this feat. With an outstanding record of nearly 75 percent victories, Habu has the best winning percentage among professional *shōgi* players. Of the seven major *shōgi* events, Habu has won a total of 99 titles. In January 2018, Habu became the first *shōgi* player given Japan's Honor Award.

HAKUHŌ SHŌ, 白鵬翔 **(1985–).** Hakuhō Shō, born in Ulan Bator, Mongolia, as Mönkhbatyn Davaajargal, is a **sumō** star. Making his debut in March 2001, he reached the top division in May 2004. At age 22, he became the second native of Mongolia, and the fourth non-Japanese overall, to be promoted to *yokozuna*, the highest rank in sumō. As of November 2010, he had won 17 tournament championships, second at that time only to the 25 wins of **Asashōryū**, his fellow Mongolian. Between March 2007 and November 2010, Hakuhō won 16 of the 22 tournaments. In November 2010, he won his fifth consecutive tournament, winning 63 straight matches. In 2009, Hakuhō won 86 of 90 bouts and repeated this feat in 2010.

Hakuhō, one of Japan's greatest sumō stars, won in July 2015 his 35th Emperor's Cup. After that he had a dry spell. However, in March 2016, he won his 36th career championship. In the following tournament, he won his 37th championship. This easily surpassed the 32 championships won by **Taihō**, who retired in 1971. In November 2016, he became only the third wrestler ever to achieve 1,000 career wins. In November 2017, Hakuhō won his 40th career title and established an all-time high of 1,062 career victories. He is said to be the best ever at sumō.

HAMADA SHŌJI, 濱田庄司 (1894–1978). Hamada Shōji was an important potter with a major international reputation. Founder of the folk-crafts (*mingei*) movement, Hamada was born in Kawasaki and educated at Tōkyō Industrial College. He studied with Itaya Hazan, a famous potter from Mashiko. Hamada became friends with Bernard Leach, the great English potter, and worked with him for five years in England. He developed his own pottery center in Mashiko where he became famous for his glazes. Experts regard Hamada as one of the most influential masters of studio pottery and assert he has probably inspired more potters than any other person. The simplicity of his designs gives his work urgency and power. The Japanese government named Hamada a Living National Treasure in 1955 and awarded him the Order of Culture in 1968.

HANEDA AIRPORT (HANEDA KŪKŌ, 羽田空港). Haneda Airport is officially known as Tōkyō International Airport (Tōkyō Kokusai Kūkō). It is located in the Ota ward of **Tōkyō**. Haneda was opened in 1931 and was Japan's leading air terminal. By passenger count, in the late 20th century, Haneda was the busiest airport in Asia and the fifth-busiest airport in the world, serving 60 million passengers annually. Haneda handled most of Tōkyō's air traffic until the opening of New Tōkyō International Airport, now known as **Narita International Airport**. Except flights to Gimpo Airport in Seoul or some international charter flights, Haneda now provides primarily domestic flights.

On 10 June 1960, the Haneda Airport incident occurred when James Haggerty, U.S. president Dwight D. Eisenhower's press secretary, arrived and was surrounded by demonstrators opposed to the **United States–Japan Security Treaty** renewal. This was a major part of the *Anpo* movement and led to the cancellation of Eisenhower's visit.

HANI GORŌ, 羽仁五郎 **(1901–1983).** Hani Gorō was a historian and social critic. Born in Gumma Prefecture, he married Hani Setsuko, daughter of the educator Hani Motoko, and adopted the Hani family name. He studied history at Tōkyō Imperial University and philosophy at Heidelberg University, after which he taught at Japan University and Jiyū Gakuen, the school founded by his mother-in-law. In the 1930s, together with Noro Eitarō, a fellow Marxist, he was a prominent contributor to the series *Nihon Shihon Shugi Hattatsu Shi Kōza* (*Studies on the History of the Development of Capitalism in Japan*). He also published studies on the Tokugawa and Meiji eras.

Hani was imprisoned briefly during World War II for his political opinions. In 1947, he was elected to the **House of Councillors** as an independent and worked to establish the National Diet Library. His writings, especially his study of cities titled *Toshi no ronri* (1968), strongly influenced the radical **student movements** of the 1960s and the 1970s. His son, **Hani Susumu**, is an important **film** director.

HANI SUSUMU, 羽仁進 **(1928–).** Hani Susumu, the son of **Hani Gorō**, is a major **film** director and theorist of the postwar era. *Te o kaku kodomotachi* (*Children Who Draw*, 1956), which introduced revolutionary camera techniques to documentary filmmaking, was his most influential early work. This film showed surprising candor and sympathy, leading to the documentary-style techniques that paralleled the French New Wave films of the 1960s.

In 1960, Hani made his first full-length film, *Furyō Shōnen* (*Bad Boys*), using almost all amateur **actors**. This film deals with young boys in a reform school. The cast consisted of actual juvenile delinquents, and the authenticity shows. It is a gritty, pseudo-docudrama of juvenile delinquency based upon a collection of papers written by the inmates of a boy's prison. *Bad Boys* is considered the first film of the Japanese New Wave.

Hani's pioneering 1960 film, *Mitasereta seikatsu* (*A Full Life*), anti–**United States–Japan Security Treaty** in subject, demonstrates the psychologically complex story of a young woman who leaves her husband to find fulfillment outside marriage. She rejoins her old acting company and becomes involved with its director, a fellow defector from polite society. The film focuses on the oppression of **women** in modern society.

Hani directed the powerful *Kanojo to kare* (*She and He*, 1963), a film that examines a common and tragic type of modern marriage. The husband is caught up in the demands of his job and seems to diminish gradually as a human being. His wife, originally less knowledgeable and interesting, is driven by the emptiness of her life to consider the world around her and is gradually educated by life itself into becoming intellectually superior to her husband. The growth of a social conscience and responsibility within a bored housewife has rarely been better explored and documented.

HANKYŪ HANSHIN TŌHŌ GROUP (HANKYŪ HANSHIN TŌHŌ GURŪPU, 阪急阪神東宝グループ). Hankyū Hanshin Tōhō Group is one of Japan's leading *keiretsu* or association of **businesses**. It is centered on Hankyū **Railways**, Hankyū **Department Store**, and Tōhō Company. This *keiretsu* historically included Sanwa Bank, now part of **Mitsubishi UFJ Financial Group**, but they are still closely linked. Originally founded by Kobayashi Ichizō, the Hankyū Hanshin Tōhō Group consists of more than 350 companies worldwide with strengths in transportation, travel, retail, entertainment, and other industries. Hanshin has numerous transportation, **construction**, and real estate enterprises. Tōhō produces and distributes motion pictures, including more than 20 Godzilla movies, theatricals, and **television** programs.

In fiscal year 2016, the Hankyū Hanshin Tōhō Group, focused primarily in the Kansai area, recorded approximately $1.3 billion in income. Transportation and real estate continue to be its major focus, but it also has investments in entertainment, communications, and travel.

HARA SETSUKO, 原節子 (1920–2015). The legendary **actress** Hara Setsuko was one of Japan's best-known **film** stars. She had the lead in classic movies such as *No Regrets for Our Youth*, *Late Spring*, *Early Summer*, *Tōkyō Story*, and 60 others.

Born in **Yokohama** to a family with film connections, Hara joined Nikkatsu Studios when she was 15 years old. She later came under the watchful eye of **Ozu Yasujirō**, under whose direction she made six films. She also worked with such famous directors as **Kurosawa Akira**, Kinoshita Keisuke, and Naruse Mikio. After Ozu's death, Hara retired from film and lived in seclusion in Kamakura. Hara Setsuko, an example of feminine beauty and demeanor, was a symbol of the golden age of Japanese film.

HARADA MASAHIKO "FIGHTING," 原田政彦 (1943–). Although several dozen Japanese fighters have won world titles, "Fighting" Harada remains Japan's greatest ring champion ever. Harada is the only Japanese boxer selected for the International Boxing Hall of Fame. He won 55 of 62 bouts in his career of more than a decade. Born in **Tōkyō**, Harada began fighting in 1960. He built a record of 26 wins (10 knockouts) against only one decision loss. He won the flyweight championship in 1962 with an 11th-round knockout. His stint as champion was brief, however, as he lost the rematch only three months later in a 15-round decision. Next trying his luck in the bantamweight division, Harada reeled off 11 victories in 12 bouts over the next two years, culminating with a challenge to the world title in **Nagoya** in 1965 when he again became a world champion, making him the only fighter ever to have won both the world flyweight and bantamweight titles.

Between 1965 and 1967, Harada won 10 fights in a row. Four of these bouts were to defend his world crown. His bantamweight title reign ended with a decision loss in early 1968. His sights set on winning the championship in a third division, Harada moved up to the featherweight class and won four out of five fights. A close fight saw Harada lose a debatable 15-round decision. He lost again by a knockout in a rematch the following year, ending his career. In 2002, Harada became president of the Japanese Boxing Association. *See also* SPORTS.

HASEGAWA ITSUKO, 長谷川逸子 **(1941–).** Hasegawa Itsuko, an outstanding female architect, graduated from Kantō Gakuin University in **Yokohama** in 1963. After working with Kikutake Kiyonori and later for Shinohara Kazuo, she established her own studio in 1976. Hasegawa's buildings are characterized by the straightforward use of industrial materials. The Shōnandai Cultural Centre is one of her outstanding works. Although not as recognized, the Sumida Culture Factory in **Tōkyō** offers a more conservative use of public space. She is perhaps best known for her Fruit Museum in Yamanashi City. This building, striking in appearance, makes use of several structures arranged in crescent shapes with dome-like structures in various sizes. Hasegawa's large, striking Shanghai Caohejing Block 3 Office Building and her distinctive, artistic Fujinokuni Senbonmatsu Forum have garnered much attention. Hasegawa's work has won a long list of prestigious **architecture** awards.

HASHIMOTO RYŪTARŌ, 橋本龍太郎 **(1937–2006).** Hashimoto Ryūtarō was a powerful **Liberal Democratic Party** (LDP) politician in the 1980s and 1990s. He served as **prime minister** of Japan from 11 January 1996 to 30 July 1998 in a coalition government and was the leader of one of the largest factions within the LDP. Hashimoto, with a forceful personality, was often outspoken in domestic meetings and international gatherings. He exercised a strong political leadership and followed his father's motto that "statesmanship should be for the weak" and worked hard to set policies in pensions, medical care, and welfare.

A native of Okayama Prefecture, Hashimoto graduated from Keiō University in 1960 and entered the **House of Representatives** three years later. He rose through the ranks of the LDP and, in 1978, became the health and welfare minister in **Ōhira Masayoshi**'s **cabinet**. In 1980, he became the LDP's director of finance and public administration. In 1986, he served as a cabinet minister in the **Nakasone Yasuhiro** administration. In 1989, he became secretary-general of the LDP, a major party leadership position. He also served as finance minister in the **Kaifu Toshiki** cabinet. In all this, Hashimoto played a major role at international **trade** meetings. He was a key figure in the **Tanaka Kakuei** faction, which eventually fell under the influence of **Takeshita Noboru**. He briefly lost power following the collapse of the bubble **economy** in 1991. In 1994, Prime Minister **Murayama Tomiichi** chose Hashimoto to lead the **Ministry of International Trade and Industry** where he made a strong impression at APEC meetings and other economic summits.

When Murayama stepped down in 1996, the LDP chose Hashimoto as the next prime minister. For two and a half years, he operated from a powerful position. As prime minister, Hashimoto attempted to stabilize and equalize the yen–dollar exchange rate with the **United States**. He sought to carry out currency reform and frequently tried to revive the Japanese **economy**. He emphasized domestic reform, particularly in administration, society, the economy, finances, and **education**. In **foreign policy**, Hashimoto met several times with President Bill Clinton to seek improvement in United States–Japan bilateral trade relations and security cooperation. He also visited **China**, Europe, Southeast Asia, and Latin America.

However, when the LDP lost its majority in the **House of Councillors** 1998 **election**, Hashimoto resigned to take responsibility for the defeat. He remained a dominant political figure until 2003 when he disagreed with the majority of the LDP over the reelection of Prime Minister **Koizumi Jun'ichirō**. In 2004, Hashimoto stepped down as faction leader when it was revealed that he had accepted a large sum of money from the Japan Dental Association. In 2005, after serving 14 terms in the **Diet**'s House of Representatives, Hashimoto retired from politics. He unexpectedly died in 2006 at age 68.

HASHIMOTO TŌRU, 橋下徹 **(1969–).** Hashimoto Tōru is a combination lawyer, politician, and **television** celebrity, as well as a provocative figure. Controversial, he is said to resemble Donald Trump, the ultimate political outsider who was inaugurated president of the **United States** in 2017. Like Trump, he is quite outspoken and seems to have little love for politicians or bureaucrats. He is a gritty, in-your-face political leader, quite unusual for Japan.

Hashimoto was born in **Tōkyō** but moved to **Ōsaka** when he was in the fifth grade. His father, said to be a gangster, died when Hashimoto was young. Hashimoto grew up in a neighborhood populated by *burakumin* but claims not to know if he is related. After failing admission twice, he succeeded on his third try and entered Waseda University. He graduated and became a lawyer. A kind of gadfly, he frequently appears on television talk shows.

Governor of Ōsaka Prefecture (2008–2011) and mayor of Ōsaka (2011–2015), Hashimoto was a key founder of the **Nippon Ishin no Kai** (Japan Restoration Party) in 2012. Hashimoto has battled labor unions, called for performance standards for teachers, and stirred up the political landscape with his new party, which became Japan's second-largest opposition party in a very short time. His appeal seemed to reflect the desire for bolder change in Japan and a general dissatisfaction with **politics** in Japan.

Hashimoto has criticized Japan's **nuclear energy** policy since the **Great East Japan Earthquake** disaster, a popular stance with many Japanese. He wants to dismantle Japan's heavily centralized government. Hashimoto appeals to the people as an outsider. In a provocative, right-wing manner, Hashimoto has claimed that **"comfort women"** were necessary for Japan's military efforts. As governor, he closed unpopular facilities. However, Hashimoto has suggested compromises with **Korea** and **China** over island claims. He has made controversial statements about U.S. military bases on **Okinawa**. The *Asahi Shimbun* has been critical of Hashimoto, and he has responded to the newspaper in kind. However, some political analysts suggested Hashimoto might be the most suitable politician to become prime minister. At one time, Prime Minister **Abe Shinzō** and former Tōkyō governor **Ishihara Shintarō** saw him as a rising star.

After eight years in politics, Hashimoto lost his reelection bid for mayor in 2015 and has since returned to television as a commentator for TV Asahi, giving him a bully pulpit for expressing his controversial views.

HATA TSUTOMU, 羽田孜 **(1935–2017).** Hata Tsutomu was **prime minister** of Japan for two months in the spring of 1994. He started out as a staunch member of the **Liberal Democratic Party** (LDP) but, after several party changes, became a leader in the **Democratic Party of Japan** (DPJ).

Born in **Tōkyō**, Hata graduated from Seijō University and took employment with the Odakyū bus company. After 10 years with the bus company, he entered LDP politics and won a seat in the **House of Representatives** in 1969 representing Nagano Prefecture. Nagano citizens would elect Hata for 14 terms before he retired in 2012. Hata quickly rose to be a major member in the **Tanaka Kakuei–Takeshita Noboru** faction in the 1980s. He was agriculture, forestry, and fisheries minister in the mid-1980s and finance minister in **Miyazawa Kiichi**'s **cabinet**.

Hata tried to assume the leadership of the Tanaka-Takeshita faction, but when **Obuchi Keizō** won, Hata led 30-some members out of the faction and started the **Japan Renewal Party** (JRP) in 1993 with his political friend **Ozawa Ichirō**. They joined with the anti-LDP coalition that formed the **Hosokawa Morihiro** government in 1993. Hata served as foreign minister in the Hosokawa cabinet and replaced him when he resigned as prime minister.

Hata accomplished little in his brief two months as prime minister. When the **Japan Socialist Party** (JSP) left the coalition, his government collapsed, and Hata resigned rather than face a no-confidence vote. **Murayama Tomiichi**, leader of the JSP, established a new coalition and became prime minister.

When the JRP merged into the **New Frontier Party**, Hata challenged Ozawa for party leadership and lost. After that, Hata and 12 other **Diet** members formed the Sun Party, which in early 1998 became part of the Good Governance Party, which in turn became part of the DPJ in April 1998. Hata became the secretary-general of the DPJ. He remained a senior adviser to the Democratic Party until his death in 2017.

HATOYAMA ICHIRŌ, 鳩山一郎 (1883–1959). Hatoyama Ichirō was a leading postwar politician and **prime minister** of Japan from 10 December 1954 until 23 December 1956. A native of **Tōkyō** and the eldest son of the lawyer and politician Hatoyama Kazuo, he graduated from Tōkyō Imperial University. Hatoyama practiced law before being elected to the **Diet** in 1915 on the Seiyūkai ticket and then became minister of education in the **cabinets** of Inukai Tsuyoshi and then Saitō Makoto but was dismissed after the 1933 Takigawa incident, where government authorities suspended Professor Takigawa for his Marxist teachings. He opposed the formation of the Imperial Rule Assistance Association and was elected to the Diet in 1942 despite being an "unofficial" candidate.

The **Liberal Party** founded by Hatoyama became the biggest **political party** in the Diet in 1946, but Hatoyama was prevented from becoming prime minister after he was purged by the Supreme Commander for the Allied Powers. When Hatoyama failed to become prime minister, **Yoshida Shigeru** assumed the office. Hatoyama was rehabilitated in 1951, but his conflict with Yoshida over leadership of the party split the Liberal Party. Hatoyama opposed Yoshida and formed the Democratic Party and became prime minister in 1954. He became the first president of the **Liberal Democratic Party** (LDP) in 1955. In his long political career, Hatoyama was elected to the Diet a total of 15 times.

Hatoyama headed three cabinets, the first as a minority party with the support of the **Japan Socialist Party**, the second as leader of the single biggest party, and the third as the head of the new conservative coalition, the LDP. Hatoyama revised various **Occupation** reforms and was criticized for strengthening the police, for centralizing the government's control over **education**, and for advocating rearmament. His attempts to revise Article 9 of the **Constitution** were unsuccessful, as were his efforts to gain electoral reform to ensure a two-party system. In 1956, Hatoyama restored diplomatic relations with **Russia** and gained Japan's entry into the **United Nations**.

HATOYAMA KUNIO, 鳩山邦夫 **(1948–2016).** Hatoyama Kunio, grandson of **Hatoyama Ichirō** and brother of **Hatoyama Yukio**, was a leading politician of the **Democratic Party of Japan** (DPJ). He graduated from the **University of Tōkyō** and became an aide to Prime Minister **Tanaka Kakuei**. He was first elected to the **House of Representatives** in 1976 as a member of the **New Liberal Club**, but he soon switched to the **Liberal Democratic Party** (LDP). He left the LDP in 1993 to form the **New Party Sakigake** and, in 1996, helped his brother, Hatoyama Yukio, form the DPJ, in which he served as vice chairman. In 1999, he ran for governor of **Tōkyō**, revealing interparty strife within the DPJ, but he lost decisively to **Ishihara Shintarō**. He served as minister of justice (2007–2008) and as minister of internal affairs and communications under Prime Minister **Asō Tarō**. In 2012, he was elected for the 12th time to the House of Representatives. *See also* POLITICAL PARTIES.

HATOYAMA YUKIO, 鳩山由紀夫 **(1947–).** Hatoyama Yukio is a fourth-generation **political party** leader, a major politician in the **Democratic Party of Japan** (DPJ), and the **prime minister** from 16 September 2009 until 2 June 2010. Part of a highly successful political family, his great-grandfather, Hatoyama Kazuo, was speaker of the House; his grandfather, **Hatoyama Ichirō**, was prime minister; his father was Japan's foreign minister; and his brother was a leading figure in the **Diet** and in the DPJ. Hatoyama's mother is the daughter of **Ishibashi Shōjirō**, the wealthy founder of Bridgestone Tires. She has provided enormous financial support for her son's political career.

Born in **Tōkyō**, Hatoyama was educated at the **University of Tōkyō** and Harvard. He received a PhD in engineering from Stanford and was a professor at both Tōkyō Institute of Technology and Senshū University for a decade. Hatoyama was elected to the ninth Hokkaidō District seat of the Diet in 1986 under the banner of the **Liberal Democratic Party** (LDP). In 1993, he left the LDP and founded the **New Party Sakigake** with his brother, **Hatoyama Kunio**, and **Kan Naoto**. In 1996, he founded another party, the DPJ, with Kan and his brother and served as its second president from 1999 until 2002 when he resigned over difficulties with a merger with **Ozawa Ichirō**'s Liberal Party.

In August 2009, Hatoyama led the DPJ in a crushing defeat of the LDP, perhaps the largest turnaround in postwar Japanese politics. As Hatoyama took the reins of Japan's government in mid-September, much was expected of him. However, Hatoyama faced continuing **economic** difficulties, swirling **defense** issues over **Okinawa**, and a tarnished **foreign policy** image. He exacerbated the situation by failing to act decisively, and his huge approval ratings plummeted. After nine months, Hatoyama resigned a dismal failure. Kan Naoto replaced him.

Hatoyama served in the Diet until December 2012 when he retired from politics. Japanese citizens had high expectations of him as his progressive program introduced state subsidies for families with young children, offered support for single mothers, increased social spending, and expanded various welfare programs. However, his image was clouded by accusations of illegal campaign funding, spending scandals, and a shift from American-centered to Asian-centered diplomacy. In 2013, he even offered an apology to China's victims of Japanese aggression. Hatoyama Yukio now spends his time gardening and practicing meditation.

HAYASHI EITETSU, 林英哲 **(1952–).** Japan's premier solo *taiko* drummer, Hayashi Eitetsu has led a revival of drum **music** in his home country as well as around the world. Born in **Hiroshima**, he grew up in a temple where he heard the daily recitation of sutra and priests chanting **Buddhist** hymns. In 1971, Hayashi founded the *taiko* group Sado-Ondekoza and 10 years later created an offshoot known as *kodō*. He has played at various places around the world including Carnegie Hall, with the Boston Symphony Orchestra and **Ozawa Seiji**, and throughout Europe. Almost single-handedly, Hayashi has brought Japanese drumming to an artistic level. *The Wings of Flightless Birds* is one of his most famous pieces.

HAYASHI FUSAO, 林房雄 **(1903–1975).** Hayashi Fusao was a novelist and literary critic. Born in Ōita Prefecture, Hayashi was attracted to Marxism while a student at Tōkyō Imperial University. After he was jailed twice for political activities in the 1930s, his views shifted profoundly to the right, and he became an outspoken champion of ultranationalism. After World War II, Hayashi established himself as a writer of apolitical family novels, such as *Musuko no seishun (My Son's Youth,* 1950), *Seinen (Youth,* 1952), and *Tsuma no seishun (My Wife's Youth,* 1954). In the 1960s, he reemerged as a polemicist against left-wing pacifism with *Daitōa sensō kōteiron (The Great East Asia War as a Just War,* 1963), an apologia for Japan's actions in World War II. In this he championed Japan's struggle against Western imperialism. *See also* LITERATURE.

HEISEI, EMPEROR, 平成天皇. *See* AKIHITO, EMPEROR, 明仁天皇 (1933–).

HEISEI ERA, 平成時代 **(1989–).** *See* AKIHITO, EMPEROR, 明仁天皇 (1933–).

HELLO KITTY, ハローキティ. Created in 1974, Hello Kitty is an icon of Japanese pop culture and a marketing magnet. She symbolizes generosity, innocence, kindness, and most important, friendship. Kitty lives in London with her Mama and Papa and her twin sister Mimi. Kitty is curious. Both Hello Kitty and Mimi are in the third grade. They have many friends at school and, together, share many adventures. When school's out, Hello Kitty travels the world making new friends. Her hobbies include **music**, reading, eating the cookies her sister bakes, and making new friends. Her generosity and kindness endear her to everyone.

Hello Kitty likes small, cute things, such as candy, stars, and goldfish. A very energetic little girl, Kitty is a cute little white kitten who has many friends. Her trademark is the red bow she always wears on her ear. Sanrio, maker of games and cute characters, produces Hello Kitty. Not only is this cultural icon seen around the world, but UNICEF named Hello Kitty a "Special Friend of Children."

HIDARI SACHIKO, 左幸子 **(1930–2001).** Hidari Sachiko was an **actress** and **film** director. Born in Toyama Prefecture, Hidari was a high school **music** and **gymnastics** teacher before becoming an actress in 1952. She achieved international recognition in 1957 when she received the award for best actress at the Cork Film Festival in Ireland for her role in *Kamisaka Shiro no hanzai* (*The Crime of Shiro Kamisaka*, 1956), directed by Hisamatsu Seiji. Hidari was an outspoken **woman** who lived by what she believed. She displayed great courage when, in 1956, she left Nikkatsu, one of the major studios, to become an independent film performer. She gained great status as an actress in the 1960s, developing her distinctive screen personality as an earthy, independent-minded woman who awakened from the passive social role that tradition assigned to Japanese women. In 1977, after directing several short films in Paris, Hidari made her debut as the director of the film *Tōi ippon no michi* (*Far Road*). Hidari Sachiko became one of the few women to have succeeded in breaking into commercial Japanese films.

HIGASHIKUNI NARUHIKO, 東久邇稔彦 **(1887–1990).** A prince and general of the army, Higashikuni Naruhiko was Japan's first postwar **prime minister**, the only member of the **imperial family** to head a **cabinet**, and the person serving the shortest term as prime minister, occupying the office only 54 days, from 17 August to 14 October 1945. Born in **Kyōto**, the ninth son of Prince Kuni no Miya Asahiko, he married one of the daughters of Emperor Meiji and was thus the uncle of **Emperor Hirohito**. He graduated from the Army Academy and the Army War College and studied in France for several years. Upon returning to Japan, he held several military posts, becoming general commander of **defense** during the war.

Higashikuni's appointment as prime minister reflected the hope that his prestige as an imperial prince would enable him to unite a defeated and demoralized country and oversee the peaceful disbanding of the military forces. He presided over the formal signing of the surrender on 2 September 1945 and oversaw the liquidation of the armed forces. Higashikuni resigned in October in opposition to an order from the **Occupation** authorities to abolish the Peace Preservation Law and the Special Higher Police. In 1947, Higashikuni formally renounced membership in the imperial family and became a **Buddhist** monk. Higashikuni, dying at 102, was the longest lived of Japan's premiers.

HIRATSUKA RAICHŌ, 平塚らいちょう**(1886–1971).** Hiratsuka Raichō was a feminist, born in **Tōkyō** as Hiratsuka Haruko. In 1911, Hiratsuka founded the Seitōsha (Bluestocking Society), which promoted **women**'s rights and published *Seitō* (*Bluestocking*), a magazine by women, for women. In 1920, together with **Ichikawa Fusae** and Oku Mumeo, she founded the Shin Fujin Kyōkai (New Woman's Association) and engaged in a battle to reform the social and legal position of women.

After World War II, Hiratsuka continued to champion her concern with broad social issues, now with increased interest in pacifism and democracy. She strongly opposed the unilateral **San Francisco Peace Treaty** and twice appealed personally to **United States** secretary of state John Foster Dulles for peaceful democracy in Japan. She campaigned for peace as president and later honorary president of the Nihon Fujin Dantai Rengōkai (Federation of Japanese Women's Societies) and as a member of several national and international organizations.

HIROHITO, EMPEROR, 裕仁天皇 **(1901–1989).** Hirohito, also known as the Shōwa Emperor, reigned over Japan for 64 years, from the prewar era, through the war, and well into the successful postwar period. The eldest son of the Taishō Emperor, Crown Prince Hirohito acted as regent for his father. Hirohito succeeded his father as **emperor** in December 1926 and took the reign name of Shōwa. Although the keystone of the "emperor system," the Shōwa Emperor's belief in democratic politics led him to play little active political role, although such inactivity could not be total. He is generally regarded as having enforced the suppression of the 26 February 1936 uprising and having made the final decision for surrender in 1945. In January 1946, the emperor publicly renounced his claim to divinity and reigned as a **constitutional** monarch, separating himself from politics but acting as "the symbol of the state."

Empress Nagako (1903–2000) graduated from the girls' middle school department of Gakushūin. She married Crown Prince Hirohito in 1924 and became empress with his ascension to the throne two years later. She served as honorary president of the Japanese Red Cross Society and was known for her Japanese-style paintings. *See also* IMPERIAL FAMILY.

HIROSHIMA, 広島. Hiroshima is the lingering image of World War II and nuclear warfare. It is a symbol of the peace movement and hosts annual events to remind people of the horrors of war. Serving as the capital of Hiroshima Prefecture, it is western Japan's biggest city and the 10th-largest city in Japan with a population of 1.1 million. Hiroshima, literally meaning "broad island," sits on the sandy shores of the Inland Sea. Historically an important port city, Hiroshima became a castle town in the early 17th century, and then a major military city at the end of the 19th century.

During World War II, Hiroshima was a regional military headquarters for both army and marine groups. It also had shipbuilding facilities and large depots of military supplies; the city was also a key shipping center. On 6 August 1945, the **United States** dropped the world's first atomic bomb on Hiroshima, killing upward of 140,000 people and ushering in the nuclear age.

Annually thousands of Japanese come to Hiroshima on 6 August for the memorial service and to express their hope for a nuclear-free world. Famous sites in Hiroshima include the Peace Memorial Park, the A-Bomb Dome, the Children's Peace Monument, the Memorial Cenotaph, the Flame of Peace, the Hiroshima National Peace Memorial Hall for Atomic Bomb Victims, and the Peace Memorial Museum.

Today, a rebuilt Hiroshima is one of Japan's most modern cities. It has a wide variety of industries, especially the **automobile industry**, mainly **Mazda**, general machinery and equipment, and ships. It also serves as an important port city and is home to the popular Hiroshima Toyo Carp **baseball** team. Hiroshima has wide, tree-lined streets, compliments of urban renewal generated by the atomic bomb disaster. Hiroshima Castle, although criticized by purists, shows a modern representation of a traditional castle. Shukkei-en is a beautiful landscape garden.

HITACHI GROUP (HITACHI GURŪPU, 日立グループ). Hitachi is one of Japan's leading electronics *keiretsu*. Created in the early 20th century around the copper smelting business, Hitachi was officially incorporated in 1920. Its line of products grew to include ships and locomotives. It produced important military equipment during World War II. Hitachi expanded dynamically in the postwar period. Hitachi began to make **computers** and business machines in the 1960s. By the 1980s, its overseas operations had grown significantly, and it had come to rank among Japan's top 10 companies in assets and employees.

Named after the city in which it is located, Hitachi is an international company with offices in many countries and is a leading supplier of technological, especially electronic, equipment. It is the largest manufacturer of electrical machinery in Japan. It also produces computers and transportation equipment. The Hitachi Group includes more than 1,000 companies and is Japan's largest employer with more than 335,000 employees worldwide. Its core subsidiaries include Hitachi Metals, Hitachi Chemicals, and Hitachi Cable. Hitachi's Maxell brand of magnetic tapes, its batteries, and its data storage media are internationally famous.

Hitachi chairman emeritus Kawamura Takashi (1939–), who commands great respect in the Japanese **business** community, has turned the Hitachi Company around when it faced great problems due to the shocks of the **Great East Japan Earthquake** and the collapse of Lehman Brothers. In 2016, sales exceeded $20 million. It is listed on the **Tōkyō Stock Exchange** and is a constituent of both the **Nikkei 225** and Topix. It is capitalized at $27 billion. Growth and development are driven by regenerative medicine, pharmaceuticals, geothermal power, internet services, and self-driving cars.

HOLIDAYS, NATIONAL. The Japanese people celebrate 13 national holidays:

1. January 1 is New Year's Day (*Ganjitsu*) or New Year Festival (*Shōgatsu*).
2. January 15 is Adults' Day (*Seijin no hi*) and celebrates young people coming of age when 20-year-olds dress up and visit a shrine or a public place to celebrate adulthood.
3. February 11 is National Foundation Day (*Kenkoku kinen-no-hi*) and was created in 1966 as a replacement for Empire Day. Empire Day or *Kigensetsu* was a national holiday inaugurated in 1868 to commemorate the accession of Japan's mythological first **emperor**.
4. March 20 or 21 is Vernal Equinox Day (*Shunbun-no-hi*).
5. April 29, the birthday of the former Shōwa Emperor, is now "Greenery Day," a holiday to encourage the planting and cultivation of trees.
6. May 3 is **Constitution** Day (*Kempō kinenbi*) and celebrates Japan's current constitution.
7. May 5 is Children's Day Festival (*Kodomo-no-hi*). Boy's Day was traditionally held on 5 May and gave families an opportunity to celebrate their male children. In 1948, this was changed to Children's Day. However, the tradition of honoring boys on this day remains strong,

and families fly carp streamers (*koinobori*), display warrior dolls, and eat rice cakes in traditional style. Greenery Day, Constitution Day, and Children's Day are referred to as Golden Week.

8. September 15 is Respect for the Aged Day (*Keirō-no-hi*) and recognizes and celebrates elderly people in Japan.
9. September 22 is the Autumn Equinox Day (*Shūbun-no-hi*).
10. October 10 is Health-Sports Day (*Taiiku-no-hi*). It promotes health and physical development and celebrates the 1964 Tōkyō **Olympics**. Schools and **businesses** hold **sports** day.
11. November 3 is Culture Day (*Bunka-no-hi*), a holiday created in 1948 to celebrate peace and freedom and to promote culture.
12. November 23 is Labor Thanksgiving Day (*Kinrō-kansha-no-hi*).
13. December 23 is the Emperor's Birthday (*Tennō tanjobi*). It celebrates the birth date of **Emperor Akihito**.

Other nonofficial holidays include Doll Festival (*Hina matsuri*), which is a festival for girls held on 3 March; Seven-Five-Three Festival (*Shichi-gosan*) takes place on 15 November and honors girls aged three and seven and boys aged five, with families visiting **Shintō** shrines to pray for the health and well-being of the children; the Bon Festival observed in mid-July is a **Buddhist** observance honoring the spirits of departed ancestors; and Tanabata is the Star Festival celebrating the annual meeting of two celestial lover gods in Japan.

HONDA MOTOR COMPANY (HONDA GIKEN KŌGYŌ KABUSHIKIGAISHA, 本田技研工業株式会社**).** Honda Motor Company, headquartered in **Tōkyō**, is an automotive manufacturer famous for its fuel-efficient **automobiles**. **Honda Sōichirō** began the company in 1946 by first producing engines that he attached to bicycles, thus beginning the Honda **motorcycle**. This led to Honda becoming a major motorcycle producer. In 1972, Honda moved on to the automobile with the introduction of the Honda Civic, a car that helped change the automobile world with its small, fuel-efficient motor.

Honda, already the world's number one manufacturer of motorcycles, has become a leading producer of cars and industrial engines. Honda also manufactures luxury cars under the Acura brand and is a world leader in hybrid automobiles. In 1959, Honda became the first Japanese carmaker to produce passenger cars in the **United States**.

With ingenuity and efficiency, Honda became the best-selling and most respected car company in North America. The Accord became the standard for top cars in all respects and the NSX, the first Japanese supercar, dominated the Formula One scene for several years. Honda has become a leader in advanced technology, dynamic performance, and high quality.

In 2000, Honda, using artificial intelligence and robotics, introduced ASI-MO, an intelligent **robot**. The company is also engaged in space research and other forward-looking ventures. In 2013, Honda invested nearly $7 billion in research and development. It spends a lot of money on the development of hybrid electric cars, fuel cell powering, and driverless cars. As of 2014, Honda has sold more than 1.35 million hybrid cars worldwide.

Hachigō Takahiro (1959–) became president of Honda in June 2015. He faced problems when the company had to recall 15 million vehicles to correct defective Takata air bags. He has restructured the company to encourage more of a team effort. By 2016, Honda Motor Company ranked sixth in the world with more than 4.5 million vehicles produced. It was Japan's third-largest carmaker after **Toyota** and **Nissan**.

Honda shares trade not only on the **Tōkyō Stock Exchange** but also on the New York Stock Exchange. It has plants around the world. In 2016, Honda sold around 56 percent of its cars in the United States (1.6 million units), 21 percent in Asia, 12 percent in Japan, and 5 percent in Europe.

HONDA SŌICHIRŌ, 本田宗一郎 **(1906–1991).** Honda Sōichirō was an industrialist and founder of **Honda Motor Company**. He was a highly successful entrepreneur who, with his engineering background and business acumen, founded the Honda **automobile** company in 1963 after he began making Honda **motorcycles** in the early postwar era. Born in Shizuoka Prefecture, Honda was the son of a poor blacksmith. Strictly a self-made man who said that a diploma was "worth less than a movie ticket," he worked as a mechanic, opened his own repair shop, raced cars, and perfected engines. Shunning Japanese management techniques, he promoted "the Honda way," which stressed personal initiative and close personal relationships between workers and management. In his work, Honda paid an almost obsessive attention to detail. In 1989, Honda became the first Japanese to be named to the **United States** Automotive Hall of Fame.

HOSOKAWA MORIHIRO, 細川護熙 **(1938–).** Born in Kumamoto as the descendant of a prominent *daimyō* family, Hosokawa Morihiro is the grandson of Prince Konoe Fumimaro. Hosokawa graduated from Sophia University in **Tōkyō** and then worked for the *Asahi Shimbun*. Elected to the **House of Councillors** in 1971, he was the youngest person ever elected to that body. He was reelected in 1977. Hosokawa served as governor of Kumamoto during 1983–1991, when he emphasized both economic growth and **environmental** concerns, while having to deal with the carryover of the **Minamata disease** issue.

A journalist, prefectural governor, and **Liberal Democratic Party** (LDP) House of Councillors member, Hosokawa was smooth and confident, and he had an appealing image. However, in 1992, Hosokawa left the LDP to help form the **Japan New Party** (JNP). Describing Japan's political system as being moribund and out of touch with reality, he called for extensive change. The JNP elected four of 16 candidates in the July 1992 upper house **election**. Hosokawa was one of four successful JNP candidates. In the summer of 1993, the LDP lost its majority in the **Diet** election, the first time in 38 years, and was replaced by an eight-party coalition headed by Hosokawa. Hosokawa's JNP ran about 50 candidates in urban and suburban districts and won 35 seats in the 1993 election. Hosokawa subsequently became **prime minister** of the first coalition government.

Hosokawa, a major voice in the coalition, served as prime minister from 9 August 1993 to 28 April 1994 in an unstable coalition government composed of eight opposition parties. His coalition was the first non-LDP government since 1955. Hosokawa initiated electoral reforms, but it was left to Prime Minister **Murayama Tomiichi** to carry them out. Suggesting the need for more gender equality, Hosokawa appointed three **women** to his **cabinet**. He apologized for Japan's conduct in World War II and called it a "war of aggression; a mistaken war," upsetting a number of nationalists. He expressed responsibility and condolences to the war victims and survivors, the first time a prime minister had made such a confession. In March 1994, he visited **China** to promote cooperation in environmental issues. He succeeded in getting a package of political reform bills passed, but confronted with financial scandals from his earlier career, he resigned as prime minister after only eight months.

The **Japan Renewal Party**, under President **Hata Tsutomu**, took over leadership of the coalition. Hosokawa joined the **New Frontier Party** in 1996 but later moved to the **Democratic Party of Japan** in 1998. Later that year, he retired from politics to enjoy his leisure time as a potter.

In 2005, Hosokawa Morihiro assumed the headship of the Kumamoto-Hosokawa clan, one of Japan's noble families. He retained his rock-star personality and used it to campaign against **nuclear power**. In 2014, he ran unsuccessfully for governor of Tōkyō.

HOUSE OF COUNCILLORS (SANGIIN, 参議院). The House of Councillors, also known as the upper house of the **Diet**, is a powerful stabilizing legislative body that resembles the **United States** Senate. On all legislation except budgetary matters, treaties, or the selection of a **prime minister**, the **House of Representatives** must generate a two-thirds majority to override any decision of the upper house.

The 242 members of the House of Councillors are elected for six-year terms, with half of the upper house facing the voters every three years. Of the 242 seats, 146 people are elected to fill district seats and 96 to fill proportional seats. The upper house, newly created after World War II, held its first **election** on 20 April 1947. (Refer to appendix E.)

In July 2007, Japan held its 21st postwar election to the House of Councillors with 59 percent of eligible voters taking part. The percentage of people voting in the upper house elections ranged from a high of 75 percent in 1980 to a low of 45 percent in the 1995 election. In that election, the **Democratic Party of Japan** (DPJ) won a significant victory and held 109 seats, or 45 percent of the positions. The **Liberal Democratic Party** (LDP) occupied 83 seats (34 percent), the **New Kōmeitō** 20 seats (8 percent), the **Japanese Communist Party** seven seats, and the **Social Democratic Party of Japan** five seats. Eighteen other people held office from minor parties or were nonparty officeholders. However, with its coalition partners, the DPJ held a razor-thin majority. This changed in the July 2010 upper house election when the LDP gained one seat and the DPJ lost three seats and its coalition partners, causing it to lose its majority.

After the elections of 10 July 2016, the LDP held 120 seats, including carryovers, and its coalition partner, Kōmeitō, held 25 seats, giving it the majority. Other parties with seats in the House of Councillors included the Democratic Party (49 seats), Japanese Communist Party (14), Initiatives from Ōsaka and Independents (12 each), **Party for Japanese Kokoro** (3), and Social Democratic Party and Peoples Life Party (2 each) and **Okinawa Social Mass** Party (1) for a total of 242 seats. *See also* POLITICAL PARTIES.

HOUSE OF REPRESENTATIVES (SHŪGIIN, 衆議院). The House of Representatives, also known as the lower house of the **Diet**, creates and approves legislation that governs Japan. It is the main voice of the people in expressing the popular will, while working in conjunction with the **House of Councillors** and the other two branches of government, specifically the **prime minister** and the executive branch as well as the **judicial** branch. The House of Representatives is more powerful than the House of Councillors, which is sometimes called the upper house, since the lower house can override an upper house veto on bills with a two-thirds majority vote. Further, the lower house has the major say in treaties, budget matters, and the selection of the prime minister, since the upper house can only delay, not block, these decisions made by the lower house. The House of Representatives, with more frequent elections and the possibility of dissolution, is considered more sensitive to public opinion.

Japan held its first House of Representatives election in 1890. In 1942, it witnessed its 21st election, albeit heavily controlled by the military. On 10 April 1946, Japan convened its first postwar election for the lower house. The following year there was a second election. Of the 24 elections held for the House of Representatives in the postwar period, a low of 60 percent and a high of 77 percent of eligible voters have participated, thus showing the enthusiasm with which the Japanese approach their civic duty. (Refer to appendix D.) The total number of seats has changed over the years with a low of 465 seats presently and a high of 512 in 1986.

All 465 members of the House of Representatives are elected to a four-year term but have the right to call an election at any time, as well as the necessity of facing the voters if the prime minister loses a vote of confidence. After the 2005 election, Japan's 44th election for the lower house, the **Liberal Democratic Party** (LDP) held 296 seats or 62 percent of the positions. The **Democratic Party of Japan** (DPJ) had 113 seats (24 percent), the **New Kōmeitō** 31 seats, the **Japanese Communist Party** (JCP) nine seats, the **Social Democratic Party of Japan** (SDPJ) seven seats, and other parties or nonaligned individuals 24 seats. However, with the 30 August 2009 election the makeup of the House of Representatives changed dramatically when the DPJ overwhelmed the LDP by a margin of 308 seats (64 percent) to 119 seats (25 percent), the most dramatic shift in Japan's postwar political history.

Japan's House of Representatives now has 465 members, with 233 seats constituting a majority. One hundred and seventy-six members are elected from 11 multimember constituencies from a list prepared by the party proportional representation, and 289 members are elected from single-member constituencies. In the 16 December 2012 election, the LDP won 294 seats, and the DPJ won only 57 seats.

In the election of 14 December 2014, the LDP won 291 seats, and its coalition partner, the Kōmeitō, won 35 seats. Other parties with seats won include the Democratic Party (73 seats); Japan Innovation Party (41); JCP (21); Party for Future Generations, SDPJ, and People's Life Party (2 each); and Independents (8).

In September 2017, Prime Minister **Abe Shinzō** called for a snap election. On 22 October 2017, Japan held its 48th general election for the House of Representatives contesting a revised 465-seat Diet. Now it requires 233 seats to have a majority, but the LDP won 284 seats, and with the 29 seats held by the Kōmeitō, the LDP has a supermajority in the Diet. The so-called Pacifist coalition made up of the JCP, the SDPJ, and the **Constitutional Democratic Party** garnered just 69 seats. Originally filled with hope, **Koike Yuriko**'s coalition won only 61 seats. Although his hold on power may be precarious in the long run, Prime Minister Abe appears to be firmly in control for the present. *See also* POLITICAL PARTIES.

HOUSING. Traditional Japanese housing has increasingly given way to modern, multiunit facilities. These multistory apartment complexes, called *danchi*, incorporate many features of Western dwellings. Nonprofit government organizations began building *danchi* in the mid-1920s under the auspices of the Dōjunkai, a nonprofit government organization, in areas such as Aoyama and Daikanyama. Spurred by the terrible hardships created by the Great Tōkyō Earthquake, *danchi* were designed to meet a specific human need.

In 1941, the government replaced the Dōjunkai with its Public Housing Agency (Jutaku Eidan). From 1955, the Japan Housing Corporation helped build *danchi* in order to meet the acute housing shortages. The 2LDK (living room, dining/kitchen, with two bedrooms) was large for the time.

Manshon are apartment buildings with rental or condominium units, having modern facilities that render them relatively luxurious and distinguish them from more utilitarian public housing, or *danchi*. The concept of *manshon* seems to suggest Western-style dwellings, but these often have some sort of Japanese amenities. Recently, the distinction between *danchi* and *manshon* has become increasingly blurred.

In 1975, the new Town Development Public Corporation began building large "bed town" communities in the suburbs of metropolitan areas to meet a need for affordable housing. In 1981, the Housing and Urban Development Corporation (HUDC, Jūtaku Toshi Seibi Kōdan) took over both the Japan Housing Corporation and the Housing and Urban Development Corporation. HUDC works to provide better and more affordable housing for people. Overall there has been an improvement in the quality and availability of housing, thanks to these agencies. *See also* ARCHITECTURE.

I

IBUKA MASARU, 井深大 **(1908–1997).** In 1946, together with **Morita Akio**, Ibuka Masaru developed a tape recorder and founded a small electronics company that became **Sony Corporation** in 1955. Born in Tochigi Prefecture and a graduate of Waseda University, Ibuka won international recognition for his invention of a modulated-light transmission system and specialized in transistor radios. He marketed the Trinitron color **television** system. Ibuka was very interested in learning theories and wrote extensively on mother-child bonding and early educational experience for infants. His Early Development Association, which he founded in 1967, seeks to find the optimum conditions for **education** in the mother-child relationship.

IBUSE MASUJI, 井伏鱒二 **(1898–1993).** Ibuse Masuji was a leading Japanese author whose short stories and novels fully and carefully describe Japanese life. His most famous book is *Kuroi ame* (*Black Rain*, 1966), a story about the effects of the bombing of **Hiroshima**. The book contrasts the beauty of the area and the tragedy of the bombing. He highlights the difficulties of the A-bomb survivors. Ibuse won the Naoki, Noma, and Order of Culture prizes and was inducted into the Japan Art Academy. *See also* LITERATURE.

ICHIKAWA FUSAE, 市川房枝 **(1893–1981).** Ichikawa Fusae was an important feminist politician who led the Japanese **women**'s suffrage movement and served five terms in the **House of Councillors**. A native of **Nagoya**, Ichikawa worked as a primary school teacher and reporter. In 1918, she went to **Tōkyō** and joined **Hiratsuka Raichō** in promoting the Yūaikai, a workers' movement. Ichikawa spent two and a half years in the **United States** where she learned about the women's rights movement. In Japan, she helped found the Women's Suffrage League in 1924.

In 1945, Ichikawa organized and became president of the Shin Nihon Fujin Dōmei (New Japan Women's League), an organization aimed at improving the legal status of Japanese women, but in 1947–1950, she was banned from public office because of her association with state-sponsored women's organizations during the war. Resigning from women's organizations in 1953, Ichikawa was elected to the House of Councillors as an independent and, except for 1971–1974, remained there until her death. Twice, Ichikawa received the highest number of votes of any candidate standing for **election**. She consistently campaigned against money politics and for "clean" elections. She wrote widely on the women's movement and her part in it, and on politics. In 1945, she founded the Nihon Fujin Yūkensha Dōmei (League of Women Voters), a national organization.

ICHIKAWA KON, 市川崑 (1915–2008). Ichikawa Kon was a **film** director of international fame. Born in Mie Prefecture, Ichikawa left school to become a cartoonist and designer. He turned to filmmaking after the war. As a film director, Ichikawa showed skillful editing, talented acting, beautiful scenes, and concern for human nature. He is best known in the West for his film *Tōkyō Olympics*, which meticulously chronicles the splendor and success of the 1964 **Olympics**.

Biruma no tategoto (*Harp of Burma*), based on a novel by Takeyama Michio, is a powerful antiwar film about a young Japanese soldier in Burma at the end of the war who tries to convince a group of holdouts that the war is over. He fails to move the fanatics, all of whom are killed. Surviving by stealing a **Buddhist** monk's robes, he begins to act out the monk's role as he tries to give proper honors to the dead, and he remains in Burma to care for them.

Nobi (*Fires on the Plain*) is another of Ichikawa's famous films with a strong antiwar sentiment. Based on the book by **Ōoka Shōhei**, the film presents a bleak picture of World War II in the Philippines. It shows retreating Japanese soldiers struggling against starvation and hostile Filipinos. These soldiers build signal fires on the plains, thus giving the name to this 1959 film.

Based on a novel by **Mishima Yukio**, the film *Enjō* (*Conflagration*) is the true story of a young acolyte who deliberately burns down Kinkakuji, a revered national shrine. Ichikawa demonstrates how this senseless act of destruction is complexly motivated, with perfect balance between personal neurosis and social conditions. Like most of his work, *Enjō* is especially remarkable for its breathtaking visuals.

In 1983, he directed *Sasameyuki* (*The Makioka Sisters*), a film based on a novel by **Tanizaki Jun'ichirō**, which chronicles the life and affairs of four sisters in the 1920s. An older, conservative sister tries to continue family traditions and has pretensions to status, while the younger sisters discover the new freedoms becoming available to them. This battle over traditional ways is set in marked contrast to social and political changes going on in Japan.

IENAGA SABURŌ, 家永三郎 **(1913–2002).** Ienaga Saburō was a historian who, in celebrated court cases, challenged the legality of the Ministry of Education's right to control the content of schoolbooks in Japan's **textbook controversy** and, specifically, to make him remove passages critical of Japan in World War II. Born in Aichi Prefecture, he graduated from Tōkyō Imperial University in 1937, taught school in Niigata during the war, and became a professor of **education** at Tōkyō University of Education and Chūō University. In the interest of a peaceful future, he strongly advocated that the report of Japan's wartime atrocities should not be watered down. For three decades, he fought government efforts to suppress details of Japan's wartime atrocities from school history **books** but won only a partial victory. In 1997, Japan's Supreme Court ruled the Ministry of Education had acted illegally when it removed references to the inhumane treatment of people in the infamous germ warfare group known as Unit 731.

Ienaga forced the government to commission a new generation of textbooks, but the Supreme Court ruled that the government could force Ienaga to delete uncomfortable details about the Japanese invasions of **Korea** and Manchuria, the rapes and killings in Japan's occupations, and to tone down the references to the Nanjing Massacre. The author of more than 40 books, Ienaga was nominated for the **Nobel Peace Prize** but took the most satisfaction in improving the textbooks of Japan.

IKEDA HAYATO, 池田勇人 **(1899–1965).** Ikeda Hayato served as **prime minister** from 19 July 1960 through 9 November 1964. A native of **Hiroshima**, Ikeda studied law at Kyōto Imperial University, entered the **Ministry of Finance**, and served as deputy finance minister during 1947–1948. In 1949, he was elected to the **Diet** and later served as finance minister and international trade and industry minister in **Yoshida Shigeru**'s third **cabinet** during 1949–1952, and he was responsible for implementing an economic stabilization program. He was close to Yoshida and attended the **San Francisco Peace Treaty** conference as a delegate. Serving briefly as the international trade and industry minister in 1952, he resigned after a no-confidence motion. Ikeda remained influential in the **Liberal Democratic Party** (LDP), and from 1956 onward, he built up his own faction. During 1956–1957, he was finance minister and headed the **Ministry of International Trade and Industry** in 1959–1960.

In 1960, Ikeda succeeded **Kishi Nobusuke** as president of the LDP and as prime minister. Domestically, Ikeda maintained a low profile as compared with Kishi and concentrated on obtaining a high rate of economic growth with his famous income-doubling plan. Ikeda announced his plan on 5 September 1960, and he promised that an individual's income as well as the nation's GNP would double in 10 years. Ikeda helped Japan achieve this phenomenal economic growth in seven years.

Ikeda's administration advocated close relations with the **United States**. It also promoted an increase of commerce and trade with the People's Republic of **China**, although formal relations were not reestablished. Known for his efforts to minimize social conflict, Ikeda played an important role in settling the **Miike Mine Strike**. Ikeda resigned as prime minister in November 1964 due to ill health. *See also* ECONOMY; FOREIGN POLICY.

IKEDA RIYOKO, 池田理代子 (1947–). Author of famous girls' comics (*shōjo manga*) and historical **manga**, Ikeda Riyoko was born in **Ōsaka** and published her first very successful manga, *Berusaiyu no bara* (*The Rose of Versailles*), in 1972. This manga, an instant hit, told the story of the nobility during the French Revolution. Its main characters were Marie Antoinette, her Swedish lover, and a French woman whose father had raised her as a man. After 82 issues, the serial came to an end. Collected into 10 volumes, it sold 12 million copies, a *shōjo manga* record.

Ikeda followed this with *Jotei Ekaterina* (*Empress Katerina*), a historical study about Catherine the Great. She continued her interest in Marie Antoinette in *Berubara*. She told the story of Napoleon's empire in *Eroika*. In 1975, Ikeda produced *Oniisama e* (*My Dearest Brother*). This, along with *Berubara*, is Ikeda's only work to become an **anime**. In 1980, Ikeda's *Oruheusu no mado* (*The Window of Orpheus*) received the ninth Japanese Manga Writers' Award. Her manga are known for their vivid color and style, meticulous detail of background and character, handsome figures, beautiful costumes, and ornate, precise architecture. Her works are popular with young **women**.

IMAMURA SHŌHEI, 今村昌平 (1926–2006). Imamura Shōhei was an outstanding **film** director whose work captured the Japanese preoccupation with superstition and irrational matters. Imamura was born in **Tōkyō**, the son of a physician. He studied Western history at Waseda University, where he fell under the influence of films. In 1951, he joined the Shōchiku Motion Picture Company but, in 1954, left Shōchiku for better wages at Nikkatsu. Leader of Japan's *Nūberu bāgu* (New Wave) movement, Imamura was the first Japanese to win the prestigious Palme d'Or at Cannes twice. As a director, he was second in popularity only to **Kurosawa Akira**.

Karayuki-san (*The Making of a Prostitute*), Imamura's 1975 docudrama, chronicles the lives of Japanese **women** abducted by their own government during World War II and taken to Southeast Asia. These women were cut off from their homeland and forced into prostitution. Using interviews and historical photographs as well as dramatization, he explores the political and economic circumstances that rendered the *karayuki-san*, or "workers abroad," victims of state-sponsored kidnapping.

In 1979, Imamura made *Fukushū suru ware ni ari* (*Vengeance Is Mine*). Based on a true story, this is a horror tale of murder and bizarre behavior. It is "a terrifying portrait of a man without a heart." Starring Ogata Ken, this film is a violent, gripping tale of a cross-country murder spree told in flashbacks.

Another of Imamura's outstanding films is his 1983 *Narayamabushi-ko* (*The Ballad of Narayama*), a film that shares the traditional legend of taking old people to the mountains to die. This powerful film commanded a large international audience.

Kuroi ame (*Black Rain*) is the story of a family that survived the nuclear bombing of **Hiroshima**. The film focuses on the ways in which their bodies and souls, though poisoned by the fallout, try to cope. Psychologically, a mushroom cloud hovers over their lives every day. Imamura won the Japanese Academy Award for the Best Film with each of these last three movies. In 1997, he again won the Cannes Palme d'Or for his film *The Eel*, a film about a man who is imprisoned for murdering his wife and meets another woman as he tries to start a new quiet life in a village. *See also* JAPAN CONGRESS AGAINST ATOMIC AND HYDROGEN BOMBS (GENSUI-KIN, 原水禁).

IMPERIAL FAMILY. The Japanese imperial family is the oldest hereditary monarchy in the world, dating back well over two millennia. However, the postwar Japanese monarchy has had only two **emperors**, **Hirohito** (r. 1926–1989) and the current **Akihito** (r. 1989–present). The 1947 Imperial Household Law identified the members of the imperial family and defined its succession order. Presently, in addition to Emperor Akihito and Empress Michiko, the following are the leading members of the family. Crown Prince Naruhito (1960–), is the eldest son of Emperor Akihito and is scheduled to become emperor in 2019. In 1978, he enrolled in the History Department of Gakushūin University, where he was active in the orchestra. In 1980, a formal ceremony marked his coming of age. In 1993, he married former diplomat Owada Masako (1963–), a Harvard-educated **Ministry of Foreign Affairs** official. They have a daughter, Princess Aiko (2001–).

Prince Akishino (1965–) is the second son of the imperial family. He graduated from Gakushūin University with a degree in political science. He studied zoology at Oxford University and received a PhD from the National University for General Research. He married Kawashima Kiko (1967–) in 1990, and they have two daughters—Princess Mako (1991–), who announced her forthcoming marriage to a commoner in September 2017 and will thus leave the imperial family, and Princess Kako (1994–)—and a son, Prince Hisahito (2006–), who is third in the imperial succession line.

Princess Sayako (1969–) is the third child of Emperor Akihito and Empress Michiko. When she married Kuroda Yoshiki, a staff member of the **Tōkyō** metropolitan government in 2005, she officially left the imperial family and took her husband's surname.

IMPERIAL SUBJECTS PARTY (NIPPON KŌMINTŌ, にっぽんコミント). The Imperial Subjects Party is a small group of ultranationalists who cruised the streets of **Tōkyō** with their loudspeakers championing the **emperor** and criticizing the regular **political parties**. This group was especially strong during the 1980s and 1990s. Members of the party attacked **Takeshita Noboru** for his supposed disloyalty to former prime minister **Tanaka Kakuei**. They disrupted the political system by supporting **Kanemaru Shin** and Watanabe Hiroyasu, the president of Tōkyō Sagawa Kyūbin. In 2004, this group rammed a bus into the gate of the consulate of the People's Republic of **China** in **Ōsaka**. Rituals of loyalty are very important in Japanese society and absurdly important to right-wing extremists.

IMPERIAL SYSTEM (*TENNŌ-SEI*, 天皇制). Japan's imperial system has generated a lot of controversy in the postwar period. Conservatives and members of the **Liberal Democratic Party** (LDP) generally support the imperial system although they do not see it as crucial to the country. They accept the **emperor** and his office as the symbol of the state and the "unity" of the people. Some members of the LDP, seeking to restore patriotism and traditional values, have been trying to use the emperor for this purpose. At worst, they characterize the emperor system as benign, anachronistic, and perhaps an unnecessary expense. Clearly, however, the Japanese have a great affection for their "royals" as is demonstrated in their public ceremonies.

From a more advanced support position, Japanese ultranationalists extend lavish praise on the emperor and glorify his role in the Japanese government. Rather than a symbolic figure, they see the emperor as an all-powerful "god." Japanese rightists, as represented in more than 800 right-wing groups, want to restore imperial control over the government and armed forces.

Conversely, Japanese leftists criticize and even condemn the imperial system and charge it with being irrelevant and dangerous. With **Emperor Hirohito** as a symbol of Japan's dark military past, leftist critics fear that the emperor may again become the focal point for right-wing military movements. Warlords and military leaders have manipulated the emperor and used him to argue legitimacy for their views. Leftists roundly condemn those who see the emperor as divine.

Today, less than 5 percent of the Japanese people believe that the emperor is divine. Most Japanese are benignly indifferent to the imperial system.

Although the cost factor is rather negligible, it is still a factor in the controversy over the imperial system. Today the emperor, his male descendants, and male siblings cost the Japanese people about $260 million dollars annually. Leftists criticized the expenditure of nearly $15 million in public funds for the enthronement ceremony of **Emperor Akihito**. The leftists, together with Christian organizations, tried unsuccessfully to block the ceremony.

The emperor of Japan is strongly controlled by the all-powerful Imperial Household Agency, which supervises every detail of his life and activities. This includes everything from where he goes, what he does, whom he meets with, what he says, to what he wears and eats. Obviously, such matters as a marriage partner and the raising of his children are carefully controlled.

A survey conducted by the *Asahi Shimbun* in 1997 revealed that 82 percent of the Japanese wanted to continue the monarchy. However, other later polls show that at least one-third of the people are "indifferent" toward the first family. While the controversies over the imperial system are not among the greatest problems facing Japan, the issue does arouse a great deal of passion among some people.

The imperial system benefits Japan by providing a symbol of the country, a sense of linkage and purpose, a spiritual core, a diplomatic role as ambassador, and a source of tradition and stability. A smaller percentage of people have argued that such views are out of date, contribute little or nothing to Japan, and should be removed or reduced. They suggest that the imperial system is out of sync with the times.

INAMINE SUSUMU, 稲嶺進 (1946–). Inamine Susumu is the fiery mayor of Nago, a small city in the northern part of **Okinawa Prefecture**. In 2010, Inamine, supported by the **Democratic Party of Japan** and its coalition partners, defeated the incumbent Yoshikazu Shimabukuro backed by the **Liberal Democratic Party** (LDP) and its **Kōmeitō** partner. He won on a campaign pledge to stop the construction of a new **United States** military base near Nago.

In January 2014, Mayor Inamine, reelected to a second term, vowed to block construction of the base by denying permits for the project. He cemented his position with a hard-fought election contest that he won against a pro-base opponent supported by Japan's ruling LDP. The people of Naha do not want the base moved to their city, and many want the base out of Okinawa. Inamine continues to be a thorn in the side for Prime Minister **Abe Shinzō**.

In May 2014, Inamine led a mission to Washington to protest the building of any American military base in Naha, or Okinawa for that matter. In May 2015, he helped organize approximately 35,000 protesters who raised placards saying "Do not yield to authority" during a rally to protest a controversial U.S. air base in Naha.

In August 2015, Mayor Inamine led the opposition to Defense Minister Nakatani Gen's plan to build an American military base in Naha. In February 2016, he helped organize a protest of at least 28,000 people who ringed the Japanese Diet Building in opposition to the building of a new American military base in Okinawa. On 4 February 2018, Inamine lost his bid for reelection.

ISHIBASHI SHŌJIRŌ, 石橋正二郎 **(1889–1976).** Ishibashi Shōjirō was a businessman and the founder of Bridgestone Tire Company. Born in Fukuoka Prefecture, Ishibashi expanded his family's footwear business by producing inexpensive goods on a mass scale. After World War I, he developed rubber-soled *tabi* for work and later produced rubber boots. In 1931, he established Bridgestone Tire in order to produce **automobile** tires. Military demand accelerated his company's prosperity during World War II. In 1950, he signed a contract for technical cooperation with Goodyear Tire and Rubber Company, which enabled him to improve the quality of domestically manufactured tires. An avid collector of art objects, Ishibashi established the Bridgestone Museum of Art in 1952.

Ishibashi's daughter, Yasuko, married **Hatoyama Ichirō**, and she became known as the "Godmother" as she bankrolled the political efforts of her sons **Hatoyama Yukio** and **Hatoyama Kunio** and their roles in the formation and operation of the **Democratic Party of Japan**.

ISHIBASHI TANZAN, 石橋湛山 **(1884–1973).** Ishibashi Tanzan, a politician, economist, and journalist, was Japan's **prime minister** for a short period from 23 December 1956 through 25 February 1957. A native of **Tōkyō**, Ishibashi became a journalist after graduating from Waseda University in 1907. In 1911, he joined the *Toyo Keizai Shimpō* (Oriental Economic Journal) and acted as its editor (1925–1946) and from 1941 also acted as its president. During the 1930s, he was one of the few critics of Japan's military endeavors. He became well known as a liberal economist and exponent of Keynesian ideals and economics. In 1946–1947, Ishibashi was finance minister under **Yoshida Shigeru** and tried to use his ideas to rebuild the **economy**.

Ishibashi was elected to the **Diet** in 1947 but was soon purged by the Supreme Commander for the Allied Powers. He served as finance minister in the first Yoshida **cabinet**. After returning to sit in the Diet in 1952–1963, conflict with Yoshida developed; Ishibashi built up his own faction and served as minister of international trade and industry under **Hatoyama Ichirō** during 1954–1956. He then became the second president of the **Liberal Democratic Party** (LDP) in the first **election** to be held at the party assembly and, consequently, became prime minister in December 1956. His policies were at the liberal end of the LDP spectrum, and he hoped to reflate the economy by tax reduction and initiate relations of friendship and commerce with the People's Republic of **China** (PRC). However, in February 1957, Ishibashi resigned due to ill health. The Ishibashi faction virtually ceased to exist after he failed to get elected in 1963, but until his death Ishibashi worked to promote relations with the PRC and the **Soviet Union**, although he argued for Japan's independent **defense** capability. *See also* FOREIGN POLICY.

ISHIHARA NOBUTERU, 石原伸晃 **(1957–).** Ishihara Nobuteru is a politician who served as secretary-general of the **Liberal Democratic Party** (LDP) from 2010 until 2016. Son of **Tōkyō** governor **Ishihara Shintarō**, the people of the Fourth District of Tōkyō elected him nine times to the **House of Representatives**. He is considered one of the rising stars of the LDP.

Following his graduation from Keiō University, Ishihara worked as a political reporter before joining the Diet. After filling a variety of LDP offices, he decided to run for president of the party in 2008 but finished a distant fourth. He served as head of the Ministry of Environment from December 2012 until September 2014. In January 2016, he became head of the Ministry of State for Economic and Fiscal Policy. Well-connected politically, he is an ally of Prime Minister **Abe Shinzō**.

ISHIHARA SHINTARŌ, 石原慎太郎 **(1932–).** Ishihara Shintarō, born in Hyōgo Prefecture, was a 1956 graduate of Hitotsubashi University where he authored a novel, *Taiyō no kisetsu* (*Season in the Sun*), which won the prestigious Akutagawa Prize. This popular novel depicted the pleasure-seeking and sexually liberated lifestyle of some of the postwar generation known as the "Sun Tribe." Throughout his life, Ishihara has penned more than 40 books.

Ishihara turned to politics where he was elected to the **House of Councillors** in 1968 with a record vote, then to the **House of Representatives** in 1972 as a **Liberal Democratic Party** (LDP) member. He joined Seirankai, an LDP fragment group, where he advocated a strong Japan. He had a high-profile career in politics as a spokesman for Japanese nationalism and traditional values and as a critic of the modern political establishment. As an LDP **Diet** member, he criticized Prime Minister **Tanaka Kakuei** over the **Lockheed scandal**. He challenged **Kaifu Toshiki** for leadership of the LDP. In 1989, Ishihara, together with **Morita Akio**, published *The Japan That Can Say No*, a book that was highly critical of the **United States** as well as Japan. He infuriated American policy makers with his challenges to the United States and his abrasive, blunt ways.

In 1995, Ishihara resigned from the House after accusing the LDP of opposing progress. He was then elected governor of **Tōkyō** in April 1999 by a large margin. Many politicians and critics consider Ishihara politically erratic. He is considered one of Japan's most prominent "right-wing" politicians, supporting various nationalistic causes, frequently visiting **Yasukuni Shrine**, and making racist, sexist, and historical revisionist statements. Ishihara served as Tōkyō's governor from 1999 to 2012, making him the second-longest-serving governor of Japan's capital city after **Suzuki Shun'ichi**. In 2012, Ishihara again won a seat in the House of Representatives but lost that seat in the next election.

Ishihara showed his involvement in right-wing politics when he helped establish the Sunrise Party Japan in 2010. He then joined **Hashimoto Tōru**, **Ōsaka**'s mayor, in forming the **Nippon Ishin no Kai** or Japan Restoration Party, which opposed Article 9 of the **Constitution**. Finally, Ishihara joined the Party for Future Generations, but after losing in the December 2014 election, he finally retired from politics. However, in 2017, government officials were raising questions about his deal to relocate the **Tsukiji Fish Market**. *See also* LITERATURE.

ISHIHARA TAKASHI, 石原隆 **(1912–2003).** Ishihara Takashi was president of **Nissan Motor Company** when Japan surged ahead of Detroit to become the world's largest **automobile** producer. As chairman of the **Japan Association of Corporate Executives** and the leader of the Japan Automobile Manufacturers Association, he was a frequent spokesman on **trade** issues before the **Diet**.

Born in **Tōkyō**, Ishihara graduated from Tōhoku University in 1937 with a law degree and then joined Nissan. He was a former **rugby** player who in his business life was not afraid to act in a burly, forceful manner. In **business**, Ishihara was a risk taker, and these risks paid off.

In the 1960s, Ishihara was the first president of Nissan's U.S. subsidiary and, in the 1970s, successfully guided Nissan's rapid expansion into the world market. In the 1980s, as president of Nissan, he built plants in the **United States** and Great Britain and exercised a hands-on approach to management. Ishihara's Nissan plant in Tennessee was one of his biggest initiatives. He was responsible for promoting the manufacturing of the Datsun Sunny model, Nissan's one-liter engine car. This car became a best-selling model. Ishihara served as president of Nissan from 1977 to 1985 and later as chairman for seven years.

ISHII SUSUMU, 石井進 **(1924–1991).** Ishii Susumu was the head and leading underworld figure of the Inagawa-kai, Japan's second-largest **crime** syndicate. He was the central figure in a stock scandal that forced the resignations of presidents of the Nomura and Nikkō **securities companies**. Ishii headed the 8,200-member crime organization in **business**, stock, and real estate deals. In 1989, he sold memberships in a **golf** course and used the proceeds to buy shares in the **Tōkyū Corporation** through the Nomura and Nikkō securities companies. Through persuasion of the securities companies, prices skyrocketed, but the authorities raised charges of improper compensation for favored clients. Ishii retired as head of the syndicate in 1990. *See also YAKUZA*, ヤクザ.

ISHIKAWA ICHIRŌ, 石川一郎 **(1885–1970).** A key leader in the **Japan Federation of Economic Organizations** (Keidanren), Ishikawa Ichirō was a businessman who graduated from Tōkyō Imperial University in 1909 and went on to become an assistant professor in the engineering faculty at his alma mater. Ishikawa later became managing director of the Dai Nippon Jinzō Hiryō Kaisha (Japan Nitrogen Fertilizer Company), the largest chemical fertilizer firm in Japan at the time, and then president of Nissan Chemical Industries in 1941. Although most other **business** leaders and corporation executives were purged after World War II, Ishikawa reorganized various economic organizations and became president of Keidanren in 1948. He played an important role in the reconstruction of the war-torn Japanese **economy** until 1956 when **Ishizaka Taizō** took over as chairman of Keidanren.

ISHIOKA EIKO, 石岡瑛子 **(1938–2012).** Ishioka Eiko was one of Japan's most famous art directors and a well-known costume and graphic designer. Her work graced the stage, screen, print media, and advertising. Highly aesthetic, Ishioka's designs were known for their eerie feeling and beautiful sensual lines.

Born into a family of graphic artists, Ishioka graduated from the Tōkyō National University of Fine Arts and Music. Her first job was with **Shiseidō**, the cosmetics company, where she had considerable success. She then moved to Parco where she developed striking commercials. The Houston Rockets, an American basketball team, hired her to design their logo. She designed clothing for several famous film directors including Paul Schrader, Francis Ford Coppola, Richard Wagner, and others. She won numerous awards for her designs. She even designed the uniforms for members of the Swiss, Canadian, Spanish, and Japanese **Olympic** teams. Finally, she designed costumes for Cirque du Soleil.

ISHIZAKA TAIZŌ, 石坂泰三 **(1886–1975).** Ishizaka Taizō was a businessman who was born in **Tōkyō**. After graduating from Tōkyō Imperial University, Ishizaka joined the Ministry of Communications but shifted to Daiichi Seimei, an insurance firm, in 1915. He served as its president from

1938 to 1946. Purged by the Allied **Occupation** authorities, he later returned to public life, and as president of Tōkyō Shibaura Electric, he reinvigorated the company. He became the second president of the **Japan Federation of Economic Organizations** (Keidanren) in 1956, leading the organization for a dozen years during the time of Japan's high economic growth. Ishizaka opposed governmental intervention in economic affairs, particularly in **trade** and capital liberalization, and led the business-industrial community toward policies conducive to good relations with the **United States**.

ISOZAKI ARATA, 磯崎新 **(1931–).** Isozaki Arata, an internationally famous architect, studied under **Tange Kenzō** at the **University of Tōkyō** and served as his apprentice for nearly a decade. Isozaki then worked with a design firm known as Urtec (Urbanists and Architects). In 1963, he formed his own architectural design firm. Always open to new ideas, Isozaki served as a visiting professor at a number of universities throughout the **United States**. He has won many awards for his creative designs that combine traditional Japanese sensibility with Western asymmetrical patterns, interestingly juxtaposed materials, eclectic styles, and technologically sophisticated details.

Isozaki, born in Ōita, has many of his commissions in three northern Kyūshū cities, Ōita, Fukuoka, and Kitakyūshū. Geography appears to be one key to Isozaki's work. He served as commissioner of Kumamoto Artpolis from 1988 to 1998. A measure of Isozaki's status is that he is frequently selected as the juror for major projects.

Isozaki's most noted buildings in Japan are the Ōita Prefectural Library; the Kitakyūshū City Museum of Art; the Civic Center of Tsukuba, a building composed of geometric shapes made from granite, artificially colored stone, and aluminum panels; and Mito's Art Tower, a masterpiece in postmodernist **architecture**. He was the chief architect for Japan's **Expo** '70. Internationally, he designed the Los Angeles Museum of Contemporary Art; the Team Disney Building in Orlando, Florida; the Olympic Stadium in Barcelona, Spain; and the Center of Science and Industry in Columbus, Ohio. Isozaki also designed the Guggenheim Museum SoHo in New York; Domus La Casa del Hombre in La Coruña, Spain; and Biennale de Firenze in Italy. Isozaki's buildings are known for bold forms and colors as well as inventive detailing.

ISUZU MOTOR COMPANY (ISUZU JIDŌSHA KABUSHIKI-GAISHA, いすゞ自動車株式会社**).** Isuzu Motor Company is a Japanese specialty **automobile** company that is headquartered in **Tōkyō**. It has both assembly and manufacturing plants in the city of Fujisawa, as well as in Tochigi and Hokkaidō prefectures. Isuzu is famous for producing commercial vehicles and diesel engines that can be found in vehicles all over the world. Isuzu is a subsidiary of Fuji Heavy Industries. In 2005, Isuzu was the world's largest manufacturer of medium-sized trucks. Isuzu Motors, known for its SUVs, has partnerships with both **Toyota** and General Motors. However, in 2008, Isuzu withdrew from the American market.

Isuzu now concentrates primarily on the manufacture of commercial vehicles and diesel engines. It continues to make some specialty cars, buses, and other "working vehicles." Its trucks are sold worldwide. Isuzu has subsidiaries in Turkey, **Russia**, **China**, India, Indonesia, Malaysia, and several other countries. Isuzu's trucks are quite prominent in Africa and Asia.

ITAMI JŪZŌ, 伊丹十三 (1933–1997). Itami Jūzō was one of Japan's leading moviemakers and **film** satirists. He was born in **Kyōto**, son of Itami Mansaku, a pioneer director, scriptwriter, and film producer. He worked as a boxer, a commercial designer, a translator, a **television** documentarist, an essayist, a talk-show host, and an **actor**. He produced the television special super-drama *Daichūshingura* (*47 Rōnin*) and wrote 26 **books** and 15 collections of essays. Itami, who is said to have committed suicide, was successful at home and abroad.

Itami directed *Osōshiki* (*The Funeral*), his first film, in 1984. This film, which won the Japanese Academy Award for the best film, is a satiric look at how a modern Japanese family endures a traditional three-day **Buddhist** funeral. Avoiding both easy sentimentality and cheap derision, Itami carefully examines the minor calamities, subtle incongruities, messy details, and awkward moments that accompany this most solemn of rituals. The family watches a video on "The ABCs of Funerals," the priest arrives by Rolls-Royce, the women get giggling fits during the sermon, and the protagonist's mistress inopportunely shows up, throws a tantrum, and drags him off into the woods for a lusty bit of lovemaking. The incidents contrast old and new ways, young and old, ritual ceremony and true feelings, sometimes comically, sometimes poignantly.

In *Minbo no onna* (*The Gentle Art of Japanese Extortion*), Itami turns his acid humor to Japan's infamous institution, the *yakuza*. This film is about a courageous attorney who rallies all the employees at a hotel in an effort to resist the *yakuza* blackmail. After this 1984 film was completed, thugs viciously attacked the director, forcing him to go into hiding. The film is a brilliant, satirical look at the underbelly of Japanese modern life.

Itami created the hilarious *Tanpopo* (*The Dandelion*) in 1986. This Japanese noodle western is one of the funniest celebrations of food ever made. Male customers patronize this nondescript roadside noodle restaurant and constantly ogle the place. A truck driver helps the struggling cook search for the perfect bowl of ramen. This film lampoons modern Japan and Japanese standards of perfection. *Tanpopo* bestows a glimpse of modern Japanese culture, cuisine, and humor.

Itami directed *Marusa no onna* (*A Taxing Woman*), which won the Japanese Academy Award for the best film in 1987. Having previously lampooned obsessions with death and food, Itami created a phenomenal success in Japan by moving on to that equally essential subject, money. With tax evasion becoming a fine art, the government employs squads of zealous tax agents. In Itami's story, the master tax-evader, an adult hotel proprietor, meets his match, a cunning woman tax agent who hunts down her quarry with resourceful determination.

ITŌ MIDORI, 伊藤みどり **(1969–).** Itō Midori is Japan's greatest figure skater, with superb ability and international recognition. A native of **Nagoya**, Itō took to the ice at age four and was competing two years later. Early on, Itō's tremendous athletic ability caught the attention of the skating world. At Paris in March 1989, Itō was the first female skater to complete a triple axel in international competition. She was also the first Japanese skater to ever win a world championship. She won the All-Japan **Figure Skating** Championships eight times. She garnered a silver medal in the following year's World Championships and another second-place finish in the 1992 Albertville **Olympic** Games. In 1996, Itō switched to professional skating after being plagued by injuries. Admired by both men and **women**, she was inducted into the World Figure Skating Hall of Fame in 2003. *See also* SPORTS.

ITŌ TOYŌ, 伊東豊雄 **(1941–).** Itō Toyō is an outstanding representative of the New Wave of Japanese **architecture**. After graduating from the **University of Tōkyō** in 1965, Itō went to work for the Metabolist architect Kiyonori Kikutake. In 1971, he opened his own office, Urban Robot, or URBOT, which he later renamed Toyō Itō Architect & Associates. Itō sought to eliminate irrelevant things in his architecture and inspire the straightforward use of **construction** materials. He designed the Tower of Winds in **Yokohama**, an innovative and inspiring creation. It uses electronic and **computer** technologies to make a complex pattern of light and wind displays.

In **Tōkyō**, Itō's main buildings are I-Building Asakusabashi, T-Building Nakameguro, F-Building in Minami Aoyama, and Kaze-no-tamago (Egg of Wind). Internationally, Itō gained a reputation for his "La Maison de la Culture de Japon" in Paris, his urban design project for Shanghai, his Eckenheim Municipal Kindergarten in Frankfurt, and his design for the Berkeley Art Museum with its honeycomb-like spaces. By infusing his design with the psychological, emotional, and social dimensions, Itō has become one of the world's leading architects.

Itō continues to be innovative and influential in the architectural world. He has trained leading architects such as **Sejima Kazuyo** and Nishizawa Ryue. He has been a guest professor at several world-renowned universities. After the **Great East Japan Earthquake** of 2011, he designed the "Home for All," a living facility for victims of the disaster, thus showing his strong sense of social responsibility. In 2013, Itō Toyō received the Pritzker Architecture Prize, the highest award in his field.

ITŌCHŪ (ITŌCHŪ SHŌJI KABUSHIKI-GAISHA, 伊藤忠商事株式会社**).** Itōchū is one of Japan's leading **general trading companies** (*sōgo shōsha*). Founded as a textile wholesaler in 1858, Itōchū Corporation consisted of C. Itoh & Company and **Marubeni** Corporation after World War II. It took its present name in 1992. Strong in the fields of machinery, **construction**, metals, textiles, and chemicals, Itōchū is one of the largest companies in the world. It has more than 1,000 branches and subsidiaries in more than 80 countries.

In 1971, C. Itoh & Company assisted in arranging a basic contract for cooperation between General Motors Corporation of the **United States** and **Isuzu Motors** of Japan. In 1972, the Chinese government welcomed C. Itoh as a friendly general trading company, the first such recognition given to a Japanese *sōgo shōsha*. In 2001, Marubeni-Itōchū **Steel** was established. In 2002, Itōchū and the government of China's Shandong Province teamed up to jointly develop businesses in the province.

In 2016, Itōchū made a profit of approximately $2.2 billion. Itōchū has approximately 120 plants in 63 countries and 4,370 employees; as one of Japan's leading *sōgō shōsha*, it engages in domestic trading, import/export, and overseas trading of various products such as textiles, machinery, metals, minerals, energy, chemicals, food, general products, realty, information and communications technology, and finance, as well as business investments.

Itōchū is building the world's largest geothermal plant as well as coal-fueled power plants in Indonesia, joint ventures in Saudi Arabia, nuclear reactors in Turkey, and oil and gas developments in Azerbaijan.

Itōchū, together with **Mitsubishi Corporation**, usually leads the Japanese trading companies for the top spot in profits among Japanese trading companies. In 2016, it made around $3.66 billion in net profit. President Okafuji Masahiro (1949–), who has led the Japanese trading house for the past seven years, is extending his tenure another year in order to see his Chinese initiative achieve success. (Refer to appendix M.)

J

J.LEAGUE (J リーグ). J.League, short for Japan Professional Football League (Nippon Puro Sakka Rigu, 日本プロサッカーリーグ), launched in 1993 and has three divisions with 53 teams. The Kashima Antlers, the current champion, and Sanfrecce **Hiroshima** have won the most titles with eight each. The J1 League has 18 teams and plays for the Emperor's Cup. The J2 League has 22 teams. The J3 League has 13 teams and is the lesser of the three leagues.

However, Japanese football, or as it is known in the United States, **soccer**, got its organized start in 1975 with the Japan Soccer League. Tōyō Industries dominated the league for its seven years. In 1972, the Japan Soccer League Division 1 started and was the major league for the next 20 years. **Yomiuri FC** and **Mitsubishi** Heavy Industries were the strongest teams during this period. J.League came into play from 1993 through 1998. In 1999, J.League Division 1 began and continues today.

The J.League boomed during its first three seasons, but during the period 1996–1999 it experienced a significant decline in attendance. The J.League encouraged expansion hoping to reach 100 teams by 2092. They realigned the teams and changed the infrastructure. In 2005, they adopted a format similar to the European club football.

The strongest teams in the J.League have been the Kashima Antlers who have won eight titles including the 2016 championships, the Sanfrecce Hiroshima who have also won eight titles, **Tōkyō** Verdy with seven titles, the Urawa Red Diamonds who have won five times, and the Kawasaki Frontale, three-time runner-up and the 2017 champions.

The J.League's most valuable players include Sanfrecce Hiroshima's Satō Hisato in 2012, **Yokohama** F. Marinos's Nakamura Shunsuke in 2013, Gamba Ōsaka's Endō Yasuhito in 2014, Sanfrecce Hiroshima's Aoyama Toshihiro in 2015, Kawasaki Frontale's Nakamura Kengo in 2016, and Kawasaki's Kobayashi Yū in 2017.

In early 2017, the J.League struck a 10-year deal for $1.88 billion with a United Kingdom online distributor of sports entertainment, making it the biggest sale of broadcasting rights in Japanese sporting history. The company will emphasize online video broadcasting. J.League soccer is expanding to other Asian markets.

JAPAN AIR SYSTEM (NIHON EA SHISUTEMU, 日本エアシステム). Japan Air System (JAS) was the smallest of Japan's Big Three airlines. Incorporated in 1964, JAS took its present name in 1988. Although involved in some international services, it operated primarily domestic flights and charter flights to several international destinations. In 2001, JAS merged with **Japan Airlines Company** (JAL). JAL and JAS established a new holding company that was called Japan Airlines System and was reborn as the new Japan Airlines Group. It is part of the **Tōkyū Corporation.** *See also* ALL NIPPON AIRWAYS (ZEN NIPPON KŪYU KABUSHIKI-GAISHA, 全日本空輸株式会社).

JAPAN AIRLINES COMPANY (KABUSHIKI-GAISHA NIHON KŌKŪ, 株式会社日本航空). Japan Airlines Company (JAL) is Japan's flagship airline company. Founded in 1951, it became a government-owned company in 1953. JAL's first international flight, from **Tōkyō** to San Francisco, began in 1954. In 1967, it initiated round-the-world service. In 1987, JAL was privatized. JAL is one of the world's largest airlines with international routes to 344 airports in more than 56 countries, as well as 143 domestic routes. In 2001, it incorporated **Japan Air System** (JAS) as a subsidiary. In 2004, JAL changed its name to Japan Airlines International, and JAS became Japan Airlines Domestic. That same year, the company adopted the name Japan Airlines Corporation. JAL has the largest fleet of Boeing 747s in the world. Ueki Yoshiharu (1952–) has been president of JAL since 2012. *See also* ALL NIPPON AIRWAYS (ZEN NIPPON KŪYU KABUSHIKI-GAISHA, 全日本空輸株式会社).

JAPAN ASSOCIATION OF CORPORATE EXECUTIVES (KEIZAI DŌYUKAI, 経済同友会). The Japan Association of Corporate Executives, composed of individual businessmen, was established in 1946 as one of Japan's three major economic organizations along with the **Japan Federation of Economic Organizations** (Keidanren) and the **Japan Federation of Employers' Association** (Nikkeiren). The Japan Association was formed by non-*keiretsu* businessmen on the rise, usually men from the managing-director level, and in its earlier years it was a vehicle for a more flexible, progressive capitalism. It took positions opposing Keidanren on issues such as **environmental** pollution, political corruption, **labor**-management rapprochement, and public responsibilities of private enterprise.

Gradually, the Japan Association of Corporate Executives abandoned its liberal-minded approach and became more anti-labor. Approximately 1,300 top executives of some 900 large corporations participate in the association. Kobayashi Yoshimitsu (1946–) became the association's chairman in 2015. The association has urged the government to tackle financial reconstruction and has opposed increased social security spending and tax grants to local government.

JAPAN BROADCASTING CORPORATION (NIPPON HŌSŌ KYŌKAI, 日本放送協会). Japan Broadcasting Corporation or NHK, began operations in 1925 under the name **Tōkyō** Broadcasting Station. It took on its present name the following year after it merged with stations in **Ōsaka** and **Nagoya**. NHK was Japan's only broadcaster until the end of World War II.

NHK is Japan's publicly funded broadcasting service. It gets nearly all of its funding through fees paid regularly by every Japanese household. The company operates five television channels, including terrestrial networks Educational TV and General TV, offering cultural and educational programming, along with news and entertainment. It also broadcasts on three public radio services. NHK has 54 stations throughout Japan. Internationally, the company offers NHK World TV and NHK World Radio Japan.

On 1 August 2016, NHK started 4K and 8K ultra-high-definition test broadcasting on its BS satellite channels, aiming to verify the technology and popularize it ahead of the 2020 Tōkyō **Olympics** and Paralympics. Viewers cannot watch 4K and 8K broadcasting with conventional television sets or tuners. NHK will demonstrate 8K televisions at its broadcasting centers nationwide.

JAPAN BUSINESS FEDERATION (NIPPON KEIZAI DANTAI RENGŌKAI, 日本経済団体連合会). The Japan Business Federation is an economic organization established in 2002 to replace the **Japan Federation of Economic Organizations** (Nippon Keidanren) by linking up with the **Japan Federation of Employers' Association** (Nikkeiren). This powerful business group represents more than 1,300 companies, 125 industrial associations, and 50 regional employers' associations. Officially, the mission of the Nippon Keidanren, its shortened name, is "to accelerate growth of Japan's and world **economy** and to strengthen the corporations to create additional value to transform Japanese economy."

The Japan Business Federation is located in the Ōtemachi section of **Tōkyō**. Canon's Mitarai Fujio (1935–) became chairman in 2005 and served until May 2010 when Yonekura Hiromasa (1937–), the chairman of Sumitomo Chemical Company, replaced him. Powerful leaders of 15 major corporations serve as vice chairmen of Nippon Keidanren. The organization has strong political ties to the **Liberal Democratic Party**.

In its 2007 vision statement, the Japan Business Federation enthusiastically called Japan "the land of hope" and pointed to its small but positive growth rates, predicting a 2 percent increase over the next decade. Admitting Japan's difficult times, it promised to pursue technological innovation vigorously, to reform Japan's economy, to counteract global warming, and to improve Japan's **labor**-management relations.

As of April 2017, the Japan Business Federation has 1,601 members, representing 1,350 companies, along with 109 industrial associations and 47 regional economic organizations. Sakakibara Sadayuki serves as chairman of the Japan Business Federation.

Keidanren's statement of purpose says, "Our mission as a comprehensive economic organization is to draw upon the vitality of corporations, individuals and local communities to support corporate activities which contribute to the self-sustaining development of the Japanese economy and improvement in the quality of life for the Japanese people."

JAPAN CHAMBER OF COMMERCE AND INDUSTRY (NIHON SHŌKŌ KAIGISHO, 日本商工会議所). Nisshō is a short form for Nihon Shōkō Kaigisho, or the Japan Chamber of Commerce and Industry (JCCI). It is devoted to encouraging **trade** both domestically and internationally. First formed in **Tōkyō** in 1878, JCCI has spread to nearly all major cities, with more than 500 chapters and a membership of 1.25 million people. Large companies dominate the Japan Chamber of Commerce. The chamber, whose chairman is Mimura Akio (1940–), and its members provide economic leadership in Japan. *See also* BUSINESS; ECONOMY.

JAPAN CONFEDERATION OF LABOR (ZEN NIHON RŌDŌ SŌDŌMEI KAIGI, 全日本労働総同盟会議). The Japan Confederation of Labor, or Dōmei, was formed in 1964 by a merger of three politically moderate federations that opposed the leftist stance of the larger and more militant **General Council of Japanese Trade Unions** (Sōhyō). Unlike the majority of Sōhyō members, who were public employees, most Dōmei members worked for private-sector firms. Dōmei was a supporter of the more moderate **Democratic Socialist Party** while Sōhyō members generally supported the **Japan Socialist Party**.

By 1967, Dōmei, with its private enterprise membership of 2.2 million members, would be larger than Sōhyō. Dōmei, with its emphasis on economic opportunities, began to challenge the strength of Sōhyō for the leadership of the labor movement. In the second half of the 1970s, Dōmei would grow to supplant Sōhyō in the leadership of the labor movement.

In 1987, with the Dōmei philosophy dominant, a new private-sector national labor union federation called the **Japanese Trade Union Confederation** (Rengō) was founded, and in 1989, Rengō expanded to embrace most of Sōhyō's public-sector unions, basically replacing Dōmei.

JAPAN CONGRESS AGAINST ATOMIC AND HYDROGEN BOMBS (GENSUIKIN, 原水禁). One of Japan's leading antinuclear and pro-peace organizations, the Japan Congress against Atomic and Hydrogen Bombs was established in 1965 when it split from the **Japan Council against Atomic and Hydrogen Bombs** (Gensuikyō). Gensuikin opposes all nuclear tests and all nuclear weapons throughout the world. It has chapters in all 47 prefectures and enjoys support from 32 nationwide **labor** unions and youth groups.

Gensuikin works to foster solidarity with antinuclear groups around the world, to support antinuclear, pro-peace campaigns, encourage various initiatives toward a nuclear-free world, and help victims of the atomic bombs. It sponsors two major annual events, the "3-1 Bikini Day" to commemorate the disaster of fallout from nuclear testing at Bikini and, in August, the World Congress against Atomic and Hydrogen Bombs in **Hiroshima** and Nagasaki.

Japan's antinuclear movement split over the issue of whether or not to support the possession of nuclear weapons by socialist countries. Gensuikin left the central movement in 1965 when it opposed nuclear weapons in all countries. *See also* COUNCIL FOR PEACE AND AGAINST NUCLEAR WEAPONS (KAKKIN KAIGI, 核禁会議); THREE NONNUCLEAR PRINCIPLES.

JAPAN CONGRESS OF INDUSTRIAL UNIONS (SANBETSU, 産別). In August 1946, **labor** groups established the Japan Congress of Industrial Unions with strong communist backing. Its membership exceeded 1.5 million members. That October, the Congress organized strikes in mining, the electrical industry, and the media sector. Some members of the Congress split because of their opposition to the close association with the **Japanese Communist Party** (JCP) and the **Japan Socialist Party**. Sanbetsu led a number of major strikes in the late 1940s, but it had entered into a period of serious decline. Its membership dropped from 1.68 million members to 0.76 million by late 1949. In 1948, some members of the Sanbetsu split from the JCP and formed the Democratization League (Mindō), where they emphasized labor issues rather than political matters.

JAPAN COUNCIL AGAINST ATOMIC AND HYDROGEN BOMBS (GENSUIKYŌ, 原水協). The Japan Council against Atomic and Hydrogen Bombs was established in 1955. Its roots stem from protests against the **United States'** testing of a hydrogen bomb in the Bikini atoll that year. The original objectives of Gensuikyō were to prevent nuclear war, ban and eliminate nuclear weapons, and support the victims of the atomic bombings. It continues to hold the same objectives today. It has members throughout Japan and has support from **labor** union members, **women** activists, student groups, and various international organizations.

Gensuikyō played a leading role in the passage of the Atomic Bomb Victims' Medical Care Law in 1957. It also played a dynamic role in the struggle against *Anpo*. Today it is a federation of 60 national organizations composed mainly of labor, women, youth, and health care workers' groups. Its total membership numbers around 2.5 million people.

Gensuikyō, calling for a "world without nuclear weapons," demands that the Japanese government stop its war cooperation and subordination to the U.S. military policy. Originally the **Liberal Democratic Party** (LDP) supported this group even though it had a strong leftist base, but in 1961, the LDP moved away and came to support a more centrist group. However, it is fitting that the world's only country to experience an atomic bomb would remain a strong leader in the world's antinuclear movement. *See also* COUNCIL FOR PEACE AND AGAINST NUCLEAR WEAPONS (KAKKIN KAIGI, 核禁会議); JAPAN CONGRESS AGAINST ATOMIC AND HYDROGEN BOMBS (GENSUIKIN, 原水禁); THREE NONNUCLEAR PRINCIPLES.

JAPAN EXTERNAL TRADE ORGANIZATION (NIHON BŌEKI SHINKŌKIKO, 日本貿易振興機構). The **Ministry of International Trade and Industry** started the Japan External Trade Organization, commonly known as JETRO, in 1958 to promote Japan's exports and secure international **trade** information to advance Japanese **businesses**. By the 1970s, JETRO and other efforts had become so successful that Japan's balance of trade shifted from a deficit to a surplus. JETRO not only sought to encourage Japan's trade but also now worked to improve Japan's trade relations with other countries. (Refer to appendix H.)

Today, JETRO gathers trade information, conducts market research and planning, and distributes trade information. It promotes direct foreign investment into Japan, facilitates economic growth in developing countries through trade promotion, assists small and medium-sized enterprises, researches developing economies, and supplies Japan with foreign economic information. In 2013, JETRO employed more than 1,500 people in its 37 domestic and 73 international offices in 55 countries. Headquartered in **Tōkyō** under its chairman Ishige Hiroyuki, JETRO's 21st-century focus is on promoting foreign direct investment into Japan and helping small and medium-sized businesses maximize their global impact. *See also* ECONOMY; FOREIGN POLICY.

JAPAN FEDERATION OF ECONOMIC ORGANIZATIONS (NIHON KEIZAI DANTAI RENGŌKAI, 日本経済団体連合会). The Japan Federation of Economic Organizations, better known by its Japanese name, Keidanren, was Japan's most important **business** organization in the second half of the 20th century. Although formed in 1946, Keidanren was descended from the prewar Japan Industrial Club and was composed of Japan's leading business figures who worked together with politicians to promote Japan's economic growth and development. More than 700 businesses and 100 manufacturers' associations participated in the organization, which had a great deal of political clout.

Key roles in Keidanren have been filled by business leaders like **Ishikawa Ichirō**, the first president of Keidanren; **Ishizaka Taizō**, president of Tōkyō Shibaura Electric and the second president of Keidanren who led the organization for a dozen years during the time of Japan's high economic growth; **Uemura Kōgorō**, Keidanren's president for six years in the early 1970s, who strengthened the economic organization's staff and established a collective management system; and his successor, **Dokō Toshio**, "Japan's business prime minister."

In 2002, Keidanren and the **Japan Federation of Employers' Association** (Nikkeiren) amalgamated into the **Japan Business Federation** (Nippon Keidanren) to become the most powerful business organization in 21st-century Japan.

JAPAN FEDERATION OF EMPLOYERS' ASSOCIATION (NIHON KEIEISHA DANTAI RENMEI, 日本経営者団体連盟). The Japan Federation of Employers' Association, an important **business** organization, was founded in 1948 to coordinate capital and **labor** and thereby ensure good relations and maximum productivity. The federation, known by the Japanese name Nikkeiren, was a national management federation that coordinated business efforts to counteract union gains in the early postwar period. It was concerned largely with labor-management relations and overseeing the annual "spring struggle" known as *shuntō*.

Sakurada Takeshi (1904–1985) helped create Nikkeiren and served as its executive director and permanent executive secretary, leading the federation in many conflicts with labor unions. Sakurada served as chairman of the federation from 1974 to 1979. A leader in the business-industrial community, he advocated for large-business concerns during **Ikeda Hayato**'s premiership and exercised strong influence in later years.

Shikanai Nobutaka (1911–1990), and after him Nemoto Jirō (1928–2014), headed Nikkeiren during the period 1995 to 1999. In 1999, Nemoto stepped down and was replaced by Okuda Hiroshi (1932–), the former chairman of **Toyota**. In 2002, Nikkeiren joined with Keidanren to form the **Japan Business Federation**.

JAPAN FOUNDATION (KOKUSAI KŌRYŪ KIKIN, 国際交流基金). The Japanese government created the Japan Foundation in 1972. The Japan Foundation supports international **education** and exchange. It also tries to improve Japan's image in the international arena. Under the auspices of the **Ministry of Foreign Affairs**, the foundation emphasizes exchanges and knowledge acquisition in the humanities and social sciences. It has invited many foreign scholars, educators, **students**, artists, journalists, and researchers to work in Japan and assists Japanese to study in other countries. It is a vital supporter of international education and exchange. *See also* FOREIGN POLICY.

JAPAN NEW PARTY (NIHON SHINTŌ, 日本新党). Announcing his desire to overturn the **Liberal Democratic Party** (LDP) government, **Hosokawa Morihiro**, a former governor of Kumamoto Prefecture, broke with the LDP and formed the Japan New Party (JNP) in May 1992. The JNP ran about 50 candidates in urban and suburban districts and won 35 seats in the 1993 **election**. Hosokawa subsequently became **prime minister** of the first coalition government, a coalition of eight parties including nearly all but the LDP, and succeeded in getting a package of political reform bills passed. But he stepped down in April 1994 to take responsibility for throwing **Diet** deliberations into confusion due to questionable loans he had received from private corporations. The JNP continued to play a role in the coalition government that followed Hosokawa's resignation but withdrew into the opposition when the **cabinet** resigned in June 1994. The JNP disbanded in 1996. *See also* POLITICAL PARTIES.

JAPAN RENEWAL PARTY (SHINSEITŌ, 新生党). The Japan Renewal Party (JRP) provided the catalyst for the ending of the long, consecutive run of power by the **Liberal Democratic Party** (LDP). In 1993, **Hata Tsutomu**, a protégé of **Tanaka Kakuei**, led a liberal faction out of the LDP and formed the JRP in a struggle against **Obuchi Keizō**. **Ozawa Ichirō**, a powerful politician, was Hata's political ally but would eventually override him.

Under Hata's leadership, 44 LDP members, who claimed to seek political reform, broke with the party. In the House of Representatives **election** in 1993, the JRP won 55 seats, making it the third-largest party in the lower house. The JRP played a central role in the establishment of the coalition government, made up of six parties, under **Hosokawa Morihiro** that ended almost four decades of LDP rule, and Hata took office as deputy **prime minister** and minister of foreign affairs. When a new administration was later formed, Hata became prime minister in the spring of 1994 but served only two months. The secession of the **Social Democratic Party of Japan** from the ruling coalition deprived the Hata administration of a parliamentary majority.

In June 1994, faced with the adoption of a no-confidence motion submitted by the LDP in a plenary session of the **House of Representatives**, the **cabinet** resigned, and the JRP withdrew to the opposition. Soon after, the JRP merged with other small parties to become the **New Frontier Party**. *See also* POLITICAL PARTIES.

JAPAN SOCIALIST PARTY (NIHON SHAKAITŌ, 日本社会党). Having close links to prewar socialist parties, the Japan Socialist Party (JSP) was founded in 1945, the first **political party** to form after the war. The JSP became the largest party in the Japanese **Diet** in the 1947 **election** but soon split into right and left factions due to an internal conflict. A JSP-led coalition governed Japan between May 1947 and March 1948.

In the April 1947 election, the JSP won the largest number of votes, forcing the formation of a coalition government, which the socialist leader **Katayama Tetsu** headed. Katayama served barely seven months before the coalition government fell. While having only a tenuous hold on power, the JSP failed to offer meaningful solutions to Japan's problems. Too involved in ideological battles and internecine struggles, the JSP did not accomplish much. However, it did try to advance progressive issues. **Labor**, former tenant farmers, discontented young white-collar workers, and intellectuals found a common ground in the JSP. Moreover, the JSP was closely linked with the **General Council of Japanese Trade Unions** (Sōhyō) and later the **Japanese Trade Union Confederation** (Rengō). Until the 1990s, the JSP was Japan's largest opposition party.

The socialists in Japan experienced many divisions and difficulties. In December 1948, a small group of the JSP split off and formed the Labor-Farmer Party (Rōdō Nōmintō). This is symptomatic of the JSP and its ideological and personality conflicts.

The early 1950s saw the JSP reach its peak of power, but increasingly left-wing elements caused internal feuding that continued for 30 years.

In 1955, the socialist factions merged again to form the main opposition to the **Liberal Democratic Party** (LDP). However, a right-wing faction, led by **Nishio Suehiro**, broke away to form the **Democratic Socialist Party** in 1960. At its high point in 1958, the JSP garnered 32.9 percent of the popular vote but never went above the "one-third barrier."

In 1970, the JSP changed its Japanese name to Minshatō but kept its English name the same. In May 1977, the Socialist Citizens' League (Shakai Shimin Rengō) group split off from the JSP. A year later it changed its name to the United Social Democratic Party (Shakai Minshu Rengō).

In the 1980s, support for the JSP declined. In the **House of Representatives** election of 1976, the JSP won 21 percent of the vote, but 10 years later the party's support had dwindled to only 17 percent. JSP support for the **student movements** and **environmental** issues in the mid-1960s moved the JSP further from the mainstream of Japanese public opinion. The JSP often followed rather dogmatic domestic and **foreign policies** and were frequently out of touch with the majority of the people, thus preventing the JSP from gaining popular support.

Under the leadership of **Doi Takako**, the charismatic speaker of the House of Representatives, the JSP had some short-lived success in the late 1980s and early 1990s. She was the first **woman** in Japanese history to hold the post of chair of a major political party and later became the first woman to be chosen speaker of the House of Representatives. The JSP began to shift its policies to more readily gain popular acceptance. However, the JSP's move toward moderation appeared to be too little, too late. The JSP, as well as other opposition parties, thus continued to decline. Even the decline in popularity of the LDP did not translate into any growth for the JSP. In fact, it was just the opposite.

In the **House of Councillors** election of July 1989, the JSP took 46 seats, 10 more than the LDP, giving the party a total of 66 upper house seats. In the February 1990 lower house election, the party gained 53 seats for a total of 136. However, in the 1992 upper house election, the JSP won only 22 seats, just enough to maintain the status quo, giving the party 71 seats in total. And in the July 1993 lower house election, the JSP had only 70 winning candidates, halving the number of seats it had held before the election.

In its party convention in 1986, the JSP abandoned the platform adopted in 1955, which was strongly influenced by Marxism-Leninism. In its new declaration, the party called for a policy line like that of the social democratic parties of Western Europe. There was still disagreement within the party over the issues of the **United States–Japan Security Treaty** and **nuclear power**, but the JSP maintained its official foreign policy stance of unarmed neutrality.

In the 19 elections from 1946 through 1993, the JSP averaged 117 seats per election with a high of 166 seats (33 percent of the vote) in 1958 and a low of 48 seats in 1949 during a split in the party. Its strongest showings were in the 1947 election when it garnered 143 seats, and in the four elections from 1958 through 1967 when it averaged 149 seats per election. From 1960 through 1993, the DSP drained off approximately 22 percent of the socialist vote from the JSP. From 1996 through the election of 2005, the JSP has averaged only 12 seats per election, with even fewer seats in the last two elections.

Several outstanding socialist leaders have contributed to the JSP. Suzuki Mosaburō helped form the JSP, serving as secretary-general from 1948 and as its chairman from 1951. After 1960, Suzuki acted as an adviser to the JSP. Eda Saburō served as secretary-general of the party several times and attempted to institute his controversial program that called for worker participation in the existing capitalist system as a way of realizing the socialist revolution. His son, Eda Satsuki, became chairman of the Socialist Citizens' League and, in 1978, worked with progressive Diet members to form the Social Democratic Party (SDP), which existed until 1994. The SDP, under the leadership of Den Hideo and Eda, elected an average of three lower house representatives during its time of existence.

Den Hideo participated in the founding of the SDP, along with Eda Satsuki, and was one of the party's key leaders. Ishibashi Masashi opposed a close alliance with the **United States** and felt shame that **Kishi Nobusuke**, a one-time war criminal, was in charge of treaty revision. However, as JSP chair, he would soften the stance against Japan's military ties with the United States. **Asukata Ichio** served as chairman of the JSP and sought to unite its various factions.

In 1994, the JSP changed its name to the **Social Democratic Party of Japan** (Nihon Shamintō, SDPJ) and joined in a coalition government headed by **Murayama Tomiichi**. However, the influence of the JSP continued to wane as the party's policies did not mesh with the people's primary goals. *See also* JAPAN CONGRESS AGAINST ATOMIC AND HYDROGEN BOMBS (GENSUIKIN, 原水禁).

JAPAN TEACHERS' UNION (NIHON KYŌSHOKUIN KUMIAI, 日本教職員組合). The Japan Teachers' Union, known as Nikkyōso, is a militant **labor** organization founded in 1947. Left-wing politicians strongly influenced this union. It sought to prevent students from falling prey to the aggressive, imperialistic **education** that they had received in the prewar period. Some of these students would go on to be supporters of the National Student Federation (Zengakuren).

The Japan Teachers' Union enabled teachers to make their voices heard in the educational world. Many of Nikkyōso's 300,000 members supported the policies of the **Japan Socialist Party** or even the **Japanese Communist Party**. The leftist tendencies of the Japan Teachers' Union were offset by the rightist attitudes and actions of some groups. Frequently, the police would have to provide union members with police protection to avoid physical disruption of their meetings by heavy-handed intimidation.

In the early postwar period, the unity of teachers was countered by skillfully responding to the dissatisfaction of high school teachers toward wages. Some high school teachers' unions, which had drifted away from Nikkyōso, formed the All-Japan High School Teachers' Union. This union, together with some independent high school teachers' unions, organized the Japan High School Teachers' Union (Nikkōkyō) in 1956. The mutual distrust between Nikkyōso and Nikkōkyō was resolved, and a basic agreement was proposed for their future unification in 1959. Ultimately, Nikkōkyō would not adopt the policy on unification because of resistance from within the union, and the effort at unification failed.

The Japan Teachers' Union was quite powerful in the early postwar period with about 86 percent of all teachers belonging to it in 1958. By 1987, membership had dropped to about 60 percent of all teachers. In the 21st century, only about one-third of teachers belong to this union.

The All-Japan Council of Teachers and Staff Union (former Zenkyō) was formed in November 1989, uniting all those teachers' unions at the prefectural level, which resolved to defend the progressive tradition of the teachers' union movement in Japan. In April 1991, a larger national teachers' union, the All-Japan Teachers and Staff Union, was inaugurated by the unification of the former Zenkyō and the Japan Senior High School Teachers and Staff Union (Nikkōkyō), both of which were under the banner of a militant trade union center, the **National Confederation of Trade Unions** (Zenrōren). *See also* STUDENT MOVEMENTS.

JAPAN TIMES. The *Japan Times* is the oldest and largest English-language **newspaper** in Japan. It is a subsidiary of Nifco, a plastics design and manufacturing company. Its headquarters is in Minato-ku, **Tōkyō**. Zumoto Motosada launched the *Japan Times* in 1897 in order to provide a source of information about Japan in English. Although influenced by the government during the war, it has been a relatively independent source of news.

Although known as the *Japan Times* at the beginning and now, it has gone by other names such as the *Japan Times and Mail* (1918–1940), the *Japan Times and Advertiser* (1940–1943), and *Nippon Times* (1943–1956). Ogasawara Toshiaki served as chairman and publisher of the *Japan Times* until his death in 2016. Tsutsumi Takeharu is now president of the newspaper.

The *Japan Times* newspaper publishes three editions, a daily broadsheet, an English-language weekly, and a weekly tabloid geared to learning English. It covers domestic and world news, editorials and opinion pieces, sports, entertainment, and feature articles. As of 2013, it has a working arrangement with the *New York Times*.

JAPAN TOBACCO COMPANY (NIHON TABAKO SANGYŌ KABU-SHIKI-GAISHA, 日本たばこ産業株式会社). Japan Tobacco Company (JT) was created in 1985 by the privatization of the Japan Tobacco and Salt Public Corporation, which until 1984 had been a state monopoly on the production and sale of tobacco. JT occupies about 80 percent of the tobacco market in Japan and sells more than 90 brands of cigarettes, including the popular Mild Seven and Caster brands. Koizumi Mitsuomi serves as president and Kimura Hiroshi as CEO of JT. The Japanese people remain heavy smokers, consuming nearly twice as many cigarettes per person as Americans.

JAPAN TRAVEL BUREAU (NIHON KŌTSŪ KŌSHA, 日本交通公社). Founded in 1912 as the Japan Tourist Bureau to attract foreign tourists and incorporated as a nonprofit organization in 1945, JTB became a private corporation in 1963. JTB is the largest travel agency in Japan. Headquartered in **Tōkyō**, it is also involved in resort development. The Japan National Tourism Organization also provides travel information to foreigners traveling in Japan or abroad. (Refer to appendix T.) *See also* TOURISM.

JAPAN WOMEN'S NATIONAL FOOTBALL TEAM (NADESHIKO JAPAN, なでしこジャパン). The Japan Women's National Football Team is one of the best in the world. It won the World Cup in 2011, the first ever for an Asian team, and finished second in the 2015 competition. It also won the silver medal in the 2012 Summer **Olympics**. The term *Nadeshiko* roughly translates into "ideal Japanese woman." Naturally, what Americans know as *soccer*, the rest of the world calls *football*.

Women's football began in the 1970s in Japan, and by the 1980s, Japan had a national team. In 1989, the Japan Women's Football League, abbreviated "L.League," came into being. The team qualified for the 1991 FIFA Women's World Cup in **China**. Nadeshiko has a large following in Japan, is financially stable, enjoys company sponsorships, and has its leading players recognized as celebrities.

Sawa Homare, playing from 1993 through 2015, is recognized as Japan's best player with 205 caps and 83 goals. Other leading players include Miyama Aya, Ohno Shinobu, and Ōgimi Yūki. Women's football has been a means of helping to achieve gender equality in Japan.

JAPANESE COMMUNIST PARTY (NIHON KYŌSANTŌ, 日本共産 党). The Japanese Communist Party (JCP) came into being in 1922, making it the oldest existing **political party** in Japan. The JCP sought to make Japan a worker's nation, free of capitalism, opposed to militarism, and devoid of the **imperial system**. In the prewar and wartime periods, as might be expected, the JCP suffered serious repression.

However, **Occupation** officials released imprisoned JCP leaders and made the party legal. Since then the JCP has proclaimed a Marxist program seeking the support of workers and the urban poor. From the late 1940s, the JCP has had close ties with the **student movement**. It has fiercely maintained its independence and ideological integrity. The party reemerged in the postwar period to be a consistent political force registering 5–10 percent of the votes in elections and an average of 15–20 seats in the **Diet**.

During most of the postwar period, the JCP sought to terminate the **United States–Japan Security Treaty**, make Japan a nonaligned country, create an economically democratic system, oppose nuclear weapons and military blocs, and lead a peaceful existence. The JCP, a moderate communist party today, is not against **religion** and does not strive to eliminate the **emperor**. It supports multiparty democracy and does not advocate the imposition of radical change on Japanese society.

The JCP enjoyed some successes in the immediate postwar period, but the Red Purge drove JCP members to acts of terrorism, which undercut its public support. Under the leadership of **Nosaka Sanzō** and **Miyamoto Kenji**, the JCP moderated its policies and began to regain popular support. Stressing a peaceful transition to communism, the JCP has adopted an independent and nationalist position. In **foreign policy**, it calls for the return of the Russian-held Northern Territories but has eased its earlier opposition to the existence of the **Self-Defense Forces** and the military alliance with the **United States**.

In the postwar period, the JCP had close association with a number of **labor** organizations. Fear of the power of labor and leftist parties prompted the Occupation leaders to undercut their power. The anticommunist sentiment that accompanied the Korean War and terrorist acts by some JCP members reduced its popularity. Support for the JCP came from union members, farmers with ties to the prewar tenant movement, discontented young white-collar workers, and intellectuals.

With the exception of the 1952 election, the JCP has elected members of the **House of Representatives** in every postwar **election**. In the 11 elections from 1946 through 1969, it elected an average of seven people to the lower house, but from 1972 through 2000, the number of successful JCP candidates rose to 25 people per election.

By the 1960s, the JCP had regained some support by breaking with the communist parties of the **Soviet Union** and **China**. The 1970s was the strongest period for the JCP. In 1976, the JCP won 10 percent of the vote in the House of Representatives election. In 1979, the JCP won 39 seats, its most seats. After this, the JCP reestablished ties with the Chinese and Soviet communist parties.

In the 1980s, the JCP advocated a neutral foreign policy, severing military ties with the United States, and improvement in social conditions for the people of Japan. In the 1986 election, the JCP vote declined to 6 percent. In the 1990 election, the JCP lost 11 of its 27 seats in the House of Representatives. In the 1996 election for the House of Representatives, the JCP increased its position to 26 seats.

Leadership of the postwar JCP came from various figures, many with prewar experience. Nosaka Sanzō worked to reconcile differences in philosophy and approach within the JCP, bridging disputes between the moderates and the extremists. Many other individuals played a major role in the JCP. **Senaga Kamejirō**, who was deeply involved in **Okinawan** social and reversion movements, served as vice chairman of the JCP. **Shiga Yoshio**, imprisoned for 18 years for his communist beliefs, and Tokuda Kyūichi, who also spent 18 years in prison, helped reorganize the postwar JCP. Miyamoto Kenji, since 1958 a central figure in the JCP, was a member of the **House of Councillors** and former chairman of the JCP's central committee. Finally, Fuwa Tetsuzō was chief secretary of the JCP until he retired in 2006.

In May 2006, the JCP chose Shii Kazuo (1954–) as its president and executive committee chair, and Ichida Tadayoshi as its secretary-general. The JCP held its 24th Congress in January 2006 and published its goals as resolutions in the 15 January 2006 issue of *Akahata* (*Red Flag*), the JCP **newspaper** and its chief source of income.

The JCP has not suffered much of a decline due to the fall of the Soviet Union. However, its overall electoral strength is declining. The JCP polled 11.3 percent of the vote (20 seats) in the 2000 House of Representatives election, 8.2 percent in 2003, 7.3 percent in 2005, and around an equal percentage in 2009.

The JCP, with approximately 305,000 members, remains one of the largest nongoverning communist parties in the world. It champions a society based on socialism, democracy, peace, and opposition to militarism.

As of the 22 October 2017 election, the JCP holds 12 seats in the House of Representatives, and with the 10 July 2016 House of Councillors election, it maintains 14 seats, making it a small, but staunchly consistent political party. Shii Kazuo remains the president of the JCP and Koike Akira its secretary-general.

JAPANESE GRAND PRIX, 日本グランプリ. The Japanese Grand Prix is a Formula One World Championship race. It has been the venue for many title-deciding races, with 13 World Champions being crowned in this race.

Fuji Speedway hosted Grand Prix races in 1976 and 1977, but soon thereafter race authorities removed Japan from the calendar. The Grand Prix returned to Japan in 1987 at Suzuka, which had hosted the Grand Prix exclusively for 20 years and gained a reputation as one of the most challenging F1 circuits. In 1994 and 1995, Japan also hosted the Pacific Grand Prix at the TI Circuit, making Japan one of only seven countries to host more than one Grand Prix in the same season. In 2007, the Grand Prix moved back to the newly redesigned Fuji Speedway. After a second race at Fuji in 2008, the race returned to Suzuka in 2009, as part of an alternating agreement between the owners of Fuji Speedway and Suzuka Circuit. However, in July 2009, Toyota announced it would not host the race at Fuji Speedway in 2010 and beyond due to a downturn in the global economy, and so the Japanese Grand Prix was held at Suzuka instead. Suzuka has hosted the Japanese Grand Prix every year since 2009.

JAPANESE TRADE UNION CONFEDERATION (NIHON RŌDŌ KUMIAI SŌRENGŌKAI, 日本労働組合総連合会 OR RENGŌ, 連合). Rengō is an umbrella organization set up for **labor** in 1987 by a combination of the **Japan Confederation of Labor** (Dōmei), the **Federation of Independent Labor Unions** (Chūritsu Rōren), and the **National Federation of Industrial Organizations** (Shinsanbetsu). In 1989, Rengō expanded to embrace most of the **General Council of Japanese Trade Unions**' (Sōhyō) public-sector unions, bringing its membership to more than seven million, the largest national trade union in Japan that speaks for labor with a moderate voice. Rengō is the world's third-largest national labor federation. Its unions represent about 60 percent of the organized workers in Japan and all are company centered. However, Rengō does not have great influence in a country dominated by big **business**, bureaucracy, and establishment politicians.

As of 2012, Rengō continues to have 6.83 million members, 54 affiliate unions, and 47 local organizations. Usually, Rengō is affiliated with the **Democratic Party of Japan** but recently has supported some **Liberal Democratic Party** candidates in local elections.

JUDICIAL SYSTEM. Japan's judicial system is divided into four basic tiers. There are 438 summary courts scattered throughout Japan. These courts handle small claims civil cases or those involving less than about ¥1.4 million as well as minor criminal offenses. At the second level, there is one district court for each of the 47 prefectures, and these have jurisdiction over felony cases and civil cases involving more than ¥1.4 million. At the next level, there are eight high courts serving the areas around the eight major cities of Japan. At the top of the judicial system is the Supreme Court located in **Tōkyō** near the **Diet** Building.

Although law plays a central role in the Japanese system, there are relatively few lawyers in the country. As of 2009, Japan had only 23,119 lawyers, or about 2 percent the number found in the **United States**. The Japanese generally try to solve issues outside the court system. The government closely oversees the legal system and strictly limits the number of lawyers. In 2009, Japan implemented a quasi-jury system.

JŪDŌ, 柔道. Jūdō originated in Japan in the late 19th century. Therefore, Japan became a world leader in jūdō, with several outstanding competitors. Among the leaders of Japan's jūdō participants was Fujii Shōzō (1950–), who won four World Jūdō Championships. Competing in 1971, 1973, 1975, and 1979, Fujii came home with gold medals each time, three at the 80-kilogram division and one at the 78-kilogram division. He competed for Tenri University and now serves as its head coach as well as Japan's national coach. Hikage Nobutoshi (1956–), a powerful jūdō wrestler, won the World Championships in 1983 and again in 1985. Another of Japan's greatest *jūdōka* was **Yamashita Yasuhiro** (1957–) who competed in three World Championships, taking home the gold in 1979, 1981, and 1983. Yamashita, the men's open-weight category gold medalist at the 1984 **Olympics**, is now the chairman of the All Japan Jūdō Federation. He replaced Muneoka Shōji (1956–) and will lead the federation into the 2020 Tōkyō Olympics.

In Japan's Jūdō Championships, Yamashita won the most titles with nine titles, and Ogawa Naoya won seven titles. For the women, Tsukada Maki won nine titles and Tanabe Yōko six titles. Recent winners include Katō Hirotaka (2012), Anai Takamasa (2013), Harasawa Hisayoshi (2015), and Ojitani Takeshi (2014 and 2016). Female winners include Tsukada Maki (2006 and 2010), Yamabe Kanae (2012, 2014, and 2016), and Asahina Sara (2017).

Minatoya Hiroshi (1943–2016) participated in four consecutive World Jūdō Championships, taking a silver in 1965 in the 68-kilogram division, a gold in 1967 in the 70-kilogram division, another gold in 1969 in the 78-kilogram division, and a silver, fighting again at 70 kilograms in the 1971 competition. Okano Isao (1944–) is perhaps the most versatile jūdō competitor ever in Japan. He could use both his right and left hands equally well and was a master technician. He became Japan's head coach, and under his leadership, Japan won all six weight categories in the 1973 World Championships. Known as "the little giant" because of his small stature, Hosokawa Shinji (1960–) won the Olympic gold medal in 1984, and in 1985, he won the World Championship. He showed great fighting spirit and ferociousness. He retired from active jūdō competition in 1988 and is now the national lightweight coach.

Yamaguchi Kaori (1964–) is one of only two Japanese women to medal in four World Jūdō Championships. In the 52-kilogram division, she won the silver medal in 1980 and again in 1982, a gold in 1984, and silver again in 1986. Yamaguchi won 10 national women's jūdō championships. She was the first Japanese woman to win a world championship. She is the coach of the Japanese national team. **Tamura Ryōko** (1975–) also participated in four Olympic Games and is one of Japan's greatest female *jūdōka*. *See also* SPORTS.

K

KABUKI, 歌舞伎. Kabuki is a traditional Japanese **theater** form that flourished from the late 17th through the mid-19th centuries among the merchants and townspeople. Its plays focus on historical events, moral conflicts, and love relationships. Speaking parts are presented in a highly stylized version with musical accompaniment. The Kabuki stage has a number of interesting devices such as trapdoors, a footbridge or *hanamichi*, and a rotating set. Men play all the roles in the Kabuki theater. Kabuki is famous for its brightly colored costumes, its lively **music** and speaking parts, and its wild and furious dancing. Highly stimulating and vigorous, Kabuki, although not as popular as during the Tokugawa era, still attracts a large number of people today, but it does not depict contemporary life in Japan nor does it take into account the degree of Westernization in Japanese society. The best place to see Kabuki today is at the Kabukiza Theater in the Ginza district of **Tōkyō** or the popular Kabuki theaters in **Ōsaka** and **Kyōto**.

KAGAWA TOYOHIKO, 賀川豊彦 **(1888–1960).** Kagawa Toyohiko was a Christian evangelist who, after controversy concerning his prewar and wartime attitude toward the state, promoted Christianity both in Japan and around the world in an effort to improve the human condition. Kagawa was a Japanese pacifist, Christian reformer, and **labor** activist. *See also* RELIGION.

KAIFU TOSHIKI, 海部俊樹 **(1931–).** Kaifu Toshiki, a highly respected **Liberal Democratic Party** (LDP) politician, served as **prime minister** for more than two years during 1989–1991. Born in **Nagoya**, he graduated from Waseda University where he excelled at public speaking and showed strong interest in politics. He was arrested for a speech criticizing the **Occupation** regulations. Kaifu, in 1960 at age 29, was elected to the **Diet** for the first of 16 consecutive terms, or for 49 years, in the lower house. He had no real independent power base but was a member of the small **Kōmoto Toshio** faction, formerly the **Miki Takeo** faction. He served twice as education minister. In 1989, after the forced resignations of **Takeshita Noboru** over the **Recruit scandal** and **Uno Sōsuke** due to a personal scandal, Kaifu, although a relatively unknown LDP figure, was elected president of the LDP and thus prime minister. Kaifu was chosen in part because of his clean image. At 58, Kaifu became the second-youngest Japanese prime minister, after **Tanaka Kakuei**, the youngest at age 54. Although he had little executive experience, he led the LDP to victory in the **House of Representatives** February 1990 **election**.

In office, Kaifu tried to end the Cold War in Asia by pressuring the **Soviet Union** to return the northern islands. He worked to improve relations with **China** and **Korea**. When South Korean president Roh Tae-woo visited Japan in 1990, Kaifu offered a sincere apology for Japan's war actions. The following year he apologized to countries in Southeast Asia. He also had to deal with the Persian Gulf crisis where he persuaded his fellow Japanese leaders to support **United Nations** Security Forces through several financial contributions, imposing economic sanctions and halting economic cooperation with Iraq. However, he refused to send Japanese troops to participate in the military action.

On the home front, Kaifu tried to push political reforms through the Diet but, lacking a power base of his own, was not successful. He sought to curb the undue influence of money in politics, reduce the disparity between rural and urban political districts, and lower the total number of seats in the lower house. Partly due to the continuing repercussions of the Sagawa scandal, Kaifu's administration was not too effective. Having lost the support of the LDP, Kaifu resigned after a little over two years as prime minister and was replaced by **Miyazawa Kiichi**.

In 1994, Kaifu left the LDP to become head of the newly formed **New Frontier Party** but resigned the following year. Since then, Kaifu has served as honorary chairman of several civil organizations. In 2003, he rejoined the LDP and continued to serve in the Diet until 2009. In June 2008, Kaifu, in a press interview, argued that Japan would not succeed in getting a permanent seat in the United Nations Security Council until it achieves reconciliation with its neighbors. He continues to speak for international and **environmental** issues.

KAINŌ MICHITAKA, 戒能通孝 **(1908–1975).** Kainō Michitaka was a lawyer and a legal scholar. He was a prominent leader in the effort to modernize the Japanese court system after the war. Born in Nagano Prefecture, Kainō studied at Tōkyō Imperial University. After graduating in 1930, he stayed on as a research assistant in the law department, immersing himself in specialized studies of civil and sociological jurisprudence. Kainō, in his legal briefs, argued that people possess fundamental **constitutional** and civil rights. After becoming acquainted with modern Anglo-American litigation procedure, he roundly criticized Japan's traditional litigation methods and juridical procedures, making a significant contribution to the modernization and democratization of the Japanese **judicial system**. Kainō was a respected teacher and prolific scholar, and his constant emphasis on people's rights had considerable effect on the study and teaching of law.

KAN NAOTO, 菅直人 (1946–). On 8 June 2010, Kan Naoto was chosen as Japan's fifth **prime minister** in less than four years. Kan, son of a working-class family, was a popular leader. He and **Hatoyama Yukio** founded the **Democratic Party of Japan** (DPJ) in 1996. Born in Yamaguchi Prefecture, Kan graduated from the Tōkyō Institute of Technology. After graduation, he took part in various grassroots citizens' movements with **Ichikawa Fusae**. In 1980, he was elected to the **Diet** under the banner of the United Social Democratic Party (Shakai Minshu Rengō). In 1993, he founded the **New Party Sakigake** with Hatoyama and served as health and welfare minister in **Hashimoto Ryūtarō**'s coalition government with the **Liberal Democratic Party** (LDP).

Kan gained great popularity when, in late 1998, he personally and passionately apologized to the HIV victims and the families of those people who received tainted blood in their medical transfusions. Kan was reinstalled in January 1999 as leader of the DPJ when he defeated Matsuzawa Shigefumi at the DPJ convention. Deputy Secretary-General Hatoyama Yukio and Secretary-General **Hata Tsutomu** of the DPJ backed him.

During the campaign of 2003, the DPJ termed the **election** a choice between the ruling LDP bloc and the DPJ with Kan as the alternative candidate to Prime Minister **Koizumi Jun'ichirō**. The DPJ used his face as its campaign trademark against the LDP. However, in 2004, Kan was accused of accepting an unpaid annuity and forced to resign the leadership of the DPJ. By 2009, his reputation was rehabilitated enough that Kan was appointed to various government positions including minister of finance in the Hatoyama government.

Indecisive and facing seemingly insurmountable problems, the Hatoyama government lasted only nine months. Kan, more decisive and charismatic than Hatoyama, was chosen leader of the DPJ and then prime minister to replace Hatoyama. The Kan government faced significant problems over Japan's sluggish **economy**, **United States** bases in **Okinawa**, and the devastating 11 March 2011 **Great East Japan Earthquake** and tsunami.

The earthquake and resulting tsunami rocked Kan's prime ministership. He resigned on 2 September 2011, less than six months later. In the 16 December 2012 general election, Kan lost his **House of Representatives** election but was continued through the proportional representation system, a situation repeated in the 14 December 2014 election. **United Nations** secretary-general Ban Ki-moon appointed him to a high-level panel on post-2015 development. Kan, along with another former prime minister, Koizumi Jun'ichirō, continues to advocate a strong antinuclear stance. *See also* POLITICAL PARTIES.

KANEDA MASAICHI, 金田正一 (1933–). Kaneda Masaichi was a professional **baseball** pitcher and manager. Born in Aichi Prefecture of **Korean** parents, he left high school before graduating and joined the Kokutetsu Swallows baseball team as a pitcher in 1950. During his 20 years as a professional player, Kaneda set a world record of 4,490 strikeouts and a new Japanese record of more than 20 victories a year for 14 consecutive seasons (1951–1964). He leads all Japanese pitchers in complete games (365) and innings pitched (5,526). From 1964, he played with the **Yomiuri Giants** until his retirement in 1969, after pitching his 400th victory. He managed the **Lotte** Orions from 1972 to 1978. Kaneda's records leave no doubt as to who is Japan's all-time premier pitcher. His 20-season career ERA of 2.34 was the 10th best ever. Along with Yoneda Tetsuya, he appeared in more than 944 games, and his 82 shutouts were only one behind the leader. *See also* SPORTS.

KANEHARA HITOMI, 金原ひとみ (1983–). Kanehara Hitomi is a young female author who has taken Japan by storm with the publication of her debut novel, *Hebi ni piasu* (*Snakes and Earrings*). Kanehara won the Akutagawa Prize at age 21, one of the youngest to win the award. This novel is the intensely private story of a young woman, Rui, who is obsessed with altering her body by getting a large tattoo and a snakelike tongue. Kanehara clicks with "freeters," those interested in unsentimental sex, and those profoundly unable to communicate verbally. Kanehara is a grammar-school dropout and writes with great explicitness in her novel, which shows the alienation of youth, much to the bewilderment of older Japanese. *See also* LITERATURE; WATAYA RISA, 綿矢りさ (1984–); WOMEN.

KANEMARU SHIN, 金丸信 (1914–1996). Kanemaru Shin was vice president of the **Liberal Democratic Party** (LDP) and a powerful political boss. He graduated from Tōkyō University of Agriculture in 1937. After working at other jobs, in 1948 he founded Nitto Kōgyō Corporation, an electronics technology company, and served as its president.

Kanemaru turned to politics and became a member of the **House of Representatives**. He served as construction minister in **Tanaka Kakuei**'s second **cabinet**, director of the National Land Agency under the **Miki Takeo** government, and director of the Defense Agency during the **Fukuda Takeo** administration. He became chairman of the **Takeshita Noboru** faction, the LDP's largest, and was a very powerful political figure, leading people to call him the "LDP's king-maker." However, in 1990, Kanemaru was caught in the Sagawa scandal, a case of corrupt backroom-style Japanese politics, when faced with accusations that he had accepted $4 million in political bribes. When investigators raided his home and office, they found hundreds of pounds of gold bars and around $50 million in cash and securities. Thus, before the 1990 general **election**, Kanemaru was forced to resign and face the humiliation of arrest and conviction. The fact that Kanemaru and the LDP amassed a fortune from illicit political donations set off a wave of public revulsion that continues to cloud the LDP into the 21st century.

KARAOKE, カラオケ. Karaoke is a form of entertainment where amateur performers sing along with recorded **music** using a microphone. Singing well-known songs, the "performers" try to synchronize with the music.

The etymology of the word comes from *kara* meaning empty and *oke* as the beginning sound of orchestra. Karaoke began in the early 1970s when the popular singer Inoue Daisuke recorded some of his favorite songs in a form that people could sing along with. Enterprising marketers created machines that ran on ¥100 coins, and the fad of "live music" was created. Special music rooms or karaoke boxes sprung up around Japan and became quite popular. Technological advances with CDs, VCRs, laserdiscs, and DVDs have given new opportunities to the karaoke international phenomenon. Starting in Japan and expanding into East Asia and then to other parts of the world, karaoke has become a major form of entertainment.

KASE TOSHIKAZU, 加瀬俊一 **(1903–2004).** A former ambassador to the **United Nations** (UN) and a pivotal diplomat during and after World War II, Kase Toshikazu was an important international figure who favored close ties with the **United States**. Educated at Amherst College and Harvard University, Kase passed the elite diplomat exam in 1925 while still a student at the Tōkyō College of Commerce (today's Hitotsubashi University) and entered the **Ministry of Foreign Affairs**. In August 1945, Kase drafted the English version of the document that said Japan would accept the terms of the Potsdam Declaration, ending the war. He was a member of the Japanese delegation accepting the surrender aboard the USS *Missouri*. He became Japan's first ambassador to the UN in 1955 and worked to gain Japan's entry the following year. Kase later served as ambassador to Yugoslavia and Bulgaria and finally as a professor at Kyōto University of Foreign Studies. *See also* FOREIGN POLICY.

KASUGA IKKŌ, 春日一幸 **(1910–1989).** Kasuga Ikkō was one of the founders and chairman of the **Democratic Socialist Party** (DSP). Born in Gifu Prefecture, Kasuga studied at a communications school and worked for the government in **Nagoya** before serving in the Aichi Prefectural Assembly. He was elected in 1952 to the **House of Representatives** as a **Japan Socialist Party** (JSP) candidate. Kasuga left the JSP in 1960 and helped form the DSP, becoming its secretary in 1967 and later its chairman from 1971 to 1977.

KATAYAMA TETSU, 片山哲 **(1887–1978).** Katayama Tetsu was a politician and socialist leader who served as **prime minister** from 24 May 1947 to 10 March 1948. Katayama was the only nonmember of the **Liberal Democratic Party** or its forerunners to be prime minister in the postwar period until 1993. A native of Wakayama Prefecture, he graduated in law from Tōkyō Imperial University in 1912. A Christian, he was a friend of Abe Isoo. From the 1920s, he acted as a legal adviser to **labor** organizations and socialist **political parties**. A leading social democrat, he helped form and became secretary of the **Japan Socialist Party** (JSP) in 1926 and was the source of its "anti-communism, anti-capitalism, anti-fascism" slogan. He was elected to the **Diet** for the first time in 1930. In 1932, the party became part of the new Social Mass Party (Shakai Taishūtō). He remained a Diet member until 1940 when his refusal to sanction the expulsion of Saitō Takao, a Diet member who had made an antiwar speech, led to his resignation.

After the war, Katayama became secretary-general of the JSP and its president in 1946. In May 1947, he headed a coalition **cabinet** with members of the Democratic Party and the Citizens' Cooperative Party (Kokumin Kyōdōtō). As a Christian, Katayama was welcomed by the Supreme Commander for the Allied Powers and with the command's backing passed laws to implement the new **constitution** as well as some aimed at economic and social democratization. However, he had insufficient strength to implement radical reform, and intra-party conflict over wage and price control measures forced him to resign in March 1948.

Katayama also lost his Diet seat in 1949 and, in 1950, declined reelection as JSP president although he remained a leading figure in the party's right wing through the 1950s. He devoted his efforts to the prevention of constitutional revision, opposed renewal of the **United States–Japan Security Treaty** in 1960, and advocated a "one **China**" policy. From 1960, he supported the new **Democratic Socialist Party** but severed his connection with it in 1965. In 1963, he failed to get elected and withdrew from the front line of politics.

KATŌ SAWAO, 加藤沢男 **(1946–).** Katō Sawao was an outstanding gymnast. Born in Niigata Prefecture, he graduated from Tōkyō University of Education. Katō took first place in the men's individual combined exercises (all-around) at the 1968 Mexico **Olympics** and then again won the gold medal at the 1972 Munich Olympics. In the 1976 Montreal Olympics, he won the gold medal in the parallel bars and led the Japanese team to its fifth consecutive team title. Katō was Japan's undisputed **gymnastics** king who, unlike other Japanese gymnasts, competed in three Olympics, taking home nine medals overall. *See also* SPORTS.

KATŌ SHIZUE, 加藤シヅエ (1897–2001). Katō Shizue was a prominent feminist and politician, known for her promotion of family planning. Born in **Tōkyō**, Katō graduated from the Joshi Gakushūin and then married Baron Ishimoto Keikichi. Following her husband to the **United States** in 1919, she met Margaret Sanger, the birth control advocate. On her return to Japan, she began to campaign for birth control and other **women**'s rights. When her husband left her, she supported herself and her two sons through writing and lecturing. Her work brought her in contact with **labor** leader Katō Kanjū whom she married in 1944. In the first postwar **election** in 1946, Katō Shizue and her husband were both elected to the **House of Representatives** as candidates of the **Japan Socialist Party**. She was elected to the **House of Councillors** in 1950, remaining a member until 1974. She led the Family Planning Federation of Japan from its founding in 1954.

KAWABATA YASUNARI, 川端康成 (1899–1972). Kawabata Yasunari won the **Nobel Prize** in **Literature** in 1968, the first Japanese ever to receive this prestigious honor. In 1994, **Ōe Kenzaburō** was the only other Japanese to win this award. Born in **Ōsaka**, the son of a talented physician, Kawabata was orphaned when he was very young and also lost his grandparents and a sister by age 15. Thus, many of his books frequently emphasize loneliness and overriding sadness, often treating death and dying. With melancholic lyricism, his works echo ancient Japanese values and attitudes. Many of his novels are formless and appear to meander aimlessly.

Kawabata graduated from Tōkyō Imperial University in 1924 and then dedicated his life to writing. With others, he helped start a new literary journal, *Bungei Jidai* (*Contemporary Literature*), which promoted new literary styles. Kawabata first gained widespread recognition with his short story "Izu no odoriko" ("The Izu Dancer," 1926).

Women were always an important part of Kawabata's stories, which focused on male-female relationships, conveyed great sensitivity to personal feelings, and showed aesthetics and eroticism. His most famous works include *Yukiguni* (*Snow Country*, 1947), which treats a lonely geisha isolated in the countryside; *Yama no oto* (*The Sound of the Mountain*, 1949) in which a young woman comforts her elderly father-in-law; *Sembazuru* (*A Thousand*

Cranes, 1952), which centers on the tea ceremony and human relations; and *Nemureru bijo* (*The House of the Sleeping Beauties*, 1961), which features an elderly man and a female artist.

People around the world still highly praise his works. He won many honors including the Japanese Academy Award. For nearly 20 years before his death, Kawabata was president of the Japanese PEN club. He helped introduce Japanese literature to Western readers. However, depressed over ill health, a possible love affair, and the death of his fellow writer **Mishima Yukio**, Kawabata apparently committed suicide at age 72 by gassing himself.

KAWAGUCHI YORIKO, 川口順子 **(1941–).** Kawaguchi Yoriko is a leading **Liberal Democratic Party** politician who served as **environment** minister (2001–2002) and foreign minister (2002–2004) in **Koizumi Jun'ichirō**'s **cabinet** and later was his adviser. A native of **Tōkyō**, she earned a BA in international relations at the **University of Tōkyō** and an MA in economics at Yale University. In 1965, she joined the **Ministry of International Trade and Industry**. She later served in the International Bank for Reconstruction and Development, in the Japanese embassy in the **United States**, and as managing director of Suntory. *See also* FOREIGN POLICY; WOMEN.

KAWAKUBO REI, 川久保玲 **(1942–).** Born in **Tōkyō**, Kawakubo Rei studied philosophy at Keiō University, but her first love was **fashion**. Kawakubo is one of the most influential people in **women**'s fashion not only in Japan but also in the world. She sells her clothes under the label "Comme des Garçons," a company she founded in 1973. She presented her first Paris show in 1981. Although having no formal design education, Kawakubo mesmerized the Parisian high-fashion world.

Kawakubo's clothes are unique and attract all ages. She uses color and fabric in a magical way to produce a spectacular line of clothing. She specializes in anti-fashion, austere, and sometimes disheveled garments. Her clothes are usually in black, dark gray, or white. Critics dubbed her early creations "Hiroshima chic" for their use of dark colors, disheveled looks, and unconventional qualities. In 1983 and again in 1988, she won the Mainichi Fashion Grand Prize and was honored again in 1987 by the Fashion Institute of Technology as one of the leading women in 20th-century design. Kawakubo is not only a top designer but also an exceptional **business** leader, as her company Comme des Garçons is quite profitable.

Mentioned in the same breath as Louis Vuitton and Prada, the reclusive Kawakubo continues to mesmerize the fashion world. Her avant-garde designs challenge conventional notions of fashion worldwide. The Metropolitan Museum of Art featured her designs in its 2017 presentation. This is only the second time that the museum has presented a solo show of a living designer, the other being Yves Saint Laurent. Fittingly, *Vogue* devoted a 2017 issue to Kawakubo Rei whose clothing line generates $220 million annually while she appears on the "most influential designer" lists.

KAWASAKI HEAVY INDUSTRIES (KAWASAKI JŪKŌGYŌ KABU-SHIKI-GAISHA, 川崎重工業株式会社**).** Kawasaki Heavy Industries (KHI), a prewar **zaibatsu**, concentrated on building ships and airplanes in the postwar period. Formed from a late 19th-century merger of industrial plants, KHI took its present name in 1939. Kawasaki, headquartered in **Kōbe**, manufactures ships, aircraft, industrial plants, and **motorcycles**. Its motorcycles are one of the top brands worldwide. It also makes Jet Ski, a world trademark. KHI has two shipyards (Kōbe and Sakaide), dating back 100 years, where the company applies its shipbuilding expertise to build and repair virtually all types of ships. KHI is also active in developing new ship designs that incorporate the latest shipbuilding **technology**, including large double-hull oil tankers.

Land, sea, or sky, KHI gets things moving. Its consumer products and machinery include motorcycles, personal watercraft, and all-terrain vehicles. Today, KHI manufactures rolling stock, **construction** machinery, electric and diesel locomotives, material handling equipment, and heavy engines. KHI's aerospace and gas turbine segments make jet engines, satellites, and structural parts for passenger aircraft. The company's other products include industrial **robots**, precision machinery, and submarines.

KDDI (KDDI KABUSHIKI-GAISHA, KDDI 株式会社**).** KDDI is Japan's second--largest telecommunications company and its chief long-distance service provider. It also operates a cellular phone system, personal hand-phone system, and internet faxing services. **Kyōcera** owns 13 percent of KDDI and **Toyota** 11 percent. It teamed with Motorola of the **United States** to develop Iridium, a worldwide cellular phone system. KDDI is the only Japanese information and communications company that comprehensively provides communications services, from fixed to mobile. It works aggressively to develop leading-edge fixed and mobile communications networks and services to support them.

Led by its president and CEO Tanaka Takashi, KDDI had revenues of $42.57 billion in 2015 and employed approximately 18,000 people. In the international arena, KDDI is working with Myanmar to improve the communications ability of that country. It also collaborates with the Taiwanese manufacturer HTC Corporation. In 2014, KDDI joined with five other global companies, including Google, to build an undersea data transmission cable link to the United States, a system that began operation in 2016. On the cutting edge, KDDI, **NTT DoCoMo**, and **SoftBank Group**, Japan's top three mobile carriers, are working to make 5G service a reality, action which would increase communication speeds 10 to 100 times.

KEIDANREN, 経団連. *See* JAPAN FEDERATION OF ECONOMIC ORGANIZATIONS (NIHON KEIZAI DANTAI RENGŌKAI, 日本経済団体連合会).

KEIRETSU, 系列. A *keiretsu* is a loose, informal grouping of affiliated companies, usually organized around a single bank, that work together to accomplish common economic objectives. The companies sometimes, but not always, own equity in each other. Major *keiretsu*, often referred to as the "Big Six," include **Mitsubishi**, **Mitsui**, **Dai-ichi Kangyō**, **Sumitomo**, **Sanwa**, and **Fuyo**. *Keiretsu* often specialize in areas such as electronics, mining, **petroleum**, **automobiles**, **steel**, heavy industry, and insurance. They are said to be horizontal types with interests extended to diverse fields and have ties with the **general trading companies** and banks. The "Big Six" have historically had a strong influence on Japan's **economy** and may control as much as 20 percent of Japan's **business**.

The *keiretsu* are often groupings with historic associations and cross-shareholdings, such that each maintains its operational independence but establishes permanent relations with other firms in its group. These groups emerged from the breakup of the **zaibatsu** or holding companies that dominated Japan's prewar economy. *Keiretsu* generally include firms in widely different sectors such as **banking**, insurance, **construction**, electronics, chemicals, and engineering.

Other types of *keiretsu* are referred to as vertical groups with an umbrella-type structure closely linked to a leading enterprise such as **Matsushita**, **Itōchū**, **Hitachi**, **Toshiba**, **Nippon Telegraph and Telephone** (NTT), **Toyota**, or **Tōkyō Electric Power**. Within the *keiretsu* in general, interlocking horizontal and vertical relationships, shareholding arrangements, personnel exchanges, common banking relationships, and executive networks, as well as many other common interests, bind the groups together. Banks and major trading companies are usually at the core of the *keiretsu*. On the periphery, less powerful firms owe a strong degree of loyalty to the main group.

While it is difficult to quantify the extent of control that members of *keiretsu* hold in Japan, it is obvious that financial, technological, transactional, and managerial ties among companies are important factors in Japan's economy. Changes in Japan's domestic markets as well as the international economy may be loosening the power of the *keiretsu*, but they still retain a powerful influence.

In 2015, Japan adopted a corporate governance code that required listed companies to disclose their cross-shareholdings. Due to this ruling, the six major *keiretsu* banks dissolved into three megabanks, the **Mitsubishi UFJ Financial Group**, **Sumitomo Mitsui Financial Group**, and **Mizuho Financial Group**. This code led to a reduction in cross-shareholding investments.

Overall, the *keiretsu* system has experienced a decline in its power over Japan's economic environment. Traditional standards have loosened with globalization, technological advances, and expanding international markets.

KIHARA NOBUTOSHI, 木原信敏 (1926–2011). Kihara Nobutoshi was known as "the wizard of Sony." An engineer at **Sony Corporation**, he is best known as the primary inventor of the Sony Walkman cassette-tape player. In the 1970s, his Walkman revolutionized the way that many people listened to **music**.

Born in **Tōkyō**, Kihara graduated from Waseda University and then joined the predecessor of Sony. He became a close friend of **Ibuka Masaru**, one of Sony's founders. He contributed to the development of magnetic tape recorders, stereo systems, the Betamax video system, Japan's first transistor radio, and many other projects. In 1988, Kihara became the president of the Sony-Kihara Research Center and oversaw the research activities of many of Sony's future products. He was very skillful at taking ideas and turning them into workable devices, ultimately having contributed to more than 700 patents. With engineering in his blood, Kihara was the genius behind many of the Sony creations.

KINUGASA SACHIO, 衣笠祥雄 (1947–2018). Japan's "iron man," Kinugasa Sachio was a **baseball** player with the Hiroshima Carp. Born in **Kyōto**, he graduated from Heian High School in 1965. In 1987, the third baseman played in his 2,131st consecutive game, breaking Lou Gehrig's record. Kinugasa never missed a game in 17 years. He went on to play in 2,215 consecutive games before retiring in 1987. He hit .270 lifetime, with 504 home runs, 2,543 hits, and 1,448 RBIs. With Kinugasa in the stands, Cal Ripken Jr. of the Baltimore Orioles broke his record in 1996.

KISENOSATO YUTAKA, 稀勢の里寛 (1986–). The first native-born person promoted to the rank of grand champion (*yokozuna*) in **sumō** since 1998, Kisenosato hails from a small town northeast of **Tōkyō**. This is exciting in a country where sumō is more popular than even **baseball**, **soccer**, and **golf**. After coming in second in 12 tournaments, Kisenosato finally won a championship in January 2017, allowing the sumō association to promote him. After winning the next tournament despite a shoulder injury, Kisenosato had to withdraw from the next three tournaments.

Kisenosato entered the top ranks of sumō at age 18, the second youngest after the great **Takanohana**. In November 2010, Kisenosato defeated **Hakuhō**, ending the sumō star's consecutive win streak at 63 victories, just short of the record 69 set by Futabayama in 1945. Being 30 years of age before gaining the highest rank in sumō makes Kisenosato part of a small group of late bloomers. In 2016, he gained the most wins in the calendar year without winning a tournament, the first wrestler to do this. More than 6 feet tall and weighing more than 380 pounds, Kisenosato is an imposing figure.

KISHI NOBUSUKE, 岸信介 (1896–1987). Kishi Nobusuke was a bureaucrat and politician who served as **prime minister** from 25 February 1957 until 19 July 1960. A native of Yamaguchi Prefecture and the biological brother of **Satō Eisaku**, Kishi graduated in 1920 from Tōkyō Imperial University where his political inclinations favored conservatism. He took the name Kishi when adopted into his uncle's family. He rose through the bureaucratic hierarchy at the Ministry of Commerce and Industry before becoming deputy head of the Manchukuo government's business section in 1936. The nominal head of the department was a Chinese, but Kishi was second only to Manchukuo's director of general affairs and played a major role in implementing a five-year plan for industrial development. He supervised Japan's economic activities in Manchuria in the 1930s. As commerce and industry minister in 1941–1943 and state and deputy munitions minister in 1943–1944, he provided economic guidance for the war.

Kishi was imprisoned for three years as a class A war criminal but was released in December 1948. His anticommunist stance and support for **constitutional** revision gradually increased his influence among conservatives, as well as his strong financial connections, meaning that he successfully achieved a base for a return to politics after being depurged in 1952. In 1953, he was elected to the **Diet** from the **Liberal Party**. He opposed **Yoshida Shigeru** within the party and subsequently promoted consolidation of the various conservative parties, becoming secretary-general of the new **Liberal Democratic Party**. He was defeated for the party presidency in 1956 but was briefly foreign minister under **Ishibashi Tanzan** before succeeding him as prime minister in February 1957.

In his capacity as prime minister, Kishi, with the strong backing of **business**, worked to promote domestic industry and Japanese commercial interests in Southeast Asia. He managed to get Japan a non-permanent seat on the **United Nations** Security Council. His strong conservative and anticommunist leanings were shown in such measures as the introduction of efficiency ratings for teachers and the proposed Police Duties Law, which aroused such opposition that it was abandoned. Kishi's efforts to forge closer links with the **United States** ended in his resignation in July 1960 after the crisis over the **United States–Japan Security Treaty**. Kishi remained in the **House of Representatives** as a staunch anticommunist and influential conservative linked with right-wing groups. *See also* FOREIGN POLICY.

KITAGAWA, JOHNNY, ジャニー喜多川 **(1931–).** "Johnny" Kitagawa is a maker or producer of male musical talent. "Johnny's Office" has cultivated some of the leading male talent in contemporary Japan. Johnny and Associates, the official English title for Johnny's Jimusho, is the undisputed leader when it comes to the creation and promotion of young Japanese male idol stars. Johnny's biggest successes over the years have been **SMAP**, Kinki Kids, Tokio, Hikaru Genji, Arashi, V6, and Johnny's Juniors. Johnny's Jimusho has been the top **music** talent agency in Japan for many years, annually making in excess of ¥3 billion. *See also* KOMURO TETSUYA, 小室哲哉 (1958–).

KITAJIMA KŌSUKE, 北島康介 **(1982–).** Kitajima Kōsuke has been one of Japan's greatest swimmers. **Swimming** in four **Olympics**, Kitajima competed in the Sydney Olympics in 2000, stormed to gold in the 100-meter and 200-meter breaststroke at the Athens Olympics in 2004, repeated this feat in the 2008 Beijing Games, and made a respectable showing in the 2012 London Games. Kitajima broke his own Japanese record by clocking 58.90 seconds in the 100 meter in **Tōkyō**. He then clung on to win the 200 meter, again edging out Tateishi Ryo. Kitajima's time of 2:08.00 eclipsed that of Hungarian Daniel Gyurta in winning gold at the 2015 World Championships in Shanghai.

Overall, Kitajima captured seven Olympic medals and 12 world championship titles. He set, lost, and regained the world record in both the 100-meter and 200-meter contests in his specialty, the breaststroke. A huge celebrity in Japan and a major figure in world swimming, Kitajima retired in April 2016.

KITANOUMI TOSHIMITSU, 北の湖敏満 **(1953–).** The famous **sumō** wrestler Kitanoumi Toshimitsu was born as Obata Toshimitsu in Usu County, Hokkaidō. He joined the Mihogaseki stable in 1967 at 13, the second-youngest age for an eventual *yokozuna* to begin training. He made his way up the sumō ranks slowly and arduously, honing his skills for seven years until he won his first title at the *Hatsu Basho* in 1974. Six months later, a second triumph in the summer tournament pushed him over the top, beginning a 10-year, six-month reign as a *yokozuna*. At 21 years and two months, Kitanoumi was the youngest *yokozuna* until **Takanohana**. An aggressive fighter, Kitanoumi took 24 *basho* over the next decade, third only to **Taihō**

Kōki and **Chiyonofuji Mitsugu** in the last half century. Kitanoumi's 804 victories are second only to Chiyonofuji's tally, and his .764 winning percentage surpasses all others but Taihō prior to the 21st century.

KITARŌ, 喜多郎 (1953–). Kitarō, whose real name is Takahashi Masanori, is famous for his New Age **music** with his lush electronic tone and meditative style. Kitarō, with his albums *Astral Voyage* (1978), *Silk Road* (1980), *Kojiki* (1990), and *Mandala* (1996), has attracted an international audience. By 1987, he had sold 10 million albums. Born to a farming family in Toyohashi, Aichi Prefecture, he started playing guitar in high school. He made the sound track for *The Silk Road*, a long-running **television** series.

KOBAYASHI YOSHINORI, 小林善範 (1953–). Kobayashi Yoshinori is a cartoonist famous for his creations Obocchamakun and Gōmanizumu Sengen. Even as a child in his hometown of Fukuoka, Kobayashi was very good at drawing cartoons, and his schoolmates showed great appreciation of his work. He drew funny cartoons like Obocchamakun and satirical **manga** like Gōmanizumu Sengen, both of which provided perceptive insights into current events. His cartoon about **Aum Shinrikyō** brought death threats. His cartoons show a social conscience, often attacking serious social problems such as AIDS.

On another side, Kobayashi has written a best-selling comic book titled *Sensōron (On War)*. In this book, Kobayashi complains that the criticisms of what the Japanese military did in World War II are cruel and unfair to his grandfather's generation. He contends that his grandfather and others like him were good men just doing their jobs. Kobayashi honors the lives of his grandfather's generation and supports the remilitarization of Japan. His far-right views suggest that the Nanjing Massacre did not occur, the kamikaze should be honored, Japan was not engaged in an imperialistic war, and the military did not force **women** into prostitution. He also upholds visits to **Yasukuni Shrine**.

KŌBE, 神戸. Kōbe, Japan's leading port city before the 1995 earthquake, is now the country's fourth-most-used port. Located in central Honshū in the heart of the Kansai region, Kōbe is hemmed in by the Rokkō Mountains to the north and the Inland Sea to the south, as it extends along an east-west axis. The capital of Hyōgo Prefecture, Kōbe, with 1.5 million people, is Japan's sixth-largest city.

One of Japan's first ports opened to Western **trade** in the 19th century, Kōbe has a strong Western influence and is one of Japan's most international cities. Cosmopolitan, Kōbe has a mosque, a synagogue, and Christian churches. Citizens from more than 100 countries make their home in Kōbe, giving the city a dynamic mix.

Kōbe has twice been destroyed in the 20th century, once by World War II bombings and again on 17 January 1995 by the **Kōbe Earthquake**. This was Japan's worst since the 1923 earthquake devastated **Tōkyō**. Kōbe has recovered remarkably, being almost completely rebuilt. In 2006, it opened a new airport on reclaimed land. It is less than three hours from Tōkyō on the Shinkansen's Nozomi. Sannomiya, at the center of the city, is the main shopping district, and Ikuta is Kōbe's liveliest entertainment district. The artificial Port Island, built on rubble removed after the earthquake, features a futuristic complex with a conference center, an exhibition hall, and several ultramodern hotels.

The **economy** of Kōbe is dominated by tertiary industries, with secondary industries making up only about one-third, and farming, fishing, and mining only a very small part. Kōbe is a leader in shipbuilding (Mitsubishi Heavy Industries), shipping, warehousing, aquaculture, **steel** production, **energy** development, and sake brewing. Its leading companies are ASICS, **Kawasaki Heavy Industries**, **Mitsubishi Motors**, and Kōbe Steel, and it hosts about 100 international companies including Procter & Gamble and Nestlé. It is a growing research center for developmental biology and medical imaging techniques, information technology, and disaster prevention. It also has made its mark on the **fashion** and furniture industries as well as hosting a thriving jazz festival. Its most famous **tourist** sites are Ikuta Shrine and the Kōbe Port Tower. And one should not forget to enjoy the delicious "Kōbe beef," which is made very tender by massage techniques and being fed heavy doses of beer.

KŌBE EARTHQUAKE (*KŌBE DAISHINSAI*, 神戸大震災). The Great Hanshin Earthquake or *Hanshin-Awaji-daishinsai*, or Kōbe Earthquake as it is more commonly known overseas, was an earthquake that measured 7.2 on the Richter scale. It occurred on 17 January 1995 at 5:46 a.m. in the southern part of Hyōgo Prefecture and lasted for approximately 20 seconds. The epicenter of the earthquake was on the northern end of Awaji Island, 12 miles from **Kōbe**. A total of 6,433 people, mainly in Kōbe, lost their lives. The earthquake caused approximately ¥10 trillion in damage. It was the worst earthquake in Japan since the Great Kantō Earthquake in 1923, which claimed 140,000 lives and was the "costliest natural disaster to befall any one country." The Japanese government was severely criticized for its delayed, inefficient handling of the 1995 earthquake issues. Unfortunately, the **Great East Japan Earthquake** of 2011 would far surpass the Kōbe Earthquake.

KODAMA YOSHIO, 児玉誉士夫 (1911–1984). A native of Fukushima, Kodama Yoshio was active in various right-wing and nationalist societies and was arrested several times for violent ultranationalist activities, including an abortive plot to kill Prime Minister Saitō Makoto. From 1937, he spent most of his time in **China** and Manchuria where he was attached in a semiofficial capacity to the Japanese army. He resigned over a disagreement with Prime Minister Tōjō Hideki but later returned to Shanghai as a navy procurement agent where he accumulated a vast fortune by allegedly purchasing looted goods.

At the end of the war Kodama was appointed adviser to Prime Minister **Higashikuni Naruhiko** but was then tried and sentenced as a class A war criminal. He was released from prison in 1948, whereupon he used some of his vast wealth to help rebuild the conservative party. He helped establish the Liberal Party and served as its backstage power broker. He then used his wealth to finance the beginnings of the **Liberal Democratic Party** (LDP). **Kishi Nobusuke** and **Tanaka Kakuei** were among his protégés.

Kodama developed close relations with conservative leaders such as Hatoyama Kazuo and **Ogata Taketora** and was highly, if sometimes surreptitiously, influential in conservative and **business** circles. He remained a leading backstage power broker in politics and a main figure of the right wing. He never held a prominent position himself but aided several LDP **prime ministers**. In 1976, Kodama, having received $7 million for his services to Lockheed, was prosecuted for his involvement in the **Lockheed scandal**.

KOIKE YURIKO, 小池百合子 (1952–). Koike Yuriko is a politician who served in the **House of Representatives** from 1993 until 2016 when she resigned to run for governor of **Tōkyō**. Elected as an independent, she serves today as Tōkyō's first female governor. In 2007, she served as Japan's **minister of defense** under the **Abe Shinzō** government but resigned in less than two months.

Koike has achieved a number of firsts. She became Japan's first-ever female defense minister in 2007. One year later she became the first woman to run for leader of the **Liberal Democratic Party** (LDP), a race she lost. In August 2016, the people of Tōkyō elected her their governor by a landslide.

Koike is a person of unusual accomplishments. She grew up in a wealthy suburb of **Kōbe**, the granddaughter and daughter of world trading company magnates. She benefited from a great deal of international contact. She studied Arabic and sociology at the University of Cairo in Egypt. She has worked as a translator and interpreter, hosted a **television** news program, supported the **environment** by organizing a dress cool campaign, and written extensively on international issues. She is quite fluent in English. Active in reform politics, she was at one time involved in the formation of the **Japan New Party**. She recently helped form a regional rival political party, the

Tōkyōites First Party (Tomin First no Kai) to challenge the LDP. In the January 2017 Tōkyō election, Koike's party soundly defeated the LDP. In the fall of 2017, she unsuccessfully challenged Abe Shinzō for the position of **prime minister**.

The third governor of Tōkyō in a short period, Koike faces a great task in carrying off the Tōkyō **Olympics**. She holds a number of interesting, but sometimes controversial positions. She supports economic liberalism and champions environmentalism but is a conservative nationalist on the issues of **textbook** reform and Article 9 of the **Constitution**. Interestingly, Koike is a big supporter of Japanese pop culture.

KOIZUMI JUN'ICHIRŌ, 小泉純一郎 **(1942–).** Koizumi Jun'ichirō was **prime minister** of Japan from 26 April 2001 to 26 September 2006, the fifth-longest term as prime minister in postwar Japan. **Abe Shinzō** replaced him. Koizumi was born in Yokosuka to a third-generation political family. A charismatic, although some say flamboyant, reformist politician, Koizumi brought Japan higher international recognition. After graduating from Keiō University where he studied economics, Koizumi began his political career as secretary to former prime minister **Fukuda Takeo**. He was then elected 11 times to the **Diet** on the ticket of the **Liberal Democratic Party** (LDP) and occupied different ministerial posts. He became health and welfare minister under Prime Minister **Takeshita Noboru**, posts and telecommunications minister under the **Miyazawa Kiichi** government, and health and welfare minister again under both **Uno Sōsuke** and **Hashimoto Ryūtarō**.

After losing the presidency of the LDP in 1995 to Hashimoto and in 1999 to **Obuchi Keizō**, Koizumi was elected president of the LDP and then Japan's 87th prime minister on 26 April 2001. As a strong advocate of political reform, he emphasized a reduction of the government's debt and the privatization of its postal service, all the while showing a colorful political style. (Refer to appendix N.)

Koizumi was quite popular with his outspoken nature and his colorful presence. Under the nicknames "Lionheart" and "Maverick," he challenged the staid Japanese political scene. He was sometimes called *henjin* (weirdo) with his gaunt looks and unruly, permed gray hair. He is a fan of opera and rock **music** including X Japan, Hide, Morning Musume, and Elvis Presley. His rancorous divorce and single-status prime minister role were unique. He rocked the political establishment when he appointed to his first **cabinet** five **women** and three nonpoliticians, both records. In the early polls, he achieved an 87 percent approval rating and brought a breath of fresh air to the rather stodgy Japanese political arena.

In the July 2004 **House of Councillors** election, Koizumi's LDP suffered a serious loss to the **Democratic Party of Japan**, causing him to experience a drop in his earlier popularity levels, but he still boosted the LDP vote share in urban areas where the LDP had been traditionally weak. In August 2005, Koizumi dissolved the **House of Representatives** and called a general **election** in September. The LDP won a decisive victory with 250 seats of the 480-seat lower house, the largest LDP victory since 1986. Together with the **New Kōmeitō**'s 34 seats, the LDP enjoyed a comfortable majority.

Reforming Japan's postal system was a key issue for Koizumi's government. In the 2005 election he campaigned under the slogan "the privatization of Japan Post is the core of our reforms." He also worked to revitalize Japan's moribund **economy**, trying to eliminate or reduce bad debts held by commercial banks and privatizing the postal savings system. Koizumi made Takenaka Heizō, an economist and a commentator, his key ally in reforming the **banking** sector, where bad debts have been curtailed. Under their leadership, the Japanese economy enjoyed a slow but steady recovery, and the stock market rebounded. Under Koizumi's leadership, the LDP began to move away from its traditional rural, agrarian base toward a more urban, liberal core, thus helping to modernize the party. (Refer to appendix N.)

In **foreign policy**, Koizumi was more assertive and international than his predecessors. He sent Japanese **Self-Defense Forces** to Iraq, openly recognized Japan's past by honoring **Yasukuni Shrine**'s war dead by six visits, traveled to and promoted relations with **North Korea**, and strived to settle the controversies with **Russia** over the northern islands. He promoted a more equal relationship with the **United States**. On 15 August 2005, the 60th anniversary of the end of World War II, Koizumi publicly expressed sadness at the suffering caused by Japan during the war. However, foreign policy issues appeared to have been less important to Japanese voters than economic policy and domestic restructuring.

Koizumi retired from politics in 2009 when his term in the Diet ended. He maintained a low political profile until 2013, when he began to play an active role in opposing **nuclear power**. The **Great East Japan Earthquake** and its attendant disasters caused Koizumi to break with the LDP and vigorously oppose any further development of nuclear power. In late 2015, Koizumi openly criticized Prime Minister Abe Shinzō for unprecedentedly "railroading everything" through the Diet and past the public. Thus, one of Japan's most colorful prime ministers remains somewhat antiestablishment and eccentric.

KŌMEITŌ, 公明党. The Kōmeitō, or the Clean Government Party as it was known in English, was a **political party** founded in 1964 by **Sōka Gakkai**, which went by the English name of Value Creation Society. In politics, the Kōmeitō took a moderate to conservative stand on most issues.

Sōka Gakkai is a lay religious organization affiliated with the Nichiren Shōshū sect of **Buddhism**. From 1955 to 1970, Sōka Gakkai backed candidates in local **Diet** elections. It decided to participate in the national **election** by forming the Kōmeitō in 1964 and won 25 lower house seats in 1967. In 1970, after a scandal over the publication of an anti–Sōka Gakkai book, the Kōmeitō declared its independence from Sōka Gakkai.

Takeiri Yoshikatsu (1926–), a faithful member of the religious organization Sōka Gakkai, entered municipal politics and, in 1961, became a central committee member of the Kōmei Political Federation, the political arm of the Sōka Gakkai. Following the formal establishment of the Kōmeitō Party in 1964, Takeiri served in several central posts. He was elected to the **House of Representatives** in 1967, and under his leadership, the Kōmeitō made significant advances on the political front. Yano Junya (1932–) was chairman of the Kōmeitō Party until he resigned in 1989. Ishida Koshirō (1930–2006) was elected chairman of the Kōmeitō in 1989 and headed the party until the mid-1990s.

Electoral support for the Kōmeitō remained very stable. Over the 10 lower house elections from 1967 through 1993, the Kōmeitō elected an average of 46 candidates, around 9 percent of the seats with a low of 25 in 1967 and a high of 58 seats in 1983. The Kōmeitō emphasized traditional Japanese beliefs and attracted religious affiliates, urban **labor**, former rural residents, **women**, and conservatives. Like the **Japan Socialist Party**, the Kōmeitō favored the gradual modification and dissolution of the **United States–Japan Security Treaty**. On the whole, Kōmeitō supporters were quite loyal and voted in consistent patterns.

After the Kōmeitō participated in the formation of a coalition government in 1993, the **New Frontier Party** absorbed it in 1994, but it again became an independent party in 1998 under the same Japanese name but with the English name **New Kōmeitō**. Since 1999, it has formed coalition governments with other political parties including the **Liberal Democratic Party** (LDP).

Over the course of several recent elections, Kōmeitō remains the third-largest political party, typically collecting 10–15 percent of the popular vote. In 1998, it changed the party name to New Kōmeitō and generally allied itself to the LDP. In 2014, the New Kōmeitō again took the name Kōmeitō. It usually supports the policies of the LDP, including a desire for the reinterpretation of the pacifist Article 9 of the **Constitution of Japan**.

As of October 2017, the Kōmeitō holds 29 seats in the House of Representatives and 25 seats in the **House of Councillors**. It remains in coalition with the LDP. Yamaguchi Natsuo (1952–) serves as its president.

KŌMOTO TOSHIO, 河本敏夫 (1911–2001). Kōmoto Toshio was director-general and economic planning minister under the **Suzuki Zenkō** government. He consistently advocated growth-oriented economic policies. He competed for **prime minister** in 1982, but **Nakasone Yasuhiro** won. Kōmoto finished second with 27 percent of the vote. He enjoyed widespread **business** support in the **Liberal Democratic Party** (LDP). He favored heavy government spending to stimulate the recovery of the **economy** and reduce **trade** friction. He favored a considerable increase in **defense** spending and strengthening of **United States**–Japan military ties. Previously president of a shipbuilding company, Kōmoto served as head of the **Ministry of International Trade and Industry** in the **cabinets** of **Miki Takeo** and **Fukuda Takeo**, posts and telecommunications minister for the **Satō Eisaku** cabinet, chairman of the **House of Representatives** cabinet committee, and chairman of the LDP policy board. Kōmoto headed the smaller Miki-Kōmoto faction, which had 31 seats in the early 1990s.

KOMURO TETSUYA, 小室哲哉 **(1958–).** Komuro Tetsuya is a producer and impresario, especially for female musicians. He is the equivalent of **Johnny Kitagawa** for **women**. Komuro produces Amuro Namie's musical presentations and is her husband. He is also credited with the development of Hitomi, MAX, Globe, and more. He produces for a company known as Avex Group. Artists in his stable are known as "TK Family." From **Tōkyō**, Komuro first achieved **music** fame as a keyboard player; he founded TMN and had a solo career in keyboard and rap.

In 2008, Komuro was arrested for fraud over copyright issues for songs. He admitted his guilt and, after paying substantial damages, resumed his music career working for Avex Group Holdings. Although less a major factor, he is still well known in the J-Pop music world, continuing to compose and play dreamy music.

KONAMI (OR KONAMI HOLDINGS CORPORATION, コナミホールディングス株式会社**).** Konami is a gigantic Japanese entertainment company that produces and sells **anime**, slot machines, arcade equipment, **video games**, and trading cards. Its famous video games include *Dance Dance Revolution, Frogger, Ganbare Goemon, Metal Gear, Yu-Gi-Oh!*, and many others. Konami is one of the world's largest **game** companies.

Founded in 1969, Konami moved from **Ōsaka** to **Tōkyō** but has major offices in the **United States** and Australia. Beginning with jukebox rental and repair, Konami moved into manufacturing amusement machines for game arcades. Konami has spun off a number of related companies with varied interests in different parts of the world. The Konami Holdings Corporation incorporates many different entertainment enterprises. Konami is a leading Japanese video game producer. Kojima Hideo and Sakuma Akira are two of its world-famous game developers.

KONISHI AYA, 小西綾 **(1903–2003).** Konishi Aya, a native of the Kansai area, was the matriarch of Japanese feminism. A junior high school dropout, she became the champion of the working **woman**. She quit her job in the

Kanebō factory office and ran her own little coffee shop. She organized women's discussion groups and rallies to celebrate International Women's Day. For 30 years, she lived and worked with an academically oriented partner, Kimi Komashaku, a retired professor at Hōsei University. Konishi started a feminist-oriented school for Japanese women. She was the embodiment of feminism in Japan.

KŌNO ICHIRŌ, 河野一郎 **(1898–1965).** Kōno Ichirō was a politician who spanned the pre- and postwar periods. Born in Kanagawa Prefecture, he graduated from Waseda University. He worked as a news reporter for the *Asahi Shimbun* before being elected to the **House of Representatives** in 1932. After the war, Kōno helped **Hatoyama Ichirō** form the **Liberal Party** in 1945. **Occupation** authorities barred him from political office until 1951. He became agriculture, forestry, and fisheries minister in 1954 and worked to restore relations with the **Soviet Union**.

Kōno was one of the founding members of the **Liberal Democratic Party**. He again became agriculture, forestry, and fisheries minister under **Ikeda Hayato** in 1961, and he served as Ikeda's construction minister on two occasions as well as filling other government positions. Kōno was a faction leader, and **Nakasone Yasuhiro** joined his faction. After Kōno's death, Nakasone inherited most of his faction. Throughout his career, Kōno had a reputation as a realist and a man of action. His son **Kōno Yōhei** is a major political figure.

KŌNO YŌHEI, 河野洋平 **(1937–).** Kōno Yōhei, a politician, was the founder and first chairman of the **New Liberal Club**. A graduate of Waseda University, he attended Stanford University in 1961. Previously a member of the ruling **Liberal Democratic Party** (LDP), he was elected to the **House of Representatives** in 1967 at age 29, succeeding his father **Kōno Ichirō**, a faction leader in the LDP. Kōno became parliamentary vice minister of education in 1972.

Kōno founded the study group Seiji Kogaku Kenkyūjo in 1974 to support his political ambitions. He revealed his political philosophy in his book, *Hakushu wa iranai: Seiji o motomete* (*I Need No Applause: Searching for a New Politics,* 1976). He rejoined the LDP in 1986.

Kōno, an 11-term member of the House of Representatives, was foreign minister in the **Obuchi Keizō** and **Mori Yoshirō** cabinets as well as chief **cabinet** secretary and deputy **prime minister** under **Murayama Tomiichi**. In 2003, he became speaker of the House of Representatives and held that office until the LDP's defeat in 2009. His six-year term as speaker is the longest on record.

In 1993 while chief cabinet secretary, Kōno issued a statement, based on a government study, that the Japanese army had forced women to work in military brothels. Over the years, this Kōno Statement has generated much controversy between right-wing nationalists and internationalists. As recently as 2014, Kōno urged Prime Minister **Abe Shinzō** to remain committed to Japan's 1993 apology to the "**comfort women**." The following year he joined former prime minister Murayama Tomiichi in urging that Japan erase any doubts about the sexual slavery tragedy.

KOREA, RELATIONS WITH. Japan's relations with the Korean peninsula go back more than two millennia, and those long connections are not always clear or comfortable. Civilization and culture flowed in both directions and included not only beneficial exchanges but also dangerous and destructive aspects. At various points in the relationship, Japanese military leaders attempted to invade Korea. By the 19th century when Japan began to expand into Korea, relations had already started to go bad, and when Japan annexed Korea in 1910, beginning a period of Japanese domination, this generated great animosity. With the long legacy of bitterness, it would take time and a great deal of effort on the part of both countries to improve relations. With the end of the Pacific War, the Korean peninsula regained its independence from Japan but was divided into a southern and a northern zone to settle the war's residue. This made the process of reconciliation with Japan even more difficult.

Japan served as an important staging area for the **United States** during the Korean War, which stimulated the **economy** and thus helped with Japan's economic recovery. In 1965, with the backing of the United States, the two East Asian countries signed the Japan–South Korea Treaty, normalizing diplomatic relations. This treaty tended to link the three countries in a military, political, and economic alliance.

Japan and the Republic of Korea (South Korea) have had a number of disputes during the postwar period. The long history of Japanese colonialism and the war experience complicated relations. Issues of war claims, failure to recognize and adequately deal with the **"comfort women"** issue, economic development and cooperation problems, the lack of an appropriate "war apology," territorial disputes, **textbook controversies**, and visits by Japanese leaders, including prime ministers **Nakasone Yasuhiro** and **Koizumi Jun'ichirō**, to **Yasukuni Shrine**, Japan's leading war memorial, all caused problems in Japanese-Korean relations. For several years after the war, Korea banned Japanese cultural products such as **books**, **music**, **films**, and **manga**.

Japan and South Korea have strong differences over the ownership of a small group of islets in the Sea of Japan or the East Sea as South Korea calls it. Korea, which controls the area, argues that the Tokdo Islands, as it refers to them, are Korean territory while Japan claims that the Takeshima, Japan's name for the islands, belongs to Japan. To further complicate matters, Europeans, who gave them this name after a French whaling crew nearly floundered there in the mid-19th century, refer to the islands as the Liancourt Rocks. Composed of two main islands and some rocks, this controversial place contains less than 50 acres in total but is the center of rich fishing grounds and, together with the focus on national pride, is the source of much difficulty.

However, leaders from both South Korea and Japan have emphasized the importance of opening a new era of Japanese–South Korean relations. In the 21st century, Korea has lifted its ban on Japanese cultural products. In 2002, Japan and South Korea cooperated in cohosting the World Cup, the world's premier **soccer** event. This cooperative effort in hosting the soccer matches contributed to a tremendous increase in popular culture exchanges. Young South Koreans and Japanese are increasingly large consumers of each other's culture. Given the bitter colonial regime Japan imposed on Korea, it is amazing how popular the mutual cultures have become. Youth may be able to accomplish what the older generation could not.

Japan and South Korea have endeavored to cooperate in facing the world economic crisis that emerged in 2008. Such new outside forces and time, along with the cultural contacts mentioned previously in this entry, may reduce the distance between the two countries.

On the other hand, the normalization of diplomatic relations between Japan and the Democratic People's Republic of Korea (North Korea) has been more difficult. Lacking official diplomatic ties and having only minimal amounts of contact between the two countries have exacerbated the problems. North Korea's failure to pay its debts, a series of media attacks, the abduction of a dozen Japanese in the late 1970s and early 1980s, the firing of rockets over Japan, and providing a safe haven for members of the Japanese **Red Army Faction** have prevented Japan and North Korea from having anything resembling friendly relations. Further, Japan's overtures toward Pyongyang tend to frustrate **Tōkyō**'s relations with Seoul.

In the 1990s, Japan conducted extensive discussions with North Korea in an effort to normalize relations. Japanese leaders gave a formal apology for their country's colonial rule and asked for forgiveness while providing various forms of economic and international assistance. However, the amount and nature of that economic assistance and the status of North Korea's nuclear program proved to be sticking points. The demands made by North Korea and its failure to resolve differences with South Korea prevent real success.

Normalization talks between Japan and North Korea have been off and on for a number of years. Unfortunately, the hard line adopted by Pyongyang frequently halts these discussions. Former prime minister Koizumi Jun'ichirō visited North Korea in 2002 and attempted to improve relations. However, as of today, Japan and North Korea have not yet normalized relations from the disaster of World War II.

A few statistics underscore the problem of relations between Japan and Korea. As of the end of the 20th century, slightly more than 15,000 Japanese lived in the Republic of Korea, but more than 636,000 Koreans lived in Japan. Looking at **trade** statistics, things are more balanced. Japan exported $24 billion in electronics, machinery, and chemicals while importing only $16 billion in textiles, machinery, metal products, and other things. Extensive programs of personal and cultural exchange have contributed to improved relations. As of 2005, South Korea was Japan's fourth-leading export country, with nearly $47 billion or 7.8 percent of Japan's exports, and seventh-leading trade partner with more than $24 billion in imports. As of 2007, the two countries are each other's third-largest trading partners with two-way trade totaling $82 billion. Trade figures with the People's Republic of Korea are unclear and, of course, much smaller.

Japan cooperates closely with the United States and participates in the six-party talks, in its efforts to encourage Pyongyang to forgo nuclear development and cooperate with the Nonproliferation Treaty and the International Atomic Energy Agency. Despite all these efforts, in 1998, Pyongyang defiantly flew missiles over Japan. Its continued missile tests show a continuation of previous patterns. The United States, Japan, and South Korea are working closely together to limit and control the activities of North Korea.

In 2013, a poll taken in Korea revealed that 94 percent of Koreans believe Japan "feels no regret for its past wrongdoings." In a similar poll taken in Japan, 63 percent of Japanese believe that Koreans expect unreasonable apologies from Japan.

In 2015, Japan and South Korea addressed the issue of "comfort women" and seemed to reach a solution. Japan's foreign minister, Kishida Fumio, pledged $8.3 million to provide care for the remaining sex slaves. Prime Minister **Abe Shinzō** made a public apology to the women. Korean leaders hailed this as a sign of progress in solving the issue.

On 2 March 2015, the Japanese **Ministry of Foreign Affairs** revised its official view of South Korea from "an important neighboring country that shares basic values with Japan such as freedom, democracy, and a market economy" to just Japan's "most important neighboring country," reflecting somewhat of a deterioration in relations.

Statues symbolizing "comfort women" were installed on five buses in Seoul in August 2017, giving passengers a constant reminder of the thorny issue between the Asian neighbors. At the same time, the dispute over ownership of the pair of rocky islets in the Sea of Japan continues to inflame relations.

Japan and North Korea do not have official relations. However, they occasionally carry on conversations concerning kidnapped Japanese citizens and nuclear armaments. Recent saber-rattling by North Korea has exacerbated Japan and frightened it into accelerating the nationwide J-Alert system. Relations between Japan and North Korea are extremely strained, and a sense of hostility prevails. In 2014, a BBC World Service poll found that 91 percent of the Japanese people view North Korea negatively. *See also* FOREIGN POLICY.

KOREEDA HIROKAZU, 是枝裕和 (1962–). Koreeda Hirokazu is a rising-star **film** director, producer, and screenwriter. Frequently compared to **Ozu Yasujirō**, Koreeda's films focus on the family, are slow moving, deeply reflective, emotional, and filled with traditional images and values.

Born in **Tōkyō** and a graduate of Waseda University, Koreeda rose quickly through the ranks to become one of Japan's most honored directors. Winner of several international awards, his work is recognized worldwide. His 2004 film *Nobody Knows* (*Dare mo shiranai*) is based on a 1988 incident where a **woman** abandoned her four children, each by a different father, and how these children survived on their own until one died in an accident. This sad, but powerful, film was an immediate blockbuster. *Still Walking* (*Aruitemo aruitemo*) debuted in 2008 and shows how the parents and family celebrate the anniversary of their son's death. This film overflows with traditional values and settings and evokes a strong feeling of *natsukashii*, or yearning for the past. The film really takes you back to an early postwar age in Japan. In 2015, Koreeda directed *Our Little Sister* (*Umimachi Dairy*), a story about three sisters in their 20s who accept a younger half sister after their father dies. At his funeral, Koreeda again presents a warm and moving treatment of family relations.

KURATA CHIKARA, 倉田力 (1889–1969). Kurata Chikara was a businessman and the second president of **Hitachi**. Born in Fukuoka Prefecture, he graduated from Sendai Higher Technical School (now Tōhoku University). Kurata joined Hitachi, then a repairing division of the Hitachi mine owned by Kuhara Mining Industry. He became its president in 1947 when Odaira Namihei, founder of the company, was purged by the **Occupation** authorities. During 20 years as president and chairman, he contributed greatly to the nation's industries by developing new **technologies**. Under Kurata's leadership, Hitachi became an important international firm widely known for its excellent products and technology.

KURODA HARUHIKO, 黒田東彦 **(1944–).** Prime Minister **Abe Shinzō** appointed Kuroda Haruhiko the 31st governor of the **Bank of Japan** on 20 March 2013. His term of office runs until 2018. Critical of the previous two governors, Kuroda has argued for looser monetary policy. He drastically cut Japan's interest rates, even into negative territory. Kuroda directs the world's third-largest economy, Japan's $4.1 trillion economy, and is a key figure in "Abenomics."

Kuroda is a native of Fukuoka Prefecture and a graduate of the **University of Tōkyō**. He also earned a master's degree from Oxford University. Kuroda has served in the **Ministry of Finance**, has been an adviser to the **cabinet**, and was the eighth president of the Asian Development Bank.

KUROKAWA KISHŌ, 黒川紀章 **(1934–2007).** A native of Aichi Prefecture, Kurokawa Kishō graduated from Kyōto University in 1957. He went on to the **University of Tōkyō** to do graduate work under the famous **Tange Kenzō**. He created a Japanese avant-garde movement called Metabolism to challenge the over-Westernization in **architecture** and renew the Japanese spirit. The Metabolists group was responsible for the architectural creations of **Expo '70** in **Ōsaka** but later disbanded.

Kurokawa's buildings explore the space between the public and the private world. Rejecting traditionalism, he exhibits interest in the culture of other countries. His firm, having achieved considerable international recognition, has affiliates all over the world and actively encourages international commissions. Internationally, Kurokawa has gained fame for his design of the Japanese-German Center Berlin in Germany, the Chinese-Japanese Youth Center in **China**, the Melbourne Center in Australia, the Pacific Tower in Paris, the new wing of the Vincent Van Gogh Museum in Amsterdam, and the Kuala Lumpur Airport. His important domestic buildings include the Nakagin Capsule Tower, the **Okinawa** Prefectural Government Headquarters, the Roppongi Prince Hotel, the National **Bunraku** Theater, and the Wacoal Kōjimachi Building.

KUROSAWA AKIRA, 黒沢明 **(1910–1998).** Kurosawa Akira was Japan's, and indeed one of the world's, leading **film** directors. Born and raised in **Tōkyō**, the Great Kantō Earthquake shaped his dramatic flair while his teachers and family recognized and encouraged his early interest in film. Perhaps being a descendant of a samurai family stimulated his interests in this genre of film. His works cover many topics, but the search for reality is one of his major themes.

The internationally acclaimed work *Rashōmon* (1950) tells a story that takes place under a great gate called Rashōmon. Clouded by rain, isolation, and separation, the film is slow moving, reflective, and imaginative. A bandit, a dead husband, the wife of the dead husband, and the woodcutter all give their account of a rape, murder, or seduction. *Rashōmon* is a classic detective story that puts the audience in the role of sleuth. Often cited as one of the world's 10 "best-ever" films, it stars **Mifune Toshirō** as the bandit, **Kyō Machiko** as the woman, and **Shimura Takashi** as a woodcutter witness to the events.

Shichinin no samurai (*Seven Samurai*, 1954) is a samurai comedy based on American westerns. It is set in 19th-century Japan where freelance swordsmen offer themselves for hire. Mifune Toshirō stars as a samurai who helps villagers. This spectacular and deeply humanistic film tells the story of a small village that hires seven unemployed samurai to defend it against bandit raids. *Ran* (*Chaos*, 1985) is the title of Kurosawa's epic tragedy where the film's theme "chaos" climaxes in an amazing fortress assault.

Other significant films are *Waga seishun ni kui nashi* (*No Regrets for Our Youth*, 1946), a historical drama that treats the famous case of Kyōto Imperial University professor Takikawa Yukitoki who was persecuted by the military government in 1933 for his liberalism; *Yoidore tenshi* (*Drunken Angel*, 1948), a film about a doctor who tries to bring spiritual and physical recovery to people who live in the poor quarter of Tōkyō immediately after the war; and *Nora inu* (*Stray Dog*, 1949) in which Kurosawa portrays Japan's postwar society as a collection of lost, hungry, solitary beasts, a powerful allegory of life in a defeated, demoralized age.

Warui yatsu hodo yoku nemuru (*The Bad Sleep Well*, 1959) is a tale of suspense and revenge set amid a sea of corporate corruption. *Yōjimbō* (*Bodyguard*, 1961) is Kurosawa's black humor, executed in the style of the American western, in a sophisticated satire on greed, violence, paranoia, and human weakness. *Kagemusha* (*The Shadow Warrior*, 1980) is an epic samurai drama that Kurosawa filled with lavish ceremonies of feudal Japan.

A perfectionist, Kurosawa's films have a polished, but authentic appearance. Although he used some Western themes and techniques, his films have a distinctive Japanese flavor. He frequently used telephoto lenses, unique camera placements, and distinctive weather conditions to heighten the mood of his films. Recipient of the Japanese Academy Award for Lifetime Achievement, the Golden Lion at the Venice Film Festival, the Palme d'Or at the Cannes Film Festival, and numerous other honors, Kurosawa created films that had a unique style and a special quality that deservedly earned him international acclaim.

KYŌ MACHIKO, 京マチ子 (1924–). Kyō Machiko was an internationally recognized **film actress** whose glamour and starring roles made her a leading performer in Japanese motion pictures for almost two decades and brought her international recognition. Born in **Ōsaka**, she was recruited by Daiei Motion Picture Company in 1949. From the outset of her motion picture career, Daiei studios publicized Kyō as something of a sex symbol. Recognition of Kyō's talent came from her much-acclaimed performance in an elaborately woven tale of rape and murder. Kyō starred in **Kurosawa Akira**'s *Rashōmon*, **Mizoguchi Kenji**'s *Ugetsu*, Kinugasa Teinosuke's *Jigokumon*, and **Ichikawa Kon**'s *Kagi*. She is known in the West for her role in *Teahouse of the August Moon*.

KYŌCERA COMPANY (KYŌSERA KABUSHIKI-GAISHA, 京セラ株式会社**).** Kyōcera Company is a **business** that focuses on information exchange and communication and also supports **environmental** preservation. It is also known as Kyōto Ceramics because it is located in **Kyōto**. Founded in 1959 by Inamori Kazuo, Kyōcera produces ceramics for electronics and printing-related devices, as well as a comprehensive line of imaging products. Kyōcera acquired Yashica Camera Company in 1983 and manufactured a line of high-quality film and digital **cameras** under the Yashica brand name until it discontinued all film and digital camera production in 2005. In 2000, Kyōcera acquired the photocopier company Mita Industrial and, a month later, bought Qualcomm, the mobile phone manufacturing operation out of San Diego. Since the 1980s, Kyōcera has marketed high-end audio components, such as CD players, receivers, turntables, and cassette decks, as well as cell phones. These feature unique **technology**, including Kyōcera ceramic-based platforms.

KYŌTO, 京都**.** Kyōto is Japan's most renowned historic and cultural center. It is also the seventh-largest city in Japan with a population of nearly 1.5 million. Kyōto was Japan's capital for more than 1,000 years until the new Meiji leaders moved the capital to **Tōkyō** in 1869. The only major city in Japan not devastated by bombs in World War II, Kyōto is filled with magnificent temples and shrines, beautiful imperial palaces, gorgeous gardens, and quaint traditional wooden houses. The city is also the home to many artisans who make textiles, dyed fabrics, pottery, bamboo ware, fans, metal works, and other arts and crafts.

Much to the disappointment of traditionalists, the area around the new Kyōto Station, completed in 1997, is filled with modern buildings and high-tech accomplishments. Extremely controversial because of its overly modern design, the station is seen by many as out of step with the more traditional architectural heritage. Kyōto has had its share of earthquakes and fires but has largely rebuilt with wood in the traditional manner, thus maintaining the city's strong romantic link with the past.

Kyōto, much of which was built in the early 1700s, is laid out on a grid pattern based on the traditional Chinese model. Known as Heian-kyō (Capital of Peace), Kyōto was a grand cultural center of the court nobility with a heavy **Buddhist** influence. The **emperor** reigned from here supported by powerful shogunal control after the late 12th century. The Ashikaga shoguns ruled from the Muromachi area of Kyōto and constructed splendid buildings including Kinkakuji (Golden Pavilion) and Ginkakuji (Silver Pavilion). Kiyomizu-dera, a traditional wooden temple supported by pillars over a mountain slope; the imposing, colorful Heian Shrine; the exquisiteness of the Imperial Palace and Nijo Castle; the scenic natural beauty of Katsura Imperial Villa; and the ambience of the Philosopher's Walk all contribute to making Kyōto a **tourist** paradise. Zen Buddhist influence such as Saihōji Temple and Ryōanji Rock Garden give the city a special ambience. Artistic accomplishments, including landscape gardening, tea ceremonies, flower arranging, and **Noh** drama, flourish in Kyōto.

Kyōto is home to 17 UNESCO World Heritage sites. It has more than 1,600 Buddhist temples, 400 **Shintō** shrines, many historical buildings and famous gardens, and a large treasure of art and **architecture**. It is known for its handicrafts and cuisine. The sylvan setting of bamboo groves, the delicate beauty of cherry blossoms in spring, and the rich red hues of maple trees in the fall all add to Kyōto's elegant beauty. The city also hosts more than 500 festivals in any given year, with the Aoi Festival and the Gion Festival the most prominent. Kyōto is indeed a beautiful and exciting place.

In 1997, Kyōto hosted an international conference that adopted an agreement on greenhouse gas emissions known as the Kyōto Protocol. This remains a guide to dealing with global warming.

The click-clack of wooden *geta* (sandals) on well-worn stones, the sight of geisha in colorful silk kimono, and traditional wooden houses define the city of Kyōto. In an effort to preserve some of Kyōto's traditional image, in 2007, the city passed an ordinance that limits the height of buildings and bans rooftop advertising. Kyōto is a cultural jewel.

L

LABOR ORGANIZATIONS. The postwar Japanese labor movement sought to improve the life of working people and promote peace and democracy. Japan's Trade Union Law of 1945 guaranteed the right of workers to organize and join unions, engage in collective bargaining, and conduct strikes. It provided these rights to both private and public unions with the exception of police and firefighters. With Allied support, trade unions experienced spectacular growth.

The Japanese government, following the guidance of the **Occupation**, passed the Labor Relations Act in 1946. In 1947, it passed the Labor Standards Law that set minimum standards for wages, limited the length of the workday, provided for unemployment insurance, mandated injury compensation, and guaranteed unemployment benefits. The law stipulated equal pay for equal work and provided 12 weeks of maternity leave for **women**.

Until the labor movement was restrained in the early 1950s by sharp deflation, revision of labor laws, and a purge of leftists, unionism enlisted more than six million members, about half of all workers. Although there were several labor organizations before World War II, trade unions became more important for the Allies' intentions for the Occupation.

In the early postwar period, the **Japan Congress of Industrial Unions** (Sanbetsu), a federated umbrella union group, pushed for major reconstruction and championed Marxist goals of industrial democracy and worker participation in management. It flourished during the late 1940s but faded thereafter as its message was seen as too radical for most Japanese.

In the 1950s, the **General Council of Japanese Trade Unions** (Sōhyō), a leading federation of unions, turned away from socialist politics and toward an economically oriented **business** unionism. Sōhyō introduced the annual spring wage offensive (*shuntō*) as its major focus but still called for support of pacifism and internationalism in **foreign policy**. The spring labor offensive was a technique used by labor unions to tie pay raises and benefits to national economic growth rates. The spring labor offensive was a highly ritualized show of force and solidarity with banners, sloganeering, and dancing in the streets, but it did not cripple businesses. While such demonstrations garnered publicity, serious discussions took place only between the union officers and corporate managers.

The number of working days lost to labor disputes peaked in the economic turmoil of the mid-1970s at around nine million. After 1975, when the **economy** began a period of slower growth, the spring wage struggle became more moderate and conciliatory. By 1979, there were fewer than one million days lost. During the 1980s and 1990s, workers received pay hikes that followed the real growth of GNP. The moderate trend continued in the early 1990s as Japan's national labor federations reorganized.

The size of Japanese union membership has varied in postwar Japan but was more significant in the early postwar period. In 1945, only 3 percent of Japanese workers were unionized, but with the establishment of workers' right to organize, unionization had exploded to more than 50 percent of the workforce in the early 1950s. Initially, the socialist and communist **political parties** controlled most unions. A pattern of frequent strikes, often violent, continued for years. Companies set up their own company unions, which resulted in violent clashes with the leftist unions.

As of 1970, the rate of labor union membership was about 35 percent but, in the 1980s, declined to an average of around 28 percent. Several factors caused the continuing long-term reduction in union membership, but the restructuring of Japanese industry away from heavy industry was a major element. In the 1990s, unionization averaged 24 percent.

Japan's enterprise unions are organized company by company instead of across industry lines and thus have much more intimate contact with management than do unions in the West. Information flows freely, and negotiations often are conducted on a more personal level. Workers are much more attuned to national interests and to those of employers than their counterparts in Europe and the United States. Japanese union members look out for one another in times of crisis.

As of 2014, Japan is about 17.5 percent unionized. Over the postwar years, the total number of union members has increased slightly, but when compared to the overall population, the percentage of membership has declined dramatically. Japan has approximately 67,737 labor unions. More than 90 percent of Japan's labor unions were enterprise-based unions or craft unions. The biggest employers were services (23.5 percent); manufacturing (22.3 percent); wholesale and retail trade (16.7 percent); **construction** (10.6 percent); **agriculture**, forestry, and fishing (7.1 percent); government (6.0 percent); transportation and communications (5.7 percent); and finance, insurance, and real estate (4.6 percent).

In the postwar period, Japan has generally had a low unemployment rate. In the mid-1980s, the unemployment rate was about 2.8 percent and then it dropped to as low as about 2.1 percent in the early 1990s. However, by 1996, it had risen to 3.3 percent. In July 2009, Japan's unemployment rate reached an all-time postwar high of 5.7 percent but has improved slightly since then. By the mid-1980s, four main labor federations represented the approximately 75,000 trade unions. The largest of these was the Sōhyō with 4.4 million members, a substantial percentage of these public-sector employees. (Refer to appendix R.)

The **Japan Confederation of Labor** (Zen Nihon Rōdō Sōdōmei Kaigi), commonly known as Dōmei, had 2.2 million members. The other two groups were the **Federation of Independent Labor Unions** (Chūritsu Rōren), with 1.6 million members, and the **National Federation of Industrial Organizations** (Shinsanbetsu), with only 61,000 members. In 1987, Dōmei and Chūritsu Rōren were dissolved and amalgamated into the newly established **Japanese Trade Union Confederation** (Rengō); in 1990, Sōhyō affiliates merged with Rengō. Local labor unions, not federations, controlled policies and actions, conducted collective bargaining, and engaged in political and public relations activities. The metamorphosis in the early 1990s of the Japan Council of Private-Sector Labor Unions (Zenmin Rōkyō) into Rengō and the dissolution of Sōhyō and Dōmei signaled the incorporation of organized labor at the national level into an enterprise movement where labor and business cooperated.

Sōhyō's leadership role in peace and democracy would continue to decline in the early 1980s with Prime Minister **Nakasone Yasuhiro**'s promotion of the **imperial system** and administrative reforms. Further, Dōmei came to adopt a policy of working with business leaders to expand foreign markets and promote Japan's international economy.

Japan is well known for harmony between labor and management, but it did not achieve this harmony until rapidly rising living standards made union militancy unnecessary. Over time, many unions cut their ties to leftist political parties and became less militant. While strike activity was in line with international norms in the 1950s and 1960s, by the mid-1990s it was comparatively low. Local labor unions and work unit unions, rather than the federations, conducted the major bargaining.

The national labor organizations are concerned mainly with such questions as wages, prices, and working conditions. Individual enterprise unions, however, retain much of their independence in dealing with employers. While the craft and national federations formulate general policy, discuss and advise on strategy, and coordinate wage offensives, individual unions and the employees usually conduct serious negotiations. One result of Japan's industrial, as opposed to craft, unionism is that demarcation disputes and interunion rivalry for members are relatively rare. Furthermore, if judged in terms of working days lost, Japanese labor relations have been noticeably more amicable and less contentious than those in other developed countries, such as Great Britain, Italy, and the **United States**.

208 • L'ARC-EN-CIEL, ラルクアンシエル

The relationship between the typical Japanese labor union and the company is unusually close. Generally, in most major companies all workers join the union. Unions exclude temporary and subcontracted workers as well as managers with the rank of section chiefs or above. However, many members of the managerial staff are former union members. Japanese unions are particularly concerned with the economic health of the company and avoid acting in such a way as to damage the company.

In the first half of the postwar period, "lifetime employment" described the situation for people who got good jobs right out of high school or university and then maintained these jobs throughout their working days. This was often misinterpreted and exaggerated. It did not apply to the majority of workers in small and medium enterprises. At any rate, "lifetime employment" has nearly disappeared today.

A shortage of labor is driving up the wages of workers. Both hourly wages and salaries are going up because there are too few people to fill the available slots. Some corporate experts have suggested that the labor shortage is so serious that it threatens to derail the country's efforts to stimulate the economy. They say Japan is running out of people to hire. They point out that in 1997, Japan had about 87 million workers, but that by 2017 that number had slipped to just over 76 million. In 2016, the number of foreigners employed in Japan rose above one million for the first time.

In early 2017, the government came out with reforms in Japan's employment practices. Government, management, and labor have agreed to cap overtime work hours, improve wages for women, and give equal treatment to regular and non-regular employees. The Japanese Trade Union Confederation has agreed to these practices. Japan is considering a four-day workweek in order to improve the balance between work and home life. *See also* EQUAL EMPLOYMENT OPPORTUNITY LAW; JAPAN TEACHERS' UNION (NIHON KYŌSHOKUIN KUMIAI, 日本教職員組合); NATIONAL CONFEDERATION OF TRADE UNIONS (ZENKOKU RŌDŌ KUMIAI SŌRENGŌ, 全国労働組合総連合); NATIONAL TRADE UNION COUNCIL (ZENKOKU RŌDŌ KUMIAI RENGŌ GIKAI, 全国労働組合連絡協議会).

L'ARC-EN-CIEL, ラルクアンシエル. L'Arc-en-Ciel is one of Japan's most popular rock **music** groups. This four-man band rocks the music world with high decibels. Combining metal and rock styles, it adds **anime**-inspired lyrics to produce a spellbinding sound. L'Arc-en-Ciel is French for "rainbow," which gives a clue to the group's music.

Founded in 1991, L'Arc-en-Ciel continues to pack venues today. Its concerts attract huge crowds of people at astronomical prices. In 2012, it sold out Madison Square Garden to celebrate its 20th anniversary with a world tour. Having sold more than 15 million albums and more than 30 million singles, the band was the first Japanese group to grace the Garden.

The band's four stars include Hyde, the lead singer; Tetsuya on base; Ken, playing guitar; and Yukihiro, banging the drums. They sport punk haircuts, wear glittery clothes, and execute fancy dance moves.

LIBERAL DEMOCRATIC PARTY (JIYŪ MINSHUTŌ, 自由民主党). The LDP, by far the most powerful **political party** in postwar Japan, was founded in November 1955 as a combination of the Liberal Party (Jiyūtō) and the **Democratic Party** (Minshutō), both of which were prewar parties. It was formed as a response to the merger of left and right socialist parties. The LDP became the dominant political force in Japan for the rest of the century and extended its power into the 21st century. From 1955 through 2009, Japan had 25 **prime ministers** with all but three of them being LDP members. Except for a short period between 1993 and 1996, the LDP has continuously controlled Japan.

Hatoyama Ichirō, a leading politician, presided over the creation of the LDP. Businessmen, white-collar workers, government employees, and farmers are the typical LDP supporters. It is closely linked to wealthy corporations and to **United States** business, political, and military interests. It supports the free enterprise system, academic freedom, social welfare programs, medical insurance, old-age pensions, and subsidies for rice farmers.

The LDP has had a number of strong leaders whose efforts have cemented the power of the party. Prime Minister **Ikeda Hayato**, with his highly successful "income doubling plan" promised in 10 years but accomplished in just seven years, gave the LDP a lot of credibility.

With the strong support of **business** circles and farmers, the LDP played a major role in the postwar Japanese economic revival, especially in **Satō Eisaku**'s administration from 1964 through 1972.

The LDP supported Japan's alliance with the United States and fostered close links between Japanese business and government. Prime ministers **Tanaka Kakuei** and **Nakasone Yasuhiro** were two of the most powerful LDP politicians in postwar Japan. From the 1960s through the 1980s, Japan prospered and grew in world stature, and LDP leaders were quick to take credit for the accomplishments.

However, political scandals and economic difficulties caused the LDP to lose its parliamentary majority in the 1993 **election**. From August 1993 through January 1996, the Japanese government was guided by three non-LDP prime ministers. Prime ministers **Hosokawa Morihiro** and **Hata Tsu-**

tomu led non-LDP coalition governments followed by **Japan Socialist Party** leader **Murayama Tomiichi**'s coalition government with the LDP at its base.

Factionalism has been a major problem for the LDP with the party often dividing along personal lines and sometimes along policy lines. Personality differences often determined the internal party struggle. Interests and policies also divide the large, rather amorphous LDP. While often having subject names, factions are more commonly referred to by their leaders' names. Naturally, the names shift over time as one party faction leader succeeds an older faction head.

Tanaka Kakuei, a key factional leader, ran the LDP with an iron hand and, after his ouster as prime minister due to the **Lockheed scandal**, was known as the "shadow shogun." **Takeshita Noboru** and **Hashimoto Ryūtarō** were other major LDP faction leaders. However, virtually all LDP prime ministers have had strong factional connections. The LDP political boss **Kanemaru Shin** was notorious for his political stronghold.

While the power and influence of factions have been reduced in recent years, they still undercut any unified political leadership in the LDP today. LDP factions, tightly organized by personal loyalty to a factional leader, stifle the open, efficient political development of issues and leadership. Today, political factions are a bit more oriented toward issues rather than personalities, but the system still prevents strong, viable political leadership.

Corruption among both politicians and bureaucrats has continually plagued the LDP. In addition to the above-mentioned Lockheed scandal (1976), major corruption scandals included the **Recruit scandal** (1988), the Sagawa Kyūbin affair (1992–1993), the Ōsaka Oil dealer Izui Jun'ichi deal (1991), the Ministry of Finance wining and dining of clients (1997–1998), Nakao Eiichi and the Ministry of Construction arrangement (2000), and the Foreign Ministry crisis (2001), as well as others. The government passed a Political Funds Control Law that obligates Diet members to report contributions of more than ¥1 million, but the law does not limit the number of fundraising organizations a politician may have. Other scandals include bid-rigging, sex and money, failure to meet construction standards, and violation of various safety regulations. Nonetheless, corruption has not precluded the LDP from being the leading party in postwar Japan.

In 1998, Prime Minister **Obuchi Keizō** formed a coalition **cabinet** and appointed Noda Takeshi, the LP's secretary-general, as home minister. Obuchi reduced the number of ministers from 20 to 18 as demanded by the **Liberal Party**. The LDP held 265 seats in the 500-seat **House of Representatives**, and the LP had 38 seats. However, in the **House of Councillors** the two parties had only 116 seats of the 252 seats needed for a majority. To get the coalition, the LDP had to agree to the LP's demand for cooperation and participation in logistic support for **United Nations** multinational armed forces. The LDP and **New Kōmeitō** (NKP) agreed to work together in a coalition government. Leaving its opposition status, the NKP got two cabinet posts in the Obuchi cabinet.

Since the interruption of its sole rule, the LDP has produced a series of weak prime ministers chosen more to maintain an alliance between party factions than for their ability or charisma. Prime Minister Takeshita Noboru's Recruit scandal, **Uno Sōsuke**'s sex scandal, and **Mori Yoshirō**'s inept handling of the Ehime incident, made LDP leaders look incompetent. However, the dynamic **Koizumi Jun'ichirō**, a former health minister, changed that when he became the LDP leader in early 2001. Koizumi served as prime minister for five and a half years, the third-longest term in postwar Japan up to that time. He provided stability and longevity for the LDP. Despite conservative opposition and inertia from his own party, he promised to reform the government and its bureaucracy. Koizumi's resurgent popularity, the continuing influence in the business and **agriculture** sectors, and the lack of a unified and strong opposition allowed the LDP to reemerge as the dominant force in Japanese politics.

The LDP faced the voters 17 times between 1958 and 2005 and averaged 267 seats per election with a low of 223 seats in the 1993 election and a high of 304 out of 512 seats (59.4 percent) and 296 out of 480 seats (61.7 percent) in the 2005 election. The LDP was particularly dominant in the six elections from 1958 through 1972 but showed weakness in the 1976 and 1979 elections. After resurgences in 1986 and 1990, the LDP suffered through four relatively weaker elections. However, in 2005, the LDP made its strongest showing in percentage of seats won. After the July 2007 House of Councillors election, the LDP held only 83 of the 242 seats, while the **Democratic Party of Japan** (DPJ) surged ahead to 109 or 45 percent of the seats.

Following Koizumi, the LDP had a succession of weak prime ministers including **Abe Shinzō**, **Fukuda Yasuo**, and **Asō Tarō**, all of whom served only one year. The LDP showed a vacuum in political leadership but continued to be conservative on social issues and **foreign policy**. Its popularity and support base quickly eroded.

The election of 30 August 2009 produced the most dramatic shift seen in postwar Japanese politics. The LDP plummeted to an incredible low of 119 seats (25 percent) while the DPJ skyrocketed to 308 seats (64 percent). Dissatisfied with the continuing economic crisis, the overriding power of the bureaucracy, and the scandals and petty infighting of the LDP, the country was ripe for change and thus overwhelmingly rejected the LDP. The **Diet** selected DPJ leader **Hatoyama Yukio** as prime minister. Coming full circle in the political carousel, Hatoyama is the grandson of Hatoyama Ichirō, the first LDP prime minister.

On 28 September 2009, the LDP selected **Tanigaki Sadakazu**, former finance minister for three years in the Koizumi Jun'ichirō cabinet, as president of the LDP, replacing Prime Minister Asō after the LDP's resounding election defeat.

Although holding power continuously since its founding in 1955, with brief exceptions in 1993–1994 and 2009–2012, the LDP is not invincible. In the 16 December 2012 general election in the lower house, the LDP, together with its ally New Kōmeitō, won a clear majority, returning to power after three years. The LDP again turned to Abe Shinzō as prime minister. Abe had previously served as president of the LDP and prime minister for a year, from 20 September 2006 to 26 September 2007. Then again, on 16 September 2012, he became both president of the party and prime minister, offices he continues to hold as of January 2018.

The election of 22 October 2017 put the LDP firmly in control as it elected 284 lower house members, and together with the Kōmeitō's 29 members, the LDP has a firm majority. It remains to be seen what it will do with that power.

LIBERAL PARTY (JIYŪTŌ, 自由党). Japan had three different Liberal Parties (LP) in the late 19th century, and **Hatoyama Ichirō** founded a fourth in 1946. In 1998, **Hatoyama Yukio** (grandson of the earlier Hatoyama), **Ozawa Ichirō**, and Fujii Hirohisa formed the fifth LP from the remnants of the **New Frontier Party**. The LP functioned for five years and pushed for reform, using the motto "Japan Renewal," but in 2003 it merged with other **political parties** to form the **Democratic Party of Japan**.

On 27 December 2012, a group of disgruntled political leaders formed another Liberal Party under the name People's Life Party but changed its name to People's Life Party & Taro Yamamoto and Friends in 2014. In October 2016, the party adopted the name Liberal Party. This center-left party emphasizes localism, environmentalism, an antinuclear position, and pacifism. Mori Yuko (1956–) was the party's president from its founding until 25 January 2013 when Ozawa Ichirō became president. Currently the Liberal Party holds two seats in the **House of Representatives** and three seats in the **House of Councillors**. In spite of losing seats since its reformation, the party is a force because of its leader.

LIFE INSURANCE. The Nippon Life Insurance Company is the largest life insurance company in the world. Incorporated in 1889, it was the first insurance company to base its system on causes of death and the first to pay dividends to its policyholders. It sells individual and group life and annuity products worldwide. It now offers **automobile**, fire, and product liability policies for individuals and corporations. Headquartered in **Ōsaka**, it has offices in many countries.

The Dai-Ichi Mutual Life Insurance Company is Japan's oldest life insurance company and one of the largest life insurance companies in the world. Created in 1902, the company has around 2,000 offices throughout the world. Mitsui Mutual Life Insurance is another of Japan's largest and oldest life insurance companies. Headquartered in **Tōkyō**, it is active worldwide. Sumitomo Life Insurance Company was founded in 1927 and became a mutual company in 1947. It, too, is one of the largest life insurance companies in the world with subsidiaries all over the world.

Other major life insurance companies include Meiji Mutual Life, Yasuda Mutual Life, Fukuoka Mutual Life, and Asahi Mutual Life.

LITERATURE. Numerous Japanese writers have achieved domestic distinction and international recognition in the postwar period. So much so that Japanese literature is recognized as a major branch of world literature and many of its works have been translated into various languages.

Japan boasts two **Nobel Prize** winners for literature: **Kawabata Yasunari** in 1968 and **Ōe Kenzaburō** in 1994. Kawabata is frequently recognized for his "delicate aesthetic sensibility" while Ōe is praised for his social conscience and political concerns in his writings.

Japanese literature can be difficult to read and understand as it is often ambiguous and subject to broad interpretation. Novels are frequently introspective and filled with mental anguish as the authors examine complex personal issues. They focus on the inner lives of their subjects and are preoccupied with the conscience of their characters. Plots are often secondary to emotional issues. Many works seek to recognize and define the national character of the Japanese. **Buddhist** themes of impermanence and self-recognition are often present. Works such as those by **Ariyoshi Sawako** and **Enchi Fumiko** sought to understand the role of **women** in contemporary Japanese society. Western readers of Japanese literature are often struck by characteristics that tend to define the style of Japanese authors. First, Japanese novels are often sparse in dialogue with the reader being forced to understand the situation, not through words, but through gestures, by key phrases or symbols, and assuming various responses. Second, those looking for dramatic physical action are likely to be disappointed since Japanese novels are usually not action packed. Finally, the reflective, introspective, and pensive nature of Japanese literature can be off-putting to some Westerners.

In the early postwar years, Japan's literature was filled with a sense of loss and the problems of coping with defeat. **Dazai Osamu**'s novel *The Setting Sun* (1951) tells the sad story of a soldier returning from the Manchurian front. **Ōoka Shōhei** describes the personal anguish he experienced in the Philippine jungles in *Fires on the Plain* (1951). The horror of the atomic bomb is dramatically portrayed in **Ibuse Masuji**'s *Black Rain* (1966). In his short story "The American School," Kojima Nobuo (1915–2006) reveals the difficulty faced by people interacting with the American **Occupation**.

Abe Kōbō was an avant-garde writer whose chilling novels *Woman in the Dunes* (1962) and *The Face of Another* (1964) shook both domestic and international readers alike.

Tanizaki Jun'ichirō, one of Japan's most renowned authors, explored the dynamics of family life, Japanese society, tradition, and love. He wrote much about the plight of women, social change, and sexual matters. Tanizaki's *Captain Shigemoto's Mother* (1949), *The Key* (1961), and *Diary of a Mad Old Man* (1965) reflect Japanese values and character.

The works of **Mishima Yukio** were numerous, versatile, and wonderfully engaging. His examination of issues from a psychological standpoint was phenomenal. His best-known works include *The Temple of the Golden Pavilion* (1956) and his last multivolume novel, *The Sea of Fertility* (1964–1970). Had it not been for his controversial sexual orientation, his ultranationalist flair, and his dramatic hara-kiri suicide, Mishima would most likely have been another Japanese Nobel Prize winner.

Writers from the 1960s through the 1980s often focused on intellectual and moral issues. Ōe Kenzaburō's *A Personal Matter* (1964) was a good example of this. Others wrote on the consequences of the atomic bomb, the nuclear age, and the impact of foreign Christianity, as in the works of **Endō Shūsaku** such as *Silence* (1966). Writings of this era dealt with psychological problems, women's issues, and postwar recovery. Inoue Mitsuaki wrote about the perplexing problems of living in the nuclear age.

Historical novels, especially those by **Shiba Ryōtarō**, Inoue Yasushi (1907–1991), and Endō Shūsaku, comment on historical aspects of Japanese life and have gained a lot of interest. Shiba's *Ryōma Mores Ahead* (1963–1966) about the ever-popular Sakamoto Ryōma, *The Last Shōgun* (1967), and *Kūkai the Universal* (1975) have been hugely successful not only as books but also on **television** and in **films**.

Popular contemporary writers include **Murakami Haruki** whose works *Norwegian Wood* (1987) and *Hard-Boiled Wonderland and the End of the World* (1991) are controversial but humorous, surreal, and lacking in gender identity. **Yoshimoto Banana**'s writings, popular with young people, treat personal loss and conflict in social relationships. Leading young female writers, including **Kanehara Hitomi** and **Wataya Risa**, have explored new subjects in new ways in contemporary Japanese literature.

Popular literature, including comic books (**manga**) of all kinds, has become quite popular among many segments of the Japanese population. Today, probably at least one-fourth of all Japanese literature falls into the manga category. Well-known manga writers include **Tezuka Osamu**, **Takahashi Rumiko**, **Akatsuka Fujio**, and **Ōtomo Katsuhiro**.

Japanese literature has a tradition of magical realism, which has continued in the postwar period. Examples of the supernatural include Kawabata's *One Arm* (1964), Abe's *The Man Who Turned into a Stick* (1967), and Murakami's *The Wind-Up Bird Chronicle* (1995). This type of "serious fantasy" adds an important dimension to Japanese literature.

Although not as well known, Japanese poets, dramatists, and short story writers make up an important part of the literary world in postwar Japan. Takamura Kōtarō (1883–1956) was known for his poetry about nature and marital love. Kinoshita Junji (1914–2006) was one of Japan's foremost playwrights who focused on a wide variety of subjects ranging from folklore to contemporary history. Betsuyaku Minoru (1937–) and Satō Makoto (1943–2007) pioneered underground theater in the late 1960s.

Postwar Japanese literature also has a dark side with special attention to illness, pain, death, and other sufferings. Ōe's *A Personal Matter* and Yoshimoto's *Kitchen* reflect this. Nakagami Kenji (1946–1992), who came from a ***burakumin*** background, shocked the world with his novels *The Cape* (1975) and *Snakelust* (1981). Personal pain and struggles strike a responsive chord in Japanese readers, where life is filled with the bad as well as the good.

Recently, a number of female writers have come to the fore. Kirino Natsuo (1951–) writes detective novels including *Out*, which focuses on murderous crimes committed by women. Miyabe Miyuki (1960–) pens crime fiction, horror, and sci-fi novels. Kakuta Mitsuyo (1967–), author of more than a dozen novels, explores women in difficult relationships. Amy Yamada (1959–) produces controversial novels that explore sexuality, interracial relationships, and xenophobia in Japan.

The cell phone novel, a recent creation, has created a new popular form of novel. Written by and for cell phone aficionados, these pulp-type novels are especially popular with young women. *Lovely Sky* has sold millions of copies and is one of the top cell phone novels. *See also* HAYASHI FUSAO, 林房雄 (1903–1975); MURAKAMI RYŪ, 村上龍 (1952–); NOMA HIROSHI, 野間宏 (1915–1991); ODAGIRI HIDEO, 小田切秀雄 (1916–2000); OSARAGI JIRŌ, 大佛次郎 (1897–1973); SAKAGUCHI ANGO, 坂口安吾 (1906–1955); YOSHIYUKI JUNNOSUKE, 吉行淳之介 (1924–1994).

LOCKHEED SCANDAL (*ROKKIIDO JIKEN*, ロッキード事件). In February 1976, the **United States** Senate subcommittee hearings revealed the outline of the Lockheed scandal involving bribes and contributions by the aircraft maker to facilitate the sale of planes manufactured by Lockheed

Aircraft to West Germany, Italy, the Netherlands, Saudi Arabia, and Japan. In Japan, Lockheed paid a series of large bribes to Prime Minister **Tanaka Kakuei** and Transport Minister Hashimoto Tomisaburō in order to sell their civil airplanes, Tristar, to **All Nippon Airways** through **Marubeni** Corporation. Tanaka was forced to resign after it was revealed that he received a donation of $3 million. The scandal was made even more unsavory when it was revealed that right-wing underworld figures like **Kodama Yoshio** had been involved.

In October 1983, the Japanese courts sentenced former prime minister Tanaka to four years in prison and fined him over the Lockheed scandal. In 1983, the court declared Tanaka guilty of violation of foreign exchange laws but not of bribery. The decision was confirmed but later appealed. In 1993, the government dropped the case when Tanaka died.

LOTTE COMPANY (ROTTEI KABUSHIKI-GAISHA, ロッテ株式会社). Incorporated in 1948, Lotte is a large international conglomerate founded in **Tōkyō** by Shin Kyuk-Ho, a South Korean national living in both **South Korea** and Japan, who is alternatively known by his Japanese name Shigemitsu Takeo. It is one of Japan's leading manufacturers of confectioneries. Its subsidiaries include Lotteria, the fast-food chain, and Chiba Lotte Marines, the professional **baseball** team. Headquartered in **Kōbe**, it operates a group of 30 companies including hotels, **department stores**, and theme parks. The company name comes from the name Charlotte, a character in a work by the German writer Goethe.

Lotte grew from selling chewing gum to children in postwar Japan to becoming a major multinational corporation with overseas branches in dozens of countries and products shipped worldwide. Lotte Group consists of more than 50 **business** units employing 38,000 people engaged in such diverse industries as candy manufacturing, beverages, hotels, fast food, retail, financial services, heavy chemicals, electronics, IT, **construction**, publishing, and entertainment. Lotte has major operations in South Korea, Japan, **China**, the Philippines, Thailand, Indonesia, Vietnam, Europe, and the **United States**.

M

MACHIMURA NOBUTAKA, 町村信孝 **(1944–2015).** Machimura Nobutaka rose through the political ranks to become the leader of the **Liberal Democratic Party**'s biggest faction, only to be stymied by factionalism itself. He never fulfilled his dream of becoming Japan's **prime minister**, though no one doubted he had the management and policy expertise for the job. His constituents elected him to the **House of Representatives** 12 times.

He attended the **University of Tōkyō** and Wesleyan University in the **United States**. Fluent in English, he twice headed the **Ministry of Foreign Affairs**, first under **Koizumi Jun'ichirō** and then under **Abe Shinzō**. Machimura was forceful in his diplomacy, pressing **China** for an apology after anti-Japanese riots broke out in 2005, and asking the Chinese for compensation for damage to Japanese businesses. On the other hand, he chided Koizumi for his repeated visits to the war-linked **Yasukuni Shrine**, a sore spot in relations with China.

Factional politics frustrated Machimura's ambition to lead the LDP. He sought to run for party president in 2007 and 2008, but deferred to **Fukuda Yasuo**, for whom he served as chief **cabinet** secretary, and **Asō Tarō**, both of whom went on to become prime minister. He later served as speaker of the House. In 2012, it seemed Machimura's time had come. However, a stroke ruled out what would prove to be his final chance to reach the prime minister's office, and he resigned in April 2015. He died shortly thereafter.

Machimura was a fitness advocate. A former high school **rugby** player, he regularly worked out at the gym. He served as vice president of the Japan-China Friendship Parliamentarians' Union.

MAINICHI SHIMBUN, 毎日新聞. The *Mainichi Shimbun*, one of Japan's three leading national **newspapers**, is also one of Japan's oldest newspapers. It has a daily circulation of more than four million copies. It was founded in **Ōsaka** in 1882 as an organ paper of the political party Nihon Rikken Seitō. Its name became *Ōsaka Mainichi* in 1888 with an emphasis on the merchant community.

218 • MAKI FUMIHIKO, 槇文彦 (1928–)

Today, the *Mainichi* has more than 3,000 employees in approximately 360 offices in Japan and 26 overseas bureaus. It is associated with 80 companies including the Tōkyō Broadcasting System (TBS), the Mainichi Broadcasting System (MBS), and the **Sports** Nippon Newspaper. It also publishes the popular *Mainichi Daily News*, an English-language edition.

MAKI FUMIHIKO, 槇文彦 (1928–). In 1993, Maki Fumihiko won the Pritzker Architecture Prize, the most prestigious recognition granted in **architecture**. He is only the second Japanese architect, the first being the famous **Tange Kenzō**, to be so honored. He also won the Raynolz Prize as well as many other awards. Born in **Tōkyō**, Maki studied under Tange at the **University of Tōkyō**. He then trained and worked at the Cranbrook Academy of Art in Bloomfield Hills, Michigan, at the Harvard School of Design, and at several famous architectural firms in New York and Great Britain. He served on the faculties of both Washington University in St. Louis and Harvard, and he later became affiliated with Keiō University.

In 1965, Maki returned to Japan and established his own firm, Maki and Associates. While the majority of his buildings are in Japan, he has creations all over the world. He is a modernist whose works are constructed out of metal, concrete, and glass. He maintains a strong interest in new **technology** and materials. His creations combine innovative use of materials with spatial depth. His buildings Spiral and the Tōkyō Metropolitan Gymnasium are outstanding examples of this.

Maki's most recognized creations include Hillside Terrace Flats in Daikanyama (1967–1992), the **Ōsaka** Prefectural Sports Center (1972), several buildings for the University of Tsukuba (1974–1976), the **Okinawa** Aquarium (1975), the Royal Danish Embassy (1977–1979), a **YKK** Guest House in Kurobe (1982), the Kyōto National Museum of Modern Art (1983–1986), the Fujisawa Municipal Gym (1984), the Wacoal Art Centre or the Spiral Building (1985), the TEPIA Science Pavilion (Tōkyō, 1989), and the Nippon Convention Center at Makuhari Messe complex (1989).

Maki, although an avowed modernist architect and an urban planner, is known for his classical modern design executed with a craftsman-like approach to technology. In 2004, the *New York Times* announced that Maki had been chosen to design one of the new office buildings at the World Trade Center. In 2009, he won the competition to design an addition for the **United Nations**.

Even at his advanced age, Maki continues to design fantastic buildings. He drew up the plans for New York's Tower 4 at the World Trade Center, which opened in 2013. Some of his other recent fantastic buildings include Aga Khan University in London and Aga Khan Museum in Toronto.

MANGA, 漫画. Manga are popular Japanese comics. There are many genres of manga. *Shōjo manga* are magazines created especially for girls. Females write these for other females. Their main themes center on mother-daughter relationships, girls rising to stardom, and love stories. *Shōjo manga* often contain Western or pseudo-Western styles and orientations. Some examples of *shōjo manga* include *Ribbon, Margaret, Shōjo Comic Nakayoshi Lala,* and *Card Captor Sakura.*

Shōnen Jump (*Boys' Jump*) is probably Japan's most famous children's comic book publisher. Colorful and full of lively action, it has a huge market in Japan. Torishima Kazuhiko edits this best-selling magazine. *Shōnen manga* are designed especially for boys and include such comics as *Jump, Mangajin, Champion,* and *Sunday.*

The "Lolita complex," or *Rorikon manga,* are named after the Nabokov novel where men have an unhealthy desire for very young girls. These erotic adult manga have a large following in Japan. Although starting much earlier, *Rorikon manga* began to flourish in the 1980s when young girls became the idealized sex objects.

Yokoyama Mitsuteru (1934–2004) was one of Japan's best manga artists. He was the author of *Sangokushi, Suikoden,* and *Shiki,* which all treated ancient China in historical themes. A prolific writer in the 1960s, Yokoyama was a contemporary of **Tezuka Osamu.** Yokoyama produced dozens of titles, but his best-known work was *Tetsujin #28* (*Iron Man 28,* a.k.a. *Gigantor*). Tetsujin was a popular **robot** who spawned a series of successors. In 1966, he created 52 **television** episodes of *Gigantor.* Yokoyama excelled at producing action figures including *Gigantor, Giant Robo,* and *Babel.*

Ishinomori Shōtarō (1938–1998) created the super-long history comic *Manga Nihon no Rekishi* (*A Manga History of Japan*), which ran to 10,000 pages and 55 volumes. He also published *A Manga Introduction to the Japanese Economy,* which first appeared in 1986. He helped lead the way in the development of "textbook manga," or what is also called "information manga." He also produced *Kamen Rider* and *Go Rangers,* which debuted in 1955. Ishinomori was the "king of manga."

Toriyama Akira (1955–2010) created the weekly manga called *Dragon Ball,* which ran from 1984 through 1995 and was collected into 42 individual **books.** The story follows the monkey-tailed boy Son Gokū who is loosely based on the Chinese folktale known as *Journey to the West.* Son fights many battles and becomes an accomplished martial arts expert. *Dragon Ball Z* is the ending of the superhero **anime** popular as a children's program. Toriyama's artwork is often used in **video games.**

Matsumoto Reiji (1938–) is famous for his *shōjo manga.* He did the manga and anime for *Galaxy Express 999* and *Queen Esmeraldas. Galaxy Express 999* is a space odyssey manga about space travel in a future world. Hoshino Tetsurō, the hero, is a boy who travels in a steam locomotive–like spaceship with a mysterious **woman** to acquire a mechanical body. This anime was directed by Nishizawa Nobutaka and produced by Tōei Animation.

Ikegami Ryōichi (1944–) is one of Japan's best manga artists. His stories such as *Crying Freeman*, an original work by Koike Kabuo, and *Sanctuary*, first written by Fumimura Shō, have gained him great fame as a cartoonist over the past 30 years. Ikegami was also the manga artist for such series as *Mai the Psychic Girl*, *Samurai Crusader*, and *Strain*. His well-known manga vividly portray man's desire, greed, and human qualities. His better-known works include *A Taste of Revenge* and *Journey to Freedom*.

Nagai Gō (1945–) is a famous manga artist who did the anime for such **films** as *Abashiri Family*, *Black Lion*, *Cutey Honey*, *Devil Man*, *Kekko Kamen*, and *Violence Jack*. *Cutey Honey* (*Kiyuchi hani*) is a television series based on Nagai's popular manga that first appeared in 1973–1974. It features the curvaceous android created by Professor Kisaragi. In this heroine action story, Cutey Honey, a female android, fights the **crime** syndicate.

There is even a style of Japanese comic books and graphic novels that aims typically at adults. **Takahashi Rumiko** produces some of the very best in the manga world and aims her work at adults. There are even manga dictionaries, a *Manga for Dummies* book, a listing of manga bestsellers in the *New York Times*, and courses and classes on manga. *See also* AKATSUKA FUJIO, 赤塚不二夫 (1935–2008); *DORAEMON*, ドラえもん; FUJIKO FUJIO, 藤子不二雄; IKEDA RIYOKO, 池田理代子 (1947–); KOBAYA-SHI YOSHINORI, 小林善範 (1953–); *SAZAE-SAN*, サザエさん; TEZU-KA OSAMU, 手塚治虫 (1928–1989).

MARUBENI (MARUBENI KABUSHIKI-GAISHA, 丸紅株式会社). Marubeni is one of Japan's most important **general trading companies** (*sōgō shōsha*). Headquartered in **Tōkyō**, but with major branches in **Ōsaka**, **Nagoya**, and other cities, Marubeni was founded in the mid-19th century but was incorporated in 1949. It is Japan's fifth-largest general trading company. In 2008, Asada Teruo (1948–) became president and CEO of Marubeni and remains in that position. Marubeni has assets of more than ¥6.9 billion and nearly 40,000 employees in 11 offices in Japan and 120 offices in 66 countries.

MARUYAMA MASAO, 丸山眞男 (1914–1996). Maruyama Masao was a famous political scientist best known for his study of the history of political thought. Born in **Ōsaka**, he graduated from the law department of Tōkyō Imperial University in 1937. He joined the faculty there, becoming a full professor in 1950 and retiring in 1971. Maruyama not only contributed greatly to the development of political science in Japan but also provided a penetrating analysis of Japan's actual social and ideological situation as seen from the viewpoint of democracy. He had a profound influence on intellectual thought in postwar Japan. A progressive thinker, Maruyama was known for his strong defense of democracy in Japan. He based his arguments in favor of democracy not only on Western philosophers but also on Japan's leading thinkers such as Fukuzawa Yukichi.

In his writings and teachings, Maruyama analyzed the social aspects and ideology of Japan and examined their impact on the country's political system. An outspoken critic of the establishment, he wrote extensively on the Japanese government, arguing that the country's postwar democracy was actually fascism in disguise. In his seminal work *Chōkokka shugi no ronri to shinri* (*The Logic and Psychology of Ultranationalism*, 1946), he examined the psychological underpinnings of Japan's antidemocratic organizations and sparked controversy with his criticism of the **imperial system**. He was praised for his ability to apply abstract concepts to actual events, and his writings, noted for their eloquence and clarity, were required reading for students of Japan's modernization. His work inspired the student antigovernment demonstrations in the 1960s. *See also* STUDENT MOVEMENTS.

MATSUDA SEIKO, 松田聖子 **(1962–).** Matsuda Seiko is one of Japan's most popular idol singers of all time. She is affectionately known as Seiko-chan. A native of Fukuoka, she is both a singer and an **actress**. She performs in Japan and the **United States**, having made her debut in 1980. Matsuda has been compared to Madonna with her scandals and reinvention of herself. Although having been married to Kanda Masaki, an actor, and being the mother of a child, she still manages to stir up controversy with near-nude appearances in **television** commercials and in **advertising**. Ever popular, as of 2009, Matsuda has had 13 albums in Oricon's Top 100 Album Chart at the same time, surpassing **Misora Hibari** who had 12. Matsuda is on the top 3 list of the most number one albums in Japan. In 2011, Oricon crowned her the number one everlasting idol of all time. *See also* MUSIC.

MATSUI HIDEKI, 松井秀喜 **(1974–).** Matsui Hideki, Japan's most popular and perhaps most talented **baseball** player, was the all-star center fielder for the **Yomiuri Giants** until he left Japan to play for the New York Yankees in 2002 for $21 million over three years. Anxious to test his abilities, Matsui joined the Yankees in 2003, becoming the first power hitter from Japan to make the move to the Major Leagues. At 6 feet, 2 inches tall and weighing 210 pounds, he hit 332 home runs in nine seasons in Japan. Known as "Godzilla," Matsui, a three-time most valuable player (MVP) in the Japanese Central League, put fear in American League pitchers.

Born in Ishikawa, Matsui participated in four National High School Baseball Tournaments at Koshien Stadium, once in the spring and three times in summer. In 1992, he drew five consecutive intentional walks in a game at Koshien tournament. Matsui graduated from Seiryo High School in Kanazawa and was drafted by the Yomiuri Giants in the first round. He played 10 years for the Giants leading them to three Japan Series Championships and was chosen the MVP three times.

After joining the New York Yankees, Matsui became the first Yankee to hit a grand slam in his first game at Yankee Stadium. He went on to hit .287 with 16 home runs and 106 RBIs in 2003. He finished 2004 with a .298 average with 31 home runs and 108 RBIs. In 2005, Matsui hit a career high .305 and 116 RBIs. He played in 1,573 consecutive games with the Yomiuri Giants and did not miss a game in his first three-plus seasons with the Yankees, putting together a streak of 519 games played before fracturing his wrist on 11 May 2006. An all-star in each of his first two seasons with New York, the soft-spoken Matsui is a Major League career .292 hitter with 141 home runs and 597 RBIs. In 2005, he signed a four-year deal for $52 million, surpassing **Suzuki "Ichirō"** as the highest-paid Japanese player in baseball. Matsui led the Yankees to the 2009 World Series title hitting .615 (8 for 13) with three home runs and eight RBIs and winning the Most Valuable Player Award.

Matsui was very popular in Japan. It is said that as many as 35 Japanese sportscasters followed Matsui while he played in the **United States**. However, after seven seasons, the Yankees seemed to lose interest in Matsui, so he played one season each with the Los Angeles Angels, the Oakland Athletics, and the Tampa Bay Rays. He retired after the 2012 season and was honored by both the New York Yankees and the Tōkyō Yomiuri Giants. At the peak of his career, Matsui earned $13 million a year. With a strong sense of philanthropy, he donated large sums of money to victims of natural disasters, giving close to $1 million to victims of the **Great East Japan Earthquake** of 2011.

MATSUI KEIKO, 松居慶子 **(1961–).** Matsui Keiko is a phenomenal female jazz performer, composer, and keyboard artist and a major figure in **music**. A native of **Tōkyō**, she graduated from Japan Women's University with a major in children's culture. She studied music at the Yamaha Music Foundation, becoming its top student and then a private teacher. She started a jazz group called Cosmos. Her most famous creation is "A Drop of Water." One database identified her as a "fusion-new age keyboard player." Matsui tours extensively in the **United States** as a composer and jazz pianist. Matsui's *Deep Blue* and *Whisper from the Mirror* are two of the top-selling jazz albums in the world. She is the only Japanese in the top 25 category.

She began performing in 1980 and since then has released 20 CDs in addition to other creations. She has been deeply influenced by the music of Stevie Wonder, Sergei Rachmaninoff, Maurice Jarre, and Chick Corea as well as other musical greats of a wide variation of styles. In 1987, she met the producer Matsui Kazu and formed a partnership, both in music and life.

Winner of many musical awards, Matsui blends both Eastern and Western musical styles. Her compositions reflect both styles and even add an ethereal, other-worldly quality. Matsui supports various charitable causes including breast cancer, bone marrow programs, and the **United Nations**. She has also contributed to various **environmental** causes.

MATSUSHITA GROUP (MATSUSHITA GURŪPU, 松下グループ). Matsushita Group is a leading *keiretsu* specializing in electrical merchandise. Its Matsushita Electric Industries is a major Japanese electronics producer, one of the world's largest, located in the **Ōsaka** area. **Matsushita Kōnosuke** founded the company in 1918 to make small batteries for bicycle lamps. During the boom years, the company produced and aggressively marketed electrical goods for the mass market, achieving huge growth both domestically and internationally. Matsushita is one of the largest manufacturers of consumer electric and electronic products in the world, with 570 companies in 45 countries producing more than 15,000 products and selling under the brand names Panasonic, Quasar, Technics, Ramsa, **Victor Company of Japan**, and National.

The Matsushita Electric Industrial Company, now identified as Panasonic Corporation, had revenue of approximately $70 billion in 2016. Panasonic is deeply involved in technological innovations such as communications, fire alarms and firefighting equipment, electric cars such as Tesla, digital images, solar power devices, plasma televisions, and power batteries, just to name a few. It is linked with leading companies in the **United States**, **China**, India, Vietnam, Slovenia, South Africa, Nigeria, and a host of other places. In early 2016, Panasonic and the City of Denver formed a formal partnership to make Denver the "smartest" city in America. As of early 2017, Panasonic president Kazuhiro is trying to make the organization profitable.

MATSUSHITA KŌNOSUKE, 松下幸之助 (1894–1989). Matsushita Kōnosuke was the founder of Matsushita Electric Industries. Born into a poor farming family in Wakayama Prefecture, Matsushita worked at various manual jobs from the age of nine. In 1918, he opened a small electric fixture shop in Ōsaka, where he had huge success in making small bicycle lamp batteries. He enlarged this into a home electric appliance plant in 1933 and reorganized it as Matsushita Electric Industries in 1935, becoming its president.

Although purged for a time by the Allied **Occupation** authorities after World War II, Matsushita returned to public life in 1947 and, after strenuous efforts, reconstructed his company. He established contractual ties with N. V. Philips's Gloeilampenfabriken in 1952 and had the highest personal income in Japan for that year. Always seeking innovations, Matsushita developed a series of home electric appliances and pushed his company to the forefront of the industry through introduction of mass-production systems and original sales tactics. He also placed special emphasis on exports and made National an internationally known brand name.

Even when American-style management swept through Japan in the post-war years, Matsushita stuck to traditional Japanese management practices. He launched the PHP (Peace and Happiness through Prosperity) movement in 1946 and advocated a management philosophy aimed at attaining peace and prosperity for society through **business** activities. This organization still serves as a philanthropic establishment. Matsushita was also involved in various cultural activities, including the establishment of the Asuka Conservation Association, the promotion of **Shintō** studies, and the creation of the Matsushita School of Government and Business. Matsushita, who served as the company's president until 1961 and chairman of the board until 1973, was the archetype of the Japanese entrepreneurial capitalist. *See also* MATSUSHITA GROUP (MATSUSHITA GURŪPU, 松下グループ).

MAZDA MOTOR COMPANY (MATSUDA KABUSHIKI-GAISHA, マツダ株式会社). Founded in 1920, the **automobile** company took its present name in 1984. It exports cars to more than 120 countries but also produces cars in the **United States** as well as in 18 other countries. Headquartered in **Hiroshima**, Mazda has a plant there that is one of the world's largest, producing more than 700,000 units a year. In 1967, Mazda Motor Company, known in Japan as Matsuda, became the world's first carmaker to manufacture cars with three types of engines, the regular piston engine, a diesel engine, and its newly developed Wankel rotary engine.

In the 1970s, Mazda linked up with Ford to help both automobile makers. By the 1980s, Mazda MX-5, or the Miata as it was known outside Japan, became a highly successful sports car that advanced the Mazda image.

The 1990s was a bad decade for Mazda with high costs and a disastrous attempt to diversify its brand image. It had been known for its economical budget car, but it attempted to do too much too quickly. Mazda held talks in 1999 with Ford Motor Company to discuss further ties between the two companies. Ford held 33 percent of Mazda's equity stake before the talks.

In 2011, Mazda raised more than $1.9 billion in a record share sale to replenish capital, as it suffered its biggest annual loss in 11 years. Mazda used part of the proceeds to jointly build an auto plant in Mexico with **Sumitomo Corporation**.

In May 2015, the company signed an agreement with **Toyota** to form a "long-term partnership" that would, among other things, see Mazda supply Toyota with fuel-efficient SkyActiv gasoline and diesel engine technology in exchange for hydrogen fuel cell systems. In 2015, Ford sold its remaining shares in Mazda when the price of the shares had sunk drastically.

Mazda's goal is to make cars that are fun to drive and yet affordable. It seeks to foster the passionate spirit of driving enjoyment. It manufactures and sells passenger cars, commercial vehicles, and automotive parts, operating in Japan, North America, Europe, and other places. It sells the majority of its vehicles overseas. In 2015, Mazda ranked 15th in the world in auto sales with more than 1.5 million units sold. As of 2016, Mazda has 40,892 employees and sales of nearly $28 billion. Kogai Masamichi serves as Mazda's CEO.

MIFUNE TOSHIRŌ, 三船敏郎 **(1920–1997).** Mifune Toshirō was one of Japan's greatest movie stars, making 170 feature **films** and achieving international fame. Mifune was born in **China** and lived there with his family until he was 19. Drafted into the Japanese army, he served in China until he was repatriated in 1946.

In 1947, Mifune entered one of the "new face" contests of the Tōhō Company and was noticed by a senior director who recommended him to a former pupil. Film director **Kurosawa Akira** later cast Mifune in an important gangster (*yakuza*) role. Mifune went on to appear in 16 of Kurosawa's pictures. Mifune's main films include *Rashōmon*, *Yōjimbō*, and *Donzoko* (*The Lower Depths*). Mifune and Kurosawa last worked together in the film *Akahige* (*Red Beard*, 1965).

Within Japan, Mifune's popularity was based mainly upon his recreation of the role of the nihilistic samurai hero. In the West, however, his apparently uninhibited performance impressed an audience not used to the grand style in film acting. Mifune gives Kurosawa full credit for his film successes, something that seems to be quite accurate. After breaking with Kurosawa, Mifune turned to **television** work and roles in foreign films. However, in these endeavors he was never as successful.

MIIKE MINE STRIKE (*MITSU TANKŌ RŌSHI FUNSŌ,*** 三池炭鉱).** The Miike Mine Strike refers to a famous Mitsui coal mine strike that occurred in 1959–1960. Lasting nearly nine months, the Miike strike involved hundreds of thousands of workers. The miners, backed by the **General Council of Japanese Trade Unions** (Sōhyō), resisted massive layoffs, and the mine responded with a lockout. Twenty-thousand Sōhyō supporters joined the miners who faced 10,000 police. Labor minister Ishida Hirohide, a progressive, tried to mediate the situation. The Miike Mine, representing

business interests, took a hard line against the workers' union, dismissing 15 percent of its 13,000 workers and lowering their benefits. In this strike, **labor** lost.

MIKI TAKEO, 三木武夫 (1907–1988). Miki Takeo, a politician who served as **prime minister** from 9 December 1974 to 24 December 1976, was known for initiating the limitation of **defense** spending to 1 percent of GNP. A native of Tokushima Prefecture, Miki was educated at Meiji University and the University of California at Berkeley. In 1937, he was elected to the **House of Representatives** as its youngest member and remained a member for 50 years, one of only five people to serve that long. As chief secretary of the Citizens' Cooperative Party (Kokumin Kyōdōtō), he was communications minister during 1947–1948 and was then transportation minister in **Hatoyama Ichirō**'s **cabinet**. He served in the National Democratic Party (Kokumin Minshutō) and the Reform Party (Kaishintō) before becoming secretary-general of the **Liberal Democratic Party** (LDP) in 1956. In 1958, Miki became state minister and head of the **Economic Planning Agency** under **Kishi Nobusuke**, but his opposition to the Police Duties Law and disagreement over revision of the **United States–Japan Security Treaty** caused him to resign in 1959.

In the early 1960s, Miki held important posts within the LDP, and although he was not regarded as belonging to the mainstream bureaucratic faction, he served as international trade and industry minister during 1965–1968. Miki was foreign minister and later international trade and industry minister in the **Satō Eisaku** cabinet. Satō defeated him in both the 1968 and 1970 **elections** for LDP president. **Tanaka Kakuei** defeated him in 1972. However, Miki was deputy prime minister from 1972 to 1974.

As prime minister from 1974 to 1976, Miki had to face the results of the economic recession caused by the 1973 oil crisis. His party base was weak, and he was elected mainly to avoid a major split between **Ōhira Masayoshi** and **Fukuda Takeo** within the party. Miki's "clean government" ticket rendered him initially very popular, but his plans to reform antimonopoly legislation failed because of **business** opposition, and he alienated party members by proposing new political funding laws, and the right wing by his **Korea** policy. His attempts to purge the party after the **Lockheed scandal** provoked even more hostility, but although Miki had lost support within the party, he battled on, supported by public opinion. In 1976, Miki announced the "1 percent of GNP" guideline for defense spending, thus setting a precedent for Japan during the next two decades. Despite his personal popularity with the public, the Lockheed scandal reflected poorly on the party, which lost its overall majority in the 1976 **Diet** election and had to make deals with minor parties to remain in power. Embarrassed by the result, Miki resigned and was succeeded by Fukuda.

MINAMATA DISEASE (*MINAMATA-BYŌ*, 水俣病). The first appearance of Minamata disease was in 1956 in Minamata City in Kumamoto Prefecture where mercury poisoning from the Chisso Corporation's chemical plant polluted the nearby sea. First fish, then animals such as cats, dogs, and pigs, and finally human beings found their nervous system disrupted, gradually lost motor skills, became deformed and paralyzed, and finally fell into a coma and died. The problem was severe for people who ate fish, shellfish, and other marine life that was contaminated by mercury. As of 2018, about 2,000 people have died of the disease, and more than 10,000 have received financial compensation from Chisso.

In 1973, Chisso Company, which had dragged its feet and refused to acknowledge responsibility for a long time, was found legally responsible for the mercury poisoning of the victims, nearly 20 years after the case began. The company made small, inadequate payments in the form of "sympathy money" to some of the victims. Chisso's domination of the political and economic scene, the victims' lack of personal assertiveness, and the reluctance of the victims to challenge authority caused the apathetic victims to more readily accept their fate. Victims of what was colloquially called the "cat dancing disease" also faced severe discrimination in their communities as people shunned them, not knowing what caused the disease.

The government indicted Chisso executives in the first **criminal** proceedings for Minamata pollution in 1976. In 1979, the Japanese **judicial system** convicted Chisso executives, holding them responsible for the Minamata pollution case. However, the government never threw its full weight behind pollution control or compensation for victims of mercury poisoning. The case of Minamata disease is a serious blot on the ecological history of Japan and remains an important issue in contemporary Japanese society and a stimulus to the Japanese environmental movement.

Driven by the desire for rapid **economic** growth, Chisso failed to take into account the **environment**. The collusion between government and industry allowed the company and its owners to profit at the expense of the people living near the plant. However, as Japan became more affluent and environmentally conscious, the country shifted its motivation from rapid industrialization to improving the quality of life.

Chisso and the government carried out a cleanup plan by covering the worst-contaminated areas with landfill, dredging mercury from the water, and installing a cement barrier in the worst part of the sea. The government, serving as "the fox watching the henhouse," declared the area safe for fishing in 1997.

There was also a second outbreak of Minamata disease in Niigata Prefecture in 1965 when mercury poisoning from Shōwa Electrical Company polluted the nearby sea. These two mercury disasters, along with the outbreak of

Yokkaichi asthma due to chemical poisoning and Itai-itai disease in mining communities of Toyama Prefecture, are considered the "Four Big Pollution Diseases of Japan."

MINISTRY OF ECONOMY, TRADE, AND INDUSTRY (KEIZAI SANGYŌSHŌ, 経済産業省). In 2001, the Japanese government reorganized the **Ministry of International Trade and Industry** by merging it with agencies from other ministries related to economic development such as the **Economic Planning Agency** to form the Ministry of Economy, Trade, and Industry (METI). Today, METI plays a central role in the development and implementation of policies on industry and international **trade**. Broadly speaking, METI is organized into the Economic and Industrial Policy Bureau, the Trade Policy Bureau, the Trade and Economic Cooperation Bureau, and the Industrial **Science and Technology** Policy and Environment Bureau.

METI compiles and publishes vast amounts of statistics on the **economy**. It issues white papers on a wide variety of international economic topics and communicates with the public through press releases. It focuses on domestic and international economic policy, assisting manufacturing, providing information and services, assisting small and medium enterprise activities, promoting **energy** conservation and development, encouraging **environmental** protection, maintaining nuclear and industrial safety, and overseeing Japanese patents.

Yet, METI controls much of Japan's economic policy including trade, industrial development, and energy policy. Its leaders are generally liberal and highly skilled officials. It is a major driving force of the Japanese government. Sekō Hiroshige (1962–) became minister of economy, trade, and industry on 3 August 2016. *See also* FOREIGN POLICY.

MINISTRY OF FINANCE (ZAIMUSHŌ, 財務省). The Ministry of Finance (MOF) is an important government agency that shapes the government budget, supervises the financial system, sets Japan's interest rates, and allocates capital in order to meet government policies. For centuries, the state treasury or the more recent MOF had been called the Ōkurashō in Japanese. However, in 2001, the government changed its Japanese name to Zaimushō.

Historically, the MOF sought to keep the cost of capital low so that Japan's industries could expand easily. It fostered close ties between **banks** and **businesses** and generally discouraged an overheating of the **Tōkyō Stock Exchange**. It encouraged businesses and the government to pursue long-term goals and cooperate with each other. By so doing, it complemented the efforts of the other crucial economic ministry, the **Ministry of International Trade and Industry**.

The **Occupation** purges dismissed only nine officials from the MOF. Left largely intact, the MOF deserves considerable credit for rebuilding Japan's postwar **economy**. Its main goal has been the growth and creation of national wealth. To illustrate the power of this ministry, 10 ministers of finance, including **Ikeda Hayato**, **Satō Eisaku**, and **Tanaka Kakuei**, have become **prime ministers** in the postwar period. The MOF has been more than a great ministry. It has been a powerful economic, political, and intellectual force unsurpassed by any other government agency.

Heavily populated by **University of Tōkyō** graduates primed for success as lawyers, politicians, and national leaders, the MOF has been deeply involved in directing Japan's economy. Cautiously following a free market philosophy, these leaders have systematically controlled Japan's macroeconomic policies.

Today, the MOF drafts and implements Japan's annual budget, oversees the collection of taxes, regulates financial markets, and manages the bank deposit insurance. However, it has less control over the securities market than is the case in some other countries. The MOF's reputation was sullied in the late 1990s when several executives were arrested for corruption and mismanagement. This was one of the reasons for the reforms in 2001.

Several powerful individuals have held the position of minister of finance. Recently, Sakakibara Eisuke was known as "Mr. Yen" due to his powers. **Kuroda Haruhiko** and Mizoguchi Zembei were called "Mr. Asian Currency" and "Mr. Dollar," respectively. As of January 2018, **Asō Tarō** is still the minister of finance, as well as the deputy prime minister. Having taken office on 26 December 2012, he is the longest-serving finance minister on record.

MINISTRY OF FOREIGN AFFAIRS (GAIMUSHŌ, 外務省). Founded in 1869, the Ministry of Foreign Affairs (MOFA) was the one ministry not affected by the large-scale ministerial reorganization of 2000. However, international and internal problems such as territorial disputes, a visit by a Taiwanese ex-president, school **textbook controversies**, and fraudulent handling of secret funds have troubled the ministry. Moreover, the assertive Tanaka Makiko declared war on her own ministry by accusing the executives of fraud in handling secret funds of the ministry. Prime Minister **Asō Tarō**, a former MOFA secretary, attempted to rebalance the ministry.

By law, the MOFA conducts **foreign policy** under the leadership of the **prime minister** and the guidance of the **Diet**. According to its legal basis, the MOFA should aim to improve the well-being of Japan and Japanese nationals, while contributing to the maintenance of a peaceful and safe international society. Through active and energetic measures, it seeks to foster a good international environment and keep and develop harmonious foreign relations. Specifically, the MOFA handles consular, immigration, communications, arms control, atomic **energy**, conflict prevention, human rights, international peacekeeping missions, security issues, official development assistance, **United Nations** connections, and cultural exchange matters.

According to the **constitution**, the prime minister has the last word in foreign policy decisions. The minister of foreign affairs acts as the prime minister's chief adviser and spokesperson. Career foreign service officers, selected through competitive examinations and rigorously trained for their assignments, represent Japan at numerous diplomatic posts around the world. Graduates of the **University of Tōkyō** frequently staff the MOFA desks, a highly prestigious career opportunity. Noted political figures such as **Yoshida Shigeru**, **Kishi Nobusuke**, and **Miyazawa Kiichi**, as well as 11 other prime ministers, have served previously as head of MOFA.

Recent difficult matters that have demanded the attention of the MOFA include the **"comfort women"** issue, the history textbook controversies, official visits to **Yasukuni Shrine**, memorial services for war dead, and bilateral relations. As Japan becomes more powerful and outgoing in the world, the MOFA has become more important. Kishida Fumio (1957–) became foreign minister on 26 December 2012. Kōno Tarō succeeded him on 3 August 2017.

MINISTRY OF HEALTH, LABOR, AND WELFARE (KŌSEI RŌDŌSHŌ, 厚生労働省). The Ministry of Health, Labor, and Welfare (MHLW), commonly known as Kōrōshō, was established in 2001 by the merger of the Ministry of Labor and the Ministry of Health and Welfare. Sakaguchi Chikara was the first head of MHLW and served for more than three years under Prime Minister **Koizumi Jun'ichirō**. Yanagisawa Hakuo, who served as minister during 2006–2007, caused a great stir when he referred to **women** as "birth-giving machines." The ministry has approximately 100,000 staff members with around 25 percent working on **labor** issues. It deals with issues of health care, children and child rearing, the elderly, disabled individuals, social security, labor policies, equal employment, and employment security. It also regulates Japan's food and drug industry. (Refer to appendix C.)

Recently, MHLW has had to face the issue of *karoshi*, or death from overwork. Given that there have been several incidents, MHLW has taken steps to avoid this problem. Shiozaki Yasuhisa (1950–) served as head of MHLW from 3 September 2014 to 3 August 2017 when Katō Katsunobu (1955–) assumed its leadership position.

MINISTRY OF INTERNATIONAL TRADE AND INDUSTRY (TSŪSHŌ SANGYŌSHŌ, 通商産業省, OR TSŪSANSHŌ). The Ministry of International Trade and Industry (MITI) was an important government agency that controlled the allocation of foreign exchange within the Japanese

economy and licensed foreign **technology** to Japanese users. MITI was created in 1949 from the former Ministry of Commerce and Industry. It was given the responsibility of coordinating Japan's international trade policy. It supervised imports and exports as well as assisting industries and businesses not overseen by other ministries. In short, MITI was a major architect of Japan's industrial and trade policies. (Refer to appendixes I and J.)

After the **Occupation** ended, MITI came to dominate the Japanese economy, directing what might be called a semi-planned economy. MITI cooperated with various **business** concerns to manage Japan's economic ship of state. Working with the **Bank of Japan** and the **Economic Planning Agency**, it offered advice to Japanese firms about all kinds of economic and technical matters. It also regulated foreign exchange and the importation of foreign technology. Thus, MITI, as one of Japan's two most powerful ministries along with the **Ministry of Finance**, directed much of Japan's postwar economic and international recovery with a tight control over foreign trade.

During the 1950s and 1960s, MITI successfully strived to protect Japan's domestic industry from international competitors. As Japanese industry became stronger, MITI tended to loosen its grasp on economic controls; it also had to respond to strong international criticism for Japan's restricted trade policies. Gradually bowing to international pressure, MITI liberalized Japan's import policies. Because MITI was such an important ministry, it was often a training ground for future **prime ministers**. With its declining influence, in 2001 MITI was reorganized into a new, larger body: the **Ministry of Economy, Trade, and Industry**. *See also* FOREIGN POLICY.

MINOBE RYŌKICHI, 美濃部亮吉 (1904–1984). Minobe Ryōkichi was an economist and politician. Born in **Tōkyō**, he was the son of the famous jurist Minobe Tatsukichi. His mother was the eldest daughter of mathematician, educator, and politician Kikuchi Dairoku. After graduating in 1927 from Tōkyō Imperial University, where he became interested in Marxist economics under **Ōuchi Hyōe**, Minobe first lectured in the agriculture faculty from 1929 to 1932 and then taught at Hōsei University. He was arrested in 1938, along with other suspected leftists, in the so-called Popular Front Incident, and was removed from the university by the government. In 1945, Minobe became an editorial writer for the centrist **newspaper** *Mainichi Shimbun*. He was chosen to head the **Cabinet** Statistics Office in 1946.

After World War II, he became a professor at the Tōkyō University of Education. He was elected governor of Tōkyō Prefecture in 1967 with the support of the socialist and communist parties. He was elected again in 1971 and 1975. As governor, Minobe stressed social welfare and opposed the government's emphasis on rapid economic growth. After retiring from the governorship, he was elected to the **House of Councillors** in 1980.

As governor of Tōkyō, Minobe's many policy achievements included providing free health care for the elderly, enacting pollution controls, converting streets in heavily trafficked areas to pedestrian-only use, allowing the construction of the Korean School in Tōkyō, and ending government sponsorship of racetracks.

MISHIMA YUKIO, 三島由紀夫 **(1925–1970).** Mishima Yukio was a talented author, some of whose **literature** championed postwar nationalism and military preparedness. Born Hiraoka Kimitake and raised by his grandmother, Mishima led a disjointed childhood. He was sickly as a child, and his health prevented him from serving in the military and possibly led to his infatuation with the military. Indeed, he even founded his own right-wing armed force group and tried to inspire a military uprising.

Mishima, a prolific and sophisticated writer, covered a wide variety of subjects. His most famous works in translation are *Confessions of a Mask* (1949), *The Sound of Waves* (1954), *Temple of the Golden Pavilion* (1956), *After the Banquet* (1960), and a group of four novels collectively called *Sea of Fertility* that included *Spring Snow* (1967), *Runaway Horses* (1968), *Temple of Dawn* (1969), and *Decay of the Angel* (1970). Although married and the father of two children, Mishima carried on homosexual affairs with his quasi-military friends. He organized a pseudo-military group called the Shield Society. He stressed bodybuilding and encouraged Japan to rearm. When the military rejected Mishima's call for a return to militarism, he committed seppuku in dramatic fashion.

MISORA HIBARI, 美空ひばり **(1937–1989).** Misora Hibari was an *enka* superstar, considered Japan's greatest postwar singer. She was called the "Queen of Japanese singers." She recorded more than 1,400 songs. She was not only an excellent popular singer but also appeared in some 160 **films** during her 30-year career. Although reflecting the essence of Japanese society and culture, Misora came from **Korean** roots. Posthumously, Misora became the first **woman** recipient of the National Prize of Honor for her long-standing contributions to the **music** industry. In 1993, the Misora Hibari Museum opened in Arashiyama, **Kyōto.** Its popularity with fans and tourists is strong. "Yawarakai," her best-selling song, sold nearly two million copies. Her song "Kawa no nagare no yō ni" (1989), was voted best Japanese song of all time in a 1997 **NHK** poll.

MITSUBISHI CORPORATION (MITSUBISHI SHŌJI KABUSHIKI-GAISHA, 三菱商事株式会社). Mitsubishi Corporation, reorganized in the early 1950s, is Japan's largest **general trading company**. A leading member of the **Mitsubishi Group**, the Mitsubishi Corporation employs more than 60,000 people in its sales and distribution of machinery, chemicals, foods, **energy**, finance, **banking**, and other enterprises.

Mitsubishi Corporation is a member of the Mitsubishi *keiretsu*. It has more than 200 offices and subsidiaries in 90 countries and affiliation with approximately 1,200 companies.

Mitsubishi Corporation is a global integrated **business** operation that creates and operates businesses throughout the world in industrial finance, energy, metals, machinery, chemicals, and products for daily life. It focuses on traditional trading operations including natural resources development, manufacturing of industrial goods, retail, new energy, infrastructure, finance, and the development of new technologies.

The corporation experienced difficulties in the 1980s and fell to fifth place among Japanese general trading companies. By 2015, it had regained the top spot based on net earnings. In 2016, with significant losses in **China**, Mitsubishi lost its top ranking to **Itōchū**.

Mitsubishi has had a number of problems in the last decade. It has been forced to apologize to Chinese workers employed during World War II. It has apologized for selling cars with defective Takata airbags. It has apologized for fudging reports on emission data.

Kobayashi Ken (1949–) is chairman of the board of Mitsubishi Corporation, and as of April 2016, Kakiuchi Takehiko (1955–) serves as its president and CEO.

MITSUBISHI GROUP (MITSUBISHI GURŪPU, 三菱グループ). The Mitsubishi Group is one of Japan's leading *keiretsu*, perhaps the largest enterprise in Japan and the one with the greatest influence on the domestic **economy**. The first Mitsubishi Company was founded by Iwasaki Yatarō in the early 1870s and made its early money from shipping. As a leading prewar **zaibatsu**, Mitsubishi concentrated on building ships, planes, and machinery.

Shortly after World War II, the Mitsubishi Group came into being and quickly came to control more than 200 companies. In the postwar period, Mitsubishi firms have been important in the chemical and **petroleum** industries along with the manufacturing of **automobiles** and ships. It has also been successful with its financial institutions, electrical manufacturing, and **consumer electronics**. This group of companies, or *keiretsu*, is led by Mitsubishi Heavy Industries with emphasis on steel **construction** and consumer products.

One of Japan's five largest chip makers, Mitsubishi Electric Corporation began in 1921 and has since become one of Japan's leading producers of electrical and electronic equipment. It has production factories and sales bases in more than 30 countries. It has developed more than half of Japan's communication satellites. Mitsubishi Electric Corporation is one of Asia's top 25 companies as of 2005.

In 2015, the Mitsubishi Group was Japan's largest **general trading company** with more than 200 bases of operations in some 80 countries worldwide. Together with its more than 500 group companies, Mitsubishi employs a multinational workforce of around 54,000 people.

The Mitsubishi Group consists of more than 500 different companies, the most important being **Mitsubishi Motors Corporation**, Mitsubishi Electric Company, the international general trading company **Mitsubishi Corporation**, and the **Mitsubishi UFJ Financial Group**, one of Japan's leading **banks**. The fact that 23 of the 29 firms belonging to the Mitsubishi Group are named Mitsubishi shows the close nature of the *keiretsu*.

The Mitsubishi Group consists of hundreds of so-called group companies, some of which, such as **Nikon Corporation**, Kirin Brewery, and Asahi Glass, do not use the Mitsubishi name. The major firms within Mitsubishi are large multinational corporations, most of which are based in Japan but have offices and subsidiaries all over the world.

MITSUBISHI MOTORS CORPORATION (MITSUBISHI JIDŌSHA KŌGYŌ KABUSHIKI-GAISHA, 三菱自動車工業株式会社). Mitsubishi Motors Corporation, started in 1917, became independent from Mitsubishi Heavy Industries in 1970. It is the eighth-largest **automobile** manufacturer in Japan and the 17th largest in the world. It also makes buses, trucks, and car parts. Its car models have been awarded many prizes for excellence. It has had cooperative ventures with Chrysler since 1971 and, more recently, with Mercedes-Benz. Since 2000, defect scandals, inflexible management, and financial problems have plagued Mitsubishi Motors. Through the leadership of President Osamu Masuko (1949–), Mitsubishi Motors has become an important component of the **Mitsubishi Group**.

In October 2016, the **Nissan Group** purchased 34 percent of Mitsubishi Motors and thus became a part of the Renault-Nissan Alliance. Mitsubishi has an international outreach in joint ventures with the Dutch-made Volvo, with France's Peugeot, and with Germany's Volkswagen. Although Mitsubishi dropped its production facilities in Australia, Europe, and North America, it still has linkages with **China**, **South Korea**, India, Malaysia, and South Africa. It also produces cars in the Philippines and Thailand. In addition to traditional cars, Mitsubishi has branched out to include electric vehicles, motorsports cars, and racing speedsters.

MITSUBISHI UFJ FINANCIAL GROUP (KABUSHIKI-GAISHA MITSUBISHI UFJ GURŪPU, 株式会社三菱UFJフィナンシャル・グループ**).** As recently as 2006, Mitsubishi UFJ Financial Group, a leading component in the **Mitsubishi Group**, was the fifth-largest bank in the world. However, by 2008, it had dropped to the world's 20th-largest financial institution but was still Japan's biggest bank. In 2008, Fortune Global 500 ranked Mitsubishi UFJ as the world's 118th-largest company and Japan's 11th-largest company, with revenues of $56 billion. Created in 2001 by a merger of Mitsubishi Tōkyō Financial Group, Japan's second-largest bank, and UFJ Holdings, Japan's fourth largest at the time, the new bank has nearly $2 trillion in assets. As of 2016, it employed 34,276 people.

Mitsubishi UFJ Financial Group has done a good job in cleansing Japan's banks of bad loans. International evaluations rank it high on asset quality. It represents the trend toward consolidation of banks. Today, three vast conglomerates, Mitsubishi UFJ Financial, along with the **Mizuho Financial Group** and the **Sumitomo Mitsui Financial Group**, dominate Japan's financial system.

Mitsubishi UFJ has become more globally competitive, first by shoring up business in Japan, and then by doing more business internationally. With innovation and daring not usually seen in Japanese banking groups, it has recently sought a major equity stake in the Bank of **China**. UFJ Holdings' former president, Tamakoshi Ryosuke (1947–), is the chairman of the new holding company while Mitsubishi Tōkyō's president, Kuroyanagi Nobuo (1941–), became the president of the new Mitsubishi UFJ Financial Group. Hirano Nobuyuki (1951–) has served as its CEO since April 2013.

Mitsubishi UFJ Financial Group (MUFG) is a holding company that engages in financial businesses and services, including commercial, investment, and trust banking and asset management services, securities businesses, credit card businesses, and related services to individual and corporate customers. As of 2016, MUFG had assets of around $2.5 trillion, making it the world's fourth-largest bank based on total assets. It is Japan's largest financial group.

MITSUI & COMPANY (MITSUI BUSAN KABUSHIKI-GAISHA, 三井物産株式会社**).** Established in 1947, Mitsui & Company, also known as Mitsui Busan, leads the **Mitsui Group** as a **general trading company**. One of Japan's largest trading companies, it specializes in machinery, **energy**, chemicals, foods, textiles, and finance. It is heavily involved in overseas trading.

By 2015, Mitsui & Company was the second-largest general trading company in Japan. Part of the Mitsui Group, it operates 140 offices in 65 countries. As of 2017, its president and CEO is Yasunaga Tatsuo (1960–), who manages assets of $26 billion and employs 48,090 people.

MITSUI GROUP (MITSUI GURŪPU, 三井グループ). The Mitsui Group is one of Japan's leading *keiretsu*. It has 26 members with 171 affiliates in which the Mitsui Group ownership of stock constitutes 10 percent or more.

Mitsui Takatoshi founded the House of Mitsui when he opened a dry goods store in Edo in 1673. His **businesses** had close ties to the Tokugawa shogunate. Continued close relations with the government in the 19th century helped the group maintain its dominance in many sectors. As a prewar **zaibatsu**, Mitsui controlled 273 companies at the end of World War II. The zaibatsu was built on three main companies, Mitsui Banking, Mitsui Trading, and Mitsui Mining.

Since the zaibatsu dissolution following World War II, the Mitsui subsidiaries have been loosely grouped in a *keiretsu*. Two presidents' clubs—the Monday Club and the Second Thursday Club—replaced the holding company.

The major partners of the Mitsui Group include Sumitomo Mitsui Banking Corporation, the **Toshiba Corporation**, Mitsui & Company, the Sumitomo Mitsui Trust Holdings, Japan Steel Works, Mitsui Chemicals, Mitsui Fudōsan, Mitsui Mining, **Mitsui O.S.K. Lines**, and others. The Mitsui enterprises focus on petrochemicals, **construction**, **energy**, engineering, **banking**, insurance, mining, metals, real estate, and shipping. The Mitsui Group maintains a global network of 140 offices in 66 countries and has 445 subsidiaries and associated companies worldwide.

MITSUI MARIKO, 三井まりこ (1948–). Mitsui Mariko is a feminist and a **Tōkyō** assemblywoman. She is a strong, vocal supporter of **women** and women's issues in the Tōkyō Metropolitan Assembly. A very liberated woman, she spent 1982 in the **United States**, studying at Columbia University on a Fulbright scholarship. Mitsui opposes beauty contests and alleged prostitution tours. She has taught at various colleges for several years.

MITSUI O.S.K. LINES (MITSUI SHŌSEN KABUSHIKI-GAISHA, 三井商船株式会社). Mitsui O.S.K. Lines is one of Japan's largest shipping companies, but it also has diversified into other areas such as real estate and **advertising**. It has the most extensive cargo shipping lines in the world, traveling to some 300 ports in more than 100 countries.

Mitsui O.S.K. Lines, an important unit of the **Mitsui Group**, is a powerful player in Japan's **economy**. Although its origins date from the late 19th century, the present configuration was created in 1964 when the Ōsaka Commercial Company and the Mitsui Steamship Company merged. After a series of reorganizations, Mitsui O.S.K. moved forward with its use of container ships, ore carriers, and **automobile** transportation. In 1970, it began an ocean-going passenger service, and in 1983 it started shipping liquefied natural gas. As of 2017, Mitsui O.S.K. Lines has more than a dozen main subsidiaries and total assets of more than ¥65 billion.

MIYAKE ISSEI (ISSEY), 三宅一生 (1938–). Miyake Issei, or Issey Miyake as he is known by his label, is the first Japanese **fashion** designer to establish an avant-garde, Japanese-Western hybrid reputation on an international level. Born in Hiroshima Prefecture, he is a graduate of Tama University of Arts in **Tōkyō**. He then spent five years working for and learning from fashion designers in Paris and New York. He founded the Miyake Design Studio in 1971 and opened a shop in Tōkyō. His fashion creations are noted for their originality and unconventional designs. In 1976, he was invited to participate in the Festival d'Automne in Paris. He was the recipient of the 1984, 1989, and 1993 Mainichi Fashion Grand Prizes.

Miyake's clothing makes use of a lot of black and dark colors and uses a full draping form. His clothes are oversized, little cut, and leave the wearer with considerable freedom. His attention to fabric and its texture is legendary. In addition to the Miyake label, Miyake also sells clothes under the I.S. line. Miyake's pleated hemp material and polyester jersey fabric "Pleats Please," which he developed in the early 1990s, is well known internationally. He also has a smaller line of men's clothing. Miyake Issei retired from the fashion world in 1997 but continues to exercise great influence over it.

Miyake Issei has received many honors. In 2012, Miyake, along with **Andō Tadao**, became codirectors of 21 21 Design Sight, Japan's first design museum. Recently, the National Art Center in Tōkyō held a large and highly successful retrospective on Miyake Issei's 45-year career.

MIYAMOTO KENJI, 宮本顕治 (1908–2007). Miyamoto Kenji was a long-time politician and leader of the **Japanese Communist Party** (JCP). He was born in Yamaguchi Prefecture and graduated from Tōkyō Imperial University. While a student, he established a reputation when his essay on the writer Akutagawa Ryūnosuke won first prize in a competition sponsored by *Kaizō* magazine. Miyamoto joined the JCP in 1931 and continued his literary activities as a member of the Proletarian Writers' Union. In 1932, he married Miyamoto Yuriko (1899–1951), a famous writer. In 1933, he became a member of the central committee of the outlawed JCP; that same year, he was arrested and sent to prison where he remained until the end of World War II. He joined the newly reorganized JCP immediately after his release, but **Occupation** authorities purged him from political participation in 1950. From 1958, Miyamoto was a central figure in the JCP.

MIYAZAKI HAYAO, 宮崎駿 **(1941–).** A leading **anime** creator, Miyazaki Hayao generates serious, high-quality **films** for children and adults alike. Born in **Tōkyō**, he graduated from Gakushūin University with majors in political science and economics. Strongly influenced by Marxism, which he abandoned in the 1990s, his films carry a social message. After graduation, he went to work for Tōei Animation where he perfected his talent as an animator. Miyazaki's films, with their breathtaking animation, compelling plots, and interesting characters, have gained Miyazaki a strong international reputation.

Miyazaki created *Kaze no tani no Nausicaa* (*Nausicaa of the Valley of Wind*) in 1984. He also did the anime for *Majo no Takkyūbin* (*Kiki's Delivery Service*) and *Mononoke hime* (*Princess Mononoke*), a big hit that set a new earnings record for Japanese films and won the Japanese Academy Award for the Best Film of 1997. He also directed the popular *Tonari to Totoro* (*My Neighbor Totoro*). In 2001, Miyazaki completed *Sen to Chihiro no Kamikakushi* (*Spirited Away*), which won the Japanese Academy Award for Best Film and again set a new earnings record. Together with Takahata Isao, he founded **Studio Ghibli**, which is a leading producer of animated films.

Miyazaki's plots are entertaining, his characters compelling, and his animation amazing. Yet, he has a political streak to his films. He is a protector of nature, a defender of women, and an opponent of militarism. He has criticized, subtly and indirectly, Prime Minister **Abe Shinzō**'s efforts to change Article 9 of the **Constitution** and his denial of war crimes.

In 2013, Miyazaki directed *The Wind Rises*, a film that garnered his third American Academy Award and his first Golden Globe award nominations. Like his other films, this blockbuster gained him international acclaim and box office success. Overall, Miyazaki is only the second Japanese, after **Kurosawa Akira**, to receive the Honorary Academy Award. Miyazaki is the world's greatest animation director. He has been nominated for and received more film awards than any other person. Following the production of *The Wind Rises*, Miyazaki announced his retirement from filmmaking. However, his retirement statement may be premature, and the creative juices continue to flow. Miyazaki Hayao, giant in anime, even has his own special museum in Mitaka.

MIYAZAWA KIICHI, 宮澤喜一 **(1919–2007).** Miyazawa Kiichi was **prime minister** of Japan from 5 November 1991 to 9 August 1993. He was born in Fukuyama, Hiroshima Prefecture, and graduated from Tōkyō Imperial University with a law degree. In 1942, he joined the **Ministry of Finance**. From 1953 until 1967, he served in the upper house of the **Diet**, and then in 1967, he moved to the **House of Representatives** where he served until 2003. He represented the citrus-growing area of **Hiroshima**.

Miyazawa held a number of prominent public positions, including international trade and industry minister (1970–1971) under **Satō Eisaku**'s **cabinet** and foreign minister (1974–1976) under the **Miki Takeo** cabinet. He had considerable international experience and was pro–**United States** in his viewpoint. His platform included careful analysis of economic and **foreign policy** problems and efforts to "double Japan's assets." He was the director-general of the **Economic Planning Agency** (1977–1978) under the **Fukuda Takeo** cabinet and used his knowledge of world economics to Japan's advantage. He was also chief cabinet secretary during 1984–1986 under the **Nakasone Yasuhiro** administration. He became finance minister under the government of **Takeshita Noboru** in 1987. As finance minister, he tried to tighten **trade** rules but got caught in the **Recruit scandal**; he promptly resigned but was shortly reelected to the Diet.

Miyazawa became prime minister in November 1991 and served in that position for almost two years, gaining brief fame in the United States when President George H. W. Bush vomited in his lap and then fainted during a state dinner on 8 January 1992. Miyazawa had to resign in 1993 after a failure to pass political reforms caused the **Liberal Democratic Party** (LDP) to face its first defeat in a national **election** since its creation in 1955.

Miyazawa later returned to the post of finance minister from 1999 to 2002 in the governments of **Obuchi Keizō** and **Mori Yoshirō**. He was a two-term member of the **House of Councillors** and a 12-term member of the House of Representatives. Miyazawa, who headed one of the largest factions in the LDP, retired from the Diet in 2003.

MIZOGUCHI KENJI, 溝口健二 **(1898–1956).** Mizoguchi Kenji was a world-renowned **film** director whose more than 90 feature films, beginning in 1922, made him the dean of Japanese film directors. Mizoguchi's films from the late 1930s are characterized by long takes, fluid camerawork, and beautiful scenery. His first films dealt with the problems of the poor and class conflict. These films showed the sacrifice, voluntary or involuntary, of a **woman** for a man's success or for the sake of the family, a theme he used in many of his later films.

In 1946, Mizoguchi, committed to women's rights, directed *Jōsei no shōri* (*The Victory of Women*), a film that stars **Tanaka Kinuyo**, Kuwano Michiko, and Miura Mitsuko. The story is about a determined young woman lawyer whose fiancé, an antiwar liberal, dies in prison during the war. She defends a former schoolmate on a murder charge, against a reactionary prosecutor who was responsible for the death of her fiancé, arguing that the **crime** was committed because of the woman's desperate destitution at war's end.

Mizoguchi made his most famous films after the war, and several won international prizes. One of his most memorable is the beautiful, surreal *Ugetsu monogatari* (*The Story of Ugetsu*, 1953). It tells of the difficulties of a woman who died in the military conflicts that devastated Japan in the 16th century.

Saikaku ichidai onna (*The Life of Oharu*, 1952) is a poignant, exquisitely filmed portrait of a woman victimized by the brutal strictures of 17th-century feudal Japan. Widely regarded as one of the world's great films, *The Life of Oharu* is Mizoguchi's self-proclaimed masterpiece. Known for his graceful directorial style and sympathetic portrayal of women, Mizoguchi risked all to tell the devastating story of one woman's fall from lady-in-waiting to concubine to prostitute. Saikaku Ihara's classic 17th-century novel is brilliantly realized through a masterful screenplay and the heart-rending performance of Tanaka Kinuyo. The film, which won top honors at the Venice Film Festival, earned Mizoguchi worldwide recognition.

Akasen chitai (*Street of Shame*) was Mizoguchi's last film. As usual, his subject was the oppression of women, in this case, women who had been forced into prostitution by economic hardships following World War II.

MIZUHO FINANCIAL GROUP (MIZUHO FINANSHARU GURŪPU, みずほフィナンシャルグループ). According to the 2008 report of *Fortune* magazine, Mizuho Financial Group is the world's 30th-largest bank holding company by assets and the third of Japan's big three financial groups, along with **Sumitomo Mitsui Financial Group** (SMFG) and **Mitsubishi UFJ Financial Group** (MUFG). Mizuho's roots go back to the late 19th century with its ties to **Dai-Ichi Kangyō Bank**, Fuji Bank, and the Industrial Bank of Japan. Maeda Terunobu served as president of Mizuho Financial Group, which was formed in 2001 from the merger of these other banks.

Mizuho was the world's first bank to acquire $1 trillion in assets. As of 2012, Mizuho employed more than 56,000 people in 900 offices. It had combined assets of $1.6 trillion, making it the second-largest financial services institution in Japan. In **banking**, Mizuho still ranks third after MUFG and SMFG. As of 2016, Mizuho is 13th in the world based on total assets. Forbes ranks Mizuho as the 106th-largest company in the world. Its shares are listed on the **Tōkyō Stock Exchange** as well as on the New York Stock Exchange. In 2016, Mizuho established Mizuho Americas LLC as a U.S. bank holding company. Satō Yasuhiro (1952–) has been Mizuho's president and CEO since 2011.

MOBILE PHONE INDUSTRY. There are more mobile phones in Japan than there are people. Mobile phones, called *keitai denwa*, first appeared in Japan in 1979. Since then the devices have incorporated many features and exploded in popularity. There are four cellular service operators in Japan, **NTT DoCoMo**, **KDDI**, **SoftBank** Mobile, and Y!mobile. Japanese cell phone technology is quite sophisticated and the envy of users around the world. Japanese manufacturers of handsets include **Fujitsu**, **Kyōcera**, NEC-Casio, Panasonic, **Sharp**, and **Sony**.

MONJU, 文殊. Monju is Japan's experimental **nuclear power** plant located in Fukui Prefecture. Construction on the **energy**-producing reactor began in 1985, and it first went into operation in 1994. On 8 December 1995, the reactor suffered a serious accident. Intense vibration caused a thermometer inside a pipe carrying sodium coolant to break. The pipe heated up and broke, allowing sodium to leak into the ventilation system. Upon coming into contact with the air, the liquid sodium ignited, filling the room with deadly fumes and producing temperatures as high as 1,500 degrees Celsius.

There was massive public outrage in Japan when it was revealed that the Power Reactor and Nuclear Fuel Development Corporation, the semigovernmental agency then in charge of Monju, had tried to cover up the extent of the accident and resulting damage. This cover-up included falsifying reports and the editing of a videotape taken immediately after the accident. In November 2000, Japan's Atomic Energy Commission announced its intention to restart the Monju reactor. However, this decision met with public resistance, resulting in a series of court battles. In January 2003, the **Nagoya** High Court's Kanazawa branch reversed its earlier ruling. Although the Japanese Supreme Court gave the green light to reopen the Monju reactor in 2005, the reactor last operated in 2010 and is scheduled for decommissioning.

MORI HANAE, 森英恵 **(1926–).** "Hanae Mori," as her label reads, is a world-famous **fashion** designer who was born in Shimane Prefecture near **Kyōto**. Following graduation from Tōkyō Women's Christian University, Mori trained as an artist and textile designer. She opened her first studio in **Tōkyō** in 1951. Most of her early work was costume design for movies, having made the clothing for more than 700 **films**. Mori designed clothes for film directors **Kurosawa Akira** and **Mizoguchi Kenji** as well as clothes for Princess Masako.

In 1965, Mori presented her first show in New York and received much acclaim for her work. Her fashion activities have become global in scope. A member of the Paris world of high fashion, she has also designed uniforms for public officials in the People's Republic of **China**. She was a recipient of the Nieman Marcus Award and played a prominent role in the world of high fashion.

"Hanae Mori" showed a wonderful blend of traditional Japanese tastes and values presented in contemporary Western-style clothes. Her creations had a classic look of sophistication, which dazzled the modern fashion world. "Hanae Mori" is the only Asian designer to be accepted as a member of La Chambre Syndicale de la Couture Parisienne, receiving this honor in 1977.

As she moved into the 21st century, Mori's fashions took on a more youthful look, thanks to the influence of her American daughter-in-law Pamela, who is the creative director for the prêt-à-porter division, Mori's ready-to-wear line.

Mori's designs continue to garner worldwide recognition. Her fashion industry, which grossed more than $500 million annually as early as the 1990s, is still highly recognized and honored. Her designs are now mainly for haute couture collections. Mori's daughter-in-law and sons now run the **business**.

Mori helped put Japan on the map as a modern fashion-producing country. She only recently retired as the head of a fashion, real estate, and publishing empire. Mori Hanae is the Grande Dame of high fashion. In the design world, her creative energy, found in her butterfly trademark, still drives the fashion industry.

MORI MINORU, 森稔 (1934–2012). Mori Minoru was one of **Tōkyō**'s and Japan's most powerful and influential real estate developers. He truly helped shape Tōkyō's skyline with his towering buildings. After graduating from the **University of Tōkyō**, he joined his father, **Mori Taikichirō**, in the real estate business. He served as president and CEO of Mori Building. Together with his brother, Mori was on Forbes' list of the world's richest men. His real estate developments included the Shanghai World Financial Center, Roppongi Hills in Tōkyō, Mori Tower, Atago Green Hills, and Omotesandō Hills, all in Tōkyō. Mori's residential developments, including Ark Towers, Roppongi First Plaza, and Moto-Azabu Hills, are numerous as well as palatial. *Fortune* magazine named him Asia Businessman of the Year in 2007.

MORI TAIKICHIRŌ, 森泰吉郎 (1904–1993). Founding father of one of Japan's richest and most economically powerful families, Mori Taikichirō started a real estate firm that now owns more than 125 office buildings in **Tōkyō** including sections of Toranomon, Kamiyachō, Ark Hills, and the new Roppongi Hills complex. Mori graduated from Tōkyō Shōka University (now Hitotsubashi University) in 1928 and pursued an academic career before taking over the two buildings of the Mori Building Company after the death of his father in 1959. An enormous growth and economic boom in real estate fueled his progress, and he was especially successful in persuading local residents to cooperate with his development plans. At the time of his death, his company controlled 83 buildings in the center of Tōkyō, the most expensive real estate in the world. Immensely successful, Forbes ranked Mori as the second-wealthiest man in the world with $15 billion in assets in 1990. With the precipitous fall in real estate prices in Japan, the Mori sons, Minoru and Akira, while still rich, have lost a sizable portion of their fortune.

Dedicated to redevelopment, replacing wooden buildings with steel-frame concrete structures, Mori transformed downtown Tōkyō from a clutter of narrow lanes populated with houses, small shops, and workshops into a modern urban center of "smart buildings" equipped with **computer**-driven heating systems, electronic "talking" elevators, and electric curtains. These sleek glass, concrete, and brick towers boast foundations secured with an intricate system of rollers designed to absorb the shock of earthquakes. The Mori family is determined to make Tōkyō an attractive city with remarkable **architecture**. Mori Hirō, the grandson, says that Tōkyō needs more areas like the stylish Omotesandō, Shiroyama Hills, and Roppongi Hills.

MORI YOSHIRŌ, 森喜朗 (1937–). Mori Yoshirō became **prime minister** in a coalition government on 5 April 2000 when **Obuchi Keizō** fell into a coma and later died. Mori, a **Liberal Democratic Party** (LDP) member and secretary-general during 1998–1999, was a multi-term member of the **House of Representatives** from Ishikawa Prefecture (1969–2012). A graduate of Waseda University's Department of Commerce, Mori served in a variety of LDP and government leadership positions including deputy director-general to Prime Minister **Miki Takeo**, deputy chief **cabinet** secretary to Prime Minister **Fukuda Takeo**, chairman of the House of Representatives standing committee on finance, **education** minister in the **Nakasone Yasuhiro** cabinet, a number of other educational posts, chairman of the Policy Research Council of the LDP, international trade and industry minister in the **Miyazawa Kiichi** cabinet, secretary-general of the LDP (1993–1995), construction minister in the **Murayama Tomiichi** cabinet, chairman of the general council of the LDP (1996–1998), and, finally, secretary-general of the LDP (1998–2000). Mori succeeded former finance minister Mitsuzuka Hiroshi as the head of the third largest of the LDP factions. **Koizumi Jun'ichirō** replaced Mori as prime minister on 26 April 2001.

Mori's time as prime minister was marred by many gaffes, unpopular decisions, and general political mistakes. One of his biggest public relations disasters was to continue his **golf** game after learning that the submarine USS *Greeneville* had accidentally sunk the Japanese fishing ship *Ehime-Maru* during a training drill on 9 February 2000, resulting in the death of nine students and teachers. Improper gestures at Obuchi's funeral, misunderstanding President Bill Clinton's English, and inappropriate remarks about the **Shintō** religion made Mori look quite inept. Although never very popular, by the end of his term, his approval rating had dropped to less than 10 percent.

Mori resigned as prime minister after only one year in office. He is known as an avid **rugby** player from his days at Waseda and still serves as president of the Japan Rugby Football Union. In 2006, Mori became head of the Asia-Pacific Water Forum, a regional network of water improvement projects, which is sponsored by the Asian Development Bank. In 2014, Mori became a member of the **2020 Summer Olympics** Committee.

MORITA AKIO, 盛田昭夫 **(1921–1999).** Morita Akio, one of Japan's major **business** leaders, was the cofounder and chairman of **Sony Corporation**, the premier Japanese electronics company. Born in **Nagoya**, he graduated from Ōsaka Imperial University in 1944 with a major in physics. In 1946, together with **Ibuka Masaru**, Morita established Tōkyō Tsūshin Kōgyō, which later became Sony Corporation. He served as president and then chairman of the board. He handled the financial and business matters of the company, marketing Sony products all over the world. He helped Sony achieve success by "Americanizing" it through the establishment of a plant in San Diego, California, as well as by starting an important export business through Sony Trading Corporation. His efforts led to Sony's internationalization in many ways.

In 1949, Morita's company invented a magnetic recording tape and, in 1950, sold the first tape recorder in Japan. In 1957, it produced a pocket-sized radio and, a year later, renamed itself Sony (*sonus* is Latin for sound). In 1960, it produced the world's first transistor **television**. In 1961, Sony Corporation of America became the first Japanese company to be listed on the New York Stock Exchange. In 1989, Sony bought Columbia Pictures.

In the 1960s, Morita, an outspoken person, wrote a book called *Never Mind School Records*, which stressed that school performance is not important in one's success or ability to do business. His book *Made in Japan* (1987) became a bestseller at home and abroad. Together with **Ishihara Shintarō**, he published *The Japan That Can Say No* (1989), which was critical of U.S. business practices and encouraged Japan to take a more independent role in business and foreign affairs.

Morita became the vice chairman of the **Japan Federation of Economic Organizations** (Keidanren) and was a member of the Japan-U.S. Economic Relations Group. He was awarded the Albert Medal from the United Kingdom's Royal Society of Arts in 1982, the first Japanese to receive the honor. Two years later, he received the prestigious National Order of the Legion of Honor and, in 1991, was awarded the First Class Order of the Sacred Treasure by the emperor of Japan.

MORIYAMA MAYUMI, 森山眞弓 (1927–). Moriyama Mayumi, a graduate of Tsuda University, was the wife of a well-known **Liberal Democratic Party** politician who held a seat in the **House of Representatives**. She had a 30-year career as a bureaucrat in the Ministry of Labor. She was elected in June 1980 to the **House of Councillors**. She served as a spokesperson for actual, not just legal, equality for **women**. Moriyama was one of the two women whom Prime Minister **Kaifu Toshiki** appointed to his first **cabinet** in August 1989. She was the first female appointed to a cabinet position, but she held that position only about a year. In all, she held four different cabinet positions. In 2007, Moriyama became president of Hakuoh University and held that position until she retired in 2013.

MOTORCYCLE INDUSTRY. With the names **Honda, Kawasaki, Suzuki**, and **Yamaha**, Japan has contributed a great deal to the world's motorcycle industry. **Honda Sōchirō** began building motorized bicycles that led to the making of motorcycles. Through his efforts, Japanese motorcycles first competed in the Isle of Man Trophy race, which gave rise to the popularity of the Japanese motorcycle. His slogan, "You meet the nicest people on a Honda," opened a real marketing bonanza.

As of 2014, Japan was the world's largest motorcycle manufacturer. The "Big Four," Yamaha, Honda, Kawasaki, and Suzuki, continue to dominate. These companies are the driving force in international racing and the leaders in innovative design. They have captured the most wins of all motorcycle manufacturing companies. In Vietnam, the fourth-largest motorcycle market in the world after **China**, India, and Indonesia, the Honda motorcycle is so popular that people call all motorbikes "Hondas."

MR. CHILDREN, ミスターチルドレン. Mr. Children is one of Japan's most popular **music** groups, rising to fame in the 1990s. The group consists of four musicians: Sakurai Kazutoshi, the vocalist; Tahara Kenichi, the guitarist; Nakagawa Keisuke, the bass player; and Suzuki Hideya, the drummer. Formed in 1988, the group adopted its name in 1989. In 1996, they won the Nihon Record Taishō Grand Prize for their best-selling song "Innocent World." Their next album, *Atomic Heart*, sold more than two million copies. After members of the group performed individually for a while, Mr. Children had a hit song, "Youthful Days," in late 2001. This record was a top 10 single on the J-Pop chart for 2001. Mr. Children was the third-best-selling J-Pop artist of the 1990s, selling 30 million units and earning ¥53 billion. By 2015, Mr. Children had sold more than 50 million units making it one of Japan's most famous pop groups ever. The group is still popular.

MUNAKATA SHIKŌ, 棟方志功 **(1903–1975).** Munakata Shikō was perhaps Japan's greatest modern woodcut artist and printmaker. He was born in the city of Aomori, the son of a poor blacksmith. In 1924, Munakata became a full-time painter in oils and moved to **Tōkyō** where, in 1928, he turned to woodcuts. After the war, his reputation spread rapidly at home and abroad as he crafted countless woodcuts, paintings in watercolor and oil, calligraphic scrolls, and illustrated **books**. Many institutional and private art collections throughout Japan, the **United States**, and Europe have collections of his works. Munakata has received many Japanese and international awards as well as having three Japanese museums named after him.

Munakata's works show a variety of influences of both Japan and the West, but at all times they display his driving vigor and dynamic personality. A deeply religious man, Munakata often found his inspiration in poetry, **religion**, or **music**. He treated extremely diverse subjects. He worked with the simplest tools but achieved spectacular compositional effects, especially in his dense black or white shapes of figures that appear to be bursting out of the picture. Munakata became one of the best-known artists of his day and, through his work, brought about the general acceptance of Japanese printmaking.

MURAKAMI HARUKI, 村上春樹 **(1949–).** As Japan's most widely read contemporary writer, the provocative Murakami Haruki advocates internationalism. Born in **Kyōto** but raised in an affluent section of **Kōbe**, Murakami taught himself English and read widely from American writers. He studied at Waseda University and delved into the unrest of the **student movement**. A prolific writer, his works have sold in the millions, have been translated into English, and have been called "easily accessible, yet profoundly complex" by the *Virginia Quarterly Review*.

After running a bar for nearly a decade, Murakami was suddenly and inexplicably inspired to write his first novel, *Kaze no uta wo kike* (*Hear the Wind Sing*, 1979), while watching a **baseball** game. This first work shows many of the basic elements of his mature writings, including Western-style idiosyncratic humor and a sense of nostalgia. A year later he published *1973-nen no pinbōru* (*Pinball, 1973*), a sequel. His third novel, *Hitsuji wo meguru bōken* (*A Wild Sheep Chase*), appeared in 1982. In 1985, he published *Sekai no owari to hādoboirudo wandārando* (*Hard-Boiled Wonderland and the End of the World*), a dreamlike fantasy that takes the magical elements in his work to a new extreme. His dreamlike stories have led people to label his writing as postmodern. When reading one of his novels, one does not usually have a clear idea of the direction in which the story is going. Everything is ambiguous, and the reader struggles to grasp the secret message the author is trying to convey.

Murakami achieved wide national recognition in 1987 when he published *Noruwei no mori* (*Norwegian Wood*), a nostalgic story of loss and sexuality. It sold millions of copies, especially to Japanese youth, giving Murakami a superstar status. In 1986, he traveled throughout Europe and settled in the **United States** where he taught at Princeton University and Tufts University. During this time, he wrote *Dansu dansu dansu* (*Dance, Dance, Dance*) and *Kokkyō no minami, taiyō no nishi* (*South of the Border, West of the Sun*).

In 1994–1995, Murakami published *Nejimaki-dori kuronikuru* (*The Wind-Up Bird Chronicle*). This novel seamlessly fuses both his realistic and fantastic tendencies, and it contains elements of physical violence. It is also more socially conscious than his previous works, dealing in part with the difficult topic of the war crimes in Manchuria. The novel, most frequently cited by critics as Murakami's greatest, won the Yomiuri Literary Award.

While Murakami was finishing *Chronicle*, the **Kōbe Earthquake** and the **Aum Shinrikyō** gas attack shook Japan. He came to terms with these events with his first nonfiction work, *Andāguraundo* (*Underground*), a collection of interviews with victims of the sarin gas attacks in the **Tōkyō** subway system.

Japan's literary establishment criticizes Murakami's fiction as humorous and surreal, referring to it as "pop" **literature**. Yet his work reflects an essential alienation, loneliness, and longing for love in a way that has touched readers in the United States and Europe, as well as in East Asia. Through his work, he is able to capture the spiritual emptiness of his generation and explore the negative effects of Japan's overemphasis on work. His writings allow him to criticize how the capitalist society in Japan has led to a decrease in human values and a loss of connection between people.

Murakami's recent novel, *Shikisai o motonai Tazaki Tsukuru to, Kare no junrei no toshi* (*Colorless Tsukuru Tazaki and His Years of Pilgrimage*), tells the story of a young man confronting the problems of youth. Published in 2013, it has become a bestseller. In February 2017, Murakami published *Kishidancho Goroshi* (*Killing Commendatore*), a two-volume work that has not yet been translated into English.

Murakami, whose writings are often compared with those of **Ōe Kenzaburō**, is internationally famous. His writings have been translated into 50 languages. Murakami, the recipient of many literary awards, is mentioned frequently as a possible **Nobel Prize** winner.

MURAKAMI RYŪ, 村上龍 (1952–). Murakami Ryū, the novelist, short story author, and filmmaker, writes with a dark side. Having a strong American influence since he grew up in Sasebo, a Japanese town dominated by an American military base, Murakami's writings are controversial, nihilistic, and sometimes frustrating and depressive.

Murakami, one of Japan's most popular and influential novelists in contemporary society, has a particularly strong following among teenagers. His novel *Kagirinaku tōmei ni chikai burū* (*Almost Transparent Blue*, 1976) deals with promiscuity and drug use among disaffected Japanese youth. In 1980, he published *Koinrokkā beibīzu* (*Coin Locker Babies*) to much critical acclaim. His 20 **books**, with their sex, violence, and drugs, give his writings a sense of flamboyance. He directed the film *Tōkyō Decadence*, which debuted in 1991. The popular media consider him an iconoclastic dandy.

In 2008, Murakami's novel, *Odishon* (*Audition*), generated a lot of attention. The novel, a psychosexual thriller, is a kind of documentary set in the upscale Aoyama section of **Tōkyō**. Murakami's conclusion is shocking and rather grisly. Murakami's writings often focus on rage and violence that fester under the surface. His protagonists are frequently young perpetrators of violence. They are often psychologically disturbed. In 2016, Kurodahan Press published *Tōkyō Decadence: 15 Stories*, a collection of his short stories. The stories are mesmerizing but seamy. In many ways, Murakami is the successor to **Dazai Osamu**. *See also* LITERATURE.

MURAKAMI TAKASHI, 村上隆 **(1962–).** Murakami Takashi is a very popular artist who is often called the Japanese Andy Warhol. His art promotes the Japanese popular fan (**otaku**) culture as well as the traditional Japanese style (*Nihonga*). A sensation both in Japan and worldwide, Murakami's pop culture art is extravagant, artificial, and mass produced, and it carries a plastic image that is recognized internationally. His work is used to sell a wide variety of products and thus creates an entrepreneurial spirit. Further, his art objects challenge the concepts of Orientalism and Western stereotypes. In 2008, Murakami appeared in *Time* magazine's "100 Most Influential People" list, the only visual artist to be included that year.

Murakami manages the careers of several young artists through his Kaikai Kiki Corporation. An art entrepreneur, he is his own best salesman for his artistic creations in paintings, sculptures, and prints. His worldwide presentations are known as being "Superflat," a term to describe his style. His works can also be described as colorful, contemporary, and inspired by **anime** and **manga**.

After showing his work internationally, in 2012 Murakami presented his first solo show in Japan in several years. Titled "Takashi Murakami: The 500 Arhats," the show appeared in Roppongi Hills, an upscale section of **Tōkyō**, and rocked the pop culture world with its otaku culture and antinuclear message. Murakami is a rock-star, pop culture artist whose works sell for very high prices.

MURATA RENHŌ, 村田蓮舫 **(1967–).** Murata Renhō, better known by just her first name, Renhō, is a journalist and politician who became leader of Japan's **Democratic Party** (DP) in September 2016.

Renhō was born in **Tōkyō**, the daughter of a Taiwanese father and a Japanese mother. She earned a law degree at Aoyama Gakuin University. She did not become a citizen of Japan until 1985. She became a **television** personality when she debuted as a Clarion Girl in 1988. She has appeared as a newscaster and popular personality on TBS and TV Asahi. She studied Chinese at Peking University from 1995 to 1997 and reported on Chinese events on television. She is married to Murata Nobuyuki, and they have twins.

Renhō was elected to the **House of Councillors** in July 2004. She has been a strong advocate for parenting issues, a critic of Japan's diplomacy with **China**, an advocate for recognizing **Taiwan** as a country, and a strong scrutinizer of fiscal policy. She served as minister for administrative reforms under Prime Minister **Kan Naoto**. She won reelection to the upper house in 2010 with a record number of votes. She has served various government positions including minister for government revitalization, minister of state for consumer affairs and food safety, and state minister of government revitalization.

Renhō, popular, charismatic, and promising to reinvigorate Japanese political culture, retained her seat in the 2016 upper house election and, soon after, became the president of Japan's DP, the first woman to hold this position as well as the first woman to head a major **political party**. However, crushed by a devastating defeat in Tōkyō's July 2017 **election**, she resigned her positions.

MURAYAMA TOMIICHI, 村山富市 **(1924–).** Murayama Tomiichi, a leader of the **Japan Socialist Party** (JSP), served as **prime minister** of Japan for a year and a half in the mid-1990s in a coalition government with the **Liberal Democratic Party** (LDP) and the **New Party Sakigake** (NPS).

Murayama was born in Ōita Prefecture, the son of a fisherman. He graduated from Meiji University and took a job as a **labor** union official in Kyūshū, soon becoming secretary of his union. Murayama joined the JSP, which his union supported. He began his political career as a member of the Ōita City Council in 1955 and served three terms. In 1963, his supporters urged him to become a candidate for the Ōita Prefectural Assembly, where he served three successive terms. In 1972, he was elected to Japan's **House of Representatives**.

Murayama was a tough negotiator but had a kind, calm demeanor. He was not assertive, but he knew how to make a good compromise. In 1991, he was appointed chairman of the **Diet** Affairs Committee of the JSP, one of the prominent posts in his **political party**. In August 1993, after the general

election, the JSP joined the **cabinet**, and Murayama was elected JSP head. He became prime minister on 30 June 1994. His cabinet was a coalition of the JSP, the LDP, and the NPS.

A representative of the **Social Democratic Party of Japan** (SDPJ), the new name for the JSP in 1996, Murayama was an unexpected choice for prime minister. For the first time since 1948, Japan had a government headed by a socialist leader. The economic approach and **foreign policy** of the former JSP had changed considerably. Murayama did a better job as prime minister than many people expected. He served as a "grandfather-type" caretaker. Coinciding with the 50th anniversary of Japan's surrender in World War II, Murayama, in a well--known speech, issued Japan's first official apology for its wartime actions. He faced a sluggish **economy** and a **banking** crisis. He also had to deal with the tragedies of the **Kōbe Earthquake** and the terrorism of the **Aum Shinrikyō** poisonous gas attacks, both in early 1995.

Because he headed a coalition government and lacked a dominating personality, Murayama's leadership was not strong. His party opposed the **United States–Japan Security Treaty**, but he stated that this pact fit within the **Constitution of Japan**, thereby disappointing many of his socialist supporters. People criticized his government for not dealing effectively with the Kōbe Earthquake or the sarin gas attack on the **Tōkyō** subway.

In the 1996 general election, the SDPJ lost many seats in the House of Representatives. Murayama expressed the wish to resign from the office of prime minister, but his supporters urged him to continue. Some months later he did resign, and **Hashimoto Ryūtarō**, the LDP president, replaced him. Murayama retired from politics in 2000.

However, Murayama continues to support his war apology statement of 1995. He has worked with **Kōno Yōhei** in opposing any backtracking on the statement. During 2015, he joined with Kōno in opposing any efforts by Prime Minister **Abe Shinzō** to walk back the apology statement.

MUSASHIMARU KŌYŌ, 武蔵丸光洋 **(1971–).** Musashimaru Kōyō is only the second foreigner to reach the ranks of *yokozuna*, which he achieved in 1999 as Japan's 67th grand champion. Born Fiamalu Penitani, an American Samoan, he moved to Hawaii at age 10. Encouraged by success in Greco-Roman **wrestling** in high school, he moved to Japan in 1989 and joined the **sumō** profession under the name Musashimaru in 1991.

Musashimaru's huge 223-kilogram (492-pound) bulk combined with his 191-centimeter (6-foot, 3-inch) height made him a formidable opponent, and his fan base was helped by a surprising facial resemblance to Japanese warrior hero Saigō Takamori. He moved up the ranks quickly and earned a majority of wins in a record 52 consecutive tournaments, but he was at that time unable to gain the successive championships needed to become a *yokozuna*.

In 1993, Hawaiian wrestler **Akebono Tarō** made history when he became the first foreign *yokozuna*, and Musashimaru became the second in 1999. Musashimaru won 12 championships and retired in 2003 due to a chronic injury to his left wrist. He became an elder in the Japan Sumō Association and, in 2013, founded Musashigawa stable.

MUSIC. Although some people may associate Japanese music only with J-Pop or youth music, Japan actually has a wide variety of distinct styles and innovative artists ranging from classical to folk, from rock to electronic, from hip hop to country music, and much more.

Japan is the world's second-largest music market just after the **United States**. In 2000, Japan sold music amounting to around $5 billion. Japanese music has an incredible influence as imitator and innovator. From huge concert halls to small intimate settings, one can hear nearly every kind of music imaginable. This setting has given rise to an impressive blend of Eastern and Western music.

Traditional Japanese music involves various Japanese instruments sometimes played by eminent performers. Miyagi Michio (1894–1956), a blind *koto* player, introduced various styles of Western music into *koto* performances. Takahashi Chikuzan (1910–1998), a *tsugaru shamisen* player, performed traditional Japanese music. Matsui Kazu (1954–) is a famous *shakuhachi* player who traveled in Europe and India when he was 20. He played *shakuhachi*, a difficult wind instrument, for several motion pictures.

Kayōkyoku refers to Japanese popular music with a blending of East and West. People not only enjoy listening to *kayōkyoku* songs in live concerts and on radio and **television** but also singing along with the taped orchestral accompaniment in **karaoke** bars or at home. This music emerged in the early 20th century and was originally composed for school **education** programs.

An *enka* is a popular ballad, a Japanese music genre that often tells the sad stories of life, the irrecoverable destiny, the loss of a lover, or some other disconcerting moment. *Enka*, perhaps Japan's equivalent of American country and western songs, are commonly sung at karaoke bars. Matsumoto Takashi is a composer of lyrics for *enka* and pop music who performs with the group named Happy Endo. Kitajima Saburō, rated one of Japan's top 20 entertainers in 1998, is a veteran *enka* star. Hosokawa Takashi is a male singing star who ranked in the top 20 entertainers in the late 1990s. Mori Shinichi has been an outstanding *enka* singer since the mid-1960s. Miyako Harumi is a female *enka* singer. In 1964, her song "Anko tsubaki wa koi no hana" ("The Anko Camellia Is the Flower of Love") won the outstanding New Artist Award and went on to make her a star. Sakamoto Fuyumi is another leading *enka* singer who is a national star. Her recording "Hotaru no chochin" ("Lantern of Firefly"), has an amazingly universal appeal.

Classical music has a long history in Japan. The Ongaku Torishirabesho or the music research institute was established in 1880 and promoted Western-style music in Japan. The Tōkyō Music School succeeded it and became the Music Department of the Tōkyō National University of Fine Arts and Music in 1949. The Tōkyō Symphony Orchestra and the NHK Symphony Orchestra are among the best in the world. The Ensemble Nipponica (Nippon Ongaku Shūdan) is another of Japan's leading orchestras.

Japan has produced many internationally famous conductors including **Ozawa Seiji**; Watanabe Akeo (1919–1990), who was founder and conductor of the Japan Philharmonic Symphony Orchestra; Wakasugi Hiroshi (1935–2009), who directed many European orchestras; Iwaki Hiroyuki (1932–2006), the **NHK** senior conductor and the chief conductor of the Melbourne Symphony Orchestra; Otaka Tadaaki (1947–), who has both taught and performed as the conductor with various orchestras and has been the principal conductor of the Tōkyō Philharmonic Orchestra; and Akiyama Kazuyoshi (1941–), internationally famous conductor of the Tōkyō Symphony. Yamada Kosaku (1886–1965) was Japan's first symphony composer. Strongly influenced by German romanticism, he studied in Berlin, Paris, and New York. Other famous Japanese composers include Ichiyanagi Toshi (1933–), Toyama Yūzō (1931–), Yuasa Jōji (1929–), **Takemitsu Tōru**, Kanno Yoshihiro (1953–), and Nishimura Akira (1953–). All of these are classical composers who use experimental techniques to blend traditional Japanese sounds with Western instrumentation. Another famous composer is Yamashita Tsutomu (1947–) who wrote the music for nearly 100 Japanese **films**.

Japan's famous international pianists include Sonoda Takahiro (1928–2004), noted for his recordings of Beethoven; Uchida Mitsuko (1948–), well known for her performance of Mozart; and **Akiyoshi Toshiko**, a jazz pianist of world fame.

Famous violinists include Etō Toshiya (1927–2008), a virtuoso instrumentalist, and Ushioda Masuko (1942–2013), an outstanding performer. Perhaps Japan's most famous violinist is **Gotō Midori** who goes by the name "Midori." A child prodigy, she trained with her mother and then at the Juilliard School of Music and performs worldwide.

Nakamaru Michie (1960–) is a world-class soprano who won the prestigious international Maria Callas Concours voice competition as well as other contests. She is a graduate of Tōhō School of Music (1985) and studied at Juilliard.

Developed in the 1920s, jazz had a modest following in prewar Japan. After the war, jazz really took off in Japan, and a number of important jazz musicians emerged. Hattori Ryōichi (1907–1993) was a great jazz player and a composer of popular songs. After the war, Hattori's jazz helped take the edge off a rather depressing era. His song "Aoi sammyaku" ("Blue Mountains") became one of Japan's best-loved songs. Hamaguchi Kuranosuke (1917–1990) was a composer who specialized in jazz. He organized an Afro-Cuban Orchestra and was its lead singer, often performing songs he wrote.

Kondō Toshinori (1948–), a jazz trumpeter, founded Kondo's Tibetan Blue Air Liquid Band. His songs include "Brainwar," "Red City Smoke," "Taihen," " Tōkyō Girl & Ima," and "Touchstone." In 1972, Kondō became a professional musician in **Tōkyō**. From 1978 to 1983, Kondō performed with various jazz groups in New York but then returned to Japan and formed his own group, International Music Activities (IMA). He disbanded IMA in 1993 and moved to Amsterdam where he lives and performs today.

Yano Akiko (1955–) is a female jazz pianist and singer as well as a songwriter. She made many albums, including several that sold in the United States. In the late 1970s, Yano toured with the Yellow Magic Orchestra. In 1980, she and her husband, **Sakamoto Ryūichi**, coproduced the highly successful album *Gohan ga dekita yo* (*Dinners Ready?*). Other famous Japanese jazz musicians include Nanri Fumio (1910–1975), "Japan's Satchmo"; Oda Satoru (1927–2016), a saxophonist who coined the term *yellow jazz*; Watanabe Sadao (1933–), a well-known jazz musician; and Yamashita Yōsuke (1942–), a leading jazz pianist.

Utada Hikaru (1983–) is a popular jazz musician with lively sounds and moving rhythms. Born in New York, she became a jazz and R&B musician. She became quite famous with her frequently played song "Dango San-Kyōdai" ("Three Dumpling Brothers"). Her works range from children's songs to songs popular with adults. Her song "Traveling" became a top 10 J-Pop single in 2001, and her album *First Love* set a domestic sales record of more than seven million copies. As of 2006, Utada had sold an astonishing 40 million units of music.

Rock music also has a strong following in Japan. Aikawa Nanase (1975–), one of the brightest names in Japanese Girl Rock, has been going strong since 1995. Her first single, "Yumemiru shōjo ja iranai," won great acclaim before her album, *Red*, won prestigious awards.

TMN was one of Japan's most popular rock bands because their style was creative and their music used **computer** enhancement. The group began in 1984 under the name TM Network, which was short for Time Machine Network. Their hit single was "Kinyōbi no Lion." In 1987, they popularized "Get Wild" and took part in a Kōhaku Uta Gassen, Japan's popular year-end singing festival.

The Yellow Magic Orchestra (YMO) began in the late 1970s and brought Japan fully into the pop rock era. Sakamoto Ryūichi on keyboard, Takahashi Yukihiro (1952–) on drums, Yano Akiko on keyboard, and Watanabe Katsumi (1959–) on guitar made up YMO. Their song "Solid State Survivor," released both in Japan and the United States, sold more than 1.4 million copies, a near record at that time. YMO became a trendsetter in the techno-pop style and a major influence on contemporary electronic music.

Inoue Yōsui (1948–) is a rocker whose song "A World of Ice" was the first to sell a million copies in Japan. Inoue helped develop the New Music style in Japan and had a significant effect on Japanese pop music in the 1970s. He founded For Life Records, an independent record company still active today. His big song "Kandore Mandore" became the most requested song in Japan in 1969.

Japanese popular music attracts millions, especially young people in Japan, Asia, and the West. Agnes-chan (1955–), born in Hong Kong, is a popular singer who had a top 10 single by age 16. She is an example of the Japanese pop star who reaches phenomenal success quickly and is called an *idoru* singer, a sweet, innocent, but seductive young performer. Agnes-chan launched her career in Japan in 1972 with the hit song "Hinageshi no hana," presenting herself as pure and cute (*kawaii*). She later outgrew this image and became an adult performer, one with brains as well as talent. Agnes studied at Sophia University, later studied psychology at the University of Toronto, and earned a PhD in education from Stanford University. She has released more than 100 albums and CDs.

Glay is a popular musical group and one of the top 20 in the late 1990s. Glay recorded *One Love*, a top album for 2001. Glay consists of four men—two guitarists, a bassist, and a vocalist. Kubo Takurō (1971–), who is the leader of the group, plays the guitar. Kobashi Teruhiko (1971–) is the vocalist. Tonomura Hisashi (1972–) is the guitarist, and Wayama Yoshihito (JIRO) (1972–) plays the bass. Their CD *Don't Worry* is spectacular. Their songs have rhythm and feeling and are catchy tunes. In 2002, the Japanese government sent Glay to **China** on a diplomatic mission.

The Pizzicato Five was a musical techno-pop group, and its members were television celebrities. It consisted of two men and one **woman**, all hailing from Tōkyō. It was one of the top 40 groups in Japan over a long time. It did television appearances and **fashion** shows and was a key part of J-Pop. The group had a great sense of style and pizzazz. In 1997, Pizzicato Five released *Happy End of the World*. Unfortunately, the group disbanded in 2001.

Chage (Shibata Shuji, 1958–) & Aska (Miyazaki Shigeaki, 1958–), J-Pop artists, debuted in 1979 with their song "Hitorizaki." Their big hits have a light, bouncy quality and include "No no darlin," "Say Yes," "Yah yah yah," "Meguriai," and "You Are Free." Internationally famous, Chage & Aska were the fifth-best-selling J-Pop artists of the 1990s, selling 26 million LPs and earning ¥54 billion.

Japan has a host of popular male musicians. Fantastic Plastic Machine is a pop musician whose most notable U.S. release was the 1998 "Sushi 3003." The Fantastic Plastic Machine is Tanaka Tomoyuki (1967–) in a solo role where he creates, arranges, and performs the music. The B'z is a popular musical group of two people, Inaba Kōshi (1964–) and Matsumoto Takahiro (1961–). The B'z debuted around 1990 and gradually grew in fame to become very popular. The B'z were the number one top-selling J-Pop artists in the 1990s. This group sold nearly 56 million units and earned ¥114 billion. Hirai Ken (1972–), who has a strong sense of rhythm, is a popular J-Pop singer with the hit record "One Love Wonderful World" in 2001.

Likewise, there are many other popular female performers. Imai Miki (1963–) is one of the most admired female singers, especially for middle-aged women. She is described as "among the bigger-name Japanese artists." She has had many careers from hostess to television **actress** but made her singing debut in 1986 and has had many hits. Morning Musume is a cutesy girl–type group from the 1990s. The group first consisted of five girls but then three more were added. Their CDs have achieved top rankings.

Pink Lady was a very popular duo who sang and danced. Mie (Nemoto Mitsuyo, 1958–) and Kei (Masuda Keiko, 1957–) were originally high school friends in Shizuoka. In 1976, they formed Pink Lady. They won success as singers and dancers. They had at least nine number one hits with some records selling more than a million copies. The Pink Lady name sold hundreds of popular items. They disbanded their group in 1981 but, in 1988, took part in the annual singing extravaganza *Kōhaku Uta Gassen*. Now they perform separately as actresses and singers. Pink Lady represents popular music in Japan and the merchandising of a perky Japanese idol.

Nakajima Miyuki (1952–) is a female singer/songwriter of popular Japanese music. She popularized a new genre of music, fittingly called "New Music," in the 1970s. Her music combines pop and folk styles with a taste of *enka*, and an emphasis on romantic relationships and emotional situations. One of her big songs was "Eikyū ketsuban." Nakajima is still popular as a singer/songwriter, DJ, and performer.

Judy and Mary Band was a popular musical group that released its first single called "Power of Love" in 1993. Its second single was "Blue Tears" in 1994. Its first album was *J.A.M*. In 1996, its eighth single, "Sobakasu," was used as the theme song for the television animation series *Rurōnikensin*. That same year they appeared on NHK's *Kōhaku Uta Gassen*. Members of the group now appear individually.

Speed was a very popular musical group with four female members. They danced as well as sang. Speed was among the top 20 entertainers in the late 1990s. Their song "White Love" was a lively, bouncy tune. They released their first album in 1996. They were very popular with young Japanese. Hitoe was the leading performer in the group.

People familiar with contemporary Japanese music will recognize the importance of J-Pop music. Furuya Hitomi (1976–), a vibrant young female J-Pop singer, transcends Eastern and Western cultures in the basic theme of love and life. **Komuro Tetsuya** promoted her musical career. In 1994, Hitomi made a CD debut titled *Let's Play Winter*. Since then, Hitomi has written all her own lyrics. She is known for her distinctively high voice, sexiness, and unusual fashion sense. Nakashima Mika (1983–), another female J-Pop performer, has a clear satiny-smooth voice providing easy listening in romantic music. Her music is popular with karaoke singers.

The Southern All Stars were the seventh-best-selling J-Pop artists of the 1990s, selling nearly 22 million units, earning ¥48 billion. Kuwata Keisuke (1956–) leads the Southern All Stars. While a student at Aoyama Gakuin University in 1974, he played with a folk song group. He organized the Southern All Stars in 1975 with five other males. Their song "Kiseki no hoshi" made them famous.

KinKi Kids is a top male J-Pop group. Cornelius (1969–) is a male techno-pop artist and is regarded as the Dave Beck of Japan. A product of the same Shibuya-area bubblegum scene that also gave rise to Pizzicato Five, Cornelius debuted in 1993. He became a national teen idol in the wake of the release of 1994's *The First Question*.

Dreams Come True formed in 1988 and made its debut record in 1989. This singing group was popular in the 1990s, especially with young females. Its songs were used in television dramas and movies, and its album *Monkey Girl/Odyssey* was a top-10 J-Pop album for 2001. Dreams Come True was the second-best-selling J-Pop group in the 1990s, selling 32 billion units and earning ¥69 billion.

Globe is a group that recorded "Genesis of Next," a top 10 J-Pop single in 2001. This song has a wild sound, with a synthesizer beat. Keiko (1972–) is the main vocalist. A Frenchman, Mark (1970–), sings and raps with Keiko. Komuro Tetsuya, who writes their lyrics and composes their music, is the third member of the group and its producer. Their songs are used on television commercials and dramas. Globe was the sixth-best-selling J-Pop artist in the 1990s, selling 22 million units and earning ¥43 billion.

Hamasaki Ayumi (1978–) is a singer/songwriter. This pop artist is from Fukuoka and has a lot of style appeal to the extent that many girls try to model their hairstyle after hers. Her hit singles "Love Destiny" and "Boys & Girls" both made Oricon's number one in 1999. Her recording "A Song Is Born" was the top J-Pop single for 2001. Her music has a sweet, pleasant sound, and she offers a nice voice, lots of background sound, rhythm and bass, and a variety of new sounds.

A final musical genre is an *idoru* or "idol," largely a product of Japanese merchandising. *Idoru* refers to the cute, girl-next-door singers who are designed, controlled, and marketed just like any other product. Talent agencies promote such starlets in **advertising**, music, television dramas, and performance tours. An actress as much as a singer, with a somewhat more mature look than most idols, Nakayama Miho (1970–) is well known for the TV series *Dorama* and movies ranging from *Be-Bop High School* to *Love Letter*. Amuro Namie (1977–) is a Japanese pop idol. Originally from **Okinawa**, she formerly performed with the girl group Super Monkeys. Namie's biggest hit was "Can We Celebrate" (1997), which is often sung at weddings. Her music is lively, frequently uses English phrases, and has a very fast tempo with staccato sounds, an electronic synthesizer, and a strong beat. Namie was a best-selling J-Pop artist in the 1990s, selling more than 21 million units at a price of more than ¥40 billion.

In 2014, Japan had the largest physical music market in the world, with sales of more than $2 billion and the second-largest overall music market with a retail value of $2.6 billion. People can hear every kind of music imaginable at any time in Japan. Classical Western music, jazz, rock or other Western forms, or Japanese popular music forms can be found anywhere, anytime. Japan has an impressive blend of Eastern and Western music.

The following Japanese musicians or musical groups have sold 50 million or more records during their careers: the B'z (1988–present), **Mr. Children** (1989–present), Hamasaki Ayumi (1998–present), and AKB48 (2005–present). These groups have a variety of sounds, but all have some form of pop and/or rock music.

Slightly less successful commercially but with 30 to 50 million records sold are the following musical groups: Southern All Stars (1975–present), Dreams Come True (1988–present), **L'Arc-en-Ciel** (1991–present), Hotei Tomoyasu (1988–present), Glay (1988–present), Zard (1991–2007), Utada Hikaru (1998–2010, 2016–present), Amuro Namie (1992–present), **SMAP** (1991–2016), Arashi (1999–present), Chage & Aska (1979–2009, 2013–present), Matsutoya Yumi (1968–present), X Japan (1982–1997, 2007–present), and **Matsuda Seiko** (1980–present). Again, pop and rock are the most dominant. *See also* ASAKURA DAISUKE, 浅倉大介 (1967–); DAN IKUMA, 團伊玖磨 (1924–2001); HAYASHI EITETSU, 林英哲 (1952–); KITAGAWA, JOHNNY, ジャニー喜多川 (1931–); KITARŌ, 喜多郎 (1953–); MATSUI KEIKO, 松居慶子 (1961–); MISORA HIBARI, 美空ひばり (1937–1989); SAKAMOTO KYŪ, 坂本九 (1941–1985); SU-ZUKI SHIN'ICHI, 鈴木鎮一 (1898–1998); YŪMING, ユーミン, OR ARAI YUMI (MATSUTŌYA YUMI, 松任谷由実) (1954–).

N

NAGASHIMA SHIGEO, 長嶋茂雄 **(1936–).** Nagashima Shigeo, known as "Mr. Giants," was a **Yomiuri Giant** for 16 of his 17 seasons (1958–1973). He led the league in home runs twice and in batting average six times, and he was a five-time most valuable player. In six different categories, Nagashima holds a claim as one of Japan's all-time **baseball** greats. In ascending order of placement, he finished 10th in average (.305), 9th in runs scored (1,270), 8th in triples (74), 7th in hits (2,471), 6th in runs batted in (1,522), and 5th in doubles, with 418. Nagashima is one of only four Japanese baseball players who stand in a career top 10 in at least six categories. He managed the Giants from 1975 to 1980 and again from 1993 to 2001. In 1988, Nagashima was inducted into the Japanese Baseball Hall of Fame.

NAGOYA, 名古屋**.** Nagoya, Japan's fourth-largest city, is located on the Pacific coast of central Honshū. It serves as the capital of Aichi Prefecture and is one of Japan's major ports. Today, 2.2 million people live in the city of Nagoya and 8.7 million in the metropolitan district.

In the early 17th century, Tokugawa Ieyasu moved the capital of Owari Province to present-day Nagoya. He built a new castle there and developed a strong base of support in the region. Located on the Tōkaidō Road, Nagoya was a strategic link between **Kyōto** and Edo, present-day **Tōkyō**.

During the 18th century, Nagoya became an important **economic** center with pottery, gunpowder, and spinning enterprises being most notable. Nagoya developed even more in the later part of the 19th century. In 1907, the harbor opened to international shipping. In the early 20th century, it became a center of industrial growth and munitions and aircraft manufacturing, including the famous Zero.

As a result of the near-total destruction of Nagoya during the war, the present-day streets are wide and straight, and the layout of the city shows strong signs of progressive urban planning.

Today, Nagoya's main economic activity centers on the **automobile** industry. **Toyota Motors** has its headquarters in Nagoya and in nearby Toyota City. **Mitsubishi Motors** has its research and development facilities in a suburb. Several automotive suppliers operate out of Nagoya or nearby areas.

Nagoya's two most famous sites are Nagoya Castle and Atsuta Shrine. The original castle was built in 1612, but most of this structure went up in flames during World War II. The castle was rebuilt in 1959, although with too many modernizations for castle aficionados, such as ferroconcrete walls and an elevator. Atsuta Shrine, probably Japan's second most important shrine after Ise, houses the imperial symbol of the sword, one of the three imperial regalia of Japan. It also contains more than 4,400 national treasures and hosts 70 festivals a year.

Nagoya is the headquarters for the world-famous Noritake chinaware. **Pachinko** also originated in this city. It has a unique open-air **architectural** museum. The Tokugawa Art Museum, the Toyota Commemorative Museum of Industry and Technology, and the Robot Museum attract many people. Nagoya is also the site of the Central Japan International Airport, Japan's newest international airport. The Chūnichi Dragons, one of Japan's leading professional **baseball** teams, makes its home in the city. Neighboring cities of Nagakute and Seto hosted **Expo** 2005, also known as the Aichi Expo, and thereby introduced Nagoya and its accomplishments to the world. Nagoya seems to combine the best of traditional and contemporary Japan.

NAKADAI TATSUYA, 仲代達矢 **(1932–).** Nakadai Tatsuya, whose real name is Nakadai Motohisa, is one of Japan's most famous **actors**. Born in **Tōkyō**, he joined the actors' training school in 1952 and performed his first stage role in 1954. His **film** debut, in 1956, was when he first received international attention. He is an adaptable actor, capable of playing all kinds of roles, whether villain, hero, or comic. He starred in **Ichikawa Kon**'s *Enjō* (*Conflagration*), Kobayashi Masaki's huge epic *Ningen no jōken* (*The Human Condition*), and **Kurosawa Akira**'s *Kagemusha* (*Shadow Warrior*) and *Ran* (*Chaos*).

Strikingly handsome, Nakadai was Japan's take-on-all action star. He played a wide range of emotions from an avenger to a *yakuza*, from a skirt-chasing boss to a very proper leader, and from a psycho to an obsessive artist. His films ranged from bloody samurai flicks to romantic heartbreakers, and from electrifying roles to highly dramatic ones in classical **theater**. Sometimes called the Japanese Marlon Brando, he played his roles with great subtlety and a definite swagger. As a screen idol, he rivaled **Mifune Toshirō**. Nakadai Tatsuya, who appeared in 160 films, has been one of the world's great actors.

Nakadai continues his acting career although well into his 80s. In 2015, the **emperor** awarded him the Order of Culture, the highest honor that can be bestowed on a person of the arts.

NAKAGAWA ICHIRŌ, 中川一郎 **(1925–1983).** Nakagawa Ichirō, a controversial politician, was elected to the **House of Representatives** in 1963. Born in **Sapporo**, he was elected seven times as Hokkaidō's representative. Prime Minister **Fukuda Takeo** appointed him agriculture, forestry, and fisheries minister in 1977. He had ties with the beef and dairy interests in Hokkaidō. Prior to Prime Minister **Suzuki Zenkō**'s resignation in 1982, Nakagawa was director-general of the **Science and Technology** Agency. He was a candidate to succeed Suzuki as **prime minister**.

A "maverick," Nakagawa was a founding member of the hawkish Blue Storm Society (Seirankai) of the **Liberal Democratic Party**. Champion of the ultraright, he wanted to abrogate the security treaty with the **United States** and build up an independent military capacity. He urged the younger generation to take a stronger military hand and root out corruption. Following the outbreak of a financial scandal, Nakagawa committed suicide by hanging himself with his kimono sash in a Sapporo hotel. *See also* DEFENSE; NAKAGAWA SHŌICHI, 中川昭一 (1953–2009).

NAKAGAWA SHŌICHI, 中川昭一 **(1953–2009).** Nakagawa Shōichi, son of **Nakagawa Ichirō**, was a member of the **House of Representatives**, having been elected seven times from his district in Hokkaidō. Nakagawa served as the chairman of the Policy Research Council of the **Liberal Democratic Party**. He held a variety of government positions including minister of agriculture, forestry, and fisheries; minister of economy, trade, and industry in **Koizumi Jun'ichirō**'s **cabinet**; and minister of finance in the cabinet of **Asō Tarō**. On 17 February 2009, Nakagawa was forced to resign his cabinet position after appearing drunk at a G-7 meeting in Rome. His fall further weakened the already tenuous position of the Asō government. Nakagawa was found dead in his **Tōkyō** apartment in October 2009, a probable suicide.

A controversial figure, Nakagawa had been critical of the bombings of **Hiroshima** and Nagasaki, calling them "truly unforgivable on humanitarian grounds," strongly opposed to Kim Jong-un's possession of nuclear weapons in **North Korea,** and disrespectful of **women**, suggesting that they should stay in their place. Like Prime Minister **Abe Shinzō**, Nakagawa supported a hard line against North Korea, a more nationalistic interpretation of Japan's history, and the revision of Article 9 of the **Constitution of Japan**.

NAKANO KŌICHI, 中野浩一 **(1955–).** Nakano Kōichi is a world cycling champion. He was born in Fukuoka Prefecture to a father who was a professional bicycle racer. After high school, he entered the Japan Bicycle Racing School in Shizuoka Prefecture where he trained diligently until he entered professional competition in 1970. Since then he has won many races and achieved international fame in bicycling. He won the world pro bicycle sprint championships from 1977 to 1986, a total of 10 times in a row. Nakano was also a *keirin* cyclist, a form of motorcycle racing, from 1975 to 1992. Today, he is a **sports** commentator and **television** personality.

NAKASONE YASUHIRO, 中曽根康弘 **(1918–).** Nakasone Yasuhiro, a strong, hawkish politician, served five years as **prime minister** from 27 November 1982 to 6 November 1987. As Japan's top leader in the 1980s, Nakasone is known for pushing through the privatization of state-owned companies and revitalizing Japanese nationalism. He was born in Gumma Prefecture where his father was a prosperous timber merchant and his mother a Christian. Nakasone graduated from Tōkyō Imperial University, served in the imperial navy although he saw no combat, worked in the Ministry of the Interior, and became Japan's 16th postwar prime minister. To become prime minister, Nakasone won 58 percent of the **Liberal Democratic Party** (LDP) vote to **Kōmoto Toshio**'s 27 percent, **Abe Shintarō**'s 8 percent, and **Nakagawa Ichirō**'s 7 percent.

Nakasone was a fiscal conservative who wanted to balance the budget. Both **Tanaka Kakuei** and **Suzuki Zenkō** supported him. An advocate of a militarily strong Japan, Nakasone defended an old-fashioned Japanese nationalism. He ardently advocated **constitutional** revision. He advocated more **defense** spending and military buildup. Nakasone was a Major League **baseball** fan and a student of English, oil painting, and old Japanese folk songs. He was politically changeable and shifted to maintain power, giving him the nickname "Mr. Political Weathervane." Tall, handsome, and trim, he was the consummate politician.

Nakasone left the Ministry of the Interior in 1947 to enter the **Diet**. He became the chief of the Defense Agency in 1970. He served as trade minister during 1972–1974 under Tanaka and the director-general of the Administrative Management Agency in the Suzuki government. Nakasone was ambitious, hawkish, and nationalistic. On some occasions, his defense budget exceeded the "1 percent of GNP" policy concept that Prime Minister **Miki Takeo** had articulated earlier. He visited **Yasukuni Shrine**, much to the dismay of pacifists and people from other East Asian countries. He showed strong leadership, ambition, and outspoken nationalism, perhaps because his brother was killed as a World War II kamikaze pilot.

Nakasone had his own political faction. His LDP faction, formally controlled by former finance minister Watanabe Michio, was implicated in the **Recruit scandal** "stock-for-favors" arrangement in July 1990 causing it to lose considerable influence.

Nakasone worked to expand the support base for the LDP to urban and white-collar members since its rural base was declining in size. He tried to revive the influence of **Shintō** in Japan and promote Japan's world status.

A conservative contemporary of Ronald Reagan and Margaret Thatcher, Nakasone was best known for privatizing the **railroad** and telephone systems, increasing Japan's military strength, helping to revitalize Japanese nationalism, establishing closer ties with the **United States** and with **China**, and promoting Japan's world role during and after his term as prime minister. His frequent and close conversations with President Ronald Reagan came to be known by the popular reference "the Ron-Yasu" talks. His close ties with the United States were seen when Nakasone referred to Japan as "an unsinkable aircraft carrier," a statement that did not sit well with many Japanese.

Nakasone dominated Japanese politics in the 1980s. Following the Recruit scandal, Nakasone was forced to leave the LDP but still kept his influence. He promoted political reform in Japan, but his tax reform proposals with the value-added tax were not popular. He also spoke out strongly for "family values," which seemed to suggest a setback for **women**'s rights.

One of Japan's strongest postwar political leaders, Nakasone was one of only five people to serve in the **House of Representatives** for 50 years. He retired from the Diet in 2003.

Although well advanced in age, Nakasone remains a revered elder statesman and still seeks to revitalize Japan's nationalism. Japan's oldest living prime minister, Nakasone has received several international honors. As early as 1987, *Time* magazine wrote, "Nakasone put Japan on the world map and the rest of the world on Japan's map." His son, Nakasone Hirofumi, also an LDP representative from Gumma Prefecture, served as **Asō Tarō**'s minister of foreign affairs and **Obuchi Keizō**'s minister of **education**. *See also* FOREIGN POLICY.

NAKATA HIDETOSHI, 中田英寿 **(1977–).** Nakata Hidetoshi was a **soccer** sensation who played for A.C. Perugia and for A.S. Romain Italy. During his first season (1998–1999), he scored nine goals. Not since the **baseball** star **Nomo Hideo** made his debut with the Los Angeles Dodgers has a Japanese athlete made such an impact on an international **sports** team. Nakata was known for his reserved, cool attitude. He became a national team member in 1997 and played for Japan's Atlanta **Olympic** team. He was also a world select member in 1997. By 1998, Nakata was a key player for Japan at the World Cup in France. He then joined the Italian soccer circuit. Playing in the world's toughest soccer league, Nakata was Japan's premier player.

NARITA INTERNATIONAL AIRPORT (NARITA KOKUSAI KŪKŌ, 成田国際空港). Known as the New Tōkyō International Airport until 2004 when it was privatized and renamed Narita International Airport, Narita is Japan's main international airport, serving 39 million passengers in 2016. Located 35 miles east of **Tōkyō** in Chiba Prefecture, Narita International Airport is the hub for **Japan Airlines** and **All Nippon Airways**.

The Japanese government began a study to find a location for a new airport in 1962. Four years later it announced plans to build the airport in Chiba. In 1968, farmers in the Sanrizuka district, unwilling to give up ancestral family holdings and spurred by socialist advocates and leftist students, began a struggle against the forced sale of farmland on which to build the airport. The government, beginning in 1971, tried to use the right of eminent domain to forcibly expropriate the land, but farmers and students initiated an intense opposition movement that lasted for more than a decade.

Construction on the airport started in 1971, with the first building completed a year later. On 16 September 1971, a violent clash resulted in the death of three policemen. Demonstrations, conflicts, and even open battles continued on a regular basis. On 8 May 1977, another major clash at the airport construction site resulted in one fatality.

Narita International Airport opened for business on 20 May 1978. Operation of the facility was conducted under the strictest surveillance possible. People opposed to the building of the airport frequently clashed with the police in violent demonstrations occurring sporadically over a decade. On 28 March 1982, Narita International Airport experienced its last massive demonstration. By the time the Narita battles had ended, 13 people had died and thousands had been injured or arrested, but by 1983, the long protest movement had splintered and lost its power.

Today, Narita International Airport is Japan's largest airport in terms of freight and second busiest after **Haneda Airport** in terms of passengers. In 2016, Narita was the world's 48th-busiest airport in terms of passengers. Only two of Narita's proposed three runways have been constructed, and the second one is shorter than originally designed. Presently there are no plans to build the third runway. The considerable controversy over Narita led Japan to build its new **Ōsaka** and **Nagoya** airports on offshore sites.

NATIONAL CONFEDERATION OF TRADE UNIONS (ZENKOKU RŌDŌ KUMIAI SŌRENGŌ, 全国労働組合総連合). Established in 1989, the National Confederation of Trade Unions, known as Zenrōren in its shortened form, is leftist, affiliated with the **Japanese Communist Party**, and working-class oriented. It is an alternative to the **Japanese Trade Union Confederation** (Rengō), the conservative trade union federation with ties to the ruling **Liberal Democratic Party**. It consists of the rank and file unions. It represents just over one million people or around 10 percent of the union members in Japan. As of 2016, its membership exceeded 1.2 million. In its 20th convention of July 2004, Zenrōren urged its workers to fight **Koizumi Jun'ichirō**'s policies of arbitrary restructuring, to encourage improved living conditions and promote the cause of peace. President Kobayashi Yoji and Secretary-General Bannai Mitsuo called for equal treatment of regular and part-time workers, elimination of unpaid overtime, improved social service benefits, and support of international peace efforts. Zenrōren opposes any misguided revision of the constitution, the military buildup of the country, and the government's effort to support big enterprises over the people's welfare.

NATIONAL DIET. *See* DIET, NATIONAL (KOKKAI, 国会).

NATIONAL FEDERATION OF INDUSTRIAL ORGANIZATIONS (ZENKOKU RŌDŌ KUMIAI RENGŌKAI, 全国産業別労働組合連合会). The National Federation of Industrial Organizations, or Shinsanbetsu as it is known, had only some 61,000 members, making it the smallest of the postwar labor confederations. Left-wing unionists and intellectuals dominated it.

Shinsanbetsu joined with the **General Council of Japanese Trade Unions** (Sōhyō) in 1991 to form the **Japanese Trade Union Confederation** (Rengō), a union federation of 7.6 million members or 61 percent of all union members.

NATIONAL HOLIDAYS. *See* HOLIDAYS, NATIONAL.

NATIONAL TRADE UNION COUNCIL (ZENKOKU RŌDŌ KUMIAI RENGŌ GIKAI, 全国労働組合連絡協議会). The National Trade Union Council, known as Zenrōkyō in its shortened form, is an independent federation with no links to the **Japanese Communist Party** or any employers. It is made up primarily of independent unions and takes a more active approach to labor issues than the **Japanese Trade Union Confederation** (Rengō) or the **National Confederation of Trade Unions** (Zenrōren).

Politically, Zenrōkyō is linked to the **Social Democratic Party of Japan**. It opposes war and the existence of **United States** military facilities and supports the peace **constitution** and peace movement. Zenrōkyō holds annual conferences, but the last one took place in September 2011, suggesting a lack of vitality. The organization claims 300,000 members, but the **Ministry of Health, Labor, and Welfare** puts its numbers at only around 130,000. It is much smaller than Rengō or Zenrōren. Kanazawa Hisashi is Zenrōkyō's chairman and Nakaoka Motoaki its general secretary.

NEC (NIPPON ELECTRIC COMPANY; NIPPON DENKI KABUSHI-KI-GAISHA, 日本電気株式会社). NEC, headquartered in **Tōkyō**, is one of the world's largest manufacturers of electronics and a top producer of semiconductors. A member of the **Sumitomo Group**, it was incorporated as Nippon Electric Company in 1899 to produce telephones and switching equipment. NEC's first microcomputer was built in 1974 and its first personal **computer** in 1979. NEC merged its PC operations with Packard Bell in the United States in 1996. It is Japan's leading semiconductor and telecommunications equipment maker. The NEC Group has hundreds of affiliates, offices, and plants and employs more than 100,000 people worldwide. Its semiconductor business unit has been one of the top 20 semiconductor sales leaders in the world. Its revenue in 2013 was approximately $25 billion. It invests heavily in research and development and new product design. It manufactures more than 15,000 different products and runs Japan's second-largest internet service called Big Globe.

Primary leaders of NEC have been Kaneko Hisashi, president until his resignation in 1999; Nishigaki Koji, who became president in 1999; and Sasaki Hajime, who was promoted to chairman of the board in 1999. As of 2017, Endō Nobuhiro (1953–) serves as chairman of the board and Niino Takashi (1954–) as president and CEO. NEC's biggest rivals are **Toshiba**, **Hitachi**, and **Fujitsu**.

In 2010, NEC Electronics Corporation merged with Renesas Technology to form Renesas Electronics, the world's fourth-largest semiconductor company holding approximately 20 percent of the market. In 2011, NEC joined with Lenovo, a Chinese PC maker. As of 2013, NEC was the largest PC manufacturer in Japan with 23.6 percent of the market. In 2014, NEC joined with others in building a super-fast undersea data transmission cable link between Japan and the **United States**. The effort also included Google, **KDDI**, and SingTel. The cable link became operational in June 2016.

NEW FRONTIER PARTY (SHINSHINTŌ, 新進党). The New Frontier Party (NFP), although having only a brief three-year existence, excited observers who mistakenly saw it as introducing a significant political restructuring in Japan. The NFP combined a strange mixture of political philosophies and varied members under the leadership of former prime minister **Kaifu Toshiki**. Several small opposition parties, ranging from moderate socialist to neoliberals and conservatives, merged into the NFP in December 1994. By early 1995, the NFP had 214 members in the **Diet**. It was second in size only to the **Liberal Democratic Party** (LDP).

The NFP was formed by six different **political parties**, including the **Japan Renewal Party** (JRP), the **Kōmeitō**, and the **Japan New Party** (JNP), all of which were dissolved in December 1994. It also included the **Democratic Socialist Party** and two other opposition parties. In the July

1995 **House of Councillors** election, the NFP won 40 seats for a total of 56. Together with its 170 seats in the lower house, this made the NFP the second most powerful party after the LDP in both chambers. Kaifu served as president of the NFP and **Ozawa Ichirō** was its secretary-general. The NFP soon became a member of the ruling anti-LDP coalition led by Prime Minister **Hosokawa Morihiro.**

In December 1995, the NFP elected Ozawa its president. It held its own in the October 1996 **election**. By 6 November 1996, three leading NFP Diet representatives had quit the party. On 18 June 1997, former prime minister Hosokawa resigned from the NFP, saying that he could no longer work with Ozawa. The NFP joined with the JNP and the JRP to govern Japan until the coalition collapsed in 1997.

The NFP quickly became defunct and its members divided into many parties, among them the **Liberal Party** (LP), but also the Good Governance Party, the New Fraternity Party (Shintō Yūai), and the Democratic Reform Party (Minshu-Kaikaku-Rengō). In 2000, dissidents of the LP formed the New Conservative Party (Hoshu shintō). In 2003, the LP merged with the relatively liberal **Democratic Party of Japan**.

NEW KŌMEITŌ (KŌMEITŌ, 公明党). The original **Kōmeitō** is now defunct, but the New Kōmeitō (NKP), as it is known in English, is an offshoot of the older party. Confusingly, the NKP is still known as Kōmeitō in Japanese. In 1998, the NKP, or as it is called by some people in English, the New Clean Government Party, grew from the older Kōmeitō but without its more fringe elements or its strong connection with **religion**, which was officially dropped in the 1970s. It merged with the New Peace Party in 1998.

The NKP was established to promote international peace, support social welfare, and eliminate political corruption. It stressed "people-centered politics," respect for human life, a reduction in government bureaucracy, greater transparency in government affairs, the elimination of nuclear arms, and a rejection of armed conflict.

But over time, the NKP has moved closer to the conservative policies of the **Liberal Democratic Party**. Kanzaki Takenori (1943–) became president of the NKP in 1998 and remained its president until September 2006 when Ōta Akihiro (1946–) replaced him. Fuyushiba Tetsuzō (1936–2011) served as secretary-general of the NKP, until Kitagawa Kazuo (1953–) succeeded him in 2006.

As president of the NKP, Ōta called for the mending of **foreign policy** ties with **China** and **Korea**, stopping the visits of the **prime minister** to **Yasukuni Shrine**, and maintaining political stability.

In the four **elections** from 2000 through 2009, the NKP elected an average of 29 members (6 percent of the seats) in the **House of Representatives**. In the 2005 lower house election, the NKP received nine million votes or nearly

15 percent of the votes, translating into 31 seats. However, in the 2009 election the NKP dropped to only 21 seats. In the four elections since its re-creation, the NKP has maintained an average of 23 seats or nearly 10 percent of the **House of Councillors**.

In the 2012 general election, the NKP won 31 seats in the lower house and 19 seats in the House of Councillors. The NKP increased its seats in the lower house to 35 in the 2014 election but dropped to 29 in the 2017 election and 25 seats in the upper house in 2016. *See also* POLITICAL PARTIES.

NEW LIBERAL CLUB (SHIN JIYŪ KURABU, 新自由クラブ). The colorful politician **Kōno Yōhei** formed the New Liberal Club (NLC) in 1976. Defectors from the **Liberal Democratic Party** (LDP), Kōno and five other politicians sought to distance themselves from the **Lockheed scandal** and present a younger image than that of the aging LDP. The NLC represented a small challenge to the LDP, but never matured into a major threat, disband-ing in 1986 after 10 years. Although the NLC participated in five **elections**, it garnered an average of only nine seats and never more than 17 seats, which it won in its first election in 1976. *See also* POLITICAL PARTIES.

NEW PARTY SAKIGAKE (SHINTŌ SAKIGAKE, 新党さきがけ). The New Party Sakigake (NPS) was also called the New Party "Initiatives" or New Harbinger Party. This relatively progressive **political party**, a faction of 10 liberal-conservative **Liberal Democratic Party** (LDP) members, broke away from the LDP on 22 June 1993. In the lower house **election** of 1993, it won 13 seats. Takemura Masayoshi (1934–) headed the party. NPS lost seats in the October 1996 **House of Representatives** election. In June 1998, it broke its coalition with the LDP.

In 1994, the NPS took part in the **Murayama Tomiichi** government, a coalition of members of the LDP and the **Social Democratic Party of Ja-pan**, which replaced the liberal coalition headed the previous year by the **Japan Renewal Party**.

In 1996, most of the NPS members joined in founding the **Democratic Party of Japan**. In 1997, the NPS had only two members in the House of Representatives and three in the **House of Councillors**. However, it decided to moderate its stance, and, because of the power of the ecologist and reform-ist factions, the conservatives decided to reform the party.

In 1998, the party began to emphasize the **environment** and was renamed the **Sakigake Party** and further retitled the Green Assembly (Midori no kaigi) in 2002, but this party dissolved on 22 June 2004, mainly because of its failure to win any seats in that year's elections, thus spelling the end of the Sakigake movement. The NPS, in its 10-year life, gained its followers mainly from white-collar bureaucrats and ecologists.

NEW RELIGIONS. Japanese new religions number between 200 and 500, with a total membership of several million people. In Japan, the concept of new religions refers to religiously oriented groups formed in the postwar period that are smaller and less well known than the more traditional religions. Some of the new religions are also being exported around the world, with **Sōka Gakkai**, Tenrikyō, and Mahikari in particular claiming strong membership abroad. **Risshō Kōiseikai** is another of these major new religions.

One of the best known of these new religions is Tenrikyō (the Religion of the Divine Wisdom), founded in the early 19th century by a **woman** named Nakayama Miki. This religion began with revelations and healings, but instead of merging into the wider pattern of **Shintō**, it affiliated more with **Buddhism**. It formulated its own independent writings, constructed its own sacred city named Tenri, and shaped its own forms of worship including a special dance. Today it has approximately 1.75 million adherents.

Mahikari is a Japanese new religion founded by businessman Okada Yoshikazu (1901–1974), who received revelations from God in 1959. After the founder's death in 1974, the movement split into two organizations, with his adopted daughter taking control of the Sūkyō Mahikari group. In Japanese, Mahikari means True Light, which is considered to be the spiritual and purifying energy along the lines of Japanese *ki*. The teachings of Mahikari explain that evil or unhappy spirits that possess the living cause problems in life, such as illness or misfortune. The purification technique of radiating True Light helps people remove these bad spirits.

The religion known as Ōmotokyō (Teaching of the Great Source) is also a major independent religious group having a Shintō background combined with belief in a new revelation of its own. Deguchi Nao (1836–1918) founded Ōmotokyō in 1892. During the war, Ōmotokyō experienced severe persecutions, but in 1950, the movement regrouped. Ōmotokyō has two major centers near **Kyōto**. The spiritual leaders of the movement have always been women. Deguchi Kurenai (1956–), the movement's fifth leader, has guided the movement since 2001.

Other new religions have moved further afield from the traditional faiths of Japan. Seichō no Ie (House of Growth) claims to overcome disease and suffering through its new teachings propounded by Taniguchi Masaharu (1893–1985), a former Ōmotokyō member who authored 20 **books** on **religion**. Its modern headquarters in **Tōkyō** sells symbols and literature expressing the unity of all religions. This 1.5-million-member religious organization, which combines Buddhism, Christianity, and Shintō, involves spiritualism and psychotherapy.

Among the numerous other new religions, one should mention Aleph (*see* AUM SHINRIKYŌ, オウム真理教); Kōfuku-no-Kagaku (Institute for Research in Human Happiness); Makuya of Christ (Kirisuto no makuya); the popularly named Dancing Religion (Odoru Shokyō); Konkōkyō, where God is seen as present in this world and centers around the betterment of human life; Pana-Wave Laboratory, an early 21st-century cult that periodically predicts the end of the world and wraps trees in white sheets; and Agonshū, a Buddhist-based belief system that teaches people to strive for enlightenment in this life and combines spiritual beliefs and traditions with high-tech presentations. PL Kyōdan (the Church of Perfect Liberty) sees the whole of life as art and religion as a means of realizing this vision in the member's experience. Reiyūkai, which has a huge central hall in Tōkyō, began as a movement to care for untended tombs and stresses gratitude and loyalty toward ancestors.

There are many different explanations for the appearance of new religions, but at least it is clear that they provide a barometer of the needs and aspirations of much of Japan's population.

NEWSPAPERS, JOURNALS, AND MAGAZINES. Due to Japan's high literacy rate and affluence, the Japanese are per capita one of the greatest readers of newspapers in the world. A typical Japanese family subscribes to a national daily and a regional or local paper. This generates a strong environment for the media with over 150 daily newspapers, hundreds of weekly publications, more than 2,000 monthly magazines, five large commercial **television** networks, a public television organization, satellite and pay-television services, a cable system, and many online news websites.

Japan has five major media groups: Yomiuri, Asahi, Mainichi, Fujisankei, and Nikkei. These five organizations control much of the news presentation in Japan. They actually operate a type of news cartel. Their newspapers, and several television stations that they operate, dramatically shape the news information that the Japanese receive.

Japan's leading national newspapers include *Yomiuri Shimbun*, *Asahi Shimbun*, and *Mainichi Shimbun*, as well as *Nihon Keizai Shimbun*, *Sankei Shimbun*, and *Nikkei Shimbun*. Japan's leading English-language newspapers are the *Japan Times* and the *Nikkei Asian Review*.

Nihon Keizai Shimbun is a leading **business**-oriented newspaper in Japan. Fourth largest in circulation of Japan's national newspapers, it resembles the *Wall Street Journal*.

Sankei Shimbun is one of Japan's largest newspapers with a circulation of around two million. Maeda Hisakichi founded it in 1933 in **Ōsaka** as a financial paper, *Nihon Kōgyō Shimbun*. During World War II, it merged with other financial papers in western Japan and became *Sangyō Keizai Shimbun*. After extending its business to **Tōkyō**, it became a general newspaper but did not prosper. In 1958, Mizuno Shigeo took over management and transformed it into a great media group, **Fujisankei Communication Group**.

Nikkei Shimbun is the world's largest newspaper specializing in business and finance with a circulation of three million. It originated from *Chūgai Bukka Shimpo*, a weekly founded by Masuda Takashi, a general manger of **Mitsui**. It absorbed other business newspapers in 1942 to become *Nihon Sangyō Keizai Shimbun*. It took the actual name *Nihon Keizai Shimbun* in 1946. The group not only publishes many dailies, weeklies, and **books** but also owns business databases available through the internet and on mobile phones.

Founded in 1923 by Kikuchi Kan, *Bungei Shunjū* (*Literary Annals*) is one of Japan's leading journals of opinion. It carries general interest articles, short fiction, and serialized novels. It has promoted investigative journalism and exposed a number of government and economic scandals. *Bungei Shunjū* has a monthly circulation of nearly a million.

Chūōkōron (*Central Review*) is a leading journal of public opinion that contains semi-scholarly articles, reports, interviews, roundtable discussions, and translations on political and social subjects. In the 1990s, its circulation was more than 100,000 copies per month, but with online publication and economic difficulties, its circulation dropped to around 25,000 in the 2000s. In 1999, Yomiuri Media Group acquired this influential opinion journal.

Of the more than 2,000 monthly magazines, the most popular ones include *Gendai*, *Ronza*, *Seiron*, *Sekai*, *Shokun*, and *Ushio*, plus *Sapio*, *Playboy*, *Modern Weekly*, and *Friday Magazine* also on the more popular side. There are also around 100 weekly news magazines. All told, the magazines issue five billion copies monthly.

Founded after World War II by replacing the disbanded Dōmei Tsūshin, Kyōdō Tsūshin (Kyōdō News) is the biggest news agency in Japan with 50 overseas bureaus. It exchanges information with more than 60 international news agencies such as AP, UPA, AFP, and Reuters. Jiji Press is Japan's second-largest news agency.

NHK (NIPPON HŌSŌ KYŌKAI). *See* JAPAN BROADCASTING CORPORATION (NIPPON HŌSŌ KYŌKAI, 日本放送協会).

NIKKEI 225 (NIKKEI HEIKIN KABUKA, 日経平均株価). The Nikkei 225 is the Japanese stock market average, which measures the movement of prices of the 225 most actively traded stocks on the **Tōkyō Stock Exchange**. It is the equivalent of the Dow Jones Industrial Average in the **United States**. When the Nikkei 225 reached its peak of 38,957 on 29 December 1989, 60 of the 100 largest companies were banks. However, the Nikkei fell to a two-decade low of 7,831 on 30 April 2003, setting off much concern in government and **banking** circles.

From 2009 through 2012, the Nikkei hovered around 10,000 and then started to rise. By mid-2013, it stood at around 16,000. However, it soon plunged by almost 10 percent before rebounding. By 2015, the Nikkei had reached 20,000, its highest mark since 1989. By 19 January 2018, the Nikkei stood at 23,808, showing a healthy market. During 2017, it rose 19 percent. (Refer to appendix G.)

The Nikkei 225 has been compiled daily by the *Nihon Keizai Shimbun* since 1950. The Nikkei is one of the most important indexes of Asian stock markets. Its stocks are reviewed every September and adjustments made so that the Nikkei will reflect the market average accurately. The listed companies include those involved in foods, textiles and apparel, pulp and paper, chemicals, pharmaceuticals, oil and coal products, rubber products, glass and ceramics, **steel** products, nonferrous metals, machinery, shipbuilding, **automobiles**, mining, **construction**, **general trading companies**, banking, **securities**, insurance, real estate, electric power, and communications.

NIKKEIREN. *See* JAPAN FEDERATION OF EMPLOYERS' ASSOCIATION (NIHON KEIEISHA DANTAI RENMEI, 日本経営者団体連盟).

NIKON CORPORATION (KABUSHIKI-GAISHA NIKON, 株式会社 ニコン). Nikon is the world-famous **camera** manufacturer that also produces telescopes, eyeglasses, binoculars, imaging lenses, microscopes, measuring instruments, steppers, scanners, and some **computer** parts. Founded in 1917 as Nippon Kōgaku Kōgyō, the company grew dramatically. During World War II, the company had 19 factories and 23,000 employees, supplying items such as binoculars, lenses, bombsights, and periscopes to the Japanese military.

After the war, Nikon, headquartered in **Tōkyō**, reverted to its civilian product range and operated with a single factory and 1,400 employees. The name Nikon, which dates from 1946, is a combination of Nippon Kōgaku (Japan Optical) and the German Zeiss Ikon. Nikon had great success with its Nikon-I camera, which it started producing in 1948, and with its Nikon-F, which it unveiled in 1959. Among its other famous products are Nikkor camera lenses, Nikonos underwater cameras, the Nikon F-series of professional 135-film SLR cameras, and the Nikon D-series digital SLRs. Nikon has helped lead the transition to digital photography with both the Coolpix line of consumer cameras as well as a number of digital cameras.

In 1988, the company was renamed Nikon Corporation, after its cameras. In early 2006, Nikon announced that it would stop making most of its film camera models, continuing only its low-end FM10 and its high-end F6 cameras, and all of its large-format lenses, in order to focus on digital cameras. As of 2015, it had more than 25,000 employees worldwide. Kariya Michio served as president and CEO. Nikon is a member of the **Mitsubishi Group**.

Nikon projected a loss of $79 million in the fiscal year ending 31 March 2017. The camera business, suffering at the hands of smartphones, is struggling to make new developments and improve quality in order to stay competitive. Nikon president Ushida Kazuo (1953–) says his company will meet the challenges.

Recently, Nikon has lost an estimated $170 million a year in its precision instruments unit. Its revenue from the camera business dropped 30 percent between 2012 and 2015. In 2013, it experienced the first drop in sales from interchangeable lens cameras since it created the first digital SLR camera. Nikon's net profit fell from a peak of $754 million in 2007 to $182 million for 2015. Nikon has reassigned more than 1,500 employees as well as adopting job cuts. As of 2017, Nikon is shifting its focus to medical and industrial devices. *See also* ECONOMY.

NINTENDO (NINTENDŌ KABUSHIKI-GAISHA, 任天堂株式会社**).** Nintendo, incorporated in 1947 and based in **Kyōto**, is the Japanese video game company that makes **games** with the same name. It evolved from a handmade card game company of the late 19th century. Nintendo is the second largest of the big three video game console makers. Its Game Boy, a portable system, was successful domestically and internationally. Nintendo features games by designer Miyamoto Shigeru like *Donkey Kong* and *Super Mario Bros*. **Pokémon** is another popular product.

In 1983, Nintendo launched Famicom, its home video game console, and, shortly thereafter, introduced *Super Mario Bros.*, the best-selling video game of all time. The handheld Game Boy was followed by Super Game Boy, Game Boy Advanced, Nintendo DS, Nintendo DS Lite, and finally Nintendo DSi, each an improvement on its predecessor. Other more advanced systems and games followed. The most recent home console, the Wii, uses motion-sensing controllers to produce a variety of exciting interactive games.

Yamauchi Hiroshi (1927–2013), grandson of the company's founder, was the leading president of the company. He transformed what was once a maker of playing cards into the world's leading video game company. He graduated from Waseda University in 1950. He created the popular *Mario Bros*. game, and then released Game Boy in 1989. Japan's richest person and one of the world's richest people, Yamauchi was the leader of a group that in 1991 purchased the Seattle Mariners **baseball** team, buying 60 percent interest but agreeing to exercise less than 50 percent of the voting rights. Iwata Satoru (1959–2015) replaced Yamauchi as president of Nintendo in 2001. With Iwata's death, Kimishima Tatsumi (1950–) became president and projects great optimism for the company. Nintendo, like **Sony**, is now trying to broaden the sale of its handheld game devices, which offer other features like **music**, video, and wireless internet.

Today, Nintendo competes with Microsoft and Sony for the lead in gaming systems. In 2006, Nintendo introduced Wii, a gaming system that got more people, especially adults, involved in **video games**. This new way of playing games catapulted Nintendo into the lead in game sales. Nintendo was the 10th-largest software company in the world in 2007. Sales figures for 2008 clearly place Nintendo at the top of the video game market. Nintendo's Wii has sold more than 50 million units in just two years. The game is immensely popular not only in Japan but also in the **United States**, Europe, Asia, and the rest of the world.

In 2011, the company launched Nintendo 3DS, a system that enables viewers to have 3D capacity without using special glasses. These and other innovations made it possible for Nintendo to continue as one of the world's largest video game companies.

As of 2014, Nintendo had sold more than 670 million hardware sets and more than four billion software units. Its most popular games have been *Mario Bros.*, *The Legend of Zelda*, and *Pokémon*. Nintendo is constantly moving forward with new hardware and games, partners with other companies worldwide, and strives to be innovative. In 2015, Nintendo partnered with DeNA, a Japanese company that makes games for mobile phones.

In early February, Nintendo raised its profit forecast for the fiscal year ending 31 March 2017. The Kyōto-based video game maker expects a large growth due to the popularity of its new games and a softening of the yen. Nintendo is experiencing a resurgence. *Pokémon* materials continue to be popular, and Nintendo's 3DS handheld systems are selling briskly.

In March 2017, Nintendo released its next game console, called the Switch. Selling for about $260, Nintendo, anxious to recover its mojo, offered it in Japan as well as the United States, Europe, Hong Kong, and elsewhere. It has new entertainment packages to go with the new hardware. The new console will give players more control and better sensors.

NIPPON HŌSŌ KYŌKAI (NHK). *See* JAPAN BROADCASTING CORPORATION (NIPPON HŌSŌ KYŌKAI, 日本放送協会).

NIPPON ISHIN NO KAI (日本維新の会**).** Nippon Ishin no Kai, or the Japan Restoration Party as it is called in English, is a political party, which started as the Initiatives from Ōsaka formed by the prefectural governor, Matsui Ichirō (1964–), and the **Ōsaka** mayor, **Hashimoto Tōru**. Being rather provincial in nature, the party has not really blossomed. As of 2018, Nippon Ishin no Kai holds 11 seats in each the **House of Representatives** and the **House of Councillors**.

NIPPON STEEL & SUMITOMO METAL CORPORATION (SHIN-NITTETSU SUMIKIN KABUSHIKI-GAISHA, 新日鐵住金株式会社**).** Nippon Steel & Sumitomo Metal Corporation is a company formed in 2012 by the merger of two leading **steel** companies. As of 2017, it is the world's second-largest producer of steel. Its predecessor, Nippon Steel, came from the merger of Fuji and Yawata steel companies. The largest commercial steelmaking enterprise in Japan, Nippon Steel became one of the world's leading steel producers by the 1980s. The spearhead of Japan's economic transformation after World War II, Nippon Steel helped the shipbuilding, **automobile**, and **construction** industries to develop and flourish.

Nagano Shigeo (1900–1984) was a major force in creating Nippon Steel. Born in Matsue, Shimane Prefecture, he graduated from Tōkyō Imperial University in 1924. After working to revitalize Fuji Iron, he became director of the purchasing department in 1934 when Fuji Iron merged with Nippon Steel Corporation. In 1941, he was a member of the Iron and Steel Control Council, but after World War II, he returned to Nippon Steel as managing director while serving as vice director of the Economic Stabilization Board. In 1950, Nippon Steel split into Fuji Iron and Steel and Yawata Iron and Steel Works in accordance with the Excessive Economic Power Decentralization Law. Nagano first became president of Fuji and then assumed the chairmanship of Nippon Steel Corporation when Yawata and Fuji joined again in 1970. An important leader of the **business**-industrial community, he served as chairman of the **Japan Chamber of Commerce and Industry** (1969–1984). Nagano has been recognized as one of the major powers in the postwar Japanese **political** and **economic** world.

In 1975, Nippon Steel passed U.S. Steel to become the world's largest steelmaker. However, soon thereafter Japan became a major developed nation and no longer needed as much steel. Likewise, developed European nations no longer needed to import as much steel. Thus, Japan's steel industry declined from its leading position.

After the 2012 merger of Nippon Steel Corporation with Sumitomo Metal to form Nippon Steel & Sumitomo Metal Corporation, the company took as its motto "to pursue world-leading technologies and manufacturing capabilities, and contribute to society by providing excellent products and services." As of the merger, the corporation had 61,000 employees and annual revenues of around $33 billion.

NIPPON TELEGRAPH AND TELEPHONE CORPORATION (NIPPON DENSHIN DENWA KABUSHIKI-GAISHA, 日本電信電話株式会社**).** Nippon Telegraph and Telephone Corporation (NTT) is not only Japan's biggest but also one of the world's largest telephone companies. Originally a state monopoly, NTT was privatized in 1985, making it the country's largest joint-stock company. In 1987, NTT was broken into three private companies and sold as public stock for the first time.

NTT DoCoMo, with more than 50 million customers, is the world's second-largest wireless carrier after Vodafone. It is Japan's largest mobile phone carrier. Although strongly promoting the latest **technology** and trying to be part of the first full-fledged third-generation telephone network, the company had a hard time financially in 2002. Shorter battery life and limited service area had restricted its opportunities. DoCoMo's leading competitors are **KDDI** and J-Phone.

Fortune Global 500 ranks NTT 65th in the world and the fourth-largest telecommunications company in the world in terms of revenue. The company is private although the Japanese government owns 32.6 percent of it. Unoura Hirō (1949–) is the company's president and CEO. Headquartered in **Tōkyō**, NTT had revenues of $144 billion and 275,000 employees in 2016.

NISHIKORI KEI, 錦織圭 **(1989–).** Nishikori Kei is a star tennis player, ranked number four in the world as of March 2015. He is the only Japanese male tennis player ever to be ranked in the top 10 by the Association of Tennis Professionals. He is the only Asian male to reach a Grand Slam singles final. In 2012, he was the first Japanese man to qualify for the French Open quarterfinals in 82 years. A tennis sensation at an early age, Nishikori has won 11 singles titles and was the runner-up at the 2014 U.S. Open. His incredible run at this title held the Japanese world in suspense, even though it was played in the middle of the night in Japan. In 2016, he finished third in the Rio **Olympics** and has set a number of such Japanese records during his tennis career. Nishikori was born in Matsue in Shimane Prefecture. He began playing tennis at an early age and soon found remarkable success in the sport. He has won $17.6 million in his career and resides and trains at the IMG Academy in Bradenton, Florida. As of January 2018, Nishikori, who suffered a wrist injury, had slipped to number 24 in the world.

NISHIO SUEHIRO, 西尾末広 **(1891–1981).** Nishio Suehiro was an important **labor** leader and politician. A native of Kagawa Prefecture, from the age of 14 Nishio worked as a lathe operator and was involved in trade union organization in **Ōsaka**. He joined the Yūaikai in 1919 and was among the leadership of various moderate proletarian parties, including the Shakai

Minshutō and the Shakai Taishūtō. In the first **election** (1928) held after the enactment of universal manhood suffrage, he was elected to the **Diet** for the first of 15 terms.

Nishio played a major part in the founding of the **Japan Socialist Party** (JSP), becoming its chief secretary in 1946. He was **cabinet** secretary under **Katayama Tetsu** and deputy premier under **Ashida Hitoshi** and served in these cabinets as minister without portfolio. But he had to resign in June 1948 after a personal no-confidence vote. Nishio's arrest, shortly after, on corruption charges concerning the **Shōwa Denkō scandal** led to his expulsion from the party, but he returned as an important figure of the right wing of the JSP in 1952. Exonerated by a trial, he was reelected in 1952. Opposed to any form of cooperation with the communists, he and his supporters left the JSP in 1959 and founded the **Democratic Socialist Party** (DSP) over the issue of the renewal of the **United States–Japan Security Treaty** in January 1960. He was DSP chairman until his retirement in 1967 although he remained active in politics until 1972.

NISSAN GROUP (NISSAN CONCERN, 日産コンツェルン). Although small compared to the **Toyota Group**, the Nissan Group is one of Japan's leading *keiretsu*. It is centered on the **Nissan Motor Company**, which has developed relations with independent companies that supply parts for its cars. There are nearly 200 companies that make up the Nissan Group, which can be divided into assembly operations companies, parts manufacturers, and distribution service companies.

The Nissan Group grew out of the prewar Nissan **zaibatsu** with its emphasis on real estate and insurance. After the decline in the real estate market in the 1990s, the Nissan Group shifted its primary emphasis to **automobiles** and industry. It recently abandoned its majority interest in real estate and now focuses mainly on manufacturing and insurance.

NISSAN MOTOR COMPANY (NISSAN JIDŌSHA KABUSHIKI-GAI-SHA, 日産自動車株式会社). In 1914, Den Kenjirō, Aoyama Rokurō, and Takeuchi Meitarō began building a small car that they called the DAT after the first initials of their last names. Thus, what would be called the first Datsun was created. In 1932, after modification of this early car company, Aikawa Yoshisuke established the Nissan Motor Company. The new Nissan Company started the mass production of small cars in **Yokohama** in 1934. Nissan is therefore one of Japan's oldest car manufacturers. The company was forced to produce military vehicles including trucks, airplanes, and engines during the war and, later, served the **Occupation** in the immediate postwar period. In the mid-1950s, Nissan began to produce the Datsun Blue-bird, its leading small car. In the late 1980s, Nissan became Japan's second-largest automaker but was overtaken by **Honda** in 2001.

However, by 2016, Nissan Motor Company had become Japan's second-largest automobile manufacturer producing more than five million cars annually. It now ranks second only to **Toyota**. Internationally, it is the fourth-largest carmaker in the world.

Katayama Yutaka (1909–2015), father of the Nissan Z-car, was inducted into the Automotive Hall of Fame in 1999. Kawamata Katsuji (1905–1986) was a **business** executive and dynamic president (1957–1973) and chairman (1973–1985) of Nissan Motor Company. Through hard work and innovation, he built Nissan into one of Japan's largest **automobile** producers. A graduate of Tōkyō University of Commerce in 1929, Kawamata joined the Nissan board in 1947 and helped rebuild the company after World War II. He served as president of the Japan Automobile Manufacturers Association (1962–1972) and then vice chairman of the **Japan Federation of Economic Organizations** (Keidanren). He retired from Nissan in 1985 but continued to advise the company until his death.

Nissan is best known for its Datsun brand automobile. In 1960, it was the first automaker in Japan to receive the annual Deming Prize for engineering excellence. In 1966, Nissan introduced the Sunny, which became a major driving force behind the rapid growth of the small-car market. After the oil crises of the 1970s, the "Datsun saves" slogan helped Nissan achieve huge sales in the **United States**. Nissan has three plants in the United States, including ones in Smyrna and Decherd, Tennessee, and in Canton, Mississippi. Over the years, Nissan partnered with Ford to make a minivan, with European companies to gain a market advantage, and with other companies to gain in worldwide market share. In addition to its 13 factories in Japan, Nissan has 15 manufacturing plants in 10 countries, including four in Southeast Asia and one in **China**, and has dealerships in more than 150 countries. In 1999, Nissan signed a partnership with Renault of France to form the world's fourth-largest automaker, but by 2008, it would drop to the sixth largest. It also manufactures trucks, machinery, boats, and aerospace components. With all this, it is only Japan's number-three carmaker.

Nissan struggled with problems in the 1990s but merged with Daimler-Chrysler in 1999. Carlos Ghosn (1954–), a Brazilian-born, French-educated Lebanese and head of Renault, became Nissan's president and CEO in 2000. Ghosn served as CEO of both Renault and Nissan and enabled Nissan to make a dramatic recovery. In February 2017, Ghosn announced he would step down as CEO of Nissan but would remain chairman of the company. Nissan named Saikawa Hiroto (1953–) to succeed Ghosn. Saikawa has called for Nissan to strengthen its diversity and achieve growth without sacrificing efficiency. He seeks to narrow the gap between Toyota and Nissan by increasing sales in the Middle East, Southeast Asia, and Japan.

Nissan, a global manufacturer, sells more than 60 models under the Nissan, Infiniti, and Datsun names. In 2015, Nissan sold more than 5.4 million cars worldwide, generating more than $100 billion in revenue. Nissan produces the Nissan LEAF, the world's best-selling all-electric vehicle. As of 2016, Nissan had sold more than 275,000 all-electric vehicles. Nissan's headquarters is in Yokohama but has joint ventures with **Russia**, India, China, and other countries. *See also* ECONOMY; TRADE.

NISSHŌ IWAI CORPORATION (NISSHŌ IWAI KABUSHIKI-GAISHA, 日商岩井株式会社). Formed in 1968 through the merger of Nisshō Company and Iwai & Company, the Nisshō Iwai Corporation ranked sixth among Japan's nine major **general trading companies** in 2005. It traded in metals, machinery, and **energy**. It also managed infrastructure projects, constructed power plants, produced lumber, built condominiums, imported consumer goods, and provided financial services. Nisshō was affiliated with 550 companies in nearly 80 countries.

The company's history reaches back to the early 20th century. Takahata Seiichi (1887–1978) was a businessman, who after graduating from what is now Kōbe University, joined the firm Suzuki Shōten in 1909, a firm that would become a leading general trading company in the course of World War I. Takahata established the general trading firm Nisshō & Company, then Nisshō lwai Company, in 1928 and served as the company's chairman from 1945 through 1963.

In 2003, Nisshō Iwai Corporation merged with Nichimen Holdings, thus integrating businesses of information and communications with building materials, and changed its name to **Sōjitz Corporation**. As of 2017, Sōjitz Corporation has 440 subsidiaries and affiliates around the world in 50 countries and a net income of around $3.2 billion. It is Japan's seventh-ranked general trading company. Satō Yōji (1951–) served as president and CEO from 2012 until June 2017 when he became chairman of the board and Fujimoto Masayoshi (1958–) took over leadership of the company.

NOBEL PEACE PRIZE. *See* NOBEL PRIZE WINNERS.

NOBEL PRIZE WINNERS. Yukawa Hideki (1907–1981), the first Japanese to receive the Nobel Prize, was a theoretical physicist renowned for his numerous pioneering works in particle physics, including the meson theory and the theory of non-local fields. Born in **Tōkyō**, he graduated from Kyōto Imperial University in 1929. In 1939, he joined the faculty of his alma mater, and in 1943, he received the Order of Culture. In 1948, a year after he introduced the theory of non-local fields, he was invited by J. Robert Oppenheimer to become a visiting professor at the Institute for Advanced Study at Princeton University. The following year he became a professor at Columbia University. Yukawa returned to Japan where he served in various government and **education** posts. In addition to his scientific recognition, Yukawa was a vocal spokesman for peace and the peaceful use of atomic **energy**.

Tomonaga Shin'ichirō (1906–1979) was a theoretical physicist and corecipient of the 1965 Nobel Prize in Physics. Known for his numerous pioneering contributions, Tomonaga was important in the world of fundamental physics, including a theory that reconciled the theory of quantum electrodynamics with the special theory of relativity. Born in Tōkyō, he graduated from Kyōto Imperial University in 1929. In 1953, along with Yukawa and Sakata, he became one of the key administrators of the newly established Research Institute for Fundamental Physics at Kyōto University. He served as president of Tōkyō University of Education from 1956 to 1962, and he was also an active participant in the worldwide crusade for peaceful use of atomic energy. His publications include an important textbook in modern physics and a highly readable account of quantum physics written for the nonspecialist.

Kawabata Yasunari won the Nobel Prize in Literature in 1968, **Ōe Kenzaburō** won it in 1994, and **Satō Eisaku** won the Nobel Peace Prize in 1974.

In 1973, Esaki Reona (1925–) won the Nobel Prize in Physics, and in 1974, he received the Order of Culture. Esaki was a physicist known for the semiconductor diode that bears his name. Born in Higashi, **Ōsaka**, he graduated from the **University of Tōkyō** in 1947. He entered Tōkyō Tsūshin Kōgyō Company, now **Sony Corporation**, in 1956, and there discovered the tunneling effects in high concentration p-n junctions, the phenomenon on which his diode was based. This Esaki diode, also called the tunnel diode, with its unique operating characteristics and excellent high-frequency performance, has revolutionized circuit design in the areas of frequency generation, amplification, and switching at ultrahigh frequencies. Esaki moved to the **United States** in 1960 to join the Watson Laboratories of International Business Machines Corporation.

Fukui Ken'ichi (1918–1998) won the Nobel Prize in Chemistry in 1981 for his work applying the theory of quantum mechanics to chemical reactions. Born in Nara Prefecture, Fukui graduated from Kyōto Imperial University where he later became a professor of chemistry.

Tonegawa Susumu (1939–) won Japan's first-ever Nobel Prize in Physiology or Medicine. Tonegawa won the award in 1987 while working at the Massachusetts Institute of Technology (MIT). He won the award for his work on specialized antibodies in the human immune system. Born in **Na-**

goya, he was educated at Kyōto University and received a PhD in biology at the University of California at San Diego in 1969. In the 1970s, he worked at the Basel Institute for Immunology in Switzerland. He came to MIT as a full professor in 1981.

Born in Tōkyō, Shirakawa Hideki (1936–) won the Nobel Prize in Chemistry in 2000. He earned his doctorate at the Tōkyō Institute of Technology in 1966. Shirakawa, together with Alan Heeger and Alan MacDiarmid, modified plastics to conduct electricity and provided an important link between plastics, electricity, and **computers**. He served as a professor of chemistry at the Institute of Materials Science at the University of Tsukuba from 1982.

Noyori Ryōji (1936–) shared the Nobel Prize in Physics with two others in 2001. The Nagoya University professor was recognized for his work with chiral catalysts.

Tanaka Koichi (1959–) was awarded the Nobel Prize in Chemistry in 2002 for his work in mass spectrometry to identify proteins. He works for the Shimadzu Corporation in **Kyōto**. He shared the prize with John Fenn. Their work has helped biologists understand the chemical processes of a cell. Tanaka is one of the youngest chemistry laureates ever.

Koshiba Masatoshi (1926–), a native of Toyohashi, won the Nobel Prize in Physics in 2002 for his work at the Kamiokande neutrino detector facility. A professor at the University of Tōkyō, Koshiba has been a leading force in molding high-energy physics.

In 2008, three Japanese won the Nobel Prize in Physics. They were Kobayashi Makoto (1944–), Masakawa Toshihide (1940–), and Nambu Yoichiro (1921–2015), a Tōkyō-born U.S. citizen who was a professor emeritus at the University of Chicago. In 2008, Shimomura Osamu (1928–), now professor emeritus at Boston University, received the Nobel Prize in Chemistry along with two other American scientists.

The Nobel Prize Committee continues to recognize Japanese citizens for their fine work. In 2010, Negishi Ei-ichi (1935–) and Suzuki Akira (1930–) won the Chemistry Prize for their work in the cross-couplings of organic synthesis. In 2012, Yamanaka Shinya (1962–) won the Physiology or Medicine Prize "for the discovery that mature cells can be reprogrammed to become pluripotent." In 2014, Akasaki Isamu (1929–), Amano Hiroshi (1960–), and Nakamura Shuji (1954–), an American citizen, shared the prize in physics "for the invention of efficient blue light-emitting diodes which has enabled bright and energy-saving white light sources."

In 2015, Ōmura Satoshi (1935–) shared the Prize for Physiology or Medicine for "discoveries concerning a novel therapy against infections caused by roundworm parasites." That same year Kajita Takaaki (1959–) shared the Prize for Physics "for the discovery of neutrino oscillations, which shows that neutrinos have mass." Finally, in 2016, Ōsumi Yoshinori (1945–) received the Prize for Physiology or Medicine for his work on the "mechanisms for autophagy."

NODA YOSHIHIKO, 野田佳彦 (1957–). Noda Yoshihiko is a member of the **Democratic Party of Japan** (DPJ) and served as Japan's **prime minister** from 2 September 2011 to 26 December 2012. The sixth prime minister in six years, Noda was attacked for his nuclear **energy** policy, his controversial sales tax increase, and his handling of the disputed Senkaku Islands with **China**. In September 2016, he survived a DPJ vote but lost in the national election to **Abe Shinzō** and the **Liberal Democratic Party**. Today, he remains a member of the **House of Representatives**.

Born in Funabashi, Chiba, Noda is the son of a paratrooper in the **Japan Self-Defense Forces**. After graduation from Waseda University, he joined the prestigious **Matsushita** Institute. He entered politics in 1987 when he won election to the Chiba Prefecture assembly. He was elected to the House of Representatives in 1993. He served as the DPJ's **Diet** affairs chief and public relations officer, as well as for the country's **Ministry of Finance**. Noda succeeded **Kan Naoto** as prime minister.

Noda faced the unenviable task of dealing with the aftermath of the **Great East Japan Earthquake**, tsunami, and **nuclear power** disaster. He was roundly criticized for restarting some of the nuclear power plants. He supported the controversial Trans-Pacific Partnership and struggled to help Japan retain control over the Senkaku Islands.

NOH, 能. Noh is a classical **theater** form that has a style of **music** unique to this theatrical genre. Noh musicians, called *hayashikata*, are responsible for "beating time and intensifying the emotional atmosphere of the play." Noh is the oldest existing form of theater in Japan but usually fails to excite the postwar generations. It is supported by a small but dedicated group of theatergoers and by people who study the ancient art. Presently, there are about 1,500 professional Noh **actors** in Japan. There are five leading Noh schools, the Kanze, Hōshō, Komparu, Kita, and Kongō schools. Each has its own organization, style, and special plays. Noh organizations are very traditional and protective of their own styles. Motoya Izumi, who has gained great popularity, represents a new generation of young, dynamic Noh actors.

NOMA HIROSHI, 野間宏 (1915–1991). Born in **Kōbe**, Noma Hiroshi was an important novelist who graduated from the French Literature Department of Kyōto Imperial University in 1938. At the university, Noma became increasingly involved with the left-wing movement. He was drafted into the army in 1941 but was arrested for vocal antimilitarism and jailed six months.

Shortly after the war, Noma began work on his first novel, *Kurai e* (*Dark Pictures*), published serially in 1946. Critics called the novel, with its descriptive account of a disturbed period, "the first voice of postwar **literature**."

Noma joined the **Japanese Communist Party** (JCP) in 1947. That same year, he published a multivolume novel that built on his experiences with **burakumin** and the *buraku* liberation movement, a work that won the Tanizaki Prize. Noma was active from 1947 in the JCP cultural activities until his expulsion from the party leadership in 1964. In 1952, he published *Shinku chitai* (*Zone of Emptiness*), which vividly recounted conditions in the wartime army and the brutalities committed by Japanese soldiers. In 1952, he published a compelling depiction of corruption and brutality in the army. Other works describe the **Tōkyō Stock Exchange** and his deepening interest in **Buddhism**, which Noma felt was the only **religion** to capture the spirit of the Japanese.

NOMO HIDEO, 野茂英雄 **(1968–).** Nomo Hideo was a star Japanese **baseball** pitcher who won a silver medal in 1988 as part of the Japanese **Olympic** baseball squad and went on to be an outstanding strikeout pitcher for the Kintetsu Buffaloes in the Japanese Leagues. He gained international fame when he joined the Los Angeles Dodgers in 1995. Nomo was the first Japanese baseball player to pitch in the Major Leagues since Murakami Masanori pitched briefly in 1965. In 1995, Nomo started the All-Star Game, was named the National League Rookie of the Year, led the National League in strikeouts, and was second in ERA with a 2.54 average. He threw a no-hitter against the Colorado Rockies on 17 September 1996.

Nomo was famous for his unorthodox "tornado" delivery, twisting his body around with hands held high before each pitch. In 1998, Nomo was traded to the New York Mets, then to the Chicago Cubs, Milwaukee Brewers, Philadelphia Phillies, Detroit Tigers, and the Boston Red Sox where on 4 April 2001 he threw another no-hitter. He became only the fourth pitcher to throw a no-hitter in both the American and National Leagues, along with Cy Young, Jim Bunning, and Nolan Ryan, some very prestigious company. Nomo pitched for 13 seasons in the Major Leagues with eight different teams before retiring in 2008.

Nomo won 123 games in the Major Leagues and 78 games in Japan. He opened the door to Major League baseball for other Japanese stars such as **Suzuki "Ichirō," Matsui Hideki,** and Matsuzaka Daisuke. In 2014, he was elected to the Japan Baseball Hall of Fame.

NOMURA KATSUYA, 野村克也 **(1935–).** Nomura Katsuya was a catcher for the Nankai Hawks and later a playing manager. Subsequently he played for the **Lotte** Orions and the **Seibu** Lions, retiring in 1980. If not for the career of **Oh Sadaharu**, Nomura would stand statistically as the greatest offensive player in Japanese **baseball** history. Hitting the ninth most doubles (397), drawing the fifth most walks (1,252), and scoring the fourth most runs (1,509), awesome feats in their own right, are among Nomura's more modest accomplishments during more than 26 years of play. His truly outstanding credits include being the second in hits (2,901), home runs (657), and RBIs (1,988). In games played, he is second to none with 3,017 games. Nomura is one of only four Japanese baseball players who stand in the all-time career top 10 in at least six categories.

NORTH KOREA. *See* KOREA, RELATIONS WITH.

NOSAKA SANZŌ, 野坂参三 **(1892–1993).** Nosaka Sanzō was a politician and a major, longtime leader of the **Japanese Communist Party** (JCP). Born in Yamaguchi Prefecture and a graduate of Keiō University, Nosaka joined the Yūaikai and edited its journal *Rōdō oyobi sangyō* (*Labor and Industry*). In 1919–1920, he studied in London but was deported because of communist activities. He returned to Japan via Moscow in 1922 and played a leading role in the founding and early activities of the JCP. On Comintern orders, Nosaka went to the **United States** twice in the 1930s to engage in underground work such as the smuggling of communist tracts into Japan. He remained involved in the communist and **labor** movements through the 1920s, was arrested several times, and eventually escaped to Moscow in 1931. In 1935, Nosaka became a member of the executive committee of the Comintern, and many Japanese communists treated his statement as "official." He spent the war years in Yenan, **China**, where he organized antiwar activities among Japanese prisoners of war.

Upon returning to Japan in 1946, Nosaka was elected to the Central Committee of the reestablished JCP. He called for a "lovable Communist Party" and advocated a nonviolent revolution. That same year he was elected to the **Diet**. In 1950, he was purged by the **Occupation** authorities and, faced with party splits, remained underground until 1955 when he appeared at the Sixth National Conference and called for unity among communists. Secretary and then president of the JCP, he was elected a member of the **House of Councillors** in 1956, a position he held until 1977. He became chairman of the central committee of the party in 1958, a position he held until 1982. Nosaka continued to dominate the party and remained on its central committee. However, in 1992, at age 100, Nosaka was dismissed from his post as honorary JCP chairman for his betrayal of Yamamoto Kenzō whom Joseph Stalin had executed in 1939.

NTT DOCOMO (KABUSHIKI-GAISHA ENU TI TI DOKOMO, 株式会社NTTドコモ). NTT DoCoMo is a powerful internet holding company. A public telecommunications corporation founded in 1991, it is headquartered in **Tōkyō**'s Nagatachō. A spinoff company of NTT, it is the largest mobile phone operator in Japan. It provides all types of telecommunications. NTT DoCoMo has more than 71 million customers, the largest market in Japan. A leader in the development of 5G **technology**, it has subsidiaries in North America, Europe, and Asia.

NTT DoCoMo is a leader in wellness mobile telephones, earthquake warning systems, civil protection systems, and other technological innovations. NTT DoCoMo created the first emoji, or pictographic language, which is widely used as a part of electronic messaging. A leader in telecommunications, NTT DoCoMo has investments and research facilities around the world. It has proposed making **Olympic** medals from metals found in old cell phones. NTT DoCoMo, whose name suggests "mobility anywhere," is listed on both the **Tōkyō Stock Exchange** and the New York Stock Exchange.

NUCLEAR POWER. Prior to the **Great East Japan Earthquake** of 2011, Japan generated 30 percent of its electrical power from nuclear reactors and planned to increase that share to 40 percent. The inability to cope with seismic destruction from this earthquake caused Japan to rethink its nuclear position.

Earthquakes have always been a factor in Japan. During the 1990s, there were several nuclear reactor accidents in Japan, and many of these were covered up. Popular distrust of **Tōkyō Electric Power Company** shocked people into numerous antinuclear protests, and opposition to new plants grew.

The earthquake and accompanying tsunami of 2011 caused the cooling system at the Fukushima Nuclear Power Plant to malfunction and produced a major nuclear emergency. More than 140,000 residents within a 12-mile radius had to be evacuated. The area remains a health risk today. The disaster forced the closing of all nuclear power plants in order to carry out inspections and necessary corrections. Stabilizing the nuclear power plants has proven to be a difficult task. Public confidence in nuclear power has plummeted.

In July 2012, the government allowed the starting of a few nuclear power plants. By January 2017, Japan's nuclear watchdog had approved 10 units for production. Not only must the Nuclear Regulation Authority approve of the plant's safety, but the local population must also approve restarting the nuclear plant.

Historically, Japan began its nuclear energy program in 1954 when it adopted the Atomic Energy Basic Law. Japan opened its first nuclear reactor in 1966. From the 1970s until today, the Japanese government has promoted and controlled the private-enterprise nuclear power sector.

Despite disasters like the Three Mile Island accident and the Chernobyl disaster, Japan's nuclear program has not been greatly affected. Japan has faced problems with the **Tōkaimura accident** and the **Monju** reactor, but these have not generated drastic changes in the Japanese nuclear program.

O

OBUCHI KEIZŌ, 小渕恵三 **(1937–2000).** Obuchi Keizō was Japan's **prime minister** in a coalition government for nearly two years near the end of the 20th century. A **Liberal Democratic Party** (LDP) member, Obuchi served 12 terms in the **House of Representatives** (1963–2000) representing Gumma Prefecture. Elected at age 26, he is said to be the youngest legislator in Japanese history. A graduate of Waseda University, he served with the Ministry of Posts and Telecommunications, Ministry of Construction, and in various other political positions including director of the Okinawa Development Agency, director-general of the prime minister's office, chairman of the House of Representatives special committee on security, deputy secretary-general of the LDP, chief **cabinet** secretary in the **Takeshita Noboru** cabinet during 1987–1989, secretary-general of the LDP in 1994, and following this, vice president of the LDP.

In 1997, Obuchi became foreign minister in the **Hashimoto Ryūtarō** cabinet. As foreign minister, he negotiated with **Russia** over Japanese claims to the Kuril Islands as well as conducted negotiations over a plan to unify **Korea**. On 3 December 1997, he signed the Convention on the Prohibition of the Use, Stockpiling, Production, and Transfer of Land Mines on behalf of the Japanese government, thus reducing the death and destruction caused by land mines. Pragmatic in approach, he invited input from others in formulating and carrying out Japan's **foreign policy**.

As prime minister, Obuchi dealt with two major issues. He oversaw the signing of a peace treaty with Russia, thus attempting to officially end World War II with that country. The other major issue was to try to revive the Japanese **economy**. Although he increased public spending, this did not seem to solve Japan's economic problems. However, Obuchi did help stabilize Japan's faltering economy and calm its divisive political situation.

In the spring of 2000, Obuchi suddenly fell into a coma, causing great consternation in the leadership of the prime minister's office. He died six weeks later. Obuchi Yuko, his daughter, won her father's seat in the 2000 **election**. **Mori Yoshirō** replaced Obuchi as prime minister.

OCCUPATION OF JAPAN, AMERICAN (1945–1952). The first appearance of the American airborne forces in **Tōkyō** and the fleet off Yokosuka brought the reality of defeat to the Japanese people. No one, Japanese or American, knew what to expect when the Americans landed. Many feared atrocities and reprisals since Japan had never been successfully invaded and the Japanese had been such ferocious fighters in the Pacific. Thus began the American Occupation of Japan.

Japan was in a state of chaos. Its political system was thoroughly discredited. Its **economy** had been destroyed and its factories bombed. Japan's transportation system was badly devastated. Much of its **housing** had been reduced to rubble, and its cities lay in ruin. Death and destruction were everywhere, and a deep sense of anxiety pervaded the country. Physical devastation and psychological damage combined to make for difficult times for the Japanese.

At the Atlantic Charter meeting in 1941, the Allies declared that they sought no territorial aggrandizement and would restore sovereign rights and self-government to the defeated countries after reforms were completed. In the Cairo Declaration of December 1943, it was decided that Japan would be stripped of all islands that it had seized in the Pacific since 1914. **Korea**, Manchuria, Formosa, and all other territories taken by violence would be freed.

The **United States** created the State-War-Navy Coordination Committee ("SWNCC") to formulate and direct general policies of the U.S. government in treating the defeated countries in the postwar period. A subcommittee on East Asia laid the basic policies for Japan on 29 August 1945 in "The United States Initial Post-Surrender Policy for Japan." This policy had two basic objectives: to prevent Japan from threatening the future peace and security of the world, and to encourage the formation of a peaceful, responsible government that would respect the rights of other countries.

The Occupation authorities sought to create a Japan friendly to the United States, willing to follow American leadership in its **foreign policy**, industrially and commercially in tune with American interests, and militarily reliant on the United States. The leaders of the Occupation tried to shape the political structure in a way favorable to the United States and to direct the educational system to reflect American objectives.

General Douglas MacArthur served as head of the Supreme Commander for the Allied Powers (SCAP) and directed the essentially American Occupation of Japan. Specifically, the United States determined to destroy all vestiges of Japanese military power, punish war criminals to demonstrate that international war is wrong, eliminate ultranationalistic thought and action, and ensure that never again would Japan make war on its neighbors.

The Occupation was strictly an American operation. Australia contributed a few troops, but these were insignificant in number. The United States rejected any joint Occupation since the war in the Pacific had been primarily an American campaign and there was fear of postwar **Russian** expansionism. Under General MacArthur, the United States Eighth Army directed 45 prefectural civil-affairs teams to supervise rice and tax collections, schools, religious activities, **elections**, courts, and local governments.

Two advisory groups theoretically assisted in the Occupation. The Far Eastern Commission was designed to give other Allies a sense of participation in the Occupation. Eleven, and later 13, nations met in Washington to formulate policy to govern postwar Japan. This commission could also review directives issued by SCAP or its action on policy matters. Yet the commission was forbidden to interfere with military matters, discuss a peace treaty or territorial problems, or reach any decision unless the big four powers unanimously approved of the decision. Thus, the United States had the right of veto over decisions of the Far Eastern Commission.

The Allied Council for Japan was a four-nation advisory body that met regularly in Tōkyō. Great Britain, the **Soviet Union**, **China**, and the United States each had veto power, but this was meaningless since the United States was authorized to deal with "urgent matters" by issuing interim directives. Such directives were to be referred to the Far Eastern Commission for approval, but the United States could use its veto against any attempt to change one of its own directives.

The Occupation leaders kept the Japanese government intact and used it to administer the country. Foreign troops did not govern Japan, but SCAP ruled through the Japanese administrative structure.

The Occupation authorities began a purge in January 1946. Under this purge, they removed all militaristic and ultranationalistic leaders from public office and forbade their future service. In so doing, they hoped to destroy militaristic leadership as well as promote the emergence of fresh leadership. By May 1948, some 220,000 individuals had been purged of their political rights; 180,000 were former military officers. The purge was unpopular and frequently unjust since it took an "across-the-board" approach. SCAP authorities rescinded the purge at the end of the Occupation.

The Occupation of Japan had three basic objectives, which could be called the "three D policies." Planners for the Occupation sought the demilitarization of Japan, the democratization of its people and institutions, and later the development of its economy.

Demilitarization was the first and most obvious objective of the Occupation forces. It was also the easiest to accomplish. SCAP supervisors completed the demobilization of the army, navy, and air force by December 1945. The Occupation officials returned two million officers and men on the home islands to civilian life. It repatriated three million overseas troops and an equal number of civilian employees by early 1948. SCAP abolished the army and navy ministries.

The Occupation authorities either destroyed arsenals and other plants engaged in war production or converted them into peacetime production. The endeavor had been simplified by the air attacks that had reduced most facilities to rubble before the war's end. Authorities destroyed the existing military stores or divided them among the Allies.

Under the auspices of the International Military Tribunal of the Far East, judges from 11 nations tried a select group of Japanese leaders who, according to the indictment, had planned the war in violation of international law. The Tōkyō War Crimes Trials began on 3 May 1946 and concluded in April 1948. The tribunal brought 28 major war criminals to trial for crimes against the peace, crimes against humanity, and conventional war crimes. The verdict found all the individuals guilty and condemned seven of them to death, including Tōjō Hideki. It gave 16 men life imprisonment and others lesser terms. In December 1957, large numbers of people sentenced for war crimes had their sentences commuted.

Other regional military courts throughout East Asia tried those people accused of war crimes. They convicted 4,200 Japanese of some type of war crime. They executed 700 people and sentenced 2,500 to life imprisonment for their war crimes. They meted out lighter sentences to the rest of those found guilty. The war crimes trials served little purpose but to provide a moral lesson. However, most Japanese had already condemned the military for waging an impossible war.

SCAP officials abolished all connections between the government and state Shintōism. It cut off all public support for **Shintō** institutions and priests. SCAP eliminated all government agencies for the control and support of Japan's national **religion**. It prohibited the teaching of Shintō doctrines in the schools and the propagating of militaristic and ultranationalistic doctrines.

The issue of what to do with the **emperor** perplexed the Occupation authorities. Some wanted to put him on trial for his responsibility for Japan's war of aggression. Others, who prevailed, thought he would be more useful as a tool to further the aims of the Occupation. The authorities retained the emperor but stripped him of his prewar influence. They made him the symbol of the state and reduced his role largely to carrying out ceremonial duties.

Directors of the Occupation sought to encourage democratization by building representative government, writing a new **constitution**, and holding free elections. They ended the stranglehold of the Home Ministry over public affairs, enacted a more liberal police law, guaranteed civil rights, and provided for increased freedoms for the people. The new constitution encouraged greater popular participation, placed control in the hands of the people, provided for extensive rights and protections, and included the famous Article 9 that denied Japan the right to engage in war as a national policy.

Revision or replacement of the Japanese constitution was essential for the development of a democratic society. SCAP officials informed the Japanese government that the Meiji Constitution must be reformed. On 1 February 1946, the Matsumoto Committee submitted to SCAP a draft constitution that retained the emperor as the source of political power, failed to provide **cabinet** responsibility to the **House of Representatives**, and lacked a basic guarantee of human rights. Frustrated, SCAP assumed responsibility for the preparation of a constitutional draft.

The development and extension of civil rights became the first step in the democratization of Japan. Under SCAP directives, Japan adopted a "bill of rights" that guaranteed fundamental freedoms, abrogated legislation restricting human rights, freed political prisoners, and forbade police to interfere with individual liberties. Japan also set forth a new civil code that provided for female equality, individual freedom, and full inheritance rights. It revised the election law to give **women** the right to vote and lowered the voting age from 25 to 20 years of age. The SCAP authorities intended the new freedoms of the Japanese people to stimulate responsible political activity.

The "MacArthur Constitution," drafted in six days by Americans, formally promulgated in November 1946, and becoming effective in May 1947, produced significant changes in the Japanese political system. Instead of being "granted" by the emperor, as was the Meiji Constitution, this constitution was "made" by the people. Sovereignty resided not with the emperor but with the people who exercised their power through the legislative, executive, and **judicial** branches of government. The new constitution guaranteed freedom of thought, religion, assembly, and speech. It allowed workers to organize and bargain collectively and even assured people the right to "maintain the minimum standards of wholesome and cultural living." It provided for free, compulsory, and equal **education** for all, and it guaranteed academic freedom. The constitution made the cabinet members collectively responsible to the elected legislature. **Prime ministers** were now selected by the **Diet**, and if they lost a vote of confidence, they had to resign or order a new general election. The constitution gave the judiciary independence from the executive branch and made the tenure of justices subject to the approval of the electorate only every 10 years.

According to Article 9 of the Constitution, Japan renounced war as a sovereign right and disavowed the threat or use of force as a method to settle international disputes. Thus, it abandoned the right to maintain land, sea, and air forces. However, this issue and its interpretation is a problem for Japan today. There had been various efforts to revise the constitution to allow for military armament, but none have been successful in changing even one word of the constitution. In January 2000, former prime minister **Nakasone Yasuhiro**, a strong voice for Japanese independence, was again unsuccessful in bringing about constitutional revision.

The Occupation authorities sought to strengthen democracy through the extension of local autonomy. By giving people greater opportunity to run their own affairs, they hoped to foster "grass-roots democracy." They abolished the Home Ministry, the central authority that held prewar Japan in its iron-fisted grip. SCAP dispersed its functions among local government units and provided prefectural assemblies, prefectural civil services, and municipal assemblies with much more local control. It made prefectural governors and other officials locally elective. It decentralized the police system and placed it under a locally elected police commission. It instituted the referendum, recall, and initiative processes at both the prefectural and municipal levels.

Since the educational system in prewar Japan instilled undue nationalism in students, the Occupation leaders decided to carry out educational reforms that would correct the situation. They purged teachers guilty of stressing ultranationalistic ideas in their classrooms, eliminated military education and ethics courses from the curriculum, and rewrote the **textbooks** to reflect a more democratic society. They adopted a new educational philosophy that sought to inculcate democracy, responsibility, and individualism. To achieve their goals, the Occupation authorities decentralized the educational administration, vesting control of the local school in the hands of the local school board whom they gave responsibility to decide educational policy, budgets, curriculum, textbooks, and teachers.

Secondary schools profited as the reforms brought a freer atmosphere, more flexibility, and less formality. University education did not fare as well since the attempt to impose an alien system did not coincide with Japanese conditions. The Occupation leaders, leaning on the American state-university system, tried to create one university per prefecture as a national school. These schools suffered greatly in quality, and many were simply not large enough to be feasible. Conservative, entrenched staffs prevented change in curriculum and methods.

Since heavy economic concentration prevented democratic development, SCAP authorities set about to eliminate the **zaibatsu**. To extend democracy to the economic realm, they planned to dissolve companies considered large enough to restrain competition. Under a SCAP directive, the Japanese government established a Holding Company Liquidation Commission in April 1946. This commission took control of securities held by the zaibatsu families and provided for their disposal. Eighty-three zaibatsu holding companies were dissolved and their securities offered for public sale. SCAP instituted laws to regulate the size and nature of intercompany holdings and forced 5,000 corporations to go through financial reorganization. Although

1,200 companies were subject to possible dissolution, only nine were actually disbanded. Such minimal application was due to the fact that this reform went too far and began to impair economic recovery.

In 1949, President Harry S. Truman sent Joseph Morell Dodge (1891–1964), president of the Bank of Detroit, to Japan as a special adviser to MacArthur. Dodge worked to curb inflation and rebuild the Japanese economy. He played a role in the successful 1947 currency reform in Germany and headed several economic missions to Japan to enforce the price stabilization program that the U.S. government ordered the **Yoshida Shigeru** cabinet to implement on 18 December 1948. Dodge prescribed severe measures such as forcing layoffs, paring public spending, and stemming inflation with a short-term recession. The Japanese government later decorated him with the Grand Cordon Order of the Rising Sun.

The SCAP authorities adopted extensive **labor** reforms not only to secure a better distribution of income and an improved consumer market but also to promote democratic ideals. They revised the labor laws with the goal of creating powerful vested interests committed to the idea of supporting and furthering democratic reforms. They enacted the Trade Union Act in December 1945 and the Labor Relations Act in 1946, both of which gave Japanese workers the right to organize, bargain collectively, and strike. The Labor Standards Act, passed in 1947, guaranteed better working conditions, a health insurance system, and accident compensation. Postwar unions flourished, and by 1948, some 34,000 unions contained nearly seven million members, representing 40 percent of the industrial labor force.

Extensive concentration of land in the hands of landlords made land reform essential in Japan. Since three-fourths of Japan's rural population was wholly or partially dependent on rented land whose annual rent ranged up to one-half of their produce, the SCAP leaders made land reform a major objective. Again, both economic and political objectives prompted such action because the creation of a vested interest group in the countryside would produce support for the Occupation's reforms. Since the widely held belief that agrarian unrest had contributed to Japan's aggression, the Occupation authorities persuaded the Diet to adopt a Land Reform Law in October 1946 as a means to eliminate this potential source of danger.

SCAP leaders forced all absentee landlords to sell all their land and limited owner-farmers and resident landlords to between eight and 30 acres depending on the type of land. Not more than one-third of this land could be rented to tenant farmers. The rest of the land was sold to the government at artificially low prices and then resold to tenant farmers at low prices on easy terms. Under the land reform program, two-and-a-half million acres of rice paddy and two million acres of upland changed hands. Some 4.7 million tenants bought land causing the tenancy rate to drop from 40 percent to about

10 percent of the total acreage cultivated. The land reform program made Japan substantially a country of peasant farm owners, a very worthwhile aspect of the Occupation reform program.

In 1948, motivated by the growth of Mao Zedong and the communists in China and the potential threat of communist power in Korea, SCAP shifted the emphasis of the Occupation to the development or rehabilitation of Japan.

The SCAP authorities now saw Japan as an "ally" rather than a defeated enemy. The United States quickly became the friendly benefactor and protector of Japan, which faced the possibility of communist encroachment. The United States encouraged Japan's economic recovery and reversed or removed reforms that might hinder its economic growth.

Several Japanese and some American leaders described the Occupation's policy as shifting to a "reverse course" (*gyaku kosu*). The concept of the reverse course implies that the Occupation was a betrayal in which the United States and its Japanese conservative supporters halted the emergence of a genuine democracy in Japan. The Occupation leaders not only softened their efforts at reform in Japan but also embraced Japan as an ally in the global war against communism.

Several areas of Occupation reforms experienced reversals. SCAP reduced and then eliminated the policy of dissolving the zaibatsu, the largest and most effective economic units in Japan. Local autonomy was fine, but it soon became evident that police power had been too decentralized. With tiny units of control, it proved too difficult to coordinate, apply, and finance the police system. SCAP strengthened the police force against radical elements and, except for the six largest cities, organized the police on a prefectural basis under a national public safety commissioner. The SCAP authorities also partially recentralized the educational system. School boards appointed by prefectural governors or municipal mayors replaced locally elected school boards. In 1957, school authorities reintroduced a moral education course to give instruction regarding human relationships, personal relations, community, and national responsibility, but without any reference to patriotism.

Finally, while Article 9 had promised "land, sea, and air forces, as well as other war potential, will never be maintained," SCAP gave permission in July 1950 to form a National Police Reserve, a paramilitary force of 75,000 to take over the responsibility for Japan's domestic security from the United States. In the intervening years, the size and function of the National Police Reserve grew. In 1954, this organization was renamed the national Self-Defense Force and by 1960 had developed as a full **defense** organization, having well-equipped land, sea, and air forces numbering approximately 150,000 troops.

Led by the United States, 48 Allied nations signed the **San Francisco Peace Treaty** on 8 September 1951. The United States prepared the draft treaty, and the other countries either approved it or offered suggestions for minor changes. This treaty, nonpunitive and nondiscriminatory, sought to restore Japan's dignity, equality, and opportunity in the family of nations. In October 1951, the Japanese Diet ratified the peace treaty. It went into effect on 28 April 1952, bringing about the official end of the Occupation. Under the terms of the peace treaty, Japan agreed to apply for membership in the **United Nations** whose principles it would support and pledged to ratify formally the territorial clauses of the Potsdam Declaration.

It was no coincidence that on the same day, 8 September 1951, Japan and the United States, the two major antagonists in the Pacific War, signed the **United States–Japan Security Treaty**. By this treaty, the United States temporarily took over the responsibility for Japan's defense. The security treaty permitted the United States to retain its forces in or near Japan for an indefinite period. Legally no longer part of the Occupation force, the American troops were to remain without infringing unnecessarily on Japan's sovereignty. However, despite the treaty, independence seemed an illusion to many Japanese whose antiforeign feelings grew with the terms and implementation of the security treaty.

The "San Francisco System" refers to the international situation introduced through the peace settlement of 1951 in that city and the accompanying security arrangement with the United States. This arrangement has dominated Japanese foreign policy since its creation. The "1955 System" characterizes the political and economic convergence of Japan in that year with the creation of the **Liberal Democratic Party**, the clash between progressive and conservative forces in Japan, and the recovery of Japan's economic system to exceed prewar capacities. In these developments, Japan became a conservative, economically driven country closely linked to American foreign policy and control. These systems set the tone for much of the postwar period in Japan.

The systems and era saw the struggle between liberal and left-wing advocates against the controlling conservative elites. During this period, Japan made the conscious decision to concentrate on economic development at the expense of everything else. Japan followed a program of conservative hegemony. It put aside politics and foreign policy in its drive to become an economic, financial, and technological superpower.

The merits of the United States–Japan Security Treaty were numerous. Surrounded by formidable and potentially hostile powers, Japan could not risk being neutral, and the security treaty guaranteed this would not happen. Japan, argued proponents of the treaty, had a moral obligation to contribute to the global balance of power necessary to prevent a major war between the communist and noncommunist world. The treaty had a political advantage since Japan, as a democracy, should align itself with countries having similar political values and institutions. The United States supported Japan's reentrance into the world scene.

Economically, extensive grants, loans, and technical aid from the United States helped launch Japan on the road to economic recovery and growth. Freed from defense responsibility for two decades, Japan could use its resources for more productive economic enterprises.

Another advantage was the ever-growing volume of **trade** between the United States and Japan. Supporters of the United States–Japan Security Treaty said it was not a subservient alliance but rather represented "an independent foreign policy within the framework of cooperation with the West." They called it an act of partnership, not a sign of subordination. Thus, for the price of the alliance, the Japanese bought defense and resources with which to rebuild the economy and create the basis for a new national self-respect.

Critics of the United States–Japan Security Treaty had their major points, too. Many Japanese viewed the American military bases in the spirit of negative acquiescence at best. The bases reminded them of their country's continued dependence on the United States and thus produced resentment in Japan. Some feared that these bases would become an invitation to retaliation from the enemies of the United States. Other Japanese saw the security treaty as an odious agreement pressed upon Japan as a condition of its recovery of national sovereignty.

The American Occupation of Japan was a massive experiment in social engineering that proved quite successful under the circumstances. While the Occupation built on earlier trends from the 1910s and 1920s, the extent, scope, and nature of the changes, as well as the speed at which they were introduced, would not have been as great without the guidance and control of the Occupation authorities. The change of direction should not be overstated since there was a relatively large degree of continuity with the past. For all the ferocity of the military conflicts of the Pacific War, the Occupation was surprisingly benevolent. Elements of vindictiveness were minimal and constructive, and reformist attitudes prevailed.

The Japanese people showed great powers of cooperation and a strong regenerative spirit. Their ability to adjust to new situations made the success of the Occupation more easily achieved. Both countries deserve credit for the success. The Japanese deserve credit for their rational, pragmatic, and friendly cooperation and efforts, and these factors complement the efforts of the United States on behalf of humanity and constructiveness.

The Occupation, a major watershed in Japanese history, not only produced a long-lasting relationship between Japan and the United States but also introduced a passive and dependent role. For many years, United States–Japan relations were that of economic interdependence and security dependence. Japan has maximized its economic development and soft-pedaled its military power. Japan's foreign policy is still driven by the United States, but this is not healthy and may not last much longer.

ODAGIRI HIDEO, 小田切秀雄 (1916–2000). Odagiri Hideo was a leading literary critic in postwar Japan. Born in **Tōkyō**, he graduated from and later became a professor at Hōsei University. In 1946, Odagiri participated in the founding of *Kindai bungaku* (*Modern Literature*), a progressive literary magazine that launched the first major wave of postwar writers. He became a literary critic writing for *Kindai bungaku*. A leader in the Marxist literary movement, Odagiri held that Marxist principles were compatible with the personal freedom of writers. His best-known writings are *Minshu shugi bungaku ron* (1948), *Kindai Nippon no sakka tachi* (1954), *Nihon kindai bungaku no shisō to jōkyō* (1965), and *Gendai bungaku shi* (1974). *See also* LITERATURE.

ŌE KENZABURŌ, 大江健三郎 (1935–). Ōe Kenzaburō was a novelist, short story writer, and essayist. Born in Ehime Prefecture, he entered middle school shortly after the beginning of the **Occupation**. In 1954, he enrolled in the **University of Tōkyō**'s Department of French Literature. In 1957, he attracted attention with a short story published in a student newspaper, but his official debut on the literary scene came with *Shisha no ogori* (*Lavish Are the Dead*), published in a magazine in the same year. By the time he graduated, he was already a leader of the new generation and was established in the forefront of new writers. His first works were a poetic probing into his own immature self, showed an increasing preoccupation with social and political questions, and had an often scathing or reverberative manner that, in the following years, was to create a rift between him and some of his contemporaries.

Ōe became a spokesman for the younger left-wing intellectuals. He published a collection of short stories including two prompted by the murder of **Japan Socialist Party** chairman **Asanuma Inejirō**, which drew vicious attacks by right-wing organizations. Two events in particular acted as catalysts in bringing about new growth: the birth in 1963 of a son with a congenital abnormality of the skull and a visit to **Hiroshima** to investigate the aftereffects of the atomic bomb. The results of these experiences left a profound mark on Ōe's imagination. His resulting novel, *Kojinteki na taiken* (*A Personal Matter*), was awarded the Shinchō Literary Prize. Several visits to North America and **Okinawa** in the years 1965 to 1968 provided new material for reflections on the course taken by Japan since the 19th century. These were embodied in the novel *Man'en gannen no futtoboru* (*The Silent Cry*), which won the Tanizaki Prize.

In the early 1970s, a growing preoccupation with the dangers of power politics in the nuclear age, the Okinawa question, and Third World issues found voice in many of his writings and is apparent in a third edition of his collected essays. The sense of cultural dislocation during his formative years, the ideas of Jean-Paul Sartre and other writers in French and English, and a number of traumatic experiences in his personal life, all influences at times difficult to reconcile, are fused by a somber, sardonic, and occasionally grotesque poetic imagination to produce works of an unusual power, written in a prose that represents a conscious attempt to enrich the expressive force of the Japanese language. In 1994, Ōe became only the second Japanese to win the **Nobel Prize** in **Literature**.

OGATA SADAKO, 緒方貞子 **(1927–).** Ogata Sadako was a Sophia University professor who served as the **United Nations** high commissioner for refugees from 1991 to 2001. From 2003 through 2012, Ogata served as president of the Japan International Cooperation Agency. Born in **Tōkyō**, she graduated from Sacred Heart University in Tōkyō. She received her MA from Georgetown University and her PhD in political science from the University of California at Berkeley. Ogata is the daughter and granddaughter of diplomats. She spent five years in the **United States** in the 1930s. She speaks English without an accent. She taught international policy at Sophia University and then became dean of the faculty of foreign studies. Her husband was a noted economist. Ogata secured a large Japanese government contribution to help Middle East refugees. She is a leading diplomat and an internationalist. Ogata Sadako has been and remains a strong spokesperson for immigrants around the world. *See also* FOREIGN POLICY.

OGATA TAKETORA, 緒方竹虎 **(1888–1956).** A native of Fukuoka and graduate of Waseda University in 1911, Ogata Taketora joined the *Tōkyō Asahi* **newspaper** and acted both as political editor and general editor before becoming vice president in 1943. As editor, Ogata had maintained a relatively liberal and antimilitarist policy, but from 1940, he participated in the Imperial Rule Assistance Association and was state minister, head of the government's information section, and **cabinet** secretary during 1944–1945. Ogata was depurged in 1951 and, in 1952, was elected to the **Diet** as a **Liberal Party** (LP) member from Fukuoka. He served as state minister, cabinet secretary, and deputy **prime minister** under **Yoshida Shigeru** and then succeeded him as president of the LP. He advocated unification of the various conservative parties and became a leading figure in the more radical wing of the new **Liberal Democratic Party**. Ogata was widely expected to succeed **Hatoyama Ichirō** as the party's president, but his sudden death precluded this.

ŌGI CHIKAGE, 扇千景 **(1933–).** Ōgi Chikage, former transport minister, became the first female president of the **House of Councillors** in the summer of 2004, serving for three years. **Doi Takako** served as the first female speaker of the **House of Representatives** during the period 1993–1996. Ōgi was elected to the House of Councillors five times. She left the **Liberal Democratic Party** (LDP) in 1994 to join the New Conservative Party but returned to the LDP in 2003. She retired from politics in 2007. Ōgi is a former **actress** with the all-female Takarazuka Revue **theater** troupe. Her real name is Hayashi Hiroko.

OH SADAHARU, 王貞治 **(1940–).** Oh Sadaharu is one of Japan's most famous professional **baseball** players. Born in **Tōkyō** with a Chinese father, Oh was a pitcher for the Waseda Jitsugyō High School team that won the National Invitational High School Baseball Tournament in 1957. He joined the **Yomiuri Giants** in 1958 and, for 19 consecutive years, hit more than 30 home runs a year. During his 22 years with the Giants, he hit 55 home runs in one year (1964) and won the triple crown for two years in succession (1973 and 1974); both are Japanese records. Oh retired in 1980. The 868 home runs he hit during his career far surpass the world's Major League record of 755 achieved by Hank Aaron, and later surpassed by Barry Bonds with 762. From 1995 to 2008, Oh managed the Fukuoka Daiei Hawks, later called the Fukuoka **SoftBank** Hawks.

The numbers clearly tell the story of Oh Sadaharu's title, "king of Japanese baseball." Of his seven top-10 statistical performances, third place in two categories (2,786 hits and 422 doubles) are exceptional accomplishments. Only **Nomura Katsuya** played in more games than Oh's 2,831. In four different measures, Oh stands alone in Japan: 1,967 runs scored, 2,170 RBIs, 2,390 walks (more than 900 greater than his nearest rival), and 868 home runs, which is more than 200 beyond his nearest rival. In 22 years with the Giants, Oh was the home run leader 15 times.

ŌHIRA MASAYOSHI, 大平正芳 **(1910–1980).** Ōhira Masayoshi, known for his astute political maneuvering, served as **prime minister** of Japan from 7 December 1978 until his sudden death on 12 June 1980. Born in Shikoku, he was the son of a Kagawa Prefecture rice farmer. Baptized a Christian, Ōhira attended Tōkyō Commercial College and worked in the **Ministry of Finance** starting in 1936. He was under the wing of **Ikeda Hayato** and, in 1949, became his private secretary. He was elected 10 times to the **House of Representatives**, the first in 1952 as a member of the **Liberal Party**.

As foreign minister in the Ikeda government (1962–1964), Ōhira normalized relations with **South Korea** and subsequently served in the **Ministry of International Trade and Industry** in 1968–1970. In 1971, Ōhira took over leadership of the Ikeda faction of the **Liberal Democratic Party** (LDP). He unsuccessfully competed for the party leadership in 1972 but gave his support to **Tanaka Kakuei** and served as foreign minister in 1972–1974, when relations with **China** were restored. On Tanaka's resignation, Ōhira again contested the leadership of the party, this time with **Fukuda Takeo**; the conflict enabled **Miki Takeo** to become prime minister, and Ōhira again served as his finance minister in 1974–1976. Fukuda defeated him for the party leadership in 1976, but Ōhira subsequently used his position as LDP chairman to build up nationwide personal support within the party, which enabled him to beat Fukuda for the presidency of the LDP and become prime minister.

Ōhira was a member of the mainstream faction of the LDP and something of a dove in **foreign policy** despite a conservative emphasis on traditional Japanese values. Ōhira's nickname of *Otochan* ("papa") suggested his relative popularity. Calls for his resignation followed the October 1979 **election**, but Ōhira appeared to have little problem in maintaining his leadership. Rivalry within the LDP came increasingly into the open, however, and the government was unexpectedly defeated in a no-confidence motion in May 1980. In the hope of rallying national LDP support and uniting the party, Ōhira called a general election rather than resign, but he died suddenly of a heart attack. Ōhira's death, the first time for a postwar prime minister to die while in office, probably aided in the stunning LDP victory.

OKABE YUKIO, 岡部幸雄 **(1948–).** One of Japan's outstanding horse racing jockeys, Okabe Yukio holds the Japanese Racing Association record for the most wins, 2,948, during his 38-year career. He also is the record holder in total G-1 wins with 27. Okabe debuted as a pro jockey when he was only 18 years old, and his long jockey career lasted 38 years until he retired at 56. One of Japan's greatest jockeys, Okabe always rode in top form, was quite colorful, added excitement to Japanese racing, and greatly contributed to horse racing in Japan. In 2004, his admiring fans thronged the stands in huge numbers when he retired.

OKADA KATSUYA, 岡田克也 **(1953–).** Okada Katsuya was the leader of the **Democratic Party of Japan** (DPJ), now known as the Democratic Party (DP). Okada was the second son of Okada Takuya, the cofounder of the ÆON Group. A graduate of the **University of Tōkyō**, he joined the **Ministry of International Trade and Industry**. He was elected to the **House of Representatives** in 1990 and joined the **Takeshita Noboru** faction of the **Liberal Democratic Party**. Following association with the **Japan Renewal Party**, the **New Frontier Party**, and the Minseitō, Okada joined the DPJ. He became president of the DPJ in 2004 and led the party to a large electoral victory in the 2004 **House of Councillors** election. However, dramatic losses in the September 2005 general **election** caused him to resign.

In 2009, Okada lost the party leadership election to **Hatoyama Yukio** who in turn appointed him to head the **Ministry of Foreign Affairs**. As foreign minister, his chief role was negotiating with the **United States** over the relocation of the Marine Corp's **Futenma Air Base** on **Okinawa**. In September 2010, he became secretary-general of the DPJ. Following the DP's September 2016 election loss, Okada resigned as party leader.

OKAWARA YOSHIO, 大河原良雄 **(1919–2018).** Okawara Yoshio was ambassador to the **United States** from 1980 to 1985 and still remained influential in Japanese political and **foreign policy** circles in the 1990s. Okawara served as executive adviser to the **Japan Federation of Economic Organizations** (Keidanren) in the early 1990s. He urged Detroit automakers to "bite the bullet" of competition and suggested that the best way for the United States to compete with Japan was to modernize its **automobile** industry.

Okawara was a 1942 graduate of Tōkyō Imperial University and was one of 480 students under the Government Aid and Relief in Occupied Areas (GARIOA), a forerunner of the Fulbright program, to travel to the United States in 1951. He later served in the **Ministry of Foreign Affairs** and was ambassador to Australia in 1976. On three occasions, he served at the Japanese embassy in Washington. He was chairman of the United States–Japan 150 Years Committee and was president of the Institute for International Policy Studies. In December 2007, Okawara published an important article praising **China** and Japan for their joint efforts to strengthen good-neighbor relations as partners working for "a strategic mutually beneficial relationship."

OKINAWA PREFECTURE (OKINAWA-KEN, 沖縄県**).** Okinawa is Japan's newest, most southern, and most controversial prefecture. With its coral-fringed islands, Okinawa means "rope along the open sea," which is an appropriate name for this chain of 140 sun-drenched islands stretching south of Kyūshū almost to **Taiwan**. Okinawa is also known as the Ryūkyū Islands. It was not until 1879 that Japan annexed the Ryūkyū Islands and made them part of Japan, although this ownership was tenuous at best. Mainland Japanese look down on people from Okinawa and consider them less than true Japanese. Most Japanese consider Okinawa a hinterland and few want to live in the area since it is still Japan's poorest prefecture.

Okinawa is a conglomeration of sea-faring peoples who have melded together to create a polyglot. It is populated by a mixture of Japanese, Chinese, Pacific Islanders, and people from various places in what is now called

Southeast Asia. Only somewhat "Japanese," the people of Okinawa have characteristics and cultural traits from a wide variety of Asian peoples. It is a lovely mix of people, language, customs, and foods.

Although far removed from the core of Japanese life, Okinawa bore the worst of the fighting in the final defeat of Japan in World War II. Caught between the Japanese soldiers making their last-ditch **defense** of Japan and the attacking **United States** military, Okinawa suffered as many as 100,000 civilian deaths, many of them forced suicides, in the Battle of Okinawa. After the war, Okinawa became the headquarters of American troops in the Pacific. Although the presence of U.S. troops is controversial, it produces significant income for the people of the islands.

At the end of the war, the United States maintained jurisdiction over the islands until 1972. Because of its strategic location, the United States established approximately 100 bases there with Okinawa being home to 70 percent of the American military in Japan. Approximately 20 percent of Okinawa's land is controlled by the U.S. military, which now numbers about 27,000 people. Although Japanese sovereignty was returned in 1972, the United States continues to maintain nearly 40 Okinawan bases in total, including Kadena Air Base and five other bases in the small city of Okinawa. Inappropriate behavior, highlighted by several incidents of rape by American troops, has strained relations between the two countries. Okinawa has been a key issue in Japanese-American relations. Two key Okinawan leaders have been Yara Chōbyō (1902–1997), a leftist politician elected chief executive of Okinawa in 1968, and Ōta Masahide (1925–2017), who was governor of Okinawa Prefecture in the mid-1990s. Both challenged the legality and advisability of U.S. military bases in Okinawa.

In spite of controversies, Japan and the United States have signed bilateral agreements to allow the United States to maintain a strong military presence in the islands. The military bases constitute a major part of Okinawa's **economy**. However, **crimes** involving disorderly conduct, drugs, rape, and burglaries continually disturb relations between the people and the large U.S. military contingent.

In July 2000, Okinawa hosted the G-8 Summit, a kind of economic reward for the economically poor prefecture. In May 2006, the United States and Japan agreed to relocate the **Futenma Air Base** from southern to northern Okinawa, but these plans have not yet been realized. Another major contingent of American troops is to be transferred to Guam.

Okinawa Prefecture and the government of Prime Minister **Abe Shinzō** clashed in 2015. Plans to relocate a United States air base from Japan's southernmost prefecture met with widespread disagreement. Okinawa governor Onaga Takeshi (1950–), elected in November 2014, promised to block the relocation of the military base. Prefectural assembly members and local business leaders regularly hold rallies to protect the relocation plan.

Japan and the United States agreed in 1996 to close the Futenma Air Base, located in the middle of the crowded city of Ginowan, and return the land after relocating troops. Japan and the United States later decided that forces stationed in Futenma would be transferred to a new base to be built near Henoko in the city of Nago.

Governor Onaga argued that the United States took land away from the people of Okinawa and they wanted it back. He and the people of Okinawa expressed outrage that they continue to be forced from their land. However, the governments of both Japan and the United States contended that there was no perfect solution to Okinawa's problems. Okinawa is the site of nearly 74 percent of all U.S. military facilities in Japan. The people of Okinawa do not want any new base built on their islands. They do not want to continue to bear the burden of exorbitant U.S. military forces.

The agreement to move the Futenma Air Base came as a result of the rape of a 12-year-old girl in 1995 by three U.S. servicemen. The overly extensive presence of American military men was seen as the cause of the incident. The air base is situated in the middle of a densely populated residential area and nearby historical and cultural sites. The issue of American military bases remains a sore spot between Japan and the United States but also between the Japanese and their politicians.

Okinawa is considered Japan's Hawaii and is thus a place of considerable **tourism**. Its warm climate, sandy beaches, and carefree ambience make it a beautiful place to vacation. Naha is not only the capital but also the center of population, historical sites, American military bases, and economic development. Okinawa is well known for its beautiful hand-painted textiles known as *bingata*. Aside from this, sugarcane, pineapples, and fish are the major products. (Refer to appendix T.) *See also* RED ARMY FACTION (SEKIGUN-HA, 赤軍派); SATŌ EISAKU, 佐藤榮作 (1901–1975); SENAGA KAMEJIRŌ, 瀬長亀次郎 (1907–2001).

OKINAWA SOCIAL MASS PARTY (OKINAWA SHAKAI TAISHŪTŌ, 沖縄社会大衆党**).** Founded 31 October 1950, the Okinawa Social Mass Party consists of liberals and leftists who struggle to help the people of the beleaguered **Okinawa Prefecture**. The party consistently campaigned for reunification with Japan and achieved this result in 1972. It has regularly supported leftist causes, sometimes joining with the **Japanese Communist Party**, but generally championed local issues. Itokazu Keiko (1947–) is the party's chairman. As of 2018, it has no members in the **House of Representatives**, but three people sit in the **House of Councillors**.

ŌKITA SABURŌ, 大来佐武郎 **(1914–1993).** Ōkita Saburō was an econo-mist and secretary of an informal group calling itself the Committee on Postwar Problems. Ōkita graduated from Tōkyō Imperial University in 1937. He served in various positions with the **Economic Planning Agency** and then was president and later chairman of the Japan Economic Research Cen-ter. One of the brains behind the government's "income-doubling" plan and the sprint for growth in the 1960s, Ōkita saw the age as "the arrival of the mass consumption society and the almost limitless desire for better living." In 1979–1980, Ōkita served as foreign minister in **Ōhira Masayoshi**'s **cabi-net**. He received several honors for his academic, economic, and internation-al roles. *See also* ECONOMY; FOREIGN POLICY.

OLYMPICS. Japan has been a regular participant in the Olympics since 1912. It was not involved in the 1948 Olympics because of the aftermath of the war or in the 1980 Moscow Olympics because of the boycott. As of 2016, Japanese athletes have won 484 medals in summer games and 45 in winter games. In the summer games, Japan has won 123 gold medals, 112 silver, and 126 bronze. By sport, Japanese athletes have won 98 medals in gymnas-tics, 84 in jūdō, 80 in swimming, and 69 in wrestling.

The 1964 Summer Olympic Games were held in **Tōkyō**. Prime Minister **Ikeda Hayato** correctly described how the Olympics would enable "the nations of the world to engage in peaceful competition on our shores and observe the progress we have made in our society." The Tōkyō Olympics proved to be a great success. **Ichikawa Kon**, a brilliant director, recorded Japan's Tōkyō Olympics in *Tōkyō Orinpikku* (*Tōkyō Olympiad*), a 1966 **film**.

The **Sapporo** Winter Olympics of 1972 opened 3 February 1972 and lasted three weeks. There Japan won only three medals. In 1998, Japan hosted the Nagano Winter Olympics where it won 10 medals. Overall, at the Winter Olympics, Japan has won 45 total medals with 10 gold, 17 silver, and 18 bronze. Fifteen medals have come in speed skating and 11 in ski jumping. *See also* SPORTS.

OLYMPICS, 2020 SUMMER (*DAI SANJŪNI-KAI ORINPIKKU KYŌGI TAIKAI,*** 第三十二回オリンピック競技大会).** The 2020 Summer Olym-pics, commonly known as **Tōkyō** 2020, offers Japan numerous opportunities as well as challenges. Scheduled for 24 July to 9 August, Tōkyō 2020 will be a major event. The Japanese capital city outbid Istanbul and Madrid in the final competition to host the 32nd Olympics. More than 200 nations are expected to participate in the Olympics that has as its motto "Discover To-morrow." The Tōkyō government has allocated more than $3 billion to pay for the event. It plans to expand airport capacity, build a new railway line, and develop other facilities.

The 2020 Olympics will use several venues from the 1964 Olympics including the National Olympic Stadium, Yoyogi National Gymnasium, the Tōkyō Metropolitan Gymnasium, and Nippon Budōkan, as well as the Tōkyō International Forum, the Imperial Palace Garden, and Ryōgoku Kokugikan Arena. The National Olympic Stadium will undergo a $1 billion upgrade. After a false start, Kengo Kuma replaced the firm of Zaha Hadid to oversee the construction. Prominent Japanese architects including **Isozaki Arata**, **Maki Fumihiko**, and **Itō Toyō** led a movement against the Hadid plan. At Itō's suggestion, the Olympic Committee will adapt and reuse the existing national stadium.

Seven of the important venues are located within the central business district. Twenty more venues are in the vicinity of Tōkyō Bay near Ariake, Odaiba, and Tōkyō's artificial islands. The 2020 Summer Olympics will include 34 sports and have 324 events; 207 nations are expected to participate with more than 12,000 athletes.

It is projected that the 2020 Summer Olympics will be the most futuristic, complex, and sophisticated to date. Since Japan is on the cutting edge of **technology**, look for **robots** to play an important role, for instant language translations to make communication easier, for self-driving taxis to move people around quickly, for broadcasting technology to make giant leaps, for alternative energy sources to advance transportation, for maglev trains to move people around quickly, for hydrogen to be a major power source, and for man-made meteors to make the opening ceremonies even more spectacular.

However, there have been problems with the proposed Olympics. There have been allegations of corruption in the awarding of the games to Tōkyō. The first logo was controversial with charges of plagiarism bringing about a demand for change. Tokoro Asao designed the new logo with an indigo-colored ring of checkerboard patterns said to "express a refined elegance and sophistication that exemplifies Japan." Under the rings are the words "Tōkyō 2020" and under that the five Olympic rings.

ŌOKA SHŌHEI, 大岡昇平 **(1909–1988).** Ōoka Shōhei was a powerful novelist best known for his war stories. Born in **Tōkyō**, he graduated from Kyōto Imperial University. After World War II, Ōoka gained prominence with an autobiographical short story. Having been drafted into the imperial Japanese army, he served in the Philippines where he saw his battalion routed and many men die; he was captured and sent to a prisoner-of-war camp. This traumatic experience shaped an autobiographical short story and the very moving novel *Nobi* (*Fires on the Plain*, 1951). This was one of the most important Japanese novels of the postwar period and won the Yomiuri Literary Prize in 1951. Ōoka wrote very much in the style of the psychological novel. His novel *Kaei* (*The Shade of Blossoms*, 1958–1959) won the 1961 Shinchōsha Prize. A literary critic and translator, Ōoka was also famous for short stories and critical essays. *See also* LITERATURE.

ŌSAKA, 大阪. Ōsaka is Japan's third-largest city with a population of 2.8 million people. A major port city and commercial center, Ōsaka is at the center of the Kansai region. It is sometimes called the "kitchen of Japan." Adventuresome cuisine such as *okonomiyaki*, a mixture of eggs, vegetables, and meats fried in a special batter; *takoyaki*, deep-fried balls made of shredded octopus and other tasty ingredients; and *udon*, a noodle dish, are among the special foods of the area. Department stores even have their own "gourmet palaces."

Approximately 1,500 years old, Ōsaka grew to prominence in the 16th century when the unifier Toyotomi Hideyoshi built a magnificent castle there and made it the center of his powerful holdings. To strengthen his economic base, Toyotomi encouraged merchants to make the city the center of their operations. As they prospered so did Ōsaka, and with this success came the cultural developments. Ōsaka was the center of the rice market, soy sauce production, and sake brewing. It housed the national rice exchange and was the main dealer in copper production. A common saying of the Tokugawa era was "70 percent of the nation's wealth comes from Ōsaka."

During the prewar period, Ōsaka was the center of Japan's chemical and heavy industries. Together with **Kōbe**, it was Japan's main seaport. Thus, it became a target of American bombers in World War II, with much of Ōsaka being flattened and more than a third of the people of the region made homeless.

After World War II, Ōsaka deserved its reputation as a drab, ugly place with lots of nondescript factories and modest houses. However, in the 1990s, Ōsaka gradually became a trendy city. It has several excellent museums, a rebuilt but important castle, and a fantastic aquarium. The **Bunraku** puppet **theater** originated in Ōsaka, and it was home to Japan's greatest **playwright**, Chikamatsu.

It is estimated that Ōsaka and its surrounding area has 30,000 factories, which produce one-fourth of all Japan's industrial output. Among its many enterprises, Ōsaka is home to Panasonic, **Sharp**, **San'yō**, Suntory whisky, and Oodles of Noodles. It is known for its electronics and high-tech enterprises. Nomura Securities, Japan's first brokerage firm, as well as several leading future exchanges, are located in Ōsaka. A 2008 study by *Fortune* magazine ranked Ōsaka ninth in cities of the world for its number of Global 500 companies, which is seven. MasterCard Worldwide identified Ōsaka as the 19th-ranked global economic city.

Ōsaka is a vigorous, boisterous metropolis, full of exciting nightlife. It is filled with amusement districts, labyrinthine shopping malls, modern **architectural** skyscrapers, covered arcades, youthful **fashion** boutiques, amusement districts, **pachinko** parlors, and risqué entertainment. The city is known for its bawdy comedy entertainers including the late "Knock" Yokoyama and Takeshi "Beat" Kitano, who is also an **actor** and **film** director.

Outstanding places to visit in Ōsaka include its large, stately Ōsaka Castle; its ultramodern aquarium; a zoo; gardens; Shitennōji, which is Japan's oldest **Buddhist** temple; Tennōji, which is an area filled with museums; Shinseikai entertainment district, which was popular in the early 20th century; Tsūtenkaku Tower, which is the symbol of postwar rebuilding; Shin-Umeda City, with its impressive floating garden observatory; and the Umeda Sky Building, with its magnificent view.

Ōsaka is known for its down-to-earth, easy-going, friendly citizens. The people, known for their zest for life, are outgoing and skilled at money making. The city is recognized for its international and progressive nature in its **business** practices and for its food, castle, port, and underground shopping arcades.

Ōsaka hosted **Expo** '70, Asia's first world exposition. It has several buildings designed by the famous architect **Andō Tadao**, including the Suntory Museum, JR Universal City Station, and the cinema at Tennōji Park.

OSARAGI JIRŌ, 大佛次郎 **(1897–1973).** Osaragi Jirō was a novelist whose writings are filled with a humanistic outlook and Westernized intellectual orientation. Born in **Yokohama**, Osaragi's real name was Nojiri Kiyohiko. After a brief period as a high school teacher and a language officer in the **Ministry of Foreign Affairs**, he turned to writing full time. He published his first story while still in high school. Osaragi wrote a variety of contemporary novels as well as historical biographies, stories, plays, and children's **books**. He stressed the entertainment value of fiction, and this attitude accounted for his enormous success as a writer of serialized novels for **newspapers**. *Kurama Tengu*, his most popular novel, was serialized in newspapers and magazines for several years, gaining him many followers. He wrote of his disapproval of the superficiality and lack of principles among contemporary Japanese as well as his own respect for tradition and his quest for a world in which order and beauty existed in harmonious balance. His last work, *Tennō no seiki* (*Century of Emperors*), was a broad assessment of the intellectual and spiritual history of Japan from the mid-19th century to the present. *See also* LITERATURE.

ŌSHIMA NAGISA, 大島渚 (1932–2013). Ōshima Nagisa was an internationally acclaimed **film** director who questioned Japan's social constraints and whose works often challenged both the political left and the right. Born in **Kyōto**, he graduated from Kyōto University. Ōshima was the leader of the French-influenced, leftist, so-called Shōchiku New Wave of young directors in the 1960s. Originally hired as an assistant director, during his first six years he also wrote substantial film criticism, discussing the issues of sex and **crime** that were to become central to the New Wave in Japanese film. He stressed the importance of self-assertion, spontaneity, and freedom of expression.

Ōshima directed *Taiyō no hakaba* (*The Sun's Burial*) in 1960. This film is Ōshima's most blatantly amoral and extravagantly violent version of a juvenile delinquency drama, set in a world of rival teenage gangs, pimps, and prostitutes. The film takes place in a hellish **Osaka** where an exquisitely cruel femme fatale vies with the gangs for control of the area's most profitable business.

Yunbogi no nikki (*Yunbogi's Diary*) is Ōshima's short film about the prejudice suffered by vast numbers of Koreans living in Japan. Focusing on one abandoned **Korean** boy living in the slums, Ōshima conveyed a fascinating picture of this boy's life.

Shinjuku dorobō nikki (*Diary of a Shinjuku Thief*) is Ōshima's romantic story of a violent, moody dropout and a disaffected young **woman** who powerfully explore the world of young Japanese radicals in the late 1960s.

Gishiki (*The Ceremony*) is an ambitious film that encompasses no less than the entire history of postwar Japan and chronicles the fortunes and the sorrows of the powerful Sakurada family from 1946 to 1971.

Ōshima directed the sexy, controversial film *Ai no koriida* (*In the Realm of the Senses*), which appeared in 1976. A similarly seductive companion movie, *Ai no bōrei* (*In the Realm of Passion*), is Ōshima's passionate film set in a Japanese village in 1895. Gisaburō, a husband, is a rickshaw driver. Seki, his wife, is 20 years younger. Toyoji, a younger male visitor, seduces Seki, who becomes his lover. The two lovers decide to kill Gisaburō and throw his body down an abandoned well. The ghost of Gisaburō visits the two murderers, leading to their confession and their subsequent execution.

Ōshima directed *Senjō no merii kurisumasu* (*Merry Christmas, Mr. Lawrence*), a World War II drama set in a Japanese prison camp in Java in 1943. Colonel Lawrence (Tom Conti) and Major Celliers (David Bowie) develop close relations with their Japanese captors. This 1983 film shows the brutality of war, the nature of authority, and the Japanese and British codes of honor.

Considered by critics to be the leading spokesman of Japanese youth in cinema throughout the 1960s and 1970s, Ōshima remained consistently controversial. One of the most innovative of Japanese film directors, his films often take their subjects from contemporary **newspaper** headlines, and even those set in the past provide commentary on present-day society.

ŌTA KAORU, 太田薫 **(1912–1998).** Ōta Kaoru was a major leader of the Japanese **labor** movement. He served as chairman of the **General Council of Japanese Trade Unions** (Sōhyō) from 1955 to 1966. Ōta graduated from Ōsaka University and, after working for a chemical company until the end of World War II, entered the labor movement. In 1950, he became chairman of the Japan Federation of Synthetic Chemical Workers' Union. In 1955, he defeated Takano Minoru and became leader of Sōhyō. He played an instrumental role in organizing the *shuntō*, the annual nationwide labor offensive. He retired in 1966 but remained an influential labor leader, expressing his opinions widely. In the early 1980s, he was a labor representative on the Central Labor Relations Commission. Meeting with Ōta in 1964, Prime Minister **Ikeda Hayato** agreed to raise public employee wages by an amount comparable to private-sector increases.

OTAKU, おたく. Otaku is a Japanese term for people obsessed with something. The most common use of the term is to describe people infatuated with **anime** or **manga**. People who are consumed by figures in these media often adopt their styles and imitate their characteristics. Oftentimes, their actions take on negative characteristics. There are different categories of otaku, and their existence has even had an impact on Japan's **economy** as people, particularly the young, race to buy things to imitate their idols. Animators, **fashion** designers, and pop artists rush to capitalize on the latest fad. Otaku can range from the light and innocent to the dark and tragic. However, frequently the term is used in a pejorative manner. Otaku has come to represent a segment of the youth culture, generally in a rather negative perspective from the older, more established members of society. Otaku also serves as a major marketing tool for companies trying to reach Japan's legions of anime and manga fans.

ŌTOMO KATSUHIRO, 大友克洋 **(1954–).** One of Japan's most famous **manga** artists and **anime** creators, Ōtomo Katsuhiro was born in Miyagi Prefecture but moved to **Tōkyō** after graduating from high school. He published his first short stories, such as "Asahi" and "Domu," in manga magazines and, in 1979, published *FireBall*, a bestseller that won the prestigious Japanese Award for Science Fiction, the first manga artist to win the award.

Ōtomo began his world-famous epic, *Akira*, in 1982, and it became an even greater success than "Domu." It sold at least 3.5 million copies. *Akira* was made into a highly successful movie in 1988. A popular website describes the **film** as having "an appetite for destruction that buries any other film made in or out of Japan," and praises it as "one of the most eloquent films about atomic afterclap." Another critic described *Akira* as "quite possibly the best animated film ever made."

In 1987, Ōtomo wrote and animated *Neo-Tōkyō*, a violent, futuristic film. In the 1990s and beyond, he has been involved in a number of films. In 2006, Ōtomo wrote and directed *Mushishi*, a film adaptation of a popular manga.

In 2012, Ōtomo became only the fourth manga artist inducted into the Eisner Award Hall of Fame, one of several awards he has recently received. In 2013, he began producing historical films starting with the Tokugawa period.

ŌUCHI HYŌE, 大内兵衛 **(1888–1980).** Ōuchi Hyōe was one of postwar Japan's most famous Marxist economists. Born in Hyōgo Prefecture, he majored in economics at Tōkyō Imperial University. After working briefly for the **Ministry of Finance**, he joined the faculty of his alma mater. From 1921 to 1923, he studied in Germany where he expanded his knowledge of Marxist economics. In 1938, he was forced from his university position due to his leftist beliefs. He returned to join the faculty of the **University of Tōkyō** after World War II and retired in 1949. From 1950 to 1959, Ōuchi served as president of Hōsei University. He also served as chairman of the Statistics Council of Japan and the Advisory Council of the Social Security System. He collaborated with several others in establishing the Socialist Association and was an ideological leader for the leftist faction of the **Japan Socialist Party**.

ŌYA SŌICHI, 大宅壮一 **(1900–1970).** Ōya Sōichi was an influential social commentator and a collector of left-wing publications. Born in **Ōsaka**, he studied at Tōkyō Imperial University. As a young man, he was influenced by socialist thought and wrote articles for journals such as *Chūō kōron* and *Kaizō* in which he criticized the establishment. He later became more conservative and was known for his sharp commentaries on social trends, especially his talent for coining phrases like *kyosai* (uxorphobia) and *ichioku sohaku-chika* (the "moronization" of 100 million, to describe the age of **television**). Ōya condemned Japanese youth for watching too much television and called them "a 100 million idiots." He founded *Ōya Sōichi Bunko*, a valuable collection of left-wing publications and pamphlets.

ŌYAMA IKUO, 大山郁夫 **(1880–1955).** Ōyama Ikuo was a scholar, politician, and writer, as well as a leader of social movements. Born in Hyōgo Prefecture, he graduated from Waseda University in 1905. He studied sociology and political science at the University of Chicago and the University of Munich. He became a professor at Waseda University and concentrated on progressive social and political movements. Ōyama became a campus symbol of opposition to the government's imperialistic policies. Before the war, he vigorously championed democracy. Under pressure, he left Japan in 1933 and worked at Northwestern University in its library and Political Science Department. Ōyama returned to Japan in 1947 and rejoined the Waseda University faculty. Politically liberal, he was quite active in the peace movement. Ōyama was elected to the **House of Councillors** in 1951.

OZAKI MASASHI "JUMBO," 尾崎将司 **(1947–).** "Jumbo" Ozaki is a top international professional golfer. He was Japan's top money winner in 1990. Ozaki has long been the Jack Nicklaus of the Japanese **golf** tour. Originally a **baseball** pitcher for the Nishitetsu Lions from 1965 to 1967, Ozaki (nicknamed "Jumbo" for his hefty 6-foot, 2-inch frame) switched to golf because of a back injury. He joined the professional tour in 1969. Since then, he has led the tour in yearly earnings on 12 occasions, and he has taken the Japan Open (1989 and 1992) and Japan Professional Golfers' Association (PGA; 1989 and 1992) twice each. Recently, Ozaki won his 110th professional golf tournament, far more than any golfer who has ever competed on the PGA tour.

Ozaki, born in Tokushima, is the most successful player of all time on the Japan Golf Tour, having topped the money list 12 times and won 94 tournaments. However, his performances outside Japan have generally been disappointing, with just two wins in minor tournaments. He finished eighth at the Masters in 1973 and sixth at the U.S. Open in 1989. He competed at the Masters 18 times, but he beat par only in 1995. Ozaki's brothers, Tateo and Naomichi ("Joe"), are also professional golfers. Ozaki played regularly on the Japan Golf Tour where he was the leading money winner in 1973, 1974, 1977, 1988, 1989, 1990, 1992, 1994, 1995, 1996, 1997, and 1998. Ozaki was elected to the Golf Hall of Fame in 2010.

OZAWA ICHIRŌ, 小沢一郎 **(1942–).** Ozawa Ichirō was the former **Liberal Democratic Party** (LDP) secretary-general and acting chairman of the **Takeshita Noboru** faction in the early 1990s. A graduate of Nihon University, Ozawa was elected to the **House of Representatives**, succeeding his father after his unexpected death in 1969. As a protégé of **Kanemaru Shin**, he became a general secretary of the LDP.

Ozawa left the LDP with **Hata Tsutomu** and other friends in 1993 and formed a coalition government with **Hosokawa Morihiro** as **prime minister**. Ozawa, defecting from the LDP in 1993, launched the **Japan Renewal Party** and then later the **New Frontier Party**. In 1999, Kobunsha Publishing Company charged that Ozawa had an affair with a 24-year-old former beauty queen, resulting in a lawsuit against the publisher. Ozawa favored sweeping policy changes in the LDP and tried to gain control of the party's leadership in 1999.

In 1998, Ozawa formed the **Liberal Party** (Jiyūtō), which was really a conservative **political party**. It had 40 seats in the House of Representatives and 12 seats in the **House of Councillors**. Ozawa seems to have been a loose cannon in the party leadership. He turned down **Obuchi Keizō**'s offer of a **cabinet** position when the LDP formed a coalition with the LP.

In 2003, Ozawa merged his shrinking LP with the **Democratic Party of Japan** (DPJ), and it came to mount a solid challenge to the LDP. In the November 2003 **election**, the DPJ picked up 40 new seats, winning 177 of the 480 seats in the House of Representatives. Meanwhile, Prime Minister **Koizumi Jun'ichirō**'s LDP dropped to 237 seats. In the lower house election of 30 August 2009, the DPJ crushed the LDP by a stunning 308 to 119 count, thus elevating Ozawa's political influence.

In July 2012, Ozawa split with the DPJ, taking 50 followers, to form the People's Life First Party in an effort to protest the Japanese consumption tax. He merged this party with the newly formed Tomorrow Party of Japan. However, Ozawa's new party suffered a crushing defeat in the 2012 general election, and he left the coalition to form the Life Party. While in the LDP, Ozawa was considered a conservative, but, showing a lot of political flexibility, he has become more liberal on domestic and international issues. He is known for making outlandish and bombastic comments. Being a bit of a political gadfly, in March 2017 Ozawa called for a merger of the Liberal Party, the Democratic Party, and the **Social Democratic Party of Japan** in order to defeat Prime Minister **Abe Shinzō** and the LDP. This move was not successful.

OZAWA SEIJI, 小澤征爾 **(1935–).** Ozawa Seiji is an internationally famous orchestra conductor. Born in Shenyang, **China**, Ozawa studied under the conductor Saitō Hideo at the Tōhō Gakuen School of Music. In 1959, he won first prize in the International Competition for Orchestra Conductors in France, and he went on to serve as assistant conductor of the New York Philharmonic and **music** director of the Toronto Symphony Orchestra. In 1970, Ozawa became conductor and music director of the San Francisco Symphony Orchestra. In 1972, he became conductor of the **Tōkyō**-based New Japan Philharmonic Orchestra and was awarded the Japan Arts Academy Prize. The Boston Symphony Orchestra appointed him music director in

1973, a position he held until his retirement in 2002 when it honored him as "music director laureate." In 2005, Ozawa became the conductor of the Vienna State Opera, a position he filled until his second retirement in 2010.

Ozawa served as conductor of the Boston Symphony for a record-setting 29 years. While in Boston, he became an avid **baseball** fan of the Boston Red Sox. Ozawa has won many awards including Japan's Order of Culture, the Suntory Music Award, and the Kennedy Center Honors. Unfortunately, suffering from various health problems, he had to cancel all concerts in 2016.

OZU YASUJIRŌ, 小津安二郎 **(1903–1963).** One of Japan's leading **film** directors, Ozu Yasujirō is noted for his works on contemporary Japanese family life and his spare, sedate style featuring low-angle camera placement. He was born in **Tōkyō** but was raised in Matsuzaka. In 1923, he obtained a job as an assistant cameraman with Shōchiku, one of Japan's most important film companies. He became an assistant director in 1926 and a full-fledged director only a year later. Except for his first film, a period piece, all his films focus on contemporary Japanese life. His subject matter eventually narrowed to the activities and problems of the Japanese family, a social unit that he saw disintegrating under the pressures of modern life.

After World War II, Ozu directed 15 films, many of them classics. The film *Banshun* (*Late Spring*, 1949) is the story of a young **woman** who lives with her father and finds herself growing past the marriageable age. It shows that sadness is a part of happiness. The film stars **Ryū Chishū** and Hara Setsuko.

Overall, Ozu's films are considered "very Japanese." *Ochazuke no aji* (*The Flavor of Green Tea*, 1952) is very poetic and universal. In this film, a middle-aged husband and wife are drifting apart. He is a solid, taciturn country-born businessman while she is a popular, outgoing movie-star-type person. She is bored with him and his country ways, particularly his eating rice flavored with green tea. The film shows the slow, subtle decay of a marriage.

Following the war, Ozu became quite critical of the corrupting influence of postwar society on the institution of the family. His famous film *Tōkyō monogatari* (*Tōkyō Story*, 1953) captures the separation of the generations as an aging couple visit their two married children in bustling postwar Tōkyō. In this touching story, the children are too busy to entertain the parents and respond with indifference, ingratitude, and selfishness.

Ozu's film *Sōshun* (*Early Spring*, 1956) is also set in Tōkyō. This classic film depicts the constraints of office life and the social limitations of modern Japan. A young clerical worker shows dissatisfaction with his bleak office life. The film examines quiet, ordinary life and shows the relentless worries over economic problems of the time.

In *Higanbana* (*Equinox Flower*, 1958), Ozu portrays unusual sympathy for the younger generation and especially for those in rebellion. He shows the struggle between traditional and modern ways. The film is implicitly critical of the Japanese family system.

In *Ohayō* (*Good Morning*, 1959), Ozu has two young boys go on a silence strike when they fail to persuade their parents to buy a **television**. Neighbors misinterpret their actions and the disagreements escalate, affecting the neighborhood. This film is a delightfully humorous look at the power struggle between children and adults.

Ozu's film *Akibiyori* (*Late Autumn*, 1960) shows social tensions and family relations. A young woman announces that she is not ready for marriage, which goes against Japanese tradition. Her elders try to marry her off, but she rejects them.

In his later films, Ozu showed a gentle resignation to the ways of the world. His characters face the problems of marriage, unruly children, retirement, and loneliness, but they deal with their disappointments with wistful good humor. His last films are his most conservative, both socially and stylistically.

During his more than 30 years as a director, Ozu gained a reputation as the filmmaker whose works were definitively Japanese in character and representative of the Japanese spirit. Each of his 53 films, created with the sparsest means, has its own distinct character and emotional power. All are characterized by an elegant simplicity. While his films are rooted in Japanese life, they have an international appeal that may be explained by their dealing with people's universal desire for security, happiness, and familial affection.

P

PACHINKO, パチンコ**.** Pachinko is an amusement **game**, a cross between a slot machine and a pinball machine. Invented after World War II, one can win balls, which can be used to continue playing or exchanged for tokens or prizes. These tokens can be exchanged for merchandise, which can be kept or sold at shops for cash. The game is played in what are called "pachinko parlors," and consists of running small steel balls through pins into various gates that determine a payout.

This quasi-gambling game is said to have links to organized **crime**, reputedly through ethnic Koreans linked to **North Korea**. Pachinko parlors, reeking with loud noise, garish lights, and foul tobacco smoke, are spread all over Japan. It is said that pachinko employs one-third of a million people or three times more than Japan's **steel industry**, has 30 million regular players, and commands 40 percent of Japan's leisure industry. Serious gamblers, a small portion of the players, are referred to as *pachi-puro*, or professional pachinko players. The game has become so modernized in some places that it uses *deji-pachi*, or digital pachinko machines. Pachinko is a big-time game in Japan. *See also YAKUZA,* ヤクザ.

PANASONIC. *See* MATSUSHITA GROUP (MATSUSHITA GURŪPU, 松下グループ).

PARTY FOR JAPANESE KOKORO (NIPPON NO KOKORO, 日本の こころ**).** Founded 1 August 2014 as the Party for Future Generations, the Party for Japanese Kokoro took its current name in December 2015. Its key leaders were **Ishihara Shintarō** and **Hashimoto Tōru**. With the December 2014 elections, the party dropped from 19 seats to just two in the **House of Representatives**. As of 2018, Nakano Masashi (1948–) is its key leader. It now has only one member in the **House of Councillors** and none in the House of Representatives. Its positions are usually nationalistic and to the conservative side.

PARTY OF HOPE (KIBŌ NO TŌ, 希望の党). Tōkyō governor **Koike Yuriko** founded the Party of Hope (PH) in 2017 as a vehicle to oppose Prime Minister **Abe Shinzō**. Generally conservative in its ideology, the PH sought to challenge Abe in the 2017 general **election**. It experienced a leadership struggle that led to a split within the party. On 10 November 2017, the party elected Tamaki Yūichirō (1969–) coleader, and four days later Koike resigned, in part because of the party's poor performance in the election. As of 2018, the PH has 50 of the 465 seats in the **House of Representatives** but holds only three seats in the **House of Councillors**. The party has little national structure, suffered when Koike herself did not run, and experiences criticism when she appears to be neglecting important duties as governor of Tōkyō.

The PH is conservative minded but called for reform. It absorbed much of the Democratic Party but works with the **Nippon Ishin no Kai**, also known as the Japan Restoration Party.

PETROLEUM COMPANIES. Japan has a small oil reserve and is the world's second-leading importer of fossil fuels after **China** but just ahead of the **United States**. Japan is only 16 percent **energy** self-sufficient. As of 2013, oil accounted for a large percentage of Japan's energy while coal and natural gas provided less energy, and **nuclear power** was way down. Hydroelectric power and wind power generate even less power. At any given time, Japan has only about a half-year of petroleum reserves.

As of 2012, Japan imported 83 percent of its oil from the Middle East with Saudi Arabia, the United Arab Emirates, and Iran leading the way. Japan imports about five million barrels per day. However, it is attempting to diversify its supply market, looking toward **Russia**, Central Asia, and Africa as possible sources, and also to develop alternative sources of energy. With the Kyōto Protocol, Japan is trying to reduce its greenhouse gas emissions by 50 percent by 2050.

Based on refining capacity in 2015, Japan's leading petroleum companies are JX Holdings, Nippon Oil, Idemitsu Kosan, JAPEX, and Cosmo Oil. These five companies refine approximately two-thirds of all Japan's petroleum. Some 31 refineries in Japan process approximately six million barrels of oil per day.

PLAYSTATION. *See* GAMES.

PLAYWRIGHTS. Postwar Japan has a number of noted playwrights. Kinoshita Junji (1914–2006) was one of Japan's foremost playwrights. Kinoshita was born in **Tōkyō** and studied English literature at Tōkyō Imperial University, specializing in Elizabethan drama. In the immediate postwar years, Kinoshita published several folktales (*minwageki*), a translation of *Othello*, and three radio plays; he also participated in the founding of a new drama (*shingeki*) group that henceforth performed all his *minwageki*. Between 1940 and the late 1970s, Kinoshita wrote more than 40 plays for stage and radio, in general taking subjects from Japanese folklore and contemporary history. He also published many important works on the theory of the stage. In addition to his many plays, Kinoshita was a prolific writer on many aspects of drama. His playwriting career was an untiring search for a new Japanese drama and a wide variety of plays.

Yashiro Seiichi (1927–1998) was a noted playwright. Born in Tōkyō, he graduated from Waseda University with a major in French literature. In 1949, he joined the Bungakuza (Literary Theater), a **theater** company organized by Kishida Kunio. He won considerable public recognition for his *Kiiro to momoiro no yugata* (*Evening of Yellow and Peach*, 1959), a play about young people and their difficulties in postwar Japan. Love, individual ego, and faith were themes in his writings. In 1968, he published a play titled *Yoake ni kieta* (*They Vanished at Dawn*), an open testament of his conversion to Catholicism. Among his best recent works were plays about famous *ukiyo-e* artists, including *Sharaku ko* (*Sharaku*, 1972), for which he won the 1972 Yomiuri Literary Prize, and *Hokusai manga* (*Hokusai Sketchbook*, 1973).

Yamazaki Masakazu (1934–) is an important playwright and philosopher in postwar Japan. He grew up in Manchuria during World War II and was educated in philosophy at Kyōto University. Yamazaki has a strong interest in contemporary philosophy, which he combines with his theater career. His first major play, *Zeami* (1963), was a modern psychological and poetic examination of the life of Zeami, the founder of the medieval **Noh** theater. The subject matter of his plays ranges from contemporary Japan to incidents in Western history. In addition to his dramas, Yamazaki is known for his writings on aesthetics, history, and literary figures such as Mori Ōgai.

Terayama Shūji (1935–1983) was a playwright best known for his avant-garde artistry and shocking effects. He used a variety of puppets, dwarfs, hunchbacks, and fat **women** in his surrealist productions. He founded Tenjō Sajiki Theater in 1967. Terayama won several prizes for his works. He made the **film** *Sho o suteyo, machi e deyō* (*Throw Away Your Books, Let's Go into the Streets*) in 1971. This is a powerful work by an iconoclastic director. He also directed *Shanhai ijin shōkan* (*The Fruits of Passion*) in 1981.

Kara Jūrō (1940–) is one of Japan's leading playwrights, directors, and **actors**. Kara graduated from the Theater Department of Meiji University. He organized a theater troupe in 1963 and began to write plays. The group used a distinctive red tent that became both the symbol and the prime vehicle for realizing Kara's goal of integrating contemporary theater with everyday life. Kara seeks to return to the time when actors wandered among people and performed without any trace of gentility or artful precocity. Kara's dialogue is highly literary, humorous, and filled with puns, slang, and unexpected images and allusions.

Kishida Kunio (1890–1954) was one of Japan's leading playwrights in the early postwar period. Inoue Hisashi (1934–2010) wrote many plays and some comic fiction. Noda Hideki (1955–) is an acclaimed playwright with more than 40 plays to his credit. *See also* LITERATURE.

POKÉMON, ポケモン. In the world of **games**, **Nintendo** has created a fantastically successful character called Pokémon. Pokémon is a **manga**, an **anime**, trading cards, and a game character that charms children worldwide. In the Pokémon anime, Ash is the main character who wants to become the number one Pokémon master. His friends Misty, Rock, and later Tracey, help him in his endeavor. Along the way, he battles the evil Team Rocket who tries to capture and steal his Pokémon. Each of the 800 or so Pokémon so far discovered has its own special powers. A Pokémon trainer's goal is to capture all 800 Pokémon and thus become a Pokémon master. To capture a Pokémon, you must battle it and weaken it to the point that you can capture it with a Pokéball. Pikachu, Ash's first Pokémon, is a pocket monster mouse.

Pokémon is a media franchise managed by the Pokémon Company, a Japanese consortium. Nintendo is the main owner. Ishihara Tsunekazu, president and codeveloper of Pokémon Company, has developed the company where 600 million people worldwide have downloaded the app to their smartphones. In Japan alone, the market worth is at least $10 billion.

The Pokémon phenomenon celebrated its 20th anniversary in 2016. The company reissued several of its leading programs. In July 2016, the company released a mobile game called *Pokémon Go*, which instantly became very popular.

POLITICAL PARTIES. Political parties first appeared in Japan in the 1870s. Their activities and involvement in the country's affairs demonstrate the importance of popular participation in government. Leading political figures campaigned for freedom and popular rights (*jiyū minken*) movements. Parties such as the **Liberal Party**, Reform Party, and Constitutional Party dominated the early political scene. In the early 20th century, leftist parties would make their appearance. While only a few people had the right to participate in the early years, eventually popular involvement increased, and the scope of power expanded.

The rise of militarism in the 1930s temporarily limited the role of political parties in Japan. However, parties continued to exist, although playing a minor part in the overall political administration. In the immediate postwar period, political parties blossomed and became quite important. Some of the parties reformed and expanded from the prewar period and new parties came into being from the merger of older parties.

Since the postwar political revisions, all members of the **House of Representatives** are elected for a four-year term with the right to call an **election** at any time, or, in the event of losing a vote of confidence, they must hold an election. Members of the **House of Councillors**, a body newly created after the war to replace the House of Peers, are elected for six-year terms with half of the upper house facing the voters every three years.

During the first 40 years of the postwar period, five parties dominated the Japanese political scene. The **Liberal Democratic Party** (LDP) has been the largest and most powerful. The **Japan Socialist Party** (JSP), the **Democratic Socialist Party**, and other socialist offshoots, as well as the **Japanese Communist Party** (JCP), have offered leftist opposition, with more success in the earlier postwar period than today. **Kōmeitō** became an important force in the mid-1960s. Many other lesser parties have played significant, although fleeting, roles. In the 1980s, there was a flourishing of new political parties showing the vitality of politics in Japan. In the late 1990s, the **Democratic Party of Japan** (DPJ) had risen to first challenge LDP dominance, and then dramatically gained a virtual stranglehold on political power with its stunning victory in the 30 August 2009 lower house election. In addition to these major parties, more than 100 minor parties have participated in the political process in postwar Japan. (Refer to appendixes B and C.)

Traditionally, rural areas have been the stronghold of the LDP. The propensity to support public works projects and agricultural subsidies in the past, and a natural conservative orientation, have given the LDP a big advantage in the countryside. Japan has had a one-party dominance in the rural areas and a competitive system in the urban areas. However, recently this has been changing as farmers have become increasingly upset with the LDP for its lack of support for agricultural subsidies. Political reforms and population shifts have hurt the LDP as well. In the July 2007 House of Councillors election, as well as the 30 August 2009 lower house election, rural voters went for the DPJ in a major way.

As in any country, there are age differences in voting patterns. In Japan, older people vote in larger numbers than their younger counterparts. Many young people in Japan have been turned off by daily politics. Also, older people have tended to vote more frequently for the more conservative candidates, usually meaning the LDP members, whereas younger people are more liberal in their voting patterns. However, these trends may be changing.

Gender differences play only a minor role in Japanese politics. **Women** are not particularly decisive in the outcome of the vote. Although women seem to be stronger than men on social issues, they are generally less supportive of **defense** issues. Women tend to be less partisan than men and more often identify with the unaffiliated voter. A few candidates, such as **Koizumi Jun'ichirō**, have been quite popular with women voters. However, in the 2007 House of Councillors election, the votes of women were not significant in determining the outcome because women tended to vote in the same pattern as men.

With the formation of the LDP, Japan entered what would be termed the "1955 System," a reference to the LDP's domination and control of politics through the next 40 years. However, in 1994, Japan undertook electoral reforms. These reforms attempted to make Japanese politics more nationally oriented and less local and particularistic. They sought to increase party and candidate competition, make Japan less factional and less personalized in its voting, and reshape the "1955 system." Its multi-seat districts contributed to personalized campaigns, factionalism, money politics, personal support groups, and pork-barrel politics. Despite the reforms, Japan still has a strong attraction for the personal campaign approach.

As of 2009, women held 45 of the 480 seats in the House of Representatives and 44 of the 242 seats in the House of Councillors. Thus, roughly 9 percent of the lower house and 18 percent of the upper house members were women. Things have not changed much in 2018 as 47 of the 465 House of Representatives members are women, thus making up 10 percent of the group. The balance is somewhat more favorable in the House of Councillors as 50 of the 242 seats (21 percent) are women.

Information on the sources of party finances makes the Japanese party system more easily understood. The party leaders, especially those of the LDP, receive large political contributions for which they are expected to deliver favors. Japan is considered one of the countries with a high level of public disclosure of political contributions since all donations over ¥50,000 must be reported. Japanese corporations are not allowed to contribute to political candidates but can give to parties that in turn give to candidates. Although Japan has strict campaign finance laws, these laws are frequently abused or not enforced. The LDP is not only well financed but also regularly underreports its contributions.

The range of political philosophies of the parties runs the gamut from the very conservative to rather extreme leftist views. Despite its name, the LDP has offered voters a solidly conservative choice. The JSP and JCP have provided leftist alternatives, but always within bounds of reason. At least 20 parties have emphasized the value of democracy, or *minshu* (民主), by using that term in their party name. An equal number have used the word *socialism*, *shakaishugi* (社会主義) in Japanese, or some variant in their name. The term *new*, or *shin* (新) in Japanese, has also been very popular with at least 16 parties trying to suggest that they have a new approach to dealing with political issues. Through their names, some parties such as the Environmental Green Political Assembly (Kankyō Sento Midori no Kaigi), Greens Japan

(Midori no Mirai), and Rainbow and Greens (Niji to Midori), make evident their interest in the **environment** although they have not seriously affected the outcome of the elections. Other party names, such as the Happiness Realization Party (Kōfoku Jitsugen-tō), Internet Breakthrough Party of Japan, Japan Wellbeing Party (Nihon Fukushintō), New Party for Salaried Men (Sarariman Shintō), New Peace Party (Shintō Heiwa), **Sports** and Peace Party (Supōtsu Heiwa-tō), and Tax Affairs Party (Zeikin-tō), are interesting but hardly significant in Japan's overall political process.

Factionalism has been a fact of life in all Japanese political parties. Factionalism has stemmed from previous party mergers and politicians who share common interests as well as more specific policies. Factionalism often causes party deadlocks and lack of effective political governance. Intra-party factional alignments stem from political issues ranging from conservative to liberal groups, but mostly it stresses different personalities. Factions dominate politics, the selection of **prime ministers**, access to key **cabinet** positions, and the selection of influential party leadership posts. Factions can vary from as few as a half dozen individuals to as many as 120 people.

Although all Japanese political parties, including even the new DPJ, have factions that to some degree shape their policies and actions, the LDP is the main factional culprit. The LDP has a complex network of patron client relationships with powerful interlinking ties. LDP Diet members have local support groups, or *koenkai* (後援会), that help with ascertaining public opinion, gaining votes, and providing financial backing for political candidates. Although centered on individual politicians, some groups are supported by farmers, construction workers, businessmen, bureaucrats, and defense industry groups.

Throughout the postwar period, there have been shifts in party strength. In the first six elections, the more conservative parties such as the LP, Japan Progressive Party, Democratic Liberal Party, and Reform Party collectively garnered the most votes. The leftist JSP was consistently the number one opposition party averaging around 125 seats in the lower house per election through 1993. Since then, the JSP and its successors have been much less of a factor. The JCP has averaged a dozen seats through all 24 elections. The LDP has been by far the dominant force in the 18 elections since its formation in 1955. However, this dramatically changed with the 2009 election. The Kōmeitō and its offshoot have averaged 41 seats in the last 14 elections, but the 2009 election saw it drop to only half of the previous average. With the election of 25 June 2000, the DPJ appeared to be the rising star with its smashing victory with 308 seats won in the 30 August 2009 election. However, since then, the DPJ has experienced a dramatic decline and, in 2016, merged with other parties.

Japan has had a healthy participation of political parties at all levels, from prefectural government to the lowest level of village and rural control. Unfortunately, Japan seems incapable of producing strong political leaders, having had a string of unpopular, colorless leaders with the exception of Koizumi Jun'ichirō. Between 2006 and 2012, Japan has had a succession of six unpopular prime ministers who served only around a year each.

In 2009, voters abandoned the LDP that had ruled Japan for 50 years. However, on 16 December 2012, those same voters stunned the DPJ and gave the LDP a landslide victory. With this vote, Japan swung back to the right and returned Abe Shinzō to power. Prime Minister **Abe Shinzō** has served as prime minister since this time. He continues his nationalistic posturing to the dismay of many people and countries.

The global financial crisis also contributed to political uneasiness. The **Great East Japan Earthquake** took its toll. The growing need for political reform stirred the people. The Japanese people are hungry for more dynamic political leadership, and **Ishihara Shintarō**, former governor of **Tōkyō**, and **Hashimoto Tōru**, the former mayor of **Ōsaka**, got a lot of attention for a while but have faded recently. Both attracted eager listeners but appeared rather radical for the more conservative Japanese voters.

As of the election of 22 October 2017, the House of Representatives has 283 LDP and 29 Kōmeitō members, giving the block a supermajority. Of the opposition parties, the **Constitutional Democratic Party** has 54 seats, the **Party of Hope** has 51 seats, the **Democratic Party** has 13 seats, and the JCP has 12 seats; other minor parties split the remaining seats. (Refer to appendix D.)

The House of Councillors held its 24th election 10 July 2016. As of that date, the LDP held 125 seats and the Kōmeitō 25 seats. Among the opposition parties, the Democratic Party held 42 seats, the JCP 14 seats, and other minority parties the rest of the seats. (Refer to appendix E.)

Well over 100 political parties have mushroomed in postwar Japan, but many of them have been small in number of supporters, short-lived, regional, the province of single leaders, and often identified with unusual names. It is hard to take seriously parties with names such as Tōkyō Tea Party, Summer Breeze Assembly, Tax Party, Sunrise Party, Dawn Club, People's Life First, Sports and Peace Party, Truth Party, Green Wind, Internet Breakthrough Party, or Rainbow and Greens. Only a dozen or so parties have had national recognition, a significant number of supporters, a sustained impact, and a broad political representation. *See also* DIET, NATIONAL (KOKKAI, 国会); LIBERAL PARTY (JIYŪTŌ, 自由党); NEW KŌMEITŌ (KŌMEITŌ, 公明党); SOCIAL DEMOCRATIC PARTY OF JAPAN (SHAKAI MINSHUTŌ, 社会民主党).

POLLUTION. *See* ENVIRONMENT.

PRESS. *See* NEWSPAPERS, JOURNALS, AND MAGAZINES.

PRIME MINISTER (*NAIKAKU SŌRI DAIJIN*, 内閣総理大臣). The members of the **Diet** select the prime minister from among its constituents and then the **emperor** officially appoints this person prime minister. The prime minister serves at the pleasure of the **House of Representatives** members. If members of the House of Representatives adopt a motion of no confidence or defeat a vote of confidence, the prime minister must resign or dissolve the house within 10 days and call an **election**. The prime minister is the head of the **cabinet**, the executive branch of the government, and appoints its members.

The office of prime minister was created in 1885, four years before the adoption of the Meiji Constitution. It took its current form under the current 1947 **Constitution**.

Both the House of Representatives and the **House of Councillors** vote for their preferred candidate for prime minister. If the two houses choose different individuals, then a joint committee of both houses tries to select a mutually agreeable prime minister. However, if the two houses cannot reach an agreement within 10 days, the decision of the House of Representatives becomes final.

Only civilians are eligible to be prime minister. No member of Japan's **Self-Defense Forces** (SDF) or any former member of the Imperial Japanese Army or Imperial Japanese Navy can serve as the executive leader of Japan. However, **Nakasone Yasuhiro** became a powerful prime minister in the mid-1980s in spite of holding a low-level army position.

The prime minister exercises control over the entire executive branch of the government, presents bills to the Diet in the name of the cabinet, signs laws, appoints and dismisses cabinet ministers, reports to the Diet on domestic and **foreign policy** matters, and must respond to questions from the Diet. The prime minister also presides over cabinet meetings, serves as commander in chief of the SDF, and, with cause, can override a court injunction against an administrative act.

During the postwar period, 33 men have served as prime minister through 2017. (Refer to appendix A.) The average time in office for these political figures has been around two years. Only six individuals have served four or more years. The longest-serving prime ministers have been **Satō Eisaku** with nearly eight years (1964–1972), **Yoshida Shigeru** with just over seven years (1946–1947, 1948–1954), the current prime minister **Abe Shinzō** for six years (2006–2007, 2012–present), **Koizumi Jun'ichirō** for five and a half years (2001–2006), Nakasone Yasuhiro for just five years (1982–1987), and **Ikeda Hayato** for just over four years (1960–1964). At the opposite end of the scale, four individuals, **Higashikuni Naruhiko** (1945), **Ishibashi Tanzan** (1956–1957), **Uno Sōsuke** (1989), and **Hata Tsutomu** (1994), served only two months each. At least four others served less than a year.

By and large, Japanese prime ministers have not been forceful personalities with the exception of such leaders as Yoshida Shigeru, Ikeda Hayato, Satō Eisaku, **Tanaka Kakuei**, Nakasone Yasuhiro, and Koizumi Jun'ichirō. Only Koizumi has shown an outgoing, flamboyant personality. Most Japanese prime ministers have been rather faceless political figures who have governed through consensus and a tendency to avoid rocking the boat. The role of prime minister has often been the function of getting Japan to bring its multiple interests into a common harness.

Political leadership in Japan has reflected consensus building and group effort. Therefore, prime ministers have focused on bringing the groups together, finding the lowest common denominator, and reluctantly reacting to issues. Many of Japan's prime ministers have not been true leaders, being neither dynamic nor innovative.

An obvious characteristic of postwar Japanese prime ministers is that the vast majority of them have come from the **Liberal Democratic** Party (LDP). Of the 28 prime ministers since 1955, a total of 23 have come from the LDP. In the mid-1990s, three non-LDP members served as prime minister of Japan for less than a total of three years. The selection of **Hatoyama Yukio** as prime minister in 2009 and **Kan Naoto** in 2010, after the overwhelming victory of the **Democratic Party of Japan**, briefly opened the door in Japan to new political leadership. *See also* ASHIDA HITOSHI, 芦田均 (1887–1959); ASŌ TARŌ, 麻生太郎 (1940–); FUKUDA TAKEO, 福田赳夫 (1905–1995); FUKUDA YASUO, 福田康夫 (1936–); HASHIMOTO RYŪTARŌ, 橋本龍太郎 (1937–2006); HATOYAMA ICHIRŌ, 鳩山一郎 (1883–1959); HOSOKAWA MORIHIRO, 細川護熙 (1938–); KAIFU TOSHIKI, 海部俊樹 (1931–); KATAYAMA TETSU, 片山哲 (1887–1978); KISHI NOBUSUKE, 岸信介 (1896–1987); MIKI TAKEO, 三木武夫 (1907–1988); MIYAZAWA KIICHI, 宮澤喜一 (1919–2007); MORI YOSHIRŌ, 森喜朗 (1937–); MURAYAMA TOMIICHI, 村山富市 (1924–); OBUCHI KEIZŌ, 小渕恵三 (1937–2000); ŌHIRA MASAYOSHI, 大平正芳 (1910–1980); POLITICAL PARTIES; SHIDEHARA KIJŪRŌ, 幣原喜重郎 (1872–1951); SUZUKI ZENKŌ, 鈴木善幸 (1911–2004); TAKESHITA NOBORU, 竹下登 (1924–2000).

R

RAILROADS. Japan National Railways (JNR, Nihon Kokuyū Tetsudō, 日本国有鉄道) was founded in 1949. JNR operated the majority of the railroads in Japan in the postwar period. It developed and operated the Shinkansen, the so-called **Bullet Train**, starting in 1964. Shimomura Sadanori was the first president of JNR. Beset by financial problems, in 1987 JNR split into 11 private railroads, six of them major passenger carriers and one large freight carrier. Japan's leading railroads are East Japan Railway, Central Japan Railway, West Japan Railway, Kinki Nippon Railway, Odakyū Electric Railway, and Nagoya Railroad. The new national network of private railways today is called Japan Railways (Nihon Tetsudō) or JR.

RECRUIT SCANDAL (*RIKURŪTO JIKEN*, リクルート事件). Incorporated in 1963, Recruit Company is an information-industry company engaged in publishing, communications, and human resources. Based in **Tōkyō**, it also deals in real estate and telecommunications. For a time, Recruit was part of the Daiei *keiretsu*, but now it is independent. In 1988, the company played a central role in the Recruit scandal, sometimes called "Recruitgate," where stock shares were given to prominent politicians, bureaucrats, and **business** tycoons in order to influence political decisions and market prices. The Recruit scandal, perhaps the biggest scandal to rock postwar Japan, was an insider trading and corruption scandal that forced many prominent Japanese politicians to resign in the summer of 1988.

Recruit chairman Ezoe Hiromasa (1936–2013) offered a number of shares in a Recruit subsidiary, Cosmos, to business leaders and senior politicians shortly before Cosmos, a publishing, telecommunications, and land development corporation, went public in 1986. Following the public offering, Cosmos's share price skyrocketed, and the individuals involved in the scheme saw average profits of $70,000 each. Ezoe, who cultivated contacts with politicians in order to advance his company, gave large financial contributions to politicians and used the stock market to shift money to them. He gave low-face-valued shares, which then soared in value when they went public.

More than 100 prominent Japanese politicians of several parties were caught up in this scandal. Ezoe resigned from Recruit in 1988, was arrested in 1989, and was finally given a three-year suspended sentence in 2003.

Although only 17 members of the **Diet** were involved in the insider trading, another 30 were later found to have received special favors from Recruit. Among the politicians involved in the scandal and forced to resign were Prime Minister **Takeshita Noboru**, former prime minister **Nakasone Yasuhiro**, finance minister and deputy prime minister **Miyazawa Kiichi**, and chief cabinet secretary Fujinami Takao. In addition to members of the **Liberal Democratic Party** (LDP) government, leaders of the **Kōmeitō**, **Democratic Party of Japan**, and **Japan Socialist Party** were also found to be involved. As a result, Takeshita's **cabinet** was forced to resign, although some of its members later returned to political prominence, including future **prime ministers** Miyazawa Kiichi and **Obuchi Keizō**. Despite the breadth of the Recruit scandal across party lines, the LDP was hurt most significantly by the scandal. It is often said to be one of the main causes of **Hosokawa Morihiro**'s opposition party victory in 1993, which ended the LDP's 38-year reign.

RED ARMY FACTION (SEKIGUNHA, 赤軍派). The Red Army Faction grew out of the radical **student movements** on Japanese university campuses in the 1960s. Its stated goals were the overthrow of the Japanese government, the elimination of the Japanese monarchy, the destruction of capitalism, and the implementation of world revolution. It mainly opposed the **United States** war in Vietnam but also objected to the **United States–Japan Security Treaty**, American military bases in **Okinawa** and elsewhere, and Japanese conservative policies in general. The Red Army Faction became involved in Middle East politics. It was responsible for the bloody terrorist attack on passengers at the Tel Aviv airport in Israel on 30 May 1972. These radical factions used the most extreme methods and quickly attracted police attention. The police arrested many members, but some fled to **North Korea** by highjacking an airplane in 1970 (Yodogo incident), while others joined the Palestinian movement. Those who remained in Japan were arrested in a bloody assault at Karuizawa. *See also* FOREIGN POLICY.

REFORM (KAIKAKU, 改革). Reform was a political coalition formed in 1994. It consisted of 187 members of the **House of Representatives** with legislators from the **Japan Renewal Party**, the **Kōmeitō**, the **Democratic Socialist Party**, and the **Japan New Party**, all small parties that broke away from the **Liberal Democratic Party**. Ozawa Tatsuo (1916–2013) was the leader of this political party. Reform had only a brief existence; formed after the 1993 **election**, it dissolved before the next election in 1996.

RELIGION. Today, many Japanese claim to have no religious affiliation. However, when questioned, they will often say they have a loose association with **Shintōism** and **Buddhism**. Like so much in Japan, the past and the present seem to blend together, folding and unfolding, linked and yet separate. Religion plays an important part, although not an all-encompassing role, in modern Japan where daily life is intertwined with rituals, superstitions, and celebrations from birth through death. Most people are married at a Shintō shrine or a Christian church, have their children dedicated at a Shintō shrine, hold their funeral at a Buddhist temple, and visit religious institutions for festivals and annual events.

Shintō is the oldest, most traditional religion in Japan. It has strong racial overtones and a rich mythology. It includes animism, ancestor worship, and a strong attachment to nature. *Kami*, (神) or gods, exist in many forms and in many places. Today, Japan has around 80,000 Shintō shrines with 25,000 priests.

Buddhism has existed in Japan since the sixth century. It brought a certain religious vitality to Japan and introduced a written language, **literature**, **architecture**, higher **education**, philosophy, and a system of government from **China**. Indeed, Japan owes much to China and its Buddhist vehicle. Although declaring themselves secular in nature, most Japanese participate in various Buddhist rituals and traditions. Japanese Buddhism has some 80,000 temples with 260,000 priests.

Christianity appeared in the 16th century but was not a significant force until the 19th century. Only around 1 percent of all Japanese are Christian, but their influence is significantly larger than their numbers. Japan has around 8,500 churches with 22,000 ministers. Today, under Article 20 of the **Constitution**, all Japanese are guaranteed freedom of religion. *See also* KAGAWA TOYOHIKO, 賀川豊彦 (1888–1960); NEW RELIGIONS; RISSHŌ KŌSEIKAI, 立正佼成会; SŌKA GAKKAI, 創価学会.

RENGŌ. *See* JAPANESE TRADE UNION CONFEDERATION (NIHON RŌDŌ KUMIAI SŌRENGŌKAI, 日本労働組合総連合会 OR RENGŌ, 連合).

RICOH COMPANY (KABUSHIKI-GAISHA RIKŌ, 株式会社リコー). Ricoh Company is one of the world's leading office equipment makers. It manufactures office automation equipment, copiers, facsimile machines, data processing systems, and related supplies. It also produces state-of-the-art electronic devices and photographic equipment. Ricoh, part of the **Fuyo Group**, has more than 300 companies that operate in Japan and abroad.

RISSHŌ KŌSEIKAI, 立正佼成会. Risshō Kōseikai is one of Japan's new religions that emerged in the 1950s. Risshō Kōseikai emphasizes the *Lotus Sutra* as the doctrinal basis of the movement. It is notable that this is a lay movement that is entirely independent of any previously existing monastic sect. It also has an impressive complex of buildings in **Tōkyō**. The main emphasis of Risshō Kōseikai is on a form of group counseling in which the individual's problems are analyzed in **Buddhist** terms and the *Lotus Sutra* recited and studied.

Niwano Nikkyō (1906–1999), founder and president of Risshō Kōseikai, strongly influenced this new **religion**. Born in Niigata Prefecture, he moved to Tōkyō in 1924 where he studied folk religious practices. In 1934, he became an active member of a new religion known as the Reiyūkai. In 1938, doctrinal differences with the Reiyūkai leadership led Niwano to leave that group and form the Risshō Kōseikai, which grew rapidly after World War II. Niwano, an active administrator, public speaker, and author of numerous books, was also honorary president of the international committee of the World Conference on Religion and Peace and the chairman of its Japanese committee, vice president of the International Association for Religious Freedom, and the chairman of the board of directors of the Union of New Religious Organizations of Japan. The Templeton Foundation awarded him its 1979 Prize for Progress in Religion for his efforts on behalf of world peace and interreligious cooperation.

ROBOTS AND ROBOTICS. Japan is the world's leader in the use of industrial robots. Most of the major **automobile**, electronics, and **science and technology** companies are involved in the research and production of robots. Indeed, industrial robots, properly programmed, are important machines that perform work that humans might otherwise have to do. Most of the world's robots are manufactured in Japan, which also is the world's leading exporter of robots. Five of the world's top 10 robot companies are Japanese, including Fanuc, Yaskawa, Kawasaki, Epson, and Nachiu Fujikoshi. Robots continue to be an important part of Japan's development. As of 2012, nearly 1.5 million robots, about 40 percent of the world's total, work in Japanese factories. Indeed, robots give Japan a competitive edge in industrial production.

With one in five Japanese now 65 or older, the development of robots is essential. In the years leading up to 2006, the government provided $42 million for robot research and development. From that year through 2010, the government spent another $10 million. In 2006, the robot industry generated $5.2 billion and the government expects that figure to quadruple by 2020. Robots are gradually taking jobs to boost productivity and overcome worker shortages. Robots are one way for Japan to counter the decline in available laborers.

The Japan Robot Association seeks to advance the development, production, and sales of domestic robots. In the middle of the 20th century, Waseda University professor Katō Ichirō (1925–1994) constructed WABOT-1, a humanoid robot that could walk and see with two camera eyes. After extensive progress, Honda had produced the P2 humanoid robot, which was an efficient working machine by the end of the century.

Robots are used as entertainment creations, pets such as Sony's Aibo, guard dogs or security systems, cleaning machines, mobility devices, and rescue mechanisms; they also serve industrial functions. They also meet transportation needs, work in space probes, serve in fire-extinguishing jobs, search out land mines, assist with nursing care, perform micro-actions, and assist with many industrial and technological processes.

A unit of the **Softbank Corporation** released its humanoid robot, named Pepper, in 2016. Softbank, working with Microsoft Japan, plans for Pepper to help boost its sales by helping customers. Pepper will help with face authentication, purchase data analysis, and coupon issuance. Since 2015, about 2,000 companies have begun to use Pepper. Softbank Robotics seems to be the growing high-tech company to watch. **Son Masayoshi**, SoftBank chairman and CEO, argues that Pepper is the first robot to understand human feelings.

Advanced Telecommunications Research Institute International, working with Ōsaka and Kyōto Universities, has developed Erica, the world's most advanced humanoid robot. Erica chats easily with people. Friendly, and even flirtatious, she can carry on a conversation with humans. She has advanced language skills and even changes facial expressions. She is so advanced that SoftBank includes a clause in its user agreement that the purchaser will not engage in sexual acts with Erica!

RUGBY. Japan is traditionally the strongest rugby union power in Asia, with only occasional losses to **Korean** rivals in the region. But it has experienced mixed results against non-Asian teams over the years since Edward Bramwell Clarke and Tanaka Ginnosuke (1873–1933) introduced the sport in 1899. The Japan Rugby Football Union, founded in 1926, administers the Rugby Union in Japan.

As a team sport, rugby is still a distant third in popularity behind Japanese **baseball** and **J.League** soccer, and this is unlikely to change until Japan's national rugby union team becomes consistently successful on the world stage, especially at the Rugby World Cup. At present, rugby union is rarely seen on **television** and is mainly shown on cable subscription channels.

Japan has the fourth-largest rugby-playing population in the world with around 126,000 players. The Japanese team is known for its speed and resourcefulness but has sometimes been at a disadvantage due to the relatively smaller size of its players.

The first Rugby World Cup was held in 1987. Australia, New Zealand, and South Africa have dominated. Japan, although trying, has yet to be a major factor. Japan will, however, host the Rugby World Cup in 2019 at a dozen locations throughout the country.

In an effort to drive up the overall standard of Japanese rugby and improve the results of the Japan national rugby union team, the Japan Rugby Football Union has recently created a new semiprofessional 12-team league, called the Top League. The first season was 2003–2004. Its teams include Kintetsu Liners, **Kōbe** Kobelco Steelers, Kubota Spears, **NEC** Green Rockets, Nihon IBM Big Blue, **Ricoh** Black Rams, **San'yō** Wild Knights, Suntory Sungoliath, **Toshiba** Brave Lupus, **Toyota** Verblitz, World Fighting Bull, and **Yamaha** Jubilo. This is Japan's first nationwide rugby league and is a first step toward professionalism. So far, the league is proving to be successful with many closely fought and exciting games, although attendances at games are generally not high.

Matsuo Yuji (1954–) was one of the best Japanese rugby players ever. In 1976, his Meiji University won the national championship. His corporate team won the national championship seven times in a row from 1979. Other rugby greats include Hayashi Toshiyuki (1960–), legendary player with Kōbe Steel; Iwabuchi Kensuke (1975–), the first Japanese to play professional rugby in England; Murata Wataru (1968–), who had a great career with Yamaha Jubilo; and Yoshida Yoshihito (1969–), a world-class Japan wing.

Dubbed "Mr. Rugby," Hirao Seiji (1963–) played rugby for Dōshisha University and won the collegiate championship three times. At 19, he became the youngest person ever to play for the All-Japan team. In 1986, he joined Kōbe Steel, a powerhouse of Japanese rugby, and in 1997 became the manager of Japan's national team. Hayashi Toshiyuki (1960–), a star rugby player, holds the most caps at 38. He played with Hirao on Dōshisha University's team and then with the Kōbe Steel club.

The Japanese university rugby championships are held annually. The 2016–2017 championship was the 52nd in the series. Teikyo University has come to dominate the sport, winning eight consecutive titles from the 2009–2010 season through 2016–2017. Other strong university rugby teams include Dōshisha, Hōsei, Kantō Gakuin, Meiji, and Waseda universities.

RUSSIA/SOVIET UNION, RELATIONS WITH. Japan's contact with Russia began in a minimal way in the 17th century, but it was only in the second half of the 19th century that interaction between the two countries increased and relations became strained. Territorial expansion, misperception, mistrust, and national pride led to clashes over territory that resulted in the Russo-Japanese War of 1904–1905. The relationship between Japan and Russia, which was already under stress, became worse with the rise of communism in Russia and the creation of the Soviet Union, the outbreak of military clashes in Mongolia and northeastern **China**, and the Soviet Union's abrogation of its neutrality pact with Japan in 1945.

After World War II, relations between Japan and the Soviet Union did not go smoothly. The Soviet Union did not sign the **San Francisco Peace Treaty** in 1951, and the following year, it vetoed the admission of Japan to the **United Nations**. As late as 1956, the Soviet Union had not accounted for some 11,000 Japanese prisoners of war. However, in October 1956, the two countries issued a joint declaration calling for the restoration of diplomatic relations and promising to continue efforts toward a peace treaty and the peaceful solution of the territorial issues.

The Northern Islands controversy, a persistent thorn in the side of Japanese-Russian relations, is the disagreement between Japan and the Soviet Union, now Russia, over ownership and control of the islands of Etorofu, Kunashiri, Shikotan, and Habomai, which are called the Kuril Islands. Japan has been contesting these islands with Russia since the end of World War II. Russia claims the islands by virtue of the peace treaty and other world conferences, while Japan claims sovereignty due to earlier control of the area.

Relations between Japan and the Soviet Union in the 1960s began with the Russian protest over the renewal of the **United States–Japan Security Treaty**. However, in 1966, Japan and the Soviet Union signed a five-year **trade** agreement.

Economic cooperation grew in the 1970s. In 1975, the Soviet Union proposed a Japan–Soviet Union treaty of good-neighborliness and cooperation. Several diplomatic exchanges took place in the 1970s. However, in 1979, Japan protested the Soviet Union's military buildup on the Northern Islands.

In the 1980s, relations between Japan and the Soviet Union hardened when the United States pressured Japan to help check Soviet expansion in Afghanistan and Western Asia. However, in 1986, Soviet foreign minister Eduard Shevardnadze came to Japan, the first Soviet foreign minister to visit in 10 years, to discuss arms control and consider the Northern Territories issue. In 1988, the two countries again met but continued to be unsuccessful in finding a solution to the controversy.

In the 1990s, Japan and the Soviet Union began to discuss the issue of the Northern Territories as well as the southern part of Sakhalin in a more constructive manner. In late 1991, Boris Yeltsin took power in Russia with the dissolution of the Soviet Union. He seemed to take a harder line toward Japan. Although Yeltsin visited Japan in October 1993, the two countries made little progress toward improving relations.

Prime Minister **Koizumi Jun'ichirō** visited **energy**-rich Russia in 2003, seeking oil. As the world's second-largest oil consumer, Japan recognizes Siberian oil as important to Japan's **economy**. After Koizumi's visit, Japan agreed to spend $22 billion in the next 10 years on foreign investment projects in Russia.

Japan and Russia, two perennial adversaries, are working hard to build real economic cooperation. Bilateral trade increased 25 percent in 2003 alone. Although the dispute over the Kuril Island chain still existed, economic interests were bringing the countries closer together.

In 2003, President Vladimir Putin and Prime Minister Koizumi signed an agreement calling for "an accelerated effort to resolve the long-standing territorial dispute over the Kuril Islands that has left Russia and Japan technically in a state of war for six decades." Although efforts have been made, the issue still persists.

In 2007, Foreign Minister **Asō Tarō** met with his Russian counterpart, and the two countries agreed to a joint development of oil resources in Russian territory. In 2008, Prime Minister **Fukuda Yasuo** and Russian president Vladimir Putin agreed on a plan for the joint development of eastern Siberia. However, that same year, Japan exacerbated the Northern Islands issue when it issued guidelines for school **textbook** publishers to indicate Japanese sovereignty over the islands. In response, Russia again laid claim to the islands. In February 2009, Prime Minister Asō Tarō met with Russian president Dmitry Medvedev in Sakhalin where they agreed to speed up efforts to resolve the territorial dispute.

Very few Russians visit or live in Japan. In 2017, approximately 71,000 Russians visited Japan, a record according to the Japan National Tourist Organization. Far fewer Japanese, only around 7,800, traveled to Russia.

Today, Japan's view of Russia has improved. Japanese **defense** plans have downgraded the military threat from the north. For Japan, the threat is shifting from Russia to **North Korea** and perhaps China. Even without a formal peace treaty and with the continuation of territorial disputes, the remembrance of the Soviet Union's last-minute entry into war against Japan, and the mistreatment of Japanese troops and citizens by Russia during the war, relations between Japan and Russia have gradually improved.

As of 2017, Japan and Russia have still not been able to sign a peace treaty officially ending World War II due to disputes over the Kuril Islands. This continues to sour relations between the two countries. Although the two countries have taken steps to improve relations, including increased investments, military cooperation, and cultural exchanges, in 2017, the Pew Global Attitudes Project survey found that 64 percent of Japanese people view Russia unfavorably.

In November 2013, Japan held its first-ever diplomatic talks with the Russian Federation, and the first with Moscow since the year 1973. On 27 April 2017, Japanese prime minister **Abe Shinzō** and Russian president Vladimir Putin held a bilateral summit where they sought to make progress toward deepening trust, resolving the issue of the disputed Northern Territories, and concluding a peace treaty.

On 7 July 2017, Abe met with Putin for the 18th time while in Hamburg, Germany, at the G-20 summit. The talks seemed to proceed well, focusing on the peace treaty issue, economic cooperation, and North Korea. Yet, despite positive appearances, recent developments highlight serious problems.

According to Interfax News Agency, on 23 August 2017, Russian prime minister Dmitry Medvedev signed a document designating disputed islands controlled by Moscow but claimed by Japan as a special economic zone. *See also* FOREIGN POLICY.

RYŪ CHISHŪ, 笠智衆 (1904–1993). Ryū Chishū, one of Japan's foremost **actors**, was born in Kumamoto Prefecture. He was one of Japan's most enduring character actors. He was best known for his long association with the acclaimed **film** director **Ozu Yasujirō**, having appeared in all but two of Ozu's 54 films. Ryū was the son of a **Buddhist** priest and was preparing to follow his father into the temple until 1925 when he went into acting. In total, Ryū appeared in 155 films with his most famous roles being in the films *Banshu* (*Late Spring*, 1949), *Tōkyō Monogatari* (*Tōkyō Story*, 1953), and *Osōshiki* (*The Funeral*, 1984). He also often played the role of a kindly Buddhist priest in the Tora-san movie series.

S

SAITŌ KIYOSHI, 斎藤清 **(1907–1997).** Saitō Kiyoshi was perhaps Japan's most famous wood-block artist of the postwar period. He was well known for his snowy landscapes, **Buddhist** temples, and beautiful gardens. Born in Fukushima Prefecture, he first studied oil painting but soon turned to printmaking. In 1938, Saitō made his first prints called "Winter in Aizu." In 1951, he won first prize at an international competition in Brazil. From then on, his work has been popular in Japan and throughout the world.

Many of Saitō's prints featured young geisha and had a distinctive grain, pose, and a special quality that only he could produce. Other of his works focused on Buddhist subjects such as the buildings and culture of **Kyōto.** One of Japan's leading wood-block artists, Saitō's prints adorn many leading museums worldwide.

SAKAGUCHI ANGO, 坂口安吾 **(1906–1955).** Sakaguchi Ango is the pen name of Sakaguchi Heigo, a writer known for his short stories and essays. He became popular in the postwar years for his works that rejected conventional values. His writings stressed the need for new ideas in order to revitalize the Japanese people. Sakaguchi became a popular cult figure, but this damaged his health and affected his work. In school, he displayed a rebellious spirit and a deep attraction to **literature**, which he studied at Tōkyō Imperial University. Sakaguchi joined literary friends in publishing two small magazines in which several of his earliest works appeared. Strong spiritual impulse and open and amoral sexuality were destined to become major themes throughout his work, as was his revolt against authority.

In his postwar stories, Sakaguchi urged the Japanese people to abandon the discredited, restrictive customs of the past and seek their salvation in a rediscovery of the basics of human nature. He rejected those who criticized as "decadent" the open expression of sexual and material desires and the rejection of traditional social values; he insisted that only through the establishment of a new order based on honesty and personal liberty could the errors of the past be prevented from reoccurring. The early postwar years stand out as the peak of his career, both in terms of popularity and in the staggering quantity of his writing. Sakaguchi was one of the principal shapers of postwar Japanese literature.

SAKAI, FRANKIE, 堺フランキー **(1929–1996).** Frankie Sakai, whose real name was Sakai Masatoshi, was one of postwar Japan's leading comedians. Born in Kagoshima Prefecture, Sakai was a heavyset comic **actor** who often appeared with Arishima Ishirō as a Japanese Laurel and Hardy–type act until Arishima died in 1987. Sakai made his motion picture debut in 1957. He contributed to the recognition of comedy as a legitimate cinematic genre. Sakai became the first comedian to receive the prestigious Blue Ribbon awarded by **newspaper film** critics and the Leading Actor Award given by *Kinema Jumpō*, the most important film journal in Japan. He continued to play comic roles but added appearances in a number of science fiction films. Sakai received an acting award for his brilliant performance in *Watashi wa kai ni naritai* (*A Clam Is What I Want to Be*), a popular **television** drama.

SAKAMOTO HARUMI, 坂本春海 **(1938–).** Sakamoto Harumi is a woman who entered the **Ministry of International Trade and Industry** in 1962. After this, she joined Seiyu **Supermarket** and became senior managing director in 1993. She became vice president of **Seibu** Department Stores in September 1997. The **Japan Association of Corporate Executives** (Keizai Dōyūkai) appointed her its first female vice chairman in 1999. As of 2018, Sakamoto still serves on the boards of directors for **Mitsubishi Motors**, TechnoPro Holdings, and several other companies.

SAKAMOTO KYŪ, 坂本九 **(1941–1985).** Sakamoto Kyū released the very popular "I'll Walk Looking Up" in the **United States** as "Sukiyaki." This 1961 music release became a million seller. His song "Itsy Bitsy Teeny Weeny Yellow Polka-Dot Bikini" was the worldwide rage. Many musicians, both Japanese and foreigners, still sing his songs. Tragically, he died in a plane crash in 1985.

SAKAMOTO RYŪICHI, 坂本龍一 **(1952–).** Sakamoto Ryūichi is a world-famous musician and composer as well as **actor**. Born in **Tōkyō**, he studied classical **music** at the prestigious Tōkyō Arts University. Sakamoto formed and played with the Yellow Magic Orchestra. He composed the sound track and acted as Captain Yonai in *Merry Christmas, Mr. Lawrence*, directed by **Ōshima Nagisa**. He played a secret service man and was the main composer in *The Last Emperor*. He has produced several albums, including *The Thousand Knives*. Sakamoto's rock and pop music have a strong international following with leading stores carrying many of his works.

In 2014, Sakamoto stopped working to seek treatment for his throat cancer, but the following year, he resumed his career and composed the score for *The Revenant*, which starred Leonardo DiCaprio as a frontiersman facing terrible dangers. He continues to compose sparkling music. Sakamoto is also involved in the antinuclear movement and is a critic of current copyright law, which he sees as antiquated in this new information age.

SAKIGAKE PARTY (SAKIGAKE, さきがけ). The Sakigake Party developed from the **New Party Sakigake** (NPS), a conservative reformist-ecology **political party** that lasted from 1998 until it was dissolved in 2004. The NPS, which served as a member of the coalition government in the mid-1990s, evolved into a conservationist party. After being renamed the Sakigake Party, it was further retitled the **Environmental** Green Political Assembly or the Green Assembly (Midori no kaigi) in 2002, but this party dissolved mainly because of its failure to win any seats in the 2004 **election**. White-collar workers, ecologists, and right-wing conservatives provided the main support for the Sakigake Party.

SAN FRANCISCO PEACE TREATY (*NIHON KOKU TO NO HEIWA JŌYAKU*, 日本国との平和条約). The San Francisco Peace Treaty, which formally ended the war between Japan and its World War II adversaries, was signed by 49 nations on 8 September 1951. Officially known as the Treaty of Peace with Japan, this treaty did much to shape Japan's relations with the **United States** as well as with the majority of the world's nations. The treaty, which came into force on 28 April 1952, officially ended the Japanese empire, provided for compensation for Allied civilians and prisoners of war, and applied the **United Nations** Charter and the Universal Declaration of Human Rights to achieve its goals.

Neither the Republic of China (**Taiwan**) nor the People's Republic of **China** was a part of this peace settlement. India, which considered the treaty too repressive, signed a separate treaty with Japan. Neither of the **Koreas** was involved. Germany and Italy, former Axis partners, did not participate. Finally, the **Soviet Union**, disagreeing with the American positions, did not sign the treaty.

Under the terms of the treaty, Japan renounced all rights to territory acquired in the 20th century, accepted the judgments of the International Military Tribunal of the Far East and other decisions of war crimes courts, officially provided for the transfer of Japanese overseas assets, compensated occupied countries, and provided payments for Allied prisoners of war.

On the same day that the peace treaty was signed, Japan and the United States also inked the **United States–Japan Security Treaty**, a **defense** agreement that provided military protection for Japan and allowed the United

States considerable military options within Japan and East Asia. The peace treaty and the security treaty together are often referred to as the "San Francisco System." *See also* FOREIGN POLICY.

SANBETSU. *See* JAPAN CONGRESS OF INDUSTRIAL UNIONS (SANBETSU, 産別).

SANWA GROUP (SANWA GURŪPU, 三和グループ). The Sanwa Group was one of Japan's leading *keiretsu*. Its main companies were the Sanwa Bank, **Kōbe** Steel, Hitachi Zōsen (shipbuilding), Sekisue Chemicals, **Nisshō Iwai Corporation**, and Nichimen Corporation. In addition to Sanwa Bank, Nippon Insurance and Nomura Securities provided part of its financial core. It was known as "the other Kansai" *keiretsu*, with the **Sumitomo Group** being the most prominent Kansai *keiretsu*. In an effort to become more nationally oriented, Sanwa moved its headquarters to **Tōkyō**. After a series of mergers, the Sanwa Group is now part of the Midori Kai.

SAN'YŌ ELECTRIC COMPANY (SAN'YŌ DENKI KABUSHIKI-GAISHA, 三洋電機株式会社). The San'yo Electric Company is one of Japan's leading electronics *keiretsu*. Founded in 1947, San'yō first produced generator-powered electrical lights for bicycles. In the early 1950s, it began producing various consumer products including radio cases, washing machines, cadmium-nickel batteries, and lithium batteries, as well as photovoltaic cells for solar batteries. San'yō's founder was Iue Toshio (1902–1969), the brother-in-law of **Matsushita Kōnosuke**, the leader of **Panasonic**.

In 2011, the company had more than 104,000 employees and generated approximately $13 billion in revenue. As of 2017, Igaki Seiichirō serves as president. Although San'yō was a member of the Fortune 500, in 2009 Panasonic bought it out and made it a subsidiary of Panasonic. Headquartered in **Ōsaka**, its chief products are semiconductors, consumer electronics, dry batteries, and cellular telephones.

SAPPORO, 札幌. Sapporo, with a population of 1.95 million people, is Japan's fifth-largest city and by far the largest city north of **Tōkyō**. Originally the site of an Ainu village, Sapporo's development began only in the 1860s, thus making it one of Japan's newest cities.

Carefully planned and constructed, Sapporo has the look of a well-organized metropolis. It is built on a grid pattern with wide avenues, trees, and nearby parks. It serves as the capital and driving force of Hokkaidō, Japan's northernmost island. Sapporo presides over what might be considered the "western frontier" of Japan with the region very much in the mode of a new, nontraditional area.

Sapporo took a major step forward in 1972 when it hosted the Winter **Olympics**. Known for its fine ski slopes and winter holidays, every February Sapporo welcomes many visitors to its annual snow festival featuring magnificent snow sculptures. Starting in 1950, it also hosts a summer festival in its wide, modern streets. In 2006, Sapporo was voted Japan's most attractive city based on its modern facilities, green parks, clean streets, and ease of conveyance. Museums and a wonderful botanical garden make Sapporo a delightful place.

The most famous Sapporo product is beer. The Sapporo Brewery started in the late 19th century and continues to be a major producer of this popular drink. The city is a major processing center for Hokkaidō's **agricultural** produce, and its Sapporo ramen noodles are famous worldwide.

Several recent events have taken place in Sapporo. In 2002, Sapporo Dome hosted three games of the FIFA World Cup; in 2004, the Nippon Ham Fighters moved to Sapporo and two years later won Japan's **baseball** championship; and in 2008, Tōyako, a suburb of Sapporo, hosted the G-8 Summit. The Hokkaidō Shinkansen or **Bullet Train** links the city with Tōkyō.

Sapporo welcomes approximately 14 million **tourists** annually. Its major attractions include scenery and natural beauty, **music** festivals, many museums, several historical buildings, the great view from Sapporo JR Tower, the nightlife of Susukino, and the Sapporo Beer Museum.

SASAKAWA RYŌICHI, 笹川良一 **(1899–1995).** Sasakawa Ryōichi was a staunch anticommunist, former fascist, war crimes suspect, political power broker, influential **business** fixer, philanthropist, and known to Japanese as "the godfather." He is most famous for his ties to the Moonies and his boast of being the world's richest fascist.

Sasakawa rose to prominence during the Sino-Japanese War by funding paramilitary forces in **China**. Using his wealth and personal influence, he established a large smuggling operation for drugs and other goods. His involvements led to his arrest at the end of World War II as a class A war criminal. While in Sugamo Prison, Sasakawa became friends with **Kodama Yoshio**, a right-wing politician with ties to the *yakuza*. The U.S. intelligence community secured their release in 1948, in exchange for their aid in fighting communism and promoting the stability and reconstruction of postwar Japan. Sasakawa then turned to bribing officials and used his paramilitary forces to break up strikes and other meetings of left-wing parties.

On the other hand, Sasakawa also made extensive contributions to world peace, especially in the area of disaster relief and development in the Third World. As the founder of the **United States**–Japan Foundation, which grew into the Nippon Foundation, Sasakawa was instrumental in many global efforts to promote the betterment of the world's people.

The Nippon Foundation has directed its efforts toward solving the world's medical and **environmental** problems. By cooperating on an ongoing basis with agencies of the **United Nations**, including the World Health Organization and UNICEF, this foundation has helped to make substantial progress on many fronts, including famine relief, aid for refugees, support for various **educational** programs, allocations for pharmaceutical and medical equipment, and international campaigns to eradicate smallpox, leprosy, drug addiction, and AIDS.

SASAKI RYŌSAKU, 佐佐木良作 **(1915–2000).** Sasaki Ryōsaku was a socialist leader and union organizer. Born in Hyōgo Prefecture, Sasaki graduated from Kyōto Imperial University. After working as a **labor** leader with the All-Japan Electric Industry Workers' Union, Sasaki was elected as a **Japan Socialist Party** (JSP) representative to the **House of Councillors** in 1947.

In 1955, he was elected to the **House of Representatives** as a JSP member, but he left the JSP to help form the **Democratic Socialist Party** (DSP) in 1960. He served as party secretary-general and chairman of the party's **Diet** Policy Committee and became vice chairman of the DSP in 1975. Sasaki succeeded **Kasuga Ikkō** to the post of chairman in 1977.

SATŌ EISAKU, 佐藤榮作 **(1901–1975).** Satō Eisaku was a leading **Liberal Democratic Party** (LDP) member and the **prime minister** who presided over Japan's emergence as a leading world power. A native of Yamaguchi Prefecture, younger brother of **Kishi Nobusuke**, and son-in-law of Matsuoka Yōsuke, Satō graduated in law from Tōkyō Imperial University in 1924. He made a study tour in the **United States** from August 1934 to April 1936. He also traveled in Japan-occupied **China** in 1938 and again in 1939. After the war, he served as **Yoshida Shigeru**'s chief **cabinet** secretary and was closely linked to that political giant. In 1948, Satō joined the Ministry of Transportation. The following year, he was elected to the **Diet** as a member of the **Liberal Party** and thereafter held several different ministerial posts.

Satō then served as posts and telecommunications minister from 1951 to 1952, where he strengthened government control of broadcasting. During 1952–1953, he served as construction minister. As party secretary, he came under suspicion for corruption over shipbuilding contracts but was never arrested. Satō joined the LDP a year after its founding and served as finance minister in 1958–1960 under the Kishi government and then held the position of international trade and industry minister in 1961–1962 in the **Ikeda Hayato** cabinet.

The increase in Satō's factional power allowed him to compete for the LDP party leadership in 1964. With bureaucratic and **business** support, Satō became prime minister, succeeding Ikeda on 9 November 1964. He served until 7 July 1972, the longest term ever for a prime minister in Japan. Satō promised and delivered on tax reductions, a balance between **economic** and social development, the advancement of **education**, and the return of the Southern Kuriles and **Okinawa**.

In 1965, Satō reestablished relations with **South Korea**. He also tried to establish ties with China, but these efforts did not prove as successful. Later in his term of office, he attempted to expand Japan's export markets in Europe and the **Soviet Union**.

Also in 1965, Satō formally asked U.S. president Lyndon Johnson to return Okinawa to Japan and, later that year, became the first postwar prime minister to visit the islands. In the Satō-Nixon Communiqué of November 1969, the United States agreed to return Okinawa to Japan with full sovereignty. Satō's maintenance of close relations with the United States and extension of the **United States–Japan Security Treaty** in 1970 assisted the return of Okinawa in 1972.

In 1967, Satō coined the idea of and promoted the phrase "the **Three Nonnuclear Principles**," which argued that Japan should adhere to non-production, nonpossession, and non-introduction of nuclear weapons. Satō also oversaw the creation and development of **Expo '70**, which brought Japan international recognition and greater world acceptance.

At home, Satō maintained close contact with the business and financial world in the pursuit of economic growth and helped stabilize the conservative hold on power, but his administration was faced with mounting problems. Confronted by the effects of the dollar crisis in 1971, problems over relations with China, opposition to Japan's tacit support for the U.S. war in Vietnam, pollution, inflation, and the more deleterious effects of economic growth, Satō resigned in 1972 and was replaced by **Tanaka Kakuei**. Satō quickly lost influence in the LDP when **Fukuda Takeo**, his protégé, did not succeed him as prime minister.

Satō Eisaku was a long-serving prime minister whose leadership helped Japan reemerge as a world power as its **economy** flourished and because his **foreign policy** had a balance between support for the United States and China and advanced Japan's national stature. In 1974, Satō received the **Nobel Peace Prize** for his antinuclear diplomacy, an award that caused considerable controversy.

SAWADA MIKI, 澤田美喜 **(1901–1980).** Sawada Miki was a social worker who founded and directed the Elizabeth Saunders Home for racially mixed orphans in Japan after World War II. Born in **Tōkyō**, she was the granddaughter of the **business** tycoon Iwasaki Yatarō. In 1922, she married Sawada Renzō, a diplomat in the **Ministry of Foreign Affairs**. Concerned about the future and well-being of interracial orphans, many of whom were abandoned by their fathers and were a social burden to their mothers, Sawada founded the Saunders Home. She was a vigorous fund-raiser for the home and later received the Prime Minister's Award for her efforts. *See also* WOMEN.

SAZAE-SAN, サザエさん. Hasegawa Machiko (1920–1992) wrote stories about Sazae-san and her family in postwar Japan. Hasegawa, one of Japan's most famous cartoonists, was born in Saga but lived most of her life in the western suburbs of **Tōkyō**. The four-panel comic strip she drew of Sazae-san made her Japan's most famous **woman manga** artist. Her comic strip appeared in the *Asahi Shimbun* from 1949 to 1974. Hasegawa's **books** and dramas are the ultimate family program and treat traditional themes. The **films** are the equivalent of *The Partridge Family* and are designed to provide a feel-good sentiment.

In 1955, a commercial **television** station began broadcasting *Sazae-san*, depicting the postwar Japanese family in *Peanuts*-like fashion. This family drama was extremely popular in Japan. *Sazae-san* continues to garner good ratings on television and is one **anime** that adults find acceptable for children. During the dark days of postwar Japan, Hasegawa's *Sazae-san* brought a glimmer of light and optimism to the war-torn country. The scatterbrained heroine brought laughter to a depressed Japan. Hasegawa's cartoons have been collected into a series of 68 books under the title *The Wonderful World of Sazae-san*. By the turn of the century, more than 65 million copies had been sold, making it Japan's most popular comic series ever. The *Sazae-san* anime has more than 2,500 episodes. The longest-running anime series in Japan, it "became so woven into the national fabric of life that nearly everyone identified with it."

SCIENCE AND TECHNOLOGY. Today, Japan is a world leader in science and technology. Several Japanese government agencies promote this development. The largest in terms of expenditures is the Ministry of Education's Science and Culture Division. In 1956, the Japanese government established the Science and Technology Agency (Kagaku Gijutsu Cho), an organization to advance the scientific and technological ambitions of Japan. Functioning under the **prime minister**'s office, the Science and Technology Agency coordinates various research and development programs. The **Ministry of Economy, Trade, and Industry**, the Japan Defense Agency, and the Ministry of Posts and Telecommunications are also major contributors.

After the war, Japanese scientists, engineers, and skilled workers led the way for a massive infusion of new technology in **steel** production, shipbuilding, electronics, electrical power, **petroleum** processing, petrochemicals, and hydroelectricity. In the 1970s, Japan successfully turned to new technology in the forms of **nuclear energy**, semiconductors, **computers**, automatic **cameras**, quartz watches, video-cassette recorders, and **environmental** technology. However, Japan is best known for its world leadership in the **automobile** and electronics industries.

Although the government took the lead in the early postwar period, today most of Japan's scientific and technological innovations come from individual scientists and people in the private sector. The Japan Technology Group, a technology-based intellectual transfer company, promotes trans-Pacific technology and intellectual property transfers between Japan and North America. Some of Japan's more significant contributors to scientific and technological development are mentioned below.

Sakata Shōichi (1911–1970), a theoretical physicist, studied structures and created the Sakata model of atomic structure. Born in **Tōkyō**, Sakata graduated from Kyōto Imperial University in 1933. Working closely with Yukawa Hideki (1907–1981) at Ōsaka University, he contributed to the discovery of the meson theory of subatomic particles. His research led to his two-meson theory in 1942 and to the Sakata model in 1956. He later became involved in the study of social problems due to his interest in science. Sakata, Yukawa, and Tomonaga Shin'ichirō (1906–1979), along with other nuclear physicists in Japan and throughout the world, campaigned tirelessly for world peace and the safe use of atomic **energy**.

Umezawa Hamao (1914–1986) was a microbiologist. Born in Fukui Prefecture, he graduated from Tōkyō Imperial University and became one of the world's foremost experts on the development of antibiotics. He taught at the **University of Tōkyō** and served as director of its Institute of Microbial Chemistry.

Yagi Hidetsugu (1886–1976) was an electrical engineer who was noted for his pioneering research in shortwave and microwave signal propagation along with Uda Shintarō (1896–1976), his junior colleague. Their efforts led to the discovery of the Yagi-Uda antenna, the basic antenna configuration used in the majority of today's outdoor **television** and radio antennas. Born in **Kyōto**, he graduated from Tōkyō Imperial University in 1909. In 1919, after studying in Europe and the **United States**, he became a professor at Tōhoku University, where he began his work with signal propagation systems. He then became president first of Ōsaka University and later of the Tōkyō Institute of Technology.

Yamazaki Yoshio (1943–) worked for Suwa Seiko where he pioneered the development of the liquid-crystal display technology. Kuwano Yukinori (1941–), a researcher and later president of **San'yō Electric Company**, invented the solar battery that powered most calculators in the late 20th century. Sasaki Tadashi (1915–2018), known as "Doctor Rocket," was an indefatigable researcher at the **Sharp Corporation**. He, more than anyone else, was responsible for the pocket calculator. Nakamura Shuji (1954–) was the chief researcher of the laser for Nichia Chemical Company. As a leading electronics engineer, he recently joined the faculty at the University of California at Santa Barbara. Japan has produced at least nine **Nobel Prize** winners in science and technology.

In the early 21st century, Japan is a world leader in earthquake and seismic studies, tsunami warnings, space exploration, satellites, and **robots**, and in genetic, stem cell, flu epidemic, and psychiatric research. Japan's leading role in technology is evident by the fact that its citizens hold more patents in the United States than any other country. Japan spends around $130 billion annually in research and development, the third-largest investment in the world.

Six of the world's 15 major automobile manufacturers and seven of the world's 20 largest semiconductor companies are Japanese. The **Bullet Train** (Shinkansen) and maglev trains make Japan a world leader in high-speed transportation. The year 2009 saw a number of scientific accomplishments in Japan including a resurgence in the country's space program, sophisticated studies in gerontology, stem cell development for organ and tissue transplantation, cell reproduction, and the advancement of brain cell studies.

Japan remains a leader in technological innovations, creativeness, and new approaches. Examples include **Sony** electronics, Sony's competition with Facebook in the virtual reality market, Sharp appliances, Fanuc's new robot factory in Ibaraki Prefecture, **Nintendo**'s new smartphone and the *Pokémon* game, **Kyōcera**'s undertaking to regenerate hair growth, **Nissan**'s development of self-driving technology for its vehicles, and **Honda** and **SoftBank**'s development of artificial intelligence for cars.

Fanuc, the Japanese manufacturer of factory automation equipment, is working with Cisco Systems, a U.S. maker of communications, to create a system that connects factory machinery of all makes. **Toshiba** readies new 3-D chips, SoftBank and Toshiba are devising signage able to speak at least four languages, and Yamato Transport and DeNa are joining forces to develop door-to-door parcel delivery service using self-driving vehicles. Finally, the Japan Patent Office announces that Japan leads the world in cutting-edge autonomous driving technologies.

NTT Data Corporation has hired more people in highly technical fields than other Japanese tech organizations. As of 2014, Softbank Corporation has more invested in technology than any other Japanese company but is closely followed by **NTT DoCoMo**, NTT Communication, **KDDI** Corporation, and Canon Inc. In 2013, the top three Japanese tech companies by sales were NTT Data Corporation, OTSUKA Corporation, and Nomura Research Institute. These three companies are also the top profit makers in Japanese technology.

The Japan Science and Technology Agency is one of the core institutions responsible for the implementation of science and technology in Japan where the emphasis is on consumer electronics, the automotive industry, biomedical products, and robotics.

In order to advance its scientific and technology capacity, in 2017 alone, Japan opened a study science abroad initiative; took new steps to advance physical health among its people; participated in the International Science Olympiad; became more involved in the International Science and Engineering Fair; participated in the Strategic Promotion of International Exchanges in the fields of science, technology, and academic research; formulated a "Plan for Creation of Future Society by Science, Technology and Innovation"; signed an agreement with the United Arab Emirates to cooperate in space exploration; and launched a successful space operation mission. *See also* ASTRONAUTS/SPACE EXPLORATION.

SECURITIES COMPANIES. In the postwar period, Japan's securities market has been largely controlled by the "Big Four," referring to four brokerage companies that have dominated Japan's investments and the financial world. They are Nomura, Nikkō, Daiwa, and the former Yamaichi, which was dissolved in 1997.

Nomura Securities Company is Japan's largest brokerage firm. Incorporated in 1925 when the securities division of Daiwa Bank became independent, it began dealing in stocks in 1938 and became the first Japanese firm to start investment trust operations in 1941.

Nomura paved the way in creating opportunities for the small investor and encouraged people to treat these as savings accounts. In 1961, Nomura pioneered again when it made the first Japanese stock offering in the **United States**. In 1962, it sold the first Japanese bond issue in the United States when it offered Mitsubishi Heavy Industries bonds. In 1965, Nomura Securities established the Nomura Research Institute, Japan's largest and most prestigious think tank.

In 1981, Nomura Securities became the first Japanese company to become a member of the New York Stock Exchange. As *The Economist* said, "What Nomura does this morning, the rest of the Japanese securities industry will do after lunch." Although its U.S. division struggled to compete with U.S.-based firms, by 1989, Nomura Securities was the largest and wealthiest securities firm in the world.

During the 1990s, Nomura, like other securities firms in Japan, was beset by scandals in which the company reimbursed favored clients for their losses and revealed a cozy relationship with **crime** syndicates (*yakuza*). In 1990 alone, Nomura stock plunged 70 percent. In 1987, investors left Nomura in droves, causing its 16.3 percent share of the market to drop to 5.8 percent by the end of 1991. However, by 2017 Nomura had recovered and now manages approximately $100 billion and employs around 28,000 people worldwide. Nomura Securities plays the central role in the Nomura Group enterprises. It provides a wide range of investment services for individual and corporate customers.

Founded in 1902 but not incorporated until 1943, today the Daiwa Securities Group engages in underwriting, brokerage and trading, providing securities, and other financial services worldwide. In 1964, Daiwa established an office in London. In 1986, it became a primary dealer in U.S. government securities. In 1988, it formed a strategic alliance with Sumitomo Bank. Finally, in 1999, it became a holding company. Today, Daiwa Securities Group is Japan's second-largest securities firm with around 15,000 employees who manage $147 billion in assets.

Nikkō Securities Company, or Nikkō Cordial, is Japan's third-biggest securities company, employing nearly 7,000 people in 130 domestic and a dozen overseas offices. It was established in 1918 and incorporated in 1944, making it the youngest of "the Big Four" investment firms. Nikkō was the first Japanese securities firm to use modern American investment methods. It worked to create a group of small investors, build its client base, and familiarize people with the role and function of the **Tōkyō Stock Exchange** (TSE). It successfully targeted **women** as investors. In 1959, Nikkō set up an office in New York and thereafter expanded its international presence. The oil crisis of 1973 caused serious problems for Nikkō investors. The leaders of Nikkō responded by going international and added offices in Frankfurt, Luxembourg, Paris, Hong Kong, and Singapore to go along with its earlier offices in New York and London. The securities market was becoming increasingly globalized, and Nikkō profits soared.

However, like Nomura, Nikkō was troubled in the early 1990s by scandals involving illegal client reimbursement. Although the TSE dropped drastically, Nikkō reimbursed some 225 favored clients nearly $1 billion. Investors lost a great deal of confidence in the market. Since then, Nikkō has corrected the problems and partially restored its reputation as a major securities firm. However, in 2007, Nikkō was fined ¥500 million, the largest fine ever levied against a Japanese business, for falsifying financial statements.

Yamaichi Securities Company, established in 1897, was the fourth of "the Big Four." It reported a sharp increase in Japanese mergers and acquisitions of foreign concerns for fiscal year 1988. However, Yamaichi Securities Company collapsed in late 1997 with a $26 billion debt. This 100-year-old company voluntarily shut down its operations, making it Japan's largest company to collapse since the end of World War II.

As of 2017, Japan's five largest securities firms are Nomura Holdings, Nikkō Securities, Daiwa Securities Group, Mitsubishi UFJ Securities, and Mizuho Securities.

The Japan Securities Dealers Association (JSDA) functions both as a self-regulatory organization and as an intermediary. JSDA members consist of securities firms and other financial institutions operating securities business in Japan. The securities firms have gained wider spreads on client activities thus contributing to the upward momentum and greater volatility. *See also* BANKING; ECONOMY.

SEIBU SAISON GROUP (SEIBU SEZON GURŪPU, 西武セゾングループ**).** The Seibu Saison Group includes the Hotel Intercontinental Tōkyō Bay, Pacific Tour Systems Corporation, Seibu Railroad Company, Seibu **Department Stores**, Ticket Saison, Seiyu Company, and the Seibu Lions (now the Saitama Seibu Lions) professional **baseball** team. Its headquarters was in **Tōkyō** but is now in Saitama. The Seibu Saison Group is one of Japan's leading operators of department stores and **supermarkets**. It also sells insurance, runs real estate and travel agencies, produces a variety of foods, imports high-grade brand goods, provides financial services, and operates one of Japan's major credit card systems. It is associated with such businesses as Mujirushi Ryōhin, Parco, FamilyMart, and Credit Saison.

Tsutsumi Yasujirō (1889–1964) established a number of companies, including Seibu Railway Company and created the Seibu Group based on railways, real estate, **tourism**, and bus transportation. Born in Shiga Prefecture, he graduated from Waseda University. He was also a politician. Beginning in 1924, he was elected 13 times to the **House of Representatives** and was speaker in 1953–1954. Tsutsumi Yoshiaki (1934–), his son, was a businessman who headed the company until 2005 when he was ousted due to a series of financial scandals. Tsutsumi Seiji (1927–2013), the elder half brother, served as president of Seibu Saison after his brother's ouster. He was the visionary who grew the company into a powerhouse retail and distribution operation. Rinno Hiroshi (1942–) now serves as the CEO.

SEJIMA KAZUYO, 妹島和世 **(1956–).** In 2010, Sejima Kazuyo and her creative colleague, Nishizawa Ryue (1966–), received the Pritzker Architecture Prize, the equivalent of the **Nobel Prize** in **Architecture**. Each year since 1979, this award has been given to one person who best represents significant contributions to humanity and the environment through architecture. Thirty-three people have received this award, with Sejima and Nishizawa being only the fourth Japanese recipient after **Tange Kenzō** (1987), **Maki Fumihiko** (1993), and **Andō Tadao** (1995). She is only the second **woman** to receive this prestigious award.

After studying at Japan Women's University, Sejima worked in the office of **Itō Toyō** where she polished her craft. In 1987, she founded her own office and, in 1995, expanded this to become the firm SANAA with her former employee Nishizawa. In particular, they have been recognized for outstanding work in the Ogasawara Museum at Nagano, the 21st Century Museum of Contemporary Art in Kanazawa, and the glass pavilion for the Toledo Museum of Art (Ohio, United States), as well as projects in Spain, Germany, Switzerland, the Netherlands, and London. Their buildings have been described as "simultaneously delicate and powerful, precise and fluid, ingenious but not overly or overtly clever" and as being in tune with the **environment** and surroundings.

SEKO TOSHIHIKO, 瀬古利彦 **(1956–).** Japan's outstanding male marathon runner, Seko Toshihiko won the Boston Marathon in 1981 and again in 1987. He is one of the most admired and most popular Japanese athletes of all time. Seko also won the Fukuoka Marathon (1978–1980, 1983), the London Marathon (1986), and the Chicago Marathon (1986). In 1981, Seko set world records at 25,000 meters (1:13:55.8) and 30,000 meters (1:29:18.8). Both records have since been broken. *See also* SPORTS.

SELF-DEFENSE FORCES. *See* DEFENSE.

SENAGA KAMEJIRŌ, 瀬長亀次郎 **(1907–2001).** Senaga Kamejirō was a politician and leader of social movements in **Okinawa**. He served as vice chairman of the **Japanese Communist Party** (JCP). Born in Okinawa, Senaga became interested in Marxism while a student and school officials expelled him for his leftist activities. Jailed for three years for subversive activities, authorities soon released him but then drafted him into military service in **China**. During the **Occupation**, Senaga was active as a leader and later as chairman of the Okinawa People's Party. He was especially involved in its campaign against **United States** military bases. In 1956, the people of Naha elected him mayor, but the American military authorities soon removed him from office. He later became active in the movement for Okinawan reversion to Japan. In 1970, under a new provision allowing participation in Japanese national **elections**, he was elected to the **House of Representatives** from the Okinawa People's Party. Senaga's party merged with the JCP in 1973, a year after the reversion of Okinawa.

SETOUCHI HARUMI, 瀬戸内晴美 **(1922–).** Setouchi Harumi is a female writer who "used her unconventional life experiences to address the possibilities for sexual liberation." Raised in Shikoku, Setouchi was the daughter of a wealthy merchant. From childhood, she had a strong interest in **literature**

and the common people. She received a degree in Japanese literature from Tōkyō Women's College in 1943 and then married a professor with whom she moved to **China**. Upon returning to Japan in 1947, Setouchi divorced her husband and abandoned her daughter. Taking up with a younger man, her behavior was scandalous for this time period. Setouchi's writings touched a raw nerve in Japanese society. Later in life, she joined a **Buddhist** nunnery and adopted the name Setouchi Jakucho.

SHARP CORPORATION (SHAAPU KABUSHIKI-GAISHA, シャープ 株式会社**).** Sharp is one of Japan's leading electronics makers and is particularly big in liquid crystal screens (LCDs), flat-screen **televisions**, VCRs, **computers**, and semiconductors. Sharp, headquartered near **Ōsaka**, is Japan's largest maker of LCD screens. It employs more than 50,000 people worldwide.

Hayakawa Tokuji (1893–1980) founded Sharp Corporation in 1912. In 1915, Hayakawa invented the Ever-Sharp mechanical pencil from which the company name is derived. Sharp pioneered the integrated-circuit **technology**, and its research and development force of more than 6,000 people continues to produce cutting-edge developments in laser and magnetic technology. Sharp's high-tech digital televisions include a 64-inch wide-screen model. Today, Sharp products are sold in more than 140 countries.

As of 2013, Sharp was the world's 10th-largest manufacturer of televisions. It was the leader in Japan but has since slipped to third place. Samsung, in partnership with Sharp, has invested more than $100 million in the company. It produces solar panels, improved television sets, and smartphones.

In 2016, Foxconn, a **Taiwan**-based company, acquired a major interest in the company. In 2017, Sharp, under the restructuring of Foxconn, announced its first operating profit in three years. Foxconn, the world's largest contract electronics manufacturer, now owns the controlling interest in Sharp. The Sharp Corporation is heavily invested in the future of electronics. After some lean years, it is now a profitable company again.

SHIBA RYŌTARŌ, 司馬遼太郎 **(1923–1996).** Shiba Ryōtarō was a famous writer whose works in the 1960s brought an "optimism boom" in their messages. His heroes were people of prosperity, achievement, and brightness. He was best known for his historical novels about East Asia, many of which were turned into **television** dramas. His most popular historical works include *Ryōma ga yuku* (*Ryōma Moves Ahead*), the saga of Japan's great samurai leader Sakamoto Ryōma, and *Tokugawa Yoshinobu* (*The Last Shogun: The Life of Tokugawa Yoshinobu*). See *also* LITERATURE.

SHIDEHARA KIJŪRŌ, 幣原喜重郎 **(1872–1951).** Shidehara Kijūrō served twice as foreign minister in the mid-1920s to early 1930s, where he favored a conciliatory policy toward **China**, and he served once as **prime minister** from 9 October 1945 until 22 May 1946. He also served as the demobilization officer and as president of the demobilization agency. As prime minister, Shidehara set in motion many of the **Occupation** reforms. Fluent in English, he was a good friend to the **United States** and cooperated with the Americans.

The son of a wealthy **Ōsaka** landlord family, Shidehara studied law at Tōkyō Imperial University, graduating in 1895. He joined the foreign service and served in **Korea**, the United States, and Europe. He served in the foreign ministry under five different ministers. After the war, Shidehara served as the president of the Progressive Party (Kaishintō) and as an adviser to **Yoshida Shigeru**'s **cabinet**. In 1947, he was elected to the **House of Representatives** and became a top adviser to the Democratic Party. In 1949, he became the speaker of the House of Representatives. After, and even before World War II, Shidehara was a leading proponent of pacifism. *See also* FOREIGN POLICY.

SHIGA NAOYA, 志賀直哉 **(1883–1971).** Shiga Naoya was a widely recognized novelist and short story writer. Born in Miyagi Prefecture, he attended Gakushūin (Peers' School) and Tōkyō Imperial University. Shiga is considered the writer who perfected the "I novel" (*watakushi shōsetsu*), or a story told from a very personal standpoint. Some of his writings are autobiographical. His most important works seem to be reconstructed partially from some of his personal experiences. His readers were extremely loyal. They were attracted to him by his tightly controlled style. Shiga apparently had little new to say once he had reached the final telling of his own experiences. Shiga had a deeply intuitive and nonintellectual sensibility, and with it he created a powerful body of writing. *See also* LITERATURE.

SHIGA YOSHIO, 志賀義雄 **(1901–1989).** Shiga Yoshio, a native of Fukuoka Prefecture, was a committed leftist politician. While a student at Tōkyō Imperial University, Shiga joined the leftist study group Shinjinkai and became a member of the newly formed **Japanese Communist Party** (JCP). Following the mass arrest of communists in 1928, he was imprisoned for 18 years. Unlike some of his colleagues, Shiga refused to abandon his communist beliefs. He was released from jail only after World War II.

Shiga helped form the postwar JCP and became editor in chief of the party organ *Akahata*. He was elected to the **Diet** in 1946 but was barred from office in the so-called Red Purge by the American **Occupation** authorities. Since the Comintern heavily criticized his party tactics, Shiga went underground.

He became publicly active again in 1955 and was elected to the Central Committee of the JCP. In 1964, however, Shiga, who had always been favorably disposed to the **Soviet Union**, was removed from the party for supporting the 1963 Nuclear Test Ban Treaty. *See also* JAPAN CONGRESS AGAINST ATOMIC AND HYDROGEN BOMBS (GENSUIKIN, 原水禁).

SHIGEMITSU MAMORU, 重光葵 **(1887–1957).** Shigemitsu Mamoru was a career diplomat who served three times as foreign minister during and after World War II. In 1948, he was convicted as a war criminal but regained his freedom and went on to prominence as a party politician.

Born in Ōita Prefecture, Shigemitsu graduated from Tōkyō Imperial University in 1911 and immediately entered the **Ministry of Foreign Affairs**. After serving in various positions in **China** and the ministry, he became foreign minister in 1943 and served until April 1945. Shigemitsu became a leader of a group seeking to achieve an early peace. He tried unsuccessfully to institute a policy that would return China to the Chinese. Although no longer in the government at the end of the war, he returned to **Tōkyō** in August to urge acceptance of the surrender proposal. As foreign minister again in **Higashikuni Naruhiko**'s **cabinet**, Shigemitsu represented Japan at the official surrender ceremony on the USS *Missouri*.

After the war, the **Occupation** authorities indicted Shigemitsu as one of 28 major war criminals. His inclusion was controversial, but he was nevertheless found guilty of waging aggressive war and failure to prevent war crimes. He was sentenced to seven years but was released from Sugamo Prison in 1950 after serving less than five years.

Shigemitsu joined the newly formed Japan Reform Party (Nihon Kaishintō) in June 1952 and became its president. Although he openly aspired to the premiership, he was not an effective party leader. In 1954, the Kaishintō merged with the **Liberal Party** (Jiyūtō) to form the Japan Democratic Party (Nihon Minshutō), and Shigemitsu became vice president under **Hatoyama Ichirō**. When the new party, with the help of the **Japan Socialist Party**, forced out the **Yoshida Shigeru** cabinet in December 1954, Shigemitsu became foreign minister and deputy premier in the Hatoyama cabinet. He disagreed with Hatoyama over relations with the **Soviet Union** and favored a cautious policy with few concessions. *See also* FOREIGN POLICY.

SHIMURA TAKASHI, 志村喬 **(1905–1982).** Shimura Takashi, one of Japan's great actors of the 20th century, had key roles in *Drunken Angel*, *Rashōmon*, *Seven Samurai*, and *Kagemusha*. He starred as the unfulfilled bureaucrat Watanabe in the famous **film** *Ikiru* (*To Live*). He appeared in many of **Kurosawa Akira**'s films. A native of Hyōgo Prefecture, Shimura was honored for his contributions to the performing arts with Japan's Medal of Honor.

SHINKANSEN. *See* BULLET TRAIN (SHINKANSEN, 新幹線).

SHINTŌ, 神道. Shintō is Japan's indigenous and largest **religion** and was the state religion in the prewar and wartime eras. In direct translation, *Shintō* means "the way of the gods." A form of animism, it practices the worship of *kami* or gods in all of nature. Shintō is characterized by great love and reverence for nature. It stresses purification and has various rites to achieve a clean state of being. Shintō does not have a founder, sacred scriptures, or "preachers." It has its origins in the earliest formation of Japan. After the war, Shintō lost its status of state religion and has declined in its influence but still is seen in everyday Japanese life in such things as visits to shrines, the purchase of *omikuji* (amulets), reliance on *ema* (horse pictures) to convey messages to the gods, and other rituals.

Although most Japanese claim not to believe in religion, many have a Shintō or **Buddhist** altar in their homes, carry an *o-mamori* (amulet for protection) on their person, show great respect for their ancestors, follow various superstitions, and participate in community *matsuri* (festivals). A distinctive gate (*torii*) made of two uprights and two crossbars mark the entrance to a Shintō shrine. Shintō can be divided into several types including Shrine Shintō, Sect Shintō, Folk Shintō, and State Shintō. Continuing Shintō influence can be seen in flower arranging, traditional **architecture**, garden design, and **sumō** wrestling. *See also* YASUKUNI SHRINE (*YASU-KUNI JINJA*, 靖国神社).

SHINTŌ HISASHI, 真藤恒 **(1910–2003).** Shintō Hisashi was one of Japan's most successful postwar industrialists. He was born in Kurume, Fukuo-ka Prefecture, and graduated from Kyūshū Imperial University.

Shintō followed **Dokō Toshio** as president of Ishikawa Heavy Industries during 1972–1979. He later served as chairman of **Nippon Telegraph and Telephone** and helped modernize the telecommunications company and then to privatize it in 1985. Accused of a bribe in the **Recruit scandal**, Shintō admitted to accepting shares of Recruit Cosmos stock and making a $142,000 profit on the deal; he was arrested in March 1989. Leaving this stain aside, Shintō helped revolutionize Japan's **business** culture.

SHIPPING. Japan is well known for its shipping industry. Its leaders, Nippon Yūsen, **Mitsui O.S.K. Lines**, and Kawasaki Kisen Kaisha, carry much of the world's maritime freight. However, globally the shipping industry has suffered from overcapacity and a weak economy.

In October 2016 while struggling to cope with a global slump, Japan's three shipping giants announced that they would merge their container-shipping operations, creating the world's sixth-largest competitor, in an effort to cope with the global decline in the container business. Shipping leaders expect this move to save about $1 billion per year. This will give the group a fleet of 256 container vessels and around 7 percent of the world shipping market. They planned to complete the merger and operations by April 2018. Some operations, like grain and iron ore, will remain independent.

Projections in early 2017 call for a modest increase in earnings, or at least a break-even, for shipping companies. However, the bottom lines are still soft.

SHIRAI YOSHIO, 白井義男 **(1923–2003).** Shirai Yoshio was the first Japanese ever to win a professional world boxing title. He was a successful amateur and began fighting professionally during the war. After winning his initial eight matches, his career was temporarily derailed by his induction into the army. Resuming boxing in 1946, Shirai fought repeatedly, quickly making a name for himself in beating Hanada Yoichiō for the Japanese flyweight crown in 1949. Eleven months later, he won the bantamweight title of Japan when he scored a decision over Hiroguchi Hiroshi. He won 10 more bouts in a row before losing this title to Nagashima by an eight-round decision in 1951. Shirai reversed this loss by beating Nagashima in 10 rounds that September and, later that year, also avenged a previous loss to Marino Dado with a seventh--round knockout in Honolulu. A 1952 rubber match with Marino in **Tōkyō** saw Shirai win the world flyweight title in May. In November, he successfully defended his new crown with his third victory in four tries over Marino. He defeated three more challengers to his title before losing it to Pascual Perez by decision in 1954, then losing the rematch six months later by a fifth-round knockout. Shirai won 53 bouts against only eight losses. *See also* SPORTS.

SHIRAKAWA MASAAKI, 白川方明 **(1949–).** Shirakawa Masaaki is a powerful figure in the Japanese economic world, having served as the 30th governor of the **Bank of Japan** (BoJ) from 2008 through 2013. He joined the BoJ in 1972 and filled numerous positions including the general manager for the U.S. office in New York. As the governor of the BoJ, Shirakawa held great power and his every deed and word effected price stability in Japan and helped ensure Japan financial stability.

While governor of the BoJ, Shirakawa sought to stem the recession of Japan's economy, the third largest in the world. He led the way in increasing government expenditures, pumping more money into the Japanese **economy**, maintaining extremely low interest rates, and inflating Japan's economy. Although not achieving spectacular results, Shirakawa led the way in maintaining and even improving Japan's economic situation.

Born in Fukuoka, he earned his BA degree at the **University of Tōkyō** and completed an MA in economics at the University of Chicago. He has taught at Kyōto University and Aoyama Gakuin University.

SHISEIDŌ COMPANY (KABUSHIKI-GAISHA SHISEIDŌ, 株式会社 資生堂**).** Shiseidō, Japan's leading cosmetics company, was founded in 1872 as a Western-style pharmacy. Shiseidō developed various skin care and cosmetics products. It is known for its high-quality products offered to the public in exquisite packaging. Its products are marketed through more than 25,000 stores in 120 countries.

Okauchi Hideo (1908–2004) was the leading figure in guiding Shiseidō into becoming the largest cosmetics company in Japan. He successfully established overseas markets for its products. Born in Kagawa Prefecture, he graduated from Takamatsu Higher Commercial School. Okauchi then joined Shiseidō, became president in 1967, and served as chairman from 1975 to 1978. Okauchi has also contributed to the overall advancement of the Ginza, the **Tōkyō** street where the company's headquarters are located.

As of 2017, Shiseidō, under the leadership of Uotani Masahiko (1954–), strives to expand the company's global outreach. Uotani, with an MBA from Columbia University, seeks to make Shiseidō an even more powerful global institution. Shiseidō, with 46,000 employees, reports its 2016 net sales at $7.78 billion and its most recent sales figures in Japan at $3.7 billion, in the **United States** at $1.5 billion, in **China** at $1.3 billion, in Europe at $1.1 billion, and $50 million in Asia Pacific. Shiseidō is the largest cosmetics company in Japan and the fifth largest in the world.

SHŌRIKI MATSUTARŌ, 正力松太郎 **(1885–1969).** Shōriki Matsutarō was a **business** leader and a politician. Born in Toyama Prefecture and a graduate of Tōkyō Imperial University, Shōriki began a career in the Tōkyō Metropolitan Police Department, from which he resigned in 1924 because of the Toranomon incident, an assassination attempt on the crown prince. Shōriki then became president of the *Yomiuri Shimbun* and developed it into Japan's most widely circulated **newspaper**. After World War II, Shōriki served as director of the **Science and Technology** Agency and chairman of the Atomic Energy Commission. He promoted the beginnings of commercial television and inaugurated professional **baseball** in Japan.

SHŌWA DENKŌ SCANDAL (*SHŌWA DENKŌ JIKEN*, 昭和電工事件). The Shōwa Denkō scandal was the first of a large number of political scandals that would shake the political establishment of postwar Japan. The coalition government under **Ashida Hitoshi**, weak by its very nature, limped along until October 1948 when the scandal broke. Government officials including Ashida and Deputy Prime Minister **Nishio Suehiro** were charged with accepting bribes from Shōwa Denkō, Japan's largest chemical fertilizer company, in exchange for favorable loans. Nishio was sentenced to prison, and Ashida was forced to resign as **prime minister**, opening the door for **Yoshida Shigeru**.

SHŌWA EMPEROR, 昭和天皇. *See* HIROHITO, EMPEROR, 裕仁天皇 (1901–1989).

SKATING, FIGURE. *See* FIGURE SKATING.

SMAP, スマップ. SMAP, standing for Sports Music Assemble People, led the band boom in Japan, starting in the top 20 entertainers in the late 1990s. Johnny's Office, a **music** entrepreneur, produced SMAP. One of their songs was included in school textbooks. There were originally six members with this group, but later only four. These four guys sold image and sex. Nakai Masahiro (1972–) was the leader of the group. Kimura Takuya (1972–) was quite popular with young **women**. Inagaki Gorō (1973–) was an **actor**. Kusanagi Tsuyoshi (1974–) was a comedian. Katori Shingo (1977–) was the youngest of the group. Mori Katsuyuki (1974–) was with the group but left to become a race car driver. SMAP was a very trendy group in Japan and internationally. Their songs "Ganbarimashō," "Yozora no Mukō," and "Munasawagi o tanomuyo" achieved great popularity. People liked their music and liked them as performers.

SMAP achieved unparalleled accomplishments: 55 top 10 singles, 22 consecutive number one singles, and 33 number one single records in total. It had 24 top 10 albums and 14 number one albums. Its record "The One and Only Flower in the World" is the best-selling single in the 21st century. Other top singles include "Beyond the Night Sky," "Lion Heart," "Shake," and "Aoi Inazuma." In total, SMAP has sold more than 10 million albums and 35 million records. However, all good things must come to an end, and SMAP, the superstars of Japanese music, officially disbanded at the end of 2016.

SOCCER. Soccer is quite popular in Japan. The British first introduced soccer to Japan in 1873, but it was not until 1888 that the first competitive match took place between the **Kōbe** Regatta and Athletic Club and the **Yokohama** Country and Athletic Club. Soccer enthusiasts formed the Japanese Football Association (JFA) in 1921 and organized a national championship competition in 1948. Japan and **South Korea**, in a unique arrangement, cohosted the highly successful 2002 World Cup soccer matches.

While not yet having as many participants as **baseball**, since the 1990s, soccer has been the most rapidly growing sport in Japan. In 1991, soccer became a professional sport when the **J.League** was created with 10 enthusiastic teams. A number of colorful stars have emerged. Kamamoto Kunishige (1944–) was the ace striker of Japan's bronze-winning national soccer team at the 1968 Mexico **Olympics**. He was the top striker in the Japan League seven times. Since 1995, Kamamoto has been a politician. In 1998, Kamamoto became vice chairman of the JFA.

Ihara Masami (1967–) was a member of the Yokohama Marinos soccer team. He was the first Japanese to play more than 100 international matches. He joined the national team in 1988 as a college student, playing until 2002.

Miura Kazuyoshi (1967–) is the first Japanese to play successfully in Brazil with Santos, the famous club team. He joined the predecessor of Verdy Kawasaki in 1990. Many young Japanese, following Miura, have tried to play soccer in Brazil. In 1993, Miura had the highest income for any **sports** figure in Japan. He became the first Japanese to join Italy's Series A in 1994 when he played with Genoa. In Japan, he plays only for Verdy Kawasaki. He became the top scorer in J.League's 1996 season and was still playing in 2017.

Called "Gon" for his humorous character, Nakayama Masashi (1967–) became a star player when he played for the national soccer team from 1990 through 2003. During this time, he scored 21 goals. He was the most valuable player (MVP) in the 1997 J.League championship and the MVP and top scorer in the 1998 season. He played for the World Cup 1998 Japanese team and kicked the team's only goal. He later played for Jubilo Iwata from 1994 through 2009. In 2010, Nakayama joined Consadole **Sapporo**.

Maezono Masakiyo (1973–) was captain of Japan's Atlanta Olympic soccer team that defeated the Brazilian team. He played for the Yokohama Flugels from 1990 to 1997, when he joined Verdy as one of its star players. At the height of his popularity, he became a **fashion** model, popular with young people.

Kawaguchi Yoshikatsu (1975–) was the goalkeeper for Japan's Atlanta Olympic soccer team and later played for the Yokohama Marinos (1994–2001), in Europe (2001–2005), and with Jubilo Iwata (2005–2009).

He is good-looking and popular, but he has suffered some injuries in his career. He also played full time as a national team goalkeeper on the World Cup 1998 team in France.

The Japan national football team, known as Sakkā Nippon Daihyō, represents the country in international soccer and is operated by the JFA. Vahid Halilhodžić has been head coach since 2015. Hasebe Makoto is captain of the team, Endō Yasuhito has the most caps with 152, and Kamamoto Kunishige was the top scorer with 80 goals.

Japan's success in soccer has been demonstrated in the Olympics. In 2012, Japan finished fourth in a strong field. In the 2016 Olympics, Japan placed 10th. Japan will host the 2020 Olympic games. Japan's Asian Games record is even better, winning the 2010 championship and finishing sixth in 2014. Japan is one of Asia's most successful teams, having qualified for all the past five FIFA World Cups and winning the AFC Asian Cup a record four times in 1992, 2000, 2004, and 2011.

Soccer is one of Japan's most popular sports. Men and women of all ages enjoy and play soccer. Japan's teams are ranked highly in the world. The men's national team is called the Samurai Blue after its jersey color, and the women's national team is known as Nadeshiko Japan, representing a flower for the ideal Japanese woman. The **Japan Women's National Football Team**, Nadeshiko Japan, won the 2011 World Cup, the first Asian team to do so, and finished runners-up in 2015.

Japanese competitive soccer is structured in a pyramidal system, with the top level of the hierarchy called the J.League. The semiprofessional level, called the Japan Football League, follows, composed of regional and prefectural leagues. More than 1,000 teams from the professional to the high school level participate for the Emperor's Cup with the championship game played annually on 1 January.

SOCIAL DEMOCRATIC PARTY OF JAPAN (SHAKAI MINSHUTŌ, 社会民主党). In 1994, the **Japan Socialist Party** (JSP) changed its Japanese name from Nihon Shakaitō to Shakai Minshutō and its English name to the Social Democratic Party of Japan (SDPJ). The SDPJ took on a more moderate philosophy. **Doi Takako** was the major leader of the party at the time of the name change.

The SDPJ was the largest party in an eight-member coalition government that ousted the **Liberal Democratic Party** (LDP) from its position of leadership in 1993. Given policy differences with the other coalition parties over the tax system, **foreign policy**, and other matters, the SDPJ left the coalition and returned to the opposition.

However, a new coalition of the SDPJ, LDP, and the **New Party Sakigake** came to power in June 1994, and SDPJ chairman **Murayama Tomiichi** became Japan's first socialist prime minister in 47 years. In September 1994, the SDPJ radically overhauled its basic platform, deciding on new policies, accepting the constitutionality of the **Self-Defense Forces**, agreeing to support the **United States–Japan Security Treaty**, and approving already operating **nuclear power** facilities.

The party lost seats in the **House of Representatives** October 1996 **election**. In June 1998, it broke its coalition with the LDP. Accepting responsibility for the poor electoral showing, Doi resigned as party chair in 2003. The party then chose Fukushima Mizuho (1955–) as its president and Mataichi Seiji (1944–) as the party secretary-general. In 1998, many Diet members left the SDPJ and joined the **Democratic Party of Japan** (DPJ). As the DPJ grew, the SDPJ declined. As of 2016, the SDPJ has two seats each in the House of Representatives and the **House of Councillors**. Yoshida Tadatomo (1956–) serves as head of the party. As of 2017, the JSP, and its successor SDPJ, is nearly defunct. Although its **environmental** policies have some appeal, the party's massive social welfare program, anticapitalism, and disarmament policies have little support. *See also* DIET, NATIONAL (KOKKAI, 国会); POLITICAL PARTIES.

SOCIETY. Socially, Japan in 2018 experiences the problems and issues of advanced countries. Japanese young people are marrying in fewer numbers and having fewer children. **Toyota** builds stylish new sports cars. The fast-fashion retailer Uniqlo has world recognition. Japanese pop culture and **films** have worldwide appeal.

For the seventh consecutive year, Japan's population has dropped. In 2017, the Ministry of Internal Affairs and Communications announced that Japan's population was recorded at 126 million people. Birth rates were up slightly, but death rates grew faster.

The average life expectancy, a measure of success, continues to grow. Between 1989 and 2009, the average Japanese life expectancy increased by 4.2 years, from 78.8 years to 83 years.

Japan has a very high literacy rate of 99 percent, tying it for 21st place in the world along with the **United States**. Unemployment stands at a relatively low 4.2 percent. (Refer to appendixes B and R.)

Japan continues to be a leader in popular culture, film, **sports (baseball, soccer,** and others), and **literature**. Art and culture flourish. Japan's internet infrastructure is the envy of most nations.

SOFTBANK CORPORATION (SOFUTOBANKU KABUSHIKI-GAI-SHA, ソフトバンク株式会社). SoftBank Corporation is a **Tōkyō**-based computer software company with operations in broadband, fixed-line telecommunications, e-commerce, internet, and other communications media. **Son Masayoshi**, an important **business** leader, founded SoftBank in 1981 and is its aggressive president. SoftBank Corporation is a major provider of information and distribution services for the digital information industry. It is Japan's largest computer publisher and distributor of packaged software and hardware, having a net income of ¥108 billion in 2007, derived from more than 100 internet-related companies such as **Yahoo Japan**, GeoCities Japan, and ZDNet Japan.

In 1999, it sold part of its equity stake in the internet directory service to Yahoo Incorporated. Since 2003, SoftBank has been at the center of Japan's broadband market. It set off a boom in building high-speed networks in 2001. It has consistently offered the lowest-cost connections in its bid to take business away from **Nippon Telegraph and Telephone**, Japan's leading phone company.

In 2005, SoftBank purchased the Fukuoka SoftBank Hawks, one of Japan's professional **baseball** teams. In 2006, it purchased Vodafone Japan. In 2008, it partnered with Apple to promote internet telephone service in Japan.

In 2015, Forbes Global 2000 ranked SoftBank as the 62nd-largest public company in the world and the third-largest public company in Japan, immediately behind **Toyota** and **Mitsubishi UFJ Financial**. Between 2009 and 2014, SoftBank's market capitalization increased by 557 percent, showing the fourth-largest relative increase in the world.

Softbank has taken over many of its competitors. It bought out eAccess, Ustream, American Sprint Nextel, and Supercell. During the period 2015–2017, SoftBank purchased significant shares in DramaFever, the Korean e-commerce website Coupang, the Chinese Alibaba Group, the British chip designer ARM Holdings, Fortress Group, and numerous other investments.

SŌHYŌ, 総評. *See* GENERAL COUNCIL OF JAPANESE TRADE UNIONS (NIHON RŌDŌ KUMIAI SŌHYŌ GIKAI, 日本労働組合総評議会, COMMONLY KNOWN AS SŌHYŌ).

SŌJITZ CORPORATION (SŌJITSU KABUSHIKI-GAISHA, 双日株式会社). In 2004, **Nissho Iwai Corporation** merged with Nichimen Holdings, thus integrating **businesses** of information and communications with building materials, and adopted the name Sōjitz Corporation. This **general trading company** (*sōgō shosha*) engages in various businesses globally, providing international trade services. It invests in various sectors and conducts many business services. Headquartered in **Tōkyō**, Sōjitz employs more than 14,000 people and, in 2016, earned around $45 billion. Fujimoto Masayoshi is president and CEO.

SŌKA GAKKAI, 創価学会. Sōka Gakkai, or the Value Creation Society, claims 12 million members in 192 countries but actually has less than half that number. Makiguchi Tsunesaburō (1871–1944), Toda Jōsei (1900–1958), and Ikeda Daisaku (1928–) founded the religious sect in 1937. The early creators opposed state oppression. During World War II, Makiguchi and Toda were jailed due to their opposition to **Shintō** rites and Makiguchi died in prison. After the war, this movement grew quickly, thanks to an association with the **Buddhist** sect, Nichiren Shōshū, and an energetic president, Ikeda.

The major teaching of Sōka Gakkai contends that the Buddha nature resides in each person and that people can experience internal peace and happiness through self-discipline and chanting the Lotus Sutra. The **religion** is relatively intolerant and aggressive. It was quite outgoing in the 1970s but has declined recently.

Toda Jōsei, the second leader of Sōka Gakkai, built it into one of the largest of Japan's **new religions**.

Ikeda Daisaku, the third president of Sōka Gakkai, contributed to bringing the religious organization into the national political arena by creating a Sōka Gakkai–related **political party**, the **Kōmeitō**, in 1964. In the 1967 general **election**, Kōmeitō candidates won 25 seats in the **Diet**. In 1970, Ikeda adopted a policy of separation of politics and religion, and then turned his attention to scholarship, international communications, and world peace. Ikeda was elected president of Sōka Gakkai International in 1975 and served until 1979. As of 2017, Ikeda remains the honorary chairman of Sōka Gakkai and president of Sōka Gakkai International. Hōjō Hiroshi (1923–1981) served a two-year term as president and was succeeded by Akiya Einosuke (1930–) who served as president from 1981 through 2006. Harada Minoru (1941–) became president in 2006 and still holds that office.

Ikeda has founded several organizations to work for world peace, **environmental** preservation, and citizen diplomacy. He has been especially interested in improving Japan's relations with **China** and in championing the cause of African Americans. He has published more than 30 **books** and many articles on the same topics.

SON MASAYOSHI, 孫正義 (1957–). Son Masayoshi, a Korean by birth, is the founder and CEO of **SoftBank** Mobile. Forbes estimates his net worth at $13.6 billion as of 2015, making him the second-richest person in Japan. Son is a Japanese of Korean descent, a fact that he has had to struggle against. While in school, Son studied computer science and English and finished high school in California. He majored in economics and studied computer science at the University of California at Berkeley. There he recognized that computer technology would shape the future of commercial exchange. He saw the microchip as the leading technological revolution. Among his many entrepreneurial ideas, he patented a translating device that he sold to **Sharp** Electronics. He developed SoftBank, which was his leading enterprise. He founded Unison, which he sold to **Kyōcera**. He owned controlling interest in Yahoo. Through SoftBank, Son bought 76 percent of Sprint. Disturbed by the **Great East Japan Earthquake** nuclear disaster in 2011, Son invested in a solar power network for Japan. He pledged to donate $120 million and his remaining salary to help support victims of the earthquake and tsunami.

Highly ambitious, Son, with SoftBank, is preparing to challenge Verizon and AT&T in the American cell phone market. Son is a controversial figure who is stirring up the internet world. In addition to being an incredibly successful businessman, Son Masayoshi has been a leader challenging ethnic discrimination against Koreans in Japan.

Son, according to business leaders from Japan, **South Korea**, and **China**, is the most closely watched Japanese corporate executive. He was one of the first international **business** leaders to meet with president-elect Donald Trump and announced a world technology investment fund.

SONY CORPORATION (SONĪ KABUSHIKI-GAISHA, ソニー株式会社). Sony Corporation is one of the world's leading manufacturers of **televisions**, radios, and electronic products. Sony is also one of Japan's leading *keiretsu*. The success of Sony stems from its founders' ability to see the potential of the transistor and apply it to technical advancements. In the 1950s, the pocket-sized transistor radio earned the company worldwide acclaim. Sony became the first Japanese company to be listed on the New York Stock Exchange. In 2009, with $124 billion in assets and 180,000 employees, Sony remains a giant in the electronics industry.

In 1946, **Ibuka Masaru** and **Morita Akio** formed the Tōkyō Telecommunications Research Institute (Tōkyō Tsūshin Kōgyō). Producing electric rice cookers, heating pads, and shortwave radios, Sony engineers designed and manufactured products useful to consumers. In 1953, Ibuka and Morita purchased the **technology** for the transistor from Western Electric. This technology would revolutionize electronics. The pocket-sized transistor radio was called "Sony," a name adopted for its ties to the Latin word for sound or the nickname for a small boy. Development of videotape recorders, televisions, portable personal stereos or the "Walkman," camcorders, DVDs, and the "memory stick Walkman" gave Sony international appeal. Morita believed that a product's identity was as important as its technology. Thus, Sony became one of the most innovative companies in the world.

Iwama Kazuo (1919–1982) was an important **business** executive and electronics expert who worked with Morita and Ibuka to build the Sony Corporation. Trained as a geophysics engineer, Iwama became a company director in

1950, director of Sony Corporation of America (1971–1973), and president of Sony (1976–1982). He helped create the first transistor radio and the first transistorized television.

Ōga Norio (1930–2011) was a businessman and electronics expert who replaced Morita when he retired. He had joined Sony after sending the company a letter denouncing the poor quality of its tape recorders. Born in Shizuoka Prefecture, Ōga studied music at the Tōkyō National University of Fine Arts and Music. However, what most interested him was making a good tape recorder. He worked his way up in the company until he became president of the CBS/Sony Group in 1970, chairman of the group in 1980, and finally CEO in 1989. Ōga promoted the $2 billion purchase of CBS Records in 1988 and the $3.4 billion takeover of Columbia Pictures in 1989.

Idei Nobuyuki (1937–) became president and co–chief executive of Sony in 1995 and replaced Ōga Norio as chairman in 2003. Although making profits, Sony was involved in a restructuring project of its own. Idei was a strong spokesperson for convergence in **music, films, games**, and communications in all forms. He argued that Sony had a big advantage over other challengers because it produced televisions, personal **computers**, game consoles, and mobile phones, all of which can be integrated. The PlayStation game consoles are Sony's crown jewel.

Sony Music Entertainment is one of the largest record companies in the world. It manufactures and sells audiovisual, informational, and communicative equipment instruments and devices; makes and sells PlayStation game consoles and related software; manufactures and distributes recorded music in all formats; develops, produces, and manufactures image-based software; and provides some financial services. In 2005, electronics accounted for 63 percent of Sony's revenues, with games at 13 percent, music at 8 percent, motion pictures at 8 percent, and financial services at 6 percent.

In the late 1990s and beyond, Sony has experienced a difficult period. Its marquee electronic products have been overtaken and undercut by low-cost rivals like Dell and Samsung. Its movie studio failed to repeat its record run in 2002, and its music unit is trying to overcome hurdles. Even sales of its once enormously popular PlayStation 2 video game console have slowed. Sony is in the awkward position of having to play catch-up in some of its product lines. In 2005, Sony appointed Howard Stringer, a Welshman, as its first non-Japanese CEO and asked him to restructure Sony. He helped revitalize the company and remained its leader until 2012.

That year, Hirai Kazuo (1960–), an executive in the company's video game division succeeded Stringer as Sony's CEO. Under his leadership, Sony concentrated on consumer electronics while undertaking numerous cost-cutting measures, including selling various real estate holdings. Notably, in 2013 Sony sold its U.S. headquarters in New York.

Sony is a leading manufacturer of electronic products for consumer and professional markets. In 2016, it ranked 113th on the Fortune Global 500 list. It was the fifth-largest television manufacturer in the world.

Sony used to rely primarily on its sale of televisions, computers, and mobile telephones. Gradually it has begun to place more emphasis on the production of camera sensors, consoles, and **video games**. Its PlayStation 4 video console and PlayStation VR, a virtual reality headset, have improved its bottom line and its semiconductors, mobile devices, and film industry have also helped improve Sony's position.

SOUTH KOREA. *See* KOREA, RELATIONS WITH.

SOVIET UNION. *See* RUSSIA/SOVIET UNION, RELATIONS WITH.

SPORTS. Many Japanese enjoy and participate in sports both as athletes and as spectators. Japan introduces its children to a variety of sports in school where they undergo training in **swimming**, exercises, and running. School programs are structured to make such training fun, improve health and fitness, and introduce the students to activities that they can enjoy throughout life. One of the more memorable days in a child's **education** is Sports Day or *Undōkai*, when for one day a year the students in an elementary school are divided into two giant teams and compete against each other in a cooperative spirit.

At the junior and senior high school levels, many students join sports clubs or school teams. The excitement generated at this level can be quite intense with, for example, the spring and fall **baseball** tournaments being televised nationally.

College-level sports involve fewer people but still generate a lot of interest among students and fans. For adults, many companies and organizations sponsor their own sports teams and engage in various levels of athletic competition.

During the Middle Ages and into the Tokugawa period (17th century through to the mid-19th century), Japanese sports consisted primarily of martial arts, hunting, the use of the bow and arrow, and **sumō** matches. Japanese sports are often divided into traditional, meaning native to Japan, and imported, meaning originating in the West. Among the traditional sports are aikido, **jūdō**, jujutsu, karate, kendō, and kyūdō. Jūdō, which had been developed in the 19th century, became an **Olympic** sport in 1964. As of 2016, Japan has won a total of 84 medals, more than any other country, in Olympic jūdō competition.

The imported sports, most of which came to Japan in the late 19th and early 20th centuries, include baseball, basketball, **soccer**, track and field, **rugby**, ice hockey, competitive swimming, tennis, gymnastics, volleyball, lacrosse, table tennis, women's softball, and skiing.

Golf was introduced to Japan in the early 20th century and has become popular with approximately 12 million Japanese. Japan has around 3,500 professional golfers and 100 professional golf tournaments each year. **Aoki Isao**, Maruyama Shigeki, Nakajima Tsuneyuki, and **Ozaki Masashi** have become internationally famous male golf professionals while Okamoto Ayako and Fukushima Akiko are well-known female professionals.

In tennis, **Date Kimiko** has been successful in international competition, ranking as high as fourth in 1995. She has achieved success at the U.S. Open and at Wimbledon. Hiraki Rika and Matsuoka Shuzo have also achieved international recognition.

Japan has achieved international prominence in **figure skating** as **Itō Midori**, known as the queen of jumps, won Japan's first figure skating medal in the 1992 Olympics. Satō Yuka, a skater with great elegance, won the world professional championships in 1994.

Gymnastics is another sport at which Japan has gained international recognition, winning a total of 98 Olympic medals from the 1920s through 2016. The Japanese men's team won the team title at the Rome, **Tōkyō**, Mexico City, Munich, and Montreal Olympics, an unprecedented five straight times. Endō Yukio was probably Japan's best gymnast ever. He won the gold medal in the individual combined events in the 1964 Olympics. Gushiken Koji won the gold medal in the individual combined event at the 1984 Los Angeles Olympics.

Volleyball became an Olympic sport in the 1964 Tōkyō Olympics with the Japanese **women** winning the first Olympic gold medal in volleyball. Japan's most outstanding female stars have been Iada Takako, Okamoto Mariko, and Shirai Takako. Japan's greatest male volleyball stars were Minami Masayuki and Nekoda Katsutoshi.

Japan has excelled at swimming, winning a total of 80 medals in the history of the Olympics through 2016. In 1949, **Furuhashi Hironoshin**, Japan's "flying fish," broke world records in both the men's 800-meter and 1,500-meter freestyle and became a national hero. Yamanaka Tsuyoshi starred at swimming, winning the silver medal in the 1,500-meter event at the 1956 Melbourne Olympics.

Recently, **Kitajima Kōsuke** has emerged as Japan's world-class swimming star. In 2008, he won both the men's 100-meter and 200-meter breaststroke at the Beijing Olympics, repeating the double he achieved at the Athens Games four years earlier. This makes him the first swimmer in Olympic history to win both events at two consecutive games.

Japan has been involved in track and field in a modest way for a long time. In August 2007, **Ōsaka** hosted the World Track and Field Championships. In 1981, **Seko Toshihiko** set world records that still stand in the men's 25,000-meter and 30,000-meter contests. Matsumiya Takayuki set a world record in the 30-kilometer race in 2003. Sunada Takahiro holds the world's record for the 100-kilometer run.

Marathon running has become popular in Japan. Seko Toshihiko won the Boston Marathon in 1981 and again in 1987. The Tōkyō Marathon features approximately 30,000 runners and tours famous sites in the capital city. Taniguchi Hiromi won the 1991 world championship in the men's marathon.

Several Japanese women, including Fukushi Kayoko, Noguchi Mizuki, and Abe Tomoe, hold world's records in road races. Arimori Yuko won the silver medal in the women's marathon at the 1992 Barcelona Olympic Games, the first Japanese woman runner to win a medal at the Olympics. She also won the bronze at the 1996 Atlanta Olympics.

Japanese athletes have achieved distinction in **wrestling** at the Olympics. As of 2016, 69 Japanese have received medals in this Olympic competition. Watanabe Osamu is probably the most famous, winning the 1964 Olympic gold medal in Tōkyō and going undefeated (186–0) through his entire wrestling career.

Japan's three most favorite professional sports are baseball, soccer, and sumō. In a survey taken in 2007, 51 percent of the people named baseball as their favorite professional sport. The remaining chose soccer (23 percent), sumō (18 percent), golf (14 percent), boxing (9 percent), motor racing (8 percent), pro-wrestling (6 percent), and other sports (4 percent); 22 percent chose "none." Obviously, the survey allowed some people to choose more than one favorite.

As a measure of the popularity of sports in Japan, the country is said to have around 240,000 sports facilities with gymnasiums, multipurpose sports stadiums, indoor and outdoor swimming pools, outdoor tennis courts, and baseball and softball fields leading the way. Japan has the Ministry of Education, Culture, Sports, Science, and Technology as a **cabinet** position, thus giving sports a certain national stature. On the second Monday of October, Japan celebrates Health and Sports Day, a **national holiday** to commemorate the 1964 Summer Olympics held in Tōkyō. Hosting the 1964 Olympics, the 1972 Winter Olympics in **Sapporo**, and the 1998 Winter Olympics in Nagano, as well as cohosting the 2002 FIFA World Cup, put Japan on the international sports map.

STEEL INDUSTRY. Steel was a major industry of Japan in the first four decades of the postwar period. Putting great efforts into its steel production and sales, Japan became a world leader in this field. Japan completely rebuilt its steel factories, using the most advanced **technology**, the strongest government-**business** partnership, the best research, and all available capital. Postwar steel production multiplied 30 times over between 1950 and 1980. At its peak in 1973, Japan produced 119 million metric tons of steel.

By 1980, Japan had surpassed the **United States** as the leading steel-producing nation. Japan also became the world's leading exporter of steel. The efficiency of its steel plants was legendary. However, in the 1990s, Japan's steel industry declined due to the increased use of other materials and the growth of international competition.

The Japanese steel industry centers on two large producers, **Nippon Steel & Sumitomo Metal Corporation** (NSSMC) and JFE Steel Corporation. In 2012, Nippon Steel and Sumitomo Metal merged to create NSSMC, the second-largest steel manufacturer in the world. It operates plants in 15 countries and employs nearly 83,000 people. This company makes steel for **construction**, **automobiles**, civil engineering, **energy**, resources, and **railroads**.

JFE Steel Corporation was founded in 1950 and is based in **Tōkyō**. This company was formerly known as Kawasaki Steel Corporation and changed its name to JFE Steel Corporation in April 2003. The company provides steel sheets, electrical sheets, shapes, pipes and tubes, stainless products, steel bars, and wire rods.

Japan remains the world's second-largest steel producer, although India is quickly gaining ground on Japan. As of 2016, **China** produced 808 million metric tons of steel, Japan 105, India 96, and the United States 79 million. Japan is also the second-leading exporter of steel. In 2015, the Japanese steel market had total revenues of $48.9 billion.

With the U.S. exit from the Trans-Pacific Partnership, Japan's steel industry fears the United States will adopt a protectionism approach and disturb the steel market. Shindō Kōsei (1949–), chairman of the Japan Iron and Steel Federation and also president of Nippon Steel & Sumitomo Metal Corporation, shared this view in a 2017 press conference. The Japanese steel industry is facing increased competition around the world.

STOCK MARKET. *See* ECONOMY; SECURITIES COMPANIES; TŌKYŌ STOCK EXCHANGE (TŌKYŌ SHŌKEN TORIHIKIJO, 東京証券取引所).

STUDENT MOVEMENTS. Japanese student movements were an important social and political force in the 1960s. Zengakuren, the All-Japan Student Federation, was founded in 1948 and was initially under strong communist influence but, by the late 1950s, was more independent and ideologically divided. In the 1970s, Zengakuren split into many different factions, some of which became supporters of various terrorist movements. Zengakuren was known for its militancy. During the *Anpo* crisis of 1960, Zengakuren organized pressure movements against Prime Minister **Kishi Nobusuke**.

Kitakoji Satoshi (1936–2010) was a leader of the militant student federation Zengakuren. He saw parliamentary politics as a failure in 1960 and tried to block the 1960 revision of the **United States–Japan Security Treaty**. He was not opposed to the **United States** as a country, but he wanted to prevent Japan's rearmament.

Zenkyōtō (All-Student Joint Struggle Council) was a loosely structured student organization to protest Japanese support for United States military and political adventure in Southeast Asia. Members of the movement opposed not only **foreign policy** matters but also rallied against domestic hierarchies, rules, ideology, and misguided leadership. They encouraged domestic reform if not revolution. This radical organization struggled against the evils that beset the more traditional Japanese society. *See also* UNIVERSITY OF TŌKYŌ (TŌKYŌ DAIGAKU, 東京大学).

STUDIO GHIBLI (KABUSHIKI-GAISHA SUTAJIO JIBURI, 株式会社スタジオジブリ). Studio Ghibli is one of the leading producers of **anime** and is the corporation with the top name recognition in Japan today. Started by **Miyazaki Hayao** and Takahata Isao (1935–2018), two highly successful anime artists, Studio Ghibli is "Japan's most critically acclaimed and financially successful anime production house." Established in 1985 and named after the hot desert winds of the Sahara, Ghibli has given anime respectability. Its outstanding **films** include *Grave of the Fireflies* (1988), *My Neighbor Totoro* (1988), *Kiki's Delivery Service* (1989), *Princess Mononoke* (1997), *Spirited Away* (2001), *Howl's Moving Castle* (2004), *Ponyo* (2008), *The Wind Rises* (2013), *The Tale of Princess Kaguya* (2013), *When Marnie Was There* (2014), and *The Red Turtle* (2016).

SUBARU, スバル. Subaru, headquartered in Gunma Prefecture, is a Japanese **automobile** company that is a division of Fuji Heavy Industries. Japan's seventh-largest car company and the world's 26th in total sales, Subaru is best known for its four-wheel drive cars and its high-performance turbocharged cars such as the Legacy. Subaru grew out of five prewar small car companies and the Nakajima Aircraft Company.

By the 1990s, Subaru had come to concentrate on the rally car models with lots of power and speed. Amazingly, Subaru won eight consecutive Safari Rally meets in the 1990s. In 2006, Subaru secured a contract to work with General Motors and then **Toyota** to increase its production in the **United States**. Subaru is famous for its popular "Scooby" and "Scooby-Doo" names as well as its Outback advertisements starring Paul Hogan. Subaru has major marketing operations in Canada, the Philippines, and the United Kingdom, as well as the United States. The company works to make all its operations environmentally friendly.

SUMITOMO CORPORATION (SUMITOMO SHŌJI KABUSHIKI-GAISHA, 住友商事株式会社**).** The Sumitomo Corporation, established in 1919, is one of Japan's leading **general trading companies** and ranks among the top trading companies in the world. With its headquarters in **Tōkyō**, Sumitomo Corporation has 22 domestic and 108 overseas offices in 66 countries. Nakamura Kunihara (1947–) serves as president and CEO of this organization that employs more than 75,000 people. As of 2016, Sumitomo Corporation had assets of more than $2 billion. Sumitomo Corporation is truly a global organization focusing on various products and services, imports and exports, and domestic and international **business** investments. (Refer to appendixes I and J.)

SUMITOMO GROUP (SUMITOMO GURŪPU, 住友グループ**).** Sumitomo Masatomo founded the original Sumitomo enterprise in the early 17th century. Sumitomo grew prosperous as the purveyor of copper to the Tokugawa family, particularly in the Kansai district. The Sumitomo enterprises were much more centrally controlled by the Sumitomo family than was the case in the other **zaibatsu**. Before World War II, the 16th-generation head of the family held more than 90 percent of the group's shares. Sumitomo expanded during World War II from 40 companies to 135.

Since the zaibatsu dissolution in postwar Japan, the 80 or so remaining Sumitomo subsidiaries have been loosely grouped in a *keiretsu*. A president's club, known as "the White Waters Club," replaced the holding company. In the postwar period, the Sumitomo Group developed as one of Japan's leading *keiretsu*. The postwar Sumitomo Group concentrates on metal industries, particularly **steel**, and electronics. The Sumitomo *keiretsu* is the third of the big four prewar zaibatsu groupings.

The **Sumitomo Mitsui Financial Group** was the second-largest bank in Japan by market value as of 2016. Involved in **banking** and financial services, it is the key component of the Sumitomo Group.

Sumitomo Chemical Company was incorporated in 1925 and became one of the pillars of the Sumitomo Group. It produces a wide range of petrochemicals and chemical products. Sumitomo Chemical has joint ventures in the **United States**, Singapore, and Brazil.

Sumitomo Heavy Industries is another important component of the Sumitomo Group. It manufactures industrial machinery, ships, steel structures, power transmissions, and molding machines.

Founded in 1907 and created as a mutual company in 1947, Sumitomo Life Insurance Company is the number three mutual **life insurance** company in the world. It has 120 branches in Japan and 11 subsidiaries abroad. Employing more than 64,000 people, it has **business** dealings in 13 countries. Its headquarters are in **Ōsaka**.

Sumitomo Metal Industries is one of Japan's oldest major corporations with roots extending to the copper refining industry of **Kyōto** in the late 16th century. Incorporated in 1950, the company is engaged in mining, smelting, and the processing of gold, copper, nickel, zinc, and other metals. Sumitomo Rubber is known worldwide under the brand name of Dunlop, a company famous for its tires, **golf** and tennis balls, and rubber products. Incorporated in 1917, Sumitomo Rubber employs approximately 4,700 people in its enterprises.

Among other important related companies in the Sumitomo Group are **NEC**, a leading multinational information technology company, and Nippon Sheet Glass, one of the world's four largest glass companies. The group's **general trading company** is the **Sumitomo Corporation**.

As of 2016, Sumitomo Life has more than $745 billion in individual life insurance and more in group insurance and annuities. It employs 42,245 people. Hashimoto Masahiro (1956–) serves as president and CEO.

SUMITOMO MITSUI FINANCIAL GROUP (MITSUI SUMITOMO FINANSHARU GURŪPU, 三井住友フィナンシャルグループ**).** The Sumitomo Mitsui Financial Group (SMFG) is a holding company established in 2002 by Sumitomo Mitsui Banking Corporation (SMBC), the second-largest bank in Japan by market value. It is one of the largest financial institutions in the world. Miyata Koichi (1953–) serves as its president. Sumitomo is trying to attract American **banking** experts to broaden its international exposure and information. It is also trying to improve its IT position and develop its artificial intelligence system.

In 2012, SMFG purchased the Royal Bank of Scotland Group Plc's aircraft leasing business for $7.3 billion, the world's largest acquisition of a leasing business up to that date. In 2014, it acquired Citigroup's consumer banking **business** for $334 million. In 2016, Sumitomo Mitsui Finance and Leasing purchased General Electric Group's leasing business in Japan.

As of early 2017, SMFG employs more than 73,000 people and has total assets of approximately $8.13 billion. It provides extensive financial services. As a bank stock, Sumitomo Mitsui trades on the **Tōkyō Stock Exchange**. It oversaw the merger of three Kansai area banks.

Mitsubishi UFJ Financial Group, **Mizuho Financial Group**, and Sumitomo Mitsui Financial Group, Japan's three megabanks, plan to modernize Japan's financial technology in the near future. They are considering a wide variety of innovative technologies. *See also* SECURITIES COMPANIES.

SUMŌ, 相撲. Sumō is Japan's traditional sport where a large man attempts to push his opponent out of the ring (around 15 feet in diameter) or force him to touch the ground with any part of his body except his feet. The sport is filled with traditions and official procedures. Wrestlers, known as *rekishi*, are ranked according to their performance in the previous tournaments. The Sumō Association hosts six tournaments a year with three held in **Tōkyō** and one each in **Ōsaka**, **Nagoya**, and Fukuoka. The highest-ranked *rekishi* are known as *yokozuna*, and there have only been 72 of these since the beginning of the sport in the mid-18th century.

The greatest postwar *yokozuna* include Futabayama Sadaji (1912–1968) with 12 championships, Tochinishiki Kiyotaka (1925–1990) with 10, Wakanohana I Kanji (1928–2010) with 10, **Taihō Kōki** (1940–2013) with 32, Kitanofuji Katsuaki (1942–) with 10, Wajima Hiroshi (1948–) with 14, **Kitanoumi Toshimitsu** (1953–2015) with 24, **Chiyonofuji Mitsugu** (1955–2016) with 31, **Akebono Tarō** (1969–) with 12, **Takanohana II Kōji** (1972–) with 22, **Musashimaru Kōyō** (1971–) with 12, and **Asashōryū Akinori** (1980–) with 25 championships. However, the all-time leader is currently **Hakuhō Shō**, with 40 grand championships and still counting.

A popular Hawaiian-born sumō wrestler, Konishiki (1963–), at 630 pounds, was also the largest sumō wrestler ever. Although lacking in technical finesse, he was very big and very powerful. He was the first non-Japanese ever promoted to sumō's second-highest rank, *ōzeki*, in 1987. Konishiki is destined to go down in history as one of sumō's greatest junior champions. Konishiki won three grand tournaments. He became a Japanese citizen in 1994 and took the Japanese name Shiota Yasokichi. He retired in November 1997 and became Sanoyama. He decided to leave the Japan Sumō Association in the fall of 1998, thus giving up his status as *oyakata*, or stable master.

Takamiyama (1944–) was a sumō star with great popularity from 1964 until his retirement in 1984. Known as "Jesse," he was the first non-Japanese to win the Emperor's Cup tournament. This 430-pound athlete spent 20 years as a sumō wrestler. He strived for but never reached the rank of *yokozuna*, grand champion. Jesse Kuhaulua was born in Hawaii and attended high school in Maui. He married a Japanese **woman** and became a Japanese citizen in 1980. He now runs a stable of sumō wrestlers. He is a protégé of Konishiki.

Hailing from Nanao City in Ishikawa, Wajima Hiroshi (1948–) entered Hanakago stable after years of competing at the high school and college levels, and began competing professionally in 1970. His first tournament victory was at the *Natsu Basho* in 1972. After another victory at the same tournament the following year, Wajima became a *yokozuna* at 25. Retiring in 1981 with 14 championships under his belt, he had reigned as a *yokozuna* for almost eight years, once winning 27 matches in a row. Wajima won almost three-quarters of his matches, with a record of 620–213. Wajima is the first college graduate *yokozuna*.

Wakanohana Masaru (1971–) became Japan's 66th *yokozuna* in 1998. His real name is Hanada Masaru. He made his sumō debut in March 1988, competing as Wakahanada. His father was the former *ōzeki* Takanohana I (1950–2005), former head of the Futagoyama *heya* that included his two sons. Together with his younger brother Takanohana, he was a popular sumō champion who won five tournaments before retiring in March 2000.

The dominant sumō star in 2017 was Hakuhō Shō, who, in November of that year, won his 40th Emperor's Cup in the Nagoya Basho. By the tournament's end, he had achieved a total of 1,062 career victories, besting the marks set by *yokozuna* Chiyonofuji (1,045) and *ozeki* Kaiō (1,047). Since 2010, Hakuhō has won 28 of the 46 tournaments, or well over half of them. Harumafuji, winning eight *basho*, is a very distant second to him. *See also* SPORTS.

SUPERMARKETS. Established in 1957, Daiei was Japan's first supermarket. Founded by Nakauchi Isao (1922–2005), it led to dramatic changes in the distribution of food in Japan. Daiei's chain and **convenience stores** altered Japanese shopping patterns. Daiei has numerous markets throughout Japan and employs nearly 7,000 people. The Daiei Peacock unit also operates more than 60 supermarkets in the Kantō and Kansai districts. Daiei, Japan's second-largest retailer, stands at 20th in the world. Jusco is 24th and MY-CAL is 28th. Daiei expanded rapidly but suffered from outstanding debts in the post-bubble 1990s and in the early part of the 21st century. Struggling on the verge of bankruptcy, it has benefited from government subsidies. Daiei owned and sponsored the Fukuoka Daiei Hawks **baseball** team.

As of 2013, Japan's leading supermarket by size of sales is Itō-Yōkadō, but it ranks only 16th in the world of supermarkets. It was established in 1920 and has 178 stores nationwide and 14,000 employees. Seven & i Holdings controls Itō-Yōkadō.

ÆON Jusco, which has roots dating to the mid-18th century, is one of Japan's largest supermarkets with 290 stores in Japan. It also has several stores in **China**, Thailand, and Malaysia.

While most of Japan's supermarkets were successful, not all were, and Yaohan was a case in point. Wada Ryōhei founded the company in 1928. Initially a single shop, it later expanded into a major supermarket chain after World War II with most retail outlets located in Shizuoka Prefecture. During the 1990s, Yaohan grew dramatically outside Japan, especially into China. At its peak, it had 450 outlets in 16 countries, including nine in Hong Kong where Yaohan moved its headquarters. But due to the 1997 Asian financial crisis and the stagnation of the Japanese retail market, Yaohan declared bankruptcy with debts of ¥161 billion. It was the biggest postwar failure in Japan's retail sector at the time. In 2000, ÆON Group bought Yaohan and changed its name to Maxvalu Tokai.

Today's Japanese supermarkets are high-tech, efficient operations. Electronic price displays appear on LCD devices. All prices can be changed electronically from a central office. These price displays are solar powered. The Japanese supermarket resembles its Western counterpart, but prices are higher, sizes are smaller, and presentations differ with DVD displays, **music**, and high-pressure **advertising**. Japanese supermarkets have a good stock of fresh vegetables and fruits, selected meats, and an excellent selection of seafood products.

SUZUKI DAISETSU TEITARŌ, 鈴木大拙貞太郎 **(1870–1966).** Suzuki Teitarō is also known as Suzuki Daisetz or D. T. Suzuki. He was a philosopher who, through his numerous **books** in both Japanese and English, was instrumental in engendering the current worldwide popularity of Zen **Buddhism**. He was born in Kanazawa, Ishikawa Prefecture, the youngest of five children. He entered Tōkyō Imperial University and concurrently undertook Zen training at Engakuji Temple in Kamakura. In 1897, he traveled to Illinois, where he spent the next 11 years assisting with the translation of Oriental philosophical and religious works into English.

Upon his return to Japan in 1909, Suzuki was appointed lecturer and later professor of English at the Peers' School. In 1911, he married an American **woman**, Beatrice Lane, who helped him with his publications until her death in 1939. In 1921, he became professor of Buddhist philosophy at Ōtani University, where he began the publication of the magazine *Eastern Buddhist*. In 1949, he was elected to the Japan Academy and received the Order of Culture the same year. After this, he spent much time lecturing on Zen outside Japan, contributing firsthand to the growth of Western interest in Zen Buddhism.

SUZUKI EITARŌ, 鈴木榮太郎 **(1894–1966).** Suzuki Eitarō was a famous sociologist. Born in Nagasaki Prefecture, he graduated from Tōkyō Imperial University. He became a professor at Hokkaidō University and the **University of Tōkyō**. Scholars highly regard Suzuki for having devised a system of rural and urban sociology, as well as an original theory of local sociology. After World War II, Suzuki did research on urban sociology and criticized urban studies for tending to focus on slums and **crime**. He then turned to the structural pattern produced by the lives of the average population of a city. Suzuki theorized that the size of a city is determined by the size of the integrative organization and class composition.

SUZUKI "ICHIRŌ," 鈴木一朗 **(1973–).** Suzuki "Ichirō" was a star **baseball** player with the Orix Blue Wave and then an all-star with the Seattle Mariners. "Ichirō," as he is known, comes from Aiichi Prefecture where he was a talented high school baseball player who became a professional player right out of high school. He played nine seasons with the Blue Wave and, in 1995, set a Japanese single-season record with 210 hits in 130 games, more than any other professional baseball player of all time. He won seven consecutive batting titles and was chosen the Pacific League's most valuable player (MVP) three times, had a career batting average of .353, and won seven Gold Glove Awards.

In 2001, Ichirō joined the Seattle Mariners as the first Japanese-born everyday position player in the Major Leagues (ML). He proceeded to get 242 hits, the most by any player since 1930 and the most as a rookie. That year he was voted the American League's MVP as well as rookie of the year. In 2004, he upped his production to 262 hits, breaking George Sisler's record set in 1920. In 2007, he was the MVP of the All-Star Game, going three for three and hitting the event's first-ever inside-the-park home run. By the end of the 2008 season, he had the second-highest lifetime batting average of all players in ML baseball, trailing Albert Pujols by only .002. In 2009, Ichirō broke Japan's all-time record of 3,085 hits held by Harimoto Isao. Known also for his incredible work ethic, Ichirō has become a hero in the **United States** as well as Japan's favorite player, generating a new level of excitement for baseball in both countries.

Ichirō is a 10-time Major League baseball all-star, the MVP of the 2007 All-Star Game, winner of 10 consecutive Rawlings Gold Glove Awards, an American League record holder of seven hitting streaks of 20 or more games, and the present leader of active players in singles with 2,440 and in stolen bases with 509. He is only the 30th player to achieve 3,000 hits in his ML baseball career. At 43, Ichirō remains a baseball phenomenon with more than 4,300 hits in his career.

After playing 11 years with the Mariners, the New York Yankees acquired Ichirō where he starred for two and a half seasons before the Miami Marlins purchased his contract. On 4 October 2016, the Marlins exercised their option with Ichirō. The option guaranteed Ichirō $2 million in 2017 and includes an option for 2018.

SUZUKI MOTOR COMPANY (SUZUKI KABUSHIKI-GAISHA, スズキ株式会社**).** Suzuki Motor Company, a leader in the **motorcycle** industry, produces a range of small **automobiles**, including the K-car and other small combustion-engine products. With production facilities in 22 countries, Suzuki has teamed up with the local Indian company Maruti, making them jointly the largest automaker in India. Suzuki Michio founded the Suzuki Loom Works in Hamamatsu in 1909. In 1952, Suzuki started making motorized bicycles. In 1954, Suzuki made its first automobile and adopted the name Suzuki Motor Corporation. Its leading models have been the Suzulight, Fronte, and Jimmy. In 1981, Suzuki sold 5 percent of its shares to General Motors (GM); by 2001, GM owned 20 percent, but in March 2006, GM reduced its stake to 3 percent. Between 2009 and 2015, Volkswagen held around 20 percent of the Suzuki shares, but an international arbitration court ordered Volkswagen to sell these back to Suzuki.

As of 2015, Suzuki was ranked as the world's ninth-largest automobile company with more than three million units produced annually. It is considered Japan's fourth-largest automobile producer after **Toyota**, **Nissan**, and **Honda**. Suzuki employs more than 45,000 people worldwide and has 35 major production facilities in 23 countries. It operates 133 distributorships in 192 countries. It also manufactures a large number of motorcycles and outboard motors. In 2012, its total assets exceeded $25 billion. Suzuki Osamu (1930–), an adopted son-in-law, is the company chairman.

SUZUKI SHIN'ICHI, 鈴木鎮一 (1898–1998). Suzuki Shin'ichi created and perfected the world-famous Suzuki violin method. Born in **Nagoya**, the son of a noted violin maker, Suzuki studied violin with Andō Ko. In 1946, while living in Nagano Prefecture, he started the Talent Education Movement with the motto "Anyone's talent can be developed through **education**." When he achieved striking results, his method spread worldwide. There are numerous Suzuki Method students in Japan and abroad. Suzuki also founded the Tōkyō String Orchestra, which introduced baroque **music** to Japan. He became president of Teikoku Music School in 1930 where he perfected his violin teaching techniques.

SUZUKI SHUN'ICHI, 鈴木俊一 (1910–2010). Suzuki Shun'ichi was the powerful governor of **Tōkyō** during the period 1979–1995. His major accomplishment was the building of a new Tōkyō metropolitan government headquarters in the Shinjuku section of Tōkyō. He created a long-term plan for Tōkyō's development. Suzuki, a conservative from the **Liberal Democratic Party**, was a high-ranking official in the Ministry of Home Affairs and represented traditional bureaucratic politics. As governor, he promoted internationalism, improved social welfare services, and encouraged **business** expansion.

SUZUKI ZENKŌ, 鈴木善幸 (1911–2004). Suzuki Zenkō served as Japan's **prime minister** in the early 1980s. A native of Iwate Prefecture, Suzuki studied at the Tōkyō University of Fisheries in 1935. Son of a fisherman, he worked in various organizations concerned with the fishing industry. In 1947, Suzuki was elected to the **Diet** and served as a member of both the

Japan Socialist Party and the Social Renovation Party (Shakai Kakushintō) before joining the **Liberal Democratic Party** (LDP). Suzuki was elected 13 times before becoming prime minister. He was a skilled political mediator and proved this by serving as chairman of the LDP for 10 terms.

As chairman of the Diet's standing committee on local administration, Suzuki's skillful handling of the problems resulting from **Kishi Nobusuke**'s attempts to reform the powers of the police began to gain him political recognition. As a leading member of the **Ikeda Hayato** faction, he served as posts and telecommunications minister in 1960, then as **cabinet** secretary and state minister in 1964–1965. As welfare minister under **Satō Eisaku** (1965–1966), Suzuki made major moves toward the improvement of health insurance provisions. His negotiating abilities and political tact meant that he was generally trusted and assigned major posts in the party machine. He served as the party's chief of general affairs in 1968–1971 and again in 1972–1974.

Following a spell as agriculture, forestry, and fisheries minister under **Fukuda Takeo** (1976–1977), Suzuki, though a power in the party, held no cabinet post, but assumed the leadership of the **Ōhira Masayoshi** faction following Ōhira's sudden death in June 1980. He was officially chosen as the LDP leader in July 1980. From 17 July 1980 to 27 November 1982, he served as prime minister. Totally unknown in the West, Suzuki was not a strong leader but, rather, a "politician's politician." He worked closely with former prime minister **Tanaka Kakuei**.

SWIMMING. Japan has excelled in the sport of swimming, with 80 Olympic medals, along with **jūdō** (84 medals), wrestling (69 medals), and **gymnastics** (98 medals).

Furuhashi Hironoshin was Japan's first male swimming star. Japan's world record holders are too numerous to list all, but one should mention Nakamura Katsumi in the 100-meter freestyle, Hagino Kosuke in the 200-meter freestyle, Koga Junya in the 50-meter backstroke, **Kitajima Kōsuke** in the 50-meter breaststroke, and Watanabe Ippei in the 200-meter breaststroke.

In 2004 at Athens, Kitajima won two individual gold medals in a single Olympics, the first Japanese to do this. He is also the only man to win both breaststroke events at the same Games. He repeated this feat at the Beijing Olympics. He is a four-time Olympic competitor.

At the 2013 World Championships in Barcelona, Spain, Hagino won two seconds, three fifths, and a seventh. Seto Daiya won gold medals in the 400-meter individual medley at the world short course championships in 2012, 2014, and 2016. He also won at the 2013 and 2015 world long course championships. Seto is the first Asian swimmer to be a world champion in the individual medley.

At the 2014 Pan Pacific Championships, Irie Ryosuke won the 100-meter backstroke, Seto Daiya won the 200-meter butterfly, Koseki Yasuhiro the 100-meter breaststroke, and Hagino Kosuke the 400-meter individual medley. Hagino was named world swimmer of the year, the only Japanese to ever receive this award in more than 50 years.

Japanese female swimmers have achieved modest success in swimming at the Olympics. Tanaka Satoko won the bronze medal in the 100-meter backstroke in 1960, Nakamura Mai the silver in 2000, and Terakawa Aya the bronze in 2012. In the 200-meter backstroke, Nakao Miki won the bronze in 2000 and Nakamura Reiko the bronze in 2004 and 2008. Suzuki Satomi won the bronze in the breaststroke in 2012. Iwasaki Kyoko won the gold medal in the 200-meter breaststroke in 1992, followed by Suzuki Satomi the silver in 2012 and Kaneto Rie the gold in 2016. In the 100-meter butterfly, Aoki Mayumi won in 1972. Nakanishi Yoko finished third in the 200-meter butterfly in 2004, 2012, and 2016. In short, Japanese female swimmers trail their male counterparts.

T

TAIHŌ KŌKI, 大鵬幸喜 **(1940–2013).** Taihō Kōki was a grand champion who remained at the top of the **sumō** mountain for a decade. Born Kōki Naya in Hokkaidō, Taihō was forced to work in manual jobs to help sustain his mother and siblings. Spotted by representatives of the Nishinoseki stable, the stable master repeatedly begged his mother to let him become a sumō wrestler. She finally gave in and sent the teenager to train in the late 1950s. In 1960, he upset a *yokozuna* and progressed rapidly thereafter.

Taihō won his first championship in 1961, and the 20-year-old was promoted to *yokozuna* in September of that year, the youngest-ever recipient of the honor. He amassed 32 championships in all, the last in 1971 when he retired at the age of 31. He demonstrated his dominance of the 1960s by winning 45 matches in a row, the postwar standard until **Chiyonofuji Mitsugu** topped this mark. He also had two other winning streaks of 34 straight. In eight of his championships, Taihō went undefeated, a mark equaled only by Futabayama. In 1962–1963 and again in 1966–1967, he won six consecutive titles, more in a row than many grand champions win in their whole careers. His final record stood at 746–146, an unparalleled winning percentage of .836.

Taihō opened his own sumō stable but was not very successful at this. In 1997, he suffered a stroke that eventually left him in a wheelchair. Suffering from poor health, he died of heart failure in 2013.

TAIWAN, RELATIONS WITH. Japan's relations with Taiwan, the neutral name Japan uses since it does not recognize the Republic of China, are shaped by a cultural commonality, a history of 50 years of colonial rule, strong economic ties, the 1972 Japan-China Joint Communiqué, and the extraordinary rise to economic power of the People's Republic of **China** (PRC).

Cultural similarities in written languages, Confucian philosophy and social mores, **Buddhism**, and artistic styles have given Japan and Taiwan a foundation on which to build a close relationship. But this was overturned by the negative experience of Japan's colonial occupation of Taiwan. While making contributions to its development, Japan's period of colonial rule generated many unfavorable images. Cultural similarities and colonial legacies form a close, although often rocky, relationship.

In 1972, President Richard Nixon visited Beijing and signed the Joint Communiqué of the **United States** of America and the People's Republic of China. Shortly thereafter, Prime Minister **Tanaka Kakuei** established Japan's diplomatic relations with the PRC. After Japan's recognition of the PRC in 1972, Japan and Taiwan maintained a working relationship on a nongovernmental basis. Like many countries, Japan severed diplomatic ties with the Republic of China in deference to Beijing's "one-China" policy.

Japan's relationship with Taiwan is also driven by its policy toward the PRC. In 1978, Japan strengthened its ties with the PRC by signing the Treaty of Peace and Friendship between Japan and the People's Republic of China. This, in turn, further weakened the diplomatic ties between Japan and Taiwan although economic and **trade** relations continued to flourish. The Tōkyō-Taipei-Beijing relationship is a tricky one.

In 1998, Japan further defined its relationship in a declaration jointly signed with the PRC called the Japan-China Joint Declaration on Building a Partnership of Friendship and Cooperation for Peace and Development. In this document, Japan stated that it "reiterates its understanding that there is one China. Japan will continue to maintain its exchanges of a private and regional nature with Taiwan." Thus, Japan affirmed the primacy of the PRC while still holding private, low-key ties with Taiwan.

On the other hand, during Prime Minister **Koizumi Jun'ichirō**'s administration, more hawkish politicians in the **Liberal Democratic Party** pushed for stronger support of Taiwan. Prime Minister **Abe Shinzō** visited Beijing in October 2006 where he reaffirmed the 1978 agreement. In 2008, Japan-Taiwan trade hit $64 billion, making Japan Taiwan's second-leading trading partner. With international travel being increasingly important, more than a million people from Japan and Taiwan visit each other's country on an annual basis. Most people in Japan and Taiwan want economic relations to flourish and diplomatic ties to be smooth.

Taiwan is popular for Japanese tourists with 1.89 million visiting there in 2016. It's convenient, comfortable, and receptive to Japanese visitors in spite of the history of a half century of occupation by Japan. Japanese culture can be found throughout Taiwan. More than 12,000 Japanese live in Taipei. Japanese **video games** and **films** along with pop culture cover the island nation.

During the administration of President Ma Ying-jeou (2008–2016), Taiwan and Japan signed 28 bilateral agreements including ones to alleviate fishing disputes and handling matters in the Senkaku/Diaoyu Islands dispute. Naturally, the PRC has complained over the growing relationship.

Taiwan's President Tsai Ing-wen (2016–) has made the advancement of Taiwan-Japan relations one of her primary goals. Prime Minister Abe has been trying to strengthen strategic relations with Taiwan as a counterweight to Japan's relations with a more assertive China. Other Japanese lawmakers have voiced similar views. Japan seems to be experiencing a pro-Taiwan movement with two-thirds of Japanese saying they "feel close" to the people of Taiwan. *See also* FOREIGN POLICY.

TAKADA KENZŌ, 高田賢三 **(1939–).** Known internationally in the **fashion** world as Kenzō, Takada has built his reputation on style and presentation. Takada was born in Himeji in Hyōgo Prefecture and, from childhood, wanted to be a dressmaker. He was one of the first males to graduate from the Bunka Fashion College. In 1961, he won the *So-en* fashion prize. He went to France in 1964 and, after a long apprenticeship, offered his first showing in Paris in 1970. He formed a company in the 1970s that made a name for him. In 1983, he started a line of men's clothing. The brand name Kenzō is known worldwide for its clothes, skincare products, and perfumes.

Takada first leaned heavily on Japanese traditional styles but then began to make use of the "big silhouette" designs that came to distinguish his works. These creations became a trendsetter for young people and made him a pioneer in world fashion. His designs show dramatic, daring, and colorful looks. His creations are sporty, use a lot of native fabrics, and show a natural look.

Takada is quite well known internationally. As proof of his success, his work is often copied, providing inspiration for other fashion creators. Although he retired in 1999 to spend more time with art, Takada is still involved with various aspects of his business, still an inspiration in the world of fashion. In 2013, Takada became the honorary president of the Asian Couture Federation.

TAKAHASHI RUMIKO, 高橋留美子 **(1957–).** Takahashi Rumiko is one of Japan's most renowned **manga** artists. She has worked on *Maison ikkoku* and *Ranma 1/2* and also contributed to *Inu Yasha, Urusei Yatsura, Mermaid Forest, Mermaid Scar, Mermaid's Gaze, Rumic Theater*, and the Rumic World trilogy.

Beautiful Dreamer (*Urusei yatsura*), a science fiction romantic comedy, is based on Takahashi's manga. The Japanese title translates as "Those Troublesome Aliens," and its 218 episodes trace many stories of struggle and demon chases. *Beautiful Dreamer* is the story of an unlucky, lecherous young man named Ataru Moroboshi. When aliens invade Earth, Ataru is randomly selected to defend his planet by playing a game of tag, the alien's

national sport. By winning, he can save the world. Ataru is strongly motivated by Lum, the curvaceous alien princess. Takahashi has become one of
Japan's richest **women** through the tremendous sales of her **books**.

TAKAKURA KEN, 高倉健 **(1931–2014).** Takakura Ken was an actor
known for his tough-guy roles in numerous gangster films. He was born in
Fukuoka Prefecture as Oda Gōichi. After graduating from Meiji University,
he joined the acting stable of Tōei Motion Picture Company in 1955. Takakura became the archetypical hero of *yakuza* movies for his performance in
an 18-segment movie series. He became one of Japan's most popular box
office stars. Takakura often played the role of chivalrous *yakuza* and the
quintessential stoic male tough guy. The breakout role for Takakura was
playing an ex-con antihero in *Abashiri Bangaichi: Bokyohen* (*Abashiri Prison: Longing for Home*) in 1965. By the time Takakura left Tōei in 1976, he
had appeared in more than 180 films.

Known as the "Clint Eastwood" of Japan, Takakura achieved his street-
wise swagger and tough-guy persona watching *yakuza* movies. He gained
international fame when he starred in the 1975 Sydney Pollack movie *The
Yakuza* with Robert Mitchum and was probably best known in the West for
his role in Ridley Scott's *Black Rain* (1989) where he surprised Americans
with his retort, "Listen, I do speak f***ing English." He again won recognition for his role in the comedy *Mr. Baseball* starring Tom Selleck. In 2005,
Takakura appeared in *Qian li zou dan ji* (*Riding Alone for Thousands of
Miles*), directed by the famous Chinese director Zhang Yimou.

Takakura, the actor with a tough-guy, rugged-individual aura about him,
won the Japan Academy Prize four times, more than any other person. He
was famous not only in Japan but widely admired in both the **United States**
and **China**. **Ishihara Shintarō**, the politician and cult figure, called him "the
last big star" in Japanese film.

TAKAMINE HIDEKO, 高峰秀子 **(1924–2010).** Takamine Hideko was
one of Japan's greatest **film** stars who represented thoroughly modern **wom-
en**. For 50 years between the late 1920s and the 1970s, Takamine appeared in
176 movies. Her memorable performance in *Onna ga kaidan o agaru toki*
(*When a Woman Ascends the Stairs*, 1960) is perhaps the best by a Japanese
actress.

TAKAMURE ITSUE, 高群逸枝 **(1894–1964).** Takamure Itsue was a historian and feminist, known for her pathfinding research in **women**'s history.
Born in Kumamoto Prefecture in 1930, she joined with several other feminists in forming the Musan Fujin Geijutsu Renmei (Proletarian Women's Art
League), a group sympathetic to anarchism. Her direct involvement with

activism was brief, however, and today she is best known for her many historical studies, especially those tracing the development of Japanese marriage patterns. Her most famous works include a study of matrilineal practices in ancient Japan, a study of the patterns of marriage, and a four-volume history of Japanese women (*Josei no rekishi*, 1954–1958).

TAKANOHANA II KŌJI, 貴乃花光司 **(1972–).** Takanohana II was Japan's 65th *yokozuna* and one of the greatest **sumō** stars of the 1990s. Takanohana, originally known as Hanada Kōji, became a *yokozuna* after winning the September 1994 *basho* with a record of 15–0, the November 1994 *basho* with the same mark, and the January 1995 *basho* with a 13–2 record. He weighed more than 300 pounds and was extremely skillful, being known as one of the best technicians of sumō. Formerly known as Takahanada, he won the January and November 1992 sumō tournament championships, both with 14–1 records. He became the youngest *ozeki* in sumō history when he reached that rank at 20 years and five months. Takanohana garnered 22 championships and finished with a 794–262 record, but he missed 201 matches due to injuries, his weak point.

TAKAYANAGI KENZŌ, 高柳賢三 **(1887–1967).** Takayanagi Kenzō was a scholar of Anglo-American law. Born in Saitama Prefecture, he graduated from Tōkyō Imperial University in 1912 and taught in its law faculty until his retirement in 1948. Takayanagi specialized in legal history and comparative law. He became a member of the House of Peers, where his legal expertise led him to be appointed to a committee to discuss Japan's new **constitution**. During the 1950s and 1960s, Takayanagi chaired the Commission on the Constitution and gained recognition as one of the most respected defenders of Japan's constitution.

TAKEMITSU TŌRU, 武満徹 **(1930–1996).** Takemitsu Tōru was one of Japan's leading composers who made a real mark on Japanese **music**. Born in **Tōkyō**, he studied with Kiyose Yasuji. He worked on experimental music but also used traditional music. He employed improvisation and the sounds of nature plus visual effects and was quite original in his music. He had more than 70 credits for **film** music scores. He was recognized internationally for his compositions, being perhaps Japan's foremost modern composer. Takemitsu not only wrote purely orchestral works but employed avant-garde techniques.

TAKESHITA NOBORU, 竹下登 **(1924–2000).** Takeshita Noboru, a lifelong politician, served as **prime minister** during the late 1980s, a period that experienced the ill health and death of **Emperor Hirohito**. Takeshita was born in Shimane Prefecture to a sake-brewing family. He attended Waseda University but was drafted into the army, delaying his graduation until 1947. He was elected to the **House of Representatives** in 1958 and served 11 terms for an unbroken period of 29 years. He served as a secretary in **Satō Eisaku**'s **cabinet**, as finance minister for five terms, and as secretary-general of the **Liberal Democratic Party** (LDP) in 1986–1987. As finance minister, Takeshita signed the Plaza Accord, which brought the world's currencies into balance in 1985. In July 1987, Takeshita became head of the LDP and then succeeded **Nakasone Yasuhiro** as prime minister from 6 November 1987 to 3 June 1989. He carried out political reforms in the **Diet** and orchestrated passage of the 3 percent consumption tax.

Takeshita was the successor to the **Tanaka Kakuei** faction. He was ambitious but closely watched by Tanaka. In the later 1980s, Takeshita was identified as one of Japan's new leaders. In June 1989, he became a political casualty of the **Recruit scandal**. He also had ties with the questionable Sagawa Express Delivery Company and **Kanemaru Shin**, the right-wing political strongman. The Takeshita faction had 69 House of Representatives seats and 37 **House of Councillors** seats for a total of 106 seats as of 1991. His constituents knew him for taking care of Shimane Prefecture and bringing in lots of "pork barrel" projects.

TAMURA RYŌKO, 田村亮子 **(1975–).** Tamura Ryōko was a female champion **jūdō** participant in four Olympic Games. Tamura's performances at the World Championships and the **Olympics** alike clearly established her as Japan's greatest female *jūdōka*. She first earned a bronze at 48 kilograms in the World Championship in 1991, and then won gold medals at this weight in 1993, 1995, and 1997. She won the silver medal in the extra-lightweight event at the 1992 Olympic Games in Barcelona, and she went the next four years and 84 matches without a loss. She won her second Olympic silver medal at the 1996 Atlanta Games. Her first Olympic gold medal came four years later at the 2000 Games in Sydney. At the 2004 Olympic Games in Athens, Tamura won her second gold medal. The popular Tamura was widely known in Japan as "Yawara-chan" after a **manga** character with whom she shares a close resemblance. In 2010, Tamura ran for and won a seat in the **House of Councillors**, but she chose not to run again in 2016.

TANAKA IKKO, 田中一光 **(1930–2002).** Born in Nara City, Tanaka Ikko studied art at the **Kyōto** City School of Fine Arts. He worked at the Sankei Shimbun and Nippon Design Center; in 1963, he established the Ikko Tanaka Design Studio.

His posters were designed to attract attention, to tempt viewers to buy or do something. Tanaka was probably one of the best graphic designers in Japan, creating unique posters with bold geometric designs that continue to influence Japanese design today. He contributed to the 1964 Tōkyō **Olympics**, creating the games' logotype, medal motif, and facility pictograms, and he was one of the creative minds behind the no-label Muji brand aesthetic.

Tanaka's work also included the design of the symbols for **Expo '85** in Tsukuba and World City Expo **Tōkyō** 1996. Among others, he has worked for the **Seibu Saison Group**, Hanae Mori (**Mori Hanae**), Issey Miyake (**Mikaye Issei**), and the **Mazda Corporation**. Tanaka designed exhibitions for London's Victoria and Albert Museum. He also designed the main logo of Ōsaka University.

TANAKA KAKUEI, 田中角栄 (1918–1993). Tanaka Kakuei, a successful contractor and a savvy politician, served as Japan's **prime minister** in the 1970s. He was the most influential member of the **Liberal Democratic Party** (LDP) until the mid-1980s. A native of Niigata Prefecture and the son of a poor farming family, he left school after the eighth grade. He received some engineering training and, at age 19, founded his own transport and **construction** companies. Tanaka served two years in the military in a cavalry corps in Manchuria but contracted pneumonia and was sent home.

Gutsy and with unbounded energy, Tanaka was first elected to the **Diet** in 1947 from the Japan Democratic Party, but then joined the **Liberal Party**. He was arrested for political corruption but, in 1949, was reelected in a landslide while still in prison. He later was acquitted.

Tanaka always seemed to have close connections with rich, influential supporters. An important support group, the Etsuzankai (Niigata Mountain Association), provided him with a powerful base, and he reciprocated by bringing lots of government-funded projects to Niigata. In the LDP, Tanaka was close to **Satō Eisaku** and, through the 1960s, held important positions in the party. He was posts and telecommunications minister in 1957–1958, finance minister in 1962–1965, and international trade and industry minister in 1971–1972.

By political maneuvering and extensive use of money, Tanaka built up the LDP's largest faction and, in July 1972, beat **Fukuda Takeo** for the post of president and thereafter became prime minister, the youngest since the war. He served as prime minister from 7 July 1972 to 9 December 1974.

Initially Tanaka had considerable support because of his unorthodox background and status as a self-made man. His *Nihon Kaizōron* (*Plan for Remodeling the Japanese Archipelago*) was a design to utilize the benefits of economic growth to improve life for the Japanese, but it was shelved due to inflation and the oil shock of 1973.

Tanaka gained popular support when he stood up to the **United States** in trade talks and helped with the repatriation of **Okinawa**. His establishment of diplomatic relations with the People's Republic of **China** in 1972 was regarded as his major achievement. When Tanaka first became prime minister, he is said to have had the highest popularity rating of any new premier in Japanese history.

Tanaka's popularity declined and criticism of him increased due to his financial dealings inside and outside politics. In December 1974, he was forced to resign. He was arrested in July 1976 and charged with taking ¥500 million in bribes in what would be called the **Lockheed scandal**, which involved attempts to promote the sale of planes to Japan. Legal proceedings against Tanaka started in 1977 and ended in 1983 with his conviction for bribery and violation of the foreign exchange law. He was sentenced to four years in jail, but through political and legal means, he managed to avoid spending any time in jail. He remained in the Diet until 1989 when he resigned due to ill health. Tanaka was tainted by scandal, "money politics," and the charge of being the "LDP king-maker." His other powerful nicknames included "the Computerized Bulldozer," "Shōgun of the Dark," and "Shadow General."

A stroke and changing political opinion cost Tanaka his influence. His faction, the largest in the LDP, was taken over by **Takeshita Noboru**, who served as prime minister from 1987 to 1989. After Takeshita encountered political difficulties with the **Recruit scandal**, the Tanaka faction came to support **Hashimoto Ryūtarō**. Tanaka's daughter, Tanaka Makiko, was elected to his seat in 1993 and eventually became Japan's first female foreign minister under **Koizumi Jun'ichirō** in 2001–2002. Tanaka is the only modern Japanese prime minister who did not finish high school or graduate from a university. Yet he was a very powerful political figure in Japan. *See also* FOREIGN POLICY.

TANAKA KINUYO, 田中絹代 (1910–1977). Tanaka Kinuyo was a popular film **actress** and director, one of only a handful of **women** in Japan's film history to work in both capacities. She is better known for her work as an actress in a career that spanned 50 years. She worked with most of Japan's leading directors, but her most famous connection came from her long association with director **Mizoguchi Kenji**. She was popular through the war years, but some of her best and most popular performances were made after the war when she played such sympathetic roles as a downtrodden wife, a working woman, and a prostitute.

Tanaka directed her first film in 1953. The six films she directed, though generally undistinguished, show Mizoguchi's style with long, sweeping, panoramic shots and stately grace. She continued to act in the 1960s and

1970s. For her last film appearance, as an old prostitute, she won the *Kinema Jumpō* Prize for best actress, the Japanese **film** industry's highest award. Her long acting career is unmatched in Japan.

TANAKA MASAHIRO, 田中将大 **(1988–).** Tanaka Masahiro, born in Hyōgo Prefecture, led his high school team to the National High School **Baseball** Tournament championship in his junior year and runner-up berth in his senior year. He was the first-round pick of the Tōhoku Rakuten Golden Eagles in 2006.

Tanaka pitched seven seasons for the Golden Eagles and won 26 consecutive games from 2012 through 2013. He was 24–0 in 2013 with a 1.27 ERA and easily won the Eiji Sawamura Award, Japan's equivalent of the Cy Young Award. The New York Yankees signed Tanaka in 2014 to a seven-year, $155 million contract, and he responded with an impressive 6–0 start with his American team. After 13 starts with the Yankees, Tanaka was 10–1. Since joining the Yankees in 2014, Tanaka has a 52–28 record as of the end of the 2017 season.

TANGE KENZŌ, 丹下健三 **(1913–2005).** A pioneer in modern Japanese **architecture**, Tange Kenzō was born in the city of Imabari in Shikoku. He graduated from Tōkyō Imperial University in 1938. He became an assistant professor in 1946 and a professor in 1949. Early in his career he won recognition for his **Hiroshima** Peace Center (1949). Within the next decade, he established himself as a major architect by designing a series of impressive public buildings. An architect and city planner of international standing, Tange is known for his boldly shaped, distinctive buildings and urban complexes that show that functionalism does not demand a rigidly geometric style. He introduced a number of modern technological developments to architecture, notably the shell structure, and he is acclaimed for his conscious blending of modern expression with traditional Japanese aesthetics.

In the 1960s, Tange began designing his buildings in a more dramatic form. For the 1964 Tōkyō **Olympic** Games, Tange designed two dynamically paired structures that made up the Yoyogi National Gymnasium, a noted example of **steel** suspension roofing. Two other striking examples of his work from this period are the Yamanashi Press and Broadcasting Center and the theme pavilion for **Expo** '70 in **Ōsaka**. Tange's works have been expressive of the continual physical transformations that cities undergo. From 1960 on, Tange devoted himself increasingly to urban planning. He has also written widely on various aspects of architecture and its history in Japan. He has been a prime mover in international architectural circles. His approach to architecture, his spatial solutions, and his attention to materials and detail have influenced many younger architects.

Tange, Japan's most famous architect, designed the Tōkyō City Hall in Shinjuku, a great example of postmodernist architecture in Japan. This grand complex of buildings, rising high on the western side of Shinjuku, covers nearly 400,000 square meters. Tōkyō City Hall is called the New Tōkyō Metropolitan Government headquarters. Conspicuously situated among the high-rise buildings of Shinjuku's west side, its Tower I was the tallest structure in **Tōkyō** at 799 feet before the erection of Midtown Tower at 813 feet and Toranomon Hills at 838 feet.

Tange Kenzō had an immense influence on world architecture. His students read like a who's who of architecture including **Maki Fumihiko**, Kamiya Koji, **Isozaki Arata**, **Kurokawa Kishō**, and Oki Taneo. In 1987, Tange was the first Japanese to be awarded the Pritzker Prize, architecture's most coveted award. As the designer of many public buildings, Tange led the urban redevelopment of several downtown areas.

TANIGAKI SADAKAZU, 谷垣禎一 **(1945–).** Tanigaki Sadakazu was finance minister for three years in **Koizumi Jun'ichirō**'s **cabinet** and briefly minister of land, infrastructure, and transportation in 2008; on 28 September 2009, he was chosen president of the **Liberal Democratic Party** (LDP), replacing Prime Minister **Asō Tarō** after the LDP's resounding **election** defeat.

Tanigaki graduated from the **University of Tōkyō** in 1974 and passed the Japanese bar examination in 1979. His father, who represented the second district in **Kyōto**, died in 1983, and Sadakazu moved to Kyōto to run for his father's seat to which he himself would be elected nine times, with a change in configuration so he now represents the fifth district. A political and social moderate, Tanigaki is only the second LDP leader not to head a cabinet. *See also* POLITICAL PARTIES.

TANIZAKI JUN'ICHIRŌ, 谷崎潤一郎 **(1886–1965).** Tanizaki Jun'ichirō was one of Japan's greatest novelists. Born in the Nihonbashi district of **Tōkyō**, he grew up in a merchant family that experienced a decline in its fortune. He studied **literature** at Tōkyō Imperial University until family finances forced him to abandon his studies.

Tanizaki's first published work, a short story about a tattoo artist who inscribes a spider on the body of a beautiful young woman, appeared in 1910. A long list of highly acclaimed works followed. Tanizaki's key novels include *Tade kuu mushi* (*Some Prefer Nettles*, 1928–1929), which stresses the clash between traditional values and modern culture; *In'ei raisan* (*In Praise of Shadows*, 1933), in which he shows his nostalgic love of Japan's past; and *Sasameyuki* (*The Makioka Sisters*, 1943), which focuses on the decline of a wealthy family (which parallels traditional Japan's decline). Although the majority of Tanizaki's works appeared before the war, it is still legitimate to recognize him for his postwar literary accomplishments and awards.

In the postwar period, Tanizaki wrote, among other things, *Shōshō Shigemoto no haha* (*Captain Shigemoto's Mother*, 1949), a novel about a son's longing for his mother; *Kagi* (*The Key*, 1961), a psychological novel about old age and sexual desire; and *Fūten rōjin nikki* (*Diary of a Mad Old Man*, 1965), an account of the travails of an older man driven by obsessive erotic desires.

Tanizaki's writings focus on the dynamics of family life, Japanese society, tradition, and love, including destructive erotic escapades. A master storyteller, he had a strong interest in the plight of **women**. Urbanization, social change, naturalism, and sexual matters were all central themes in Tanizaki's writings. His works were uniquely Japanese. They showed a sensuous quality and occasionally even some sadomasochistic traits. Much of his writing shows men's obsessive sexual desire for women.

Japanese critics of his day regarded him as one of the best, if not the greatest, living Japanese writer. The Japanese government awarded him the Order of Culture, and the American Academy and Institute of Arts and Letters elected him to honorary membership, the first Japanese author so honored. He also won the Mainichi Publishing Culture Award and the Asahi Award. In 1965, the distinguished publishing company Chūō Kōronsha (Central Review) named what would become Japan's most highly recognized literary award after Tanizaki. Since 1965, the Tanizaki Prize has been awarded annually to one of Japan's most accomplished novelists. Although he never won it, many knowledgeable people believe that Tanizaki was deserving of the **Nobel Prize** in Literature.

TANKAN SURVEY, 短観. The **Bank of Japan** conducts a quarterly survey of **business** confidence called the Tankan Survey. It is the most comprehensive and influential measure of business confidence in Japan. The survey samples more than 10,000 companies of a broad range of small, medium, and large enterprises across a wide spectrum of industries. The Tankan Survey provides an accurate picture of business trends in Japan, thus helping guide Japan's monetary policy. The government releases the report four times a year, in April, July, October, and December. The December 2015 report showed that the job market was the tightest since 1992. The April 2016 survey revealed business sentiment at its lowest in three years. The December 2016 and September 2017 reports showed modest improvement.

TATSUMI YOSHIHIRO, 辰巳ヨシヒロ (1935–2015). Tatsumi Yoshihiro was Japan's premier **manga** artist who developed an alternative comic style starting in the late 1950s. His works have been translated into many languages. Tatsumi received the Japan Cartoonist Association Award in 1972, the **Tezuka Osamu** Cultural Prize in 2009, and the Eisner award many times. His cartoons often show the darker side of life and helped establish the genre of adult comics and graphic novels. Eric Khoo directed a full-length animated film, *Tatsumi*, on his life in 2011. Tatsumi is best known in the **United States** for his memoir, *A Drifting Life*, translated into English in 2009. He was an innovator and influenced the works of young writers and illustrators. Tatsumi's works, often called *gekiga*, or dramatic pictures, dealt with subjects such as sex, violence, greed, and betrayal.

TECHNOLOGY. *See* SCIENCE AND TECHNOLOGY.

TELEVISION. Although Japan began experimenting with television broadcasting as early as 1939, it was not until 1951 that it started regular television broadcasting. By the 1960s, the culture of television was beginning to boom in Japan. In the next several decades, television would become a major force in the lives of virtually all Japanese. Today, according to a popular survey, about 95 percent of all Japanese watch some television daily.

Japan has six major national television stations, all located in **Tōkyō**, but there are also many regional outlets throughout the country. In addition to Tōkyō, there are a dozen other regional outlets, most being regional affiliates with the six national stations but also with their own local stations. In addition, there are nearly 80 local television stations spread throughout Japan.

The **Japan Broadcasting Corporation** (Nippon Hōsō Kyōkai, or NHK) is financed through fees charged to viewers. NHK, which uses the English pronunciation of its initials, is a public service broadcaster supported by the people. NHK began the first color broadcasting in 1960. It produced Japan's first digital satellite broadcast in 2000. It carries a wide variety of the usual TV programs including news and news analysis; **sports**, including the six **sumō** tournaments, high school **baseball** championships, the **Olympic** Games, and Japan's National Sports Festival; a wide variety of drama programs; documentaries such as *The Silk Road*; children's programs such as the popular *Okaasan to issho* (*Together with Mother*); weather reports, **music** programs such as *Minna no uta* (*Everyone Sings*), which has run since 1961; **educational** programs led by *Tensai Terebikun Max* (*Reproduction Television Little Max*); and emergency reports. As a public station, NHK attempts to be impartial and tries to avoid making political comments.

Nippon News Network (NNN) runs NTV, a conservative station affiliated with the **newspaper** *Yomiuri Shimbun*. It began broadcasting in 1952 as Japan's first commercial station. In 1960, it started broadcasting in color and, in 1987, added a cable news channel. NTV produces a steady diet of news, drama, variety, sports, animation, and special TV programs. NTV has a special connection with **Studio Ghibli** and **Miyazaki Hayao** to broadcast their motion pictures. In recent years, it has been plagued by bribery scandals over ratings and charges of staging news events.

Japan News Network, led by the Tōkyō Broadcasting System (TBS), was founded in 1951. Liberal to left wing in its slant, TBS was well known for its news program *Chikushi Tetsuya's News 23*, named after its main anchor in 1989. TBS's **game** show *Takeshi's Castle* was dubbed and rebroadcast in a dozen countries worldwide.

Fuji News Network (FNN) heads Fuji Television or Fuji TV. Fuji was founded in 1957 and began broadcasting in 1959. Linked with the **Fujisan-kei Communication Group**, it often espouses the views of the conservative newspaper *Sankei Shimbun*. Fuji Television is perhaps best known for its unusual headquarters building designed by **Tange Kenzō** in Tōkyō's Odaiba, its sponsorship and broadcasting of Formula One racing, its wide range of dramas, its *Iron Chef* cooking program, and its reality television programs. Japanese dramas (*dorama*) are usually most popular on Fuji TV and on TBS. Theme music provides identity for dramas and helps maintain viewer loyalty.

The All-Nippon News Network (ANN) heads tv asahi, a left-wing or liberal station affiliated with the newspaper *Asahi Shimbun*. Writing its name in lowercase letters, tv asahi started in 1957. It was established as a for-profit educational television station, an unusual operation. However, it has now become more of a regular commercial station. Kume Hiroshi, news anchor for nearly two decades, headed the popular news program called *News Station*. Programs showing World Cup football matches, international swimming competition, and popular late-night TV programs have raised the ratings of tv asahi from a typical fourth place standing to a sometime second place status. **Maki Fumihiko**, one of Japan's leading architects, designed the tv asahi headquarters, which is located in the Roppongi area of Tōkyō.

Finally, TV Tōkyō Network heads TV Tōkyō, a balanced, middle-of-the-road station, which focuses on economic news. TV Tōkyō began in 1964. It has ties to the newspaper *Nihon Keizai Shimbun*. TV Tōkyō is the smallest of the major networks and is known for its special attention to **anime**. Its week-ly variety shows and annual historical drama (*jidaigeki*) enhance its viewing numbers.

Television programs can be divided largely into variety shows, serial dramas, and news reports. A typical weekday television broadcast consists mainly of news programs from the early morning until about 9:00 a.m. During the rest of the morning and into the early afternoon, the stations target housewives with programs of interest to them. Television stations show reruns of dramas and information programs during the mid-afternoon. From 4:00 p.m. to 6:00 p.m. in the afternoon, the stations show children's programs and popular anime. News programs dominate the 6:00 p.m. to 7:00 p.m. time slot. Prime time, or the "Golden Hour," is the period from 7:00 p.m. to 9:00 p.m. with stations presenting their top programs. Variety shows such as *Music Station* and *Utahan* (a music variety program) continue to enjoy great popularity. After 9:00 p.m., television stations run dramas and programs for older age groups. Television dramas and series generally consist of a 13-week series about popular topics. Japanese game shows are not only popular in Japan but also have an international appeal.

Popular TV programs include *KFA Music Fair*, *FNS Music Festival*, *Panel Quiz Attack 25*, *Downtown no Gaki no Tsukai ya Arahende!!*, *Sasuke*, **Doraemon**, *Nintama Rantarō*, *Ojarumaru*, *Music Station*, *Super Sentai*, *Utaban*, *Kimba the White Lion*, and many others. Much of Japanese television is driven by ratings, which are conducted on a weekly basis.

However, Japanese television is on the decline as young people do not watch as much television. Its programs are filled with cooking shows accompanied by lots of innocuous banter, variety shows with lots of celebrities, rather dull programs with talking heads. Baseball, sumō, and anime fill the time slots. *Tarento* (celebrities) occupy endless hours. *See also* SONY CORPORATION (SONĪ KABUSHIKI-GAISHA, ソニー株式会社).

TEXTBOOK CONTROVERSY. In Japan, the Ministry of Education approves a limited number of textbooks. Schools are then free to choose from this limited offering. The manner in which Japanese textbooks present the interpretation of Japan's war with **China** has been controversial abroad and even at home. On 26 July 1982, China first protested the wording of Japanese textbooks that appeared to play down Japanese aggression in World War II. The two countries reached an agreement on 9 September 1982 on the issue. On 28–30 July 1986, **South Korea** and China demanded apologies for revisions in Japanese textbooks. The historian **Ienaga Saburō** led the struggle to make the textbooks reflect the reality of wartime events.

Tsukuru-kai is a conservative group that seeks to "correct" Japanese textbooks, particularly as they present the "facts" of World War II. Tsukuru-kai, founded in 1997, argues that left--wing educators prepared school manuals in order to denigrate Japan and wrote materials that frequently echoed the opinion of Koreans and Chinese about Japanese war crimes and colonialism. In 2001, its manual of history passed the control of a commission and was published by Fusōsha. The "revised" textbook provoked a large protest in China and Korea as well as in Japan. The Tsukuru-kai text, known as *Atarashii rekishi kyōkashō* (*New History Textbook*, 2001), is said to glorify Japan's history, sanction the **imperial system**, and downplay Japan's aggressive war of imperialism. It lacks sensitivity, is politically naive, has many factual errors, and distorts other historical facts. Fortunately, only special schools in **Tōkyō** and Ehime Prefectures adopted the maligned text. The textbook controversy clouds Japan's **foreign policy** with its leading neighbors.

TEZUKA OSAMU, 手塚治虫 **(1928–1989).** Tezuka Osamu is Japan's, and perhaps the world's, most outstanding cartoonist. Tezuka grew up in Takarazuka, the hometown of the famous all-women **theater**. He studied to become a physician, but his first love was cartoons. He produced more than 150,000 pages of story cartoons, including *Tetsuwan Atomu* (*Astro Boy*, 1951–1968), and became the pioneer of postwar Japanese **manga** and created a revolution in **anime**.

Tezuka created his first manga in 1948 while a student at Ōsaka University. Four years later he published *Jungle Emperor* or *Jungle Taitei* (also known as *Kimba the White Lion*) in *Manga-shōnen*. Tezuka's most famous cartoon was *Astro Boy*. The first-ever Japanese animated series, it is action packed and full of interesting characters. It became a classic **television** series in the mid-1960s.

In 1982, Tezuka established his own animation studio, which he named Mushi (Beetle) Production. This studio became very professional and quite gifted. Many people regard Tezuka as the force behind the postwar explosion of comics in Japan. He has been called "the most influential animator in Japan" because his career parallels the rise of the Japanese animation industry.

THEATER. Japan has a rich array of theater styles starting with the classical **Noh** presentation. Rich in tradition and symbolism, Noh is slow moving and highly stylized. Most postwar Japanese are not attracted to this form of theater. **Bunraku** is a highly sophisticated form of puppetry that originated in the 17th century and typically treats conflicts between social obligations and human emotions. **Kabuki** flourished from the late 17th through the mid-19th centuries within the emerging urban culture. Highly stimulating and filled with beautiful, colored costumes, lively dance and action, provocative music, and verbal interplay, Kabuki still maintains a strong following.

Modern Japanese theater grew on the base of these earlier theater styles. Seeking a realistic presentation of themes, modern Japanese theater started in the 1890s. In the early 20th century, Japan experienced a "new theater" or *shingeki*. In the postwar period, *shingeki* led to experimental and avant-garde plays. Western **playwrights** were translated into Japanese, and Western materials came to dominate.

Postwar Japanese theater saw an extensive growth in new creative dramatic presentations. While building on the traditional base, today's Japanese theater reveals greater complexity, more complicated plots, and an international flavor. Avant-garde concepts abound and bring a strong critical aspect to the Japanese stage.

Recognized playwrights of the 1980s include Kara Jūrō (1940–), a leader in the avant-garde theater movement; Shimizu Kunio (1936–), who was also a professor of theater; Betsuyaku Minoru (1937–), a promoter of the "nonsense" theater; and Murai Shimako (1928–2018), a person strongly influenced by the bombing of **Hiroshima**. They helped promote a resurgence of modern Japanese theater. Some of their works found roots in classical Noh and Kabuki theater while other artists leaned heavily on Western influences.

Hirata Oriza (1962–) enjoys great renown across the country's theater scene, particularly for his works in original Japanese. Amateur theatrical groups flourish and bring a new twist to Japanese theater. Nylon 100, Gekidan Shinkansen, Tōkyō Sunshine Boys, and Halaholo Shangrila are some of the popular theatrical troupes. Leading artists include Okada Toshiki (1973–), known for his colloquial style and unique dances; Maeda Shirō (1977–), screenwriter and director for several films and drama series; Tanino Kurō (1976–), with his highly surrealistic plays; Miura Daisuke (1975–), known for his directing and music; and Maekawa Tomohiro (1974–), with his imaginative plays featuring aliens, the future, parallel realities, and occult powers.

THREE NONNUCLEAR PRINCIPLES. In 1967, Prime Minister **Satō Eisaku** formulated the three nonnuclear principles: that Japan will not possess, use, or allow nuclear weapons within its country. Such principles became one of the bedrocks of Japan's **defense** and **foreign policies**. *See also* JAPAN CONGRESS AGAINST ATOMIC AND HYDROGEN BOMBS (GENSUIKIN, 原水禁).

TŌHOKU EARTHQUAKE. *See* GREAT EAST JAPAN EARTHQUAKE (*HIGASHI NIHON DAISHINSAI*, 東日本大震災).

TŌKAIMURA ACCIDENT (*TŌKAIMURA JIHEN*, 東海村事変). Tōkaimura has a uranium processing plant 90 miles northeast of **Tōkyō**. On 30 September 1999, the plant had an incident that killed two workers and exposed hundreds of people to radiation. The Tōkaimura accident is the third most serious **nuclear power** accident in the late 20th century, after the 1986 Chernobyl accident and the 1979 Three Mile Island accident. Unlike these other cases, the Tōkaimura accident did not involve a nuclear power station but a nuclear fuel factory where no nuclear chain reaction should ever happen, yet due to gross negligence it did. Since there was no mechanical system to interrupt the reaction, it was sustained for nearly 20 hours. For several days, the ventilation system in the factory was left running, blowing contaminated air from the inside of the building into the surrounding village.

The accident happened when workers preparing nuclear fuels mixed uranium oxide with nitric acid using a stainless-**steel** container instead of a mixing apparatus. This shortcut was described in an illegal operating manual drafted by the company. The manual had never been approved by the supervising ministry, as was legally required. The procedure violated some of the most basic safety requirements that were well known in the nuclear industry since the early 1940s.

The company did not have any emergency plans in place for handling such critical accidents. The **Science and Technology** Agency later revoked the operating license of the plant owner. Families living near the plant were temporarily evacuated, and 300,000 people were asked to stay indoors for a day. Authorities tested neighbors and employees for radioactive contamination, identifying 63 people as having been exposed. *See also* ENERGY.

TŌKYŌ, 東京. Tōkyō is Japan's largest, most dynamic city. Huge in size, it incorporates 23 wards, 26 smaller cities, seven towns, and eight villages. From east to west, the city covers 55 miles, and from north to south, it is 15 miles. In the larger metropolitan area made up of nearly 38 million people, the average person's daily commute is one hour each way. It is the world's largest metropolitan area.

Originally Tōkyō was known as Edo, a fishing village. In 1457, Ōta Dōkan built a small castle there. In the early 17th century, Tokugawa Ieyasu established his military capital there and constructed a large, impressive castle to house his shogunal regime. The Tokugawa administration expanded the city dramatically, making it, with 1.3 million people, probably the largest city in the world in the late 18th century. The shogunal officials and the leading military lords lived in the *Yamanote* or upland area, and the artisans, merchants, and workers lived in the lowland area or *Shitamachi*. There are still some distinctions today between the "high" and "low" city.

In 1869 during Japan's great transformation of the Meiji period, Edo was renamed Tōkyō, "eastern capital," and it became the engine of economic modernization. During the second half of the 19th century, Tōkyō quickly embraced Western technology and ways and dramatically changed to a modern metropolitan area.

In the first half of the 20th century, Tōkyō suffered two catastrophic disasters with the 1923 Great Kantō Earthquake and the firebombings of World War II. Both destroyed a major part of the city and killed more than 100,000 people each. Yet both times Tōkyō recovered and experienced a dramatic rebirth.

Tōkyō serves as the capital of the country in every conceivable way. It is the political capital as the center of the national government with all three branches of government as well as most of its agencies and foreign embassies centered there. It is the capital with about nine million people (7 percent of Japan's 126 million people) in the central Tōkyō district, nearly 13 million people (10 percent) in Tōkyō Prefecture itself, and 38 million (27 percent) in the greater metropolitan region, making the Tōkyō region the world's most populous metropolitan area.

Tōkyō is also the economic capital of Japan. Its state-of-the-art financial centers move billions of dollars around the globe electronically. Tōkyō is the home to 51 Global 500 companies, nearly twice that of Paris at 25, and more than double London at 22, Beijing at 21, and New York at 20. Japan's capital also has many mammoth **department stores** that are modern merchandizing meccas.

Tōkyō's **economy** boomed through the late 1980s, and land prices reached dizzying heights. However, in 1991, the economic bubble burst, and the overinflated land prices helped trigger an economic crisis.

In the intervening years, Tōkyō has made significant strides toward recovery. Along with New York and London, Tōkyō is considered one of the world's major financial centers. It has the largest metropolitan economy in the world. It has one of the world's largest groups of investment **banks**, **securities companies**, insurance companies, and collective GDP rankings. The **Tōkyō Stock Exchange** is the world's second largest ranked by market capitalization and fourth largest ranked by share turnover. Tōkyō is one of the world's most expensive cities but is ranked as being very livable by the Michelin Guide. It ranks near the top of the world's cities in nearly every measure of urban vitality.

Tōkyō is the academic capital of Japan with 17 national universities, 127 private universities, and 59 junior colleges. The most prestigious are the **University of Tōkyō**, Tōkyō Institute of Technology, Waseda University, and Keiō University. Famous schools with international study programs include International Christian University, Sophia University, Temple University Japan, and Waseda. Tōkyō is also the home of numerous research institutes.

Not surprisingly, Tōkyō is the cultural capital of Japan. It is home to many art, **architecture**, **theater**, **film**, **music**, entertainment, pop culture, and **sports** centers as well as the Imperial Palace. Tōkyō hosted the 1964 **Olympics**, the first ever held in Asia. Tōkyō plays host to every imaginable type of international cultural event and entertainment. In 2020, it will again host the Summer Olympics.

Tōkyō has literally hundreds of museums. They range from the large famous ones like the Tōkyō National Museum, the National Museum of Western Art, and the Museum of Contemporary Art, all located in the Ueno section of Tōkyō, to historical museums like the Edo-Tōkyō Museum and the Fukagawa Edo Museum. There are many special museums like the Japan Folk Crafts Museum, the Takagi Bonsai Museum, the Kite Museum of Tōkyō, and the Miraikan (Future Science Museum). Less well known but interesting are the sports museums like the Tōkyō Sumō Museum, the Prince Chichibu Memorial Sports Museum, and the Toyota History Garage. Even slightly bizarre are a ramen museum (technically in **Yokohama**) and a parasite museum.

Tōkyō's network of rivers, canals, and other waterways, although barely visible today, once linked the city together. Nowadays, most of these are hidden underground, giving way to the vast network of roads, train lines, and subways, as well as the seemingly always active **construction** sites for Tōkyō's huge modern buildings. Spreading out across the Kantō Plain, Tōkyō retains some of its Edo layout. The large green area in the middle of the city is the site of the former castle and now the Imperial Palace. Surrounding the castle is the moat and, farther out, remnants of another moat. The oblong Yamanote Railway Line loops the city and corrals the major part of Tōkyō government, **business**, entertainment, and shopping areas.

Although having relatively few historically significant buildings, Tōkyō is home to many skyscrapers, defined as buildings that are at least 590 feet tall. Tōkyō's first modern skyscraper, completed in 1968, was the Kasumigaseki Building at 512 feet. The Midtown Tower, completed in 2007, stretches 814 feet into the sky. The Tōkyō Metropolitan Government Building, the NTT DoCoMo Yoyogi Building, the Sunshine 60 Building, and the Roppongi Hills Mori Tower round out the top five, all more than 780 feet. All told, Tōkyō presently has 46 skyscrapers. The **Tōkyō Skytree** is the world's tallest tower, rising to 2,080 feet.

Tōkyō is a world leader in public transportation. The three major forms of public transportation are trains, subways, and buses. The first two are the quickest and most reliable since they run on a precise timetable and are not slowed by surface transportation. With heavy traffic, streets and even express highways can come to a virtual standstill. Tōkyō's subways and commuter railway systems are among the busiest in the world. Being the center for national trains and suburban railways allows for a heavy concentration of people near the center of Tōkyō and thus contributes to its high population density.

On a national level, many of Japan's major **railways** pass through Tōkyō or have it as their originating point, including the high-speed **Bullet Train**. Airplane flights, buses, and ferries all carry people to their desired destination in or near the city as well as to places in Japan and abroad. One should not forget the plethora of **automobiles** that plug the streets of Tōkyō. All in all, Tōkyō does a remarkable job of daily moving several million people through the city with speed and efficiency.

For anyone interested in logistics, the movement of goods and services, the disposal of waste materials, and landfill developments, Tōkyō is a fascinating place to study. In social organization, the city opens many avenues for exploration. Even its festivals, Sanno at Hie Shrine, Sanja at Asakusa Shrine, and the Kanda Festival, to mention only a few, offer a major avenue for exploration of the city's culture and traditions.

Not a particularly attractive city, some people see Tōkyō as a huge cluster of unimaginative concrete structures with people and buildings closely crowded together. With a crush of people, the sidewalks are packed, the subways and trains jammed, and the streets clogged with cars and buses. Even the air is filled with noise and pollution. However, this possible negative impression is quickly offset when one experiences the alluring quality, the energy and vitality of the city, and the importance of Tōkyō in Japan's everyday life.

Recent development projects have sprouted all over Tōkyō. Revitalization efforts at Ebisu Garden Place, Tennōzu Isle, Shiodome, Roppongi Hills, Shinagawa, and the Marunouchi side of Tōkyō Station have brought new life to formerly rundown places. Odaiba, also known as Tōkyō Teleport Town, is built on a man-made island and offers the most modern in architecture, transportation, and commercial, residential, and leisure areas.

Tōkyō has a gigantic collection of people but with a small-town, local community atmosphere. It is made up of numerous small towns and neighborhoods grouped together with each having its own atmosphere, customs and historic places, winding streets, restaurants and bars, small shops, shrines and temples, schools, festivals and celebrations, and other distinct markings.

For all its excitement and allure, Tōkyō is one of the safest cities in the world. It has the lowest murder and robbery rates of any major city in the world. One can walk virtually anywhere in the city, day or night, without fear.

In order to absorb the flavor of Tōkyō, one can stroll through the old Asakusa district; take in an auction at the **Tsukiji Fish Market**; see the latest in electronics at Akihabara; view the city from Tōkyō Tower or any of the high-rise buildings in Shinjuku; visit any one of Tōkyō's numerous museums; watch a **sumō** tournament; shop at the huge department stores, boutiques, small shops, or the many flea markets; watch the young people in Harajuku on Sunday; be carried away by a **Kabuki** play; go nightclubbing in Roppongi; or eat at one of Japan's 5-Star restaurants or its smallest *yakitori* stands. *See also* HANEDA AIRPORT (HANEDA KŪKŌ, 羽田空港); ISHIHARA SHINTARŌ, 石原慎太郎 (1932–); MINOBE RYŌKICHI, 美濃部亮吉 (1904–1984); NARITA INTERNATIONAL AIRPORT (NARITA KOKUSAI KŪKŌ, 成田国際空港); SUZUKI SHUN'ICHI, 鈴木俊一 (1910–2010); TŌKYŌ DISNEYLAND (TŌKYŌ DEISUNII LANDO, 東京ディズニーランド).

TŌKYŌ DISNEYLAND (TŌKYŌ DEISUNII LANDO, 東京ディズ ニーランド). Tōkyō Disneyland opened in 1983 in Chiba Prefecture near **Tōkyō.** This was the first Disney Park outside the **United States** that the Walt Disney Company created, although it does not own the park. Along with the classic Disney theme parks of Adventureland, Westernland, Fantasyland, and Tomorrowland, Tōkyō Disneyland also includes the World Bazaar, Critter Country, and Mickey's Toontown. Tōkyō Disneyland has been the single-most-visited theme park in the world. Tōkyō Disneyland has a distinctly American flair to it. With the exception of the use of Japanese, the park is the same as one would find in the United States.

TŌKYŌ ELECTRIC POWER COMPANY (TŌKYŌ DENRYOKU KABUSHIKI-GAISHA, 東京電力株式会社). Tōkyō Electric Power Company, or TEPCO as it is better known, is one of the world's largest electric utilities, supplying electricity to more than 25 million customers in the Kantō region. Established in 1883, it took its present name in 1951. Approximately 56 percent of its power comes from thermoelectricity, 30 percent from nuclear plants, and 14 percent from hydroelectric plants. TEPCO is also involved in generating electric power in several other Asian locations.

Kikawada Kazutaka (1899–1977) was a **business** leader from Fukushima Prefecture who graduated from Tōkyō Imperial University. He devoted himself to obtaining private ownership of the electric power industry in cooperation with nine regional companies under the leadership of Matsunaga Yasuzaemon. He became director of TEPCO in 1951 and president in 1961. Kikawada became chairman of the **Japan Association of Corporate Executives** in 1963. He also served as chairman of the Economic Council, an advisory organ of the **Economic Planning Agency**, during 1966–1977.

In 2002, TEPCO was forced to close its nuclear reactor plants due to shoddy inspection reports. Its then president, Minami Nobuya, was forced to resign. TEPCO cleaned up its operations and restarted the nuclear plants in 2005. In 2008, the effects of an earthquake caused TEPCO to close another nuclear plant.

Following the **Great East Japan Earthquake** of March 2011, TEPCO's plant at Fukushima Daiichi became one of the world's most serious nuclear disasters. TEPCO faced $24 billion in losses and strict government oversight. With 50,000 households forced to evacuate and air, soil, and water damages, the power company faced a disastrous situation. In July 2012, TEPCO received nearly $78 billion from the government to help clean up the damage, and the company became partially nationalized.

As of 2015, TEPCO had more than 38,000 employees and an annual income of around $53 billion. It is under the leadership of President Hirose Naomi. TEPCO is Japan's largest electric utility and the world's fourth-largest electric company. *See also* ENERGY.

TŌKYŌ SKYTREE, 東京スカイツリー. Tōkyō Skytree is a futuristic tower, housing **television** and radio broadcasting stations, restaurants, and an observation deck. Located in the Sumida district of **Tōkyō**, it is recognized as the world's tallest tower at 2,080 feet. It is the second-tallest structure in the world after the Burj Khalifa in Dubai. Tōbu Railway Company and several broadcasting stations led by **NHK** underwrote the large commercial development. Nikken Sekkei designed the tower to be earthquake resistant. The exterior lattice has a paint that reflects light and, through the use of LED panels, presents a spectacular illumination. Eight TV channels broadcast from this tower. Completed in February 2012, the tower opened to the public in May 2012. The Tōkyō Skytree makes the statement that Japan and its centerpiece, Tōkyō, intends to remain competitive as other Asian cities grow and reach for the stars.

TŌKYŌ STOCK EXCHANGE (TŌKYŌ SHŌKEN TORIHIKIJO, 東京証券取引所**).** The Tōkyō Stock Exchange (TSE) was first established in 1878 under the leadership of Finance Minister Ōkuma Shigenobu and entrepreneur Shibusawa Eiichi. It reopened in 1949, pursuant to a new Securities Exchange Act. In 1982, it accepted foreign firms. In 1999, it switched to electronic trading for all transactions.

Although Japan has five stock exchanges, the TSE is by far the largest. On an average day, 1.5 billion shares exchange hands. Most of the more than 2,292 companies are domestic, but some 30 are foreign-based companies. The main indexes tracking the TSE are the **Nikkei 225**, a stock market index of companies selected by the *Nihon Keizai Shimbun*, and the Tōkyō Stock Price Index, commonly called TOPIX, an index based on share prices of major companies. TSE is the world's second-largest stock exchange.

In 2013, the Tōkyō Stock Exchange merged with the **Ōsaka** Stock Exchange making it even stronger. It is now known as the Japan Exchange Group (JPX).

As of 2015, TSE listed 2,292 companies with a market value of more than $4.1 trillion, which makes it the largest in Asia and the third largest in the world. Saitō Atsushi serves as president and CEO while Nishimuro Taizō acts as chairman. (Refer to appendix G.) *See also* SECURITIES COMPANIES.

TŌKYŌITES FIRST PARTY (TŌMIN FIRST NO KAI, 都民ファーストの会**).** **Tōkyō** governor **Koike Yuriko** and her newly formed Tōkyōites First Party, a regional party, won an overwhelming victory in the 2 July 2017 Metropolitan **election**. Her party won 49 of the 127 assembly seats, far more than the **Liberal Democratic Party** (LDP), which managed only 23 seats. Together with the **Kōmeitō**, they controlled 79 of the 127 seats.

The Tōkyōites First Party, citing the LDP as an antireform "old boys' club," campaigned on a reformist agenda with a focus on open government and cost cutting. These measures struck a responsive chord with the people of the capital city.

On one level, the election showed great approval of Governor Koike and, on another level, the severe dissatisfaction with the LDP's "arrogance" during the recent past. Koike has served as **environment** minister and **defense** minister in the **cabinet**. She has tackled problems such as overspending for the **2020 Summer Olympics**, a scandal over the relocation of the **Tsukiji Fish Market**, and other citizens' problems.

TŌKYŪ CORPORATION (TŌKYŪ KYŪKŌ DENTETSU KABUSHI-KI--GAISHA, 東京急行電鉄株式会社**).** Tōkyū Corporation, the core member of the Tōkyū Group, is made up of some 360 companies, including Tōkyū Land Corporation, Tōkyū Hotel Chain, Tōkyū Department Stores, and **Japan Air System**. Incorporated as a local railway company in 1922, Tōkyū operates train and bus transportation routes in south-central Japan. Its railways carry nearly one billion passengers annually. It is also Japan's largest real estate developer. It operates 36 hotels in Japan as well as 18 internationally. With its headquarters in the Shibuya section of **Tōkyō**, Tōkyū operates seven heavily used local **railroads**. All told, it employs nearly 25,000 people. In 2017, the Tōkyū Corporation, under the leadership of President Koshimura Toshiaki, had a net income of around $900 million.

TOMITA ISAO, 冨田勲 **(1932–2016).** Tomita Isao was a pioneer in synthesizer **music** and helped spread electronic music in Japan after importing a Moog III synthesizer in 1971, when the instruments were expensive and rarely used. He was a major influence on the nation's other noted electronic music pioneers, including **Sakamoto Ryūichi** of the techno-pop group Yellow Magic Orchestra. With the use of the synthesizer, Tomita composed the score for **Tezuka Osamu**'s **anime** *Kimba the White Lion* and the **NHK** drama *Hana no Shōgai*. With his album *Snowflakes Are Dancing*, Tomita was the first Japanese nominated for a Grammy Award. In 2014, the American film *Heaven Knows What* used four of his tracks: "Clair de Lune," "Gardens in the Rain," "The Engulfed Cathedral," and "Snowflakes Are Dancing."

TOSHIBA CORPORATION (KABUSHIKI-GAISHA TŌSHIBA, 株式会社東芝**).** The Toshiba Corporation, or Toshiba Group of Japan, is one of Japan's leading electronics *keiretsu*. Toshiba is a famous manufacturer of electric machinery, home appliances, industrial electronic products, and telecommunications equipment.

One of Japan's first electronics companies, the **Tōkyō Electric Power Company** and the Shibaura Electric Company combined in the late 1930s to form Toshiba, the nickname of the future company. Toshiba established itself in Japan before attempting to move abroad. Its goal was to produce inexpensive, efficient goods through technological advancement and control of the Japanese market.

In 1978, Toshiba introduced the world's first computerized compressor unit. This did much to propel Toshiba into world leadership in the air conditioning markets. Today, Toshiba is one of Japan's largest industrial electronics companies. It is a major producer of personal computers, communication systems, consumer goods, and electronic devices. Toshiba introduced the SmartMedia and Secure Digital Memory Card, both popular as memory media for digital devices.

In 2015, Toshiba undertook a variety of reforms. It faced a serious accounting scandal but made efforts to correct the situation. Toshiba, struggling to stay afloat, sold off a chunk of its memory chip business. The deal was controversial. The company wanted to avoid a negative net worth. President Tsunakawa Satoshi, appointed CEO in May 2016, denied that the company was in major financial trouble.

Today, Toshiba has four main groupings: the Digital Products Group, the Electronic Devices Group, the Home Appliances Group, and the Social Infrastructure Group. It is listed on the **Tōkyō Stock Exchange** and is a factor in the **Nikkei 225**. In February 2017, Toshiba revealed unaudited details of a $3.4 billion corporate-wide loss, mainly arising from its **United States**–based Westinghouse nuclear construction subsidiary. However, Toshiba is still the seventh-largest semiconductor manufacturer in the world. In 2016, it had total assets of $48 billion with sales of $50 billion and employed nearly 188,000 people.

In January 2017, Toshiba announced an investment of $10 billion in new plant construction in the United States. This is a nod toward pressure from President Donald Trump. As of July 2017, Toshiba, the technology conglomerate, continues to struggle over the sale of its $18 billion microchip business. It needs to sell the business to keep the company's finances from unraveling. The legal wrangling remains complicated.

TOURISM. Tourism has become an important part of Japan's **economy** and its outreach to the world. While the Tokugawa shogun forcing the local domain lords periodically to go to Edo, later known as **Tōkyō**, cannot really be considered tourism, it did introduce a small segment of Japanese leaders to the world outside their own locality. Later in the 19th century, the Meiji government encouraged tourism by building **railroads**, opening an agency to promote tourism, and passing a bill to promote the **construction** of hotels. However, it was only in the postwar period that tourism began to flourish in Japan. (Refer to appendix T.)

During the **Occupation**, it was not until 1950 that a few Japanese businessmen were allowed to travel abroad. In the early 1950s, Japan began to invest substantially in the promotion of a tourist infrastructure by building hotels and developing airlines. In 1947, both Northwest Airlines and Pan American opened flights to Japan. In 1954, **Japan Airlines** began service to San Francisco.

In 1912, the Japanese government, together with private initiatives, founded the **Japan Travel Bureau** (JTB) to promote and facilitate travelers visiting Japan. Today, JTB Global Marketing & Travel, a spinoff of that organization, is the leader in the Japanese tourist industry. In 1948, a commercial firm established Nihon Tourist, which would become Kinki Nippon Tourist, and another group formed the Hankyū Tourist Company.

The Japan National Tourism Organization (JNTO), established in 1964 as a Japanese government-affiliated corporation, is the major government promoter of tourism abroad. It maintains 13 offices in key cities around the world, which conduct a wide range of tourism promotions designed to get people to visit Japan. In 2003, JNTO launched a Visit Japan Campaign and has 113 offices throughout Japan to help travelers. It sponsors a Goodwill Guide Program with more than 47,000 volunteers and 1,550 bilingual guides to assist travelers.

The Tōkyō **Olympics** of 1964 stimulated travel to Japan and showcased Japan's reemergence into international society. Prior to the Tōkyō Olympics, travel abroad for Japanese was quite restricted, but with the Olympics the government loosened its foreign travel bans.

Today, tourism is an important part of the Japanese economy and a leading way to build better international relations. Tourism includes both domestic and international travel for Japanese, as well as foreign guests visiting Japan.

Within Japan, schools make travel a small but important part of their curriculum. Most schools hold an annual field trip to a local site such as **Tōkyō Disneyland** or some historical or cultural landmark. Some high schools travel as far as **Okinawa** or Hokkaidō. A few schools even travel abroad. Japan's extensive network of railroads and its frequent air flights make travel in Japan quick and relatively inexpensive.

Tōkyō is obviously the place that most people visit. In 2006, nearly five million foreigners visited Japan's capital. Government estimates suggest that this brought nearly ¥10 trillion to the city's economy. The second most popular destination is **Kyōto**, followed by Nara, **Ōsaka**, and **Hiroshima**.

In 2016, 24 million international travelers visited Japan. Japan is one of the world's popular tourist destination and the top place to visit in Asia. It scored especially high as being a healthy place, a safe destination, and rich in cultural resources. Tourism is a vital part of Japan's economy. Most of Japan's tourists come from East Asia. More than six million Chinese, five million South Koreans, and four million Taiwanese visitors came to Japan in 2016. More than one million Americans visited Japan that year.

Although much smaller in population, Japan ranks just behind **China** in the number of outbound travelers with more than 17 million Japanese traveling abroad in 2013. Of that number, 3.7 million traveled to the **United States**, the most popular destination. China, **South Korea**, **Taiwan**, Hong Kong, and Europe are the other places attracting a lot of Japanese tourists.

In 2008, more than eight million foreigners visited Japan, but almost twice as many Japanese traveled abroad. Thus, Japan experienced a negative balance of payments in the tourist industry. China, with more than a million visitors to Japan, accounted for the largest number of tourists, followed by South Korea and Taiwan. The countries sending visitors to Japan parallel that of Japanese traveling abroad, but international visitors to Japan number only about half those of Japanese going abroad.

According to the World Tourism Organization, Tōkyō Disneyland is one of the world's top 10 attractions with 12.9 million visitors a year. Festivals, hot springs baths, technology fairs, ninja classes, and **manga** museums are some of the attractions for foreigners. Indeed, the Japan of today is more than beautiful scenery, coy geishas, and the ephemeral cherry blossoms. *See also* FOREIGN POLICY.

TOYODA EIJI, 豊田英二 (1913–2013). Although it is spelled Toyoda, this name is pronounced Toyota. Toyoda Eiji was the son of Toyoda Keiichi and a successor in the **Toyota Motor Corporation**. He helped develop the Toyota auto industry. Born in Aichi Prefecture, he was a 1936 graduate of Tōkyō Imperial University. He spent three months at Ford in Detroit studying production techniques. He was sometimes identified as Japan's Henry Ford. In 1967, he became president of Toyota Motor Company. Branching into real estate, he also headed the Towa Real Estate Development Company. Although it was his cousin, Toyoda Kiichirō, who founded the **automobile** plant in the 1930s, it is Toyoda Eiji who was largely credited with its success. David Cole, former chairman of the Center for Automotive Research, called Toyoda "a real visionary and inspirational leader who understood what it would take to make Toyota a successful company."

TOYOTA GROUP (TOYOTA GURŪPU, トヨタグループ). The **Toyota Motor Corporation** is a major part of the Toyota Group, the leading Japanese automotive *keiretsu*. One of the largest companies in the world and the single largest firm in Japan, its annual sales are approximately $72 billion. It employs some 340,000 workers. Toyota's total value is said to be more than

$200 billion. While it is primarily involved in the automotive industry, producing nearly 17 million units in 2015, the Toyota Group has major holdings in telecommunications, **computers**, aircraft, automobile insurance, real estate, finance, **energy**, biotechnology, and agriculture. In contrast with other *keiretsu*, the Toyota Group is not oriented around a bank. It controls many other companies in a pyramidal arrangement with most related to the **automobile** industry. There are close to 300 automotive supply companies in the Toyota Group. Toyoda Akio (1956–) became CEO of Toyota in 2009. *See also* TOYODA EIJI, 豊田英二 (1913–2013).

TOYOTA MOTOR CORPORATION (TOYOTA JIDŌSHA KABU-SHIKI-GAISHA, トヨタ自動車株式会社). In 2016, Toyota Motor Corporation and Volkswagen were virtually tied for the top spot as the world's largest automobile manufacturers. Each company produced just over 10 million vehicles. It is regularly one of *Fortune* magazine's top companies in the Global 500. Based on its high-quality technology, its prescience in promoting the hybrid car, its styling, and its marketing techniques, Toyota is one of Japan's, and indeed the world's, most respected companies.

Established in 1933, Toyota Motor Corporation took its present name in 1937. However, the company really did not take off until after the war when it introduced the Toyopet Crown. The Crown model became the company's flagship model. During the Korean War, Toyota profited by selling motor vehicles to the American forces.

Toyoda Kiichirō (1894–1952) founded the company, but his cousin **Toyoda Eiji** made the company a success. The Toyota Company began exporting autos in the early 1960s. In 1987, Toyota became the first Japanese company, and the fourth in the world, to pass the 60-million-unit production figure. As of 2016, Toyota has 53 overseas factories in 28 countries and sells vehicles in 170 countries. Toyota is one of the world's most profitable **automobile** manufacturers and has a top brand-name recognition in Japan and worldwide.

Toyota established the Toyota Motor Foundation in 1974 to promote research into the effects of technological change on society and foster relations between Japan and other countries, especially in Southeast Asia. Toyota is jointly headquartered in **Nagoya** and Toyota City.

Other Toyota leaders contributed to the success of the company. Ōno Taiichi (1912–1990), an engineer for Toyota, revolutionized the "just-in-time system" and helped rebuild Toyota. He became executive vice president of Toyota in 1975, and he retired in 1978 but remained as a consultant until 1982. Okuda Hiroshi (1932–) became president and then chairman of both Toyota Motor Corporation in 1999 and, later, of the **Japan Federation of Economic Organizations** (Keidanren), Japan's most powerful **business** organization. Okuda became the first non-Toyoda family member to head the corporation in 28 years. He showed creative and dramatic leadership while heading Toyota. Watanabe Katsuaki (1943–) replaced Okuda and was adept at setting a favorable international image for Toyota but encountered difficulties with the world recession. In January 2009, Toyota named Toyoda Akio (1956–), grandson of Toyoda Kiichirō, as its new president. He is fluent in English, having earned a master's degree in business administration in the **United States**. He has urged Toyota to focus on green technology, and the company does have a lead in the international sale of its Prius, the hybrid environmentally friendly car.

As of 2014, Toyota had 338,875 employees worldwide, and by 2016, it was the 13th-largest company in the world by revenue. It was the world's first automobile manufacturer to produce more than 10 million vehicles per year. As of 2014, Toyota was the largest listed company in Japan, more than twice the second-ranked **SoftBank**.

Toyota Motor Corporation has subsidiaries including Lexus, **Daihatsu**, Hino, Toyota Tsūshō, Toyota Financial Services, **Japan Airlines**, Fuji Heavy Industries, **KDDI**, and many others. It is part of the **Toyota Group**, one of the largest conglomerates in the world. Toyota Motor Corporation sells 70 different car models and is a leader in the manufacture of hybrid electric cars having sold 10 million as of January 2017. It has sold more than six million Prius cars alone. Like other automotive companies, Toyota has had its share of recalls to fix malfunctioning power windows and defective Takata air bags.

TRADE. International trade was, is, and will continue to be the lifeblood of the Japanese **economy**. Weak in natural resources but strong in capital development, **technology** skills, and entrepreneurial ability, Japan, within little more than a decade of its crushing defeat, regained its prewar level of trade standing. The people of Japan see themselves as a "processing nation" where they import raw materials and produce high-quality goods not only for domestic consumption but also for export. Indeed, Japan, one of the world's first export-oriented economies, has become an international trade powerhouse.

In the first two decades after the war, Japan improved its trade position through a series of government measures to provide tax relief and give assistance to leading export industries. The **Japan External Trade Organization** (JETRO) acted to assist smaller firms with overseas marketing and worked to give Japan trade advantages. The growth of Japanese exports in the 1960s and 1970s was phenomenal.

In the 1970s and 1980s, the Japanese government used policies to restrain exports in certain sectors of the economy. The government imposed various tariffs and quotas. This produced an international backlash and a series of trade disputes causing the **United States** and other countries to push for quotas or "voluntary" restraints of their own on such products as textiles, **steel**, **television** sets, and **automobiles**. Japan has provoked considerable trade controversies, some going as far as to produce the "Nixon shocks" dealing with trade and the SII legislation policing trade practices. However, these issues were decreased as Japan's 490 import items under quota in 1962 dropped to only 27 import items by the mid-1980s. Controversial quotas on beef and citrus fruits ended in 1991. Even rice, Japan's sacred food, which had long been protected by heavy tariffs, has become more open to imports. (Refer to appendixes I and J.)

In the 1990s, Japan's trade markets became even more open, but it is not unusual to still hear complaints of unfair trading. Today there still remain some unresolved trade disputes.

Japan's 6,000 **general trading companies**, at least the largest ones, are a driving force for international trade and have played a large role in promoting Japan's economic growth. They strengthen the ties of companies to their suppliers, assist in international marketing, orchestrate and direct major trade deals, and thus have expanded and made international trade a much larger feature in Japan.

The **Ministry of International Trade and Industry** (MITI) organized JETRO to promote Japan's economic growth and development and encourage exports and secure international trade information to assist businesses. In 2001, MITI later reorganized to become the **Ministry of Economy, Trade, and Industry**. Several other organizations promoted Japan's international trade interests. The **Japan Chamber of Commerce and Industry** worked to encourage trade internationally. The **Japan Federation of Economic Organizations** grouped most of Japan's leading **business** figures with politicians who promoted trade. The **Japan Business Federation**, the successor to the Japan Federation of Economic Organizations, represents companies, industrial associations, and regional employers' associations in an effort to accelerate the growth of Japan's international trade.

According to the **Ministry of Finance** (MOF), Japan's trade balance for fiscal year 2008 marked the first deficit in 28 years. This deficit was due to rises in commodity prices and slower exports to the United States and other major economies. The nation's trade deficit hit a negative $7.38 billion in fiscal 2008, according to the MOF. Japan last registered a trade deficit in 1980, when soaring crude oil prices skewed the balance. Japan uses its trade surpluses with the United States to pay for its trade deficits with OPEC.

The MOF reported Japan's 2008 exports at ¥81 trillion and its imports at ¥79 trillion, making a surplus of ¥2 trillion. By component, exports consisted of 24.8 percent transport equipment, 19.7 percent general machinery, 19 percent electrical machinery, 12.6 percent manufactured goods, 9 percent chemicals, and 15.1 percent other. Overall, Japan's exports were of high-value-added products such as motor vehicles, integrated circuits, and advanced technology products. On the import side, Japan's purchases consisted of 35 percent mineral fuels, 10.9 percent electrical machinery, 9.3 percent manufactured goods, 7.9 percent foodstuffs, 7.7 percent general machinery, 7.3 percent chemicals, 7 percent raw materials, 2.9 percent transport equipment, and 12 percent other. In imports, energy resources and raw materials dominated.

Areas or countries of Japan's exports in order of size were Asia (excluding China, ¥27 trillion), the United States (¥14,2 trillion), **China** (¥12.9 trillion), the European Union (¥11.4 trillion), and the Middle East (¥3.5 trillion), in total an export worldwide of ¥81 trillion. In imports, the leading countries or regions were the Middle East with ¥17,4 trillion, Asia (excluding China), ¥17.2 trillion, China (¥14.8 trillion), the United States (¥8 trillion), and the European Union (¥7.3 trillion), with total imports at ¥79 trillion.

Motor vehicles, semiconductors, and iron and steel topped Japan's 2008 export charts. The top three countries of export in motor vehicles were the United States (30.9 percent), **Russia** (9.5 percent), and Australia (5.8 percent). The top three in semiconductors were China (22.5 percent), **Taiwan** (13.6 percent), and Hong Kong (12.8 percent). In iron and steel, the Republic of **Korea** led the way with 21.2 percent, followed by China (18.9 percent) and Thailand (11 percent).

Petroleum was by far the major import, followed at a distance by clothing and nonferrous metals. Not surprisingly, Middle Eastern countries dominated the petroleum source with Saudi Arabia supplying 28.8 percent, the United Arab Emirates at 24.9 percent, Iran at 11.2 percent, Qatar at 10 percent, and Kuwait at 7.3 percent. China dominated clothing imports with 82.7 percent. Nonferrous metals came primarily from South Africa (21.8 percent), Russia (11.2 percent), Australia (9.5 percent), and China (8.7 percent).

The value of the yen directly affects the trade balance. In the spring of 1995, the yen reached a high of 79 to the US$1. Thereafter, the yen progressively weakened to about 145 to the US$1 in July 1998. Between 1999 and 2008, the yen hovered between 100 to 120 yen to the US$1, but in late 2008, it appreciated sharply to about 90 yen to the US$1. In June 2010, the yen stood at about 90 yen to the US$1. As of 31 January 2018, the US$1 equaled ¥109.

The increase in Japanese imports has been due to many factors. The general growth of the Japanese income and economy level has been a key factor. Increased dependence on imported raw materials, especially **energy** sources, has also been important. The relative low price of imports is another. Trade liberalization made the importing of goods easier. Finally, a favorable exchange rate played to Japan's advantage.

For the month of April 2010, the trade balance recorded a surplus of ¥8.25 billion. Exports surged 40.4 percent to ¥4.2 trillion, and imports fell 36.7 percent to ¥5.89 trillion. As of 2017, Japan's trade balance, while slipping, was still ¥2.99 trillion.

With the United States, Japan's trade surplus in April 2010 plunged 76.7 percent to ¥154 billion. Exports dropped 51.4 percent to ¥666 billion, and imports declined 27.6 percent to ¥511 billion. On 6 July 2009, the United States trade envoy's office issued a report saying that progress has been made in opening Japan's markets to foreign investors. Both countries seemed pleased with the recent developments.

In the first six months of 2009, China became Japan's largest trading partner. This is the first time that Japan's exports to China have surpassed those to the United States. In trade with China, Japan logged a deficit of ¥174.55 billion, against the year before deficit of ¥62.24 billion. Exports shrank 31.5 percent to ¥790 billion, and imports fell 20.7 percent to ¥965 billion. In 2016, Japan's trade deficit with China was about ¥1,951 billion.

Japan and South Korea agreed on 27 June 2009 to work more closely to weather the economic crisis that has affected not only their circumstances but also the world's economy. Japanese finance minister Yosano Kaoru said, "We have reached a joint understanding that to ride out the current economic and financial crisis, Japan and South Korea will cooperate in a variety of settings." Without doubt, international trade is a vital part of Japan's economy.

In 2016, the United States imported approximately $271 billion in goods and services from Japan while exporting $108 billion, making for a $163 billion deficit. The United States is Japan's largest trading partner while Japan is the fourth-largest trading partner of the United States.

Japan's top export destinations in order are the United States, China, and South Korea followed by other Asian countries. Its top countries of import origins are China, the United States, Australia, South Korea, and the United Arab Emirates.

According to the Economic Complexity Index, Japan is the world's fourth-largest export economy and the most complex one. It reports that in 2015, Japan imported $589 billion in materials and exported $670 billion in products, making for a $81 billion positive trade balance. *See also* FOREIGN POLICY; HASHIMOTO RYŪTARŌ, 橋本龍太郎 (1937–2006); IKEDA HAYATO, 池田勇人 (1899–1965); ISHIHARA TAKASHI, 石原隆 (1912–2003); ISHIZAKA TAIZŌ, 石坂泰三 (1886–1975); KŌMOTO TO-SHIO, 河本敏夫 (1911–2001); LABOR ORGANIZATIONS; MIKI TA-KEO, 三木武夫 (1907–1988); MINISTRY OF FOREIGN AFFAIRS (GAIMUSHŌ, 外務省); MIYAZAWA KIICHI, 宮澤喜一 (1919–2007);

SATŌ EISAKU, 佐藤榮作 (1901–1975); SECURITIES COMPANIES; TA-NAKA KAKUEI, 田中角栄 (1918–1993); UEMURA KŌGORŌ, 植村甲午郎 (1894–1978).

TREATY OF MUTUAL COOPERATION AND SECURITY BE-TWEEN THE UNITED STATES AND JAPAN (*NIPPON-KOKU TO AMERIKA-GASSHŪKOKU TO NO AIDA NO SŌGO KYŌRYOKU OYO-BI ANZEN HOSHŌ JŌYAKU,* 日本国とアメリカ合衆国との間の相互協力及び安全保障条約). The Treaty of Mutual Cooperation and Security between the United States and Japan, signed 19 January 1960 in Washington, superseded the **United States–Japan Security Treaty** of nearly a decade earlier.

This new treaty made both Japan and the **United States** responsible for the **defense** of Japan and its surrounding territory. It established a guarantee of mutual defense support should a military crisis arise. However, the treaty created an inherent conflict because, although it called for Japan to come to the aid of the United States, Japan could not legally maintain military forces. This became a source of later controversy. The treaty reiterated Japan's Article 9 "no-war" clause from the **constitution** but did not clarify the situation. The treaty did include a 10-year term after which the agreement could be revoked although this has never been applied.

Many Japanese objected to the proposed treaty and, led by members of the **Japan Socialist Party** and the **Japanese Communist Party** as well as pacifist opponents, mounted a strong opposition to the ratification of the treaty.

Pressured by the United States, Japan agreed to this revised treaty. Prime Minister **Kishi Nobusuke** pushed the treaty ratification through the **House of Representatives** on 19 May 1960 with the revised treaty going into effect on 19 June 1960. This treaty gave the United States a strong hand in Japan's **foreign policy** and extended its role in the Japanese **economy**. Some critics go so far as to argue that it made Japan a ward of the United States. The treaty provides the major military linkage between the two countries and today is the determining factor in Japan's U.S. relations.

TSUKIJI FISH MARKET. The Tsukiji wholesale market in central **Tōkyō** was scheduled to close on 2 November 2016 and to reopen in a new location a couple of kilometers away in Toyosu. However, **environmental** problems postponed the move until at least 2018. The Tsukiji Fish Market has been in constant use since its opening in 1935, and for many market regulars and outside observers alike, the place is inseparable from the buying and selling of fish and from the images of what constitutes an idealized market. The Tsukiji Fish Market is said to be "the world's largest fish market." It sells approximately 2,000 tons of seafood from around the world, estimated at several million dollars, every morning. The market, known for its high-quality marine life, is a cultural landmark in Japan.

TSUTSUMI YOSHIAKI, 堤義明 **(1934–).** Tsutsumi Yoshiaki was one of the world's richest people with a $16 billion net worth in 1990. His wealth was based on landholdings amassed by his grandfather, Tsutsumi Yasujirō, since the 1920s. Born in Shiga Prefecture, he graduated from Waseda University in 1957. He headed Kokudo Keikaku, a family holding company, and ran Seibu Railways, which is part of the larger **Seibu Saison Group.** His father built the chain of Prince Hotels. He is an active **sports** figure. He was instrumental in getting the 1998 **Olympics** to be held in Nagano, but he was accused of giving expensive gifts to influence this choice. He was president of the Japan Olympic Committee in 1989 but resigned due to pressure from environmentalists against building a new ski slope and **golf** course in Nagano.

In 2005, Tsutsumi was arrested on charges of violating the securities trading laws. Convicted, authorities gave him a suspended sentence, but he still remains an indirect major shareholder in Seibu. Today, his net worth is estimated at $1.2 billion.

2020 SUMMER OLYMPICS. *See* OLYMPICS, 2020 SUMMER (*DAI SANJŪNI-KAI ORINPIKKU KYŌGI TAIKAI,* 第三十二回オリンピック競技大会).

U

UCHIMURA KŌHEI, 内村航平 **(1989–).** Uchimura Kōhei is an outstanding figure in the international world of **gymnastics**, a five-time **Olympic** medalist and a 19-time World Championships medalist. He is the first gymnast to win all six titles in a single Olympics. In the 2016 Rio de Janeiro Olympics, Uchimura anchored the Japan team to win a gold medal with a score of 274.094, claiming the title for Japan. Two days later Uchimura won the Olympic all-around crown. He is the first man to achieve back-to-back victories in the Olympic all-around since fellow countryman **Katō Sawao** did it in 1968 and 1972. He holds 10 gold medals in the World Championships and 19 medals in all. He went undefeated from the 2008 Beijing Olympics through both the London and Rio Olympics until he finally lost in 2017.

Born in Fukuoka Prefecture to parents who were both competitive gymnasts, Uchimura moved to **Tōkyō** to train with Tsukahara Naoya (1977–), the gold medalist at the Athens Olympics. He joined the national team in 2007 and competed in the Paris World Cup. He helped Japan win the silver medal at the 2008 Olympics in Beijing. With his success in Rio de Janeiro, Uchimura, arguably the world's best gymnast ever, brings grace and artistry to his precise routines.

UEMURA KŌGORŌ, 植村甲午郎 **(1894–1978).** Uemura Kōgorō, a prominent **business** leader, was born in **Tōkyō**. After graduating from Tōkyō Imperial University, Uemura immediately joined the Ministry of Agriculture and Commerce. He became director of the Coal Control Board in 1941 and focused on coal production and procurement during the war. He was one of Japan's top civilian planners of the war effort and was purged by the Allied **Occupation** after the war but was asked to become vice president of the **Japan Federation of Economic Organizations** (Keidanren) after being rehabilitated.

Uemura tried to avoid collusion between big businesses and the government by attempting to abolish the practice of direct corporate contributions to **political parties**. He became Keidanren's president in 1968, serving in that position for six years. Uemura strengthened the economic organization's staff and established a collective management system. While in office, he devoted himself to negotiations regarding textile **trade** between Japan and the **United States** and overcoming pollution problems. Uemura skillfully combined the roles of businessman and bureaucrat.

UEMURA NAOMI, 植村直己 **(1941–1984).** Uemura Naomi, a fearless and daring adventurer, was a mountaineer and polar explorer. Born in Hyōgo Prefecture, he was active in Meiji University's Alpine Club, although shy and diffident. Uemura scaled Mount Everest in Asia, Mount Kilimanjaro in Africa, Mont Blanc in Europe, Aconcagua in South America, and Mount McKinley in North America, and, with the exception of Everest, he climbed them alone. In 1970, he was the first member of a Japanese team of 39 climbers to reach the summit of Mount Everest, the highest point on earth. In 1968, Uemura made the first recorded solo trip by raft down the Amazon. In 1978, after 57 harrowing days and nights, he reached the North Pole by dogsled, said to be the first person in history to have made an overland traverse of Greenland's midsection. Although he was the first climber to reach the summit of Mount McKinley in the winter of 1970, Uemura died in that climb, and his body was not recovered.

UFJ HOLDINGS (KABUSHIKI-GAISHA YŪEFUJEI HŌRUDINGUSU, 株式会社UFJホールディングス**).** UFJ Holdings was a financial group, the weakest among the four major **banking** groups in postwar Japan. The name *UFJ* is an abbreviation of "United Financial of Japan," which was, however, almost never used. On 1 October 2005, the company merged with the Mitsubishi Tōkyō Financial Group to form the **Mitsubishi UFJ Financial Group**.

ULTRAMAN, ウルトラマン**.** Created in the 1960s by Tsuburaya Eiji (1901–1970), the Ultraman series resembled America's Superman. Ultraman came from the Land of Light, which resided in the M-78 nebula, to help the people of Earth battle space monsters. Ultraman assumed human form as Hayata, a member of the Science Special Search Party, but became Ultraman, a 40-meter-tall hero in a skintight red-and-silver suit who struggled against evil monsters. In times of need, Hayata would enter the Beta capsule to transform into Ultraman, who could run at Mach 5 (700 kilometers per hour) and possessed a host of ultimate weapons. When Ultraman crossed his hands, they emitted deadly rays.

Ultraman, one of the Starman-type superheroes serialized on Japanese **television**, had an international life, being popular in many countries. Its originators produced at least seven Ultraman movies. By the mid-1990s, they had created at least 23 Ultraman characters. In 1995, Tsuburaya Noboru

(1935–1995), son of the company founder and its second president, constructed an Ultramanland Theme Park in Kumamoto Prefecture. The park operated until 2013.

UNITED NATIONS. A Cold War casualty, the **Soviet Union** vetoed Japan's admission to the United Nations (UN) in 1952. However, Japan was admitted on 18 December 1956 with support from the **United States**.

Since its admission to the UN, Japan has followed a policy of international cooperation; stressing multilateral action; aid to developing nations; **educational**, cultural, and technical exchange; nuclear disarmament; and world peace. Having been the world's only atomic bomb sufferer, Japan has been quite active in the nuclear test ban and nonproliferation treaties. Japan provides valuable service on nearly all the UN committees. In 1980, Japan was elected to a non-permanent seat on the UN Security Council where it played an important role as a contributor to world development and peace. Several UN agencies operate in Japan with the United Nations University, a research facility, located in **Tōkyō**.

Japanese senior **foreign policy** makers suggest that Japan, the second-largest financial contributor to the UN, reduce its support by one-quarter. Japanese diplomats calculate that Japan's GDP accounts for 14.4 percent of the global **economy**. But, in 2016, Japan paid 9.68 percent of the UN budget. Yet Japan, the world's third-largest economy, remains frustrated in its bid to win a permanent seat on the UN Security Council.

Japan has unsuccessfully sought a permanent seat on the UN Security Council. **Russia** and **China** have offered strong opposition, arguing that Japan has not made adequate apologies for its role in World War II. Japan has been elected nine times, more than any other nation, to a non-permanent seat on the Security Council. Japan has taken the lead in peace-building efforts and argues that a permanent seat would increase Asia's influence in the UN.

Some Japanese have assumed leadership positions with the UN. Akashi Yasushi (1931–), a veteran diplomat, became Japan's first undersecretary-general of the UN. He also served as the chief of the UN peacekeeping mission in Cambodia and in the former Yugoslavia. Matsuura Kōichirō (1937–) was elected to a six-year term as director-general of United Nations Educational, Scientific and Cultural Organization (UNESCO) in 1999 and reelected to a four-year term in 2005. He has been responsible for a modest reshaping of the organization. He helped get the United States to rejoin UNESCO in 2002, after an 18-year absence. **Ogata Sadako** served as the UN high commissioner for refugees from 1991 until 2001. Finally, in July 2009, the International Atomic Energy Agency, the UN's agency to combat the proliferation of nuclear weapons and promote the peaceful use of atomic **energy**, chose Amano Yukiya (1947–) as its fifth director-general. Yoshikawa Motohide (1951–) is Japan's ambassador to the United Nations.

On 29 September 2016, Prime Minister **Abe Shinzō** spoke to the UN General Assembly, where he stressed **North Korea**'s nuclear threat as a matter of particular sensitivity to Japan. He also emphasized that, for the past 30 years, Japan has been the second-largest donor to the UN. He reaffirmed his country's pledge of ¥1.3 trillion of assistance to developing countries by 2020 and its commitment to the work of the Paris Climate Change Agreement.

UNITED STATES, RELATIONS WITH. The most important organization in Japan during the immediate postwar period was the Supreme Commander for the Allied Powers (SCAP). From 1945 until 1951, General Douglas MacArthur was the head of SCAP, which had its headquarters in **Tōkyō** in the Dai-Ichi Insurance Building overlooking the Imperial Palace grounds. In 1951, General Matthew B. Ridgway replaced MacArthur.

Two advisory bodies assisted General MacArthur. The Far Eastern Commission, composed of the 11 nations that had won the war, met in Washington and supervised SCAP. The Allied Council for Japan, consisting of the United States, Great Britain, **China**, and the **Soviet Union**, met in Tōkyō and advised SCAP on policy. However, the **Occupation** of Japan was primarily an operation controlled by the U.S. 8th Army. The supreme commander oversaw the war crimes trials of the International Military Tribunal of the Far East, directed the military staff, and supervised 17 nonmilitary sections that dealt with various issues. SCAP did not function as a military government but worked through the Japanese political bureaucracy to govern and transform Japan.

But things did not always run smoothly. The Sunagawa Case, also called the Tachikawa Air Base Struggles, involved the extension of the Tachikawa Air Base runway. The incident started in September 1955 when locals struggled against the expansion of U.S. military control. In July 1957, extensive demonstrations against the extension of the Tachikawa Air Base runway and against the constitutionality of the bases and the security issues disrupted much of Japan, although they did not prevent the extension of the runway. In March 1959, the defendants in the Sunagawa Case were found innocent of interfering with American efforts.

On 8 September 1951, the United States and Japan signed both the **San Francisco Peace Treaty** and the **United States–Japan Security Treaty**. The security treaty enabled the United States to legitimately maintain a strong military force and military bases in Japan, an important factor during the Korean War. This security arrangement, with major modifications, continues today. In 1960, the United States forced revisions in the treaty and created the **Treaty of Mutual Cooperation and Security between the United States and Japan**. Prime Minister **Kishi Nobusuke** pushed the treaty ratification through the **Diet** in May 1960 with the revised treaty going into effect the next month.

In the late 1960s, Japan's relations with the Nixon administration were promising. President Richard Nixon and Prime Minister **Satō Eisaku**, in a meeting on Guam, first announced the Nixon Doctrine, also known as the Guam Doctrine. Later on, the "Nixon shocks" disturbed American-Japanese relations. On 15 July 1971, the first "Nixon shock" struck Japan with the announcement that President Nixon would visit the People's Republic of China, without any advance notice to Japan. The second "Nixon shock" struck on 15 August, when the president issued a 10 percent surcharge on imports into the United States from Japan and the nonconvertibility of the dollar. In October 1971, with the third "Nixon shock" the president compelled Prime Minister Satō to accept voluntary restraints on Japanese synthetic textile exports to the United States. These "Nixon shocks" destroyed Satō's credibility and precipitated his resignation.

During the 1970s, three issues largely shaped Japanese-American relations. The first was a security-related matter in which the United States sought to involve Japan more in its own **defense** and help the United States with East Asian regional security. The second focus was economic power as Japan built an increasing **trade** surplus and improved its world economic ranking. The third issue was the need for Japan to expand its regional security role as the United States withdrew from Vietnam. These issues made Japan a more important player on the world scene.

Prime Minister **Nakasone Yasuhiro** did his best to patch up Japanese-American relations. However, while in Washington during a January 1983 meeting with President Ronald Reagan, he unwisely used the phrase "an unsinkable aircraft carrier" to describe Japan. The use of this phrase set off a wave of protest by people who were frightened by possible military action. However, the term "Ron-Yasu talks" became a popular phrase to describe the chummy conversations, on a more equal level, between Reagan and Nakasone in the mid-1980s.

U.S.-Japan relations have often been exacerbated by "Japan bashing." This phenomenon, particularly strong in the United States in the 1980s and 1990s, displayed a sense of paranoia and xenophobia that put Japan in a bad light. From the mid-1980s, various American journalists, politicians, and businessmen increasingly viewed Japan suspiciously and considered it a hostile economic superpower. Japan was seen as separate from the rest of the world and concerned only with its own economic well-being. Many of these same critics also suggested that Japan's economic success in the postwar period rested primarily, if not exclusively, on the largess of the United States.

The 1980s witnessed sweeping change in the relative economic power of Japan and the United States. U.S. trade and budget deficits produced a need for currency realignment. As the Japanese yen grew stronger, Japan made important investments in the United States, giving some people the view that Japan was buying up key U.S. properties. When Japan became the second-largest investor after Great Britain, many people complained of a Japanese economic invasion.

The United States has used its trade commission against Japan to secure more favorable relations. They have also turned to international organizations such as the GATT and the WTO to protest and resolve trade issues with Japan. Mutō Kabun (1926–2009), international trade and industry minister during **Kaifu Toshiki**'s **cabinet**, strove to improve United States–Japan relations. Of the trade imbalance, he said, "Japan is certainly not forcibly exporting. It is merely selling products that are demanded by the U.S. market." The Federal Trade Commission, an American organization, attempted to protect U.S. interests in international trade.

The SII refers to talks between Japan and the United States to police trade conditions. This is sometimes called the Japan-U.S. Structure Conference. The Super 301 Clause is a United States law that justifies trade sanctions against any country that the United States believes is taking unfair advantage in trade matters. This trade law has frequently been aimed at Japan, particularly in the late 1980s.

In the 1990s, Japanese-American relations improved as the long-time military allies and the two major world economic powers found it advantageous to grow closer together. As leading trading partners, their economic ties grew more comfortable while they grew larger. As military allies, the relationship became more equal, more stable, and more mature. The people of both countries saw the ties between the two countries as more balanced, more essential, and more normal. Most Japanese came to see the United States as Japan's main security ally and leading trade partner, while Americans were beginning to acknowledge Japan for its accomplishments not only in the **economy** but also in many other capacities.

There were, however, thorny issues in Japanese-American relations in the 1990s. Growing U.S. deficits in bilateral trade, trade restrictions, technological competition, and military matters all presented problems for the two countries.

During the opening years of the 21st century, President George W. Bush encouraged Japan to play a more active role in international affairs, and Japan responded positively. Under Prime Minister **Koizumi Jun'ichirō**, Japan made its first-ever military deployments in a noncombat role supporting the United States in Afghanistan. In 2005, Japan sent troops to Iraq in spite of strong domestic opposition. That same year Japan and the United States strengthened their military cooperation. As the world's economic problems become more acute, Japan is likely to pay less attention to U.S.-Japan military affairs.

Since the end of World War II, the United States has maintained military forces in Japan, first as an Occupation force and then as allied troops under the auspices of the United States–Japan Security Treaty.

As of 2017, the United States maintains around 45,000 troops in Japan and has its 7th Fleet stationed there. Associated with these troops are 40,000 dependents and 5,500 civilian employees. With concerns over **North Korea** and China, the United States employs a major surveillance operation near Japan. In addition, the 7th Fleet is based in Yokosuka, the 3rd Marine Expeditionary Force is in **Okinawa**, and some 130 U.S. Air Force fighters are at Misawa and Kadena air bases. Japan paid the United States around $2 billion in support of these forces.

As of 2017, the U.S. Air Force has 20 installations in Japan; the U.S. Army, 15 bases; the Marine Corps, 17 installations; and the U.S. Navy, 32 stations. However, many of these are small, and a significant number have been closed in recent years. Japan not only provides bases but gives financial and material support to the U.S. forces.

In the half century since the Occupation, U.S. military personnel have committed nearly 200,000 accidents and crimes, but more than 90 percent of these were vehicle accidents or traffic violations. However, some cases have gained much notoriety, such as the rape of a 12-year-old Okinawan schoolgirl by three U.S. soldiers in 1995, several helicopter crashes that killed Japanese citizens, and a number of murders committed by American military personnel.

Japan and the United States are key economic partners, with Japan exporting more to the United States than any country except Canada and importing more from the United States than any other country except China. Japan is the second-largest investor in the United States after Great Britain. Although Chinese investments have grown, Japanese investors remain the largest holders of U.S. treasury bills, helping to finance the U.S. trade deficit.

Trade friction has frequently been a problem for U.S.-Japanese relations. However, in 2000, China eclipsed Japan as the country with the biggest trade surplus with the United States, although Japan's trade surplus with the United States is still huge.

President Barack Obama made relations with Japan a high priority in his administration. Prime Minister **Asō Tarō** was the first foreign leader to visit the White House during Obama's term, and Secretary of State Hillary Rodham Clinton made Japan the first country she visited. Leaders of both countries have used such phrases as "irreplaceable partnership," "the most important bilateral relationship in the world," and "the cornerstone of our diplomacy." Japan has supported the United States in its efforts to recover from the world recession.

In 2015, Japan and the United States bolstered their relationship by strengthening their defense guidelines. Japan agreed to provide bases as well as financial and material support while the United States confirmed its support for Japan. The two countries signed a new five-year pact in January 2016. In December of that year, the United States returned some 10,000 acres of land occupied in Okinawa to Japanese control.

The United States and Japan claim to have very strong political, economic, and military relations. Each considers the other a strong ally with citizens of both countries calling the other country its best world partner.

The United States has had a number of outstanding people as its ambassador to Japan. Leading postwar ambassadors to Japan include Edwin Reischauer (1961–1966), Mike Mansfield (1977–1988), Walter Mondale (1993–1996), and Howard Baker Jr. (2001–2005). The 14 postwar ambassadors have served an average of four years each. President Barack Obama appointed John V. Roos, CEO of a Silicon Valley law firm, as his ambassador to Japan. Katō Ryōzō served with distinction as Japan's ambassador to the United States from 2001 to 2008 when he was replaced by Fujisaki Ichirō who served from 2008 through 2012. Sasae Ken'ichirō served as Japanese ambassador to the United States until early 2018 when Sugiyama Shinsuke replaced him.

The election of Donald Trump as president of the United States has caused much apprehension in Japan. Prime Minister **Abe Shinzō**, who previously enjoyed a positive working relationship with the Obama administration, has gone out of his way to work with the new president. Time will tell how relations between the two strong allies will unfold. Trump nominated William F. Hagerty, a Tennessee businessman and consultant, as the new ambassador to Japan. He replaces the popular Ambassador Caroline Kennedy.

In a January 2017 speech to the **House of Representatives**, Prime Minister Abe emphasized the importance of Japan-U.S. relations, calling it the "linchpin of Japan's foreign diplomacy and national security." In a September 2017 statement, the United States emphasized its commitment to further cooperation with Japan in the areas of national security and economic development. *See also* FOREIGN POLICY.

UNITED STATES–JAPAN SECURITY TREATY (*NICHIBEI ANZEN HOSHŌ JŌYAKU,* 日米安全保障条約**). The United States–Japan Security Treaty was signed by the **United States** and Japan on 8 September 1951, the very same day the **San Francisco Peace Treaty** was signed. The security treaty enabled the United States to legitimately maintain a strong military force and military bases in Japan, an important factor during the Korean War and a continuing factor in Japan's U.S. relations. This treaty gave the United States a major military stronghold in Japan, playing a significant role in Japan's **defense** and also shaping its **foreign policy**.

Specifically, the treaty forced Japan to allow the United States to establish and maintain military forces in Japan, prohibited other countries from gaining any bases or military rights in Japan, and provided for administrative agreements to determine the status of forces.

Emerging in the late 1950s, a Japanese movement against the treaty brought about the 1960 struggle against continuation and revision of the treaty. During the late 1960s, the anti-security movement, known as *Anpo*, generated strong opposition against the security treaty. After 1970, the *Anpo* movement died out, but opposition to military ties with the United States still remains.

In 1960, the security treaty was revised to become the **Treaty of Mutual Cooperation and Security between the United States and Japan**. Prime Minister **Kishi Nobusuke** pushed the treaty ratification through the **House of Representatives** on 19 May 1960 with the revised treaty going into effect the next month.

UNIVERSITY OF TŌKYŌ (TŌKYŌ DAIGAKU, 東京大学). Japan's most prestigious university, the University of Tōkyō began in 1877 under its present name but was soon renamed Tōkyō Imperial University. In the postwar period, it again became the University of Tōkyō. One of Japan's leading research universities, it has five campuses, 10 faculties, a full-time staff of more than 2,500 people, and around 30,000 students. It is especially well known for its faculties of law and **literature** and has produced many of Japan's political leaders and outstanding scholars. *Akamon* (Red Gate), the ginkgo leaf symbol, and Yasuda Auditorium are landmarks that identify the university. "Tōdai," as the school is known, is an outstanding public university.

In the University of Tōkyō incident, Japanese students occupied the University of Tōkyō on two occasions for more than seven months starting on 2 July 1968. A Tōdai class for 1968 was not formed. On 18–19 January 1969, riot police evicted leftist **students** from the University of Tōkyō.

UNO SŌSUKE, 宇野宗佑 (1922–1998). Uno Sōsuke was briefly **prime minister** of Japan. Born into a wealthy sake-brewing family in Moriyama in Shiga Prefecture, Uno enrolled at the Kōbe University of Commerce but was conscripted into the army. He was captured and became a prisoner of war in Siberia. After returning from two years of **Russian** captivity, he entered local politics being elected to the **House of Representatives** in 1960 for the first of eight times. A leading **Liberal Democratic Party** (LDP) member, Uno was a long-time political ally of **Nakasone Yasuhiro**. Uno served as vice minister of the **Ministry of International Trade and Industry** (MITI) during 1966–1968, becoming head of MITI in June 1983. He was director of the Defense Agency under **Tanaka Kakuei** and director of the **Science and Technology** Agency under **Fukuda Takeo**.

Never a popular political figure, Uno served as prime minister for only two months, from 3 June to 10 August 1989, the second-shortest term ever in Japan. More than an issue of morality, Uno's irresponsibility in failing to provide appropriately for his mistress was the main issue. The scandal over his affair with a former geisha led to his political ouster. The sex scandal contributed to the LDP's poor showing in the **House of Councillors** July 1989 **election**, causing Uno to be a real political liability. In addition to the sex scandal, Uno's administration is remembered for the institution of the country's first consumption tax, the lingering effects of the **Recruit scandal**, and his being the first postwar LDP prime minister without a faction of his own.

V

VENDING MACHINES. Vending machines first appeared in the 1890s, but it was not until the postwar period that they came to flourish in Japan. Today, they can be found in every conceivable place. They carry an unbelievable variety of items including the usual soft drinks, cigarettes, ice cream, snacks, and train and subway tickets, and these machines also dispense such items as alcoholic beverages, cooked foods, batteries, comic books, pornography, condoms (including designer ones), **video games**, and even whiffs of oxygen.

Japan has the highest number of vending machines in the world with nearly one machine for every 20 people. This amounts to 5.5 million vending machines, literally "automatic-vending-machine" (*jidō-hanbaiki*) in Japanese. Cell phones can now be used to pay for things from vending machines, and smart cards are used to control the purchase of cigarettes and liquor from vending machines.

Vending machines are popular in Japan because of the country's lack of space, high cost of shop facilities, and security. People also appreciate the convenience, 24-hour availability, and anonymous quality of vending machines.

VICTOR COMPANY OF JAPAN (NIPPON BIKUTĀ KABUSHIKI-GAISHA, 日本ビクター株式会社). Victor Company of Japan (JVC) was established in 1927 as a subsidiary of RCA. A member of the **Matsushita Group**, Victor produces VCRs, **televisions**, audio equipment, CDs, and **computers**. It is known overseas under the popular brand name JVC. The company employs more than 30,000 people and is headquartered in **Yokohama**.

A key leader in Victor Company was Takayanagi Kenjirō (1899–1990), an electrical engineer who produced the first television transmission in Japan in 1926 and who started working for the company in 1946, creating the video recorder. Inventor of more than 120 patents, Takayanagi is sometimes called "the father of Japanese television." Takano Shizuo (1923–1992), an electronics engineer, headed JVC in its development of VHS during the period 1970–1976. Eguchi Shōichirō (1955–) is the current president of JVC.

VIDEO GAMES. Japan, while not the original creators of video games, has made them a preeminent form of entertainment. Ask gamers and they will say that Japan dominates the industry. One popular list includes at least 1,500 games developed by Japanese game makers. Video games have taken the **games** industry far beyond the thrills offered by **pachinko**.

While there may be some arguments among game aficionados, *Super Mario*, *Space Invaders*, *Pac-Man*, **Pokémon**, *The Legend of Zelda*, *Street Fighter*, *Sonic the Hedgehog*, *Final Fantasy*, *Resident Evil*, and *Silent Hill* generally rank among the most popular. *Donkey Kong* and *Dragon Quest* fans will have to enter their objections.

Nintendo, Sega, Taito, Namco, Capcom, and **Konami** are the most famous game maker companies. Several of these companies started in the early 1970s, but it was not until the mid-1980s that Japan became the dominant country in the games industry.

At first, games were played primarily on consoles. However, in the early 2000s Japan's **mobile phone** culture gave rise to a series of games that could be played anywhere. In 2002, Japanese video game makers controlled around 50 percent of the global market; however, as the market became worldwide, Japan produced only around 10 percent of the video games. However, as of 2009, that still amounted to around $20 billion in sales. Today, Japan is the largest market for mobile games, generating in excess of $5 billion annually.

Now in the eighth generation of video games, the leading console or home video game makers are **Sony**'s PlayStation 4 (PS4) launched in 2013, Nintendo's Wii U, and Microsoft's Xbox One. Leaders in portable systems are Nintendo's 3DS and PlayStation Vita (PS Vita) made by Sony. Video games are big business in Japan.

VOLLEYBALL. Volleyball is one of the so-called minor **sports** that has a large following and a number of participants in Japan. Between 1962 and 1974, Japanese **women** won the World Championships five times and finished in the top three 12 times. The men's team finished in the top three on six occasions, winning in 1972. Japan has produced many famous players. Iida Takako (1946–) was one of Japan's greatest female volleyball players. In the Munich **Olympics**, she helped Japan win the silver medal, and in Montreal, the gold.

Saitō Mayumi (1971–) was a member of Japan's national volleyball team from 1989 until 2004. She won the most valuable player (MVP) award at age 18 when her team, Itō-Yōkado, clinched the Japan League title in 1989. She quit Itō-Yōkado in 1997 and joined Daiei where she again won the MVP title. She was the winner of the highest number of votes for the 1998 All-Star Game. Two other of Japan's greatest female volleyball players, Shirai Takako (1952–) and Okamoto Mariko (1951–), participated in several Olympics with great success. They helped Japan win the silver medal in Munich and the gold medal at Montreal.

Minami Masayuki (1941–2000) was one of Japan's greatest male volleyball stars. One of only two men to represent Japan in three consecutive Olympics, Minami was a member of medal-winning squads each time. In the 1964 Tōkyō Games, Japan won a bronze medal. Four years later, in Mexico City, Minami returned as a veteran, leading his team to the silver medal. Continuing his spiking and setting career well beyond that of most Olympic athletes, Minami played yet again in the 1972 Munich Games. His long international experience paid dividends, as Japan won its only men's gold medal. Nekoda Katsutoshi (1944–1983) was another of Japan's greatest-ever male volleyball stars. He also represented Japan in three consecutive Olympics and was one of the members of the medal-winning squads each time. Nekoda's athletic career was quite similar to that of Minami, culminating with the 1972 Munich Games.

WAKAO AYAKO, 若尾文子 **(1933–).** Wakao Ayako is a film **actress**. Born in **Tōkyō**, she moved to Sendai during World War II and, as a high school student, was inspired to become an actress after seeing a stunning performance. After participating in a local **theater** troupe, she joined Daiei Motion Picture Company. She portrayed many roles of a strong sexual nature. After Daiei went bankrupt, Wakao performed on stage and on **television**, and she made occasional appearances in the Shōchiku film series *Otoko wa tsurai yo* (*It's Tough Being a Man*) with its star, the late Atsumi Kiyoshi (1928–1996). Stylish and sensual, Wakao has appeared in 160 **films** since her debut in 1952.

WATAYA RISA, 綿矢りさ **(1984–).** Wataya Rise, as a 19-year-old female writer, shared the Akutagawa Prize in 2003 for her novel *Keritai senaka* (*The Back You Want to Kick*). **Kanehara Hitomi**, another outstanding young writer, and Wataya's **books** have been analyzed profusely in publications and on the internet and the authors hailed as voices of a new generation. Their books have broken sales records, and the young women have become very popular. *See also* LITERATURE; WOMEN.

WOMEN. The status of women has advanced dramatically in postwar Japan with the women's movement being an important factor in improving the life and position of women. In addition, women in the postwar period are living longer, marrying later, having fewer children, and getting more divorces. The average lifespan for a Japanese woman is now 87 years. The average age of marriage for women is presently 27; the average age for women to give birth to their first child is 30. In the early postwar period, the average Japanese woman gave birth to four children. By 2009, the average had plummeted to 1.4 children per couple, well below the replacement rate of 2.1 children. Japanese annual birth rates have been decreasing for almost two decades, and Japan's current population of about 126 million is expected to decline even further. (Refer to appendixes B and C.) The average divorce rate is 1.4

divorces per 1,000, but this number is rising. Almost half of all Japanese women with children in school now work outside the home at some point during their children's schooling.

Women in Japan got the right to vote for the first time on 10 April 1946. With this they truly became citizens and full members of the nation. The new **constitution** of 1946 stipulated equality between the sexes. In 1979, the Japanese government held a Convention on the Elimination of All Forms of Discrimination against Women and ratified it in 1985.

In 1986, the Women's Bureau of the Ministry of Labor enacted an **Equal Employment Opportunity Law** (EEOL), the first "gender equality law formulated mainly by Japanese women." The EEOL sought to improve the welfare of women workers and guarantee equal opportunity and treatment for them. However, as of 2016, Japanese women earned only 73 percent of what men were paid for comparable jobs. Today, although the EEOL does not have strong enforcement power, Japanese women have greater, but not fully equal, opportunities. Despite these changes by the EEOL, Japan still received low marks from the *World Human Rights Guide* on the status of women.

The worst contemporary example of public discrimination against women in Japan occurred in 2007 when **Nakagawa Shōichi**, chairman of the **Liberal Democratic Party**'s Policy Research Council, told a newspaper that "women have their proper place: they should be womanly. They have their own abilities and these should be fully exercised, for example, in flower arranging, sewing, or cooking. It's not a matter of good or bad, but we need to accept reality that men and women are genetically different." Unsurprisingly, Prime Minister **Abe Shinzō** promptly dismissed him.

Although women were involved in the **labor** movement, few women were allowed to hold political office, even in unions with primarily female membership. Further, until at least the 1980s unions often signed contracts that required women workers, but not men, to retire early.

As part of the Japanese Civil Code, marriages in Japan require that the couple share a surname because they must belong to the same *koseki* or household. Although it has been possible since 1976 for the husband to join the wife's family, more than 90 percent of the time it is the woman who must join the man's family and, therefore, change her surname. Men may take the wife's surname only when the bride has no brother and the bride's parents adopt the bridegroom as the successor of the family.

Japan has a strong consensus regarding gender roles and the appropriate division of labor within the family. A man's primary focus is the workplace, but this often includes extensive socializing with male colleagues during evening hours. In contrast, a woman's chief focus is her home, family, and the rearing of children. The family-centered role and their relative lack of opportunities outside the home impede women's long-term careers.

While most Japanese accept the view that a woman's place is in the home and that work should not interfere with her primary responsibilities to children and husband, women nevertheless make up almost 43 percent of the labor force as of 2017. More than half of these women are married. Many mothers with small children work only part-time so they can be at home when their children are not in school. Although fathers provide children with certain role models and many take an active interest in **education** matters, the task of attending to the child's upbringing and education is usually left to the mother.

Japanese women are among the best educated in the world. However, in a survey conducted by the Inter-Parliamentary Union, Japan ranked only 127th out of 190 countries in terms of the proportion of women to men in the **House of Representatives**. In the 2017 election, the number of female legislators was only 47, or just 10 percent of the seats. After the 2016 election for the **House of Councillors**, women held 50 seats, or 21 percent of the body. Less than 1 percent of Japan's mayors are women. Japan also lacks female role models like Hillary Clinton or Angela Merkel. Even as women become more active and vocal, they continue to encounter strong resistance to their political aspirations.

Japanese women have increased their role in politics, although they have a long way to go to gain equality. Leading postwar feminists and political leaders such as **Hiratsuka Raichō**, **Ichikawa Fusae**, and **Katō Shizue** made important contributions to the political fate of Japanese women. In 2001, **Doi Takako** became the first female speaker of the House of Representatives, and she also served as chair of the **Japan Socialist Party**. Fukushima Mizuho succeeded her as chair of the renamed **Social Democratic Party of Japan** in 2003. To date, 20 Japanese women have served as ministers of state, including **Kawaguchi Yoriko**, Japan's first female minister of defense; Moriya Mayumi; **Ogi Chikage**; and Tanaka Makiko, the first-ever female minister of foreign affairs.

Only seven women have served or are serving as prefectural governors, including Ota Fusae (1951–) of **Ōsaka**, Shiotani Yoshiko (1939–) of Kumamoto, Dōmoto Akiko (1932–) of Chiba, Takahashi Harumi (1954–) of Hokkaidō, Kada Yukiko (1950–) of Shiga, Yoshimura Mieko (1951–) of Yamagata, and **Koike Yuriko** of Tōkyō. Hayashi Fumiko (1946–), a former president of BMW Tōkyō and later vice chairperson of Daiei **Supermarket**, was elected mayor of **Yokohama** in 2009 and then reelected in 2013 and 2017. Kōri Kazuko (1957–) was elected mayor of Sendai in 2017. They are the only female mayors of major cities.

Some Japanese women have made their mark in business. However, in the corporate world, women fill only about 15 percent of the managerial posts in 2017 as compared to 42.5 percent in the **United States**. In government, only 7 percent of the leadership positions are filled by women. Even though Japan enacted the EEOL in 1985, female executives are still fairly rare due to the expectation that women will leave the workforce when they marry or at least when they have children. Prime Minister Abe has called for 30 percent of the corporate management to be female by 2020. There is no way he will meet this goal.

Among successful women leaders, one should focus on Horiuchi Mitsuko, the Asia Pacific regional director for the International Labour Organization; Nakanishi Tamako (1919–), the president of the Women's Solidarity Foundation; **Ogata Sadako**, who has held several important **United Nations** positions; Okutani Reiko (1950–), the founder and CEO of The R, a temporary personnel service company; Nonaka Tomoyo (1954–), a television personality and CEO of **San'yō Electric** (2005–2007); Katsuma Kazuyo (1968–), a businesswoman and author of many business management books; and **Sakamoto Harumi**, vice president of **Seibu** Department Stores and the first female vice chairperson of the **Japan Association of Corporate Executives**. Other strong feminist leaders include **Konishi Aya**, **Mitsui Mariko**, and **Sawada Miki**.

Women are still expected to stay at home and care for the house and children. They are expected to be modest and passive. And Japanese law still requires that married couples use one surname, which almost always means the man's. But as women work to move into the male world of politics, they are not merely imitating men. They speak as women whose concerns have not been adequately addressed by government.

Japanese women are increasingly involved in the country's entrepreneurship. Japan maintains a traditional economic system that is deeply rooted in a male-dominant society. Societal expectations toward women are low, regardless of a woman's education, ability, or career aspirations. Women are expected to stay home and take care of their families. In recent years, however, the Japanese economic system has begun to accept women who take an active part in the business world. Entrepreneurship rather than employment in large companies particularly offers Japanese women an improved chance of advancing in their careers.

Most Japanese universities are coeducational. Approximately 37 percent of women receive education beyond high school as compared to 43 percent of men. However, most women go to junior colleges and technical schools as opposed to universities. As of 2016, women students accounted for around 43 percent of all university undergraduates, and this percentage is growing. However, two of three women enroll in education, social sciences, or humanities programs, and many fewer study science or engineering. While 66 percent of females enroll in the humanities, only 14 percent study science or engineering. More than 90 percent of students enrolled in junior colleges are women, many of whom see such as preparation for marriage or short-term careers. Graduate schools are largely for men with women accounting for only about 13 percent of all doctoral program participants.

It is more common to see women making their mark in such areas as **literature, music** (including pop idols), **sports**, and **film**. Leading female writers in the postwar period include **Enchi Fumiko, Setouchi Harumi, Ariyoshi Sawako, Yoshimoto Banana, Kanehara Hitomi**, and **Wataya Risa**. All these women have given creative voice to women in Japan.

Important female musical figures include **Misora Hibari**, the *enka* superstar; **Akiyoshi Toshiko**, the world-renowned jazz pianist; **Matsuda Seiko**, the popular idol singer; **Yūming**, a favorite J-Pop star; **Matsui Keiko**, the world-famous jazz performer; and **Gotō Midori**, the internationally known violinist.

In sports, Japanese female stars of world caliber include **Tamura Ryōko** (**jūdō**), **Itō Midori** and **Arakawa Shizuka** (**figure skating**), **Date Kimiko** (tennis), and **Fukuhara Ai** (table tennis). Star **actresses** include **Tanaka Kinuyo, Kyō Machiko, Takamine Hideko, Hidari Sachiko**, and **Wakao Ayako**.

Mori Hanae and **Kawakubo Rei** are internationally recognized for their **fashion** designs. **Hasegawa Itsuko** and **Sejima Kazuyo** are world-class **architects**. Hasegawa Michiko, **Takahashi Rumiko**, and **Ikeda Riyoko** are highly recognized **manga** artists.

Although the actual status of women has not reached one of equality in Japan, women have made and are increasingly making important contributions to their country.

WRESTLING. Western-style wrestling has enjoyed modest interest in Japan. Uetake Yōjirō (1943–) was an outstanding freestyle wrestler who won gold medals in the freestyle wrestling competition in the 1964 and 1968 **Olympics**. A native of Yamanashi Prefecture, Tsuruta Tomomi (1951–2000), better known as Jumbo, was a member of the national basketball team, but he transferred to wrestling to participate in the 1972 Munich Olympics. He became a professional wrestler and the first to win all three titles in professional wrestling. He was probably the greatest Japanese wrestler of his time.

Popularly regarded as the greatest pro-wrestler in Japan, Rikidōzan (1924–1963) started out as a **sumō** wrestler. He transferred to Western-style pro-wrestling and boosted its presence in Japan. Rikidōzan, also a popular figure in the entertainment world, was stabbed to death in 1963.

Inoki Antonio (1943–) was a wrestling star brought into the sport by Rikidōzan. Known for his aggressiveness, Inoki often makes a pose with his chin sticking out. Inoki became the first International Wrestling Grand Prix champion and defended the title four times. He established the Shin Nippon

Pro-Wrestling organization in 1972. He went into politics in 1989 as a member of the **House of Councillors** but failed in his 1995 reelection bid. However, he again joined the upper house after winning a seat in the 2013 **election**. *See also* SPORTS.

YAHOO JAPAN CORPORATION (YAFŪ KABUSHIKI-GAISHA, ヤ フー株式会社). Japan's largest internet portal, Yahoo Japan is headquartered in **Tōkyō**. Its largest stockholder and parent company is **SoftBank Corporation**. Founded in 1996, it is listed on both the **Nikkei 225** and on the TOPIX 100. As with its parent company, Yahoo Japan is best known for its web portal, search engine, directory, and e-mail service. In 2015, it had 5,518 employees, sales of more than $3.3 billion, and a net income of $835 million. **Son Masayoshi** serves as the chairman of the board, and Miyasaka Manabu (1967–) is president and CEO of Yahoo Japan.

YAKULT HONSHA COMPANY (KABUSHIKI-GAISHA YAKURO-TO HONSHA, 株式会社ヤクルト本社). Yakult produces dairy products, foods, and cosmetics. It owns the Yakult Swallows, a professional **baseball** team. The company is famous for its Yakult drink and its "Yakult Ladies" who sell the drinks door to door. Yakult is Japan's third-largest producer of dairy products.

Kyōto Imperial University pediatrics professor Shirota Minoru invented Yakult in 1930. In 1955, he founded the Yakult Honsha Company to market his beverage. Since then, Yakult has also introduced a broader line of beverages. More recently, Yakult Honsha played a major role in developing a chemotherapy drug. Today, Yakult is manufactured and sold in Japan, Asia, Australia, Latin America, and Europe.

YAKUSHO KOJI, 役所広司 (1956–). Yakusho Koji is a prolific **actor** who has played the lead in several **films**. In 1996, Yakusho's career blossomed with the romantic comedy *Shall We Dance?*, a huge hit that caught the public imagination and started a social dance craze. He also starred in **Imamura Shōhei**'s *Hanabi*. Yakusho first became popular in the early 1980s when he appeared on an **NHK** drama series and then in **Itami Jūzō**'s *Tanpopo*.

Born Hashimoto Koji in Nagasaki, Yakusho was a 20-year-old working at a municipal ward office when a visit to see the Gorky play *The Lower Depths* convinced him that he wanted to pursue an acting career. He was one of four chosen out of 800 applicants to the Mumeijuku acting studio.

Unagi (*The Eel*), a darker, more intense movie, won critical plaudits and the Palme d'Or Prize at Cannes; *Shitsurakuen* (*Lost Paradise*, 1997) gained instant cult status in Japan with its sexually charged portrayal of middle-aged forbidden love and also made a star of actress Kuroki Hitomi; *Kyua* (*Cure*, 1997) was an intelligent thriller; and another lesser-known film, *Bounce ko gyals* (*Bounce Young Girls*), while less successful, showed his ability to play a darker, more sinister character. Suddenly, Yakusho was everywhere, **advertising** Kirin beer and curry rice, appearing in Shakespeare, and adorning every magazine cover. These hits were followed by critical successes in *Karisuma* (*Charisma*, 1999), *Kinyu Fushoku Retto: Jubaku* (*Spellbound*, 1999), *Eureka* (2000), and *Korei* (*Séance*, 2000), which brought even more awards to this talented and versatile actor. In 2005, Yakusho made his Hollywood debut in *Memoirs of a Geisha*.

Yakusho's acting career continues to blossom, and he has also developed his talents as a writer and director. He appeared in two of Miike Takashi's films. He played the role of Admiral Yamamoto Isoroku in a popular World War II drama. Since 2010, Yakusho has appeared in 15 films and five television dramas, and he has won or has been nominated for 10 film awards.

YAKUZA, ヤクザ. A *yakuza* is a member of one of Japan's organized **crime** syndicates. *Yakuza* have existed since the mid-19th century, being especially involved in gambling, drugs, petty crime, and prostitution. Violence is a way of life for the *yakuza*, especially for the *yakuza* who violates the code of behavior. Although *yakuza* have generally operated independently, some of them have had ties with political figures and **business** and financial interests. *Yakuza* also provide a strong social support system for their members and for the public at large as witnessed by the help provided by the *yakuza* to victims of the **Kōbe Earthquake** in 1995.

Reputedly, there are around 80,000 *yakuza* members belonging to 3,000 separate groups, with three major groups most well known. The largest group is the Yamaguchi-gumi, which is centered in **Kōbe** and has more than 20,000 members. This group has close ties with the **construction industry**. The second-largest group is the Sumiyoshi-kai with an estimated 10,000 members. The Inagawa-kai, the third-largest *yakuza* group, has ties with more than 300 organizations.

In the late 1980s, *yakuza* began to move away from petty crimes and began to extort large sums of money from stockholders of large businesses. As of the early 1990s, 40 percent of the major corporations were asked to make financial contributions to a *yakuza* group.

Traditionally, the police have looked the other way where matters of *yaku-za* have been concerned. When the police have taken a more active role against them, the *yakuza* have effectively claimed a violation of their **constitutional** rights.

YAMADA YŌJI, 山田洋次 **(1931–).** Yamada Yōji is one of Japan's leading **film** directors. Graduating from the **University of Tōkyō** in 1954, he joined the Shōchiku Company in the same group with director **Ōshima Nagisa**. Yamada was the creator of the popular Tora-san series known as *Otoko wa tsurai yo* (*It's Tough Being a Man*), and the first of these comedies, made in 1969, vaulted him to national prominence. Thereafter, Yamada turned out two Tora-san episodes each year in addition to his several other films.

Yamada directed the film *Shiawase no kiiroi hankachi* (*The Yellow Handkerchief*, 1977). The plot is a simple one, but the characterizations and travel episodes are the focus of the movie. The film shows the travelers' affection for small towns as they see the old houses and their residents from the car window.

Yamada dominated the Japanese film world in the 1970s and after, winning two *Kinema Jumpō* awards and numerous other honors. His films not only have a high level of artistic achievement but are popular commercial successes. They are also noted for promoting the virtues of small-town or rural family life. Yamada adeptly depicts the difficulties ordinary people face in coping with the expansion of **technology** and urbanization. His characters are often at odds with progress, and yet they try, often unsuccessfully, to accommodate themselves to the times. The Japan Film Academy has honored Yamada four times, an impressive record. He won the academy's award for outstanding film with *The Yellow Handkerchief* in 1977, *Musuko* (*My Sons*) in 1991, *Gakkō* (*A Class to Remember*) in 1993, and *Tasogare Seibei* (*Twilight Samurai*) in 2002.

In his 50-year career, Yamada has directed around 80 films. Since 2010, he has directed five new films, all involving family relationships and having a warm feeling. Yamada even has a museum devoted to him and Tora-san in the Katsushika Shibamata section of **Tōkyō**.

YAMAGUCHI YOSHIKO, 山口淑子 **(1920–2014).** Yamaguchi Yoshiko was an actress, singer, and politician whose career blossomed in Japan, **China**, and the **United States**. Born to Japanese parents who were settlers in Manchuria, Yamaguchi starred in Japanese propaganda **films** during Japan's occupation of China in the 1930s and 1940s. Narrowly escaping execution by the Chinese after the war, Yamaguchi helped normalize relations between the two countries.

As an 18-year-old, Yamaguchi, known by her Chinese name Li Xianglan, starred in films promoting the Japanese occupation of China. After the war, she returned to Japan and starred in a variety of films. She also worked in American films. She played the role of a beautiful Chinese woman who falls in love with the handsome Japanese soldier or sailor. She helped make Japan look good in these films. After the war, Chinese officials arrested her and condemned her for her actions. She apologized for her role as a propagandist and fled back to Japan.

Yamaguchi embarked on a political career and became a cosmopolitan voice for better Japanese-Chinese relations. She campaigned for greater public awareness of **"comfort women"** and advocated paying them reparations. She became a talk-show host on Japanese **television** in the 1960s and was elected to the **House of Councillors** in 1974. She served in the House until 1992. She worked tirelessly to improve relations with the People's Republic of China. Her life and career inspired two Japanese television dramas, a novel by Ian Buruma, and an opera. She is said to have considered China her "home country" and Japan her "ancestral country."

YAMAHA CORPORATION (YAMAHA KABUSHIKI-GAISHA, ヤマハ株式会社). Yamaha Corporation is the world's largest manufacturer of musical instruments. Yamaha Torakusu established the company in Hamamatsu in 1887 initially to produce superb-quality pianos, guitars, and, more recently, synthesizers and audio equipment. Yamaha is also widely recognized for its **music** program started in the 1980s. *See also* YAMAHA MOTOR COMPANY (YAMAHA HATSUDŌKI KABUSHIKI--GAISHA, ヤマハ発動機株式会社).

YAMAHA MOTOR COMPANY (YAMAHA HATSUDŌKI KABU-SHIKI--GAISHA, ヤマハ発動機株式会社). Yamaha Motor Company separated from **Yamaha Corporation** in 1955 and started manufacturing **motorcycles**, snowmobiles, car engines, boats, and outboard motors as well as all-terrain vehicles. Yamaha has become world renowned for road and racing motorcycles and for its snowmobiles, car engines, and industrial **robots**. It manufactures products in 45 countries. Yamaha Motors, with its headquarters in Shizuoka Prefecture, sponsors the Jubilo Iwata **J.League** professional **soccer** team.

YAMAKAWA HITOSHI, 山川均 (1880–1958). Yamakawa Hitoshi, born in Kurashiki, was a Marxist writer and theoretician who was active in much of Japanese socialist history. Like other Japanese socialists of his time,

Yamakawa first became interested in social reform when he came into contact with Christianity. Because of articles in his paper criticizing the arranged marriage of the crown prince, he and others were arrested for lèse-majesté.

Yamakawa began to study socialism while in prison and joined the newly founded **Japan Socialist Party** (JSP) in 1906. In 1907, he went to **Tōkyō** to participate in the fledgling socialist movement just as the mainstream was turning from Christian socialism to anarcho-syndicalism. After the revival of the socialist movement in 1916, Yamakawa soon became its intellectual leader. During the years 1916 to 1937, he wrote prodigiously, mainly on Marxism and contemporary Japan. He helped found and edit various socialist journals. In his shift toward political action, he was greatly influenced by the Bolsheviks' success in **Russia**. From 1918 to 1921, he was the foremost writer in Japan on Vladimir Lenin and the Bolsheviks and participated in founding the **Japanese Communist Party** (JCP) in 1922.

After World War II, Yamakawa promoted the formation of a "democratic united front" to include Marxist socialists and communists, but he refused to join the JCP and helped found the JSP. He was critical of the right-wing socialist **cabinet** of **Katayama Tetsu** of 1947–1948 and doubted its truly socialist character. He encouraged the split of the JSP in 1951. People like Suzuki Mosaburō and Sakisaka Itsurō led the new left wing of the JSP. Although the move was opposed by Yamakawa, **Arahata Kanson**, and others, the JSP reunited in 1955 but came under the Rōnōha (Workers-Farmers Faction) leadership as its left wing did increasingly well in **elections**. Yamakawa, together with **Ōuchi Hyōe**, was a representative to the Socialist Association. Since Yamakawa's death, the Rōnōha has split over the question of the extent to which socialists should cooperate with popular democratic governments.

YAMAMOTO YŌJI (YOHJI), 山本耀司 (1943–). Yamamoto Yōji is one of the world's top **fashion** designers. Yamamoto's clothes are large in size and have a flowing quality. Black is the dominant color he uses in his creations. Yamamoto will use a lot of black, navy, and white, and then add a splash of color for effect. His creations have a timeless, classic look to them.

Yamamoto was born in **Yokohama** and graduated from Keiō University in 1966. After this, he spent three years at Bunka Fashion College, Japan's most famous design school, where he graduated in 1969. In 1972, he formed the company Y's. He presented his first show in Paris in 1981 and won wide acclaim. He has been in numerous international shows and won multiple awards. He is the only Japanese fashion designer to have been awarded the French Chevalier de l'Ordre des Arts et des Lettres. He also won the Mainichi Fashion Grand Prize in 1986 and again in 1994. His main store is his headquarters in Minami Aoyama.

YAMASHITA YASUHIRO, 山下泰裕 (1957–). Commonly thought of as the greatest Japanese *jūdōka* in recent memory, Yamashita Yasuhiro competed in three World Jūdō Championships, taking home the gold in 1979, 1981, and 1983, as well as another top finish in the Open event in 1981. His most cherished victory for his fans was his winning the Open division in the 1984 Los Angeles **Olympics**, taking the final despite a painful calf muscle tear from an earlier fight. While other **jūdō** champions have medal hauls roughly comparable to Yamashita, no one has ever duplicated his string of 203 straight victories over eight years (1977–1985) in various international competitions. He continues as a jūdō instructor and is head coach and assistant professor at Tōkai University.

YAMAUCHI HIROSHI, 山内溥 (1927–2013). Yamauchi Hiroshi was a powerful businessman who served as Nintendo's third president. He transformed **Nintendo** from a card-making company into a multibillion-dollar **video game** company. In 1992, Yamauchi became the majority owner to the Seattle Mariners **baseball** team. Shortly before his death, Forbes estimated Yamauchi's net worth at $2.1 billion, placing him among the world's 500 richest people.

Born in **Kyōto**, Yamauchi was too young for military service in World War II but worked in a military factory. In 1945, he enrolled at Waseda University and studied law. However, in 1947 he left school to assume the leadership responsibilities at Nintendo when his grandfather became incapacitated. Yamauchi's grandparents raised him after his father abandoned the family. Yamauchi soon exerted himself and led the company with an iron hand. His main contribution was to determine which products had maximum market potential, a role that he filled quite well. His plastic playing cards, Ultra Hand, and electronic toys became the base for a powerful video game company, Nintendo. Yamauchi made *Donkey Kong*, *Mario Bros.*, Nintendo 64, Nintendo Game Cube, and Game Boy world famous and enabled Nintendo to dominate the video game world.

When the Seattle Mariners fell on hard times, Yamauchi bought a majority stake in the team. He later turned his interest in the Mariners over to the city of Seattle. In 2001, the Mariners signed **Suzuki "Ichirō,"** thus opening a new era in Major League baseball.

YANAGIYA KOSAN, 柳家小さん (1914–2002). Yanagiya Kosan was an outstanding teller of traditional Japanese stories (*rakugo*) who in 1995 became the first *rakugo* storyteller to be designated as a living national treasure. Born in Nagano Prefecture but raised in the Asakusa and Kōjimachi sections of **Tōkyō**, Yanagiya, whose real name was Kobayashi Morio, became an apprentice to Yanagiya Kosan IV in 1933. After nearly a generation of practice, he became Yanagiya Kosan V in 1950. His best-known stories focused on the people of Edo's row houses (*nagaya*) where he told stories of urban life of the common people. Yanagiya became the top adviser to the Rakugo Kyōkai (Storytelling Association), which he chaired from 1972 to 1996. Yanagiya received various decorations including the Order of the Rising Sun, Gold Rays with Rosette, in 1986.

YANAIHARA TADAO, 矢内原忠雄 (1893–1961). Yanaihara Tadao was a famous economist and educator. He was born in Ehime Prefecture, the son of a doctor. He was educated at First Higher School and then at Tōkyō Imperial University. His academic detachment and his keen sense of justice based on his Christian faith made him increasingly critical of Japan's official policies with the Manchurian incident and Japan's aggression in **China**. He gradually became a target of attack from right-wing scholars backed by militarists. His teaching specialized in the field of colonial policy in Japan and elsewhere; his standpoint was a Christian Socialist one, strongly influenced by the ideas of Uchimura Kanzō, Nitobe Inazō, and Yoshino Sakuzō. In 1937, Yanaihara came under attack both from right-wing colleagues and from the government for articles in *Chūō Kōron* critical of Japan's **foreign policy**. He was eventually forced to resign from the university.

In 1945, Yanaihara returned to **Tōkyō** where he taught international economics and founded and became head of the Social Science Research Institute. He served as the president of the **University of Tōkyō** from 1951 to 1957 and was widely regarded as its intellectual and spiritual leader. He wrote extensively on imperialism, colonial policy, and Christianity.

YASUKUNI SHRINE (*YASUKUNI JINJA*, 靖国神社). Yasukuni Shrine, Japan's leading **Shintō** shrine, is dedicated to nearly 2.5 million war dead and military heroes from the Meiji civil wars to the present. Controversial, it is the source of much internal conflict. Prime Minister **Suzuki Zenkō** and 18 **cabinet** members visited Yasukuni Shrine on 15 August 1981, to commemorate the end of the war. This caused a lot of flak. Prime Minister **Nakasone Yasuhiro**, playing to Japan's right wing, later participated in a Founding Day ceremony at Yasukuni Shrine. Again, this created big problems. Then, on 21 April 1983, Nakasone visited Yasukuni Shrine and signed his name as **prime minister**, thereby indicating an official function.

Okuno Seisuke (1913–2016) served as justice minister under the Suzuki cabinet in 1980. A **Liberal Democratic Party Diet** member and previous holder of ministerial positions, Okuno produced quite a stir. He had been a member of the *Kempeitai* (military police) in **China** during the war yet was appointed by Nakasone to examine the issue of whether it was proper for a prime minister to visit Yasukuni Shrine. His report and remarks that Japan was not the aggressor in World War II led to his forced resignation in May 1988.

Fujio Masayuki (1917–2006), a controversial politician, was **labor** minister also under the Suzuki government in 1980. A graduate of Sophia University, Fujio was previously a *Yomiuri Shimbun* reporter. Fujio served in various political roles. In 1986, as **education** minister under Nakasone, he caused a stir by justifying Japanese colonization of **Korea** in a *Bungei Shunjū* interview when he said Korean officials had agreed to the annexation and, in part, were responsible for the colonization. Fujio went on to claim that "killing people in war is not murder in terms of international law" and that the Tōkyō War Trial "cannot be considered correct." He equated Japanese visiting Yasukuni Shrine with Chinese visiting Confucian temples, and that the Nanjing Massacre was a fabrication. The controversial Fujio refused to retract his remarks, and Nakasone dismissed him.

Since 2010, Yasukuni Shrine has continued to be a source of controversy for Japan and its leaders. On 26 December 2013, Prime Minister **Abe Shinzō** visited the shrine bringing forth loud criticisms from more liberal groups. He declined to visit in 2015 and thereafter. Tokugawa Yasuhisa (1948–), the great-grandson of the last Tokugawa shogun, has served as the head of the shrine since 2013. *See also* FOREIGN POLICY.

YKK (YOSHIDA KŌGYŌ KABUSHIKI-GAISHA, 吉田工業株式会社). YKK takes its name from Yoshida Kōgyō Kabushiki-gaisha. YKK is the world's number one manufacturer of zippers and fasteners. Founded in 1934 by Yoshida Tadao (1908–1993), a native of Toyama Prefecture, the company is not listed on the **Tōkyō Stock Exchange** but issues stocks to employees who take part in the management of the firm. YKK was first registered as a trademark in 1946. By 1983, YKK had sales of more than $1 billion. It exported to more than 120 countries and had plants in more than 50 countries.

Today, the YKK Group is a Japanese group of manufacturing companies. YKK Group is most famous for making zippers, although it also does business in other fastening products, architectural objects, and industrial machinery. Yoshida succeeded in making YKK-brand products widely known throughout the world by using a highly mechanized production system, from raw materials to finished products.

In 2017, chairman and CEO Yoshida Tadahiro (1947–), an MBA graduate of Northwestern University, announced YKK's four-year plan to invest $2.41 billion in capital improvements with the hope of selling 12.9 billion zippers around the world. YKK presently produces zippers and fasteners at 109 factories in 71 countries.

YOKOHAMA, 横浜. Located on the southern edge of **Tōkyō** and home to 3.6 million people, Yokohama, Japan's second-largest city, is also its leading port. It has many international historical ties since it was one of the first ports opened to Westerners in the mid-19th century. Today, Yokohama is Japan's most multicultural city. Early on, government authorities created a special settlement for merchants, traders, missionaries, and other foreigners. Thus, a large number of foreigners, including many **Chinese**, live there, especially in an area called the Bluff. Yokohama holds the record for many of Japan's firsts, including the first **railroad** line, gas-powered street lamp, power plant, bakery, photo studio, brewery, public restroom, cinema, daily **newspaper**, and ice cream factory, all in the 1860s and 1870s.

Like Tōkyō, the Kantō Earthquake of 1923 devastated Yokohama. Yokohama lagged behind Tōkyō in its redevelopment. However, it grew as an industrial city. Again, World War II brought great devastation when American B-29 bombers leveled half the city. After the war, it became the center of the American **Occupation**.

By the 1970s, Yokohama had grown dramatically. In an effort to revitalize, Yokohama's first and largest urban development program started in the early 1980s with its future-oriented Minato Mirai 21 (Harbor Future 21) project. This thoroughly modern development has high-rise office buildings including the 70-story Landmark Tower (Japan's tallest building), a state-of-the-art conference center, great museums, first-class hotels, shopping centers, and a myriad of restaurants. Minato Mirai 21 was the site of the first public operation of a maglev train in Japan and is the home of Cosmo Clock 21, which was the world's largest Ferris wheel in the 1980s, and the 860-meter Yokohama Bay Bridge. Maritime museums and harbor facilities constitute a special feature and historical attraction of Yokohama. In Yokohama one can visit one of the world's largest Chinatowns, see the world's tallest lighthouse and the largest clock, and tour the famous Anpanman Museum.

Yokohama's **economy** centers on shipping, biotechnology, and semiconductor industries. **Nissan** moved its headquarters there in 2010. Today, Yokohama is a modern, thriving industrial, commercial, and service city. In 2009, it celebrated its 150th anniversary as an international port.

YOMIURI GIANTS (YOMIURI JAIANTSU, 読売ジャイアンツ). The Yomiuri Giants are Japan's most powerful **baseball** team. The Giants are the oldest and one of the few profitable baseball franchises in professional baseball in Japan. Like the New York Yankees, some people love them, and an equal number hate them.

The Yomiuri Giants are the oldest professional team in Japan. They were founded in 1936 and joined the new Japanese Baseball League. The Giants play in **Tōkyō** Dome and are in the Central League. A media conglomerate that includes two **newspapers** and a **television** network owns the Giants.

Starting in 1965, the Giants won nine consecutive Central League pennants and Japan Series titles, in large part because of the hitting of **Nagashima Shigeo** and **Oh Sadaharu**. In all, the Yomiuri Giants have won 34 league and 22 Japan Series championships. The Yomiuri Giants have won more pennants and Japan Series titles than any other team, with their last pennant and series win in 2012. In 2016, former star Takahashi Yoshinobu managed the Giants. He succeeded Hara Tatsunori (2002–2003, 2006–2016) as manager. *See also YOMIURI SHIMBUN*, 読売新聞.

YOMIURI SHIMBUN, 読売新聞. The *Yomiuri*, labeled a conservative daily, is a popular national **newspaper**. As Japan's oldest and the world's biggest commercial newspaper with a circulation of 10 million copies, it is Japan's largest circulating paper. It was founded in 1874 as a small daily with *furigana* characters. The chief editor, Takahashi Sanae (1860–1938), transformed *Yomiuri* into an important newspaper. The Great Kantō Earthquake of 1923 damaged it, but **Shoriki Matsutarō** took over the management. In 1942, it merged with *Hōchi Shimbun*. The Yomiuri Company owns the **baseball** team **Yomiuri Giants**, Yomiuri TV, and many other publications.

YOSHIDA SHIGERU, 吉田茂 **(1878–1967).** Probably Japan's most prominent early postwar politician, Yoshida Shigeru served as Japan's **prime minister** from 22 May 1946 to 24 May 1947 and then again from 15 October 1948 to 10 December 1954, the second-longest term in postwar Japan. Born in **Tōkyō** to a Kōchi family, Yoshida was the son of Takenouchi Tsuna but was soon adopted by Yoshida Kenzo. Yoshida later became the son-in-law of the early 20th-century political leader Makino Nobuaki. After graduating from Tōkyō Imperial University in 1906, he became a diplomat. Yoshida entered the **Ministry of Foreign Affairs** and, after various assignments abroad, was appointed consul general at Mukden in 1925. In this capacity, he attended the Eastern Conference where he advocated a strong policy in **China**.

In 1928, Yoshida became deputy foreign minister and was subsequently ambassador to Italy and then Great Britain during 1936–1938. He was strongly identified in military eyes with liberalism and friendship with Great Britain and the **United States** and, on one occasion during the war, was arrested by the military police. From 1938, Yoshida avoided political participation, but in September 1945, he became foreign minister. Strongly interested in international affairs, Yoshida served as foreign minister in both the **cabinets** of **Higashikuni Naruhiko** and **Shidehara Kijūrō**. He then served as foreign minister during his own first three cabinets.

In May 1946, following the sudden purge of **Hatoyama Ichirō**, Yoshida succeeded him as president of the **Liberal Party** and prime minister. Supported by various conservative parties, Yoshida remained in power until October 1954, with the exception of May 1947–October 1948. As prime minister for much of the **Occupation** period, Yoshida initially complied with major reforms such as the new **constitution** and land reform. During the years after his resumption of power in 1948, he allied with the more conservative elements among the Occupation authorities. While he did not always agree with Occupation policy, and although it is difficult to assess the degree of his influence, he appeared to have possessed considerable power, exercised through his personal dynamism and domination. Yoshida strongly backed the economic stabilization program and promoted the so-called reverse course policies from the late 1940s. He supported Japan's rearmament by setting up what later became the **Self-Defense Forces**, and supported the **security treaty** with the United States, which accompanied the conclusion of the **San Francisco Peace Treaty**. After the end of the Occupation, Yoshida depurged many Japanese, further strengthened Japan's armed forces, and increased government centralization.

Yoshida was strongly opposed by Hatoyama after the latter returned to politics, and a combination of opponents within the conservative parties combined with a decline in his popular appeal eventually brought about Yoshida's resignation. However, he remained a powerful influence on conservative politics, with something of the status of an elder statesman. The policies followed by Yoshida during his period in office in effect established the guidelines for the policies followed by subsequent **Liberal Democratic Party** governments.

Yoshida had a grating personality and was not afraid to speak out against what he saw as American errors in running the Occupation. This earned him a degree of respect from General Douglas MacArthur and some popularity with the Japanese public. But with the conclusion of the peace treaty, his combativeness, while appreciated when Japan was prostrate, became increasingly distasteful. Yoshida, however, did not fade away. Although a powerful leader, Yoshida was not very popular among Japanese since he was abrasive, overconfident, tactless, and autocratic. His style of politics was confrontation rather than consensus.

Yoshida's administration, while seminal in Japan's postwar transformation, was filled with violent confrontation with leftist parties, **labor** unions, and intellectuals. Very closely aligned with the United States, Yoshida was strongly anticommunist and sought to curb communist influence and prevent antisubversive activities. He was described as "tactless, cocksure, and autocratic" and was said to have operated a "one-man" government.

Yoshida Shigeru dominated Japanese politics during and after the Occupation. He stressed Japan's **economic** recovery and reliance on U.S. military protection even if it meant some loss of independence in Japan's **foreign policy**. His influence, through what became known as the Yoshida Doctrine, continued beyond his life.

YOSHIDA TAMAO, 吉田玉男 **(1919–2006).** Yoshida Tamao was a master puppeteer whose inspired performances breathed life into the declining **Bunraku** puppet **theater**. Apprenticed to the theater at age 13, Yoshida spent his life in perfecting and developing the theater. He added creativity and insight into the Bunraku performances. A great stage artist, he helped revitalize the Bunraku theater arts. In 1997, the Japanese government designated Yoshida a Living National Treasure.

YOSHIMOTO BANANA, 吉本ばなな **(1964–).** An unconventional female writer, Yoshimoto Banana is the author of *Kitchen*, a sensation that has gone through 60 printings. Her real name is Yoshimoto Mahoko, but she uses the pseudonym "Banana," which she considers androgynous and cute. She graduated from Nihon University with a major in **literature**. Yoshimoto's offbeat style is popular with young readers. Her writings depict personal loss and the nature of social relationships among the young, wealthy patrons of urban Japan. Some people consider her writings superficial and commercial, but many other readers, especially young **women**, see her as capturing the spirit of young Japan. She is the daughter of Yoshimoto Takaaki (1924–2012), one of Japan's leading intellectuals.

YOSHIMOTO KŌGYŌ COMPANY (YOSHIMOTO KŌGYŌ KABU-SHIKI-GAISHA, 吉本興業株式会社**).** Yoshimoto Kōgyō is Japan's largest talent agency whose chief product is laughter. Started in **Ōsaka** in 1912, Yoshimoto controls nearly 700 *tarento*, or TV personalities who do comic routines. The Japanese entertainment conglomerate Yoshimoto Kōgyō is the major company promoting *manzai*, a comedy style popularized after World War II.

By 1961, Yoshimoto Kōgyō was listed on the **Tōkyō Stock Exchange**. In the 1970s and 1980s, Yasu-Kiyo was the most popular *manzai* duo. Now Downtown, a comedy duo (*owarai kombi*), generally tops the charts. Yoshimoto is so popular that it owns a comedy theme park in Hokkaidō, has offices and theaters throughout Japan, and even has its own FM radio station. Truly, Yoshimoto Kōgyō dominates Japan's comedy industry. Yoshimoto has even branched out to other Asian countries and has partnered with Second City, the Chicago-based comedy group.

YOSHIYUKI JUNNOSUKE, 吉行淳之介 **(1924–1994).** Yoshiyuki Junnosuke was a novelist and short story writer. In his novels, Yoshiyuki pursued the theme of human sexual experience but did it with a refined prose style and sparkling wit. Near the end of the war, he briefly studied **literature** at Tōkyō Imperial University. In 1947, Yoshiyuki began to write for a scandal magazine called *Modan Nihon* (*Modern Japan*), and for six years was bound up with its declining fortunes. Here he received an education in the darker side of society that reinforced his antipathy to conformity and his sympathy for social outcasts. *Anshitsu* (*The Dark Room*, 1969), his prize-winning novel, best exemplifies the main elements of his writing where his protagonist struggles through the war, overcomes poverty, and survives illness but is unable to keep from thinking that his life is in vain.

In 1978, Yoshiyuki's *Yugure made* (*Until Dusk*) won the Noma Literary Prize. This story is considered his second most important work after *Anshitsu*. Yoshiyuki produced popular fiction for a clearly conceived mass audience. In his serious writing, Yoshiyuki writings show clarity of expression, crispness of style, and the objectivity of an independent mind.

YŪMING, ユーミン, OR ARAI YUMI (MATSUTŌYA YUMI, 松任谷 由実**) (1954–).** Yūming is the short name for Arai Yumi or Matsutōya Yumi. Arai is her maiden name, and Matsutōya is her married name. In 1990, Yūming's *The Gates of Heaven* became Japan's first album to sell two million copies. Her hit songs include "Haru yo, kui," an all-time bestseller, and "Sweet, Bitter Sweet," a top 10 J-Pop in 2001. She began recording in 1969 and since has sold 42 million records.

The number of her record sales has grown yearly since the early 1990s. She is among the leaders in career album sales. She writes most of the words and **music** to the songs she sings. Yūming's music has a smooth, sweet, gentle sound. Her music combines folk, rock, pop, and *enka* styles. A favorite J-Pop star, Yūming is one of Japan's most popular culture icons.

Z

ZAIBATSU, 財閥**.** In prewar years and also during the war, a zaibatsu was a financial clique or conglomerate with large commercial, financial, and industrial enterprises controlled by powerful families or by small groups of people. Convinced that the zaibatsu were strong supporters of Japan's military aggression in World War II, **Occupation** leaders set out on a course of zaibatsu busting. These authorities tried to dissolve huge conglomerates like **Mitsui**, **Mitsubishi**, **Sumitomo**, and Yasuda, which authorities said controlled up to one-fourth of the Japanese **economy** before the war. In all, the Occupation dissolved 45 holding companies. Although the Occupation authorities came to question the wisdom of zaibatsu busting and stopped the policy, some 1,200 companies were affected.

During the "reverse course" policy adopted by the Occupation in the Korean War, the zaibatsu began to reemerge. These revised conglomerates became known as *keiretsu*, or enterprise groups. A *keiretsu* is a group of firms in different industries that maintain close relationships by owning shares in each other's companies and through interlocking directorates, intra-group financial commitments, special leadership clubs, and various customer-supplier interlocking agreements. In addition to the prewar zaibatsu, new conglomerates were also formed including **Nissan**, **Nippon Steel**, Oji Paper, **Matsushita**, **Sony**, and **Honda**.

445

Appendix A

Postwar Japanese Prime Ministers

Name	Date	Party
1. Higashikuni Naruhiko	17 August 1945–9 October 1945	None
2. Shidehara Kijūrō	9 October 1945–22 May 1946	None
3. Yoshida Shigeru	22 May 1946–24 May 1947	JLP
4. Katayama Tetsu	24 May 1947–10 March 1948	JSP
5. Ashida Hitoshi	10 March 1948–15 October 1948	LP
6. Yoshida Shigeru	15 October 1948–10 December 1954	DLP
7. Hatoyama Ichirō	10 December 1954–23 December 1956	LDP
8. Ishibashi Tanzan	23 December 1956–25 February 1957	LDP
9. Kishi Nobusuke	25 February 1957–19 July 1960	LDP
10. Ikeda Hayato	19 July 1960–9 November 1964	LDP
11. Satō Eisaku	9 November 1964–7 July 1972	LDP
12. Tanaka Kakuei	7 July 1972–9 December 1974	LDP
13. Miki Takeo	9 December 1974–24 December 1976	LDP
14. Fukuda Takeo	24 December 1976–7 December 1978	LDP
15. Ōhira Masayoshi	7 December 1978–12 June 1980	LDP
16. Suzuki Zenkō	17 July 1980–27 November 1982	LDP
17. Nakasone Yasuhiro	27 November 1982–6 November 1987	LDP
18. Takeshita Noboru	6 November 1987–3 June 1989	LDP
19. Uno Sōsuke	3 June 1989–10 August 1989	LDP
20. Kaifu Toshiki	10 August 1989–5 November 1991	LDP
21. Miyazawa Kiichi	5 November 1991–9 August 1993	LDP
22. Hosokawa Morihiro	9 August 1993–28 April 1994	JNP
23. Hata Tsutomu	28 April 1994–30 June 1994	JRP
24. Murayama Tomiichi	30 June 1994–11 January 1996	SDPJ
25. Hashimoto Ryūtarō	11 January 1996–30 July 1998	LDP
26. Obuchi Keizō	30 July 1998–5 April 2000	LDP
27. Mori Yoshirō	5 April 2000–26 April 2001	LDP
28. Koizumi Jun'ichirō	26 April 2001–26 September 2006	LDP
29. Abe Shinzō	26 September 2006–26 September 2007	LDP

30. Fukuda Yasuo	26 September 2007–24 September 2008	LDP
31. Asō Tarō	24 September 2008–16 September 2009	LDP
32. Hatoyama Yukio	16 September 2009–8 June 2010	DPJ
33. Kan Naoto	8 June 2010–2 September 2011	DPJ
34. Noda Yoshihiko	2 September 2011–26 December 2012	DPJ
35. Abe Shinzō	26 December 2012–present	LDP

Appendix B

Japan's Population Trend

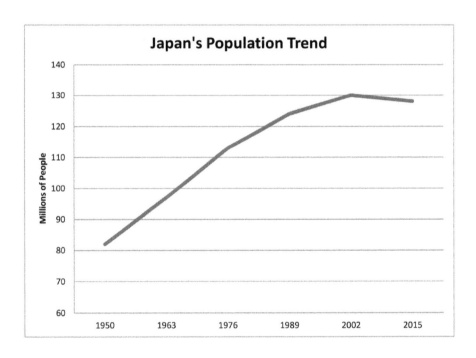

Appendix C

Births and Deaths

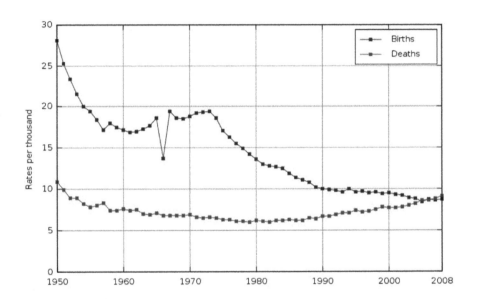

House of Representatives
October 22, 2017 election

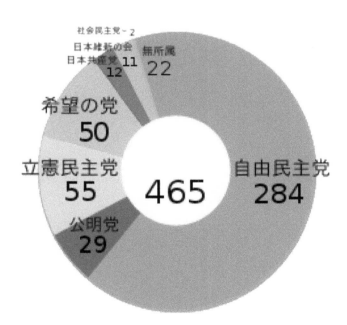

House of Councillors
July 18, 2016 election

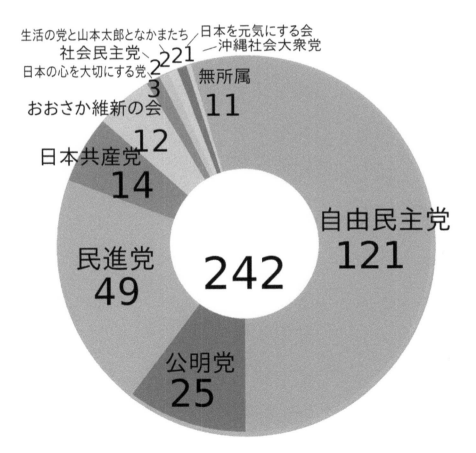

生活の党と山本太郎となかまたち
社会民主党
日本の心を大切にする党
おおさか維新の会
日本共産党
民進党
49
日本を元気にする会
沖縄社会大衆党
2 2 1
無所属
11
2
3
12
14
242
自由民主党
121
公明党
25

Appendix F

Gross National Income

JAPAN GROSS NATIONAL INCOME

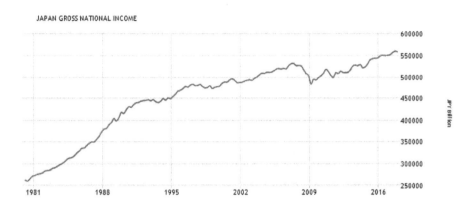

Appendix G

Nikkei 225 Index, 1950–2015

Nikkei 225 Index, 1950-2015

Appendix H

Balance of Trade

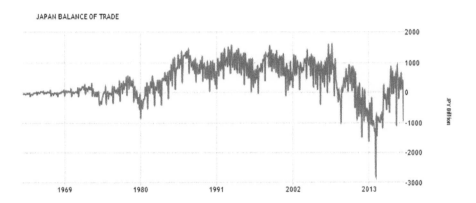

JAPAN BALANCE OF TRADE

Appendix I

Imports

Appendix J

Exports

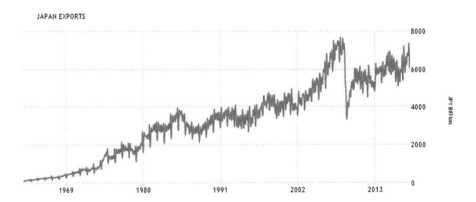

Appendix K

GDP Annual Growth Rate

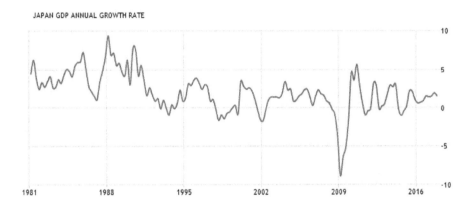

JAPAN GDP ANNUAL GROWTH RATE

Appendix L

GDP per Capita

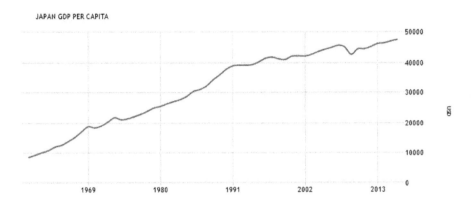

JAPAN GDP PER CAPITA

Appendix M

Corporate Profits

Appendix N

Government Debt to GDP

JAPAN GOVERNMENT DEBT TO GDP

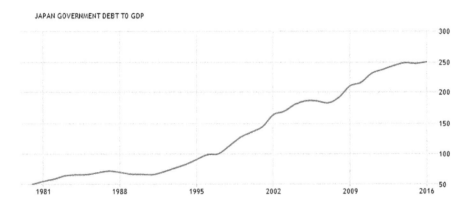

Appendix O

Countries with Highest Incomes

Countries with highest incomes:

Rank	Country	GNI per capita (US$)[1]	Year
1	Norway	82,390	2016
2	Switzerland	81,240	2016
3	Luxembourg	71,590	2016
4	Denmark	57,020	2016
5	United States	56,810	2016
6	Iceland	56,790	2016
7	Sweden	54,480	2016
8	Australia	54,230	2016
9	Ireland	52,010	2016
10	Singapore	51,880	2016

11	Netherlands	46,610	2016
12	Austria	45,870	2016
13	Finland	45,050	2016
14	Germany	43,940	2016
15	Canada	43,680	2016
16	United Kingdom	42,360	2016
17	Belgium	41,860	2016
18	United Arab Emirates	40,480	2016
19	New Zealand	38,740	2016
20	France	38,720	2016
21	Japan	37,930	2016

Appendix P

Foreign Aid

Foreign aid: These countries are most generous
Net overseas development assistance, total (million US$), 2015

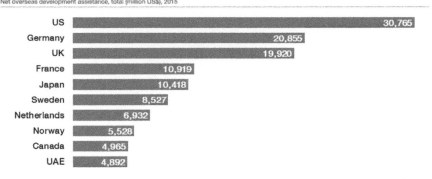

US	30,765
Germany	20,855
UK	19,920
France	10,919
Japan	10,418
Sweden	8,527
Netherlands	6,932
Norway	5,528
Canada	4,965
UAE	4,892

Public Debt Compared to GDP

Public debt compared to GDP

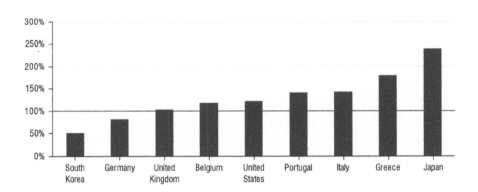

Appendix R

Unemployment Rate

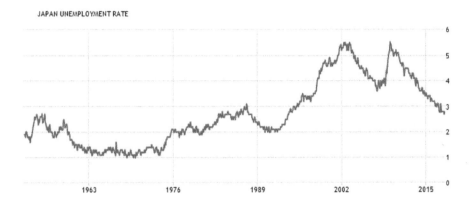

JAPAN UNEMPLOYMENT RATE

Appendix S

Military Expenditures

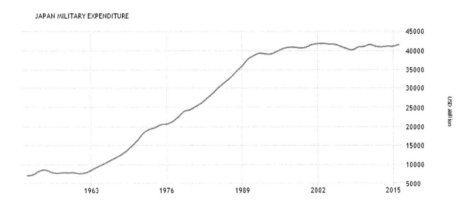

JAPAN MILITARY EXPENDITURE

Appendix T

Tourist Arrivals

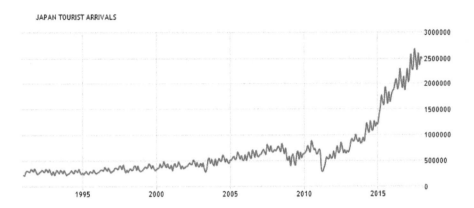

JAPAN TOURIST ARRIVALS

Bibliography

CONTENTS

INTRODUCTION

There are more publications about postwar Japan than there are books on most other countries. Literally thousands of books have appeared in the last 70 years. This bibliography focuses primarily on books published since 1980. It excludes journal and newspaper articles, conference papers, dissertations, novels, popular works, literature, most social and cultural books, biographies, travel, arts and crafts, and martial arts publications. It contains only English-language books.

One can offer a variety of observations concerning publications on postwar Japan. A single entry could well fall into two or more categories. While there is a vast diversity of subjects, the fields of society, economy, politics, and international relations dominate. Science and technology merit separate categories. Women and gender issues have attracted more attention. Popular culture has become a distinct category. Film and popular culture generate increasing numbers of scholarly publications.

World War II sparked the beginning of Japanese studies. The first studies focused primarily on history and culture, the reasons for the war, and early postwar conditions. As their knowledge of Japan grew, scholars turned to various topics and produced a wide variety of books in the later part of the 20th century.

General Introductions

Standard general assessments of the period include Frank Gibney's *The Fragile Superpower*, which contrasts U.S. and Japanese cultural and business traditions; Edwin O. Reischauer's *The Japanese*, which shows sensitivity in explaining the paradoxes of Japan; Roger Buckley's *Japan Today*, which is an excellent introductory survey of contemporary Japan; Patrick Smith's *Japan: A Reinterpretation*, which challenges the Chrysanthemum Club's uncritical assessment of Japan; John Nathan's *Japan Unbound: A Volatile Na-*

tion's Quest for Pride and Purpose, which uses interviews to reveal a sense of malaise; and Kenneth B. Pyle's *Japan Rising*, which presents Japan with a new vitality and changing international role.

Recent general treatments of Japan are plentiful. Frank Baldwin and Anne Allison edited the works of several scholars, *Japan: The Precarious Future*, which discusses Japan's erosion of global economic and political power, the growing shadow of China, and other major problems. Keiko Hirata and Mark Warschauer critique various issues from the economy and politics to immigration, education, and the increasing alienation of Japanese youth in their book *Japan: The Paradox of Harmony*. Christopher Hood, in his book *Japan: The Basics*, provides a readable introduction to Japanese culture and society.

Alex Kerr, an old Japan hand, introduces the culture and values of traditional Japan in a nostalgic way in his reissued book, *Lost Japan: Last Glimpse of Beautiful Japan*. Jeffrey Kingston has put together a book of interdisciplinary articles, *Critical Issues in Contemporary Japan*, written by leading scholars for the general reader seeking to understand postwar Japan. Timothy Iles and Peter Matanle, in their edited work *Researching Twenty-First Century Japan: New Directions and Approaches for the Electronic Age* have woven together 15 diverse articles that capture the key trends of postwar Japan.

Clyde Prestowitz, following in the pattern of Ezra Vogel's *Japan as Number One*, has written a book that visions Japan in the year 2050 when it is a world leader in virtually every area of human endeavor. The provocative book *Japan Restored: How Japan Can Reinvent Itself and Why This Is Important for America and the World* is a useful study.

Rien T. Segers, in his edited book *A New Japan for the Twenty-First Century: An Inside Overview of Current Fundamental Changes and Problems*, sees Japan in a transition period resembling the vast changes of the Meiji era or the Occupation transformation. He offers some provocative interpretations. B. Youngshik and T. J. Pempel, in *Japan in Crisis: What Will It Take for Japan to Rise Again?*, argue that Japan must not only overcome the triple disaster of the 2011 earthquake, tsunami, and nuclear meltdown, but it must free itself from more than 20 years of economic stagnation, political fumbling, and decline in regional and global influence.

In terms of assessment of the books, most earlier works praised and admired Japan. Favorable words appearing in titles include *alliance*, *ally*, *cooperation*, *friend*, *lessons* or *lesson from*, *miracle*, and *partner*. Iconic scholars such as the late Edwin O. Reischauer in *The Japanese* praised Japan for its tremendous accomplishments, and Ezra Vogel, in *Japan as Number One: Lessons for America*, proclaimed Japan the leading country for the 21st century, thus sparking great controversy.

Chief among those challenging the idealistic predictions of Vogel has been Jon Woronoff. His thought-provoking book *Japan as—anything but—Number One* corrects the idealized views of Japan. Woronoff recognizes the many accomplishments of Japan but systematically reveals the limitations and the shortcomings of the Japanese system.

Unfortunately, a certain amount of emotion has entered into the assessment of contemporary Japan. To an extent, things have polarized into two camps, the Japan-apologists and the Japan-bashers. Criticism of Japan by the Japan-bashers is condemned as racist, and Western defense of Japan is seen as being unpatriotic. However, in the last 30 years, there has been an increase in the number of works critical of Japan. Negative references in titles are found in the words *challenge, competition, conflict, confrontation, crisis, dysfunctional, friction, hegemony, myth, struggle, threat,* and *trade friction.*

History

It was not until the 1990s that the first systematic historical treatment of the postwar era appeared. Andrew Gordon's edited work *Postwar Japan as History* is a useful collection of scholarly articles covering many topics. Mikiso Hane's *Eastern Phoenix: Japan since 1949* provides a valuable topical survey of postwar Japan. Gary D. Allinson's *Japan's Postwar History* is the best short analysis of Japan since the war.

Recent historical treatment has been rich in information and analysis. Makoto Iokibe provides us with a comprehensive treatment of Japan's international relations in *The Diplomatic History of Postwar Japan.* Jeff Kingston's *Contemporary Japan: History, Politics, and Social Change since the 1980s* gives us excellent coverage of the history of recent Japan. Mizuki Shigeru's autobiographical *Showa 1953–1989: A History of Japan* has received a lot of praise.

American Occupation of Japan

The American Occupation has been a popular topic for scholars of postwar Japan. Among the best general studies are Kazuo Kawai's journalistic account *Japan's American Interlude*; Roger Buckley's *Occupation Diplomacy*, whose multiple editions focus on British and American roles in the Occupation; Michael Schaller's *The American Occupation of Japan*, which helps explain the connection between the Occupation and the Cold War; and Robert E. Ward and Yoshikazu Sakamoto's frequently cited scholarly collection *Democratizing Japan.*

Several scholars have examined war crimes with Arnold Brackman's eyewitness, journalistic account *The Other Nuremberg*; Richard Minear's *Victor's Justice*, which charges unfair and racist treatment; and Tim Maga's

Judgment at Tokyo: The Japanese War Crimes Trials, which argues that the Japanese trials were warranted and fair, providing the best interpretations. The development of democracy received scholarly attention in Kyoko Inoue's *MacArthur's Japanese Constitution*, Dale M. Helleger's *We the Japanese People*, and Mark E. Caprio and Yoneyuki Sugita's *Democracy in Occupied Japan*.

Several new books on the Occupation have appeared recently. In *Architects of Occupation: American Experts and Planning for Postwar Japan*, Dayna L. Barnes treats the process by which the United States successfully transformed a military enemy into a democratic ally while forging a strong alliance. Seymour Morris, in his book *Supreme Commander: MacArthur's Triumph in Japan*, tells a story of the Occupation from a military, political, and business perspective while combining it with a biography. Charles River's *The Postwar Occupation of Japan: The History of the Transition from World War II to Modern Japan* presents various interpretations of the Occupation from "a revolution from above" and outside Japanese control to one in which the Japanese people supported and endorsed the political transformation.

Several works of history focus on Emperor Hirohito, with Daikichi Irokawa's *The Age of Hirohito*, which condemns Hirohito for prolonging the war and its suffering; Stephen Large's *Emperor Hirohito and Showa Japan* with its objective assessment of the late emperor's personality; and Herbert P. Bix's *Hirohito and the Making of Modern Japan*, which shows the emperor as an active participant in Japan's aggressive war, being among the best. John W. Dower's *Empire and Aftermath* is both sweeping and impressively analytical. Edwin M. Reingold's *Chrysanthemums and Thorns* and Elise K. Tipton's *Modern Japan* provide useful, interpretive introductions.

For an interesting and useful study of the history and role of Japan's dynamic capital city, see Roman Cybriwsky's impressive *Historical Dictionary of Tokyo*.

Government and Politics

Of the many entries on government and politics, one can single out a few important categories. For general party politics, the classical works include Robert E. Ward's *Political Development in Modern Japan*, Bradley M. Richardson's *Political Culture of Japan*, Takeshi Ishida's *Political Culture*, Junnosuke Masumi's *Contemporary Politics in Japan*, Masaru Kohno's *Japan's Postwar Party Politics*, J. A. A. Stockwin's *Governing Japan*, Ian Neary's *The State and Politics in Japan*, and Louis D. Hayes's *Introduction to Japanese Politics*.

For important insights into contemporary Japanese politics, one should consult Jon Woronoff's *Politics the Japanese Way*, Kent Calder's *Crisis and Compensation*, Gerald Curtis's *The Japanese Way of Politics*, Chalmers Johnson's *Who Governs?*, and Yasumasa Kuroda's *The Core of Japanese Democracy*. For a negative view, one should read Karel van Wolferen's *The Enigma of Japanese Power*, which criticizes both Japan's political and economic system.

The best sources about the Liberal Democratic Party are the books by Nathaniel B. Thayer (*How the Conservatives Rule Japan*), Haruhiro Fukui (*Party in Power*), and Roger Bowen (*Japan's Dysfunctional Democracy*). On the Japan Socialist Party, see Allen Burnett Cole's *Socialist Parties in Postwar Japan*. For the Japan Communist Party, Robert A. Scalapino's *The Japanese Communist Movement*, although old, remains useful.

For new treatment on the Liberal Democratic Party, see Ellis S. Krauss and Robert J. Pekkanen's *The Rise and Fall of Japan's LDP: Political Party Organization as Historical Institutions*. For the best explanation of the Kōmeitō party, see George Ehrhardt, Axel Klein, Levi McLaughlin, and Steven R. Reed's *Kōmeitō: Politics and Religion in Japan*.

Several recent studies focus on individual political parties including Karol Zakowski's *Decision-Making Reform in Japan: The DPJ's Failed Attempt at a Politician-Led Government*, Kenji E. Kushida and Phillip Y. Lipscy's *Japan under the DPJ: The Politics of Transition and Governance*, Aurelia George Mulgan's *Ozawa Ichirō and Japanese Politics: Old Versus New* and her account of Prime Minister Abe Shinzō, *The Abe Administration and the Rise of the Prime Ministerial Executive*.

For an understanding of the Japanese constitution, one should examine Dan Fenno Henderson's *The Constitution of Japan*, Junji Banno's *The Establishment of the Japanese Constitutional System*, Theodore McNelly's *The Origins of Japan's Democratic Constitution*, and Lawrence W. Beer and John M. Maki's *From Imperial Myth to Democracy: Japan's Two Constitutions*.

Among a large body of recent work on Japanese politics, see Amy Catalinac's *Electoral Reform and National Security in Japan: From Pork to Foreign Policy*; Yoichi Funabashi's *Examining Japan's Lost Decades*; Sigal Ben-Rafael Galanti, Nissim Otmazgin, and Alon Levkowitz's *Japan's Multilayered Democracy*; Dagfinn Gatu's *The Post-war Roots of Japanese Political Malaise*; Ronald J. Hrebenar and Akira Nakamura's *Party Politics in Japan: Political Chaos and Stalemate in the 21st Century*; Leonard J. Schoppa's *The Evolution of Japan's Party System: Politics and Policy in an Era of Institutional Change*; and Arthur Stockwin and Kweku Ampiah's *Rethinking Japan: The Politics of Contested Nationalism*.

Recent useful studies of individual political leaders include Akio Watanabe's edited volume *The Prime Ministers of Postwar Japan, 1945–1995: Their Lives and Times*, Junji Banno and Jirō Yamaguchi's *The Abe Experiment and the Future of Japan: Don't Repeat History*, and Yu Uchiyama's *Koizumi and Japanese Politics: Reform Strategies and Leadership Style*.

For a good treatment of elections, see Robert J. Pekkanen, Ethan Scheiner, and Steven R. Reed's *Japan Decides 2014: The Japanese General Election*. On elections and an important individual, see Takashi Oka's *Policy Entrepreneurship and Elections in Japan: A Political Biography of Ozawa Ichirō*.

The disaster of Fukushima generated several political-related studies including Dominic Al-Badri and Gijs Berends's *After the Great East Japan Earthquake: Political and Policy Change in Post-Fukushima Japan*; Richard Krooth, Morris Edelson, and Hiroshi Fukurai's *Nuclear Tsunami: The Japanese Government and America's Role in the Fukushima Disaster*; Tsujinaka Yutaka and Hiroaki Inatsugu's *Aftermath: Fukushima and the 3.11 Earthquake*; and even a personal account by Kan Naoto, *My Nuclear Nightmare: Leading Japan through the Fukushima Disaster*.

Economy and Business

Japan's economic and business success has fascinated scholars, especially since the 1970s. Among the more successful general economic studies are Hugh T. Patrick's *The Japanese Industrialization and Its Social Consequences*, Herman Kahn's *The Japanese Challenge: The Success and Failure of Economic Success*, George C. Allen's *A Short Economic History of Modern Japan*, Richard J. Samuels's *The Business of the Japanese State*, Kent E. Calder's *Strategic Capitalism*, and James C. Abegglin's *21st-Century Japanese Management*.

Although the quantity of books published on the Japanese economy has slowed somewhat in the last decade, economic and business studies on Japan still hold a strong place in the literature. In his book *Circles of Compensation: Economic Growth and the Globalization of Japan*, Kent E. Calder identifies the crucial variables that shape social, political, and economic organizations in Japan. David Flath's third edition of *The Japanese Economy* continues to demolish the idea that Japan's economic development is an exception to modern economic history.

For a useful compendium of Japanese business firms, one should turn to Stuart D. B. Picken's updated *Historical Dictionary of Japanese Business*. Parissa Haghirian and her contributors provide a useful overview of Japanese management and business practices in *Routledge Handbook of Japanese Business and Management*. Kenji E. Kushida and his fellow editors use their book, *Syncretism: The Politics of Economic Restructuring and System Reform in Japan*, to describe the first decade of the 21st century as a period of broad transformation in Japan's political economy. W. Miles Fletcher and fellow scholars see the period after Japan's "lost decade" of the 1990s as a transformative period and offer a wide range of international perspectives on Japan in their book *Japan's "Lost Decade": Causes, Legacies and Issues of Transformative Change.*

Masatomi Wakatabe's *Japan's Great Stagnation and Abenomics: Lessons for the World* does an excellent job of treating Japan's economic crisis and Abe Shinzō's campaign to resolve the issues. He argues that Japan has experienced and overcome the burst of their bubble economy, financial crisis, tepid recovery, and a decade-long deflation and stagnation to become one of the world's most stable economies today. Aaron Forsberg offers an arresting account of Japan's postwar economic resurgence in a world polarized by the Cold War in his book *America and the Japanese Miracle: The Cold War Context of Japan's Postwar Economic Revival, 1950–1960.* He offers a fresh interpretation of the connections between Japan's economic revival and worldwide changes of the 1950s.

Hiroshi Mikitani and his late father, Ryoichi Mikitani, have written a thoughtful, lively response to the question of why Japan has fallen behind recently in *The Power to Compete: An Economist and an Entrepreneur on Revitalizing Japan in the Global Economy* and offer suggestions for addressing the problems. In *Stealth Japan: The Surprise Success of the World's First Infomerc Economy*, Scott Foster argues that Japan's economy is not on the verge of collapse but, rather, is a remarkable success story.

Social Issues

Publications on social topics are so numerous and varied to make identification of categories, as well as identifying leading works, difficult. Older classics on postwar Japanese society include Beardsley, Hall, and Ward's *Village Japan*; Ronald P. Dore's *City Life in Japan*; Ezra F. Vogel's *Japan's New Middle Class*; David W. Plath's *The After Hours*; Chie Nakane's *Japanese Society*; Takeshi Ishida's book by the same title; Robert E. Cole's *Japanese Blue Collar*; Takeo Doi's *Amae: The Anatomy of Dependence*; and Robert J. Smith's *Japanese Society*.

Other studies of special merit include Theodore C. Bestor's *Neighborhood Tokyo* on neighborhoods and *Tsukiji* on the fish market, Jonathan Rauch's interpretative work *The Outnation*, and John Creighton Campbell and Naomi Ikegami's *Containing Health Care Costs in Japan*. Susan Long's *Caring for the Elderly in Japan*, David R. Leheny's *The Rules of Play: National Identity and the Shaping of Japanese Leisure*, Brian J. McVeigh's *Nationalisms of Japan*, and Gregory J. Kasza's *One World of Welfare* also have much to teach us about social issues.

Yoshio Sugimoto's *An Introduction to Japanese Society*, now in its fourth edition, is a sophisticated, yet readable, exploration of Japanese society. He challenges the traditional notion that Japan is a very uniform culture by pointing out its subcultural diversity and class competition. Hiroshi Ishida and David H. Slater's edited book, *Social Class in Contemporary Japan*, traces the dynamics of social structure, institutional socialization, and class culture in postwar Japan.

Equality, or the lack thereof, is a common subject in the Japanese social order. Sawako Shirahase, in *Social Inequality in Japan*, raises doubt about the degree of social equality in contemporary Japan. In the degree of female participation in the labor market, income inequality, the nature of the family, generational change, single-person households, and income distribution among the aged, Japan has its own distinct inequality. David Chiavacci and Carola Hommerich's edited book, *Social Inequality in Post-growth Japan: Transformation during Economic and Demographic Stagnation*, sees Japan as having a declining economy, fraught with social inequality and facing a shrinking population with a very high proportion of elderly people. Andrea Germer, Vera Mackie, and Ulrike Wöhr's edited volume, *Gender, Nation and State in Modern Japan*, focuses on the gendering of the modern Japanese nation-state from the late 19th century to the present. They contend that gender differences are deeply embedded in the Japanese state.

Debito Arudou contends that racism is pervasive in Japan in his book, *Embedded Racism: Japan's Visible Minorities and Racial Discrimination*, and contends that Japan's economic and demographic decline cannot be corrected unless Japan honestly and fully accepts immigrants.

Robert Pekkanen, Yutaka Tsujinaku, and Hidehiro Yamamoto write about Japan's numerous, active neighborhood associations in their book, *Neighborhood Associations and Local Governance in Japan*. Japan's numerous civic organizations and neighborhood associations make important contributions to the governance of Japan.

Anne Allison examines the question of how the Japanese experience insecurity in their daily lives in her book *Precarious Japan*. She argues that Japan has not only economic problems to solve but also social issues that must be confronted.

In *Sustainability in Contemporary Rural Japan: Challenges and Opportunities*, Stephanie Assmann contends that rural communities suffer from significant depopulation and economic downturn. Low birth rates, aging populations, agricultural decline, and youth migration to large cities have destroyed farming and fishing communities.

Tomoko Aoyama, Laura Dales, and Romit Dasgupta have edited a book, *Configurations of Family in Contemporary Japan*, which explores the "family" in Japan, and combines the scholarly research on literature, gender studies, media and cultural studies, sociology, and anthropology.

As might be expected, women have been the center of numerous studies in postwar Japan. Suzanne Hall Vogel traces the evolution of women in Japanese society through the lives of three ordinary yet remarkable women, as well as their daughters and granddaughters, in her book *The Japanese Family in Transition: From the Professional Housewife Ideal to the Dilemmas of Choice*. Vogel contends that the role of the professional housewife constrained Japanese middle-class women in the postwar era but also empowered them. Yoko Tokuhiro explores the state of marriage in Japanese society in her book *Marriage in Contemporary Japan*. She argues that by delaying marriage and child rearing, young women can be seen as "rebels" challenging Japanese patriarchal society.

Alisa Freedman, Laura Miller, and Christine R. Yano present an edited work that treats Japanese women from a multiplicity of disciplines in *Modern Girls on the Go: Gender, Mobility, and Labor in Japan*. Aya Ezawa examines the difficult living conditions facing single mothers in Japan including hardship in earning an adequate wage, managing the work-family balance, and class distinctions in family life in her book, *Single Mothers in Contemporary Japan: Motherhood, Class, and Reproductive Practice*.

On the distaff side, Sabine Frühstück and Anne Walthall have edited a book, *Recreating Japanese Men*, which explores the meanings of manhood in Japan from the 17th to the 21st centuries. They look at what today is considered proper masculine pursuits and modes of behavior.

Simon Andrew Avenell shows how activists, intellectuals, and movements played a crucial role in shaping civil society and civic thought throughout Japan's postwar period in his book *Making Japanese Citizens: Civil Society and the Mythology of the Shimin in Postwar Japan*. He outlines the development of a new vision of citizenship based on political participation, self-reliance, popular nationalism, and commitment to daily life.

With Japan facing difficulties as its economy globalizes, its political establishment stalemates, and its people experience alternative lifestyles, Wolfram Manzenreiter and Barbara Holthus in their edited book, *Happiness and the Good Life in Japan*, see Japanese society as confronting new challenges to answer the fundamental question of how to live a good life with meaning, purpose, and value. Akiko Takeyama explores the host clubs of Tōkyō's Kabuki-chō red-light district where young men seek their fortunes by selling love, romance, companionship, and sometimes sex to female consumers. In *Staged Seduction: Selling Dreams in a Tokyo Host Club*, Takeyama provides a provocative look at the fantasy world for wealthy women seeking an escape from everyday life.

Public housing has been an issue of concern in postwar Japan. Laura Lynn Neitzel examines life in the high-rise public housing projects (*danchi*) in her book *"The Life We Longed For": Danchi Housing and the Middle Class Dream in Postwar Japan*. Christoph Brumann and Evelyn Schulz have edited a book, *Urban Spaces in Japan: Cultural and Social Perspectives*, which explores the workings of power, money, and the public interest in the planning and design of Japanese space.

Rebellious youth have caught the attention of many scholars in Japan. Carl Cassegärd's *Youth Movements, Trauma and Alternative Space in Contemporary Japan* provides a detailed study of social movements among young Japanese from the 1980s until the present. He examines antiwar mobilizations, freeter unions, artists in the homeless movement, campus protests, antinuclear protests, and social withdrawers. Roger Goodman, Yuki Imoto, and Tuukka Toivonen have edited an interesting study of youth culture, *A Sociology of Japanese Youth: From Returnees to NEETs*, which treats NEETs ("not in education, employment or training"), bullying, corporal punishment, compensated dating, and withdrawn youth. Sharon Kinsella explores the cult of girls in contemporary Japanese media and culture in her book *Schoolgirls, Money and Rebellion in Japan*.

Turning from youth to the aged, Satsuki Kawano has examined end-of-life procedures in her book *Nature's Embrace: Japan's Aging Urbanites and New Death Rites*. She examines Japan's changing death rites from the perspective of those who elect to have their cremated remains scattered and celebrate their return to nature, a process that requires neither a grave nor a caretaker.

Scholars of Japan have examined a wide range of social topics. Carolyn S. Stevens charts the history and nature of disability in Japan, discusses policy and law relating to disability, examines caregiving and accessibility, and explores how disability is viewed in her book *Disability in Japan*. Ruth Taplin and Sandra J. Lawman examine the issue of mental health, including widespread depression, a high suicide rate, and institutionalization in their book *Mental Health Care in Japan*.

In 1995, Japan was shaken by the "double disaster" of a major earthquake and a sarin gas attack while in 2011 it was devastated by the "triple disaster" of earthquake, tsunami, and nuclear meltdown. Mark R. Mullins and Koichi Nakano have edited a book, *Disasters and Social Crisis in Contemporary Japan: Political, Religious, and Sociocultural Responses*, where an international, multidisciplinary group of scholars examines the way Japanese people respond to such disasters.

Stigmatized throughout Japanese history as an outcaste group, being from the *burakumin* group is still "risky." Marginalized, they experience many disadvantages. Japan's largest minority group numbers perhaps as many as three million. Christopher Bondy examines how *burakumin* function in their society in his interesting book *Voice, Silence, and Self: Negotiations of Buraku Identity in Contemporary Japan*. Ian Neary treats the subject in *The Buraku Issue and Modern Japan: The Career of Matsumoto Jiichirō*, a leading *burakumin* activist in the 1950s and 1960s.

For an interesting phenomenon in Japanese sports life, see the importance attached to marathon running as presented in Thomas R. H. Havens's *Marathon Japan: Distance Racing and Civic Culture*. Merry White's *Coffee Life in Japan* is a fascinating book about Japan's vibrant café society. She examines themes as diverse as gender, privacy, and urbanism as seen in the coffee culture.

Religion

For general studies of Japanese religion, see H. Byron Earhart's *Religion in Japan: Unity and Diversity*, Joseph Kitagawa's *On Understanding Japanese Religion*, Ian Reader's *Religion in Contemporary Japan*, Winston B. Davis's *Japanese Religion and Society*, and Klaus J. Antoni's *Religion and National Identity in the Japanese Context*. For Shintōism, see John Breen and Mark Teeuwen's *Shintō in History*, C. Scott Littleton's *Shintō: A Short History*, and Thomas P. Kasulis's *Shintō: The Way Home*. For works on Buddhism, see Helen Hardacre's *Lay Buddhism in Contemporary Japan* and Esben Andreasen's *Popular Buddhism in Japan*.

Barbara R. Ambros examines the roles that women have played in the religions of Japan in her book *Women in Japanese Religions*, providing an important corrective to the male-centered narratives of Japanese religious history.

Stuart D. B. Picken's *Historical Dictionary of Shintō* (2nd ed.) relates the history of Shintō through a chronology, an introductory essay, an extensive bibliography, and more than 800 cross-referenced entries on Shintō concepts, individuals, places, activities, and periods.

Education

Some general works on Japanese education are William K. Cummings's *Education and Equality in Japan* and Edward R. Beauchamp's *Education in Modern Japan*. Much has been made of Japanese education as a model accomplishment. For books in this vein, see Richard Lynn's *Educational Achievement in Japan*, Robert Leestma and Herbert J. Walberg's *Educational Productivity*, and Catherine C. Lewis's *Educating Hearts and Minds*. For books that question the possible embellishment of Japanese education, see Robert L. Cutts's *An Empire of Schools*, a revisionist treatment of the University of Tōkyō; Kaori Okano and Motonori Tsuchiya's *Education in Contemporary Japan*; Shoko Yoneyama's *The Japanese High School*; Brian J. McVeigh's *Japanese Higher Education*; and Gary Decoker's *Japanese Education in an Era of Globalization: Culture, Politics, and Equality*.

Akiko Hayashi and Joseph Tobin examine early education in Japan's preschools to gain perspective on how teachers embody their lessons and present their findings in *Teaching Embodied: Cultural Practice in Japanese Preschools*. Christopher Bjork presents an ethnography of Japanese elementary and middle schools in his study *High-Stakes Schooling: What We Can Learn from Japan's Experiences with Testing, Accountability, and Education Reform*. Peter Cave shows how junior high schools try to balance the development of autonomy with that of social interdependence in his book *Schooling Selves: Autonomy, Interdependence, and Reform in Japanese Junior High Education*. Robert W. Aspinall analyzes the ways in which Japanese government policies on English-language education and the promotion of Study Abroad have been implemented in schools and universities in his book *International Education Policy in Japan in an Age of Globalisation and Risk*.

Japan's need to internationalize its higher education system has been a recent goal in Japan. John Mock and Hiroaki Kawamura offer an empirically grounded, culturally nuanced analysis of how universities are attempting to internationalize their educational system in their book, *The Impact of Internationalization on Japanese Higher Education: Is Japanese Education Really Changing?* In his book *The Organisational Dynamics of University Reform in Japan*, Jeremy Breaden shows that although Japan has tried to internationalize its higher educational system, it remains a somewhat reclusive member of the global academic community. Brian J. McVeigh draws on his own experience of teaching at a women's junior college to show how young women are socialized to fit the role of a low-level employee and future mother in his interesting book *Life in a Japanese Women's College: Learning to be Ladylike*.

Labor

The role of labor and unions has been important in the development of postwar Japan. Good general studies of labor include Jon Woronoff's *Japan's Wasted Workers*, which shows less than eager workers, overstaffed enterprises, hidden unemployment, and overdeveloped bureaucratization; Joe B. Moore's *The Other Japan*; Andrew Gordon's *The Wages of Affluence*, which argues that Japan's economy owes as much to coercion as to consensus; and Michael H. Gibbs's *Struggle and Purpose in Postwar Japanese Unionism*. Christena Turner's *Japanese Workers in Protest*, Edward Fowler's *San'ya Blues*, Tom Gill's *Men of Uncertainty*, and Reiko Kosugi's *Escape from Work* are useful specialized studies on workers.

In her book *Migrant Workers in Contemporary Japan: An Institutional Perspective on Transnational Employment*, Kiyoto Tanno focuses on Brazilian migrant workers in Japan to provide a comprehensive picture of the forces driving transnational labor migration to Japan and the situations they experience. Gracia Liu-Farrer sheds light on all facets of Chinese labor migration to Japan in her book *Labor Migration from China to Japan: International Students, Transnational Migrants*.

Insecure employment practices have disrupted Japan's fixed employment practices of the past and have given rise to the existence of the phenomenon of day laborers. In her book *Reconstructing Adult Masculinities: Part-Time Work in Contemporary Japan*, Emma E. Cook argues that, in the past two decades, Japan's socioeconomic environment has undergone considerable changes prompted by both a long recession and the relaxation of labor laws that gave rise to the phenomenon of "freeters," or part-time workers, a development that has disrupted the Japanese labor system. In *Lost in Transition: Youth, Work, and Instability in Postindustrial Japan*, Mary C. Brinton tells the story of the "lost generation" that came of age in Japan's economic recession of the 1990s. She argues that Japan has experienced an era of profound changes that have strongly impacted the young generation, causing many young workers to have only temporary, insecure forms of employment. Huiyan Fu's *An Emerging Non-Regular Labour Force in Japan: The Dignity of Dispatched Workers* treats the rise of non-regular workers who are organized and supplied by employment agencies.

In his book *Yokohama Street Life: The Precarious Career of a Japanese Day Laborer*, Tom Gill presents a one-man ethnography of a single Japanese day laborer from his wartime childhood in Kyūshū through a brief military career to a lifetime spent working on the docks and construction sites. Jiyeoun Song focuses on Japan and South Korea with their advanced labor markets and confronts the rapid rise of a split in labor markets between protected regular workers and under-protected, underpaid non-regular workers in her book *Inequality in the Workplace: Labor Market Reform in Japan and Korea*.

In his study of youth in the labor force titled *Japan's Emerging Youth Policy: Getting Young Adults Back to Work*, Tuukka Toivonen is one of the first people to investigate in detail how the state, experts, and the media, as well as youth workers, have been affected by the rise of youth joblessness in 21st-century Japan.

Women

Studies on women and their role in postwar Japan have grown dramatically in the past three decades. Among the earlier studies, Dorothy Robbins-Mowry's *The Hidden Sun*, Takie Sugimura Lebra's *Japanese Women*, Mary C. Brinton's *Women and the Economic Miracle*, Janet Hunter's *Japanese Women Working*, and Barbara Molony and Kathleen S. Uno's *Gendering*

Modern Japanese History are important. For specialized studies, see Anne Allinson's *Nightwork*, Anne E. Inamura's *Re-Imaging Japanese Women*, and Gail Bernstein's *Haruko's World*.

In more recent studies, Anne Stefanie Aronsson's *Career Women in Contemporary Japan: Pursuing Identities, Fashioning Lives* examines what motivates Japanese women to pursue professional careers, explores how they reconfigure notions of selfhood, and analyzes how professional women contest conventional notions of femininity and negotiate new gender roles and cultural assumptions.

Ayako Kano, in her book *Japanese Feminist Debates: A Century of Contention on Sex, Love, and Labor*, traces the origins and development of the feminist movement in Japan from the late 19th century to the present. Justin Charlebois's *Japanese Femininities* explores how women's gender roles are both confirmed and undermined in Japan today. It shows that old held concepts are simultaneously resisted and transformed by contemporary women. Susan Holloway attempts to answer the questions of why Japanese women are postponing marriage and bearing fewer children in her stimulating book *Women and Family in Contemporary Japan*.

Kumiko Nemoto, in her book *Too Few Women at the Top: The Persistence of Inequality in Japan*, argues that the number of women in positions of power in Japanese companies remains small despite the increase in the number of educated women and the passage of legislation on gender equality. Anne Zacharias-Walsh provides an in-depth look at the rise of women-only unions in Japan, the challenges they face, and a firsthand account of an ambitious, and sometimes contentious, women's labor union in her book *Our Unions, Our Selves: The Rise of Feminist Labor Unions in Japan*.

Environment

To understand Japan's postwar treatment of the environment, one should consult Jeffrey Broadbent's *Environmental Politics in Japan*, Brendan F. D. Barrett's *Ecological Modernization and Japan*, and Pradyumna Prasad Karan's *Japan in the Twenty-First Century*. To comprehend trends in science and technology, one would do well to read Daniel K. Okimoto's *Between MITI and the Market*, Samuel Coleman's *Japanese Science from the Inside*, and Morris Low's *Science and the Building of a New Japan*.

In the most recent scholarship, Conrad Totman, the leading scholar on Japan's environment, provides us with a major guide to Japan's environmental history in his book *Japan: An Environmental History*. Brett L. Walker's powerful book *Toxic Archipelago: A History of Industrial Disease in Japan* tells the story of Minamata and the disastrous impact of unfettered industrial growth in 20th-century Japan.

Bruce L. Batten and Philip C. Brown, in *Environment and Society in the Japanese Islands: From Prehistory to the Present*, describe various environmental problems and challenges confronting Japan and try to draw some understandings about the relationship between human society and the natural environment.

Simon Avenell, in his book *Transnational Japan in the Global Environmental Movement*, combines local, national, regional, and global historical narratives about contemporary Japanese environmental movements from Japanese industrial pollution in the 1960s to more recent movements addressing global environmental problems.

Ian Jared Miller, Julia Adeney Thomas, and Brett L. Walker edited a book, *Japan at Nature's Edge: The Environmental Context of a Global Power*, which provides a broad introduction to Japan's environmental history in light of Japan's March 2011 disaster. For an interesting perspective on Japan's environment, see Bruce Allen and Yuki Masami's edited work *Ishimure Michiko's Writing in Ecocritical Perspective*. They have collected essays by one of Japan's most famous writers on the environment, including issues from the Minamata disease catastrophe to the Fukushima disaster.

As one might expect, the Fukushima disaster spawned a plethora of studies. Michael C. Brannigan, in his study *Japan's March 2011 Disaster and Moral Grit: Our Inescapable In-Between*, attempts to explain Japan's cultural mind-set and its relationship to the terrible catastrophe in Fukushima. He sees Japanese ethics as a major factor in how the Japanese people have responded to this terrible disaster. Richard Hindmarsh's *Nuclear Disaster at Fukushima Daiichi: Social, Political and Environmental Issues* provides a useful account of the earthquake, tsunami, and Fukushima Daiichi nuclear meltdown along Japan's northeast coastline on 11 March 2011. Hindmarsh, with the help of Rebecca Priestly, edited another book on the disaster in northeast Japan, titled *The Fukushima Effect: A New Geopolitical Terrain*. Combining the research and thoughts of several international scholars, they present a study of how such a series of events would be understood in various countries.

Richard J. Samuels offers a broad scholarly assessment of the Fukushima disaster's impact on Japan's government and society in his book *3.11: Disaster and Change in Japan*. The event came at a very inopportune time as Japan had experienced two decades of social and economic malaise as well as considerable political and administrative turmoil.

Susan Carpenter's *Japan's Nuclear Crisis: The Routes to Responsibility* analyzes and explores the impact of Japan's 2011 nuclear crisis including why Daiichi was constructed in an earthquake-prone zone and continued to operate despite problems known since 1989.

Koichi Hasegawa penned a powerful condemnation of nuclear power in Japan in his book *Beyond Fukushima: Toward a Post-nuclear Society*. He asks why Japan continued its use of the nuclear power plant when problems were already projected. With convincing analysis, Hasegawa argues passionately for denuclearization.

Peter Wynn Kirby treats the handling of waste in Japan from a broad ethical perspective in his book *Troubled Natures: Waste, Environment, Japan*. His anthropological study of two Tōkyō neighborhoods is quite instructive.

Midori Kagawa-Fox examines the link between government policy and environmental risks in her book *The Ethics of Japan's Global Environmental Policy: The Conflict between Principles and Practice*. She looks at nuclear energy, whaling, and forestry management from a universal perspective and argues the Japanese government has failed to follow adequate ethical policies.

Jeff Kingston and several other scholars examine Japanese life in the second decade of the 21st century from multiple perspectives in their book *Natural Disaster and Nuclear Crisis in Japan: Response and Recovery after Japan's 3/11*. This useful book enables the reader to view Japan in a more sophisticated way.

Saadia M. Pekkanen and Paul Kallender-Umezu's book, titled *In Defense of Japan: From the Market to the Military in Space Policy*, provides the first complete, up-to-date, English-language account of the history, politics, and policy of Japan's space program.

International Relations

International relations have been a major focus of Japanese studies in the postwar period. Foreign policy in general has been well examined by Robert A. Scalapino's *The Foreign Policy of Modern Japan*, Shirao Saito's *Japan and the Summit*, Gerald L. Curtis's *Japan's Foreign Policy after the Cold War*, Reinhard Drifte's *Japan's Foreign Policy in the 1990s*, Warren S. Hunsberger's *Japan's Quest: The Search for International Role, Recognition, and Respect*, and Kevin Cooney's *Japan's Foreign Policy since 1945*.

Japan in the world is the theme of Tsuneo Akaha and Frank Langdon's *Japan in the Posthegemonic World*, Walter Hatch and Kozo Yamamura's *Asia in Japan's Embrace*, Ronald P. Dore's *Japan, Internationalism and the UN*, Bert Edstrom's *Japan's Evolving Foreign Policy Doctrine*, Akiko Fukushima's *Japanese Foreign Policy*, John Clammer's *Japan and Its Others*, and Michael J. Green's *Japan's Reluctant Realism*.

Glenn D. Hook and Hiroko Takeda's edited book, titled *Ending the Postwar in Japan: Structure, Actors, Norms and Challenges*, tries to answer the question as to whether the postwar period has ended. Various scholars argue that Japan is more heterogeneous than homogeneous. Hook, Ra Mason, and Paul O'Shea use the theory of risk as a tool for understanding international relations in their book *Regional Risk and Security in Japan: Whither the Everyday*. This book utilizes the concept of risk to provide an innovative perspective on Japan's relations with China, North Korea, and the United States.

Hidekazu Sakai and Yoichiro Sato challenge the idea that Japan has slipped from being a major power but, rather, argue that Japan is one of the leading forces in the world today in their book *Re-rising Japan: Its Strategic Power in International Relations*. Yasutami Shimomura, John Page, and Hiroshi Kato, in their edited book *Japan's Development Assistance: Foreign Aid and the Post-2015 Agenda*, argue that although Japan has slipped from being the world's largest ODA provider and seems less visible in international development, it has its own aid philosophy, experiences, and models of aid, and offers the international community new perspectives on international aid.

In his new book *Koizumi Diplomacy: Japan's Kantei Approach to Foreign and Defense Affairs*, Tomohito Shinoda analyzes the prime minister's role in policy making, focusing on the assistance he receives from the *Kantei*, or cabinet secretariat, the Japanese equivalent of the U.S. president's White House cabinet. Japan's policy-making strategy in foreign and defense affairs changed dramatically in 2001 after Prime Minister Koizumi Jun'ichirō took the helm of the long-ruling Liberal Democratic Party.

Michael J. Green and Zack Cooper, in their edited book *Postwar Japan: Growth, Security, and Uncertainty since 1945*, reflect on the evolution of political, economic, and defense policies in Japan and draw lessons for the coming decades. They assert the continuing viability of Japan's postwar strategic choices.

Yoneyuki Sugita's edited work *Toward a More Amicable Asia-Pacific Region: Japan's Roles* contends that President Barack Obama's "pivot to Asia" strategy shows that the region is an engine for the world economic growth, but instability in the region comes from many sources of conflicts such as disputes on the Senkaku/Diaoyu Islands, the unsettled Exclusive Economic Zone (EEZ) borders, and many others. Jing Sun's *Japan and China as Charm Rivals: Soft Power in Regional Diplomacy* focuses on the competition between China and Japan for the allegiance of South Korea, Taiwan, and other states in the region. Sun finds that China and Japan apply customized charm campaigns in each country, while taking into consideration the target's culture, international position, and political values, to gain a major advantage in the area.

The Japan Exchange and Teaching (JET) Program, launched in 1987, has had more than 60,000 participants. Emily T. Metzgar's *The JET Program and the US-Japan Relationship: Goodwill Goldmine* argues that JET functions as much more than an opportunity for young people to spend a year or more teaching in Japanese schools or working in municipal offices across the Japanese archipelago. As she contends, the JET program is a form of public diplomacy and soft power.

Paul Midford, in his book *Rethinking Japanese Public Opinion and Security: From Pacifism to Realism*, argues that since 9/11 Japanese public opinion has moved away from pacifism and toward supporting a normal level of military power.

Sebastian Maslow, Ra Mason, and Paul O'Shea offer new insights into the analysis of contemporary foreign policy in East Asia and Japan's post–Cold War international relations in particular in their book *Risk State: Japan's Foreign Policy in an Age of Uncertainty*.

Timur Dadabaev provides insights into the security, political, and economic aspects of cooperation between countries in Central Asia and Japan and the features that characterize these relations in his book *Japan in Central Asia: Strategies, Initiatives, and Neighboring Powers*.

Guibourg Delamotte's edited book *Japan's World Power: Assessment, Outlook and Vision* examines the nature of Japan's power today, showing how Japan appears to be shifting from economic and financial, to more political and military power. Yet this book argues that despite recent developments and changes, Japan exercises its power differently from other major powers as it is still guided by its pacifist identity.

H. P. D. Envall's *Japanese Diplomacy: The Role of Leadership* questions the role of individual leadership styles, personalities, perceptions, and beliefs in shaping Japan's diplomacy. Various prime ministers have played different roles. In his book *Japan's Foreign and Security Policy under the "Abe Doctrine": New Dynamism or New Dead End?* Christopher W. Hughes argues that Japan is shifting onto a more muscular national security policy, with the U.S.-Japan alliance acting as a base for regional and global security. In a second book, *Japan's Re-emergence as a "Normal" Military Power*, he concludes that Japan is moving along the trajectory of becoming a more assertive military power, and that this trend has accelerated since 9/11. Hughes believes that Japan's defensive shield of the U.S. offensive sword bolsters U.S. military hegemony.

Yasukuni Shrine, Japan's memorial to its war dead, has generated a great deal of controversy in the Asian world. Akiko Takenaka's *Yasukuni Shrine: History, Memory, and Japan's Unending Postwar* is the first extensive study in English of the Yasukuni Shrine issue. It explores the controversial shrine's role in waging war, promoting peace, honoring the dead, and building Japan's modern national identity. In *Political Survival and Yasukuni in Japan's Relations with China*, Mong Cheung looks at the role prime ministers have played in Japan's relations with China over the Yasukuni issue.

Terence Roehrig provides a comprehensive look at the nuclear umbrella in northeast Asia in the broader context of deterrence theory and U.S. strategy in his book *Japan, South Korea, and the United States Nuclear Umbrella*. Roehrig argues that the nuclear umbrella is most important as a political signal demonstrating commitment to the defense of allies and as a tool to prevent further nuclear proliferation in the region.

Carin Holroyd and Ken Coates, in their edited book *Japan in the Age of Globalization*, look at the way multiple and diverse forces of globalization have significantly affected Japan in the last few decades. This collection examines the impact of globalization on Japan. Ross Mouer and fellow scholars contend, in their book *Globalizing Japan: Striving to Engage the World*, that Japan is being forced to grapple with the problems of the world.

Yoshihide Soeya and David A. Welch, in their edited work *Japan as a "Normal Country"? A Nation in Search of Its Place in the World*, argue that most scholars have seen Japan's foreign relations as abnormally weak and limited in relation to its size and level of sophistication. These scholars question what is normal and urge a reassessment of Japan's foreign policy.

Gerald Figal's *Beachheads: War, Peace, and Tourism in Postwar Okinawa* explores Okinawa's transformation to a tourist destination despite the long historical shadow and among the physical ruins of the Pacific War's most devastating land battle. He shows how a place burdened by a history of semi-colonialism, memories of war and occupation, economic hardship, and contentious current political affairs have reshaped itself into a resort destination.

With the United States

The leading books covering Japan's relations with the United States include Roger Buckley's *U.S.-Japan Alliance Diplomacy*, William R. Nester's *American Power, the New World Order and the Japanese Challenge*, Harrison M. Holland's *Japan Challenges America*, Michael H. Armacost's *Friends or Rivals?*, Chihiro Hosoya and Tomohito Shinoda's *Redefining the Partnership: The United States and Japan in East Asia*, Masashi Nishihara's *The Japan-U.S. Alliance*, C. Fred Bergsten's *No More Bashing*, and Akira Iriye's *Partnership: The United States and Japan*.

Kent E. Calder, a highly respected scholar, provides a comparative analysis of the transpacific alliance and its political, economic, and social foundations in his book *Pacific Alliance: Reviving U.S.-Japan Relations*. He asserts that bilateral relations between the two countries seem to be eroding as both countries are following broader options in a globally oriented world.

Michael R. Auslin presents an interesting treatment of cultural exchanges from the mid-19th century through the 1970s in his book *Pacific Cosmopolitans: A Cultural History of U.S.-Japan Relations*. Of special interest is the ambivalence Auslin points out between Japan and the United States in their cultural exchanges.

Peter Duus and Kenji Hasegawa, in their edited work *Rediscovering America: Japanese Perspectives on the American Century*, present a collection of writings, covering the period from 1878 to 1989, by various Japanese visitors to the United States in which they give their perspective on Americans and American society.

Historical dictionaries are becoming more prominent. John Van Sant, Peter Mauch, and Yoneyuki Sugita published their *Historical Dictionary of United States–Japan Relations* about a decade ago. They trace the 150-year relationship through a chronology, an introduction, appendixes, a bibliography, and cross-referenced entries on key persons, places, events, institutions, and organizations. Mayako Shimamoto, Koji Ito, and Yoneyuki Sugita wrote the *Historical Dictionary of Japanese Foreign Policy* where they provide over 400 cross-referenced entries on important personalities, politics, economy, foreign relations, religion, and culture.

Frederik L. Schodt, in his book *America and the Four Japans: Friend, Foe, Model, Mirror*, aptly characterizes Japan and its relations with America in his title. Warren S. Hunsberger, in his book titled *Japan's Quest: The Search for International Role, Recognition, and Respect*, goes further and, in the title, describes Japan's desire to find a role, recognition, and respect.

Sheila Smith argues that Japan's new politics challenge some basic assumptions about U.S.-Japan alliance management in her book *Japan's New Politics and the U.S.-Japan Alliance*. She contends political changes have tended to reshape alliance cooperation and policy reform.

With China

In the last two decades, Japan and China have begun to explore a new relationship. Important studies of recent Japanese-Chinese interaction include Akira Iriye's *China and Japan in the Global Setting*, which relates power, economics, and culture in three eras; Caroline Rose's *Interpreting History in Sino-Japanese Relations*, which recounts the diplomatic storm generated by the textbook controversy of the 1980s; Greg Austin and Stuart Harris's *Japan and Greater China*, which discusses the political economy and military power as Asia matures; Margaret Sleeboom's *Academic Nations in China and Japan*, which examines the descriptions Japanese and Chinese attribute to themselves; and Linus Hagstrom's *Japan's China Policy*, which challenges conventional views of Japan's defense policy.

Robert Hoppens, in his book *The China Problem in Postwar Japan: Japanese National Identity and Sino-Japanese Relations*, treats the history of Sino-Japanese relations in the 1970s, a period of dramatic developments between Japan and the PRC.

In a powerful, timely book, Richard McGregor reveals the fissures that are severely disturbing the Pacific region. The American security umbrella is weakening as toxic rivalry between China and Japan worsens, China's economic power grows, regional ambitions grow, and Donald Trump seems intent on upsetting old alliances. *Asia's Reckoning: China, Japan, and the Fate of U.S. Power in the Pacific Century* suggests that East Asian relations are falling apart.

Claude Meyer poses a challenging question in his book *China or Japan: Which Will Lead Asia?* Meyer sees Asia, with three of the four largest economies, as the dominant place in the 21st century. Both, along with India, will do well, but Meyer gives the edge to Japan based on its leadership, productivity, competitiveness, and technological edge.

Anna Costa examines the foreign and security policies adopted by China and Japan since the 1970s in their competition over the Senkaku/Diaoyu Islands in the East China Sea. In *The China-Japan Conflict over the Senkaku/Diaoyu Islands: Useful Rivalry*, she sees increasing nationalism in both China and Japan as a triggering factor and suggests that the leaders of both countries find competition over the islands to be a convenient vehicle to support their foreign and security policies, as they are becoming increasingly assertive and potentially belligerent.

Tim F. Liao and Kimie Hara offer a provocative analysis of the territorial dispute between Japan and China over the Diaoyu/Senkaku Islands. *The China-Japan Border Dispute: Islands of Contention in Multidisciplinary Perspective* helps us understand the complexity of the dispute and to consider peaceful solutions from multiple perspectives.

James Manicom challenges the orthodox view that the strategic rivalry between China and Japan will escalate into military conflict but sees instead the East China Sea as a likely place for Sino-Japanese military rivalry and pressing tensions in his book *Bridging Troubled Waters: China, Japan, and Maritime Order in the East China Sea.*

With Korea

Korea has increasingly become the focus of Japan's attention. Celeste L. Arrington, in her book *Accidental Activists: Victim Movements and Government Accountability in Japan and South Korea*, examines the dynamics of interaction between the two countries and treats the various avenues of redress. Brad Glosserman and Scott A. Snyder, in *The Japan-South Korea Identity Clash: East Asian Security and the United States*, argue that, despite their shared interests, common values, and geographic proximity, Japan and South Korea, while having Western-style democracies with open-market economies and a commitment to the rule of law, have divergent national identities that drive a wedge between them.

Alexis Dudden's *Troubled Apologies: Among Japan, Korea, and the United States* looks at the role of apologies in history, focusing on the problematic relationship binding Japanese imperialism, South Korean state building, and American power in Asia. She argues that apologies have created problems from which the two countries cannot escape.

Chaihark Hahm and Sung Ho Kim question the making of Japan and Korea's constitutions in their book *Making We the People: Democratic Constitutional Founding in Postwar Japan and South Korea*. They cast doubt on the "we the people" concept.

Marie Söderberg, in her edited book *Changing Power Relations in Northeast Asia: Implications for Relations between Japan and South Korea*, analyses the Japanese–South Korean relationship from the standpoint of politics, security, economics, culture, and immigration. She argues that the two countries are natural partners as both are democratic societies, economically strong, and members of the OECD. Both have security treaties with the United States and share security concerns when it comes to the North Korean nuclear threat as well as the rise of China. Japan and South Korea also share similar values, customs, cultures, and languages. It would seem they should have a strong bilateral relationship, but this is still not the case.

Seung Hyok Lee, in *Japanese Society and the Politics of the North Korean Threat*, sees North Korean ballistic missile tests as provoking Japanese alarm and severely constrained action. Such action has provoked Japan to use coercion against a neighboring state.

Japan is not very multicultural, as is seen in the lack of acceptance of Koreans in Japanese society. David Chapman's *Zainichi Korean Identity and Ethnicity* addresses the broad notions and questions of citizenship, identity, ethnicity, and belonging through investigation of Japan's Korean population known as *Zainichi*.

With Southeast Asia

Peng-Er Lam's edited *Japan's Relations with Southeast Asia: The Fukuda Doctrine and Beyond* argues that the Fukuda Doctrine has been the official blueprint to Japan's foreign policy toward Southeast Asia since 1977. This book questions whether this doctrine is still in effect.

Taizo Miyagi analyzes the importance of Japan's relationship with Southeast Asia in *Japan's Quest for Stability in Southeast Asia: Navigating the Turning Points in Postwar Asia*. This book tries to show the hidden trail left by Japan during its military involvement that has shaped Southeast Asia today.

Ernest Z. Bower, Murray Hiebert, Phuong Nguyen, and Gregory B. Polling, in their book *Southeast Asia's Geopolitical Centrality and the U.S.-Japan Alliance*, examine the force that developments in Southeast Asia has had and presently has on the alliance between the United States and Japan.

With Russia

Japan's relationship with Russia continues to be of central interest to Japan. James D. J. Brown, in his book *Japan, Russia and Their Territorial Dispute*, sees the dispute between Japan and Russia over four islands off the northeast coast of Hokkaidō as an enduring obstacle to good relations between the two powers. Despite efforts to solve the issue, the problem continues to fester.

Joseph Ferguson surveys Japanese-Russian relations from the Russo-Japanese War until the 2000s in his book *Japanese-Russian Relations, 1907–2007*. He sees the late 1990s as a hopeful period in their relationship and a general trend toward *rapprochement*, a condition he argues that was not unique in the two countries' relationship.

With the European Union

Since the 1950s, Japan-Europe relations have been characterized by a mutual coldness in terms of diplomatic dialogue, punctuated by a number of trade disputes. Before 2010, scholars published a half dozen books on Japan-EU relations, but since then the topic has generated more interest. Oliviero Frattolillo, in *Diplomacy in Japan-EU Relations*, analyzes the development of the political and diplomatic relationship between Japan and Europe, and shows that, especially during the Cold War years, the quality of diplomatic relations has often been sacrificed to both overcome trade issues and as a result of systemic factors. He traces the historical development of the relationship from the postwar years to the signing of the Japan-EU action plan in 2001, which marked a key turning point in the relationship.

Jörn Keck, Dimitri Vanoverbeke, and Franz Waldenberger, in their book *EU-Japan Relations, 1970–2012: From Confrontation to Global Partnership*, present a comprehensive overview of EU-Japan relations. They analyze key areas of importance to the relationship and speculate on how the relationship will probably develop.

With India

Bilateral relations between Japan and India have grown dramatically in the 21st century. Rohan Mukherjee and Anthony Yazaki have edited *Poised for Partnership: Deepening India-Japan Relations in the Asian Century*, a book that attempts to analyze contemporary bilateral relations between India and Japan, from the 1990s onward. The authors treat four major topics: economic cooperation; energy and climate change; security and defense; and global governance.

With Africa

Once unrecognized by Japan, Africa has increasingly come into focus since the 1990s. Jun Morikawa, a scholar-activist, wrote one of the first books on Japanese-African relations. In *Japan and Africa: Big Business and Diplomacy*, Morikawa aimed to unmask the true nature of Japan's Africa policy and to influence its development and implementation. Howard P. Lehman edited *Japan and Africa: Globalization and Foreign Aid in the 21st Century*. Japan's primary influence has been through its foreign aid policies with emphasis on changing global conditions related to aid to Africa, including the consolidation of the poverty reduction agenda and China's growing presence in Africa. Pedro Amakasu Raposo has studied Japan's foreign aid policy toward Africa and reports his finding in the book *Japan's Foreign Aid Policy in Africa: Evaluating the TICAD Process*. His central conclusion is that, while Tōkyō's International Conferences on African Development lack the agencies to support Japanese companies in Africa, Japan's partnerships with Africa have expanded.

Defense and Military

For books that focus on defense and the military, one should consult Richard J. Samuels's *"Rich Nation: Strong Army": National Security and the Technological Transformation of Japan*, which treats the role of national defense in economic development; Peter J. Katzenstein's *Cultural Norms and National Security*, which links defense to cultural norms; Glenn D. Hook's *Militarization and Demilitarization*, which warns of an arms race in East Asia; and Kent E. Calder's *Pacific Defense*, which challenges conventional views of Japan's defense policy.

For a recent comprehensive summary of Japan's postwar military system, see David Hunter-Chester's *Creating Japan's Ground Self-Defense Force, 1945 to 2015: A Sword Well Made*. This book will appeal to people interested in security studies and alliance studies. Colonel Frank Kowalski, who served with the Occupation's military advisory group, provides an important history of Japan's postwar army in his book *An Inoffensive Rearmament: The Making of the Postwar Japanese Army*. First published in Japanese in 1969, this 2014 English edition is important for understanding Japan's contemporary military.

Robert D. Eldridge and Paul Midford, in their edited work *The Japanese Ground Self-Defense Force: Search for Legitimacy*, provide the first major English-language study of the primary branch of Japan's military as it plays its role in defense and disaster relief. Lindsay Black's *Japan's Maritime Security Strategy: The Japan Coast Guard and Maritime Outlaws* gives insight into Japan's political, ethical, and international perspective as well as an understanding into the history and perspectives of the force and its role in both defense and disaster relief.

Okinawa is a major focal point in Japanese-American military relations. Yuko Kawato examines conflict at several U.S. military bases in Asia with a special emphasis on Japanese bases in her book *Protests against U.S. Military Base Policy in Asia: Persuasion and Its Limits*. Kawato's comprehensive study of anti-U.S. base protests in Asia, offers brilliant insights into the key elements of successful protests against largely unresponsive policy makers. Mire Koikari's study *Cold War Encounters in US-Occupied Okinawa: Women, Militarized Domesticity and Transnationalism in East Asia* sees the U.S. occupation of Okinawa as a major example of Cold War cultural interaction, which sparked various women's grassroots activities to reshape the controversies of U.S. and Japanese disagreements. Finally, Gavan McCormack and Satoko Oka Norimatsu provide a detailed, critical study of U.S. military involvement in Okinawa in their revised study *Resistant Islands: Okinawa Confronts Japan and the United States*.

Akihiro Sado's book *The Self-Defense Forces and Postwar Politics in Japan* reviews the history of Japan's Self-Defense Force (JSDF) and then explores the financial constraints placed on the JSDF in the form of a percentage of the GNP. It looks at U.S.-Japan relations and Japan's defense policy, attempting to shine light on the JSDF in the face of challenges including post-9/11 international terrorism, North Korean nuclear development, and increased Chinese military involvement in East Asia. In *Japan's Postwar Military and Civil Society: Contesting a Better Life*, Tomoyuki Sasaki details the interactions between the SDF and civil society over several decades. These interactions include recruitment, civil engineering, disaster relief, anti-SDF litigation, state financial support for communities with bases, and a fear-mongering campaign against the Soviet Union. Takao Sebata's book *Japan's Defense Policy and Bureaucratic Politics, 1976–2007* examines Japan's military expansion and the decision making in a crucial period and focuses on the National Defense Program and guidelines for United States–Japan Defense Cooperation.

Arts, Culture, and Literature

Outstanding books on arts, culture, and literature are Makoto Ueda's *Modern Japanese Writers and the Nature of Literature*, J. Thomas Rimer's *Modern Japanese Fiction and Its Traditions*, Donald Keene's *Appreciations of Japanese Culture*, Thomas R. H. Havens's *Artist and Patron in Postwar Japan*, Leith Morton's *Modern Japanese Culture*, and Melinda Takeuchi's *The Artist as Professional in Japan*.

In the last decade, there has been an outpouring of books on Japanese arts, culture, and literature. These specialized studies include works on such topics as Japanese gardens, *taiko* drumming, *butō* dancing, manga, music, Kabuki, and tea culture to name just a few.

Samuel L. Leiter's *Historical Dictionary of Japanese Traditional Theatre* (2nd ed.) offers a detailed coverage of the most important terms, people, and plays in Japan's principal traditional Japanese theatrical forms of *nō*, *kyōgen*, Bunraku, and Kabuki. In the *Routledge Handbook of Japanese Culture and Society*, Victoria and Theodore C. Bestor, along with others, provide a useful interdisciplinary resource that focuses on contemporary Japan and the social and cultural trends.

Michael Lucken uses a representative work from four modern genres—painting, film, photography, and animation—in his book *Imitation and Creativity in Japanese Arts: From Kishida Ryūsei to Miyazaki Hayao* to portray the range of approaches that Japanese artists use to represent contemporary influences. Vera Mackie, in her study *The Politics of Visual Culture in Japan*, takes an original approach to examine visual culture by looking at a poster, a cartoon, a postage stamp, a photograph, a painting, and a digital collage and then discusses their artistic, cultural, and political milieu.

In *Japan's Cold War: Media, Literature, and the Law*, Ann Sherif rejects the idea of insularity in postwar Japan and argues that nuclear anxiety, polarized ideologies, gender issues, and myths of progress shaped Japanese literature, criticism, and art and encouraged Japan's democratic institutions. Daniel Sosnoski's edited work *Introduction to Japanese Culture* presents more than 60 short articles that treat various cultural aspects in Japan such as religion, art, foods, and recreation.

Film and Popular Culture

The best introductions to film and popular culture can be found in Keiko I. McDonald's *Cinema East*, with its cultural insights; Frederik Schodt's *Dreamland Japan*, which illustrates the rising significance of Japanese comics; John Whittier Treat's *Contemporary Japan and Popular Culture*; D. P. Martinez's *The Worlds of Japanese Popular Culture*; Donald Ritchie's authoritative presentation *A Hundred Years of Japanese Film*; Douglas Slaymaker's useful collection *A Century of Popular Culture in Japan*; and Susan J. Napier's *Anime from Akira to Howl's Moving Castle*, which shows anime as an important part of Japanese culture.

Publications on film and popular culture have literally exploded in the last decade. There are so many of them that only a few can be mentioned. E. Taylor Atkins has one of the best books on popular culture. His *A History of Popular Culture in Japan: From the Seventeenth Century to the Present* treats trends from the mid-Tokugawa period until the present. Matthew Allen and Rumi Sakamoto's edited work *Japanese Popular Culture* provides a comprehensive overview of Japanese popular culture.

William M. Tsutsui's *Japanese Popular Culture and Globalization* is an excellent, concise overview of the amazing impact of Japanese popular culture around the world. Tsutsui surveys Japanese popular culture from anime and manga to monster movies and Hello Kitty paraphernalia in a style that has appeal.

In film, one should look at Jasper Sharp's *Historical Dictionary of Japanese Cinema*, an introduction to and overview of the long history of Japanese cinema. It provides useful information for the novice and important facts even for the specialist. It is organized so people can find specific information through its detailed chronology, introductory essay, and appendixes of films, film studios, directors, and performers.

David Elliott's *Bye Bye Kitty!!!: Between Heaven and Hell in Contemporary Japanese Art* tries to help non-Japanese overcome the superficiality and infantilism in manga and anime. This book offers a more incisive and wide-ranging view of the contemporary Japanese art scene, as seen in the works of 15 artists who work in painting, sculpture, photography, video, and other media.

Manami Okazaki and Geoff Johnson tackle a popular topic among the young in Japan, particularly girls, in their book *Kawaii!: Japan's Culture of Cute*. They provide a written as well as a visual tour through all things cute or *kawaii*. The concept of *kawaii* blossomed in the 1970s and continues to have a strong hold on young Japanese females. Manga, Hello Kitty, and Harajuku are focal points in the world of *kawaii*.

Timothy Perper and Martha Cornog edited *Mangatopia: Essays on Manga and Anime in the Modern World*, a book that provides a sophisticated anthology of varied commentary from leading authors in both formats. These essays provide in-depth information well beyond the simple comic book level. This volume is useful for people who teach and write about manga and anime.

Mia Consalvo, in her book *Atari to Zelda: Japan's Videogames in Global Contexts*, analyzes video games made in Japan to determine if they are universal or reveal a trace of Japanese culture. She finds a great deal of cross-cultural interchange in the video games coming from Japan and those from other countries.

In *Anime: A Critical Introduction*, Rayna Denison traces the types of Japanese animation that have flourished in Japan and shows how different commentators have interpreted anime. She sees anime as a complex cultural phenomenon that has had a strong effect on Japanese society as well as on countries around the world.

Mizuko Ito, Daisuke Okabe, and Izumi Tsuji have edited a book that attempts to explain *otaku*, excessively devoted fans. In *Fandom Unbound: Otaku Culture in a Connected World*, they investigate how this once marginalized popular culture has come to play a major role in Japan's identity at home and abroad.

Patrick W. Galbraith has shown great interest in Japanese popular culture. He has written or coedited at least four books on the subject. *The Otaku Encyclopedia: An Insider's Guide to the Subculture of Cool Japan* (2014); *Idols and Celebrity in Japanese Media Culture* (2012); *Media Convergence in Japan* (2016); and *Debating Otaku in Contemporary Japan: Historical Perspectives and New Horizons* (2015).

Roman Rosenbaum's edited book *Manga and the Representation of Japanese History* explores how graphic art, especially Japanese manga, represents Japanese history. The teaching of history via manga is controversial, but Rosenbaum attempts to make it respectable.

Excellent bibliographical materials can be found in the following:

Allinson, Gary D. *The Columbia Guide to Modern Japanese History*. New York: Columbia University Press, 1999.

Basic Bibliography for Research on Japanese History. http://www.columbia.edu/~hds2/BIB95/basicbib.html.

Bolger, Karl. *Postwar Industrial Policy in Japan: An Annotated Bibliography*. Metuchen, N.J.: Scarecrow Press, 1988.

Center for Japanese Studies Publications, University of Michigan. https://quod.lib.umich.edu/c/cjs/aae0325.0001.001/--bibliography-of-reference-works-for-japanese-studies-edited?rgn=main;view=fulltext.

Dower, John W., and Timothy S. George. *Japanese History and Culture from Ancient to Modern Times*. Princeton, N.J.: Markus Wiener, 1995.

Fukuda, Naomi, ed. *Bibliography of Reference Works for Japanese Studies*. Ann Arbor: Center for Japanese Studies, University of Michigan, 1979.

Japan Bibliography, DePauw University. http://acad.depauw.edu/~mkfinney/teaching/Com227/culturalportfolios/japan/bibliography.htm.

Japan Studies: Bibliographies, George Washington University. https://lib-guides.gwu.edu/japan/bibliographies.

Kodansha Encyclopedia of Japan. Tōkyō: Kodansha, 1983.

National Diet Library, Japan. http://www.ndl.go.jp/en/data/data_service/jnb/index.html.

Perren, Richard, comp. *Japanese Studies from Pre-History to 1990: A Bibliographical Guide*. Manchester, U.K.: Manchester University Press, 1992.

Selected Interdisciplinary Bibliography on Japan. http://dark-wing.uoregon.edu/~gwf/japan_bibliography.html.

Shulman, Frank J. *Japan*. World Bibliography Series 103. Oxford, U.K.: Clio Press, 1989.

GENERAL

Allinson, Gary D. *The Columbia Guide to Modern Japanese History*. New York: Columbia University Press, 1999.

———. *Japan's Postwar History*. 2nd ed. Ithaca, N.Y.: Cornell University Press, 2004.

Bailey, Paul J. *Postwar Japan: 1945 to the Present*. Cambridge: Blackwell, 1996.

Baldwin, Frank, and Anne Allison, eds. *Japan: The Precarious Future*. New York: New York University Press, 2015.

Buckley, Roger. *Japan Today*. 3rd ed. New York: Cambridge University Press, 1998.

Buckley, Sandra, ed. *Encyclopedia of Contemporary Japanese Culture*. London: Routledge, 2002.

Dougill, John. *Japan's World Heritage Sites: Unique Culture, Unique Nature*. North Clarendon, Vt.: Tuttle, 2014.

Duus, Peter, ed. *The Cambridge History of Japan*. Vol. 6, *The Twentieth Century*. New York: Cambridge University Press, 1988.

Field, Norma. *In the Realm of a Dying Emperor: A Portrait of Japan at Century's End*. New York: Pantheon Books, 1991.

Gibney, Frank. *Japan: The Fragile Superpower*. 3rd ed. Tōkyō: Tuttle, 1996.

Gluck, Carol, and Stephen R. Graubard, eds. *Showa: The Japan of Hirohito*. New York: Norton, 1992.

Gordon, Andrew, ed. *Postwar Japan as History*. Berkeley: University of California Press, 1993.

Hall, Ivan P. *Cartels of the Mind; Japan's Intellectual Closed Shop*. New York: Norton, 1998.

Hane, Mikiso. *Eastern Phoenix: Japan since 1945*. Boulder, Colo.: Westview, 1996.

Hirata, Keiko, and Mark Warschauer. *Japan: The Paradox of Harmony*. New Haven, Conn.: Yale University Press, 2014.

Hood, Christopher. *Japan: The Basics*. New York: Routledge, 2015.

Huffman, James L., ed. *Modern Japan: Encyclopedia of History, Culture, and Nationalism*. New York: Garland, 1998.

Iles, Timothy, and Peter Matanle, eds. *Researching Twenty-First Century Japan: New Directions and Approaches for the Electronic Age*. Lanham, Md.: Lexington Books, 2012.

Kerr, Alex. *Lost Japan: Last Glimpse of Beautiful Japan*. London: Penguin, 2016.

Kingston, Jeffrey, ed. *Critical Issues in Contemporary Japan*. New York: Routledge, 2013.

———. *Japan in Transformation, 1952–2000*. New York: Longman, 2001.

Lucken, Michael, Anne Bayard-Sakai, and Emmanuel Lozerand, eds. *Postwar Japan*. New York: Routledge, 2014.

McCargo, Duncan. *Contemporary Japan*. New York: St. Martin's, 2000.

Murakami, Haruki. *Underground: The Tokyo Gas Attack & the Japanese Psyche*. London: Harvill Secker Press, 2000.

Nathan, John. *Japan Unbound: A Volatile Nation's Quest for Pride and Purpose*. Boston: Houghton Mifflin, 2004.

———. *Living Carelessly in Tokyo and Elsewhere: A Memoir*. New York: Free Press, 2008.

Norbury, Paul. *Japan—Culture Smart!: The Essential Guide to Customs & Culture*. London: Kuperard, 2011.

Packard, George P. *Edwin O. Reischauer and the American Discovery of Japan*. New York: Columbia University Press, 2010.

Pilling, David. *Bending Adversity: Japan and the Art of Survival*. London: Allen Lane, 2014.

Prestowitz, Clyde. *Japan Restored: How Japan Can Reinvent Itself and Why This Is Important for America and the World*. North Clarendon, Vt.: Tuttle, 2015.

Pyle, Kenneth B. *Japan Rising: The Resurgence of Japanese Power and Purpose*. New York: PublicAffairs, 2007.

Reischauer, Edwin O. *Japan: The Story of a Nation*. New York: Knopf, 1989.

Reischauer, Edwin O., and Marius B. Jansen. *The Japanese Today: Change and Continuity*. Cambridge, Mass.: Harvard University Press, 1995.

Segers, Rien T., ed. *A New Japan for the Twenty-First Century: An Inside Overview of Current Fundamental Changes and Problems*. New York: Routledge, 2012.

Smith, Patrick. *Japan: A Reinterpretation*. New York: Pantheon Books, 1997.

Steel, Gill, ed. *Power in Contemporary Japan*. New York: Palgrave Macmillan, 2016.

Sugimoto, Yoshio, and Ross E. Mouer, eds. *Constructs for Understanding Japan*. London: Kegan Paul, 1989.

van Wolferen, Karel. *The Enigma of Japanese Power: People and Politics in a Stateless Nation*. New York: Vintage, 1989.

Vogel, Ezra F. *Is Japan Still Number One?* Subang Jaya, Malaysia: Pelanduk, 2000.

————. *Japan as Number One: Lessons for America*. Cambridge, Mass.: Harvard University Press, 1979.

Youngshik, B., and T. J. Pempel, eds. *Japan in Crisis: What Will It Take for Japan to Rise Again?* New York: Palgrave Macmillan, 2012.

Zengage, Thomas R., and C. Tait Ratcliffe. *The Japanese Century: Challenge and Response*. London: Longman, 1988.

AMERICAN OCCUPATION OF JAPAN

Barnes, Dayna L. *Architects of Occupation: American Experts and Planning for Postwar Japan*. Ithaca, N.Y.: Cornell University Press, 2017.

Brackman, Arnold. *The Other Nuremberg: The Untold Story of the Tokyo War Crimes Trials*. New York: Morrow, 1987.

Broinowski, Adam. *Cultural Responses to Occupation in Japan: The Performing Body during and after the Cold War*. London: Bloomsbury Academic, 2016.

Buckley, Roger. *Occupation Diplomacy: Britain, the United States, and Japan, 1945–1952*. New York: Cambridge University Press, 1982.

Burkman, Thomas W., ed. *The Occupation of Japan: The International Context*. Norfolk, Va.: MacArthur Memorial, 1984.

Caprio, Mark E., and Yoneyuki Sugita, eds. *Democracy in Occupied Japan: The U.S. Occupation and Japanese Politics and Society*. London: Routledge, 2007.

Cohen, Theodore. *Remaking Japan: The American Occupation as New Deal*. New York: Free Press, 1987.

Dore, Ronald P. *Land Reform in Japan*. London: Oxford University Press, 1959.

Dorman, Benjamin. *Celebrity Gods: New Religions, Media, and Authority in Occupied Japan*. Honolulu: University of Hawai'i Press, 2012.

Finn, Richard B. *Winners in Peace: MacArthur, Yoshida, and Postwar Japan*. Berkeley: University of California Press, 1992.

Goodman, Grant K., ed. *The American Occupation of Japan*. Lawrence: University Press of Kansas, 1968.

Gordon, Beate Sirota. *The Only Woman in the Room*. Tōkyō; New York: Kodansha International, 1997.

Harries, Meirion, and Susie Harries. *Sheathing the Sword: The Demilitarization of Japan*. New York: Macmillan, 1987.

Hellegers, Dale M. *We the Japanese People: World War II and the Origins of the Japanese Constitution*. Stanford, Calif.: Stanford University Press, 2002.

Inoue, Kyoko. *MacArthur's Japanese Constitution: A Linguistic and Cultural Study of Its Making*. Chicago: University of Chicago Press, 1991.

Kage, Reiko. *Civil Engagement in Postwar Japan: The Revival of a Defeated Society*. London: Cambridge University Press, 2010.

Kawai, Kazuo. *Japan's American Interlude*. Chicago: University of Chicago Press, 1960.

Kawashima, Yasuhide. *The Tokyo Rose Case: Treason on Trial*. Lawrence: University Press of Kansas, 2013.

Kitamura, Hiroshi. *Screening Enlightenment: Hollywood and the Cultural Reconstruction of Defeated Japan*. Ithaca, N.Y.: Cornell University Press, 2010.

Koshiro, Yukiko. *Trans-Pacific Racism and the U.S. Occupation of Japan*. New York: Columbia University Press, 1999.

Kovner, Sarah. *Occupying Power: Sex Workers and Servicemen in Postwar Japan*. Redwood City, Calif.: Stanford University Press, 2012.

Maga, Timothy P. *Judgment at Tokyo: The Japanese War Crimes Trials*. Lexington: University Press of Kentucky, 2001.

McLelland, Mark. *Love, Sex, and Democracy in Japan during the American Occupation*. New York: Palgrave Macmillan, 2012.

Minear, Richard H. *Victor's Justice: The Tokyo War Crimes Trial*. Princeton, N.J.: Princeton University Press, 1971.

Morris, Seymour, Jr. *Supreme Commander: MacArthur's Triumph in Japan*. New York: HarperCollins, 2014.

River, Charles, ed. *The Postwar Occupation of Japan: The History of the Transition from World War II to Modern Japan*. Mansfield, Mass.: Charles River Press, 2014.

Saeki, Chizuru. *U.S. Cultural Propaganda in Cold War Japan: Promoting Democracy 1948–1960*. Lewiston, N.Y.: Edwin Mellen, 2008.

Schaller, Michael. *The American Occupation of Japan: The Origins of the Cold War in Asia*. New York: Oxford University Press, 1985.

Schonberger, Howard B. *Aftermath of War: Americans and the Remaking of Japan, 1945–1952*. Kent, Ohio: Kent State University Press, 1989.

Sugita, Yoneyuki. *Pitfall or Panacea: The Irony of US Power in Occupied Japan, 1945–1952*. New York: Routledge, 2003.

Takemae, Eiji. *Inside GHQ: The Allied Occupation of Japan and Its Legacy*. Translated by Robert Ricketts and Sebastian Swann. New York: Continuum, 2002.

Totani, Yuma. *The Tokyo War Crimes Trial: The Pursuit of Justice in the Wake of World War II*. Cambridge, Mass.: Harvard University Press, 2008.

Trefalt, Beatrice. *Post-war Repatriation to Defeated Japan*. New York: Routledge, 2012.

Tsutsui, William M. *Banking Policy in Japan: American Efforts at Reform during the Occupation*. London: Routledge, 1988.

Ward, Robert E., and Yoshikazu Sakamoto, eds. *Democratizing Japan: The Allied Occupation*. Honolulu: University of Hawai'i Press, 1987.

HISTORY

Andrews, William. *Dissenting Japan: A History of Japanese Radicalism and Counterculture from 1945 to Fukushima*. London: Oxford University Press, 2016.

Asahi Shimbun Company. *Media, Propaganda and Politics in 20th-Century Japan*. Translated by Barak Kushner. London: Bloomsbury Academic, 2015.

Banno, Junji, and Jirō Yamaguchi. *The Abe Experiment and the Future of Japan: Don't Repeat History*. Translated by Arthur Stockwin. Honolulu: University of Hawai'i Press, 2017.

Bix, Herbert P. *Hirohito and the Making of Modern Japan*. New York: HarperCollins, 2000.

Brinckmann, Hans. *Showa Japan: The Post-war Golden Age and Its Troubled Legacy*. North Clarendon, Vt.: Tuttle, 2008.

Cybriwsky, Roman. *Historical Dictionary of Tokyo*. 2nd ed. Lanham, Md.: Scarecrow Press, 2011.

Dower, John W. *Embracing Defeat: Japan in the Wake of World War II*. New York: Norton, 1999.

———. *Empire and Aftermath: Yoshida Shigeru and the Japanese Experience, 1878–1954*. Cambridge, Mass.: Harvard University Press, 1979.

Dunscomb, Paul E. *Japan since 1945*. Ann Arbor, Mich.: Association for Asian Studies, 2014.

Fogel, Joshua, ed. *The Nanjing Massacre in History and Historiography*. Berkeley: University of California Press, 2000.

Funabashi, Yoichi, ed. *Examining Japan's Lost Decades*. New York: Routledge, 2015.

Gayle, Curtis Anderson. *Marxist History and Postwar Japanese Nationalism*. New York: Routledge, 2015.

Gerteis, Christopher, and Timothy S. George, eds. *Japan since 1945: From Postwar to Post-bubble*. London: Bloomsbury Publishing, 2013.

Hane, Mikiso, and Louis G. Perez. *Modern Japan: A Historical Survey*. 5th ed. Boulder, Colo.: Westview, 2012.

Hashimoto, Akiko. *The Long Defeat: Cultural Trauma, Memory, and Identity in Japan*. New York: Oxford University Press, 2015.

Henshall, Kenneth. *A History of Japan: From Stone Age to Superpower*. Basingstoke, U.K.: Macmillan, 1999.

Hoyt, Edwin P. *Hirohito: The Emperor and the Man*. New York: Praeger, 1992.

Ienaga, Saburō. *Japan's Past, Japan's Future: One Historian's Odyssey*. Translated by Richard H. Minear. Lanham, Md.: Rowman & Littlefield, 2001.

Iokibe, Makoto, ed. *The Diplomatic History of Postwar Japan*. New York: Routledge, 2011.

Irokawa, Daikichi. *The Age of Hirohito: In Search of Modern Japan*. Translated by Mikiso Hane. New York: Free Press, 1995.

Karatani, Kojin. *History and Repetition*. Edited by Seiji M. Lippit. New York: Columbia University Press, 2011.

Kawahara, Toshiaki. *Hirohito and His Times: A Japanese Perspective*. Tōkyō: Kodansha International, 1990.

Kingston, Jeff. *Contemporary Japan: History, Politics, and Social Change since the 1980s*. Hoboken, N.J.: Wiley-Blackwell, 2010.

Large, Stephen. *Emperor Hirohito and Showa Japan: A Political Biography*. London: Routledge, 1992.

Maclachlan, Patricia L. *The People's Post Office: The History and Politics of the Japanese Postal System, 1871–2010*. Cambridge, Mass.: Harvard University Asia Center, 2011.

McCargo, Duncan. *Contemporary Japan*. 3rd ed. New York: Palgrave Macmillan, 2012.

Minear, Richard H. *Through Japanese Eyes*. 4th ed. Lanham, Md.: Apex Press, 2008.

Mizuki, Shigeru. *Showa 1953–1989: A History of Japan*. Translated by Zack Davisson. Montreal, Canada: Dawn and Quarterly, 2015.

Morris-Suzuki, Tessa. *Showa: An Inside History of Hirohito's Japan*. London: Athlone, 1984.

Murphy, R. Taggart. *Japan and the Shackles of the Past*. New York: Oxford University Press, 2014.

Nakamura, Takafusa. *A History of Showa Japan, 1926–1989*. Tōkyō: University of Tōkyō Press, 1998.

Nakazato, Nariaki. *Neonationalist Mythology in Postwar Japan: Pal's Dissenting Judgment at the Tokyo War Crimes Tribunal*. Lanham, Md.: Lexington Books, 2016.

Nozaki, Yoshiko. *War Memory, Nationalism and Education in Postwar Japan: The Japanese History Textbook Controversy and Ienaga Saburo's Court Challenges*. New York: Routledge, 2008.

Otmazgin, Nissim, and Rebecca Suter, eds. *Rewriting History in Manga: Stories for the Nation*. New York: Palgrave Macmillan, 2016.

Reingold, Edwin M. *Chrysanthemums and Thorns: The Untold Story of Modern Japan*. New York: St. Martin's, 1992.

Rosenbaum, Roman, and Yasuko Claremont, eds. *Legacies of the Asia-Pacific War: The Yakeato Generation*. New York: Routledge, 2015.

Saito, Hiro. *The History Problem: The Politics of War Commemoration in East Asia*. Honolulu: University of Hawai'i Press, 2016.

Sasaki, Fumiko. *Nationalism, Political Realism and Democracy in Japan: The Thought of Masao Maruyama*. New York: Routledge, 2015.

Schodt, Frederik L. *America and the Four Japans: Friend, Foe, Model, Mirror*. Berkeley, Calif.: Stone Bridge Press, 1994.

Seaton, Philip A. *Japan's Contested War Memories: The "Memory Rifts" in Historical Consciousness of World War II*. New York: Routledge, 2007.

Seraphim, Franziska. *War Memory and Social Politics in Japan, 1945–2005*. Cambridge, Mass.: Harvard University Press, 2006.

Shillony, Ben-Ami. *Enigma of the Emperors: Sacred Subservience in Japanese History*. Folkestone, Kent, U.K.: Global Oriental, 2005.

Southard, Susan. *Nagasaki: Life after Nuclear War*. New York: Viking, 2015.

Sugita, Yoneyuki, ed. *Japan Viewed from Interdisciplinary Perspectives: History and Prospects*. Lanham, Md.: Lexington Books, 2015.

Takenaka, Akiko. *Yasukuni Shrine: History, Memory, and Japan's Unending Postwar*. Honolulu: University of Hawai'i Press, 2015.

Tipton, Elise K. *Modern Japan: A Social and Political History*. New York: Routledge, 2002.

Toyama, Kiyohiko. *War and Responsibility in Japan: The Role of the Emperor and the War Occupation Debates*. New York: Routledge, 2005.

Tsurumi, Shunsuke. *A Cultural History of Postwar Japan, 1945–1980*. London: Kegan Paul International, 1986.

Van Sant, John, Peter Mauch, and Yoneyuki Sugita. *Historical Dictionary of United States–Japan Relations*. Lanham, Md.: Scarecrow Press, 2007.

Walker, Brett L. *A Concise History of Japan*. New York: Cambridge University Press, 2015.

Watt, Lori. *When Empire Comes Home: Repatriation and Reintegration in Postwar Japan*. Cambridge, Mass.: Harvard University Press, 2009.

Yoneyama, Lisa. *Cold War Ruins: Transpacific Critique of American Justice and Japanese War Crimes*. Durham, N.C.: Duke University Press, 2016.

Zwigenberg, Ran. *Hiroshima: The Origins of Global Memory Culture*. New York: Cambridge University Press, 2016.

GOVERNMENT AND POLITICS

Abe, Hitoshi, Muneyuki Shindō, and Sadafumi Kawato. *The Government and Politics of Japan*. Translated by James W. White. Tōkyō: University of Tōkyō Press, 1994.

Al-Badri, Dominic, and Gijs Berends, eds. *After the Great East Japan Earthquake: Political and Policy Change in Post-Fukushima Japan*. Honolulu: University of Hawai'i Press, 2013.

Allinson, Gary D., and Yasunori Sone, eds. *Political Dynamics in Contemporary Japan*. Ithaca, N.Y.: Cornell University Press, 1993.

Amyx, Jennifer, and Peter Drysdale, eds. *Japanese Governance: Beyond Japan Inc*. London: Routledge, 2003.

Ando, Takemasa. *Japan's New Left Movements: Legacies for Civil Society*. New York: Routledge, 2013.

Andrews, William. *Dissenting Japan: A History of Japanese Radicalism and Counterculture from 1945 to Fukushima*. London: Oxford University Press, 2016.

Apter, David E., and Nagayo Sawa. *Against the State: Politics and Social Protest in Japan*. Cambridge, Mass.: Harvard University Press, 1984.

Babb, James. *Tanaka: The Making of Postwar Japan*. New York: Longman, 2000.

Baerwald, Hans H. *Party Politics in Japan*. London: Allen and Unwin, 1986.

Banno, Junji. *The Establishment of the Japanese Constitutional System*. Translated by J. A. A. Stockwin. London: Routledge, 1992.

Beer, Lawrence W., and John M. Maki. *From Imperial Myth to Democracy: Japan's Two Constitutions, 1889–2002*. Boulder, Colo.: University Press of Colorado, 2002.

Bingman, Charles F. *Japanese Government Leadership and Management*. New York: Palgrave Macmillan, 1989.

Bowen, Roger W. *Japan's Dysfunctional Democracy: The Liberal Democratic Party and Structural Corruption*. Armonk, N.Y.: M. E. Sharpe, 2003.

Bronson, Adam. *One Hundred Million Philosophers: Science of Thought and the Culture of Democracy in Postwar Japan*. Honolulu: University of Hawai'i Press, 2011.

Calder, Kent E. *Crisis and Compensation: Public Policy and Political Stability in Japan 1949–1986*. Princeton, N.J.: Princeton University Press, 1988.

Campbell, John Creighton. *How Policies Change: The Japanese Government and the Aging Society*. Princeton, N.J.: Princeton University Press, 1992.

Carlson, Matthew. *Money Politics in Japan: New Rules, Old Practices*. Boulder, Colo.: Lynne Rienner, 2007.

Catalinac, Amy. *Electoral Reform and National Security in Japan: From Pork to Foreign Policy*. New York: Cambridge University Press, 2016.

Christensen, Ray. *Ending the LDP Hegemony: Party Cooperation in Japan*. Honolulu: University of Hawai'i Press, 2000.

Cole, Allen Burnett, George O. Totten, and Cecil H. Uyehara. *Socialist Parties in Postwar Japan*. New Haven, Conn.: Yale University Press, 1966.

Curtis, Gerald L. *Election Campaigning, Japanese Style*. New York: Columbia University Press, 1971.

———. *The Japanese Way of Politics*. New York: Columbia University Press, 1988.

———. *The Logic of Japanese Politics: Leaders, Institutions, and the Limits of Change*. New York: Columbia University Press, 2000.

Ehrhardt, George, Axel Klein, Levi McLaughlin, and Steven R. Reed, eds. *Kōmeitō: Politics and Religion in Japan*. Berkeley: University of California Press, 2014.

Feldman, Ofer. *Politics and the News Media in Japan*. Ann Arbor: University of Michigan Press, 1993.

Flanagan, Scott C., Shinsaku Kohei, Ichiro Miyake, Bradley M. Richardson, and Jōji Watanuki. *The Japanese Voter*. New Haven, Conn.: Yale University Press, 1991.

Fukui, Haruhiro. *Party in Power: The Japanese Liberal-Democrats and Policy-Making*. Berkeley: University of California Press, 1970.

Funabashi Yoichi, and Koichi Nakano, eds. *The Democratic Party of Japan in Power: Challenges and Failures*. New York: Routledge, 2017.

Galanti, Sigal Ben-Rafael, Nissim Otmazgin, and Alon Levkowitz, eds. *Japan's Multilayered Democracy*. Lanham, Md.: Lexington Books, 2015.

Garon, Sheldon. *Molding Japanese Minds: The State in Everyday Life*. Princeton, N.J.: Princeton University Press, 1997.

Gatu, Dagfinn. *The Post-war Roots of Japanese Political Malaise*. New York: Routledge, 2015.

Gaunder, Alisa. *Political Reform in Japan: Leadership Looming Large*. New York: Routledge, 2011.

———, ed. *The Routledge Handbook of Japanese Politics*. New York: Routledge, 2011.

Hadd, Mary Alice. *Building Democracy in Japan*. London: Cambridge University Press, 2012.

Hahm, Chaihark, and Sung Ho Kim. *Making We the People: Democratic Constitutional Founding in Postwar Japan and South Korea*. London: Cambridge University Press, 2015.

Hayao, Kenji. *The Japanese Prime Minister and Public Policy*. Pittsburgh, Pa.: University of Pittsburgh Press, 1993.

Hayes, Louis D. *Introduction to Japanese Politics*. 4th ed. Armonk, N.Y.: M. E. Sharpe, 2005.

Henderson, Dan Fenno, ed. *The Constitution of Japan: Its First Twenty Years, 1947–1967*. Seattle: University of Washington, 1968.

Herzog, Peter J. *Japan's Pseudo-Democracy*. New York: New York University Press, 1993.

Higuchi, Yoichi, ed. *Five Decades of Constitutionalism in Japanese Society*. New York: Columbia University Press, 2000.

Hirata, Keiko. *Civil Society in Japan: The Growing Role of NGOs in Tokyo's Aid Development Policy*. New York: Palgrave Macmillan, 2002.

Hook, Glenn D., ed. *Contested Governance in Japan: Sites and Issues*. New York: Routledge, 2005.

Hori, Harumi. *The Changing Japanese Political System: The Liberal Democratic Party and the Ministry of Finance*. London: Routledge, 2005.

Horiuchi, Yusaku. *Institution, Incentives and Electoral Participation in Japan: Cross-Level and Cross-National Perspectives*. New York: Routledge, 2005.

Hrebenar, Ronald J. *Japan's New Party System*. Boulder, Colo.: Westview, 2000.

———, ed. *The Japanese Party System: From One-Party Rule to Coalition Government*. 2nd ed. Boulder, Colo.: Westview, 1991.

Hrebenar, Ronald J., and Akira Nakamura, eds. *Party Politics in Japan: Political Chaos and Stalemate in the 21st Century*. New York: Routledge, 2014.

Ike, Nobutaka. *Japanese Politics: Patron-Client Democracy*. New York: Knopf, 1972.

Ikeda, Ken'ichi, and Sean Richey. *Social Networks and Japanese Democracy: The Beneficial Impact of Interpersonal Communication in East Asia*. New York: Routledge, 2014.

Ikuta, Tadahide. *Kanryō: Japan's Hidden Government*. New York: Weatherhill, 1995.

Inoguchi, Takashi, ed. *Japanese Politics Today: From Karaoke to Kabuki Democracy*. New York: Palgrave Macmillan, 2011.

Ishida, Takeshi. *Japanese Political Culture: Change and Continuity*. New Brunswick, N.J.: Transaction Books, 1983.

Ishida, Takeshi, and Ellis S. Krauss, eds. *Democracy in Japan*. Pittsburgh, Pa.: University of Pittsburgh Press, 1989.

Jain, Purnendra, and Takashi Inoguchi, eds. *Japanese Politics Today: Beyond Karaoke Democracy?* New York: St. Martin's, 1997.

Johnson, Chalmers. *Japan: Who Governs? The Rise of the Developmental State*. New York: Norton, 1995.

Johnson, Stephen. *Opposition Politics in Japan: Strategies under a One-Party Dominant Regime*. New York: Routledge, 2000.

Kabashima, Ikuo, and Gill Steel. *Changing Politics in Japan*. Ithaca, N.Y.: Cornell University Press, 2010.

Kan, Naoto. *My Nuclear Nightmare: Leading Japan through the Fukushima Disaster*. Translated by Jeffery S. Irish. Ithaca, N.Y.: Cornell University Press, 2017.

Kataoka, Tetsuya, ed. *Creating Single-Party Democracy: Japan's Postwar Political System*. Stanford, Calif.: Hoover Institution Press, 1992.

———. *The Price of a Constitution: The Origin of Japan's Postwar Politics*. New York: Crane Russak, 1991.

Kersten, Rikki. *Defeat and the Intellectual Culture of Postwar Japan*. Leiden, the Netherlands: Leiden University, 2003.

———. *Democracy in Postwar Japan: Maruyama Masao and the Search for Autonomy*. London: Routledge, 1996.

———. *Turning to the Nation in Postwar Japan*. New York: Palgrave Macmillan, 2006.

Kimura, Shunsuke. *Regional Administration in Japan: Departure from Uniformity*. New York: Routledge, 2016.

Kobayashi, Yoshiaki. *Malfunctioning Democracy in Japan: Quantitative Analysis in a Civil Society*. Lanham, Md.: Lexington Books, 2012.

Kohno, Masaru. *Japan's Postwar Party Politics*. Princeton, N.J.: Princeton University Press, 1996.

Koseki, Shōichi. *The Birth of Japan's Postwar Constitution*. Edited and translated by Ray A. Moore. Boulder, Colo.: Westview, 1997.

Krauss, Ellis S. *Broadcasting Politics in Japan: NHK and Television News*. Ithaca, N.Y.: Cornell University Press, 2000.

Krauss, Ellis S., and Robert J. Pekkanen. *The Rise and Fall of Japan's LDP: Political Party Organization as Historical Institutions*. Ithaca, N.Y.: Cornell University Press, 2010.

Krooth, Richard, Morris Edelson, and Hiroshi Fukurai. *Nuclear Tsunami: The Japanese Government and America's Role in the Fukushima Disaster*. Lanham, Md.: Lexington Books, 2015.

Kuroda, Yasumasa. *The Core of Japanese Democracy: Latent Interparty Politics*. New York: Palgrave Macmillan, 2005.

Kushida, Kenji E., and Phillip Y. Lipscy, eds. *Japan under the DPJ: The Politics of Transition and Governance*. Redwood City, Calif.: Stanford University Press, 2013.

LeBlanc, Robin M. *The Art of the Gut: Manhood, Power, and Ethics in Japanese Politics*. Berkeley: University of California Press, 2010.

Maclachlan, Patricia L. *Consumer Politics in Postwar Japan: The Institutional Boundaries of Citizen Activism*. New York: Columbia University Press, 2002.

Mann, Thomas E., and Takeshi Sasaki, eds. *Governance for a New Century: Japanese Challenges, American Experience*. Tōkyō: Japan Center for International Exchange, 2002.

Martin, Sherry L. *Popular Democracy in Japan: How Gender and Community Are Changing Modern Electoral Politics*. Ithaca, N.Y.: Cornell University Press, 2011.

Masamori, Sase. *Changing Security Policies in Postwar Japan: The Political Biography of Japanese Defense Minister Sakata Michita*. Edited and translated by Robert D. Eldridge with Graham B. Leonard. Lanham, Md.: Lexington Books, 2017.

Masumi, Junnosuke. *Contemporary Politics in Japan*. Translated by Lonny E. Carlile. Berkeley: University of California Press, 1995.

———. *Postwar Politics in Japan, 1945–1955*. Translated by Lonny E. Carlile. Berkeley: University of California Press, 1985.

McCormack, Gavan, and Yoshio Sugimoto, eds. *Democracy in Contemporary Japan*. Armonk, N.Y.: M. E. Sharpe, 1986.

McNeil, Frank. *Democracy in Japan: The Emerging Global Concern*. New York: Crown Publishers, 1994.

McNelly, Theodore. *The Origins of Japan's Democratic Constitution*. Lanham, Md.: University Press of America, 2000.

Miyamoto, Masao. *Straitjacket Society: An Insider's Irreverent View of Bureaucratic Japan*. Tōkyō: Kodansha, 1994.

Moore, Ray A., and Donald L. Robinson. *Partners for Democracy: Crafting the New Japanese State under MacArthur*. Oxford: Oxford University Press, 2002.

Morris-Suzuki, Tessa. *Beyond Computopia: Information, Automation, and Democracy in Japan*. London: Kegan Paul International, 1988.

Mulgan, Aurelia George. *The Abe Administration and the Rise of the Prime Ministerial Executive*. New York: Routledge, 2017.

———. *Japan's Failed Revolution: Koizumi and the Politics of Economic Reform*. Canberra, Australia: Asia Pacific Press, 2002.

———. *Japan's Interventionist State: The Role of the MAFF*. London: Routledge, 2005.

———. *Ozawa Ichirō and Japanese Politics: Old versus New*. New York: Routledge, 2014.

Muramatsu, Michio. *Local Power in the Japanese State*. Berkeley: University of California Press, 1997.

Nakano, Koichi. *Party Politics and Decentralization in Japan and France: When the Opposition Governs*. New York: Routledge, 2010.

Narramore, Terry. *Rethinking Modern Japan: Politics, Economics, Identity*. New York: Routledge, 2005.

Neary, Ian. *The State and Politics in Japan*. Cambridge: Blackwell, 2002.

Oka, Takashi. *Policy Entrepreneurship and Elections in Japan: A Political Biography of Ozawa Ichiro*. New York: Routledge, 2011.

Oros, Andrew L. *Japan's Security Renaissance: New Policies and Politics for the Twenty-First Century*. New York: Columbia University Press, 2017.

Overby, Charles M. *A Call for Peace: The Implications of Japan's War-Renouncing Constitution*. Tōkyō: Kodansha, 1997.

Pekkanen, Robert J., Ethan Scheiner, and Steven R. Reed, eds. *Japan Decides 2014: The Japanese General Election*. New York: Palgrave Macmillan, 2016.

Pempel, T. J. *Regime Shift: Comparative Dynamics of the Japanese Political Economy*. Ithaca, N.Y.: Cornell University Press, 1998.

———. *Uncommon Democracies: The One-Party Dominant Regimes*. Ithaca, N.Y.: Cornell University Press, 1990.

Pharr, Susan J. *Losing Face: Status Politics in Japan*. Berkeley: University of California Press, 1990.

———. *Political Women in Japan: The Search for a Place in Political Life*. Berkeley: University of California Press, 1981.

Pharr, Susan J., and Ellis S. Krauss, eds. *Media and Politics in Japan*. Honolulu: University of Hawai'i Press, 1996.

Ramseyer, J. Mark. *Second-Best Justice: The Virtues of Japanese Private Law*. Chicago: University of Chicago Press, 2015.

Ramseyer, J. Mark, and Frances McCall Rosenbluth. *Japan's Political Marketplace*. Cambridge, Mass.: Harvard University Press, 1993.

Reed, Steven R. *Japanese Electoral Politics: Creating a New Party System*. London: Routledge, 2003.

———. *Making Common Sense of Japan*. Pittsburgh, Pa.: University of Pittsburgh Press, 1993.

Richardson, Bradley M. *Japanese Democracy: Power, Coordination, and Performance*. New Haven, Conn.: Yale University Press, 1997.

———. *Political Culture of Japan*. Berkeley: University of California Press, 1974.

Richardson, Bradley M., and Scott C. Flanagan. *Politics in Japan*. Boston: Little, Brown, 1984.

Rothacher, Albrecht. *The Japanese Power Elite*. New York: St. Martin's, 1993.

Ruoff, Kenneth J. *The People's Emperor: Democracy and the Japanese Monarch, 1945–1995*. Cambridge, Mass.: Harvard University Press, 2001.

Sakamoto, Takayuki. *Building Policy Legitimacy in Japan: Political Behaviour beyond Rational Choice*. New York: St. Martin's, 1999.

Scalapino, Robert A. *The Japanese Communist Movement, 1920–1966*. Berkeley: University of California Press, 1967.

Scalapino, Robert A., and Junnosuke Masumi. *Parties and Politics in Contemporary Japan*. Berkeley: University of California Press, 1962.

Scheiner, Ethan. *Democracy without Competition in Japan: Opposition Failure in a One-Party Dominant State.* New York: Cambridge University Press, 2006.

Schlesinger, Jacob M. *Shadow Shoguns: The Rise and Fall of Japan's Postwar Political Machine.* New York: Simon & Schuster, 1997.

Schoppa, Leonard J., ed. *The Evolution of Japan's Party System: Politics and Policy in an Era of Institutional Change.* Toronto: University of Toronto Press, 2011.

Schwartz, Frank J., and Susan J. Pharr, eds. *The State of Civil Society in Japan.* New York: Cambridge University Press, 2003.

Shinoda, Tomohito. *Contemporary Japanese Politics: Institutional Changes and Power Shifts.* New York: Columbia University Press, 2013.

————. *Leading Japan: The Role of the Prime Minister.* Westport, Conn.: Praeger, 2000.

Smith, Roger D. *Japan's International Fisheries: Policy: Law, Diplomacy and Politics Governing Resource Security.* New York: Routledge, 2015.

Söderberg, Marie, and Patricia A. Nelson, eds. *Japan's Politics and Economy: Perspectives on Change.* New York: Routledge, 2009.

Steiner, Kurt, Ellis S. Krauss, and Scott C. Flanagan, eds. *Political Opposition and Local Politics in Japan.* Princeton, N.J.: Princeton University Press, 1981.

Steslicke, William E. *Doctors in Politics: The Political Life of the Japan Medical Association.* New York: Praeger, 1973.

Stockwin, Arthur, and Kweku Ampiah. *Rethinking Japan: The Politics of Contested Nationalism.* Lanham, Md.: Lexington Books, 2017.

Stockwin, J. A. A. *Governing Japan.* Oxford, U.K.: Blackwell, 1999.

Stronach, Bruce. *Beyond the Rising Sun: Nationalism in Contemporary Japan.* Westport, Conn.: Praeger, 1995.

Suzuki, Takaaki. *Japan's Budget Politics: Balancing Domestic and International Interests.* Boulder, Colo.: Lynne Rienner, 2000.

Thayer, Nathaniel B. *How the Conservatives Rule Japan.* Princeton, N.J.: Princeton University Press, 1969.

Tsujinaka, Yutaka, and Hiroaki Inatsugu, eds. *Aftermath: Fukushima and the 3.11 Earthquake.* Balwyn, North Victoria, Australia: Trans-Pacific, 2018.

Uchiyama, Yu. *Koizumi and Japanese Politics: Reform Strategies and Leadership Style.* New York: Routledge, 2010.

Ward, Robert E., ed. *Political Development in Modern Japan.* Princeton, N.J.: Princeton University Press, 1968.

Watanabe, Akio, ed. *The Prime Ministers of Postwar Japan, 1945–1995: Their Lives and Times.* Supervisory translation by Robert D. Eldridge. Lanham, Md.: Lexington Books, 2016.

Watanabe, Tsuneo. *Japan's Backroom Politics: Factions in a Multiparty Age.* Translated by Robert D. Eldridge. Lanham, Md.: Lexington Books, 2013.

Watanuki, Jōji. *Politics in Postwar Japanese Society.* Tōkyō: University of Tōkyō Press, 1977.

Winkler, Christian G. *The Quest for Japan's New Constitution: An Analysis of Visions and Constitutional Reform Proposals 1980–2009.* New York: Routledge, 2013.

Woodall, Brian. *Japan under Construction: Corruption, Politics, and Public Works.* Berkeley: University of California Press, 1996.

Woronoff, Jon. *Politics the Japanese Way.* London: Macmillan; New York: St. Martin's, 1987.

Zakowski, Karol. *Decision-Making Reform in Japan: The DPJ's Failed Attempt at a Politician-Led Government.* New York: Routledge, 2015.

ECONOMY AND BUSINESS

Abegglen, James C. *21st-Century Japanese Management: New Systems, Lasting Values.* New York: Palgrave, 2006.

Abegglen, James C., and George Stalk, Jr. *Kaisha: The Japanese Corporation.* New York: Basic Books, 1985.

Alexander, Arthur J. *In the Shadow of the Miracle: The Japanese Economy since the End of High-Speed Growth.* Lanham, Md.: Lexington Books, 2003.

Alexander, Jeffrey W. *Brewed in Japan: The Evolution of the Japanese Beer Industry.* Honolulu: University of Hawai'i Press, 2011.

Allen, George C. *A Short Economic History of Modern Japan.* 4th ed. New York: St. Martin's, 1981.

Amyx, Jennifer A. *Japan's Financial Crisis: Institutional Rigidity and Reluctant Change.* Princeton, N.J.: Princeton University Press, 2004.

Anchordoguy, Marie. *Reprogramming Japan: The High Tech Crisis under Communitarian Capitalism.* Ithaca, N.Y.: Cornell University Press, 2005.

Aoki, Masahiko, and Ronald P. Dore, eds. *The Japanese Firm: Sources of Competitive Strength.* Oxford, U.K.: Oxford University Press, 1994.

Aoki, Masahiko, and Hugh Patrick, eds. *The Japanese Bank System: Its Relevance for Developing and Transforming Economies.* Oxford, U.K.: Oxford University Press, 1995.

Babb, James. *Business and Politics in Japan.* Manchester, U.K.: Manchester University Press, 2001.

Beason, Dick, and Jason James. *The Political Economy of Japanese Financial Markets: Myth versus Reality.* New York: St. Martin's, 1999.

Beason, Dick, and Dennis Patterson. *The Japan That Never Was: Explaining the Rise and Decline of a Misunderstood Country*. Albany: State University of New York Press, 2004.

Beck, John C., and Martha N. Beck. *The Change of a Lifetime: Employment Patterns among Japan's Managerial Elite*. Honolulu: University of Hawai'i Press, 1994.

Blomstrom, Magnus, Byron Gangnes, and Summer La Croix, eds. *Japan's New Economy: Continuity and Change in the Twenty-First Century*. New York: Oxford University Press, 2001.

Blomstrom, Magnus, and Sumner La Croix, eds. *Institutional Change in Japan*. New York: Routledge, 2006.

Blumenthal, Tuvia. *Savings in Postwar Japan*. Cambridge, Mass.: Harvard University Press, 2006.

Boyer, Robert, and Toshio Yamada, eds. *Japanese Capitalism in Crisis: A Regulationist Interpretation*. New York: Routledge, 2000.

Brown, J. Robert. *The Ministry of Finance: Bureaucratic Practices and the Transformation of the Japanese Economy*. Westport, Conn.: Quorum Books, 1999.

Burstein, Daniel. *Yen! Japan's New Financial Empire and Its Threat to America*. New York: Simon & Schuster, 1988.

Bytheway, Simon James. *Investing Japan: Foreign Capital, Monetary Standards, and Economic Development, 1859–2011*. Cambridge, Mass.: Harvard University Press, 2014.

Calder, Kent E. *Circles of Compensation: Economic Growth and the Globalization of Japan*. Redwood City, Calif.: Stanford University Press, 2017.

———. *Strategic Capitalism: Private Business and Public Purpose in Japanese Industrial Finance*. Princeton, N.J.: Princeton University Press, 1993.

Callon, Scott. *Divided Sun: MITI and the Breakdown of Japanese High-Tech Industrial Policy, 1975–1993*. Stanford, Calif.: Stanford University Press, 1995.

Cargill, Thomas F., Michael M. Hutchinson, and Takatoshi Ito. *Financial Policy and Central Banking in Japan*. Cambridge, Mass.: MIT Press, 2001.

Carlile, Lonny E., and Mark C. Tilton, eds. *Is Japan Really Changing Its Ways? Regulatory Reform and the Japanese Economy*. Vancouver: University of British Columbia Press, 2005.

Coffey, Dan. *The Myth of Japanese Efficiency: The World Car Industry in a Globalizing Age*. Northampton, Mass.: Edward Elgar, 2007.

Cohen, Stephen D. *Cowboys and Samurai: Why the United States Is Losing the Industrial Battle and Why It Matters*. New York: Harper Business, 1991.

Colignon, Richard A., and Chikako Usui. *Amakudari: The Hidden Fabric of Japan's Economy*. Ithaca, N.Y.: Cornell University Press, 2003.

Crump, John. *Nikkeiren and Japanese Capitalism*. New York: Routledge, 2003.

Czinkota, Michael R., and Masaaki Kotabe. *The Japanese Distribution System: Opportunities & Obstacles, Structure & Practices*. Chicago: Probus, 1992.

Dore, Ronald P. *Stock Market Capitalism: Welfare Capitalism: Japan and Germany versus the Anglo-Saxons*. New York: Oxford University Press, 2000.

————. *Taking Japan Seriously: A Confucian Perspective on Leading Economic Issues*. Stanford, Calif.: Stanford University Press, 1987.

Dore, Ronald P., and D. Hugh Whittaker. *Social Evolution, Economic Development, and Culture: What It Means to Take Japan Seriously*. Northampton, Mass.: Edward Elgar, 2001.

Eli, Max. *Japan Inc.: Global Strategies of Japanese Trading Corporations*. Chicago: Probus, 1991.

Emmott, Bill. *Japanophobia: The Myth of the Invincible Japanese*. New York: Crown, 1993.

————. *The Sun Also Sets: The Limits to Japan's Economic Power*. London: Simon & Schuster, 1989.

Estevez-Abe, Margarita. *Welfare and Capitalism in Postwar Japan: Party, Bureaucracy, and Business*. New York: Cambridge University Press, 2010.

Fallows, James. *Looking at the Sun: The Rise of the New East Asian Economic System and Political System*. New York: Pantheon Books, 1994.

Fingleton, Eamonn. *Blindside: Why Japan Is Still on Track to Overtake the U.S. by 2000*. New York: Houghton Mifflin, 1995.

Flath, David. *The Japanese Economy*. 3rd ed. New York: Oxford University Press, 2014.

Fletcher, W. Miles, III, and Peter W. von Staden, eds. *Japan's "Lost Decade": Causes, Legacies and Issues of Transformative Change*. London: Routledge, 2013.

Forsberg, Aaron. *America and the Japanese Miracle: The Cold War Context of Japan's Postwar Economic Revival, 1950–1960*. Chapel Hill, N.C.: University of North Carolina Press, 2014.

Foster, Scott. *Stealth Japan: The Surprise Success of the World's First Infomerc Economy*. Friday Harbor, Wash.: FiReBooks, 2016.

Francks, Penelope. *Japanese Economic Development: Theory and Practice*. 2nd ed. London: Routledge, 1999.

Fransman, Martin. *Japan's Computer and Communications Industry: The Evolution of Industrial Giants and Global Competitiveness*. Oxford, U.K.: Oxford University Press, 1995.

Freedman, Craig, ed. *Economic Reform in Japan: Can the Japanese Change?* Northampton, Mass.: Edward Elgar, 2001.

————, ed. *Why Did Japan Stumble? Causes and Cures*. Northampton, Mass.: Edward Elgar, 1999.

Friedman, David. *The Misunderstood Miracle: Industrial Development and Political Change in Japan*. Ithaca, N.Y.: Cornell University Press, 1988.

Fruin, W. Mark. *The Japanese Enterprise System: Competitive Strategies and Comparative Structures*. New York: Oxford University Press, 1994.

————. *Knowledge Works: Managing Intellectual Capital at Toshiba*. New York: Oxford University Press, 1997.

Fukutake, Tadashi. *The Japanese Social Structure: Its Evolution in the Modern Century*. Translated by Ronald P. Dore. Tōkyō: Tōkyō University Press, 1980.

Fuss, Melvyn A., and Leonard Waverman. *Costs and Productivity in Automobile Production: The Challenge of Japanese Efficiency*. New York: Cambridge University Press, 1992.

Gao, Bai. *Japan's Economic Dilemma: The Institutional Origins of Prosperity and Stagnation*. New York: Cambridge University Press, 2001.

Garside, W. R. *Japan's Great Stagnation: Forging Ahead, Falling Behind*. Cheltenham, U.K.: Edward Elgar, 2012.

Genther, Phyllis Ann. *A History of Japan's Government-Business Relationship: The Passenger Car Industry*. Ann Arbor: Center for Japanese Studies, University of Michigan, 1990.

Gerlach, Michael L. *Alliance Capitalism: The Social Organization of Japanese Business*. Berkeley: University of California Press, 1992.

Gibney, Frank. *Miracle by Design: The Real Reasons behind Japan's Economic Success*. New York: Times Books, 1982.

————, ed. *Unlocking the Bureaucrat's Kingdom: Deregulation and the Japanese Economy*. Washington, D.C.: Brookings, 1998.

Graham, Fiona. *A Japanese Company in Crisis: Ideology, Strategy, and Narrative*. New York: Routledge, 2005.

Grimes, William W. *Unmaking the Japanese Miracle: Macroeconomic Politics, 1985–2000*. Ithaca, N.Y.: Cornell University Press, 2001.

Haak, Rene, and Markus Pudelko, eds. *Japanese Management: The Search for a New Balance between Continuity and Change*. New York: Palgrave Macmillan, 2005.

Haghirian, Parissa, ed. *Routledge Handbook of Japanese Business and Management*. New York: Routledge, 2016.

Harner, Stephen M. *Japan's Financial Revolution and How American Firms Are Profiting*. Armonk, N.Y.: M. E. Sharpe, 2000.

Hartcher, Peter. *The Ministry: How Japan's Most Powerful Institution Endangers World Markets*. Cambridge, Mass.: Harvard Business School Press, 1997.

Hasegawa, Harukiyo, and Glenn D. Hook, eds. *Japanese Business Management: Restructuring for Low Growth and Globalization*. London: Routledge, 1997.

Hayami, Yujiro, and Saburō Yamada. *The Agricultural Development of Japan: A Century's Perspective*. Tōkyō: University of Tōkyō Press, 1991.

Hayes, Declan. *Japan's Big Bang: The Deregulation and Revitalization of the Japanese Economy*. North Clarendon, Vt.: Tuttle, 2000.

Hein, Laura E. *Fueling Growth: The Energy Revolution and Economic Policy in Postwar Japan*. Cambridge, Mass.: Harvard University Press, 1990.

Hodgson, James D., Yoshiro Sano, and James L. Graham. *Doing Business with the New Japan*. Lanham, Md.: Rowman & Littlefield, 2000.

Hoshi, Takeo, and Anil Kashyap. *Corporate Financing and Governance in Japan: The Road to the Future*. Cambridge, Mass.: MIT Press, 2001.

Hunter, Janet, and Cornelia Storz, eds. *Institutional and Technological Change in Japan's Economy: Past and Present*. New York: Routledge, 2005.

Ibata-Arens, Kathryn. *Innovation and Entrepreneurship in Japan: Politics, Organization, and High Technology Firms*. New York: Cambridge University Press, 2005.

Ikeo, Aiko, ed. *Japanese Economics and Economists since 1945*. New York: Routledge, 2000.

Imai, Kenichi, and Ryutaro Komiya, eds. *Business Enterprise in Japan: Views of Leading Japanese Economists*. Cambridge, Mass.: MIT Press, 1995.

Inkster, Ian. *The Japanese Industrial Economy: Late Development and Cultural Causation*. New York: Routledge, 2001.

———. *Japanese Industrialisation: Historical and Cultural Perspectives*. New York: Routledge, 2001.

Ishi, Hiromitsu. *Making Fiscal Policy in Japan: Economic Effects and Institutional Settings*. New York: Oxford University Press, 2000.

Ishinomori, Shōtarō. *Japan Inc.: An Introduction to Japanese Economics: The Comic Book*. Berkeley: University of California Press, 1988.

Ito, Takatoshi, Hugh Patrick, and David E. Weinstein, eds. *Reviving Japan's Economy: Problems and Prescriptions*. Cambridge, Mass.: MIT Press, 2005.

Itoh, Makoto. *The Japanese Economy Reconsidered*. New York: Palgrave, 2000.

Jackson, Keith, and Miyuki Tomioka. *The Changing Face of Japanese Management*. New York: Routledge, 2003.

Johnson, Chalmers. *MITI and the Japanese Miracle: The Growth of Industrial Policy, 1925–1975*. Stanford, Calif.: Stanford University Press, 1982.

Johnstone, Bob. *We Were Burning: Japanese Entrepreneurs and the Forging of the Electronics Age*. New York: HarperCollins, 1999.

Kahn, Herman. *The Japanese Challenge: The Success and Failure of Economic Success*. New York: Crowell, 1979.

Kase, Kimio, Francisco J. Saez-Martinez, and Hernan Riquelme. *Transformational CEOs: Leadership and Management Success in Japan*. Northampton, Mass.: Edward Elgar, 2005.

Katayama, Osamu. *Japanese Business into the 21st Century: Strategies for Success*. London: Athlone, 1996.

Katz, Richard. *Japan: The System That Soured: The Rise and Fall of the Japanese Economic Miracle*. Armonk, N.Y.: M. E. Sharpe, 1998.

———. *Japanese Phoenix: The Long Road to Economic Revival*. Armonk, N.Y.: M. E. Sharpe, 2002.

Kensy, Rainer. *Keiretsu Economy—New Economy? Japan's Multinational Enterprises from a Postmodern Perspective*. New York: Palgrave, 2001.

Kinzley, W. Dean. *Industrial Harmony in Modern Japan: The Invention of a Tradition*. London: Routledge, 1991.

Kohama, Hirohisa. *Industrial Development in Postwar Japan*. London: Routledge, 2007.

Koike, Kazuo. *Understanding Industrial Relations in Modern Japan*. New York: St. Martin's, 1988.

Komiya, Ryutaro. *The Japanese Economy: Trade, Industry, and Government*. Tōkyō: University of Tōkyō Press, 1990.

Kono, Toyohiro, and Stewart Clegg. *Trends in Japanese Management: Continuing Strengths, Current Problems and Changing Priorities*. New York: Palgrave, 2001.

Kuroda, Yoshimi. *Rice Production Structure and Policy Effects in Japan: Quantitative Investigations*. New York: Palgrave Macmillan, 2016.

Kushida, Kenji E., Kay Shimizu, and Jean C. Oi, eds. *Syncretism: The Politics of Economic Restructuring and System Reform in Japan*. Redwood City, Calif.: Stanford University Press, 2013.

Lathan, John. *Japanese Industrialization and the Asian Economy*. New York: Routledge, 1994.

Lechevalier, Sebastien. *The Great Transformation of Japanese Capitalism*. Translated by J. A. A. Stockwin. New York: Routledge, 2011.

Levine, Solomon B., and Koji Taira, eds. *Japan's External Economic Relations: Japanese Perspectives*. Newbury Park, Calif.: Sage Periodicals Press, 1991.

Lincoln, Edward J. *Arthritic Japan: The Slow Pace of Economic Reform*. Washington, D.C.: Brookings, 2001.

Lincoln, James R., and Michael L. Gerlach. *Japan's Network Economy: Structure, Persistence, and Change*. New York: Cambridge University Press, 2004.

Malcolm, James P. *Financial Globalisation and the Opening of the Japanese Economy*. London: Routledge, 2001.

Maswood, S. Javed. *Japan in Crisis*. Houndmills, U.K.: Palgrave Macmillan, 2002.

Matanle, Peter. *Japanese Capitalism and Modernity in a Global Era: Refabricating Lifetime Employment Relations*. New York: Routledge, 2003.

Matsumoto, Koji. *The Rise of the Japanese Corporate System: The Inside View of a MITI Official*. Translated by Thomas I. Elliott. London: Kegan Paul International, 1991.

Metzler, Mark. *Capital as Will and Imagination: Schumpeter's Guide to the Postwar Japanese Miracle*. Ithaca, N.Y.: Cornell University Press, 2013.

Mikitani, Hiroshi, and Ryoichi Mikitani. *The Power to Compete: An Economist and an Entrepreneur on Revitalizing Japan in the Global Economy*. Hoboken, N.J.: Wiley, 2014.

Milhaupt, Curtis J., and Mark D. West. *Economic Organizations and Corporate Governance in Japan: The Impact of Formal and Informal Rules*. Oxford, U.K.: Oxford University Press, 2004.

Milly, Deborah J. *Poverty, Equality, and Growth: The Politics of Economic Need in Postwar Japan*. Cambridge, Mass.: Harvard University Asia Center, 1999.

Miwa, Yoshiro. *State Competence and Economic Growth in Japan*. New York: Routledge, 2004.

Miwa, Yoshiro, and J. Mark Ramseyer. *The Fable of the Keiretsu: Urban Legends of the Japanese Economy*. Chicago: University of Chicago Press, 2006.

Miyazaki, Hirokazu. *Arbitraging Japan: Dreams of Capitalism at the End of Finance*. Berkeley: University of California Press, 2013.

Morris-Suzuki, Tessa. *A History of Japanese Economic Thought*. London: Routledge, 1989.

Morris-Suzuki, Tessa, and Takuro Seiyama, eds. *Japanese Capitalism since 1945: Critical Perspectives*. Armonk, N.Y.: M. E. Sharpe, 1989.

Mulgan, Aurelia George. *Japan's Agricultural Policy Regime*. New York: Routledge, 2006.

Mulgan, Aurelia George, and Masayoshi Honma, eds. *The Political Economy of Japanese Trade Policy*. New York: Palgrave Macmillan, 2015.

Nakamura, Masao, ed. *Changing Japanese Business, Economy and Society: Globalization of Post-bubble Japan*. New York: Palgrave Macmillan, 2004.

———, ed. *The Japanese Business and Economic System: History and Prospects for the 21st Century*. New York: Palgrave, 2001.

Nakamura, Takafusa. *The Postwar Japanese Economy: Its Development and Structure, 1937–1994*. New York: Columbia University Press, 1995.

O'Byran, Scott. *The Growth Idea: Purpose and Prosperity in Postwar Japan*. Honolulu: University of Hawai'i Press, 2009.

Ogura, Takekazu. *Agricultural Development in Modern Japan: Japanese Economic History*. London: Routledge, 2000.

Okazaki, Tetsuji, and Masahiro Okuno-Fujiwara, eds. *The Japanese Economic System and Its Historical Origins*. Oxford, U.K.: Oxford University Press, 1999.

Ōkita, Saburō, ed. *The Postwar Reconstruction of the Japanese Economy*. Tōkyō: University of Tōkyō Press, 1991.

Oppenheim, Phillip. *Japan without Blinders: Coming to Terms with Japan's Economic Success*. Tōkyō: Kodansha, 1992.

Paprzycki, Ralph. *Japanese Interfirm Networks: Adapting to Survive in the Global Electronics Industry*. New York: Routledge, 2005.

Partner, Simon. *Assembled in Japan: Electrical Goods and the Making of the Japanese Consumer*. Berkeley: University of California Press, 2004.

Patrick, Hugh T., ed. *Japanese Industrialization and Its Social Consequences*. Berkeley: University of California Press, 1976.

Pesek, William. *Japanization: What the World Can Learn from Japan's Lost Decades*. Hoboken, N.J.: Wiley, 2014.

Picken, Stuart D. B. *Historical Dictionary of Japanese Business*. Lanham, Md.: Scarecrow Press, 2007.

Porter, Michael E., Hirotaka Takeuchi, and Mariko Sakakibara. *Can Japan Compete?* Basingstoke, U.K.: Macmillan, 2000.

Preston, Peter Wallace. *Understanding Modern Japan: A Political Economy of Development, Culture and Global Power*. Thousand Oaks, Calif.: Sage, 2000.

Prestowitz, Clyde V., Jr. *Trading Places: How We Allowed Japan to Take the Lead*. New York: Basic Books, 1998.

Reading, Brian. *Japan: The Coming Collapse*. New York: Harper Business, 1992.

Rebick, Marcus. *The Japanese Employment System: Adapting to a New Economic Environment*. Oxford, U.K.: Oxford University Press, 2005.

Rosenbluth, Frances McCall. *Financial Politics in Contemporary Japan*. Ithaca, N.Y.: Cornell University Press, 1989.

Rosenbluth, Frances McCall, and Michael F. Thies. *Japan Transformed: Political Change and Economic Restructuring*. Princeton, N.J.: Princeton University Press, 2010.

Rothacher, Albrecht. *Japan's Agro-Food Sector: The Politics and Economics of Excess Protection*. New York: St. Martin's, 1990.

Rowland, Diana Kathleen. *Japanese Business: Rules of Engagement*. Angola, Ind.: Rowland & Associates, 2015.

Sakakibara, Eisuke. *Beyond Capitalism: The Japanese Model of Market Economics*. Lanham, Md.: University Press of America, 2005.

Samuels, Richard J. *The Business of the Japanese State: Energy Markets in Comparative and Historical Perspective*. Ithaca, N.Y.: Cornell University Press, 1987.

Sato, Kazuo, ed. *The Transformation of the Japanese Economy*. Armonk, N.Y.: M. E. Sharpe, 1999.

Schaede, Ulrike. *Choose and Focus: Japanese Business Strategies for the 21st Century*. Ithaca, N.Y.: Cornell University Press, 2008.

Schmiegelow, Michele, ed. *Japan's Response to Crisis and Change in the World Economy*. Armonk, N.Y.: M. E. Sharpe, 1986.

Schmiegelow, Michele, and Henrik Schmiegelow. *Strategic Pragmatism: Japanese Lessons in the Use of Economic Theory*. New York: Praeger, 1989.

Shibata, Tsutomu, ed. *Japan, Moving toward a More Advanced Knowledge Economy*. Herndon, Va.: World Bank, 2006.

Shimokawa, Koichi. *The Japanese Automobile Industry: A Business History*. London: Athlone Press, 1994.

Smitka, Michael. *Japan's Economic Ascent: International Trade, Growth, and Postwar Reconstruction*. London: Routledge, 1998.

Stern, Robert M., ed. *Japan's Economic Recovery: Commercial Policy, Monetary Policy, and Corporate Governance*. Northampton, Mass.: Edward Elgar, 2003.

Stewart, Paul. *Beyond Japanese Management: The End of Modern Times?* London: Routledge, 1997.

Storz, Cornelia, ed. *Small Firms and Innovation Policy in Japan*. New York: Routledge, 2006.

Suzuki, Yoshio. *Japan's Economic Performance and International Role*. Tōkyō: University of Tōkyō Press, 1989.

Szymkowiak, Kenneth. *Sōkaiya: Extortion, Protection, and the Japanese Corporation*. Armonk, N.Y.: M. E. Sharpe, 2002.

Tabb, William K. *The Postwar Japanese System: Cultural Economy and Economic Transformation*. New York: Oxford University Press, 1995.

Tachi, Ryuichiro. *The Contemporary Japanese Economy: An Overview*. Translated by Richard Walker. Tōkyō: University of Tōkyō Press, 1994.

Tachibanaki, Toshiaki. *Capital and Labour in Japan: The Functions of Two Factor Markets*. London: Routledge, 2000.

———, ed. *The Economics of Social Security in Japan*. Northampton, Mass.: Edward Elgar, 2004.

———, ed. *Who Runs Japanese Business? Management and Motivation in the Firm*. Northampton, Mass.: Edward Elgar, 1998.

Takayama, Noriyuki. *The Greying of Japan: An Economic Perspective on Public Pensions*. Tōkyō: Kinokuniya, 1992.

Takenaka, Heizō. *Contemporary Japanese Economy and Economic Policy*. Ann Arbor: University of Michigan Press, 1991.

Tandon, Rameshwar. *The Japanese Economy and the Way Forward*. New York: Palgrave Macmillan, 2005.

Teranishi, Juro. *Evolution of the Economic System in Japan*. Northampton, Mass.: Edward Elgar, 2005.

Tilton, Mark. *Restrained Trade: Cartels in Japan's Basic Materials Industries*. Ithaca, N.Y.: Cornell University Press, 1996.

Trevor, Malcolm. *Japan—Restless Competitor: The Pursuit of Economic Nationalism*. New York: Routledge, 2016.

Tsuru, Shigeto. *Japan's Capitalism: Creative Defeat and Beyond*. New York: Cambridge University Press, 1993.

Tsurumi, Yoshi. *Sōgōshōsha: Engines of Export-Based Growth*. Montreal: Institute for Research on Public Policy, 1980.

Tsutsui, William M. *Manufacturing Ideology: Scientific Management in Twentieth-Century Japan*. Princeton, N.J.: Princeton University Press, 1998.

Turner, Charlie G. *Japan's Dynamic Efficiency in the Global Market: Trade, Investment, and Economic Growth*. New York: Quorum Books, 1991.

Uriu, Robert M. *Troubled Industries: Confronting Economic Change in Japan*. Ithaca, N.Y.: Cornell University Press, 1996.

Usui, Kazuo. *Marketing and Consumption in Modern Japan*. London: Routledge, 2014.

Vogel, Steven K. *Japan Remodeled: How Government and Industry Are Reforming Japanese Capitalism*. Ithaca, N.Y.: Cornell University Press, 2007.

Wakatabe, Masatomi. *Japan's Great Stagnation and Abenomics: Lessons for the World*. New York: Palgrave Macmillan, 2015.

Werner, Richard A. *Princes of the Yen: Japan's Central Bankers and the Transformation of the Economy*. Armonk, N.Y.: M. E. Sharpe, 2003.

Whitehill, Arthur M. *Japanese Management: Tradition and Transition*. London: Routledge, 1992.

Whittaker, D. Hugh. *Small Firms in the Japanese Economy*. New York: Cambridge University Press, 1997.

Wilks, Stephen, and Maurice Wright, eds. *The Promotion and Regulation of Industry in Japan*. New York: St. Martin's, 1991.

Witt, Michael A. *Changing Japanese Capitalism: Societal Coordination and Institutional Adjustment*. New York: Cambridge University Press, 2006.

Wood, Christopher. *The Bubble Economy: The Japanese Economic Collapse*. Tōkyō: Tuttle, 1993.

Woronoff, Jon. *Japan: The Japanese Economic Crisis*. London: Macmillan; New York: St. Martin's, 1993.

———. *The Japanese Management Mystique: The Reality behind the Myth*. Chicago: Probus, 1992.

Wright, Maurice. *Japan's Fiscal Crisis: The Ministry of Finance and the Politics of Public Spending, 1975–2000*. Oxford, U.K.: Oxford University Press, 2002.

Yamamura, Kozo, ed. *The Economic Emergence of Modern Japan*. New York: Cambridge University Press, 1997.

Yamazawa, Ippei. *Economic Development and International Trade: The Japanese Model*. Honolulu, Hawaii: East-West Center, 1990.

Yoda, Tomiko, and Harry Harootunian, eds. *Japan after Japan: Social and Cultural Life from the Recessionary 1990s to the Present*. Durham, N.C.: Duke University Press, 2006.

Yorozu, Chie. *Narrative Management in Corporate Japan: Investor Relations as Pseudo-Reform*. New York: Routledge, 2015.

Yoshihara, Kunio. *Sogo Shosha: The Vanguard of the Japanese Economy*. Oxford, U.K.: Oxford University Press, 1981.

Yoshimura, Noboru, and Philip Anderson. *Inside the Kaisha: Demystifying Japanese Business Behavior*. Cambridge, Mass.: Harvard University Press, 1997.

Yoshino, Michael Y., and Thomas B. Lifson. *The Invisible Link: Japan's Sogo Shosha and the Organization of Trade*. Cambridge, Mass.: MIT Press, 1986.

Young, Alexander K. *The Sogo Shosha: Japan's Multinational Trading Companies*. Boulder, Colo.: Westview, 1979.

SOCIAL ISSUES

Aldrich, Daniel P. *Site Fights: Divisive Facilities and Civil Society in Japan and the West*. Ithaca, N.Y.: Cornell University Press, 2008.

Allinson, Gary D. *Suburban Tokyo: A Comparative Study in Politics and Social Change*. Berkeley: University of California Press, 1979.

Allison, Anne. *Precarious Japan*. Durham, N.C.: Duke University Press, 2013.

Ambaras, David R. *Bad Youth: Juvenile Delinquency and the Politics of Everyday Life in Modern Japan*. Berkeley: University of California Press, 2006.

Ames, Walter L. *Police and Community in Japan*. Berkeley: University of California Press, 1981.

Anderson, Stephen J. *Welfare Policy and Politics in Japan: Beyond the Developmental State*. New York: Paragon, 1993.

Aoyama, Tomoko, Laura Dales, and Romit Dasgupta, eds. *Configurations of Family in Contemporary Japan*. New York: Routledge, 2015.

Arai, Andrea Gevurtz. *The Strange Child: Education and the Psychology of Patriotism in Recessionary Japan*. Redwood City, Calif.: Stanford University Press, 2016.

Arudou, Debito. *Embedded Racism: Japan's Visible Minorities and Racial Discrimination*. Lanham, Md.: Lexington Books, 2016.

Ashkenazi, Michael, and John R. Clammer. *Consumption and Material Culture in Contemporary Japan*. New York: Kegan Paul, 2000.

Assmann, Stephanie, ed. *Sustainability in Contemporary Rural Japan: Challenges and Opportunities*. New York: Routledge, 2015.

Avenell, Simon Andrew. *Making Japanese Citizens: Civil Society and the Mythology of the Shimin in Postwar Japan*. Berkeley: University of California Press, 2010.

Bachnik, Jane M., ed. *Roadblocks on the Information Highway: The IT Revolution in Japanese Education*. Lanham, Md.: Lexington Books, 2003.

Bass, Scott A., Robert Morris, and Masato Oka, eds. *Public Policy and the Old Age Revolution in Japan*. New York: Haworth Press, 1996.

Bayley, David H. *Forces of Order: Policing Modern Japan*. Berkeley: University of California Press, 1991.

Beardsley, Richard K., John W. Hall, and Robert E. Ward. *Village Japan*. Chicago: University of Chicago Press, 1959.

Bebenroth, Ralf, and Toshihiro Kanai, eds. *Challenges of Human Resource Management in Japan*. New York: Routledge, 2011.

Belderbos, Rene A. *Japanese Electronics Multinationals and Strategic Trade Policies*. Oxford, U.K.: Clarendon Press, 1997.

Bellah, Robert H. *Imaging Japan: The Japanese Tradition and Its Modern Interpretation*. Berkeley: University of California Press, 2003.

Ben-Ari, Eyal, Brian Moeran, and James Valentine, eds. *Unwrapping Japan: Society and Culture in Anthropological Perspective*. Manchester, U.K.: Manchester University Press, 1990.

Bestor, Theodore C. *Neighborhood Tokyo*. Stanford, Calif.: Stanford University Press, 1989.

———. *Tsukiji: The Fish Market at the Center of the World*. Berkeley: University of California Press, 2004.

Bestor, Theodore C., and Victoria Bestor, eds. *Routledge Handbook of Japanese Culture and Society*. New York: Routledge, 2010.

Bondy, Christopher. *Voice, Silence, and Self: Negotiations of Buraku Identity in Contemporary Japan*. Cambridge, Mass.: Harvard University Press, 2015.

Botsman, Daniel V. *Punishment and Power in the Making of Modern Japan*. Princeton, N.J.: Princeton University Press, 2005.

Brumann, Christoph, and Evelyn Schulz, eds. *Urban Spaces in Japan: Cultural and Social Perspectives*. New York: Routledge, 2012.

Campbell, John Creighton, and Naoki Ikegami. *The Art of Balance in Health Policy: Maintaining Japan's Low-Cost, Egalitarian System.* New York: Cambridge University Press, 1998.

———, eds. *Containing Health-Care Costs in Japan.* Ann Arbor: University of Michigan Press, 1996.

Cassegärd, Carl. *Youth Movements, Trauma and Alternative Space in Contemporary Japan.* Leiden, the Netherlands: Global Oriental, 2014.

Castro-Vázquez, Genaro. *Intimacy and Reproduction in Contemporary Japan.* New York: Routledge, 2016.

Cather, Kirsten. *The Art of Censorship in Postwar Japan.* Honolulu: University of Hawai'i Press, 2012.

Chalmers, Norma J. *Industrial Relations in Japan: The Peripheral Workforce.* New York: Routledge, 1989.

Chan, Yeeshan. *Abandoned Japanese in Postwar Manchuria: The Lives of War Orphans and Wives in Two Countries.* New York: Routledge, 2013.

Chaplin, Sarah. *Japanese Love Hotels: A Cultural History.* New York: Routledge, 2007.

Chiavacci, David, and Carola Hommerich, eds. *Social Inequality in Postgrowth Japan: Transformation during Economic and Demographic Stagnation.* New York: Routledge, 2016.

Christensen, Paul A. *Japan, Alcoholism, and Masculinity: Suffering Sobriety in Tokyo.* Lanham, Md.: Lexington Books, 2015.

Clammer, John. *Difference and Modernity: Social Theory and Contemporary Japan.* London: Kegan Paul International, 1995.

Colby, Mark. *Japan's Healthcare Debate: Diverse Perspectives.* Folkestone, Kent, U.K.: Global Oriental, 2004.

Cole, Robert E. *Japanese Blue Collar: The Changing Tradition.* Berkeley: University of California Press, 1971.

Cornyetz, Nina, and J. Keith Vincent, eds. *Perversion and Modern Japan: Psychoanalysis, Literature, Culture.* New York: Routledge, 2011.

Croydon, Silvia. *The Politics of Police Detention in Japan: Consensus of Convenience.* London: Oxford University Press, 2016.

Cwiertka, Katarzyna J. *Modern Japanese Cuisine: Food, Power and National Identity.* London: Reaktion Books, 2006.

Cybriwsky, Roman. *Tokyo: The Changing Profile of an Urban Giant.* Boston: G. K. Hall, 1991.

Dasgupta, Romit. *Re-reading the Salaryman in Japan: Crafting Masculinities.* London: Routledge, 2012.

De Vos, George A., and Hiroshi Wagatsuma, eds. *Japan's Invisible Race: Caste in Culture and Personality.* Berkeley: University of California Press, 1966.

Di Marco, Francesca. *Suicide in Twentieth-Century Japan.* New York: Routledge, 2016.

Doane, Donna L. *Cooperation, Technology, and Japanese Development: Indigenous Knowledge, the Power of Networks, and the State.* Boulder, Colo.: Westview, 1998.

Doi, Takeo. *Amae: The Anatomy of Dependence.* Translated by John Bester. Tōkyō: Kodansha International, 1973.

————. *The Anatomy of Self: The Individual versus Society.* Translated by Mark A. Harbison. Tōkyō: Kodansha, 1986.

Dore, Ronald P. *City Life in Japan: A Study of a Tokyo Ward.* Berkeley: University of California Press, 1959.

Ducke, Isa. *Civil Society and the Internet in Japan.* New York: Routledge, 2007.

Dusinberre, Martin. *Hard Times in the Hometown: A History of Community Survival in Modern Japan.* Honolulu: University of Hawai'i Press, 2012.

Ezawa, Aya. *Single Mothers in Contemporary Japan: Motherhood, Class, and Reproductive Practice.* Lanham, Md.: Lexington Books, 2016.

Farrell, William R. *Blood and Rage: The Story of the Japanese Red Army.* Lexington, Mass.: Lexington Books, 1990.

Freedman, Alisa, Laura Miller, and Christine R. Yano, eds. *Modern Girls on the Go: Gender, Mobility, and Labor in Japan.* Redwood City, Calif.: Stanford University Press, 2013.

Frost, Dennis J. *Seeing Stars: Sports Celebrity, Identity, and Body Culture in Modern Japan.* Cambridge, Mass.: Harvard University Press, 2010.

Frühstück, Sabine, and Anne Walthall, eds. *Recreating Japanese Men.* Berkeley: University of California Press, 2011.

George, Timothy S. *Minamata: Pollution and the Struggle for Democracy in Postwar Japan.* Cambridge, Mass.: Harvard University Press, 2001.

Germer, Andrea, Vera Mackie, and Ulrike Wöhr, eds. *Gender, Nation and State in Modern Japan.* New York: Routledge, 2014.

Goodman, Roger. *Children of the Japanese State: The Changing Role of Child Protection Institutions in Contemporary Japan.* Oxford, U.K.: Oxford University Press, 2000.

Goodman, Roger, Yuki Imoto, and Tuukka Toivonen, eds. *A Sociology of Japanese Youth: From Returnees to NEETs.* New York: Routledge, 2012.

Gottlieb, Nanette. *Linguistic Stereotyping and Minority Groups in Japan.* New York: Routledge, 2006.

Goulding, Matt. *Rice, Noodle, Fish: Deep Travels through Japan's Food Culture.* New York: Harper Wave, 2015.

Greenfeld, Karl Taro. *Speed Tribes: Days and Nights with Japan's Next Generation.* New York: HarperCollins, 1994.

Guttmann, Allen, and Lee Thompson. *Japanese Sports: A History.* Honolulu: University of Hawai'i Press, 2001.

Hankins, Joseph D., and Carolyn S. Stevens, eds. *Sound, Space and Sociality in Modern Japan.* New York: Routledge, 2016.

Hashimoto, Kenji. *Class Structure in Contemporary Japan*. Melbourne, Australia: Trans-Pacific, 2003.

Havens, Thomas R. H. *Marathon Japan: Distance Racing and Civic Culture*. Honolulu: University of Hawai'i Press, 2015.

Hayes, Peter, and Toshie Habu. *Adoption in Japan: Comparing Policies for Children in Need*. New York: Routledge, 2006.

Hein, Carola, and Philippe Pelletier, eds. *Cities, Autonomy, and Decentralization in Japan*. New York: Routledge, 2006.

Heinrich, Patrick, and Christian Galan, eds. *Language Life in Japan: Transformations and Prospects*. New York: Routledge, 2013.

Hendry, Joy. *Interpreting Japanese Society: Anthropological Approaches*. 2nd ed. New York: Routledge, 1998.

———. *Understanding Japanese Society*. 3rd ed. London: Routledge, 2003.

———. *Wrapping Culture: Politeness, Presentation, and Power in Japan and Other Societies*. New York: Oxford University Press, 1993.

Hill, Peter B. E. *The Japanese Mafia: Yakuza, Law, and the State*. Oxford, U.K.: Oxford University Press, 2003.

Hood, Christopher P. *Dealing with Disaster in Japan: Responses to the Flight JL123 Crash*. New York: Routledge, 2013.

———. *Shinkansen: From Bullet Train to Symbol of Modern Japan*. New York: Routledge, 2006.

Hopson, Nathan. *Ennobling Japan's Savage Northeast: Tōhoku as Japanese Postwar Thought, 1945–2011*. Cambridge, Mass.: Harvard University Press, 2017.

Hutchinson, Rachael, ed. *Negotiating Censorship in Modern Japan*. New York: Routledge, 2013.

Inagami, Takeshi, and D. Hugh Whittaker. *The New Community Firm: Employment, Governance and Management Reform in Japan*. New York: Cambridge University Press, 2005.

Inkster, Ian, and Fumihiko Satofuka, eds. *Culture and Technology in Modern Japan*. New York: Tauris, 2000.

Ishida, Hiroshi, and David H. Slater, eds. *Social Class in Contemporary Japan*. New York: Routledge, 2010.

Ishida, Takeshi. *Japanese Society*. New York: Random House, 1971.

Ishikawa, Yoshitaka, ed. *International Migrants in Japan: Contributions in an Era of Population Decline*. Balwyn, North Victoria, Australia: Trans-Pacific, 2015.

Ishimure, Michiko. *Paradise in the Sea of Sorrow: Our Minamata Disease*. Translated by Livia Monnet. Kyoto: Yamaguchi Publishing House, 1990.

Itasaka, Gen. *Gates to Japan: Its People and Society*. Translated by Jon H. Loftus. Tōkyō: 3A Corporation, 1989.

Johnson, David T. *The Japanese Way of Justice: Prosecuting Crime in Japan*. Oxford, U.K.: Oxford University Press, 2002.

Kaplan, David E., and Alec Dubro. *Yakuza: The Explosive Account of Japan's Criminal Underworld*. New York: Macmillan, 1986.

Karan, Pradyumna P., and Kristin Stapleton, eds. *The Japanese City*. Lexington: University Press of Kentucky, 1997.

Kasza, Gregory J. *One World of Welfare: Japan in Comparative Perspective*. Ithaca, N.Y.: Cornell University Press, 2006.

Kawano, Satsuki. *Nature's Embrace: Japan's Aging Urbanites and New Death Rites*. Honolulu: University of Hawai'i Press, 2010.

Kerr, Alex. *Dogs and Demons: Tales from the Dark Side of Japan*. New York: Hill & Wang, 2001.

Kingston, Jeff. *Japan's Quiet Transformation: Social Change and Civil Society in the Twenty-First Century*. New York: Routledge, 2004.

Kinsella, Sharon. *Schoolgirls, Money and Rebellion in Japan*. London: Routledge, 2014.

Koschmann, J. Victor. *Revolution and Subjectivity in Postwar Japan*. Chicago: University of Chicago Press, 1996.

———, ed. *Authority and the Individual in Japan: Citizen Protest in Historical Perspective*. Tōkyō: University of Tōkyō Press, 1978.

Krauss, Ellis S. *Japanese Radicals Revisited: Student Protest in Postwar Japan*. Berkeley: University of California Press, 1974.

Krauss, Ellis S., Thomas P. Rohlen, and Patricia G. Steinhoff, eds. *Conflict in Japan*. Honolulu: University of Hawai'i Press, 1984.

Krech, Gregg. *The Art of Taking Action: Lessons from Japanese Psychology*. Monkton, Vt.: ToDo Institute, 2014.

Kumagai, Fumie. *Unmasking Japan Today: The Impact of Traditional Values on Modern Japanese Society*. Westport, Conn.: Praeger, 1996.

Lebra, Takie Sugiyama. *Above the Clouds: Status Culture of the Modern Japanese Nobility*. Berkeley: University of California Press, 1993.

———. *The Japanese Self in Cultural Logic*. Honolulu: University of Hawai'i Press, 2004.

———, ed. *Japanese Social Organization*. Honolulu: University of Hawai'i Press, 1992.

Lee, A. Robert. *Tokyo Commute: Japanese Customs and Way of Life Viewed from the Odakyu Line*. Honolulu: University of Hawai'i Press, 2011.

Leheny, David R. *The Rules of Play: National Identity and the Shaping of Japanese Leisure*. Ithaca, N.Y.: Cornell University Press, 2003.

———. *Think Global, Fear Local: Sex, Violence, and Anxiety in Contemporary Japan*. Ithaca, N.Y.: Cornell University Press, 2006.

Leonardsen, Dag. *Japan as a Low-Crime Nation*. New York: Palgrave Macmillan, 2004.

Lie, John. *Multiethnic Japan*. Cambridge, Mass.: Harvard University Press, 2001.

Long, Susan Orpett. *Family Change and the Life Course in Japan*. Ithaca, N.Y.: Cornell University Press, 1987.

———. *Final Days: Japanese Culture and Choice at the End of Life*. Honolulu: University of Hawai'i Press, 2005.

———, ed. *Caring for the Elderly in Japan and the U.S.: Practices and Policies*. London: Routledge, 2000.

MacKellar, Landis. *The Economic Impacts of Population Ageing in Japan*. Northampton, Mass.: Edward Elgar, 2004.

Mackie, Vera C., Ulrike Wöhr, and Andrea Germer, eds. *Gender, Nation and State in Modern Japan*. London: Routledge, 2006.

Mackintosh, Jonathan D. *Homosexuality and Manliness in Postwar Japan*. New York: Routledge, 2011.

Maguire, Joseph, and Masayoshi Nakayama, eds. *Japan, Sport and Society: Tradition and Change in a Globalizing World*. New York: Routledge, 2006.

Manzenreiter, Wolfram, and Barbara Holthus, eds. *Happiness and the Good Life in Japan*. London: Routledge, 2017.

March, Robert C. *Reading the Japanese Mind: The Realities behind Their Thoughts and Actions*. Tōkyō: Kodansha International, 1996.

Matanle, Peter, and Anthony S. Rausch, eds. *Japan's Shrinking Regions in the 21st Century: Contemporary Responses to Depopulation and Socioeconomic Decline*. Amherst, N.Y.: Cambria Press, 2011.

Mathews, Gordon, and Bruce White, eds. *Japan's Changing Generations: Are Young People Creating a New Society?* New York: Routledge, 2006.

Matsumoto, David. *Unmasking Japan: Myths and Realities about the Emotions of the Japanese*. Stanford, Calif.: Stanford University Press, 1996.

McCormack, Gavan. *The Emptiness of Japanese Affluence*. Armonk, N.Y.: M. E. Sharpe, 1996.

McCormick, Kevin. *Learning from Japan*. New York: Routledge, 2006.

McKnight, Anne. *Nakagami, Japan: Buraku and the Writing of Ethnicity*. Minneapolis: University of Minnesota Press, 2011.

McLauchlan, Alastair. *Prejudice and Discrimination in Japan: The Buraku Issue*. Lewiston, N.Y.: Edwin Mellen, 2003.

McVeigh, Brian J. *Nationalisms of Japan: Managing and Mystifying Identity*. Lanham, Md.: Rowman & Littlefield, 2004.

———. *The Nature of the Japanese State: Rationality and Rituality*. London: Routledge, 1998.

Meli, Mark. *Craft Beer in Japan: The Essential Guide*. Atlanta, Ga.: Bright Wave Media, 2013.

Metraux, Daniel A. *Aum Shinrikyo's Impact on Japanese Society*. Lewiston, N.Y.: Edwin Mellen, 2000.

Miller, Alan S., and Satoshi Kanazawa. *Order by Accident: The Origins and Consequences of Conformity in Contemporary Japan*. Boulder, Colo.: Westview, 2000.

Mishima, Akio. *Bitter Sea: The Human Cost of Minamata Disease*. Tōkyō: Kosei, 1992.

Mitchell, Louise, ed. *The Cutting Edge: Fashion from Japan*. London: Ashgate, 2005.

Mizuta, Kazuo. *The Structures of Everyday Life in Japan in the Last Decade of the Twentieth Century*. Lewiston, N.Y.: Edwin Mellen, 1993.

Moeran, Brian. *A Japanese Advertising Agency: An Anthropology of Media and Markets*. Honolulu: University of Hawai'i Press, 1996.

Morris-Suzuki, Tessa. *Re-inventing Japan: Time, Space, Nation*. Armonk, N.Y.: M. E. Sharpe, 1998.

Mosk, Carl. *Japanese Industrial History: Technology, Urbanization, and Economic Growth*. Armonk, N.Y.: M. E. Sharpe, 2001.

Mouer, Ross E., and Hirosuke Kawanishi. *A Sociology of Work in Japan*. New York: Cambridge University Press, 2005.

Mouer, Ross E., and Yoshio Sugimoto. *Images of Japanese Society: A Study in the Structure of Social Reality*. London: Kegan Paul International, 1986.

Mullins, Mark R., and Koichi Nakano, eds. *Disasters and Social Crisis in Contemporary Japan: Political, Religious, and Sociocultural Responses*. New York: Palgrave Macmillan, 2016.

Nakane, Chie. *Japanese Society*. Berkeley: University of California Press, 1970.

Nakano, Lynne. *Community Volunteers in Japan: Everyday Stories of Social Change*. London: Routledge, 2004.

National League for Support of the School Textbook Screening Suit. *Truth in Textbooks, Freedom in Education, and Peace for Children: The Struggle against the Censorship of School Textbooks in Japan*. Tōkyō: NLSTS, 1995.

Neary, Ian. *The Buraku Issue and Modern Japan: The Career of Matsumoto Jiichirō*. New York: Routledge, 2015.

Neitzel, Laura Lynn. *"The Life We Longed For": Danchi Housing and the Middle Class Dream in Postwar Japan*. Honolulu: University of Hawai'i Press, 2016.

Norbeck, Edward, and Margaret M. Lock, eds. *Health, Illness, and Medical Care in Japan: Cultural and Social Dimensions*. Honolulu: University of Hawai'i Press, 1987.

Norgren, Christiana A. E. *Abortion before Birth Control: The Politics of Reproduction in Postwar Japan*. Princeton, N.J.: Princeton University Press, 2001.

Oblas, Peter B. *Perspectives on Race and Culture in Japanese Society: The Mass Media and Ethnicity*. Lewiston, N.Y.: Edwin Mellen, 1995.

Ochiai, Emiko. *The Japanese Family System in Transition: A Sociological Analysis of Family Change in Postwar Japan*. Tōkyō: LTCB International Library Foundation, 1997.

Ogawa, Akihiro. *The Failure of Civil Society? The Third Sector and the State in Contemporary Japan*. Albany: State University of New York Press, 2009.

Ohnuki-Tierney, Emiko. *Rice as Self: Japanese Identities through Time*. Princeton, N.J.: Princeton University Press, 1993.

Osborne, Stephen P., ed. *The Voluntary and Non-Profit Sector in Japan*. New York: Routledge, 2003.

Parker, L. Craig, Jr. *The Japanese Police System Today: An American Perspective*. Tōkyō: Kodansha, 1984.

Parry, Richard Lloyd. *Ghosts of the Tsunami: Death and Life in Japan's Disaster Zone*. Montclair, N.J.: MCD Books, 2017.

Partner, Simon. *Toshie: A Story of Village Life in Twentieth-Century Japan*. Berkeley: University of California Press, 2004.

Pekkanen, Robert. *Japan's Dual Civil Society: Members without Advocates*. Stanford, Calif.: Stanford University Press, 2005.

Pekkanen, Robert, Yutaka Tsujinaku, and Hidehiro Yamamoto. *Neighborhood Associations and Local Governance in Japan*. New York: Routledge, 2014.

Plath, David W. *The After Hours: Modern Japan and the Search for Enjoyment*. Berkeley: University of California Press, 1964.

Powell, Margaret, and Masahira Anesaki. *Health Care in Japan*. London: Routledge, 1990.

Rath, Eric C. *Japan's Cuisines: Food, Place and Identity*. Chicago: University of Chicago Press, 2016.

Rauch, Jonathan. *The Outnation: A Search for the Soul of Japan*. Boston: Little, Brown, 1992.

Rausch, Anthony S. *Japan's Local Newspapers: Chihoshi and Revitalization Journalism*. New York: Routledge, 2012.

Rebick, Marcus, and Ayumi Takenaka, eds. *The Changing Japanese Family*. New York: Routledge, 2006.

Richie, Donald, and Roy Garner. *The Image Factory: Fads and Fashions in Japan*. London: Reaktion Books, 2003.

Richter, Franz-Jürgen, ed. *The Dynamics of Japanese Organization*. London: Routledge, 1996.

Rupp, Katherine. *Gift-Giving in Japan: Cash, Connections, Cosmologies*. Stanford, Calif.: Stanford University Press, 2003.

Ryang, Sonia. *Japan and National Anthropology: A Critique*. New York: Routledge, 2004.

Saaler, Sven. *Politics, Memory and Public Opinion: The History Textbook Controversy and Japanese Society*. Munich, Germany: Iudicium, 2005.

Sand, Jordan. *Tokyo Vernacular: Common Spaces, Local Histories, Found Objects*. Berkeley: University of California Press, 2013.

Sargent, John. *Perspectives on Japan: Towards the Twenty-First Century*. London: Routledge-Curzon, 2007.

Sasaki-Uemura, Wesley. *Organizing the Spontaneous: Citizen Protest in Postwar Japan*. Honolulu: University of Hawai'i Press, 2001.

Satō, Ikuya. *Kamikaze Biker: Parody and Anomy in Affluent Japan*. Chicago: University of Chicago Press, 1991.

Schoppa, Leonard J. *Race for the Exits: The Unraveling of Japan's System of Social Protection*. Ithaca, N.Y.: Cornell University Press, 2006.

Schwartz, Frank J., and Susan J. Pharr, eds. *The State of Civil Society in Japan*. London: Cambridge University Press, 2003.

Seaton, Philip. *Japan's Contested War Memories: The "Memory Rifts" in Historical Consciousness of World War II*. New York: Routledge, 2007.

Seward, Jack. *The Japanese: The Often Misunderstood, Sometimes Surprising, and Always Fascinating Culture and Lifestyles of Japan*. Lincolnwood, Ill.: Passport Books, 1995.

Shirahase, Sawako. *Social Inequality in Japan*. New York: Routledge, 2013.

Smil, Vaclav, and Kazuhiko Kobayashi. *Japan's Dietary Transition and Its Impacts (Food, Health, and the Environment)*. Cambridge, Mass.: MIT Press, 2012.

Smith, Robert J. *Ancestor Worship in Contemporary Japan*. Stanford, Calif.: Stanford University Press, 1974.

———. *Japanese Society: Tradition, Self, and the Social Order*. New York: Cambridge University Press, 1983.

Solt, George. *The Untold History of Ramen: How Political Crisis in Japan Spawned a Global Food Craze*. Berkeley: University of California Press, 2014.

Steele, Valerie, et al. *Japan Fashion Now*. New Haven, Conn.: Yale University Press, 2010.

Steinhoff, Patricia G., ed. *Going to Court to Change Japan: Social Movements and the Law in Contemporary Japan*. Ann Arbor, Mich.: Center for Japanese Studies Publications, 2014.

Steven, Rob. *Classes in Contemporary Japan*. New York: Cambridge University Press, 1983.

Stevens, Carolyn S. *Disability in Japan*. London: Routledge, 2013.

———. *On the Margins of Japanese Society: Volunteers and the Welfare of the Urban Underclass*. New York: Routledge, 2013.

Sugimoto, Yoshio. *An Introduction to Japanese Society*. 4th ed. New York: Cambridge University Press, 2015.

———. *Popular Disturbance in Postwar Japan*. Hong Kong: Asian Research Service, 1981.

Sugiyama, Haruko, Ayaka Yamaguchi, and Hiromi Murakami. *Japan's Global Health Policy: Developing a Comprehensive Approach in a Period of Economic Stress*. Edited by Katherine E. Bliss. Lanham, Md.: Rowman & Littlefield, 2013.

Suzuki, David T., and Keibo Oiwa. *The Other Japan: Voices beyond the Mainstream*. Golden, Colo.: Fulcrum, 1999.

Szczepanska, Kamila. *The Politics of War Memory in Japan: Progressive Civil Society Groups and Contestation of Memory of the Asia-Pacific War*. New York: Routledge, 2014.

Takahashi, Mutsuko. *The Emergence of Welfare Society in Japan*. Aldershot, Hants, U.K.: Avebury, 1997.

Takeyama, Akiko. *Staged Seduction: Selling Dreams in a Tokyo Host Club*. Redwood City, Calif.: Stanford University Press, 2016.

Takezawa, Shōichirō. *The Aftermath of the 2011 East Japan Earthquake and Tsunami: Living among the Rubble*. Lanham, Md.: Lexington Books, 2016.

Taplin, Ruth, and Sandra J. Lawman, eds. *Mental Health Care in Japan*. New York: Routledge, 2016.

Tasker, Peter. *Inside Japan: Wealth, Work and Power in the New Japanese Empire*. London: Sidgwick & Jackson, 1987.

Tatsuno, Sheridan. *Created in Japan: From Imitators to World-Class Innovators*. New York: Harper & Row, 1990.

Tobin, Joseph J., ed. *Re-made in Japan: Everyday Life and Consumer Taste in a Changing Society*. New Haven, Conn.: Yale University Press, 1992.

Toivonen, Tuukka. *Japan's Emerging Youth Policy: Getting Young Adults Back to Work*. New York: Routledge, 2013.

Tokuhiro, Yoko. *Marriage in Contemporary Japan*. New York: Routledge, 2011.

Traphagan, John W., and John Knight, eds. *Demographic Change and the Family in Japan's Aging Society*. Albany: State University of New York Press, 2003.

Upham, Frank. *Law and Social Change in Postwar Japan*. Cambridge, Mass.: Harvard University Press, 1987.

Vanoverbeke, Dimitri. *Juries in the Japanese Legal System: The Continuing Struggle for Citizen Participation and Democracy*. New York: Routledge, 2015.

Vogel, Ezra F. *Japan's New Middle Class: The Salary Man and His Family in a Tokyo Suburb*. Berkeley: University of California Press, 1963; 3rd ed., Lanham, Md.: Rowman & Littlefield, 2013.

Vogel, Suzanne Hall, with Steven K. Vogel. *The Japanese Family in Transition: From the Professional Housewife Ideal to the Dilemmas of Choice*. Lanham, Md.: Rowman & Littlefield, 2013.

Wardell, Steven. *Rising Sons and Daughters: Life among Japan's New Young*. Cambridge, Mass.: Plympton Press, 1995.

Waswo, Ann, and Yoshiaki Nishida, eds. *Farmers and Village Life in Twentieth-Century Japan*. New York: Routledge, 2003.

Weiner, Michael, ed. *Japan's Minorities: The Illusion of Homogeneity*. London: Routledge, 1997.

———, ed. *Race, Ethnicity and Migration in Modern Japan: Japan, Race and Identity*. 3 vols. London: Routledge, 2004.

White, Merry. *Coffee Life in Japan*. Berkeley: University of California Press, 2012.

———. *Perfectly Japanese: Making Families in an Era of Upheaval*. Berkeley: University of California Press, 2002.

Wolff, Leon, Luke Nottage, and Kent Anderson, eds. *Who Rules Japan? Popular Participation in the Japanese Legal Process*. Cheltenham, U.K.: Edward Elgar, 2015.

Woronoff, Jon. *Japan as—anything but—Number One*. London: Macmillan; Armonk, N.Y.: M. E. Sharpe, 1990.

———. *Japan: The Japanese Social Crisis*. London: Macmillan; New York: St. Martin's, 1997.

Yamagishi, Takakazu. *War and Health Insurance Policy in Japan and the United States: World War II to Postwar Reconstruction*. Baltimore, Md.: Johns Hopkins University Press, 2011.

Yamamoto, Beverley Anne. *The Sexual Behaviour of Japanese Youth*. New York: Routledge, 2003.

Yasuoka, Maria-Keiko. *Organ Donation in Japan: A Medical Anthropological Study*. Lanham, Md.: Lexington Books, 2015.

Yoda, Tomiko, and Harry D. Harootunian, eds. *Japan after Japan: Social and Cultural Life from the Recessionary 1990s to the Present*. Durham, N.C.: Duke University Press, 2006.

Yoder, Robert Stuart. *Deviance and Inequality in Japan: Japanese Youth and Foreign Migrants*. Chicago: University of Chicago Press, 2011.

———. *Youth Deviance in Japan: Class Reproduction of Non-Conformity*. Melbourne, Australia: Trans-Pacific, 2004.

Zielenziger, Michael. *Shutting Out the Sun: How Japan Created Its Own Lost Generation*. New York: Nan A. Talese, 2006.

RELIGION

Ambros, Barbara R. *Women in Japanese Religions*. New York: New York University Press, 2015.

Andreasen, Esben. *Popular Buddhism in Japan: Shin Buddhist Religion and Culture*. Honolulu: University of Hawai'i Press, 1998.

Antoni, Klaus J., Hiroshi Kubota, Johann Nawrocki, and Michael Wachutka, eds. *Religion and National Identity in the Japanese Context*. New Brunswick, N.J.: Transaction, 2003.

Baffelli, Erica, Ian Reader, and Birgit Staemmler, eds. *Japanese Religions on the Internet: Innovation, Representation, and Authority*. New York: Routledge, 2013.

Breen, John, and Mark Teeuwen. *A New History of Shinto*. Hoboken, N.J.: Wiley Blackwell, 2010.

———, eds. *Shinto in History: Ways of the Kami*. Richmond, Surrey, U.K.: Curzon, 2000.

Bremen, Jan van, and D. P. Martinez, eds. *Ceremony and Ritual in Japan: Religious Practices in an Industrialized Society*. New York: Routledge, 1995.

Cali, Joseph, and John Dougill. *Shinto Shrines: A Guide to the Sacred Sites of Japan's Ancient Religion*. Honolulu: University of Hawai'i Press, 2012.

Carter, Robert E. *Encounter with Enlightenment: A Study of Japanese Ethics*. Albany: State University of New York Press, 2001.

Chryssides, George D. *Historical Dictionary of New Religious Movements*. Lanham, Md.: Scarecrow Press, 2001.

Davis, Winston B. *Japanese Religion and Society: Paradigms of Structure and Change*. Albany: State University of New York Press, 1992.

Dumoulin, Heinrich. *Zen Buddhism in the 20th Century*. New York: Weatherhill, 1992.

Earhart, H. Byron. *Japanese Religion: Unity and Diversity*. Belmont, Calif.: Wadsworth, 1982.

———. *Mount Fuji: Icon of Japan*. Columbia: University of South Carolina Press, 2011.

———. *Religion in Japan: Unity and Diversity*. 5th ed. Independence, Ky.: Wadsworth, 2013.

Ellwood, Robert. *Introducing Japanese Religion*. New York: Routledge, 2007.

Hardacre, Helen. *Kurozumikyo and the New Religions of Japan*. Princeton, N.J.: Princeton University Press, 1986.

———. *Lay Buddhism in Contemporary Japan: Reiyukai Kyodan*. Princeton, N.J.: Princeton University Press, 1984.

———. *Shinto and the State, 1868–1988*. Princeton, N.J.: Princeton University Press, 1989.

Harding, Christopher, Iwata Fumiaki, and Yoshinaga Shin'ichi, eds. *Religion and Psychotherapy in Modern Japan*. New York: Routledge, 2014.

Holtom, Daniel Clarence. *The National Faith of Japan: A Study in Modern Shinto*. New York: Paragon Book Reprint, 1965.

Hori, Ichiro. *Folk Religion in Japan: Continuity and Change*. Edited by Joseph M. Kitagawa and Alan L. Miller. Chicago: University of Chicago Press, 1968.

Inoue, Nobutaka, Satoshi Ito, Jun Endo, and Mizue Mori, eds. *Shinto: A Short History*. Translated by Mark Teeuwen and John Breen. London: Routledge, 2003.

Isomae, Jun'ichi. *Religious Discourse in Modern Japan: Religion, State, and Shinto*. Leiden, the Netherlands: Brill Academic Publishers, 2014.

Josephson, Jason Ananda. *The Invention of Religion in Japan*. Chicago: University of Chicago Press, 2012.

Kasulis, Thomas P. *Shintō: The Way Home*. Honolulu: University of Hawai'i Press, 2004.

Kisala, Robert J. *Prophets of Peace: Pacifism and Cultural Identity in Japan's New Religions*. Honolulu: University of Hawai'i Press, 1999.

Kisala, Robert J., and Mark R. Mullins, eds. *Religion and Social Crisis in Japan: Understanding Japanese Society through the Aum Affair*. New York: Palgrave Macmillan, 2001.

Kitagawa, Joseph M. *On Understanding Japanese Religion*. Princeton, N.J.: Princeton University Press, 1987.

Lifton, Robert Jay. *Destroying the World to Save It: Aum Shinrikyo, Apocalyptic Violence, and the New Global Terrorism*. New York: Henry Holt, 1999.

Littleton, C. Scott. *Shinto: Origins, Rituals, Festivals, Spirits, Sacred Places*. Oxford, U.K.: Oxford University Press, 2002.

Lobetti, Tullio Frederico. *Ascetic Practices in Japanese Religion*. New York: Routledge, 2013.

McMahan, David L. *The Making of Buddhist Modernism*. Oxford, U.K.: Oxford University Press, 2008.

McVeigh, Brian J. *Spirits, Selves, and Subjectivity in a Japanese New Religion: The Cultural Psychology of Belief in Shukyo Mahikari*. Lewiston, N.Y.: Edwin Mellen, 1997.

Metraux, Daniel Alfred. *Aum Shinrikyo's Impact on Japanese Society*. Ann Arbor: University of Michigan Press, 2000.

———. *The History and Theology of Sōka Gakkai: A Japanese New Religion*. Lewiston, N.Y.: Edwin Mellen, 1988.

Miyake, Hitoshi. *Shugendō: Essays on the Structure of Japanese Folk Religion*. Ann Arbor: University of Michigan, Center for Japanese Studies, 2007.

Miyamoto, Yuki. *Beyond the Mushroom Cloud: Commemoration, Religion, and Responsibility after Hiroshima*. New York: Fordham University Press, 2012.

Nelson, John K. *Enduring Identities: The Guise of Shinto in Contemporary Japan*. Honolulu: University of Hawai'i Press, 2000.

————. *A Year in the Life of a Shinto Shrine*. Seattle: University of Washington Press, 1996.

Picken, Stuart D. B. *Historical Dictionary of Shinto*. 2nd ed. Lanham, Md.: Scarecrow Press, 2010.

Reader, Ian. *Religion in Contemporary Japan*. London: Macmillan Academic, 1991.

————. *Religious Violence in Contemporary Japan: The Case of Aum Shinrikyo*. Honolulu: University of Hawai'i Press, 2000.

Richey, Jeffrey L., ed. *Daoism in Japan: Chinese Traditions and Their Influence on Japanese Religious Culture*. New York: Routledge, 2015.

Shimazono, Susumu. *From Salvation to Spirituality: Popular Religious Movements in Modern Japan*. Melbourne, Australia: Trans-Pacific, 2004.

Thomas, Jolyon Baraka. *Drawing on Tradition: Manga, Anime, and Religion in Contemporary Japan*. Honolulu, Hi.: University of Hawai'i Press, 2012.

EDUCATION

Aspinall, Robert W. *International Education Policy in Japan in an Age of Globalisation and Risk*. Folkestone, Kent, U.K.: Global Oriental, 2012.

————. *Teachers' Unions and the Politics of Education in Japan*. Albany: State University of New York Press, 2001.

Beauchamp, Edward R., ed. *Education in Modern Japan: Old Voices, New Voices*. Armonk, N.Y.: M. E. Sharpe, 2002.

Bjork, Christopher. *High-Stakes Schooling: What We Can Learn from Japan's Experiences with Testing, Accountability, and Education Reform*. Chicago: University of Chicago Press, 2015.

Breaden, Jeremy. *The Organisational Dynamics of University Reform in Japan*. New York: Routledge, 2012.

Cave, Peter. *Schooling Selves: Autonomy, Interdependence, and Reform in Japanese Junior High Education*. Chicago: University of Chicago Press, 2016.

Cummings, William K. *Education and Equality in Japan*. Princeton, N.J.: Princeton University Press, 1980.

Cutts, Robert L. *An Empire of Schools: Japan's Universities and the Molding of a National Power Elite*. Armonk, N.Y.: M. E. Sharpe, 1997.

Decoker, Gary. *Japanese Education in an Era of Globalization: Culture, Politics, and Equality*. New York: Teachers College Press, 2013.

Decoker, Gary, and Thomas P. Rohlen. *National Standards and School Reform in Japan and the United States*. New York: Teachers College Press, 2002.

Dierkes, Julian. *Postwar History Education in Japan and the Germanys: Guilty Lessons*. New York: Routledge, 2010.

Duke, Benjamin C. *Education and Leadership for the Twenty-First Century: Japan, America, and Britain*. New York: Praeger, 1991.

Eades, J. S., Roger Goodman, and Yumiko Hada, eds. *The "Big Bang" in Japanese Higher Education: The 2004 Reforms and the Dynamics of Change*. Melbourne, Australia: Trans-Pacific, 2005.

Goodman, Roger. *Japan's "International Youth": The Emergence of a New Class of Schoolchildren*. Oxford, U.K.: Oxford University Press, 1990.

Goodman, Roger, and David Phillips, eds. *Can the Japanese Change Their Education System?* Providence, R.I.: Symposium Books, 2003.

Hayashi, Akiko, and Joseph Tobin. *Teaching Embodied: Cultural Practice in Japanese Preschools*. Chicago: University of Chicago Press, 2015.

Hendry, Joy. *Becoming Japanese: The World of the Pre-School Child*. Honolulu: University of Hawai'i Press, 1986.

Leestma, Robert, and Herbert J. Walberg, eds. *Japanese Educational Productivity*. Ann Arbor: Center for Japanese Studies, University of Michigan, 1992.

LeTendre, Gerald K. *Learning to Be Adolescent: Growing Up in U.S. and Japanese Middle Schools*. New Haven, Conn.: Yale University Press, 2000.

LeTendre, Gerald K., and Rebecca Erwin Fukuzawa. *Intense Years: How Japanese Adolescents Balance School, Family and Friends*. London: Routledge, 2001.

Lewis, Catherine C. *Educating Hearts and Minds: Reflections on Japanese Preschool and Elementary Education*. New York: Cambridge University Press, 1995.

Lynn, Richard. *Educational Achievement in Japan: Lessons for the West*. Armonk, N.Y.: M. E. Sharpe, 1988.

Marshall, Byron K. *Learning to Be Modern: Japanese Political Discourse on Education*. Boulder, Colo.: Westview, 1995.

McVeigh, Brian J. *Japanese Higher Education as Myth*. Armonk, N.Y.: M. E. Sharpe, 2002.

———. *Life in a Japanese Women's College: Learning to Be Ladylike*. New York: Routledge, 2014.

Mock, John, and Hiroaki Kawamura, eds. *The Impact of Internationalization on Japanese Higher Education: Is Japanese Education Really Changing?* Rotterdam, the Netherlands: Sense Publishers, 2016.

Okano, Kaori, and Motonori Tsuchiya. *Education in Contemporary Japan: Inequality and Diversity*. New York: Cambridge University Press, 1999.

Roesgaard, Marie Højlund. *Japanese Education and the Cram School Business: Functions, Challenges and Perspectives of the Juku*. Honolulu: University of Hawai'i Press, 2006.

Rohlen, Thomas P. *Japan's High Schools*. Berkeley: University of California Press, 1983.

Rohlen, Thomas P., and Gerald K. LeTendre, eds. *Teaching and Learning in Japan*. New York: Cambridge University Press, 1996.

Sato, Nancy. *Inside Japanese Classrooms: The Heart of Education*. New York: Routledge, 2003.

Schoppa, Leonard J. *Education Reform in Japan: A Case of Immobilist Policies*. London: Routledge, 1991.

Thurston, Donald R. *Teachers and Politics in Japan*. Princeton, N.J.: Princeton University Press, 1973.

Tsukada, Mamoru. *Yobikō Life: A Study of the Legitimation Process of Social Stratification in Japan*. Berkeley: University of California Press, 1991.

White, Merry. *The Japanese Educational Challenge: A Commitment to Children*. New York: Free Press, 1987.

Yoneyama, Shoko. *The Japanese High School: Silence and Resistance*. London: Routledge, 1999.

LABOR

Brinton, Mary C. *Lost in Transition: Youth, Work, and Instability in Postindustrial Japan*. New York: Cambridge University Press, 2010.

Cook, Emma E. *Reconstructing Adult Masculinities: Part-Time Work in Contemporary Japan*. New York: Routledge, 2016.

Fowler, Edward. *San'ya Blues: Laboring Life in Contemporary Japan*. Ithaca, N.Y.: Cornell University Press, 1996.

Fu, Huiyan. *An Emerging Non-regular Labour Force in Japan: The Dignity of Dispatched Workers*. London: Routledge, 2011.

Gibbs, Michael H. *Struggle and Purpose in Postwar Japanese Unionism*. Berkeley: University of California Press, 2000.

Gill, Tom. *Men of Uncertainty: The Social Organization of Day Laborers in Contemporary Japan*. Albany: State University of New York Press, 2001.

———. *Yokohama Street Life: The Precarious Career of a Japanese Day Laborer*. Lanham, Md.: Lexington Books, 2015.

Gordon, Andrew. *The Wages of Affluence: Labor and Management in Postwar Japan*. Cambridge, Mass.: Harvard University Press, 1998.

Hamada, Koichi, and Hiromi Kato, eds. *Ageing and the Labour Market in Japan: Problems and Policies*. Northampton, Mass.: Edward Elgar, 2007.

Hanami, Tadashi A., and Fumito Komiya. *Labour Law in Japan*. 2nd ed. Alphen aan den Rijn, the Netherlands: Wolters Kluwer, 2015.

Kosugi, Reiko. *Escape from Work: Freelancing Youth and the Challenge to Corporate Japan*. Melbourne, Australia: Trans-Pacific, 2007.

Kume, Ikuo. *Disparaged Success: Labor Politics in Postwar Japan*. Ithaca, N.Y.: Cornell University Press, 1998.

Liu-Farrer, Gracia. *Labor Migration from China to Japan: International Students, Transnational Migrants*. New York: Routledge, 2013.

Matsumura, Wendy. *The Limits of Okinawa: Japanese Capitalism, Living Labor, and Theorizations of Community*. Durham, N.C.: Duke University Press, 2015.

Moore, Joe B., ed. *The Other Japan: Conflict, Compromise, and Resistance since 1945*. Armonk, N.Y.: M. E. Sharpe, 1996.

Mosk, Carl. *Competition and Cooperation in Japanese Labour Markets*. New York: St. Martin's, 1995.

Price, John. *Japan Works: Power and Paradox in Postwar Industrial Relations*. Ithaca, N.Y.: Cornell University Press, 1996.

Roberson, James E. *Japanese Working Class: An Ethnographic Study of Factory Workers*. London: Routledge, 1998.

Sako, Mari. *Japanese Labour and Management in Transition: Diversity, Flexibility and Participation*. London: Routledge, 1997.

Song, Jiyeoun. *Inequality in the Workplace: Labor Market Reform in Japan and Korea*. Ithaca, N.Y.: Cornell University Press, 2014.

Tanno, Kiyoto. *Migrant Workers in Contemporary Japan: An Institutional Perspective on Transnational Employment*. Melbourne, Australia: Trans-Pacific, 2013.

Toivonen, Tuukka. *Japan's Emerging Youth Policy: Getting Young Adults Back to Work*. New York: Routledge, 2016.

Turner, Christena L. *Japanese Workers in Protest: An Ethnography of Consciousness and Experience*. Berkeley: University of California Press, 1995.

Watanabe, Hiroaki Richard. *Labour Market Deregulation in Japan and Italy: Worker Protection under Neoliberal Globalisation*. London: Routledge, 2014.

Williamson, Hugh. *Coping with the Miracle: Japan's Unions Explore New International Relations*. London: Pluto Press, 1994.

Woronoff, Jon. *Japan's Wasted Workers*. Totowa, N.J.: Allanheld, Osmun, 1983.

WOMEN

Allison, Anne. *Nightwork: Sexuality, Pleasure, and Corporate Masculinity in a Tokyo Hostess Club*. Chicago: University of Chicago Press, 1994.

Aronsson, Anne Stefanie. *Career Women in Contemporary Japan: Pursuing Identities, Fashioning Lives*. New York: Routledge, 2014.

Bardsley, Jan. *Women and Democracy in Cold War Japan*. London: SOAS Japan Research Centre, 2014.

Bernstein, Gail. *Haruko's World: A Japanese Farm Woman and Her Community*. Stanford, Calif.: Stanford University Press, 1997.

Bishop, Beverley. *Globalisation and Women in the Japanese Workforce*. New York: Routledge, 2004.

Borovoy, Amy. *The Too-Good Wife: Alcohol, Codependency, and the Politics of Nurturance in Postwar Japan*. Berkeley: University of California Press, 2006.

Brinton, Mary C. *Women and the Economic Miracle: Gender and Work in Postwar Japan*. Berkeley: University of California Press, 1993.

Bullock, Julia D. *The Other Women's Lib: Gender and Body in Japanese Women's Fiction*. Honolulu: University of Hawai'i Press, 2010.

Charlebois, Justin. *Japanese Femininities*. New York: Routledge, 2016.

Dalton, Emma. *Women and Politics in Contemporary Japan*. New York: Routledge, 2015.

Frühstück, Sabine. *Colonizing Sex: Sexology and Social Control in Modern Japan*. Berkeley: University of California Press, 2003.

———. *Playing War: Children and the Paradoxes of Modern Militarism in Japan*. Berkeley: University of California Press, 2017.

Fujimura-Fanselow, Kumiko, and Atsuko Kameda, eds. *Japanese Women: New Feminist Perspectives on the Past, Present and Future*. New York: Feminist Press, 1995.

Gayle, Curtis Anderson. *Women's History and Local Community in Postwar Japan*. London: Routledge, 2010.

Gerteis, Christopher. *Gender Struggles: Wage-Earning Women and Male-Dominated Unions in Postwar Japan*. London: Routledge, 2010.

Hansen, Gitte Marianne. *Femininity, Self-harm and Eating Disorders in Japan: Navigating Contradiction in Narrative and Visual Culture*. New York: Routledge, 2015.

Holloway, Susan. *Women and Family in Contemporary Japan*. New York: Cambridge University Press, 2010.

Hunter, Janet, ed. *Japanese Women Working*. London: Routledge, 1993.

Imamura, Anne E., ed. *Re-Imaging Japanese Women*. Berkeley: University of California Press, 1996.

Iwao, Sumiko. *The Japanese Woman: Traditional Image and Changing Reality*. New York: Free Press, 1993.

Kano, Ayako. *Japanese Feminist Debates: A Century of Contention on Sex, Love, and Labor*. Honolulu: University of Hawai'i Press, 2016.

Kodate, Naonori, and Kashiko Kodate. *Japanese Women in Science and Engineering: History and Policy Change*. New York: Routledge, 2015.

Kondo, Dorinne K. *Crafting Selves: Power, Gender, and Discourses of Identity in a Japanese Workplace*. Chicago: University of Chicago Press, 1990.

LeBlanc, Robin M. *Bicycle Citizens: The Political World of the Japanese Housewife*. Berkeley: University of California Press, 1999.

Lebra, Takie Sugiyama. *Japanese Women: Constraint and Fulfillment*. Honolulu: University of Hawai'i Press, 1984.

Liddle, Joanna, and Sachiko Nakajima. *Rising Suns, Rising Daughters: Gender, Class, and Power in Japan*. New York: Zed Books, 2000.

Lo, Jeannie. *Office Ladies, Factory Women: Life and Work at a Japanese Company*. Armonk, N.Y.: M. E. Sharpe, 1990.

Loftus, Ronald P. *Changing Lives: The "Postwar" in Japanese Women's Autobiographies and Memoirs*. Ann Arbor, Mich.: Association for Asian Studies, 2013.

Lowy, Dina. *The Japanese "New Woman": Images of Gender and Modernity*. New Brunswick, N.J.: Rutgers University Press, 2007.

Mackie, Vera C. *Feminism in Modern Japan: Citizenship, Embodiment and Sexuality*. New York: Cambridge University Press, 2003.

———. *Gender in Japan: Power and Public Policy*. London: Routledge, 2005.

Macnaughtan, Helen. *Women and Work in Postwar Japan*. London: Routledge, 2005.

McVeigh, Brian J. *Life in a Japanese Women's College: Learning to Be Ladylike*. London: Routledge, 1996.

Miller, Laura, and Jan Bardsley, eds. *Bad Girls of Japan*. New York: Palgrave Macmillan, 2005.

Molony, Barbara, and Kathleen S. Uno, eds. *Gendering Modern Japanese History*. Cambridge, Mass.: Harvard University Press, 2005.

Murase, Miriam Yuko. *Cooperation over Conflict: The Women's Movement and the State in Postwar Japan*. New York: Routledge, 2006.

Nemoto, Kumiko. *Racing Romance: Love, Power, and Desire among Asian American/White Couples*. New Brunswick, N.J.: Rutgers University Press, 2009.

———. *Too Few Women at the Top: The Persistence of Inequality in Japan*. Ithaca, N.Y.: Cornell University Press, 2016.

Ogasawara, Yuko. *Office Ladies and Salaried Men: Power, Gender, and Work in Japanese Companies*. Berkeley: University of California Press, 1998.

Renshaw, Jean R. *Kimono in the Boardroom: The Invisible Evolution of Japanese Women Managers*. New York: Oxford University Press, 1999.

Robins-Mowry, Dorothy. *The Hidden Sun: Women of Modern Japan*. Boulder, Colo.: Westview, 1983.

Roberts, Glenda S. *Staying on the Line: Blue-Collar Women of Contemporary Japan*. Honolulu: University of Hawai'i Press, 1994.

Rosenberger, Nancy Ross. *Gambling with Virtue: Japanese Women and the Search for Self in a Changing Nation.* Honolulu: University of Hawai'i Press, 2001.

Shigematsu, Setsu. *Scream from the Shadows: The Women's Liberation Movement in Japan.* Minneapolis: University of Minnesota Press, 2012.

Siden, Kyoko. *More Stories by Japanese Women Writers: An Anthology.* New York: Routledge, 2011.

Skov, Lise, and Brian Moeran, eds. *Women, Media, and Consumption in Japan.* Honolulu: University of Hawai'i Press, 1995.

Soh, C. Sarah. *The Comfort Women: Sexual Violence and Postcolonial Memory in Korea and Japan.* Chicago: University of Chicago Press, 2009.

Tanaka, Yukiko, and Elizabeth Hanson, eds. and trans. *This Kind of Woman: Ten Stories by Japanese Women Writers, 1960–1976.* Redwood City, Calif.: Stanford University Press, 1982.

White, Merry I., and Kristina R. Huber. *Challenging Tradition: Women in Japan.* New York: Japan Society, 1991.

Zacharias-Walsh, Anne. *Our Unions, Our Selves: The Rise of Feminist Labor Unions in Japan.* Ithaca, N.Y.: Cornell University Press, 2016.

ENVIRONMENT

Allen, Bruce, and Yuki Masami, eds. *Ishimure Michiko's Writing in Ecocritical Perspective: Between Sea and Sky.* Lanham, Md.: Lexington Books, 2016.

Avenell, Simon. *Transnational Japan in the Global Environmental Movement.* Honolulu: University of Hawai'i Press, 2017.

Barrett, Brendan F. D., ed. *Ecological Modernization and Japan.* London: Routledge, 2005.

Barrett, Brendan F. D., and Riki Therivel. *Environmental Policy and Impact Assessment in Japan.* London: Routledge, 1991.

Batten, Bruce L., and Philip C. Brown, eds. *Environment and Society in the Japanese Islands: From Prehistory to the Present.* Corvallis, Ore.: Oregon State University Press, 2015.

Brannigan, Michael C. *Japan's March 2011 Disaster and Moral Grit: Our Inescapable In-between.* Lanham, Md.: Lexington Books, 2015.

Brecher, W. Puck. *An Investigation of Japan's Relationship to Nature and Environment.* Lewiston, N.Y.: Edwin Mellen, 2000.

Broadbent, Jeffrey. *Environmental Politics in Japan: Networks of Power and Protest.* New York: Cambridge University Press, 1998.

Carpenter, Susan. *Japan's Nuclear Crisis: The Routes to Responsibility.* New York: Palgrave Macmillan, 2012.

Hasegawa, Koichi. *Beyond Fukushima: Toward a Post-nuclear Society*. Translated by Minako Sato. Balwyn, North Victoria, Australia: Trans-Pacific, 2015.

———. *Constructing Civil Society in Japan: Voices of Environmental Movements*. Balwyn, North Victoria, Australia: Trans-Pacific, 2004.

Hindmarsh, Richard, ed. *Nuclear Disaster at Fukushima Daiichi: Social, Political and Environmental Issues*. New York: Routledge, 2013.

Hindmarsh, Richard, and Rebecca Priestly, eds. *The Fukushima Effect: A New Geopolitical Terrain*. New York: Routledge, 2015.

Huddle, Norie, and Michael Reich. *Island of Dreams: Environmental Crisis in Japan*. 2nd ed. Rochester, Vt.: Schenkman Books, 1987.

Imura, Hidefumi, and Miranda A. Schreurs, eds. *Environmental Policy in Japan*. Northampton, Mass.: Edward Elgar, 2005.

Kagawa-Fox, Midori. *The Ethics of Japan's Global Environmental Policy: The Conflict between Principles and Practice*. New York: Routledge, 2014.

Kalland, Arne. *Unveiling the Whale: Discourses on Whales and Whaling*. New York: Berghahn Books, 2009.

Karan, Pradyumna P. *Japan in the 21st Century: Environment, Economy, and Society*. Lexington: University Press of Kentucky, 2005.

Karan, Pradyumna P., and Unryu Suganuma, eds. *Local Environmental Movements: A Comparative Study of the United States and Japan*. Lexington: University Press of Kentucky, 2008.

Kingston, Jeff, ed. *Natural Disaster and Nuclear Crisis in Japan: Response and Recovery after Japan's 3/11*. Oxford, U.K.: Routledge, 2012.

Kirby, Peter Wynn. *Troubled Natures: Waste, Environment, Japan*. Honolulu: University of Hawai'i Press, 2011.

Kühr, Rüdiger. *Japan's Transnational Environmental Policies: The Case of Environmental Technology Transfer to Newly Industrializing Countries*. Bern, Switzerland: Peter Lang, 2012.

Lam, Peng-Er. *Green Politics in Japan*. New York: Routledge, 1999.

Lesbirel, S. Hayden. *NIMBY Politics in Japan: Energy Siting and the Management of Environmental Conflict*. Ithaca, N.Y.: Cornell University Press, 1998.

MacDonald, Deanna. *Eco Living Japan: Sustainable Ideas for Living Green*. North Clarendon, Vt.: Tuttle, 2016.

McKean, Margaret A. *Environmental Protest and Citizen Politics in Japan*. Berkeley: University of California Press, 1981.

Miller, Ian Jared, Julia Adeney Thomas, and Brett L. Walker, eds. *Japan at Nature's Edge: The Environmental Context of a Global Power*. Honolulu: University of Hawai'i Press, 2013.

Morikawa, Jun. *Whaling in Japan: Power, Politics, and Diplomacy*. New York: Columbia University Press, 2009.

Samuels, Richard J. *3.11: Disaster and Change in Japan*. Ithaca, N.Y.: Cornell University Press, 2013.

Shelton, Barrie. *Learning from the Japanese City: Looking East in Urban Design*. 2nd ed. New York: Routledge, 2012.

Smil, Vaclav, and Kazuhiko Kobayashi. *Japan's Dietary Transition and Its Impacts*. Cambridge, Mass.: MIT Press, 2012.

Smith, Joseph Wayne. *The High Tech Fix: Sustainable Ecology or Technocratic Megaprojects for the 21st Century?* Brookfield, Vt.: Avebury, 1991.

Sorensen, André, and Carolin Funck, eds. *Local Empowerment? Citizens' Movements, Machizukuri and Living Environments in Japan*. New York: Routledge, 2006.

Totman, Conrad. *Japan: An Environmental History*. New York: I. B. Tauris, 2016.

Tsuru, Shigeto. *The Political Economy of the Environment: The Case of Japan*. Vancouver: University of British Columbia Press, 1999.

Vivoda, Vlado. *Energy Security in Japan: Challenges after Fukushima*. Farnham, Surrey, U.K.: Ashgate, 2014.

Walker, Brett L. *Toxic Archipelago: A History of Industrial Disease in Japan*. Seattle: University of Washington Press, 2011.

Wong, Anny. *The Roots of Japan's Environmental Policies*. New York: Routledge, 2017.

SCIENCE AND TECHNOLOGY

Coleman, Samuel. *Japanese Science from the Inside*. London: Routledge, 1999.

Collins, Steve W. *The Race to Commercialize Biotechnology: Molecules, Markets and the State in the United States and Japan*. New York: Routledge, 2004.

Cusumano, Michael A. *The Japanese Automobile Industry: Technology and Management at Nissan and Toyota*. Cambridge, Mass.: Harvard University Press, 1985.

———. *Japan's Software Factories: A Challenge to U.S. Management*. New York: Oxford University Press, 1991.

Dearing, James W. *Growing a Japanese Science City: Communication in Scientific Research*. London: Routledge, 1995.

Fransman, Martin. *The Market and Beyond: Cooperation and Competition in Information Technology in the Japanese System*. New York: Cambridge University Press, 1990.

Hayashi, Takeshi. *The Japanese Experience in Technology: From Transfer to Self-Reliance*. Tōkyō: United Nations University Press, 1990.

Hemmert, Martin, and Christian Oberländer. *Technology and Innovation in Japan: Policy and Management for the Twenty-First Century.* London: Routledge, 1998.

Holroyd, Carin, and Ken Coates. *Innovation Nation: Science and Technology in 21st Century Japan.* New York: Palgrave Macmillan, 2007.

Kimura, Aya Hirata. *Radiation Brain Moms and Citizen Scientists: The Gender Politics of Food Contamination after Fukushima.* Durham, N.C.: Duke University Press, 2016.

Kirsch, Griseldis, Dolores P. Martinez, and Merry White. *Assembling Japan: Modernity, Technology and Global Culture.* Bern, Switzerland: Peter Lang, 2015.

Kodama, Fumio. *Emerging Patterns of Innovation: Sources of Japan's Technological Edge.* Boston: Harvard Business School Press, 1995.

Low, Morris. *Science and the Building of a New Japan.* New York: Palgrave Macmillan, 2005.

Low, Morris, Shigeru Nakayama, and Hitoshi Yoshioka. *Science, Technology and Society in Contemporary Japan.* New York: Cambridge University Press, 1999.

Minami, Ryōshin, Kwan S. Kim, Fumio Makino, and Joung-Hae Seo, eds. *Acquiring, Adapting and Developing Technologies: Lessons from the Japanese Experience.* New York: St. Martin's, 1995.

Mizutani, Fumitoshi. *Regulatory Reform of Public Utilities: The Japanese Experience.* Cheltenham, U.K.: Edward Elgar, 2012.

Moreno, T., S. R. Wallis, T. Kojima, and W. Gibbons, eds. *Geology of Japan.* London: Geological Society, 2016.

Morris-Suzuki, Tessa. *The Technological Transformation of Japan: From the Seventeenth to the Twenty-First Century.* New York: Cambridge University Press, 1994.

Nakayama, Shigeru. *Science, Technology and Society in Postwar Japan.* London: Kegan Paul International, 1991.

Odagiri, Hiroyuki, and Akira Gotō. *Technology and Industrial Development in Japan.* Oxford, U.K.: Oxford University Press, 1996.

Okimoto, Daniel I. *Between MITI and the Market: Japanese Industrial Policy for High Technology.* Stanford, Calif.: Stanford University Press, 1989.

Robertson, Jennifer. *Robo Sapiens Japanicus: Robots, Gender, Family, and the Japanese Nation.* Berkeley: University of California Press, 2017.

Smits, Gregory. *When the Earth Roars: Lessons from the History of Earthquakes in Japan.* Lanham, Md.: Rowman & Littlefield, 2014.

Takashima, Tetsuo. *Megaquake: How Japan and the World Should Respond.* Edited and translated by Robert D. Eldridge. Lincoln, Neb.: Potomac Books, 2015.

Tyson, Laura D'Andrea. *Who's Bashing Whom? Trade Conflict in High-Technology Industries*. Washington, D.C.: Institute for International Economics, 1992.

INTERNATIONAL RELATIONS

Akaha, Tsuneo, and Frank Langdon, eds. *Japan in the Posthegemonic World*. Boulder, Colo.: Lynne Rienner, 1993.

Arase, David, ed. *Japan's Foreign Aid: Old Continuities and New Directions*. London: Routledge, 2005.

Armacost, Michael H. *Friends or Rivals? The Insider's Account of U.S.-Japan Relations*. New York: Columbia University Press, 1996.

Arrington, Celeste L. *Accidental Activists: Victim Movements and Government Accountability in Japan and South Korea*. Ithaca, N.Y.: Cornell University Press, 2016.

Auslin, Michael R. *Pacific Cosmopolitans: A Cultural History of U.S.-Japan Relations*. Cambridge, Mass.: Harvard University Press, 2011.

Austin, Greg, and Stuart Harris. *Japan and Greater China: Political Economy and Military Power in the Asian Century*. Honolulu: University of Hawai'i Press, 2001.

Barclay, Kate. *A Japanese Joint Venture in the Pacific: Foreign Bodies in Tinned Tuna*. New York: Routledge, 2012.

Barnet, Richard J. *The Alliance—America, Europe, Japan: Makers of the Postwar World*. New York: Simon & Schuster, 1983.

Berger, Thomas U., Mike M. Mochizuki, and Jitsuo Tsuchiyama, eds. *Japan in International Politics: The Foreign Policies of an Adaptive State*. Boulder, Colo.: Lynne Rienner, 2007.

Bergsten, C. Fred, Takatoshi Ito, and Marcus Noland. *No More Bashing: Building a New Japan–United States Economic Relationship*. Washington, D.C.: Institute for International Economics, 2001.

Bower, Ernest Z., Murray Hiebert, Phuong Nguyen, and Gregory B. Polling. *Southeast Asia's Geopolitical Centrality and the U.S.-Japan Alliance*. Lanham, Md.: Lexington Books, 2015.

Breaden, Jeremy, Stacey Steele, and Carolyn S. Stevens, eds. *Internationalising Japan: Discourse and Practice*. London: Routledge, 2014.

Bridges, Brian. *Japan and Korea in the 1990s: From Antagonism to Adjustment*. Northampton, Mass.: Edward Elgar, 1993.

Brown, James D. J. *Japan, Russia and Their Territorial Dispute*. New York: Routledge, 2016.

Brown, James D. J., and Jeff Kingston, eds. *Japan's Foreign Relations in Asia*. London: Routledge, 2017.

Buckley, Roger. *U.S.-Japan Alliance Diplomacy, 1945–1990*. New York: Cambridge University Press, 1992.

Calder, Kent E. *Pacific Alliance: Reviving U.S.-Japan Relations*. New Haven, Conn.: Yale University Press, 2010.

Cha, Victor D. *Alignment Despite Antagonism: The US-Korea-Japan Security Triangle*. Stanford, Calif.: Stanford University Press, 1999.

Cheung, Mong. *Political Survival and Yasukuni in Japan's Relations with China*. New York: Routledge, 2016.

Clammer, John. *Japan and Its Others: Globalization, Difference, and the Critique of Modernity*. Melbourne, Australia: Trans-Pacific, 2001.

Collingwood, Dean W. *Japan and the Pacific Rim*. Guilford, Conn.: McGraw-Hill/Dushkin, 2001.

Conte-Helm, Marie. *The Japanese and Europe: Economic and Cultural Encounters*. London: Athlone, 1996.

Cooney, Kevin. *Japan's Foreign Policy since 1945*. Armonk, N.Y.: M. E. Sharpe, 2006.

Costa, Anna. *The China-Japan Conflict over the Senkaku/Diaoyu Islands: Useful Rivalry*. London: Routledge, 2017.

Curtis, Gerald L., ed. *Japan's Foreign Policy after the Cold War: Coping with Change*. Armonk, N.Y.: M. E. Sharpe, 1993.

———, ed. *New Perspectives on U.S.-Japanese Relations*. Tōkyō: Japan Center for International Exchange, 2000.

Dadabaev, Timur. *Japan in Central Asia: Strategies, Initiatives, and Neighboring Powers*. New York: Palgrave Macmillan, 2015.

Delamotte, Guibourg, ed. *Japan's World Power: Assessment, Outlook and Vision*. London: Routledge, 2018.

Dobson, Hugo. *Japan and the G7/8: 1975 to 2002*. London: Routledge, 2004.

———. *Japan and UN Peacekeeping: New Pressures and New Responses*. New York: Routledge, 2003.

Dore, Ronald P. *Japan, Internationalism and the UN*. London: Routledge, 1997.

Drifte, Reinhard. *Japan's Foreign Policy in the 1990s: From Economic Superpower to What Power?* New York: St. Martin's, 1996.

———. *Japan's Security Relations with China since 1989: From Balancing to Bandwagoning?* London: Routledge, 2003.

Drohan, Thomas A. *American-Japanese Security Agreements, Past and Present*. Jefferson, N.C.: McFarland, 2007.

Drysdale, Peter, and Dong Dong Zhang, eds. *Japan and China: Rivalry or Cooperation in East Asia?* Canberra, Australia: Asia Pacific Press, 2000.

Dudden, Alexis. *Troubled Apologies: Among Japan, Korea, and the United States*. New York: Columbia University Press, 2014.

Dujarric, Robert. *Japan and Korea's Future: A Japanese-Korean-US Trilateral Dialogue*. Vancouver: University of British Columbia Press, 2005.

Duus, Peter, and Kenji Hasegawa, eds. *Rediscovering America: Japanese Perspectives on the American Century*. Berkeley: University of California Press, 2011.

Edstrom, Bert. *Japan's Evolving Foreign Policy Doctrine: From Yoshida to Miyazawa*. New York: St. Martin's, 1999.

Ellison, Herbert J., ed. *Japan and the Pacific Quadrille: The Major Powers in East Asia*. Boulder, Colo.: Westview, 1987.

Emmerson, John K., and Harrison M. Holland. *The Eagle and the Rising Sun: America and Japan in the Twentieth Century*. Reading, Mass.: Addison-Wesley, 1988.

Encarnation, Dennis J. *Rivals beyond Trade: America versus Japan in Global Competition*. Ithaca, N.Y.: Cornell University Press, 1993.

Envall, H. P. D. *Japanese Diplomacy: The Role of Leadership*. Albany: State University of New York Press, 2015.

Ferguson, Joseph. *Japanese-Russian Relations, 1907–2007*. New York: Routledge, 2011.

Figal, Gerald. *Beachheads: War, Peace, and Tourism in Postwar Okinawa*. Lanham, Md.: Rowman & Littlefield, 2012.

Fingar, Thomas, ed. *Uneasy Partnerships: China's Engagement with Japan, the Koreas, and Russia in the Era of Reform*. Redwood City, Calif.: Stanford University Press, 2017.

Finn, Richard B., ed. *United States–Japan Relations: A Surprising Partnership*. New Brunswick, N.J.: Transaction, 1987.

Frattolillo, Oliviero. *Diplomacy in Japan-EU Relations*. New York: Routledge, 2016.

Fukushima, Akiko. *Japanese Foreign Policy: The Emerging Logic of Multilateralism*. New York: St. Martin's, 1999.

Gilson, Julie. *Japan and the European Union: A New Partnership for the Twenty-First Century?* New York: Palgrave, 2000.

Glaubitz, Joachim. *Between Tokyo and Moscow: The History of an Uneasy Relationship, 1972–1990s*. Honolulu: University of Hawai'i Press, 1995.

Glosserman, Brad, and Scott A. Snyder. *The Japan–South Korea Identity Clash: East Asian Security and the United States*. New York: Columbia University Press, 2015.

Gourevitch, Peter, Takashi Inoguchi, and Courtney Purrington, eds. *United States–Japan Relations and International Institutions: After the Cold War*. San Diego: University of California, 1995.

Graham, Euan. *Japan's Sea Lane Security, 1940–2004: "A Matter of Life and Death?"* New York: Routledge, 2006.

Grant, Richard L., ed. *Strengthening the U.S.-Japan Partnership in the 1990s: Ensuring the Alliance in an Unsure World.* Honolulu, Hawaii: Pacific Forum/CSIS, 1992.

Green, Michael J. *Japan's Reluctant Realism: Foreign Policy Challenges in an Era of Uncertain Power.* New York: Palgrave, 2001.

Green, Michael J., and Zack Cooper. *Strategic Japan: New Approaches to Foreign Policy and the U.S.-Japan Alliance.* Lanham, Md.: Lexington Books, 2015.

————, eds. *Postwar Japan: Growth, Security, and Uncertainty since 1945.* Lanham, Md.: Rowman & Littlefield, 2017.

Green, Michael J., and Patrick M. Cronin, eds. *The U.S.-Japan Alliance: Past, Present, and Future.* New York: Council on Foreign Relations, 1999.

Hagström, Linus. *Japan's China Policy: A Relational Power Analysis.* New York: Routledge, 2005.

Hara, Kimie. *Cold-War Frontiers in the Asia-Pacific: Divided Territories in the San Francisco System.* New York: Routledge, 2007.

————. *Japanese-Soviet/Russian Relations since 1945.* New York: Routledge, 2003.

Hara, Kimie, and Geoffrey Jukes, eds. *Northern Territories, Asia-Pacific Regional Conflicts and the Aland Experience: Untying the Kurillian Knot.* New York: Routledge, 2009.

Hasegawa, Tsuyoshi, Jonathan Haslam, and Andrew C. Kuchins, eds. *Russia and Japan: An Unresolved Dilemma between Distant Neighbors.* Berkeley: University of California Press, 1993.

Hatch, Walter, and Kozo Yamamura. *Asia in Japan's Embrace: Building a Regional Production Alliance.* New York: Cambridge University Press, 1996.

Havens, Thomas R. H. *Fire across the Sea: The Vietnam War and Japan 1965–1975.* Princeton, N.J.: Princeton University Press, 1987.

Hayes, Declan. *Japan: The Toothless Tiger.* 2nd ed. North Clarendon, Vt.: Tuttle, 2014.

Hayes, Louis D. *Japan and the Security of Asia.* Lanham, Md.: Lexington Books, 2002.

Hein, Laura, and Mark Selden, eds. *Censoring History: Citizenship and Memory in Japan, Germany, and the United States.* Armonk, N.Y.: M. E. Sharpe, 2000.

————, eds. *Living with the Bomb: American and Japanese Cultural Conflicts in the Nuclear Age.* Armonk, N.Y.: M. E. Sharpe, 1997.

Hilpert, Hanns-Günther, and René Haak, eds. *Japan and China: Co-operation, Competition and Conflict.* Basingstoke, U.K.: Palgrave, 2002.

Hogan, Michael J., ed. *Hiroshima in History and Memory.* New York: Cambridge University Press, 1996.

Holgerson, Karen M. *The Japan-U.S. Trade Friction Dilemma: The Role of Perception*. Burlington, Vt.: Ashgate, 2002.

Holland, Harrison M. *Japan Challenges America: Managing an Alliance in Crisis*. Boulder, Colo.: Westview, 1992.

Holroyd, Carin, and Ken Coates, eds. *Japan in the Age of Globalization*. New York: Routledge, 2014.

Holstein, William J. *The Japanese Power Game: What It Means for America*. New York: Charles Scribner's Sons, 1990.

Honda, Katsuichi. *The Impoverished Spirit in Contemporary Japan: Selected Essays of Honda Katsuichi*. New York: Monthly Review Press, 1993.

———. *The Nanjing Massacre: A Japanese Journalist Confronts Japan's National Shame*. Edited by Frank Gibney. Translated by Karen Sandness. Armonk, N.Y.: M. E. Sharpe, 1999.

Hook, Glenn D., Julie Gilson, Christopher W. Hughes, and Hugo Dobson. *Japan's International Relations: Politics, Economics and Security*. 3rd ed. New York: Routledge, 2011.

Hook, Glenn D., and Harukiyo Hasegawa, eds. *Political Economy of Japanese Globalization*. New York: Routledge, 2001.

Hook, Glenn D., Ra Mason, and Paul O'Shea. *Regional Risk and Security in Japan: Whither the Everyday*. New York: Routledge, 2015.

Hook, Glenn D., and Hiroko Takeda, eds. *Ending the Postwar in Japan: Structure, Actors, Norms and Challenges*. New York: Routledge, 2017.

Hoppens, Robert. *The China Problem in Postwar Japan: Japanese National Identity and Sino-Japanese Relations*. London: Bloomsbury Academic, 2016.

Hosoya, Chihiro, and Tomohito Shinoda. *Redefining the Partnership: The United States and Japan in East Asia*. Lanham, Md.: University Press of America, 1998.

Hughes, Christopher W. *Japan's Economic Power and Security: Japan and North Korea*. New York: Routledge, 1999.

———. *Japan's Foreign and Security Policy under the "Abe Doctrine": New Dynamism or New Dead End?* New York: Palgrave Pivot, 2015.

———. *Japan's Re-emergence as a "Normal" Military Power*. London: International Institute for Strategic Studies, 2015.

Hunsberger, Warren S. *Japan's Quest: The Search for International Role, Recognition, and Respect*. Armonk, N.Y.: M. E. Sharpe, 1996.

Ibe, Hideo. *Japan, Thrice-Opened: An Analysis of Relations between Japan and the United States*. Translated by Lynne E. Riggs and Manabu Takechi. New York: Praeger, 1992.

Igarashi, Yoshikuni. *Bodies of Memory: Narratives of War in Postwar Japanese Culture, 1945–1970*. Princeton, N.J.: Princeton University Press, 2000.

Ikenberry, G. John, and Takashi Inoguchi, eds. *The Uses of Institutions: The U.S., Japan, and Governance in East Asia.* New York: Palgrave Macmillan, 2007.

Inoguchi, Takashi. *Global Change: A Japanese Perspective.* New York: Palgrave, 2001.

Inoguchi, Takashi, and Purnendra Jain, eds. *Japanese Foreign Policy Today.* London: Palgrave Macmillan, 2000.

Iriye, Akira. *China and Japan in the Global Setting.* Cambridge, Mass.: Harvard University Press, 1992.

———, ed. *Partnership: The United States and Japan 1951–2001.* Tōkyō: Kodansha International, 2002.

Iriye, Akira, and Warren I. Cohen, eds. *The United States and Japan in the Postwar World.* Lexington: University of Kentucky Press, 1989.

Ishihara, Shintarō. *The Japan That Can Say NO: Why Japan Will Be First among Equals.* Translated by Frank Baldwin. New York: Simon & Schuster, 1989.

Ito, Go Tsuyoshi. *Alliance in Anxiety: Détente and the Sino-American-Japanese Triangle.* New York: Routledge, 2003.

Itoh, Mayumi. *The Origins of Contemporary Sino-Japanese Relations: Zhou Enlai and Japan.* New York: Palgrave Macmillan, 2016.

Ivanov, Vladimir I., and Karla S. Smith, eds. *Japan and Russia in Northeast Asia: Partners in the 21st Century.* Westport, Conn.: Praeger, 1999.

Iwabuchi, Koichi. *Resilient Borders and Cultural Diversity: Internationalism, Brand Nationalism, and Multiculturalism in Japan.* Lanham, Md.: Lexington Books, 2015.

Iwashita, Akihiro. *Japan's Border Issues: Pitfalls and Prospects.* New York: Routledge, 2015.

Jacob, Jo Dee Catlin. *Beyond the Hoppo Ryodo: Japanese-Soviet-American Relations in the 1990s.* Washington, D.C.: AEI Press, 1991.

Japan Center for International Exchange. *New Dimensions of China-Japan-U.S. Relations.* Washington, D.C.: Brookings, 1999.

Kamikaze, Shoichi, and Richard L. Grant, eds. *Strengthening the U.S.-Japan Partnership in the 1990s: Ensuring the Alliance in an Unsure World.* Honolulu, Hawaii: Pacific Forum/CSIS, 1992.

Kawashima, Yutaka. *Japanese Foreign Policy at the Crossroads: Challenges and Options for the Twenty-First Century.* Washington, D.C.: Brookings, 2005.

Keck, Jörn, Dimitri Vanoverbeke, and Franz Waldenberger. *EU-Japan Relations, 1970–2012: From Confrontation to Global Partnership.* New York: Routledge, 2016.

Kendall, Harry H., and Clara Joewono, eds. *Japan, ASEAN, and the United States.* Berkeley, Calif.: Institute of East Asian Studies, 1991.

Kim, Jemma. *Japan and East Asian Integration: Trade and Domestic Politics*. London: Routledge, 2018.

King, Amy. *China-Japan Relations after World War Two: Empire, Industry and War, 1949–1971*. London: Cambridge University Press, 2016.

Kishida, Shu. *A Place for Apology: War, Guilt, and U.S.-Japan Relations*. Translated by Yukiko Tanaka. Lanham, Md.: University Press of America, 2004.

Krauss, Ellis S., and Ben Nyblade, eds. *Japan and North America*. New York: Routledge, 2004.

Krauss, Ellis S., and T. J. Pempel, eds. *Beyond Bilateralism: U.S.-Japan Relations in the New Asia-Pacific*. Stanford, Calif.: Stanford University Press, 2004.

Kunkel, John. *America's Trade Policy towards Japan: Demanding Results*. New York: Routledge, 2003.

Lam, Peng-Er, ed. *Japan's Relations with China: Facing a Rising Power*. New York: Routledge, 2006.

———, ed. *Japan's Relations with Southeast Asia: The Fukuda Doctrine and Beyond*. London: Routledge, 2015.

Lauren, Paul Gordon, and Raymond F. Wylie, eds. *Destinies Shared: U.S.-Japanese Relations*. Boulder, Colo.: Westview, 1989.

Lee, Seung Hyok. *Japanese Society and the Politics of the North Korean Threat*. Toronto: University of Toronto Press, 2016.

Leheny, David, and Kay Warren, eds. *Japanese Aid and the Construction of Global Development: Inescapable Solutions*. New York: Routledge, 2009.

Lehman, Howard P., ed. *Japan and Africa: Globalization and Foreign Aid in the 21st Century*. New York: Routledge, 2010.

Leitch, Richard D., Jr., Akira Kato, and Martin E. Weinstein. *Japan's Role in the Post–Cold War World*. Westport, Conn.: Greenwood, 1995.

Liao, Tim F., and Kimie Hara. *The China-Japan Border Dispute: Islands of Contention in Multidisciplinary Perspective*. London: Routledge, 2015.

Lincoln, Edward J. *Troubled Times: U.S.-Japan Trade Relations in the 1990s*. Washington, D.C.: Brookings, 1999.

Loo, Tze May. *Heritage Politics: Shuri Castle and Okinawa's Incorporation into Modern Japan, 1879–2000*. Lanham, Md.: Lexington Books, 2014.

Makin, John H., and Donald C. Hellmann, eds. *Sharing World Leadership? A New Era for America and Japan*. Washington, D.C.: American Enterprise Institute, 1989.

Manicom, James. *Bridging Troubled Waters: China, Japan, and Maritime Order in the East China Sea*. Washington, D.C.: Georgetown University Press, 2014.

Maslow, Sebastian, Ra Mason, and Paul O'Shea. *Risk State: Japan's Foreign Policy in an Age of Uncertainty*. New York: Routledge, 2016.

Mason, Mark. *American Multinationals and Japan: The Political Economy of Japanese Capital Controls, 1899–1980*. Cambridge, Mass.: Harvard University Press, 2002.

———. *Europe and the Japanese Challenge: The Regulation of Multinationals in Comparative Perspective*. New York: Oxford University Press, 1997.

Mason, T. David, and Abdul M. Turay. *U.S.-Japan Trade Friction: Its Impact on Security Cooperation in the Pacific Basin*. New York: St. Martin's, 1991.

Masuda, Wataru. *Japan and China: Mutual Representations in the Modern Era*. London: Routledge, 2000.

Maswood, Syed Javed, ed. *Japan and East Asian Regionalism*. London: Routledge, 2001.

McConnell, David L. *Importing Diversity: Inside Japan's JET Program*. Berkeley: University of California Press, 2000.

McCraw, Thomas K., ed. *America versus Japan*. Boston: Harvard Business School Press, 1986.

McGregor, Richard. *Asia's Reckoning: China, Japan, and the Fate of U.S. Power in the Pacific Century*. New York: Viking, 2017.

McKinnon, Ronald I., and Kenichi Ohno. *Dollar and Yen: Resolving Economic Conflict between the United States and Japan*. Cambridge, Mass.: MIT Press, 1997.

Mendl, Wolf. *Japan's Asia Policy: Regional Security and Global Interests*. London: Routledge, 1995.

———, ed. *Japan and South East Asia: International Relations*. London: Routledge, 2001.

Metzgar, Emily T. *The JET Program and the US-Japan Relationship: Goodwill Goldmine*. Lanham, Md.: Lexington Books, 2017.

Meyer, Claude. *China or Japan: Which Will Lead Asia?* New York: Columbia University Press, 2011.

Midford, Paul. *Rethinking Japanese Public Opinion and Security: From Pacifism to Realism?* Redwood City, Calif.: Stanford University Press, 2011.

Mikuni, Akio, and R. Taggart Murphy. *Japan's Policy Trap: Dollars, Deflation, and the Crisis of Japanese Finance*. Vancouver: University of British Columbia Press, 2004.

Miller, John H. *American Political and Cultural Perspectives on Japan: From Perry to Obama*. Lanham, Md.: Lexington Books, 2016.

Miyagi, Taizo. *Japan's Quest for Stability in Southeast Asia: Navigating the Turning Points in Postwar Asia*. London: Routledge, 2018.

Miyagi, Yukiko. *Japan's Middle East Security Policy: Theory and Cases*. London: Routledge, 2008.

Miyashita, Akitoshi. *Limits to Power: Asymmetric Dependence and Japanese Foreign Aid Policy*. Lanham, Md.: Lexington Books, 2003.

Miyashita, Akitoshi, and Yoichiro Sato, eds. *Japanese Foreign Policy in Asia and the Pacific: Domestic Interests, American Pressure, and Regional Integration*. New York: Palgrave, 2001.

Miyoshi, Masao. *Off Center: Power and Culture Relations between Japan and the United States*. Cambridge, Mass.: Harvard University Press, 1991.

Miyoshi, Masao, and Harry D. Harootunian, eds. *Japan in the World*. Durham, N.C.: Duke University Press, 1993.

Mochizuki, Mike M., ed. *Toward a True Alliance: Restructuring U.S.-Japan Security Relations*. Washington, D.C.: Brookings, 1997.

Morikawa, Jun. *Japan and Africa: Big Business and Diplomacy*. Trenton, N.J.: Africa World Press, 1997.

Morris, Narrelle. *Japan-Bashing: Anti-Japanism since the 1980s*. New York: Routledge, 2013.

Morris, Paul, Naoko Shimazu, and Edward Vickers, eds. *Imagining Japan in Post-war East Asia: Identity Politics, Schooling and Popular Culture*. New York: Routledge, 2014.

Morris-Suzuki, Tessa. *Exodus to North Korea: Shadows from Japan's Cold War*. Lanham, Md.: Rowman & Littlefield, 2007.

Mouer, Ross, ed. *Globalizing Japan: Striving to Engage the World*. Balwyn, North Victoria, Australia: Trans-Pacific, 2015.

Mukherjee, Rohan, and Anthony Yazaki, eds. *Poised for Partnership: Deepening India-Japan Relations in the Asian Century*. London: Oxford University Press, 2016.

Murphy, R. Taggart. *The Weight of the Yen: How Denial Imperils America's Future and Ruins an Alliance*. New York: Norton, 1996.

Nagatani, Keizō, and David W. Edgington, eds. *Japan and the West: The Perception Gap*. Burlington, Vt.: Ashgate, 1998.

Nester, William R. *American Power, the New World Order, and the Japanese Challenge*. New York: St. Martin's, 1993.

———. *European Power and the Japanese Challenge*. New York: New York University Press, 1993.

———. *Japan and the Third World: Patterns, Power, Prospects*. New York: St. Martin's, 1992.

Nimmo, William F. *Japan and Russia: A Reevaluation in the Post-Soviet Era*. Westport, Conn.: Greenwood, 1994.

Nishihara, Masashi. *The Japan-U.S. Alliance: New Challenges for the 21st Century*. Washington, D.C.: Japan Center for International Exchange, 2000.

Nishikawa, Yukiko. *Japan's Changing Role in Humanitarian Crises*. New York: Routledge, 2005.

Orr, James J. *The Victim as Hero: Ideologies of Peace and National Identity in Postwar Japan*. Honolulu: University of Hawai'i Press, 2001.

Orr, Robert M., Jr. *The Emergence of Japan's Foreign Aid Power.* New York: Columbia University Press, 1990.

Packard, George B. *Protest in Tokyo: The Security Treaty Crisis of 1960.* Princeton, N.J.: Princeton University Press, 1966.

Pan, Liang. *The United Nations in Japan's Foreign and Security Policymaking, 1945–1992.* Cambridge, Mass.: Harvard University Press, 2006.

Penn, Michael. *Japan and the War on Terror: Military Force and Political Pressure in the US-Japanese Alliance.* New York: I. B. Tauris, 2014.

Raposo, Pedro Amakasu. *Japan's Foreign Aid Policy in Africa: Evaluating the TICAD Process.* New York: Palgrave Pivot, 2014.

Régnier, Philippe, and Daniel Warner, eds. *Japan and Multilateral Diplomacy.* Burlington, Vt.: Ashgate, 2001.

Reimann, Kim D. *The Rise of Japanese NGOs: Activism from Above.* New York: Routledge, 2011.

Rix, Alan. *The Australia-Japan Political Alignment: 1952 to the Present.* New York: Routledge, 1999.

———. *Japan's Foreign Aid Challenge: Policy Reform and Aid Leadership.* London: Routledge, 1993.

Roehrig, Terence. *Japan, South Korea, and the United States Nuclear Umbrella.* New York: Columbia University Press, 2017.

Rose, Caroline. *Interpreting History in Sino-Japanese Relations: A Case Study in Political Decision-making.* London: Routledge, 1998.

———. *Sino-Japanese Relations: Towards a Future-Oriented Diplomacy.* London: Routledge, 2005.

Rozman, Gilbert F., ed. *Japan and Russia: The Tortuous Path to Normalization, 1949–1999.* New York: St. Martin's, 2000.

———. *Japan's Response to the Gorbachev Era, 1985–1991: A Rising Superpower Views a Declining One.* Princeton, N.J.: Princeton University Press, 1992.

———. *Japanese Strategic Thought toward Asia.* New York: Palgrave Macmillan, 2007.

Saito, Shiro. *Japan at the Summit: Its Role in the Western Alliance and in Asian Pacific Cooperation.* New York: Routledge, 1990.

Sakai, Hidekazu, and Yoichiro Sato. *Re-rising Japan: Its Strategic Power in International Relations.* Bern, Switzerland: Peter Lang, 2017.

Satō, Ryūzō. *The Chrysanthemum and the Eagle: The Future of U.S.-Japan Relations.* New York: New York University Press, 1994.

Satō, Ryūzō, and Julianne Beth Nelson. *Beyond Trade Friction: Japan-U.S. Economic Relations.* New York: Cambridge University Press, 1989.

Satō, Yōichirō, and Satu Limaye, eds. *Japan in a Dynamic Asia: Coping with the New Security Challenges.* Lanham, Md.: Rowman & Littlefield, 2006.

Scalapino, Robert A. *Economic Development in the Asia Pacific Region: Appropriate Roles for Japan and the United States*. Berkeley: University of California Press, 1986.

———, ed. *The Foreign Policy of Modern Japan*. Berkeley: University of California Press, 1977.

Schaede, Ulrike, and William Grimes, eds. *Japan's Managed Globalization: Adapting to the Twenty-First Century*. Armonk, N.Y.: M. E. Sharpe, 2003.

Schaller, Michael. *Altered States: The United States and Japan since the Occupation*. New York: Oxford University Press, 1997.

Schoppa, Leonard J. *Bargaining with Japan: What American Pressure Can and Cannot Do*. New York: Columbia University Press, 1997.

Sharpe, Michael O. *Postcolonial Citizens and Ethnic Migration: The Netherlands and Japan in the Age of Globalization*. New York: Palgrave Macmillan, 2014.

Shibusawa, Naoko. *America's Geisha Ally: Reimagining the Japanese Enemy*. Cambridge, Mass.: Harvard University Press, 2006.

Shibuya, Hiroshi, Makoto Maruyama, and Masamitsu Yasaka, eds. *Japanese Economy and Society under Pax-Americana*. New York: Columbia University Press, 2002.

Shimamoto, Mayako, Koji Ito, and Yoneyuki Sugita. *Historical Dictionary of Japanese Foreign Policy*. Lanham, Md.: Rowman & Littlefield, 2015.

Shimizu, Kosuke, and William S. Bradley, eds. *Multiculturalism and Conflict Reconciliation in the Asia-Pacific: Migration, Language and Politics*. New York: Palgrave Macmillan, 2014.

Shimomura, Yasutami, John Page, and Hiroshi Kato, eds. *Japan's Development Assistance: Foreign Aid and the Post-2015 Agenda*. New York: Palgrave Macmillan, 2015.

Shinoda, Tomohito. *Koizumi Diplomacy: Japan's Kantei Approach to Foreign and Defense Affairs*. Seattle: University of Washington Press, 2017.

Sleeboom, Margaret. *Academic Nations in China and Japan: Framed in Concepts of Nature, Culture and the Universal*. New York: Routledge, 2003.

Smith, Sheila A. *Intimate Rivals: Japanese Domestic Politics and a Rising China*. New York: Columbia University Press, 2016.

———. *Japan's New Politics and the U.S.-Japan Alliance*. New York: Council on Foreign Relations Press, 2014.

Söderberg, Marie, ed. *Changing Power Relations in Northeast Asia: Implications for Relations between Japan and South Korea*. New York: Routledge, 2011.

———, ed. *Chinese-Japanese Relations in the Twenty-First Century: Complementarity and Conflict*. London: Routledge, 2002.

Soeya, Yoshihide, and David A. Welch, eds. *Japan as a "Normal Country"? A Nation in Search of Its Place in the World.* Toronto: University of Toronto Press, 2011.

Stallings, Barbara. *Common Vision, Different Paths: The United States and Japan in the Developing World.* Baltimore, Md.: Johns Hopkins University Press, 1993.

Starrs, Roy, ed. *Japanese Cultural Nationalism: At Home and in the Asia-Pacific.* Folkestone, Kent, U.K.: Global Oriental, 2004.

Steven, Rob. *Japan and the New World Order: Global Investments, Trade and Finance.* New York: St. Martin's, 1996.

Sudō, Sueo. *The International Relations of Japan and South East Asia: Forging a New Regionalism.* London: Routledge, 2001.

Sugita, Yoneyuki, ed. *Toward a More Amicable Asia-Pacific Region: Japan's Roles.* Lanham, Md.: University Press of America, 2015.

Sun, Jing. *Japan and China as Charm Rivals: Soft Power in Regional Diplomacy.* Ann Arbor: University of Michigan Press, 2012.

Takamine, Tsukasa. *Japan's Development Aid to China: The Long-Running Foreign Policy of Engagement.* New York: Routledge, 2005.

Tamaki, Taku. *Deconstructing Japan's Image of South Korea: Identity in Foreign Policy.* New York: Palgrave Macmillan, 2010.

Taylor, Robert. *Greater China and Japan: Prospects for an Economic Partnership in East Asia.* London: Routledge, 1996.

Thorsten, Marie. *Superhuman Japan: Knowledge, Nation and Culture in US-Japan Relations.* New York: Routledge, 2012.

Togo, K., ed. *Japan and Reconciliation in Post-war Asia: The Murayama Statement and Its Implications.* New York: Palgrave Pivot, 2013.

Tsutsui, Wakamizu. *The Changing Postwar International Legal Regime: The Role Played by Japan.* Boston: Kluwer Academic Publishers, 2002.

Vernon, Raymond. *Two Hungry Giants: The United States and Japan in the Quest for Oil and Ores.* Cambridge, Mass.: Harvard University Press, 1983.

Vogel, Steven K., ed. *U.S.-Japan Relations in a Changing World.* Washington, D.C.: Brookings, 2002.

Wan, Ming. *Japan between Asia and the West: Economic Power and Strategic Balance.* Armonk, N.Y.: M. E. Sharpe, 2001.

———. *Sino-Japanese Relations: Interaction, Logic, and Transformation.* Stanford, Calif.: Stanford University Press, 2006.

Wang, Qingxin Ken. *Hegemonic Cooperation and Conflict: Postwar Japan's China Policy and the United States.* New York: Praeger, 2000.

Welfield, John B. *An Empire in Eclipse: Japan in the Postwar American Alliance System: A Study in the Interaction of Domestic Politics and Foreign Policy.* London: Athlone Press, 1988.

Wilkinson, Endymion P. *Japan versus the West: Image and Reality*. New York: Penguin, 1990.

Williams, Brad. *Resolving the Russo-Japanese Territorial Dispute: Hokkaido-Sakhalin Relations*. New York: Routledge, 2007.

Yamada, Haru. *Different Games, Different Rules: Why Americans and Japanese Misunderstand Each Other*. Oxford, U.K.: Oxford University Press, 1997.

Yamamoto, Mari. *Grassroots Pacifism in Post-war Japan: The Rebirth of a Nation*. London: Routledge, 2004.

Yamashita, Shōichi, ed. *Transfer of Japanese Technology and Management to the ASEAN Countries*. Tōkyō: University of Tōkyō Press, 1991.

Yamazaki, Jane. *Japanese Apologies for World War II: A Rhetorical Study*. New York: Routledge, 2012.

Yasutomo, Dennis T. *The New Multilateralism in Japan's Foreign Policy*. New York: St. Martin's, 1995.

Yokoi, Noriko. *Japan's Postwar Economic Recovery and Anglo-Japanese Relations, 1948–1962*. New York: Routledge, 2016.

Yoshitsu, Michael M. *Japan and the San Francisco Peace Settlement*. New York: Columbia University Press, 1983.

Yuzawa, Takeshi. *Japan's Security Policy and the ASEAN Regional Forum: The Search for Multilateral Security in the Asia-Pacific*. New York: Routledge, 2006.

Zhao, Quansheng. *Japanese Policymaking: The Politics behind Politics: Informal Mechanisms and the Making of China Policy*. Westport, Conn.: Praeger, 1993.

DEFENSE AND MILITARY

Barshay, Andrew E. *The Gods Left First: The Captivity and Repatriation of Japanese POWs in Northeast Asia, 1945–1956*. Berkeley: University of California Press, 2013.

Black, Lindsay. *Japan's Maritime Security Strategy: The Japan Coast Guard and Maritime Outlaws*. New York: Palgrave Macmillan, 2014.

Calder, Kent E. *Pacific Defense: Arms, Energy, and America's Failure in Asia*. New York: William Morrow, 1996.

Chinworth, Michael W. *Economic Strategy and U.S.-Japan Defense Collaboration*. Cambridge, Mass.: MIT, 1990.

———. *Inside Japan's Defense: Technology, Economics and Strategy*. Washington, D.C.: Brasseys, 1992.

DiFilippo, Anthony. *The Challenges of the U.S.-Japan Military Arrangement: Competing Security Transitions in a Changing International Environment.* Armonk, N.Y.: M. E. Sharpe, 2002.

Drifte, Reinhard. *Arms Production in Japan: The Military Applications of Civilian Technology.* Boulder, Colo.: Westview, 1986.

Eldridge, Robert D., and Paul Midford, eds. *The Japanese Ground Self-Defense Force: Search for Legitimacy.* New York: Palgrave Macmillan, 2017.

Friedman, Edward, and Sung Chull Kim, eds. *Regional Co-operation and Its Enemies in Northeast Asia.* New York: Routledge, 2006.

Green, Michael J. *Arming Japan: Defense Production, Alliance Politics, and the Postwar Search for Autonomy.* New York: Columbia University Press, 1995.

Hein, Laura, and Mark Selden, eds. *Islands of Discontent: Okinawan Responses to Japanese and American Power.* Lanham, Md.: Rowman & Littlefield, 2003.

Holland, Harrison M. *Managing Defense: Japan's Dilemma.* Lanham, Md.: University Press of America, 1988.

Hook, Glenn D. *Militarization and Demilitarization in Contemporary Japan.* London: Routledge, 1996.

Hughes, Christopher W. *Japan's Re-emergence as a "Normal" Military Power.* New York: Routledge, 2006.

———. *Japan's Security Agenda: Military, Economic, and Environmental Dimensions.* Boulder, Colo.: Lynne Rienner, 2004.

Hunter-Chester, David. *Creating Japan's Ground Self-Defense Force, 1945 to 2015: A Sword Well Made.* Lanham, Md.: Lexington Books, 2016.

Inoue, Masamichi S. *Okinawa and the U.S. Military: Identity Making in the Age of Globalization.* New York: Columbia University Press, 2006.

Kataoka, Tetsuya, and Ramon H. Myers. *Defending an Economic Superpower: Reassessing the U.S.-Japan Security Alliance.* Boulder, Colo.: Westview, 1989.

Katzenstein, Peter J. *Cultural Norms and National Security: Police and Military in Postwar Japan.* Ithaca, N.Y.: Cornell University Press, 1996.

Kawato, Yuko. *Protests against U.S. Military Base Policy in Asia: Persuasion and Its Limits.* Redwood City, Calif.: Stanford University Press, 2015.

Keddell, Joseph P., Jr. *The Politics of Defense in Japan: Managing Internal and External Pressures.* Armonk, N.Y.: M. E. Sharpe, 1993.

Kliman, Daniel M. *Japan's Security Strategy in the Post 9/11 World: Embracing a New Realpolitik.* Westport, Conn.: Praeger, 2006.

Koikari, Mire. *Cold War Encounters in US-Occupied Okinawa: Women, Militarized Domesticity and Transnationalism in East Asia.* New York: Cambridge University Press, 2015.

Kowalski, Col. Frank. *An Inoffensive Rearmament: The Making of the Post-war Japanese Army*. Annapolis, Md.: Naval Institute Press, 2014.

McCormack, Gavan, and Satoko Oka Norimatsu. *Resistant Islands: Okinawa Confronts Japan and the United States*. 2nd ed. Lanham, Md.: Rowman & Littlefield, 2018.

Pekkanen, Saadia M., and Paul Kallender-Umezu. *In Defense of Japan: From the Market to the Military in Space Policy*. Stanford, Calif.: Stanford University Press, 2010.

Sadō, Akihiro. *The Self-Defense Forces and Postwar Politics in Japan*. Translated by Makito Noda. Tōkyō: Japan Publishing Industry, 2017.

Samuels, Richard J. *"Rich Nation, Strong Army": National Security and Technological Transformation of Japan*. Ithaca, N.Y.: Cornell University Press, 1994.

Sasaki, Tomoyuki. *Japan's Postwar Military and Civil Society: Contesting a Better Life*. London: Bloomsbury, 2015.

Sebata, Takao. *Japan's Defense Policy and Bureaucratic Politics, 1976–2007*. Lanham, Md.: University Press of America, 2010.

Swaine, Michael D., Rachel M. Swanger, and Takashi Kawakami. *Japan and Ballistic Missile Defense*. Santa Monica, Calif.: Rand Corporation, 2001.

ARTS, CULTURE, AND LITERATURE

Akagawa, Natsuko. *Heritage Conservation and Japan's Cultural Diplomacy: Heritage National Identity and National Interest*. New York: Routledge, 2014.

Anan, Nobuko. *Contemporary Japanese Women's Theatre and Visual Arts: Performing Girls' Aesthetics*. New York: Palgrave Macmillan, 2016.

Aoyagi, Hiroshi. *Islands of Eight Million Smiles: Idol Performance and Symbolic Production in Contemporary Japan*. Cambridge, Mass.: Harvard University Press, 2005.

Atkins, E. Taylor. *Blue Nippon: Authenticating Jazz in Japan*. Durham, N.C.: Duke University Press, 2001.

Baird, Bruce. *Hijikata Tatsumi and Butoh: Dancing in a Pool of Gray Grits*. New York: Palgrave Macmillan, 2012.

Befu, Harumi. *Hegemony of Homogeneity: An Anthropological Analysis of "Nihonjinron."* Melbourne, Australia: Trans-Pacific, 2001.

Bender, Shawn. *Taiko Boom: Japanese Drumming in Place and Motion*. Berkeley: University of California Press, 2012.

Bestor, Victoria Lyon, and Theodore C. Bestor, eds., with Akiko Yamagata. *Routledge Handbook of Japanese Culture and Society*. London; New York: Routledge, 2011.

Bognar, Botund. *Contemporary Japanese Architecture: Its Development and Challenge*. New York: Van Nostrand Reinhold, 1985.

Calichman, Richard F. *Beyond Nation: Time, Writing, and Community in the Work of Abe Kōbō*. Redwood City, Calif.: Stanford University Press, 2016.

————, ed. *Contemporary Japanese Thought*. New York: Columbia University Press, 2005.

Chonghwa, Lee, ed. *Still Hear the Wound: Toward an Asia, Politics, Art to Come*. Translations edited by Rebecca Jennison and Brett de Bary. Cornell East Asia Series. Ithaca, N.Y.: Cornell University, East Asia Program, 2015.

Clancy, Judith. *Kyoto Gardens: Masterworks of the Japanese Gardener's Art*. North Clarendon, Vt.: Tuttle, 2015.

Claremont, Yasuko. *The Novels of Oe Kenzaburo*. New York: Routledge, 2011.

Coaldrake, A. Kimi. *Women's Gidayū and the Japanese Theatre Tradition*. New York: Routledge, 1997.

Coaldrake, William H. *Architecture and Authority in Japan*. London: Routledge, 1996.

Dale, Peter N. *The Myth of Japanese Uniqueness*. New York: St. Martin's, 1986.

Davies, Roger J., and Osamu Ikeno. *The Japanese Mind: Understanding Contemporary Japanese Culture*. North Clarendon, Vt.: Tuttle, 2002.

De Mente, Boye Lafayette. *Etiquette Guide to Japan: Know the Rules That Make the Difference!* 3rd ed. North Clarendon, Vt.: Tuttle, 2015.

Denson, Abby. *Cool Japan Guide: Fun in the Land of Manga, Lucky Cats and Ramen*. North Clarendon, Vt.: Tuttle, 2015.

Furukawa, Hideo. *Horses, Horses, in the End the Light Remains Pure: A Tale That Begins with Fukushima*. Translated by Doug Slaymaker and Akiko Takenaka. New York: Columbia University Press, 2016.

Galliano, Luciana. *Yōgaku: Japanese Music in the Twentieth Century*. Lanham, Md.: Scarecrow Press, 2002.

Geilhorn, Barbara, and Kristina Iwata-Weickgenannt, eds. *Fukushima and the Arts: Negotiating Nuclear Disaster*. New York: Routledge, 2016.

Gessel, Van C., and Tomone Matsumoto, eds. *The Showa Anthology: Modern Japanese Short Stories*. 2 vols. Tōkyō: Kodansha, 1985.

Goodman, Roger, and Kirsten Refsing, eds. *Ideology and Practice in Modern Japan*. London: Routledge, 1992.

Graham, Patricia J. *Japanese Design: Art, Aesthetics & Culture*. North Clarendon, Vt.: Tuttle, 2014.

Hall, Ivan P. *Bamboozled! How America Loses the Intellectual Game with Japan and Its Implications for Our Future in Asia*. Armonk, N.Y.: M. E. Sharpe, 2002.

Havens, Thomas R. H. *Artist and Patron in Postwar Japan: Dance, Music, Theatre, and the Visual Arts, 1955–1980*. Princeton, N.J.: Princeton University Press, 1982.

Hein, Laura. *Reasonable Men, Powerful Words: Political Culture and Expertise in Twentieth-Century Japan*. Berkeley: University of California Press, 2004.

Hein, Laura, and Rebecca Jennison, eds. *Imagination without Borders: Feminist artist Tomiyama Taeko and Social Responsibility*. Ann Arbor: University of Michigan, 2010.

Hibbett, Howard, ed. *Contemporary Japanese Literature: An Anthology of Fiction, Film, and Other Writing since 1945*. New York: Knopf, 1977.

Isaka, Maki. *Onnagata: A Labyrinth of Gendering in Kabuki Theater*. Seattle: University of Washington Press, 2015.

Jodidio, Philip. *Contemporary Japanese Architects*. Vol. 2. New York: Taschen, 1997.

Kato, Shuichi. *A History of Japanese Literature*. Vol. 3, *The Modern Years*. Translated by Don Sanderson. New York: Kodansha, 1983.

Keene, Donald. *Appreciations of Japanese Culture*. Tōkyō: Kodansha International, 1981.

———. *Dawn to the West: Japanese Literature in the Modern Era, Fiction*. New York: Holt, Rinehart and Winston, 1984.

Kojin, Karatani. *The Origins of Modern Japanese Literature*. Edited by Brett de Bary. Durham, N.C.: Duke University Press, 1993.

Kondo, Dorinne K. *About Face: Performing Race in Fashion and Theater*. New York: Routledge, 1997.

Kurabayashi, Yoshimasa, and Yoshiro Matsuda. *Economic and Social Aspects of the Performing Arts in Japan: Symphony Orchestras and Opera*. Tōkyō: Kinokuniya, 1988.

Leiter, Samuel L. *Historical Dictionary of Japanese Traditional Theatre*. 2nd ed. Lanham, Md.: Scarecrow Press, 2014.

Levy, Indra, ed. *Translation in Modern Japan*. New York: Routledge, 2010.

Lucken, Michael. *Imitation and Creativity in Japanese Arts: From Kishida Ryūsei to Miyazaki Hayao*. New York: Columbia University Press, 2016.

Mackie, Vera. *The Politics of Visual Culture in Japan*. New York: Routledge, 2016.

Maddox, Amanda. *Ishiuchi Miyako: Postwar Shadows*. Los Angeles, Calif.: Getty Publications, 2015.

Marcus, Marvin. *Japanese Literature: From Murasaki to Murakami*. Ann Arbor, Mich.: Association for Asian Studies, 2015.

Marotti, William. *Money, Trains, and Guillotines: Art and Revolution in 1960s Japan*. Durham, N.C.: Duke University Press, 2013.

Martinez, D. P. *Modern Japanese Culture and Society*. New York: Routledge, 2007.

Maruyama, Masao. *Thought and Behavior in Modern Japanese Politics*. Edited by Ivan Morris. London: Oxford University Press, 1963.

Masami, Yuki. *Foodscapes of Contemporary Japanese Women Writers: An Ecocritical Journey around the Hearth of Modernity*. New York: Palgrave Macmillan, 2015.

Matsue, Jennifer Milioto. *Focus: Music in Contemporary Japan*. New York: Routledge, 2015.

Matthew, Robert. *Japanese Science Fiction: A View of Changing Society*. New York: Routledge, 1989.

Miller, J. Scott. *Historical Dictionary of Modern Japanese Literature and Theater*. Lanham, Md.: Scarecrow Press, 2009.

Mitsios, Helen, ed. *New Japanese Voices: The Best Contemporary Fiction from Japan*. New York: Atlantic Monthly Press, 1991.

Mitsui, Toru. *Made in Japan: Studies in Popular Music*. New York: Routledge, 2015.

Miyoshi, Masao. *Accomplices of Silence: The Modern Japanese Novel*. Berkeley: University of California Press, 1974.

Morton, Leith. *Modern Japanese Culture: The Insider View*. New York: Oxford University Press, 2003.

Mostow, Joshua S., Norman Bryson, and Maribeth Graybill, eds. *Gender and Power in the Japanese Visual Field*. Honolulu: University of Hawai'i Press, 2003.

Murakami, Ryu. *Popular Hits of the Showa Era*. Translated by Ralph McCarthy. New York: Norton, 2011.

———. *Tokyo Decadence*. Translated by Ralph McCarthy. Tōkyō: Kurodahan, 2016.

Nagahara, Hiromu. *Tōkyō Boogie-Woogie: Japan's Pop Era and Its Discontents*. Cambridge, Mass.: Harvard University Press, 2017.

Nakazawa, Keiji. *Hiroshima: The Autobiography of Barefoot Gen*. Translated by Richard H. Minear. Lanham, Md.: Rowman & Littlefield, 2010.

Napier, Susan J. *The Fantastic in Modern Japanese Literature: The Subversion of Modernity*. New York: Routledge, 1996.

Novak, David. *Japanoise: Music at the Edge of Circulation*. Durham, N.C.: Duke University Press, 2013.

Ohkura, Shunji. *Kabuki Today: The Art and Tradition*. Tōkyō: Kodansha, 2001.

Paramore, Kiri. *Japanese Confucianism: A Cultural History*. London: Cambridge University Press, 2016.

Powell, Brian. *Japan's Modern Theatre: A Century of Change and Continuity*. New York: Palgrave, 2001.

Ridgely, Steven C. *Japanese Counterculture: The Antiestablishment Art of Terayama Shuji*. Minneapolis: University of Minnesota Press, 2010.

Rimer, J. Thomas. *Modern Japanese Fiction and Its Traditions: An Introduction*. Princeton, N.J.: Princeton University Press, 1978.

Rimer, J. Thomas, and Van C. Gessel, eds. *The Columbia Anthology of Modern Japanese Literature: From 1945 to the Present*. New York: Columbia University Press, 2007.

Rimer, J. Thomas, Mitsuya Mori, and M. Cody Poulton, eds. *The Columbia Anthology of Modern Japanese Drama*. New York: Columbia University Press, 2014.

Roquet, Paul. *Ambient Media: Japanese Atmospheres of Self*. Minneapolis: University of Minnesota Press, 2016.

Rubin, Jay, ed. *Modern Japanese Writers*. New York: Scribner, 2001.

Salz, Jonah. *A History of Japanese Theatre*. New York: Cambridge University Press, 2016.

Sas, Miryam. *Experimental Arts in Postwar Japan: Moments of Encounter, Engagement, and Imagined Return*. Cambridge, Mass.: Harvard University Press, 2011.

Sato, Shozo. *Shodo: The Quiet Art of Japanese Zen Calligraphy: Learn the Wisdom of Zen through Traditional Brush Painting*. North Clarendon, Vt.: Tuttle, 2014.

———. *Sumi-e: The Art of Japanese Ink Painting*. North Clarendon, Vt.: Tuttle, 2010.

Seats, Michael Robert. *Murakami Haruki: The Simulacrum in Contemporary Japanese Culture*. Lanham, Md.: Lexington Books, 2006.

Sherif, Ann. *Japan's Cold War: Media, Literature, and the Law*. New York: Columbia University Press, 2016.

Shirane, Haruo. *Japan and the Culture of the Four Seasons: Nature, Literature, and the Arts*. New York: Columbia University Press, 2013.

Snyder, Stephen, and Philip Gabriel, eds. *Oe and Beyond: Fiction in Contemporary Japan*. Honolulu: University of Hawai'i Press, 1999.

Sosnoski, Daniel, ed. *Introduction to Japanese Culture*. North Clarendon, Vt.: Tuttle, 2014.

Stahl, David C. *Trauma, Dissociation and Re-enactment in Japanese Literature and Film*. New York: Routledge, 2017.

Sterling, Marvin D. *Babylon East: Performing Dancehall, Roots Reggae, and Rastafari in Japan*. Durham, N.C.: Duke University Press, 2010.

Stewart, David B. *The Making of a Modern Japanese Architecture: 1868 to Present*. Tōkyō: Kodansha, 1987.

Strecher, Matthew Carl. *The Forbidden Worlds of Haruki Murakami*. Minneapolis: University of Minnesota Press, 2014.

Sugimoto, Yoshio, ed. *The Cambridge Companion to Modern Japanese Culture*. London: Cambridge University Press, 2009.

Surak, Kristin. *Making Tea, Making Japan: Cultural Nationalism in Practice*. Redwood City, Calif.: Stanford University Press, 2012.

Takeshi, Matsuda. *Soft Power and Its Perils: U.S. Cultural Policy in Early Postwar Japan and Permanent Dependency*. Washington, D.C.: Woodrow Wilson Center Press, 2007.

Takeuchi, Melinda, ed. *The Artist as Professional in Japan*. Stanford, Calif.: Stanford University Press, 2004.

Tanaka, Motoko. *Apocalypse in Contemporary Japanese Science Fiction*. New York: Palgrave Macmillan, 2014.

Tezuka, Miwako, ed. *Rebirth: Recent Work by Mariko Mori*. New York: Japan Society, 2013.

Thornbury, Barbara E. *The Folk Performing Arts: Traditional Culture in Contemporary Japan*. Albany: State University of New York Press, 1997.

Treat, John Whittier. *Writing Ground Zero: Japanese Literature and the Atomic Bomb*. Chicago: University of Chicago Press, 1995.

Tsurumi, Shunsuke. *A Cultural History of Postwar Japan: 1945–1980*. New York: Routledge, 2013.

Ueda, Makoto. *Modern Japanese Writers and the Nature of Literature*. Stanford, Calif.: Stanford University Press, 1976.

Van Compernolle, Timothy J. *Struggling Upward: Worldly Success and the Japanese Novel*. Cambridge, Mass.: Harvard University Press, 2016.

Wade, Bonnie C. *Composing Japanese Musical Modernity*. Chicago: University of Chicago Press, 2014.

———. *Music in Japan: Experiencing Music, Expressing Culture*. New York: Oxford University Press, 2004.

Wakabayashi, Bob Tadashi, ed. *Modern Japanese Thought*. New York: Cambridge University Press, 1997.

Wake, Hisaaki, Keijuro Suga, and Yuki Masami, eds. *Ecocriticism in Japan*. Lanham, Md.: Lexington Books, 2017.

Washburn, Dennis C. *The Dilemma of the Modern Japanese Fiction*. New Haven, Conn.: Yale University Press, 1995.

Yamada, Shoji. *Shots in the Dark: Japan, Zen, and the West*. Translated by Earl Hartman. Chicago: University of Chicago Press, 2009.

Yano, Christine R. *Tears of Longing: Nostalgia and the Nation in Japanese Popular Song*. Cambridge, Mass.: Harvard University Press, 2002.

Yoneyama, Lisa. *Hiroshima Traces: Time, Space, and the Dialectics of Memory*. Berkeley: University of California Press, 1999.

Young, David, and Michiko Young. *The Art of Japanese Architecture*. North Clarendon, Vt.: Tuttle, 2007.

FILM AND POPULAR CULTURE

Allen, Matthew, and Rumi Sakamoto, eds. *Japanese Popular Culture*. New York: Routledge, 2014.

⸻, eds. *Popular Culture and Globalisation in Japan*. New York: Routledge, 2006.

Allison, Anne. *Millennial Monsters: Japanese Toys and the Global Imagination*. Berkeley: University of California Press, 2006.

Anderson, Joseph L., and Donald Richie. *The Japanese Film: Art and Industry*. Princeton, N.J.: Princeton University Press, 1982.

Atkins, E. Taylor. *A History of Popular Culture in Japan: From the Seventeenth Century to the Present*. London: Bloomsbury, 2017.

Ashcraft, Brian, and Shoko Ueda. *Japanese Schoolgirl Confidential: How Teenage Girls Made a Nation Cool*. North Clarendon, Vt.: Tuttle, 2014.

Balmain, Colette. *Introduction to Japanese Horror Film*. Edinburgh: Edinburgh University Press, 2008.

Berra, John, ed. *Directory of World Cinema: Japan*. Bristol, U.K.: Intellect, 2010.

Brown, Steven T. *Tokyo Cyberpunk: Posthumanism in Japanese Visual Culture*. New York: Palgrave Macmillan, 2010.

Clements, Jonathan, and Helen McCarthy. *The Anime Encyclopedia: A Guide to Japanese Animation since 1917*. Rev. ed. Berkeley, Calif.: Stone Bridge Press, 2006.

Condry, Ian. *The Soul of Anime: Collaborative Creativity and Japan's Media Success Story*. Durham, N.C.: Duke University Press, 2013.

Consalvo, Mia. *Atari to Zelda: Japan's Videogames in Global Contexts*. Cambridge, Mass.: MIT Press, 2016.

Craig, Timothy J., ed. *Japan Pop! Inside the World of Japanese Popular Culture*. Armonk, N.Y.: M. E. Sharpe, 2000.

Davis, Blair, and Robert Anderson, eds. *Rashomon Effects: Kurosawa, Rashomon and Their Legacies*. New York: Routledge, 2015.

Davisson, Zack. *Kaibyo: The Supernatural Cats of Japan*. Seattle, Wash.: Chin Music Press, 2017.

Denison, Rayna. *Anime: A Critical Introduction*. London: Bloomsbury Academic, 2015.

du Gay, Paul, Stuart Hall, Linda Janes, et. al. *Doing Cultural Studies: The Story of the Sony Walkman*. Thousand Oaks, Calif.: Sage, 2013.

Elliott, David. *Bye Bye Kitty!!!: Between Heaven and Hell in Contemporary Japanese Art*. New Haven, Conn.: Yale University Press, 2011.

Frühstück, Sabine, and Sepp Linhart, eds. *The Culture of Japan as Seen through Its Leisure*. Albany: State University of New York Press, 1998.

Furuhata, Yuriko. *Cinema of Actuality: Japanese Avant-Garde Filmmaking in the Season of Image Politics*. Durham, N.C.: Duke University Press, 2013.

Galbraith, Patrick W. *The Otaku Encyclopedia: An Insider's Guide to the Subculture of Cool Japan*. New York: Kodansha, 2014.

Galbraith, Patrick W., Thiam Huat Kam, and Björn-Ole Kam, eds. *Debating Otaku in Contemporary Japan: Historical Perspectives and New Horizons*. London: Bloomsbury, 2015.

Galbraith, Patrick W., and Jason G. Karlin, eds. *Idols and Celebrity in Japanese Media Culture*. New York: Palgrave Macmillan, 2012.

———, eds. *Media Convergence in Japan*. Tōkōyo Kinema Club, 2016.

Garcia, Hector. *A Geek in Japan: Discovering the Land of Manga, Anime, Zen, and the Tea Ceremony*. North Clarendon, Vt.: Tuttle, 2011.

Gibbs, Michael H. *Film and Political Culture in Postwar Japan*. New York: Peter Lang, 2012.

Harris, Blake J. *Console Wars: Sega, Nintendo, and the Battle That Defined a Generation*. New York: IT Books, 2014.

Ito, Mizuko, Daisuke Okabe, and Izumi Tsuji, eds. *Fandom Unbound: Otaku Culture in a Connected World*. New Haven, Conn.: Yale University Press, 2012.

Iwata-Weickgenannt, Kristina, and Roman Rosenbaum, eds. *Visions of Precarity in Japanese Popular Culture and Literature*. New York: Routledge, 2014.

Kajiyama, Sumiko. *Cool Japan: A Guide to Tokyo, Kyoto, Tohoku and Japanese Culture Past and Present*. New York: Museyon, 2013.

Kelly, William W., ed. *Fanning the Flames: Fans and Consumer Culture in Contemporary Japan*. Albany: State University of New York Press, 2004.

Kinsella, Sharon. *Adult Manga: Culture and Power in Contemporary Japanese Society*. Honolulu: University of Hawai'i Press, 2000.

Ko, Mika. *Japanese Cinema and Otherness: Nationalism, Multiculturalism and the Problem of Japaneseness*. London: Routledge, 2011.

Martinez, D. P., ed. *The Worlds of Japanese Popular Culture: Gender, Shifting Boundaries and Global Cultures*. New York: Cambridge University Press, 1998.

McClure, Steve. *Nippon Pop: Sounds from the Land of the Rising Sun*. North Clarendon, Vt.: Tuttle, 1998.

McDonald, Keiko I. *Cinema East: A Critical Study of Major Japanese Films*. Rutherford, N.J.: Fairleigh Dickinson University Press, 1983.

McKevitt, Andrew C. *Consuming Japan: Popular Culture and the Globalizing of 1980s America*. Chapel Hill: University of North Carolina Press, 2017.

McLelland, Mark, ed. *The End of Cool Japan: Ethical, Legal, and Cultural Challenges to Japanese Popular Culture*. New York: Routledge, 2016.

McLelland, Mark, and Nanette Gottlieb, eds. *Japanese Cybercultures*. New York: Routledge, 2003.

Moeran, Brian. *Language and Popular Culture in Japan*. New York: Routledge, 2010.

Murakami, Takashi, ed. *Little Boy: The Arts of Japan's Exploding Subculture*. New Haven, Conn.: Yale University Press, 2005.

Murguía, Salvador Jimenez. *The Encyclopedia of Japanese Horror Films*. Lanham, Md.: Rowman & Littlefield, 2016.

Napier, Susan J. *Anime from Akira to Howl's Moving Castle, Updated Edition: Experiencing Contemporary Japanese Animation*. New York: Palgrave Macmillan, 2005.

Nygren, Scott. *Time Frames: Japanese Cinema and the Unfolding of History*. Minneapolis: University of Minnesota Press, 2007.

Okazaki, Manami, and Geoff Johnson. *Kawaii!: Japan's Culture of Cute*. New York: Prestel Publishing, 2013.

Okuyama, Yoshiko. *Japanese Mythology in Film: A Semiotic Approach to Reading Japanese Film and Anime*. Lanham, Md.: Lexington Books, 2015.

Otmazgin, Nissim Kadosh. *Regionalizing Culture: The Political Economy of Japanese Popular Culture in Asia*. Honolulu: University of Hawai'i Press, 2013.

Perper, Timothy, and Martha Cornog, eds. *Mangatopia: Essays on Manga and Anime in the Modern World*. Santa Barbara, Calif.: Libraries Unlimited, 2011.

Powers, Richard Gid, Hidetoshi Kato, and Bruce Stronach. *Handbook of Japanese Popular Culture*. New York: Greenwood, 1989.

Ragone, August. *Eiji Tsuburaya: Master of Monsters: Defending the Earth with Ultraman, Godzilla, and Friends in the Golden Age of Japanese Science Fiction Film*. San Francisco, Calif.: Chronicle Books, 2014.

Richie, Donald. *A Hundred Years of Japanese Film: A Concise History, with a Selective Guide to Videos and DVDs*. Tōkyō: Kodansha International, 2001.

Rosenbaum, Roman, ed. *Manga and the Representation of Japanese History*. New York: Routledge, 2016.

Schilling, Mark. *The Encyclopedia of Japanese Pop Culture*. New York: Weatherhill, 1997.

Schodt, Frederik L. *Dreamland Japan: Writings on Modern Manga*. Berkeley, Calif.: Stone Bridge Press, 1996.

Seaton, Philip A., and Takayoshi Yamamura, eds. *Japanese Popular Culture and Contents Tourism*. New York: Routledge, 2016.

Sepp, Linhart, and Sabine Frühstück, eds. *The Culture of Japan as Seen through Its Leisure*. Albany: State University of New York Press, 1998.

Shamoon, Deborah, and Chris McMorran, eds. *Teaching Japanese Popular Culture*. Ann Arbor, Mich.: Association for Asian Studies, 2016.

Sharp, Jasper. *Historical Dictionary of Japanese Cinema*. Lanham, Md.: Scarecrow Press, 2011.

Slaymaker, Douglas, ed. *A Century of Popular Culture in Japan*. Ann Arbor: University of Michigan Press, 2001.

Standish, Isolde. *Politics, Porn and Protest: Japanese Avant-Garde Cinema in the 1960s and 1970s*. London: Bloomsbury Group, 2011.

Steinberg, Marc. *Anime's Media Mix: Franchising Toys and Characters in Japan*. Minneapolis: University of Minnesota Press, 2012.

Suan, Stevie. *The Anime Paradox: Patterns and Practices through the Lens of Traditional Japanese Theater*. Leiden, the Netherlands: Global Oriental, 2013.

Swale, Alistair D. *Anime Aesthetics: Japanese Animation and the "Post-cinematic" Imagination*. New York: Palgrave Macmillan, 2015.

Thornton, S. A. *The Japanese Period Film: A Critical Analysis*. Jefferson, N.C.: McFarland, 2008.

Toku, Masami, ed. *International Perspectives on Shojo and Shojo Manga: The Influence of Girl Culture*. New York: Routledge, 2015.

Treat, John Whittier, ed. *Contemporary Japan and Popular Culture*. Honolulu: University of Hawai'i Press, 1996.

Tsutsui, William M. *Japanese Popular Culture and Globalization*. Ann Arbor, Mich.: Association for Asian Studies, 2010.

Tsutsui, William M., and Michiko Ito, eds. *In Godzilla's Footsteps: Japanese Pop Culture Icons on the Global Stage*. New York: Palgrave Macmillan, 2006.

Ueda, Atsushi. *The Electric Geisha: Exploring Japan's Popular Culture*. Tōkyō: Kodansha International, 1994.

West, Mark I., ed. *The Japanification of Children's Popular Culture: From Godzilla to Miyazaki*. Lanham, Md.: Scarecrow Press, 2008.

Wild, Peter. *Akira Kurosawa*. Chicago: University of Chicago Press, 2014.

Wong, Yoke-Sum. *The Aesthetics of Cute in Contemporary Japanese Art*. New York: Palgrave Macmillan, 2016.

Yokota, Masao, and Tze-Yue G. Hu. *Japanese Animation: East Asian Perspectives*. Jackson: University Press of Mississippi, 2013.

NEWSPAPERS

Asahi Shimbun
Daily Yomiuri Online
Japan Forward

Japan News
Japan Real Time
Japan Times
Japan Today
Kyodo News
Mainichi
New York Times
New York Times (International edition)
News on Japan
Nikkei Asian Review
Nikkei, Nihon Keizai Shimbun
Sankei Shimbun
Wall Street Journal (Asian edition)
Yomiuri Shimbun

JOURNALS

Asia-Pacific Journal: Japan Focus
Asian Affairs
Asian Pacific Perspectives
Asian Profile
Asian Survey
Bank of Japan Quarterly
Bibliography of Asian Studies (Association for Asian Studies)
Bulletin of the School of Oriental and African Studies
Business in Asia
Contemporary Japan
Contemporary Religions in Japan
Critical Asian Studies (formerly *Bulletin of Concerned Asian Scholars*)
East Asia Forum
East Asian History
Electronic Journal of Contemporary Japanese Studies
European Association for Japanese Studies
Far Eastern Quarterly (now *Journal of Asian Studies*)
Foreign Affairs
Foreign Press Center, Japan
Gaikō Forum: Journal of Japanese Perspectives on Diplomacy
Harvard Asia Quarterly
Harvard Journal of Asiatic Studies
Hitotsubashi Journal of Arts and Sciences
International Journal of Japanese Sociology

JALT Journal
Japan Book News (Japan Foundation)
Japan Christian Quarterly
Japan Forum
Japan Labor Review
Japan Review: Bulletin of the International Research Center for Japanese Studies
Japan Society Review
Japan Today
Japanese Economic Studies
Japanese Economic Review
Japanese Journal of Labour Studies
Japanese Journal of Political Science
Japanese Journal of Religious Studies
Japanese Language and Literature
Japanese Literature Today
Japanese Studies
Journal of American-East Asian Relations
Journal of Asian Affairs
Journal of Asian Economics
Journal of Asian History
Journal of Asian Security and International Affairs
Journal of Asian Studies
Journal of Contemporary Asia
Journal of Japanese & Korean Cinema
Journal of Japanese Philosophy
Journal of Japanese Studies
Journal of Religion in Japan
Journal of the Japanese and International Economies
Modern Asian Studies
Monumenta Nipponica
New Voices in Japanese Studies
Nikkei Asian Review
Pacific Affairs
Pacific Historical Review
Review of Japanese Culture and Society
Shashi: The Journal of Business and Company History
Social Science Japan Journal
Stanford Journal of East Asian Affairs
Tokyo Journal
Transactions of the Asiatic Society of Japan
U.S.-Japan Women's Journal

INTERNET RESOURCES

General

Jim Becker's (U of Northern Iowa) Website: http://www.uni.edu/becker/japanese222.html

Jim Breen's Japanese Page: http://nihongo.monash.edu//Japanese.html

Central Intelligence Agency, World Factbook, Japan: https://www.cia.gov/library/publications/the-world-factbook/geos/ja.html

H-Japan: https://networks.h-net.org/h-japan

Japan Guide: http://www.japan-guide.com/ (travel, living, and general information)

Japan Information Network: http://www.jinjapan.org/

Japan National Tourist Organization: http://www.jnto.go.jp/

Japan Reference: http://www.jref.com/

Japan Today: http://www.japantoday.com/

Japan Zone: http://www.japan-zone.com/ (Japan travel guide; information on Japan and Japanese culture)

Japan-Related Websites: http://tronweb.super-nova.co.jp/japanwebsites.html

Library of Congress: A Country Study: Japan: http://lcweb2.loc.gov/frd/cs/jptoc.html

National Archives of Japan: http://www.archives.go.jp/english/index.html

National Diet Library: http://www.ndl.go.jp/en/index.html

Stanford Guide to Japan Information Resources: http://jguide.stanford.edu/site/reference_130.html

TripSavvy: https://www.tripsavvy.com/japan-4138866 (general information and travel guide)

Web Japan; Japan Links: http://web-japan.org/links/ (a comprehensive list of useful websites sponsored by the Japanese Ministry of Foreign Affairs)

Welcome to Keiko Schneider's Bookmarks: http://www.sabotenweb.com/bookmarks/

History

Contemporary Japan in Historical Perspective (by Lee A. Makela): http://academic.csuohio.edu/makelaa/history/courses/his373/index.html

Edo-Tokyo Museum: http://www.edo-tokyo-museum.or.jp/english/index.html

An Encyclopedia of Japanese History (compiled by Chris Spackman): http://www.openhistory.org/jhdp/encyclopedia/index.html

Institute of Social Science, University of Tokyo: http://www.iss.u-to-kyo.ac.jp/
Internet East Asian History Sourcebook (Fordham University): http://www.fordham.edu/halsall/eastasia/eastasiasbook.html
National Museum of Japanese History: http://www.rekihaku.ac.jp/english/index.html

Government and Politics

Cabinet Office, Government of Japan: http://www.cao.go.jp/index-e.html
Government of Japan: https://www.japan.go.jp/japan/
Governments on the WWW: Japan: http://www.gksoft.com/govt/en/jp.html (links to Japanese governmental sites)
Japanese Cabinet Office: http://www.gov-online.go.jp/eng/publicity/book/hlj/index.html (online magazine of articles favorable to Japan)
Japanese Communist Party: http://www.jcp.or.jp/english/
Liberal Democratic Party: https://www.jimin.jp/english/
Ministry of Justice: http://www.moj.go.jp/ENGLISH/index.html
National Diet of Japan, House of Councillors: http://www.sangiin.go.jp/eng/
National Diet of Japan, House of Representatives: http://www.shugiin.go.jp/internet/index.nsf/html/index_e.htm
Online dictionary of politics and media in Japan: http://www.docoja.com/dico/poltxtg0.html
Political Resources: Japan: http://www.politicalresources.net/japan.htm (links to Japanese political sites)
Prime Minister of Japan and His Cabinet: http://japan.kantei.go.jp/index.html

Economy and Business

Bank of Japan: http://www.boj.or.jp/en/index.htm
Japan Center for Economic Research: http://www.jcer.or.jp/eng/index.html
Japan Exchange Group: http://www.jpx.co.jp/english/
Japan External Trade Organization: http://www.jetro.go.jp/
Keizai Koho Center, Japan Institute for Economic and Social Affairs: http://www.kkc.or.jp/english/
Ministry of Economy, Trade and Industry: http://www.meti.go.jp/english/index.html
Ministry of Finance: http://www.mof.go.jp/english/index.htm
Mizuho Securities Company: https://www.mizuho-sc.com/english/index.html (links to English-language websites of companies)
Nippon Keidanren: http://www.keidanren.or.jp/
Nomura Research Institute: http://www.nri.co.jp/english/

Toyo Keizai: http://corp.toyokeizai.net/en/

Society

International Research Center for Japanese Studies: http://www.nichibun .ac.jp/welcome_e.htm

International Shinto Foundation: http://www.internationalshinto foundation.org

Japan Institute for Labor Policy and Training: http://www.jil.go.jp/english/ index.html

Jinja Honcho (Association of Shinto Shrines): http://www.jinjahoncho.or.jp/ en/

Ministry of Agriculture, Forestry, and Fisheries: http://www.maff.go.jp/ein-dex.html

Ministry of Education, Culture, Sports, Science, and Technology: http:// www.mext.go.jp/english/index.htm

Ministry of Health, Labor, and Welfare: http://www.mhlw.go.jp/english/in-dex.html

Ministry of Land, Infrastructure, Transport, and Tourism: http:// www.mlit.go.jp/english/

Ministry of the Environment: http://www.env.go.jp/en/

National Christian Council in Japan: http://ncc-j.org/english/profile.htm

National Confederation of Trade Unions (Zenrouren): http:// www.zenroren.gr.jp/jp/english/index.html

National Institute for Educational Policy Research in Japan: http:// www.nier.go.jp/English/index.html

National Institute of Population and Social Security Research: http:// www.ipss.go.jp/index-e.html

National Women's Education Center, Japan: http://www.nwec.jp/en/

Rengo (Japanese Trade Union Confederation): http://www.jtuc-rengo.org/

Statistics Bureau (Director-General for Policy Planning & Statistical Re-search): http://www.stat.go.jp/english/index.htm

Supreme Court of Japan: http://www.courts.go.jp/english/

International Relations

Aneki.com: http://www.aneki.com/Japan.html (comparative rankings of countries in various categories)

Japan International Cooperation Agency: http://www.jica.go.jp/english/

Ministry of Defense: http://www.mod.go.jp/e/index.html

Ministry of Foreign Affairs of Japan: http://www.mofa.go.jp/

Ministry of Foreign Affairs of Japan (Diplomatic Record Office): http://www.mofa.go.jp/about/hq/record/index.html

National Clearinghouse for U.S.-Japan Studies: http://spice.stanford.edu/docs/clearinghouse/

Permanent Mission of Japan to the United Nations: http://www.un.emb-japan.go.jp/itprtop_en/index.html

Culture

AnimeNation: http://www.animenation.net/category/anime-news/

Crafts of Japan: http://kougeihin.jp.e.oo.hp.transer.com

Fashion in Japan: http://www.fashioninjapan.com/

Japan Fashion Association: http://www.japanfashion.or.jp/english/index.html

Japan Football Association (soccer): http://www.jfa.or.jp/eng/

Japanese Baseball: http://www.japanesebaseball.com/

Japanese baseball information (by Jim Allen): http://www2.gol.com/users/jallen/jimball.html

J.League (soccer): https://www.jleague.jp/en/

Kinema Club: http://kinemaclub.org (a database for films)

Mark Schilling's *Tokyo Ramen*: http://japanesemovies.homestead.com/

Midnight Eye Guide to New Japanese Films: http://www.midnighteye.com/features/midnighteye_guide.shtml

Nihon Sumo Kyokai: http://www.sumo.or.jp/En/

Professional Golfers' Association of Japan: http://www.pga.or.jp/english/index.html

Tokyo Street Style: http://www.style-arena.jp/en/tokyo-streetstyle

Newspapers and Media

Asahi Shimbun and *International Herald Tribune*: http://www.asahi.com/english/

Fuji Media Holdings: http://www.fujimediahd.co.jp/en/

Fuji News Network: http://www.fnn-news.com

Fujisankei Communications International: http://www.fujisankei.com/en/

Japan News (by the *Yomiuri Shimbun*): http://the-japan-news.com

Japan News.Net: http://www.thejapannews.net

Japan Times Online: http://www.japantimes.co.jp/

Mainichi: https://mainichi.jp/english/

News on Japan: http://www.newsonjapan.com

NHK Online: http://www.nhk.or.jp/english/

Nikkei Asian Review: https://asia.nikkei.com

Nippon Television Network: http://www.ntv.co.jp/english/index.html

NIPPONIA: http://web-japan.org/nipponia/archives/en/index.html (quarterly online magazine on modern Japan)

About the Author

William D. Hoover was fascinated by his freshman Muskingum College world civilization history course and attracted to the life of a professor early in his undergraduate experience, so he enrolled in a Japanese studies graduate program at the University of Michigan, where his interest in things Japanese grew even stronger. He claims he has had the best job in the world: reading, studying, researching, writing, and teaching about Japan for the past 40 years.

The recipient of National Defense Language, Fulbright, and Japan Foundation fellowships, Hoover has been privileged to live in Tōkyō for three extended periods (1966–1967, 1977–1978, and 1994–1996), and has visited Japan on numerous other occasions. He has also taken local groups on tours through the heart of Japan.

Hoover has written articles on Japanese businessmen Godai Tomoatsu, Shibusawa Eiichi, and Furukawa Ichibei, as well as the internationalist Nitobe Inazō. He was the regional editor of *Biographical Dictionary of Modern Peace Leaders* (1985); editor (with Melvin Small) of *Give Peace a Chance: Exploring the Vietnam Antiwar Movement* (1992); and author of numerous articles on the Japanese journalist K. K. Kawakami, about whom he is finishing a book.

During his career, Hoover has been a visiting professor at the University of Michigan and Bowling Green State University as well as a visiting researcher at the University of Tokyo and Aoyama Gakuin University. He offered a "Seminar on Teaching about Asia" for the National Consortium for Teaching about Asia on several occasions and was chair of the History Department at the University of Toledo for 15 years.

In retirement, Professor Emeritus Hoover and his wife, a retired mathematics professor, continue to enjoy international travel and also find time to visit their mountain house in western North Carolina. An avid reader of newspapers, he maintains several large files of clippings on Japan. He scours book reviews and samples many publications in order to remain current on Japan. He has traveled to approximately 60 countries in order to educate himself and thus better understand Japan as well as his own country. Since the edition of the first edition of *Historical Dictionary of Postwar Japan*, Hoover has traveled to Japan five times and read material on all kinds of Japanese topics. Japan is never far from his mind. He has enjoyed writing this second edition.

595